Routledge Handbook of New Media in Asia

While a decade ago much of the discussion of new media in Asia was couched in Occidental notions of Asia as a "default setting" for technology in the future, today we are seeing a much more complex picture of contesting new media practices and production. As "new media" becomes increasingly an everyday reality for young and old across Asia through smartphones and associated devices, boundaries between art, new media, and the everyday are transformed.

This Handbook addresses the historical, social, cultural, political, philosophical, artistic and economic dimensions of the region's new media. Through an interdisciplinary revision of both "new media" and "Asia" the contributors provide new insights into the complex and contesting terrains of both notions.

The *Routledge Handbook of New Media in Asia* will be the definitive publication for readers interested in comprehending all the various aspects of new media in Asia. It provides an authoritative, up-to-date, intellectually broad, conceptually cutting-edge guide to the important aspects of new media in the region – as the first point of consultation for researchers, and advanced level undergraduate and postgraduate students in fields of new media and Asian studies.

Larissa Hjorth is an artist, digital ethnographer and Professor in the Games Programs, and codirector of RMIT's Digital Ethnography Research Centre (DERC), Melbourne, Australia.

Olivia Khoo is Senior Lecturer in Film and Screen Studies at Monash University, Australia.

Routledge Handbook of New Media in Asia

Edited by Larissa Hjorth and Olivia Khoo

LONDON AND NEW YORK

First published 2016
by Routledge
2 Park Square, Milton Park, Abingdon, Oxon OX14 4RN

and by Routledge
711 Third Avenue, New York, NY 10017

Routledge is an imprint of the Taylor & Francis Group, an informa business

British Library Cataloguing in Publication Data
A catalogue record for this book is available from the British Library

Library of Congress Cataloging-in-Publication Data
The Routledge handbook of new media in Asia / eds., Larissa Hjorth &
  Olivia Khoo.
    pages cm
  Includes bibliographical references and index.
  1. Information technology—Social aspects—Asia. 2. Mass media
and technology—Asia. 3. Mass media—Technological innovations—
Asia. 4. Social media—Asia. I. Hjorth, Larissa. II. Khoo, Olivia.
  HN655.2.I56R68 2016
  302.23095—dc23
  2015016524

ISBN: 978-1-138-02600-1 (hbk)
ISBN: 978-1-315-77462-6 (ebk)

Typeset in Bembo
by Apex CoVantage, LLC

Printed and bound in Great Britain by
TJ International Ltd, Padstow, Cornwall

Contents

Contents

Illustrations

Figures

Table

Acknowledgements

The editors would like to thank the authors for their contributions, the Routledge editorial team Leanne Hinves, Helena Hurd and Lucy McClune, RMIT University, Monash University and the Asia Research Institute (ARI) at the National University of Singapore. Larissa Hjorth would like to acknowledge the Australian Research Council Linkage with Intel Locating the Mobile (LP130100848). The editors also wish to send a big thanks to Esther Pierini.

Larissa and Olivia would like to dedicate this collection to the next generation of new media users, Sebastian Khoo and Jesper Hjorth.

Every effort has been made to contact copyright holders for their permission to reprint material in this book. The publishers would be grateful to hear from any copyright holder who is not here acknowledged and will undertake to rectify any errors or omissions in future editions of this book.

Glossary

agencement	Arrangement in Actor-Network Theory
Aliran, Aliran Kesedaran Negara	National Consciousness Movement in Malaysia
anime	Japanese word for animation
ANT	Actor-Network Theory
app	Mobile phone application
ASEAN	Association of Southeast Asian Nations
Bangsa Malaysia	Malaysian race
Barisan Nasional (BN)	National Front (Malaysia)
BBS	Bulletin Board Services
big-character poster	Handwritten posters using large Chinese characters
BL	Boys' Love; female-authored homoerotic genre
CCP	Chinese Communist Party
CCTV	China Central Television
chaebol	South Korean form of business conglomerate
CNNIC	China Internet Network Information Center
cosplay	Costume play (especially of Japanese characters)
DIY	Do it yourself
FDI	Foreign direct investment
FTM	Female-to-male transgender
GPS	Global Positioning System of radio navigation
Hallyu	Korean popular culture wave
hawala	Informal banking system used in the Indian subcontinent, the Middle East, and parts of Africa
ICTs	Information and Communication Technologies
IRC	Internet Relay Chat
J-pop	Japanese popular culture
jugaad	Hindi word for "making things happen," referring to innovative use of limited resources and infrastructure to create new processes and structures of functioning. It has a strong resonance with shanzhai cultures in China, which also operate on similar principle
K-pop	Korean popular culture
KBS	Korean Broadcasting System
keiretsu	Japanese system of corporate governance
keitai	Japanese word for mobile phone

les	Hong Kong term for women with same-sex desires
LGBT	Lesbian, gay, bisexual and transgender
Lion Rock	Prominent hill above Kowloon in Hong Kong
locative media	Media of communication bound to a location
manga	Japanese comic culture
MMOB	Multi-Media on Board (Hong Kong public transport)
MMORPG	Massively Multiple Player Online Role Playing Games
MMS	Multimedia Messaging Service
mouh liuh	Cantonese for "doing nothing, a state of wandering"
MSC	Multimedia Super Corridor (Malaysia)
MTR	Mass Transit Railway in Hong Kong
MUDs	Multi-User Dungeons
NGOs	Non-governmental Organisations
otaku	Game and Japanese media obsessed users (literally "your home" and an honorific "you" in Japanese)
Pakatan Rakyat (PR)	People's Alliance (Malaysia)
Parti Islam Se-Malaysia (PAS)	Pan-Islamic Malaysia Party
PC bangs	Korean Internet cafés
PSB	Public Service Broadcasting
SARS	Severe Acute Respiratory Syndrome, viral
shanzhai	Chinese imitation and pirate brands and goods, particularly electronics
SMS	Short Message Service (text messaging)
SNS	Social Networking Service
Suara Rakyat Malaysia (SUARAM)	Voice of the Malaysian People
UCC	User-created content
UGC	User-generated content
VCD	Video Compact Disc
VPN	Virtual Private Network
www	World Wide Web

Intimate entanglements: new media in Asia

Larissa Hjorth and Olivia Khoo

When we think of new media today, an image of the ubiquitous smartphone user comes to mind. New media, entangled with gestures of intimacy, are increasingly becoming mainstream as mobile devices further embed within our everyday spaces. In each location, new media is shaping, and being shaped by, place in different ways. Haunted with traces of older media, what constitutes new media today is changing as mobile devices afford new access to multimedia tools and networks once unimagined. This is especially the case in Asia, the world's largest and most populous continent, where the consumption and production of new media has been the most palpable.

The undulating growth of ICTs (Information and Communication Technologies) has accompanied the uneven, multiple and contested "soft power" of the region. ICTs have played a key role in the rise of the region as well as its transnational collaborations and reframing of national boundaries (Berry et al. 2009; Otmazgin 2013). In India, one can find the third biggest group of users of Facebook with over 57 million users. In Indonesia, there are nearly 43 million Facebook users in a nation that has been dubbed "Twitter Nation." In China, where Facebook is banned everywhere except in Shanghai's newly demarcated free-trade zone (FTZ), a healthy diet of QQ, Weibo, WeChat and Jiepang dominate, highlighting the diversity of media-rich social networks and the significance of mobile media. For many of the older Chinese users, the mobile phone has been their only portal for the online, especially through QQ, which for many is synonymous not just with the social media but also the Internet. With a strong *shanzhai* (copy) phone culture that keeps smartphone prices down, we see over 420 million of China's total of 564 million online users accessing the Internet from their mobile. Chinese artist Ai Weiwei has deployed the power of Twitter (with over 220,000 followers) to fuse art and politics with new media. In Vietnam, art space Sán Art questions the governmental regulations of the online while the media-savvy strategies of "The Propeller Group" challenge governmental historical "truths."

Against the backdrop of Asia's high consumption and innovative uses of new media, the region is also home to much of the world's production of online and mobile technologies, as witnessed in the exposé of Foxconn's inhumane working conditions in Chinese factories producing the world's Apple products. The impact of ICT e-waste has brought about new narratives concerning media and the environment. In recent years a visual culture of environmental deterioration has emerged intertwined with the accelerated rate of ICTs. Artists such as China's

Figure 1.1 Yao Lu, *The Beauty of Kunming* (2010), from the "New Landscapes Part III" series (Courtesy of the artist)

Yao Lu have intercepted the new media visualizations of accelerated climate change by overlaying the traditional with the contemporary. At first glance, Yao Lu's photographs of landfill look like traditional Chinese paintings. But instead they are the reality of post-industrial new media consumption where the impact of material and immaterial waste and storage is yet to be fully acknowledged.

While a decade ago much of the discussion of new media in Asia was couched in Occidental notions of Asia as a "default setting" for technology in the future (Morley and Robins 1995), today we are seeing a much more complex picture of contesting new media practices and production. Asia is home to the world's first example of mainstream mobile Internet in Japan over 15 years ago. With strong production and consumption patterns the region's various and contesting social and mobile media cultures play a pivotal role in everyday life. As "new media" becomes increasingly an everyday reality for young and old across Asia through smartphones and their copies, boundaries between art, new media, and the everyday are transformed. From divergent gaming cultures in China, South Korea and Japan (Hjorth and Chan 2009) to new media artists like China's Cao Fei and India's Gigi Scaria, Asia's diverse new media practices are as uneven as they are dynamic.

This Handbook seeks to address the historical, social, cultural, political, philosophical, artistic and economic dimensions of the region's new media. Through an interdisciplinary revision of

Figure 1.2 Gigi Scaria, *Face to Face* (2010), inkjet print on archival paper, 63 x 44 inches
(Courtesy of the artist)

both "new media" and "Asia" the Handbook seeks to provide new insights into the complex and contesting terrains of both notions.

New media in Asia

Chapters in the Handbook explore new media politics, practices and paradigms across South, Southeast and East Asia. We do not define Asia according to strict geographical demarcations or boundaries but follow the flows and circuits of new media production and consumption between and across the region considered expansively. While often referred to as a geographic reality, Asia is a discursively constructed entity with a "historically invented geography" (Ching 2000, 238). Taking cognizance of longstanding as well as newly emergent regional dynamics, we seek to explore and problematize theories around place and locality, especially through notions such as diaspora and transnationalism, which continue to impact on how "Asia" has been and is today conceptualized.

From the Asian financial crisis of the late 1990s to the rise of China and India, the last two decades have seen increased trade and cultural connections between Southeast Asian nations (ASEAN) and China, India, Hong Kong, Japan, Korea and Taiwan. Prasenjit Duara notes that while Asia was historically linked terrestrially, and later by maritime silk routes, the new trade and cultural linkages across contemporary Asia "represent a kind of networked region" (2015, 15). Duara's description of Asia as a networked region made up of "overlapping, intersecting networks, hubs and hinterlands" (2015, 15), is especially appropriate for encapsulating the forms of digital connectivity we are interested in exploring in this volume, together with their attendant political, economic, and socio-cultural implications. This network model is not underpinned by a notion of territorial homogenization—economic, political or cultural—in the way that Europe as a region is conceived, for instance. Rather, it enables a rethinking of various connected nodes within a wider system of global capitalism.

The pitfalls of regionalist thinking have been well noted by a range of scholars. Leo T.S. Ching (2000), for example, cautioned against a reflexive tendency towards regionalist thinking regarding Asia, suggesting that regionalism "represents a mediatory attempt to come to terms with the immanent transnationalization of capital and the historical territorialization of national economies," on the one hand, while it also underscores "deeper structural and historical changes in the ways Asia is perceived as both a mode of production and a regime of discursive practice in the Japanese imaginary" (236). Regionalist thinking can distort or even eradicate internal differences and conflicts, including ongoing conditions of internal colonizing practices between various Asian nations.

As a contemporary networked region in Duara's description, however, Asia represents an intermediate stage between the global and the national that might enable forms of collective engagement with a range of issues tied to the development of global capitalism, including the environmental concerns we earlier noted. It also provides a useful framework for considering the interlinked struggles between the various Occupy Movements across Asia (and the rest of the world), and other political and social protests taking place throughout the region, including the Umbrella Revolution in Hong Kong and Taiwan's Sunflower Movement. Considering Asia as "networked," then, is one way to confront the problems of what Ulrich Beck calls "methodological nationalism" (2005, 43), which has stymied collaborative efforts across parts of the social sciences and the humanities.

In this Handbook, the particularity of Asia, for otherwise ubiquitous or "global" new media, is that far from homogenizing the region, we acknowledge the specificity of local contexts and communities as they exist within wider flows of globalization. Attention is paid to how local sites, and the flows between them, are impacted upon by censorship, varying levels of political control, alternative formations of kinship, tradition and culture, and divergent technological capabilities and capacities.

China assumes prominence in several chapters as an important node within a networked Asia due to its sheer size and influence. In China, the Internet is run on hardware controlled by state-owned entities, which gives the Chinese government a larger degree of control over and access to Internet data than anywhere else. The rise of China as a new media production center highlights the sometimes significant level of state control over the media in Asia, as well as the dichotomy between what is considered "public" or "private" in relation to new media practices, consumption and use. Related to issues of censorship, surveillance and privacy, are rapid changes in technology that afford users of new media in Asia the ability to participate more inclusively in what might otherwise be a more constrained political environment.

When Rey Chow wrote her seminal essay on the Sony Walkman in China, "Listening Otherwise, Music Miniaturized: A Different Type of Question about Revolution," she called for a "history of listening"—"a history of how listening and how the emotions that are involved in listening change with the apparatuses that make listening possible" (1990–1991, 143). Chow notes that while listening is traditionally public, with the portability of music wrought by devices such as the Walkman and the invention of headphones, "privacy" becomes possible as listening is interiorized. As a new technological device of the time, Chow argued that the Walkman provided a decisive break from the forms of listening in the past:

> If music is a kind of storage place for the emotions generated by cultural conflicts and struggles, then we can, with the new listening technology, talk about the production of such conflicts and struggles *on the human body* at the press of a button. . . . In the age of the Walkman . . . the emotions have become portable.
>
> *(Chow 1990–1991, 144)*

It is the ability to listen privately that

> leads to a certain freedom. This is the freedom to be deaf to the loudspeakers of history. We do not return to individualized or privatized emotions when we use the Walkman: rather the Walkman's artificiality makes us aware of the impending presence of the collective, which summons us with the infallibility of a sleepwalker.
>
> *(Chow 1990–1991, 145)*

Beijing-based new media artist Liu Ding encapsulates Chow's discussion of the Walkman as part of a new epoch in different approaches to listening. In the work *1999* (2014), 1990s popular culture music and quotes in China can be listened to from public phones.

In *1999* audiences can pick up a landline phone (pre mobile phone) to listen to music and quotes. A hybrid between headphones and mobile phone they are instead stationary receptors that transport the listener to another time. The work embodies Chow's discussion of rendering personal and private the act of listening which had been historically always public. *1999* inverts this history of listening by deploying a non-mobile media (the landline) to blur the public with the private, and the intimate with the social, in ways that are both culturally specific and also cross-cultural. Rather than listening being mobile and private as with the Walkman, audiences are frozen in space and also in time (stuck in the nineties). The play with old and new media also evokes the importance of co-presence (especially across time) while being both mobile and still.

Figure 1.3   Liu Ding, *1999* (2014), installation view, Shanghai Biennale
(Courtesy of the artist)

Chow's essay on the Walkman provides for us a lynchpin for how we hope the chapters in the Handbook can collectively be viewed as an attempt to historicize a field, new media in Asia, which, precisely because of its newness, is often left unhistoricized. We invited key thinkers including Chow and Leo T.S. Ching to provide reconsiderations of their earlier work, at the same time as we present a new generation of scholars and thinkers who bring their own voices and methods of "listening" to the histories and practices of new media in Asia.

The Handbook does not only provide surveys of different national contexts, although there are focused essays on national perspectives and case studies. Chapters also offer overviews of regional and sub-regional formations, as well as examinations of the interconnections and flows between local and national boundaries that have intensified with the advent and development of digital technologies, in particular the Internet since the late 1990s. Media content from throughout Asia and the rest of the world is now readily accessible through mobile phones, computers and gaming devices, which means that neither a regional nor a national approach alone are adequate in providing a picture of the rich and complex terrain that has developed across the region in the last three decades. New media in Asia, as it is conceived in this Handbook, is therefore primarily concerned with inter-Asian flows, networks and connections, rather than in perceiving how "Asia" has been constructed by and is connected to other formations outside it.

Organization

The Handbook seeks to be the definitive publication for readers interested in comprehending all the various aspects of new media in Asia. We hope it will provide a crucial reference text to inform students and scholars interested in this quickly expanding, far-reaching field of new media within the context of Asia. In this authoritative collection we seek to not only provide new insights into understanding "Asia" as a geographically, philosophically, and culturally divergent term but also the changing role of new media within the everyday lives of those who live in the region.

The Handbook is organized into six parts pertinent to the on-going theoretical and methodological development of new media in Asia. These are: "New media in Asia"; "New media cultures, politics and literacies"; "Intimate publics, screen and haptic cultures"; "Mapping mobile, diasporic and queer Asia"; "Creative industries: new producers, performativity and production paradigms"; and "Mobile, play and game ecologies in Asia." There is slippage between the sections and they are not meant to be silos but rather more like different paralleling playgrounds for conceptual meandering. Through these six parts we seek to not only consolidate the multiple and interdisciplinary ways for understanding the region but also new media. In addition to this broad, inclusive approach, we include as comprehensive as possible authors from various locations globally including the Asia-Pacific and Europe alongside Britain and the United States—this is crucial to an understanding of new media in Asia as constituted through local, situated practices and as global technology.

Part I asks key scholars in the area to reflect upon "New media in Asia" drawing from their various disciplinary backgrounds. The first chapter in Part I, by Ani Maitra and Rey Chow, reflects on the productive epistemic contradiction that shapes the title of this anthology: "New Media in Asia." By teasing out the tensions around new media as placeless or ubiquitous, this chapter questions the relationship between "Asia" and "new media" constructs. Underscoring their chapter are queries such as: What does the putative "Asian-ness" of new media and new media practices—if there could be such a thing—have to contribute to contemporary scholarship on new media? And when does the phrase "in Asia" stop being an adequate description for new media practices in Asia? As they argue, cultural readings of media practices can fall into another form of essentialism.

Probing cultural and situated definitions of new media is further extended by Lina Tao and Stephanie Hemelryk Donald's "Migrant youth and new media in Asia" in which they discuss the use of new media amongst migrant youth in the Asia-Pacific region. Drawing upon extensive fieldwork conducted in China, Tao and Hemelryk Donald question who the "migrant" is and how this figure is being defined in contemporary Asian media politics. The next chapter is Leo T.S. Ching's "Neo-regionalism and neoliberal Asia," in which he argues that regionalism in Asia (Asianism) has been historically constructed by and associated with Japanese colonial design and postwar economic and cultural imperialism. Ching argues that such a Japan-centric regionalism is no longer feasible in describing the changing geopolitical and economic dynamism under post-Cold War neoliberal capitalism. Instead, neo-regionalist formations, characterized less by "imagined geographies" as configured through "virtual geographies," have emerged as the new structure of feelings, especially among the digital youth.

We then turn to the role of new media during crisis through a case study of Japan in Love Kindstrand, Keiko Nishimura and David H. Slater's "Mobilizing discontent: social media and networked activism since the Great East Japan Earthquake." Starting with the earthquake, tsunami and Fukushima nuclear disaster known as 3/11, Kindstrand, Nishimura and Slater tease out the ways in which social media like Twitter took on a central role after the 3/11 disaster and how this marks a new form of politics and public debate in Japan. This is followed by Japanese new media scholar Machiko Kusahara in her chapter "Bridging art, technology, and pop culture: some aspects of Japanese new media art today." By focusing upon key artists—Maywa Denki (Novmichi Tosa), Kazuhiko Hachiya, Ryota Kuwakubo, and Daito Manabe—Kusahara reflects upon how artists in an age of YouTube can work outside conventional gallery or museum structures.

In the following chapter, "Staying relevant: the impact of the new media on Asia's media industries," Nissim Otmazgin examines the strategies employed by media industries to cope with the rapidly dynamic nature of the market whereby social media is transforming old distribution and consumption channels. Drawing on interviews with professionals from Japanese advertising, music, and video game industries, this chapter considers some of the challenges for media industry especially around online piracy and changes to consumption models.

The chapters in Part II, "New media cultures, politics and literacies," are concerned with the cultural policies, politics, and various ways of understanding and comprehending new media across a range of sites in Asia. Sophie Ping Sun and Jack Linchuan Qiu take as their focus the relationship between new media and migrant workers in China. Eschewing the dominant tendency to focus on "elite" consumption practices, Sun and Qiu note that working-class populations, including migrant workers with little or no education, are the biggest users of new media in China. Through a survey of the literature (in both Chinese and English) that has been produced on Chinese workers and their role in developing new media cultures, the authors attend to the fact that migrant workers not only provide labor to new media industries, they are also important to the formation of new consumer markets and new grassroots cultures, especially in terms of collective action. For Chinese migrant workers today, new media cultures are where collective formations take place.

The following chapter by Shobha Vadrevu examines the relationship between youth, citizenship and new media, particularly in Singapore. Vadrevu notes that online political activity opens up new spaces for public debate of otherwise restricted topics, although this must be carefully balanced against the Singapore government's continued control of online spaces. Mark McLelland's chapter continues an important comparative debate by tracing the regulation of obscenity in Japan and China, particularly in terms of the production and fandom surrounding Boys' Love

(BL in Japan) and *danmei* (in China) texts. Through an examination of recent examples where young women have been implicated in pornography debates and anti-obscenity prosecutions, McLelland investigates how the terms obscenity and pornography have come to develop divergent local meanings that have been used by the State and other groups not to "protect" young people from an inherent moral danger but rather to restrict or deny women's speech.

In the growing field of study on the relationship between new media and sport in Asia, Younghan Cho suggests that the Internet is crucial to Asian sportscapes because it enables sport as a commodity to be globalized with great rapidity. Providing a case study of Major League Baseball in South Korea, Cho conducts participant observation and face-to-face interviews with users of the MLBPARK website (www.mlbpark.com) in order to determine how Korean fans utilize online spaces to obtain information about baseball and to communicate with one another. Cho theorizes that the materiality of this online community is constituted through these fans' complex uses of time and space online, fluctuating between virtual and real, online and offline, and the local, national, and global.

In the following chapter, Pui-lam Law considers the case of *Passion Times*, a new media platform in Hong Kong established in 2012 by Civic Passion, a political group with a mission to fight for democracy and political autonomy in Hong Kong. Through this example, Law demonstrates the power of new media in facilitating political action, in this case to present a localist point of view against the dominance of Mainland-centric or pro-communist sentiments in the traditional (print) and mainstream media in Hong Kong. Law notes that *Passion Times* does more than facilitate political communication and online (and offline) political action; it is also a critique of ideology conducive to a new praxis.

Also offering a case study of an independent online news site, Malaysiakini, Susan Leong explores the ramifications involved in Malaysiakini's application for a press permit to add print to its digital editions. Malaysiakini was started in 1999 in Malaysia, a year after the government's undertaking not to censor the Internet so as to attract foreign technological investments into its newly established technology zone, the Multimedia Super Corridor. Leong notes that while Malaysia has a youthful population, with over 73 percent between the ages of 15–39 years (in 2013), a press permit would allow Malaysiakini access to the quarter of Malaysia's 29.3 million population that are not internet users and the three-quarters of mobile phone owners who do not own smartphones. Access and literacy become essential preconditions to an evaluation of the political interventions new media can facilitate.

The chapters in Part III, "Intimate publics, screen and haptic cultures," explore the relationship between the public nature of digital technologies and the emergence of new communities, uses, and intimacies forged through new media practices. They pay attention to the particular role that screens and screen cultures play in facilitating these intimacies.

Gloria Davies explores the changes digital technology and online communications have brought to China by showing how Chinese netizens are able to "speak back" to the Chinese Communist Party via social media. The centralizing power of the Chinese government's ability to intervene into the lives of citizens and to suppress the media and public debate has become less tenable with the spread of online communications. Focusing on the use of blogs and microblogs in China, in particular Sina Weibo, Davies notes that these technologies have again transformed the nature of publicness in China. A 140-character microblog in Chinese can convey far more than its 140-character counterpart on Twitter in English, reminding us of the specific interplay between freedom and technology in different contexts.

Jo Tacchi and Tripta Chandola examine the relationship between technology and progress in developing areas through their ethnographic work, spanning a decade, on smartphone use in the Indian slum of Govindpuri in Delhi. The authors focus on the use of smartphones by women—non-elite, "invisible" users—who must navigate their double marginalization as both slum-dwellers and women. Arguing that the inherent potential (or alternatively, threat) of mobile technologies to challenge the social order needs to be treated with caution, either for providing an overly deterministic view of the technology or because it suggests that the social order and traditions are unchangeable, the authors complicate arguments about the transformational possibilities of new media and in particular smartphones, and in so doing provide a different perspective on the relationships between new media, globalization and development.

In the next chapter David Kurt Herold describes what he terms as the "blended lives" of young Chinese online, outlining some of the unique ways in which young people in China use the Internet in order to create blended lives that consist of both online and offline elements that interact with and complement each other. Highlighting two main examples—making purchases on Taobao (the Chinese equivalent of eBay), and describing how the simple act of going out to dinner in China has now increasingly become a blended experience—Herold provides an interesting point of departure for a comparison of the online/offline relationship and practices of youth in China with those of youth elsewhere.

Continuing an exploration of social intimacies through online technologies, Kana Ohashi and Fumitoshi Kato's chapter aims to understand the ways in which social media practices influence relationships among family members, in particular mother–daughter relationships in Japan. Through a study of the various uses of *keitai* (the Japanese term for mobile phones) the authors illustrate both specific and diverse practices of how social media use among family members is influenced by gender, generation and place. It is fitting to follow this chapter with Helen Grace's overview of the theoretical work on mobility and intimacy, focusing on the everyday creative uses of mobile communications and quotidian forms of expression, including user-created content (UCC). Grace notes that the tendency towards *public* expression in media studies assumes this is of greater importance than the more widespread and typical *private* and intimate forms of expression. As a corrective, Grace maps the emotional landscape of mobility and intimacy, considering the key methodological issues and themes that emerge. Baohua Zhou and Miao Xiao's "Locative social media engagement and intergenerational relationship in China" is based on an ethnographic study of locative social media use on applications such as *WeChat, Weibo* and *Renren*, carried out with six families in Shanghai in 2013. The authors examine how parents and children sharing each other's location either by communicating directly or by tracking uploads of "moments" which display locative information, has affected intergenerational relationships, interacting with virtual co-presence and long-distance intimacy shared between parents and children who are geographically apart.

Olivia Khoo's chapter provides a case study of Viddsee, an online social viewing platform for short films developed in Singapore in 2012. Khoo is interested in the role played by Viddsee in the formation of a regional viewing community that is growing online alongside the official festival circulation of Southeast Asian cinema. Khoo argues that Viddsee's most distinguishing feature is how the founders of the site "curate" its contents, marking out Viddsee's distinction from other sites such as Vimeo and YouTube. This curation is coordinated with the social aspect of the website, which is heavily integrated with social media, in particular Facebook and Twitter. The combination of curation and social interaction allow us to contemplate the use of digital media, in this case digital short films, in the building of an online community of viewers in Southeast Asia. In this way Viddsee precipitates different audience consumption practices as filmmakers in Southeast Asia continue to seek ways of making and marketing films that have relevance beyond local audiences.

Part IV of the Handbook, "Mapping mobile, diasporic and queer Asia," explores multiple and divergent ways of conceiving of Asia as a terrain that is mobile and made up of increasingly intensifying patterns of both inward and outward migration, and diasporic and transnational flows of people and markets, and how this shifting and uneven terrain has the ability to either make visible or altogether erase the presence of marginalized groups and communities, including queer communities in Asia.

Sun Sun Lim, Becky Pham and Kakit Cheong provide an examination of the crucial role played by new media in the processes of migration within Asia. From sustaining emotional bonds with families left behind in home countries to the creation of new communities in the host country, the use of technological devices (from landline and mobile phones to computers) and Internet services (including social media and online chatting) are integral in maintaining, fulfilling and forging bonds across a transnational terrain. Lim, Pham and Cheong provide an important overview of the roles played by new media in the everyday lives of migrants, be they low-wage migrant workers, professionals or students.

Larissa Hjorth, Heather Horst, Sarah Pink, Baohua Zhou, Fumitoshi Kato, Genevieve Bell, Kana Ohashi, Chris Marmo and Miao Xiao explore how location-based new media services like Google Maps and practices of geo-tagging have become an integral part of everyday life across three sites—Shanghai, Tokyo and Melbourne—in which the authors have conducted short-term ethnographic studies with families. In particular, the research carried out by Hjorth et al. is interested in how locative media are shaping, and being shaped by, practices of intimacy and privacy in intergenerational families. Using the theme of "digital kinship," the authors suggest that formations of intimacy, family and place are being transformed in an age of locative media, and develop the theme of "intimate co-presence" as a way of describing how family members maintain mediated relationships in the face of shifting family and kinship structures across cultural, generational and temporal articulations.

Denise Tse-Shang Tang is also concerned with the development and maintenance of online intimacies and co-presence in her study of the Hong Kong lesbian mobile phone application, *Butterfly*. Tang conducts participant observation and ethnographic interviews with users of this site, built for the *les* community (a term used in Hong Kong for women with same-sex desires) in March 2013. Through these interviews Tang investigates the changing nature of gender politics and social meanings of gendered identities in Hong Kong lesbian communities. In his examination of queer mobile use in India, Nishant Shah points to the tensions and anxieties between technology and the representation of sexual identities and desires—from seemingly providing greater acceptance and permissiveness towards sexual diversity to ongoing discrimination and marginalization. Shah outlines a conception of the mobile as queer and of the queer mobile in order to offer a new framework through which to understand the lived reality of sexuality and digital technology in globalizing India. Exploring how queer and mobile intersect at points of disadvantage and discrimination, Shah delinks queerness from sexuality to characterize the mobile as a queer technology as it transcends, transgresses, and renders different bodies and events queer.

Sean Metzger's chapter brings the themes of this section together by providing a nuanced reading of Isaac Julien's nine-screen work, *Ten Thousand Waves*, in order to contemplate how we might understand aesthetic renderings of migration, in particular human trafficking. Julien's formidable installation, first exhibited in 2010, was inspired by the deaths of 23 Chinese workers, cockle pickers in England's Morecambe Bay, who placed calls to their loved ones from mobile phones before their deaths by drowning. Metzger notes that the form of the installation captures some of the fractured experience of migrancy and describes his experiencing of viewing the installation through the logic of "ebbing," a logic of return that describes not only the physical act of having to turn one's body and reorient oneself in order to take in the installation's circle of screens, but that also characterizes how the different scenes advance and transition at a regular tempo. Joining Shah's calls for the mobile as queer and queer as mobile, Metzger provides a complex reading that also situates the transnational circuits of labor and human trafficking reflected in Julien's work within the realm of globalized aesthetic production, in particular an aesthetic genealogy of queer cinema. Together, the chapters in Part VI highlight the ways in which "Asia," as it is defined through mobility, migration, and practices of intimacy, requires a range and re-orientation of perspectives, frameworks, and theoretical considerations.

In Part V, "Creative industries: new producers, performativity, and production paradigms," Michael Keane and Elaine Jing Zhao explore the changes in TV in China in "TV or not TV? Re-imagining screen content in China." In this chapter they examine the advent of post-broadcasting in China and TV's attempts to win back its youth audience through alternative forms of programming that blend East Asian celebrity with the market appeal of the Mainland. The following chapter by Audrey Yue investigates "New media in Singapore's creative economy: the regulation of illiberal pragmatism." In this chapter Yue explores the transformations of Singapore's creative economy through the shifts in the new media landscape. In particular, this chapter examines these policy changes and regulations over new media in general, and in film, television and the Internet specifically, to define a new media ecology.

Critiques of the creative industry continue but shift their focus to Japan in the next chapter by Shinji Oyama. In "Japanese creative industries in globalization," Oyama discusses the rise of the creative industries in Japan. In particular, Oyama examines underscoring fundamental contradictions in the form old media and new media tensions, alongside gender and labor issues.

In the next chapter Yeran Kim continues the focus on South Korea in her "Globalization of the privatized self-image: the reaction video and its attention economy on YouTube." This chapter studies "reaction videos" on YouTube as part of "a vernacular form of visual production." As Kim notes, "people use a webcam to record themselves while watching certain media content." The chapter seeks to account for the cultural implication of "reaction" in the contemporary global and apparently active and interactive digital mediascape. Hye-Kyung Lee follows with a chapter on "Public broadcasting, the Korean Broadcasting System (KBS), and its online services" whereby the impacts of new media and participatory consumption on the cultural sector are studied. This chapter addresses some of the questions around the cultural sector through a case study of KBS's development of online services.

The next chapter turns our focus to China. Kwai-Cheung Lo's "The struggle between subaltern nationalisms and the nation-state in the digital age: China and its ethnic minorities" examines how the Chinese state's concept of ethnic unity is challenged on the Internet by looking at various case studies such as the nationalist-separatist competitions between Chinese state media and the Uyghur and the Tibetan diaspora online communities have led each party seek to influence international perception of Xinjiang and Tibet.

In the last chapter of Part V, Katrien Jacobs discusses the digital sex cultures of Hong Kong Chinese and Mainland Chinese women in "Mainland Chinese women's homo-erotic databases and the art of failure." Jacobs explores the fantasies of homoerotic narratives in BL (boys' love animation); in particular, she considers fandom's ability to produce and reflect on compulsive queer fantasies that are little understood in the mainstream world through a redeployment of Jack Halberstam's *Queer Art of Failure*.

In Part VI of the Handbook, "Mobile, play and game ecologies in Asia," we explore the ubiquitous rise of mobile media and application (app) culture as part of play and game cultures in the region. We see how app culture—from an embodied part of quantified (monitoring) self to gamified practices— is becoming an all-pervasive part of new media experience. Through the lens of game and app culture, we can see the divergent ways in which new media practice moves in and through the rhythms of everyday life.

Part VI begins with Anthony Y.H. Fung and Vicky Ho's "Game industries in Asia: towards an Asian formation of game culture." For Fung and Ho, new media in Asia has expanded rapidly in the case of online game market. In contrast to the United States and Europe, the study of games and game production, distribution and marketing in Asia demonstrates a form of non-economic and instrumental logic of development of new media in this specific region.

The following chapter, "Online games and society in China: an exploration of key issues and challenges," is by Matthew M. Chew. This chapter identifies and overviews a number of research problematics and issues that have arisen out of distinctive cultural and social game contexts of China. Chew talks about the importance of developing a nuanced understanding of game studies that takes into account the different cultural practices within each locality. For example, gaming cultures in North America are not aligned with gaming cultures in China. The chapter covers key areas within gaming cultures in China such as gold-farming, virtual property, game addiction and game addiction treatment, gamer rights protection movement, "grieving" in Chinese game culture, commercialization of gamer groups, gamer and social protests against pay-to-win game designs, and government-sponsored public games. The next chapter by Peichi Chung examines "The globalization of game art in Southeast Asia." By focusing upon the important and yet often overlooked area of Southeast Asian game artists, Chung brings to the foreground the significant role Southeast Asia plays within global creative industry flows.

We then turn our focus to South Korea and gaming in Dal Yong Jin's "From a cottage to the symbol of creative industries: the evolution of Korea's online game industry." As Jin notes, the Korean game industry was a cottage industry until the mid-1990s because video games were not considered as a major part of culture or business. But by the mid-2000s, videogaming had become a key creative industry and an integral part of South Korean popular culture. In this chapter, Jin provides an overview of the key issues relating to online games in Korea in tandem with the creative industries.

The following chapter is by Meaghan Morris (with Elaine Lally and Catherine Driscoll), entitled "Getting a life: expatriate uses of new media in Hong Kong." In this evocative piece, Morris weaves an ongoing relationship between the three contributors carried out over many years over computer-based social games *Happy Farm*, *Farmville*, and *Cityville*, with observations and insights into new media usage in Hong Kong. Developing her concept of "fashioning" (defined as "a way of evolving a locality-based frame of reference that is also a stable field of parochially shared *affect* that happily absorbs ideas from all over") Morris describes a genre of new media usage that is local at the same time as it exceeds localism. This expansive piece rethinks the forms of temporality associated with social gaming (including moralizing discourses of how adults should productively use their time) to suggest that the sharing of new media, and the complex work of memory and nostalgia that are bound up with these practices, can in fact create new possibilities, insights and ways of confronting social transformation.

We then turn to the role of mobile media as part of emergent forms of literacy and creativity. In her chapter "The everydayness of mobile media in Japan," Kyounghwa Yonnie Kim discusses the legacy of mobile media as embedded within the "mundane" problem and how this banality can be used to deploy the device as not just a social but also a creative tool.

Conclusion: getting connected

By no means exhaustive, this Handbook seeks to unpack the various ways in which "new media" and "Asia" has been defined, experienced and conceptualized. The chapters highlight how new media is a divergent rubric subject to location, discipline and context. The academic field of research on new media in Asia is expanding rapidly to accommodate the range of critical perspectives attendant upon the growing social, cultural and technological developments in this area. To give just a few examples of new academic forums that have emerged in recent years, in 2014 Brill published its inaugural issue of the new journal *Asiascape: Digital Asia* (Volumes 1–2). In the same year, the *International Journal of Cultural Studies* (Volume 17, Number 5) published a special issue edited by Chua Beng Huat and Sun Jung on "Social Media and Cross-Border Cultural Transmissions in Asia: States, Industries, Audiences."

At the Asia Research Institute (ARI), National University of Singapore, an Inter-Asia Round-table was organized in 2012 on "Methodological and Conceptual Issues in Cyber Activism Research," adding the interdisciplinary perspectives of medical epidemiologists, mathematicians and biostatisticians to work being done by scholars in the Humanities and social sciences on social media, mobile activism and collective action in China, Korea, and elsewhere in the region. Much of this work is carried out by scholars working in institutions in Asia, in anglophone contexts, although there is a greater mass of work on local contexts being conducted in a range of Asian languages, contributing to the productive cross-fertilization in this field.

Adding to this rich and growing area, we hope the chapters in this Handbook will provide fresh and insightful ways in which to imagine and reimagine new media and Asia.

References

Beck, U. (2005) *Power in the Global Age: A New Global Political Economy*, Cambridge, MA: Polity Press.

Berry, C., Liscutin, N. and Mackintosh, J.D. (eds) (2009) *Cultural Studies and Cultural Industries in Northeast Asia: What a Difference a Region Makes*, Hong Kong: University of Hong Kong Press.

Ching, L.T.S. (2000) 'Globalizing the Regional, Regionalizing the Global: Mass Culture and Asianism in the Age of Late Capital', *Public Culture* 12(1): 233–257.

Chow, R. (1990–1991) 'Listening Otherwise, Music Miniaturized: A Different Type of Question about Revolution', *Discourse* 13(1): 129–148.

Duara, P. (2015) 'The Agenda of Asian Studies and Digital Media in the Anthropocene', Asiascape: *Digital Asia* 2: 11–19.

Hjorth, L. and Chan, D. (eds) (2009) *Gaming Cultures and Place in the Asia-Pacific*, New York: Routledge.

Morley, D. and Robins, K. (1995) 'Techno-Orientalism: Japan Panic'. In *Spaces of Identity: Global Media, Electronic Landscapes and Cultural Boundaries*, London: Routledge: 147–174.

Otmazgin, N. (2013) *Regionalizing Culture: The Political Economy of Japanese Popular Culture in Asia*, Hawaii: University of Hawaii Press.

Part I

New media in Asia

2

What's "in"? Disaggregating Asia through new media actants

Ani Maitra and Rey Chow

The future of the IT industry, many would argue, lies in Asia. In the 2014 figures released by the International Telecommunication Union (a UN agency for communication and information technology), Asia stands out as an untapped new media market for manufacturers of mobile and wireless communication devices. The ITU predicts that,

> Mobile-cellular subscriptions [globally] will reach almost 7 billion by end 2014, and 3.6 billion of these will be in the Asia-Pacific region. (. . .) By end 2014, fixed-broadband penetration will have reached almost 10 per cent globally. Forty-four per cent of all fixed-broadband subscriptions are in Asia and the Pacific, and 25 per cent are in Europe. In contrast, Africa accounts for less than 0.5 per cent of the world's fixed-broadband subscriptions . . .
>
> *(ITU 2014, n.p.)*

Arguably, as demonstrated by these numbers as well as current research on the proliferation of Internet and cell phone use in Japan, South Korea, Taiwan, Singapore, Hong Kong, mainland China, India, and the Philippines, digital and wireless technology is, and will be, transforming markets, industries, and social and political life in Asia.

While acknowledging the importance of these major shifts in Asia since the birth of the Internet in the West in the wake of the Cold War, this chapter will reflect on the productive epistemic contradiction that shapes the title of this anthology: "New Media in Asia." On the one hand, the rhetoric of "new media" often emphasizes notions of rootlessness and placelessness, as borne out by the decentered nature of rhizomatic networks that transcend spatial and temporal constraints. The "newness" of new media, we have been told, lies in its capacity for stealthy penetration and deterritorialization, exemplified by "packet-sniffers" that insidiously monitor network traffic, and by competing hacking technologies that repeatedly outsmart such watchful monitors.

On the other hand, the qualifying phrase "in Asia" suggests a geographical and geopolitical circumscription, a territorial cordoning-off so that the spotlight is on "Asia." The linguistic entity that makes this contradiction possible is the preposition "in." It is, we believe, crucial to reflect on this little and seemingly inconsequential word precisely because it goes under the radar so often. If, by definition, digital media is that which resists being clearly defined, held, or captured, how can we fully "capture," so to speak, the effects of new media "in" Asia? Why has it become necessary to speak of new media "in Asia" if digital media is everywhere? What does the putative Asian-ness of digital media practices—if there could be such a thing—have to contribute to contemporary discourse on new media? And when does the phrase "in Asia" *stop* being an adequate description for digital media practices in Asia?

1 What difference does "in" make?

The reason for the use of the preposition in the phrase "new media in Asia" is somewhat obvious: "In" announces and makes clear our focus on a particular geographical area. In this context, it is important to acknowledge that contemporary scholarship on emerging mobile media practices in Asia has advanced powerful arguments about space and locality, enabling media-makers and critics to rethink the history of the Internet and ahistorical notions of space initially associated with the technoculturalist celebration of the Internet, virtual realities, and data flows. For instance, Madanmohan Rao has pointed out that the development of the Internet must be historicized transnationally, taking into account not just the story of ARPANET in the United States but also the birth of early computing infrastructures in Asia, such as the creation of premier research and educational institutes in the region (such as the Indian Institute of Technology and the Indian Institute of Management in India), and early corporate structures such as the *keiretsu* of Japan and *chaebols* of South Korea (Rao and Mendoza 2005, 16). More recently, Larissa Hjorth and Michael Arnold have emphasized the need to examine media ecologies as a dynamic interaction between the electronic/virtual space and geographic space, the mobile and the stationary, the technological and the cultural. Through case studies carried out in Seoul, Tokyo, Shanghai, Manila, Singapore, and Melbourne, Hjorth and Arnold explore how mobile media and their sites of operation shape each other in the Asia-Pacific region, paying attention, in particular, to "the difference that place makes" (Hjorth and Arnold 2013, 2).

In this chapter, however, we seek to interrogate the recent emphasis on local difference. We argue that, while such attention to "place" is important, an unqualified emphasis on the local or the regional often gives rise to ethnoculturalist approaches that, while resisting technoculturalism, tend to overlook differences *within* these apparently homogeneous spaces. Ethnoculturalist arguments typically take two contradictory forms in new media discourse. The first, often articulated as a diffuse cultural identitarianism, is associated with an Asian country, region, or bloc like "East Asia." In this instance, new media appears as a distinctively "non-Western" platform through which a regional or pan-Asian identity is maintained. For example, in Hjorth and Arnold's analysis, it is the South Korean repurposing of the Korean language and traditions in new digital contexts that constitutes the locality of mobile media practices in Seoul (Hjorth and Arnold 2013, 30). Also, the authors identify *cultural* variations and specificities in the region, noting that the Japanese, as a people, are more "stoic" than Koreans on Twitter (Hjorth and Arnold 2013, 39), and that the Asia-Pacific on the whole is a region where "Western" notions of family, privacy, and self do not apply (Hjorth and Arnold 2013, 141). Similarly, in her analysis of mobile cultures in East Asia, Jaz Hee-Jeong Choi makes a case for the simultaneous "East Asian-ness" and "Korean-ness" of mobile media in Korea by contending that the Korean social networking site Cyworld's success lies in its appeal to "traditional attributes of collective Korean culture" and that social networking in Korea shows "strong collective in-group tendencies" (Choi 2007). Choi's main rationale is the assumption that social networking in Korea is *less individualistic* than it is in the West: "Korea, China, and Japan share a traditionally collective, interdependent, and high-contextual culture, as opposed to individual, independent, and low-contextual cultures, which are predominantly evident in the West" (Choi 2007).

In our view, this kind of emphasis on national tradition and regional cultural specificity (introduced by way of the "in" or "@" or "of") cannot go unexamined, not least because such an emphasis, which is traceable to the politics of Cold War area studies, often relies on a monolithically binary opposition between the "relational" East and the "autonomous" West.[1] Paradoxically, the same East/West binary engenders a second culturalist argument, one that is equally homogenizing even as it contradicts the first argument. In this second argument, digital media in Asia is not an ancillary platform on which Asian interdependence and sociality are rehearsed and safeguarded. Instead, as "eccentricities," the individualism and self-absorption promoted by new forms of mobile privatization threaten to take over the national social community. Historically, Japan has occupied a special place in this discursive regime of technophilia gone awry. Japanese culture is seen as being technologically "too advanced" and "too materialistic" from the Western perspective; Japan's technological prowess is seen both as ideal and an "Eastern" aberration. To describe this Western ambivalence toward Japan and other Asian countries, David Morley and Kevin Roberts coined the term "techno-orientalism" (Morley and Roberts 1992).

Importantly, once it acquires currency as a discursive operation, techno-orientalism is not sustained only as an external imposition whereby outsiders (Westerners) stereotype Asian subjects. As Toshiya Ueno reminds us, the Japanoid—Ueno's neologism for an image of "Japaneseness" that functions as a mirroring surface or an interface—exists neither inside nor outside Japan. Yet, it is through the Japanoid that the West disidentifies with Japan *and that Japan identifies with and (mis)recognizes itself* (Ueno 1996). But why should Japan identify with the Japanoid, given its (often derogatory) meanings of being "robotic," "obsessed with technology," etc.?

A brief excursion through the schizophrenic construction of the Japanese figure of the *otaku* reveals why embracing the Japanoid can be a strategic gesture that is used to commoditize all things Japanese, especially a highly technologized culture whose vilification and exoticization, in fact, add to its "market value." Coined in the 1980s to refer to *anime* fans in Japan, the word *otaku* literally means "your home" as well as "you" as a formal address. It has been suggested that the fans themselves developed the term to address each other politely at *anime* conventions, fanzine meetings, and film releases (Murakami 2001). However, the term has, from the outset, also gathered pejorative connotations of social awkwardness, self-centeredness, and even criminality in mainstream Japanese media. The arrest of the serial killer Tsutomu Miyazaki in 1989 was an important moment in the history of the pathologization of the *otaku*. The mass media linked Miyazaki's impressive collection of *anime* and slasher films to his misogynist and criminal tendencies, labelling him the "Otaku Murderer." Ironically, this national pathologization of *otaku* behavior as deviant and un-Japanese also reinvigorated Western interest in Japan and Japan studies in the 1990s. Scholars both within and outside Japan sought to explain how the anti-social behavior of the *otaku* was atypical of Japanese national culture. At the same time, it was and continues to be profitable to maintain that *otaku* culture is *made (only) in Japan*, so that it is not just a subfield of scholarly "expertise" but also a vendible national commodity.

In his astute ethnographic study of Akihabara—an electronic shopping district in Tokyo that is more popular than Disneyland as a tourist destination—Patrick Galbraith demonstrates how *otaku* culture is peddled and consumed simultaneously as deviant behavior and as a national treasure. He notes that, on the one hand, Akihabara perpetuates images of the digital misfit by advertising reports of social crimes committed by those identified as *otaku*. On the other hand, as a tourist destination, Akihabara actively sells itself as a paradise for the *otaku* and the aspiring. Tourists (Eastern and Western) are invited to see themselves in the (Japanoid mirror) ideal of the otaku-consumer: "In essence, Akihabara is an otaku's room blown up to city scale, sexy *anime*-girls posters and all" (Galbraith 2010, 211). The image of the *otaku* therefore functions as a kind of *pharmakon*: it is Japan's "poison," but it also embodies Japanese "cool." Above all, it is a commodity bearing the sign of Japanese-ness that can be sold to the entire world.

Given these forms of techno-orientalism and self-orientalization spawned by the East/West binary that are often lurking behind the phrase "in Asia," it is crucial that we move beyond culturalist arguments to more critically transnational perspectives on the localization of digital habits and habitats. Underscoring the need to study the *otaku* phenomenon as a fan culture that includes American as well as Japanese consumers of *manga* and *anime*, Thomas Lamarre notes that the "otaku is not only ordinary but also transnational at heart" (Galbraith and Lamarre 2010, 370). Even if we identify regional variations, "the otaku mode is not entirely localizable, and thus entails a constant deterritorialization" (Galbraith and Lamarre 2010, 370). Additionally, for Lamarre, the *otaku* phenomenon highlights the manner in which the nation-state plays an active role in policing and transnationalizing national culture.

However, even as we depathologize and de-essentialize the *otaku* and see it as a global tendency or potentiality, we cannot entirely ignore the question of locality that is introduced by the expression "in Asia." How should we approach this question and argue for its political and cultural significance without slipping into culturalism? What mediates or distinguishes digitally supported "social publics" and "intimate publics" (Hjorth and Arnold 2013, 12) more fundamentally than the familiar East/West divide?

As Gregory Staple and others argue, there is a divisive logic that characterizes the information economy in general, whereby collectivities converge around similar interests, often excluding those who do not have the resources to share those interests or form comparable collectivities (Staple and Dixon 1992). This form of localization is not always constituted by geographical proximity or ethnic kinship. A different approach to locality emerges if we think of the material conditions governing the level of access to digital media—conditions that compel us to *disaggregate* Asia instead of turning it into a homogeneous geopolitical entity—especially in the context of the unevenness of technological and economic development in the region. For example, according to data released in 2013 by the Indian research firm Juxt, India has 554.8 million mobile users and 143.2 million Internet users (Indian Digital Review 2013). Given that the Indian population is currently a little over one billion, it would appear that about 46 percent have mobile phones and approximately 12 percent have access to the Internet. As the same report shows, however, these figures do not give us the whole picture: "access" to the Internet needs qualification.

Of the 143.2 million, about 94 million (only about 8 percent of the national population) have access to the Internet from their desktop/ laptop, smart TV, or mobile data connections. The rest are capable of accessing the Internet through cell phone operators' portals. These latter users are called "on-deck users" (comparable to what Carolyn Cartier et al. call "the information-have-less") (Cartier et al. 2005) and they only have access to limited data services such as ringtone downloads, game downloads, and video downloads. Most important, these users lack the means (and often the basic literacy required) to "browse" the Internet like digitally savvy smartphone or iPad owners. We may thus safely conclude that, for the vast majority in India, the Internet and wireless technology do not constitute "continuous fields of presence" (Mitchell 2003, 81) that the user can "log onto" wherever and whenever. The lack of access and low digital literacy reveal that the logic of "perpetual (voluntary) contact"—often touted as the logic of the *apparatgeist* or "the spirit of the (mobile) machine" (Katz and Aakhus 2003, 65–68)—is a presumed ideal available still to only a minority.

In contrast, even though the number of Internet users in India has surpassed the population of its neighbor Japan (127.6 million as of 2012), it is not an exaggeration to claim that mobile media and wireless technology have a much older history in Japan. In 2004, more than half the Japanese population subscribed to mobile phone-based Internet services (Akiyoshi and Ono 2008, 293). In 2013, over 86 percent of the Japanese population had access to the Internet (ITU Statistics 2014). The most cursory India/Japan comparison will show that not only is the digital infrastructure of Bangalore (the capital of Karnataka and India's IT hub) vastly different from that of Tokyo, but that only a minuscule minority of users in Bangalore (those connected to the IT industry, for instance) are able to emulate the digital habits of the residents of Tokyo. A WiFi-equipped café in Kolkata (the capital of West Bengal, India) catering to clients with the latest smartphones may be right next to a village or a slum whose inhabitants have little or no access to the Internet.

This is to say that, "in Asia," if we must so speak, locality must be examined through the *material and infrastructural differences between digital multiplicities, differences that separate the urban from the rural, and the urban privileged from the urban underprivileged*. Some urban zones are capable of being "always online" while others in the same city or outside it may be in interstitial "off-line" and "lag-time" spaces (Graham 1998, 100) where connectivity is intermittent and frequently interrupted, perpetually deferred, or heavily controlled.

This digital disparity and heterogeneity between geographically proximate spaces and people—a phenomenon by no means unique to but perhaps most glaringly visible in Asia—can, we suggest, be better understood through the Actor-Network Theory (ANT) developed by the French social theorists Michel Callon, Bruno Latour, and others. While making use of networks (that include but are not restricted to digital networks), ANT proposes the concept of the "actor" or "actant" to indicate that both *human and non-human entities* participate in networks of power. Refusing liberal-humanist anthropocentrism as well as speculations on so-called intrinsic qualities of materials, technologies, humans, and cultures, ANT focuses instead on their *agencement*: the *effects* generated as a result of different kinds and durations of combinations or associations between actants (Latour 1996; Munro 2009). However, even as ANT emphasizes the motility and degrees of durability of actor-networks—their capacity to recombine, disappear, and reappear—and firmly refuses to privilege the human over the non-human, it does not ignore the question of human agency. Rol-land Munro, for instance, has called for a deeper examination of "asymmetries in power" produced not just by the distribution of materials but also by *local* human roles or "identities" resulting from human-machine associations. The production and circulation of these identities (that can be stable or unstable), Munro argues, require human intervention, planning and/or manipulation, and often represent the interests of a particular class, gender, or ethnicity: "Materials, for example, are not always ready to hand . . . their consumption can be impeded by hierarchical devices, such as the denial of access as well as by shifts in accountability" (Munro 2009, 136).

In the following section, we consider two structurally distinct *agencements* of being online "in Asia." Both cases involve the production of local identities that help us rethink the myth of perpetual contact as well as the ethnocultural specificity of digital habits. Both demonstrate (in different ways) why the local as such needs to be examined through the techno-social fragmen-tation of Asia and the causes for such fragmentation: infrastructure, governmentality, literacy, livelihood, and economic inequity.

2 Human/machine asymmetries and intermittent networks: two examples from India

The Aadhaar project

Even though the vast majority of Indians is yet to acquire the economic means to socialize over Facebook or lounge in their virtual "apartments," Indian e-governance is determined to produce and manage digital identities for the entire nation, and especially the poorest of the poor. In

February 2009, the Unique Identification Authority of India (UIDAI), an agency of the Indian government, began its unique biometric identification project called *Aadhaar* (meaning "foundation" or "support" in Hindi). The UIDAI aimed to create a "foundational" identity for every resident in India. Notably, *Aadhaar* is not a card but a *number* generated against limited personal information (name, address, gender, age, and name of parent/guardian if the applicant is below five years) and extensive biometric data—a photograph, two iris scans, and ten finger prints. Unlike the passport, the driver's license, or the social security number, the *Aadhaar* number does not prove citizenship status or bestow any rights on the resident. It is simply a number that can be used to verify the resident's identity, and this identity must be authenticated electronically each time the resident avails of a service that requires his or her *Aadhaar* number (Chaganti 2013, 26).

Now, why did India embark on this gargantuan project when there were several existing forms of IDs in the country? The implementation of *Aadhaar* is one of the 27 projects identified in India's National e-Governance Plan (NeGP) and is funded by a loan from the World Bank. One of the main goals of this project is to make public and private services available across the country, especially in remote rural areas. More than 100,000 Internet-equipped service centers serving over 600,000 Indian villages have been planned as *access points* for a variety of services such as obtaining birth/death certificates, paying utility bills, carrying out bank transactions, and making use of social sector schemes. Bureaucrats supporting the UID project also argue that the system will prevent the waste or "leakage" of Public Distribution System subsidies that currently have many "ghost" beneficiaries, as they are distributed by counting "households" and not individuals (Rajadhyaksha 2013, xxix). 640 million residents are already under *Aadhaar*'s digital umbrella (Tikku 2014) and the authentication process has been coupled with a wide variety of schemes by different state governments. *Aadhaar* has, however, also generated a lot of controversy in India. Its most vociferous critics (including the Indian Supreme Court) have questioned its constitutional validity, its violation of individual privacy, and the accuracy of the technology used.[2] Objections from civil society and the judiciary notwithstanding, the recently-elected Indian Prime Minister, Narendra Modi, has given his new government the go-ahead to meet the one billion enrolment target by linking passports, public services, and utilities (like cooking gas) to the *Aadhaar* number (Tewari 2014).

Of particular interest to us are the ethical and political concerns introduced by *Aadhaar*, especially by the associations among biometric devices, the digitally literate, and the illiterate and economically disadvantaged. First, at the level of entering the electronic database, *Aadhaar* poses a fundamental problem of *consent*. Ethnographic research carried out at enrolment centers suggest that residents who are illiterate and/or are not "digital natives" have little or no knowledge about the technology behind biometric data and its uses before they agree to the process. In her study of *Aadhaar* enrolment in Jharkhand in Eastern India, Sruti Chaganti notes, "the successful recording of iris scans is often impeded . . . by the resident's discomfort in looking into the scanner at the appropriate angle" (Chaganti 2013, 33). Chaganti goes on to mention the case of an old woman who "constantly fails various tests, until she is finally, almost forcibly enrolled" (Chaganti 2013, 33). In Andhra Pradesh, researchers noted that applicants who could not read either English or Telugu (the state language) were falling prey to brokers who were charging money to fill out forms and "help" the applicants complete the biometrics (Centre for the Study of Culture and Society 2013, 217). At the Chhotiyal enrolment center in Palam Village in Delhi, neither the enrolment agency nor the residents had a clear idea about the benefits of *Aadhaar* (Centre for the Study of Culture and Society 2013, 289). Hundreds of *Aadhaar* enrollees in rural India complained that they did not know how to alter/manage the information they supplied at the registration centers. Many were also not sure if adding personal information like their bank account numbers was optional or mandatory. These various moments of biometric capture are illuminating in that they demonstrate the hierarchical relationship between digitally challenged human actors and the non-human digital actors, managed largely by other (digitally literate) human actors. These conflicts, dysfunctions, and asymmetries of power lead us to insist that any theorization of digital identity or of being online in Asia cannot confine itself to the ethno- or technocultural habits of urban "digital natives" or to dominant narratives of the "ubiquity" of mobile devices. Indeed, they point to the necessity of scrutinizing the underside of that apparent, smooth ubiquity: the coercive digitization of the digitally "exiled." Under these circumstances, the concept of a digital identity is fast becoming a social necessity manufactured by the enumerative politics of the Indian state. For those who are digitally disenfranchised, the most mundane activities (such as withdrawing or depositing money, cooking, or buying subsidized groceries) have become contingent on a willingness to be digitally enrolled and monitored by the state-as-actor on a daily basis.

Finally, if we have pointed out the collectivizing and deterritorializing tendencies of new media in the previous section, we would like to note here that, by encountering the digital ecosystem through *Aadhaar*, certain human actors like migrant laborers, refugees, and the homeless in urban India, in fact, risk being profiled and targeted by having unique identities attached to them. As several critics have pointed out, in the case of these "surplus" populations, Indian e-governance is more interested in surveillance and regulation than in reaching out with viable social services. From that perspective, *Aadhaar* joins the compulsory registration in the National Population Register (NPR) and the Immigration Visa and Foreigner's Registration and Tracking (IVFRT), tasked to constantly sift through migrants' and refugees' records for potential terrorists. In the case of the homeless in Delhi, the UID proves "residence" by locating individuals in "homeless pockets" on an Eicher map, completely ignoring the histories of these individuals who are often made homeless because of slum demolition drives organized by the state government (Centre for the Study of Culture and Society 2013, p. 285). Here, too, digital identities are part of the state's attempt to count bodies and plan displacement so as to further "develop" the city.

From Gulf to Gulf to Gulf

Our second example of a digital actor-network also comes from disaggregated Asia and resists being read in terms of ethnoculturalism or technoculturalism, but for rather different reasons. *From Gulf to Gulf to Gulf* (2013) is a collaborative video made by the CAMP, a media-making collective based in Mumbai, India. The video is primarily a collection of fragments from the everyday lives of Indian sailors on their boats and at the ports they visit, as they ferry a wide variety of merchandise (plastic drinking straws, used cars, and even livestock) from the Gulf of Kutch, to the Persian Gulf, to the Gulf of Aden, to the Somali coast and back. There are no voiceovers or interviews in the entire video. The camera moves from one boat to another, catching the sailors working, cooking, sleeping, and dancing in moments of leisure. Following the merchandise, snippets of conversations, and the geography navigated by the boats, we get the impression that the sailors often carry smuggled goods, encounter storms and pirates en route, and facilitate informal *hawala* transactions (that bypass conventional banking systems) involving traders in India, the UAE, Somalia, and Iran. Shaina Anand and Ashok Sukumaran, the CAMP members who oversaw the video's production, describe it as an expression of what the media critic Ravi Sundaram calls India's "pirate modernity" (Anand and Sukumaran 2012), a modernity constituted by illegal and unacknowledged networks that move "everyday goods, media, clothing, and medicine, 'reassembling' bits of local regional and transnational space" (Sundaram 2010, 14).

As an *agencement* of atypical associations among several (groups of) human and material actants, *From Gulf* was produced over four years through a remarkable collaboration between CAMP members and sailors from the Kutch district in Western India. As viewers, we immediately notice that the video is an edited collage of images shot by different individuals using different kinds of cameras. While explaining the origins of the three kinds of footages, Anand and Sukumaran mention how *From Gulf* began in the context of a larger project on the creek trade called *Wharf-age* in 2009:

> We also began to collect a particularly ephemeral form of records of these journeys [of the sailors]: cellphone videos that often did not survive a sailing year, because they were easily deleted or lost. And which did not make it to YouTube, because they circulated in a blue-tooth economy fueled largely by face to face and boat to boat meetings. . . . In 2010 we gave DV cameras to sailors who were interested in filming what could be described as the opposite of the imperial "view from the boat." . . . The songs heard in the film were all found, married to cellphone videos and used in sync.
>
> *(CAMP 2013)*

Even on first viewing, the three kinds of footages can be easily distinguished: videos taken by the sailors themselves, which are often handheld and jerky; "well-composed," glossier, and steadier videos taken at several ports by CAMP members; and, last but not least, low-resolution cell phone videos (frequently of one or two boats taken from another boat) that have as their background "score" a combination of Hindi film and regional Muslim religious songs.

In light of our ongoing discussion, the form, circulation, and ephemerality of these low-res cell phone videos, which the credits describe as anonymously created "music videos shared across many boats and many years," are particularly thought-provoking. Examining "small screen realities" captured by DV, computer, and cell phone cameras in contemporary China, the media theorist Paola Voci has compellingly demonstrated how these seemingly inconsequential and often eccentric videos are worthy of critical attention precisely because they remain outside the purview of the state-promoted creative industry and the scholarly field of "Chinese cinema studies."

In her analysis, Voci develops the simple but richly evocative concept of "lightness": a marker of these small screen realities' minimal "production costs, distribution ambitions, economic impact, limited audiences, quick and volatile circulation, and resistance to being framed into and validated by either market, art or political discourses" (Voci 2010, xx). For Voci, the "lightness" of these unpopular videos also needs to be understood through their desire to reclaim the ("insub-stantial") personal over the ("weighty") collective, and to share with the interested viewer highly personalized but deeply suggestive and luminous views of the world.

Similarly, analyzing the innovations of low-res cell phone cameras among the "information-have-less" in contemporary Hong Kong, the photographer and new media artist Helen Grace argues that such images should be understood as products of *mouh liuh*—the Cantonese idiom for "a sense of wandering, doing nothing, in between more important events, a state of being without consequence" (Grace 2014, 2). Produced in a general state of distraction, boredom, and leisure, these "useless" images generate "ephemeral value. . .that has no economic function, producing a contradiction at the heart of all market value" (Grace 2014, 4). Grace also suggests that, unlike images that can be commoditized, mundane cell phone images (of people, landscapes, animals etc.) that may or may not be uploaded need to be read less in terms of their content and more in terms of

> the *act* of production—or the act of "capture"—as a register of *affective* engagement in a moment of *expressiveness*, having deep local significance but which subsequently fails to be

communicative, beyond the instant of production, for anyone other than those who have been involved.

(Grace 2014, 32)

In other words, as viewers, what we can learn to value in these ephemeral images are embodied affects that cannot be re-presented and that may ultimately become unavailable. However, insofar as these images offer us snatches of the everyday in Hong Kong, they embody a kind of "particulate vision" that is antithetical to the imperial, homogenizing images of national life and culture produced by the Chinese government and nationalist propaganda (Grace 2014, 132).

Voci's and Grace's observations on these ubiquitous but marginalized acts of digital image production and circulation can be fruitfully extended to the cell phone videos included in *From Gulf*. Like the tens of thousands of cell phone images taken in China and Hong Kong every day, the sailors' videos are both "light" and a product of some kind of *mouh liuh* (albeit forced sometimes) while their producers and consumers are at sea, waiting to reach their destination. These videos are also not mainstream commodities in that they circulate only among the sailors and their boats. As Anand and Sukumaran's comments make clear, these videos are shared via Bluetooth and frequently deleted at sea, cannot be found on YouTube, and do not fall into the category of "popular" videos that are monetized on the basis of the number of "hits" on particular websites. CAMP's inclusion of these videos in *From Gulf* therefore allows us to catch a glimpse of a *local* network of the sailors that cannot be assimilated into the world of high-speed Internet, instant Facebook posts, Instagram photos, or even fleeting Snapchat images. This is a social public in which the unpredictable sea route, the boat, its varying cargo, low-end mobile phones, and the sailors themselves are all actors that trace and maintain the wireless, contingent, and continuously shifting network.

By the same logic, it becomes difficult to describe the locality of these cell phone videos made by the Indian sailors in terms of new media practices "in" India or Asia. For one thing, as we already mentioned, these videos stand out because of a particularly destabilizing effect created by the disjunction between the sound and the image. The songs chosen by the sailors—often taking the place of ambient sound and evoking Bollywood romances, melodramatic Hindi cinema, religious devotion, and more generally "South Asian" music—are literally *out of place* since they have no immediate logical connection with the images recorded at sea. (For instance, we are not told why the video of a capsized boat shot in an unknown location is matched to a Hindi love song; or why another video following dolphins under water in another unknown location is tied to a song about missing loved ones.)

At the same time, following Voci's and Grace's arguments, and within the larger context of the shooting and sharing of what is utterly prosaic and personal, these videos have a profoundly sensuous and aesthetic quality. The disjunction between the sound and the image, in that sense, is also the *connection* between them, offering viewers traces of those moments that produced the affective, idiosyncratic coupling between the recording of a contingent event at sea and a vernacular song originating hundreds, and sometimes thousands, of miles away. The fact that these videos are passed from boat to boat also suggests that these subjective image/song couplings acquire certain communal significance for some of these sailors. Lastly, these digitally fostered associations among the boats, nameless locations, and Bollywood songs mark the unexpected forms of physical proximity among the various actors that characterize (CAMP's representation of) pirate modernity: "Goats crowd the inside of boats, charcoal catches fire. Ethiopian discotheques, sinkings off Oman, and boardings by the US navy are all recorded on the sailors' cellphones. Even if the goods are all Chinese, one state 'feels' another" (CAMP 2013). The "particulate vision" and "lightness" represented by these videos therefore urge us to reconsider the local not in terms of rigid geographic regions and boundaries but rather in terms of fragmentary networks that are quotidian yet accidental, culturally and socially complex yet not permanently bound. The videos may be produced by Gujarati sailors. The conditions of their production, however, bring to the fore a quality of the local that is not exactly place-bound.

Finally, despite the parallels between CAMP's, Voci's, and Grace's reflections on ephemeral cell phone videos, we should note that *From Gulf* emphasizes not so much the *ubiquity* of new media technologies as the *collaboration* between human actants who do not usually participate in proximate networks—media-makers based in metropolitan Mumbai and sailors from Kutch who spend nine months at sea. By juxtaposing low-res and high-res images in the video, the editors do not gloss over but rather draw our attention to the differences between the technological (and socio-economic) infrastructures inhabited by the networking actors. Simultaneously, the various acts of collaboration—giving cameras to the sailors, incorporating music videos that precede the production of *From Gulf*, and, importantly, inviting one of the sailors to be a co-editor of the final piece (Zhou and Anand 2014)—prompt us to move away from a celebration of (imposed) ubiquitous access and to focus instead on endeavors to *share and democratize access*, however briefly or intermittently. Such a gesture of partnership and self-divestiture, we submit, is politically and ethically urgent in the age of biometrically captured identities and a pervasive neo-liberal logic of competitive individualism promoted by social media.

Notes

1 For an anthropological critique of this distinction, see Hollan (1992). For a discussion of the relationship between mass media and the rise of individualism under neoliberalism in China, see Rofel (2007).
2 In September 2013, the Supreme Court passed an interim order stating that *Aadhaar* cannot be regarded mandatory for essential government services. And in March 2014, the Court directed the central government not to share biometric data with any private agency without the authorization of the card holder.

References

Akiyoshi, M. and Ono, H. (2008) 'The Diffusion of Mobile Internet in Japan', *Information Society*, vol. 24: 292–303.
Anand, S. and Sukumaran, A. (2012) 'CAMP: The Boat Modes', in *Universes in Universe*. Available at: http://universes-in-universe.org/eng/magazine/articles/2012/camp_documenta (Accessed on July 11, 2014).
CAMP (2013) *CAMP: A Portfolio of Selected Work* (unpaginated). Available at: www.experimenter.in/web/artists/camp/folio.pdf (Accessed on August 5, 2014).
Cartier, C., Castells, M., and Linchuan Qiu, J. (2005) 'The Information-Have-Less: Inequality, Mobility, and Translocal Networks in Chinese Cities', *Studies in Comparative International Development*, 40(2): 9–34.
Centre for the Study of Culture and Society (2013) 'Field Visits'. In Ashish Rajadhyaksha (ed.) *In the Wake of Aadhaar: Digital Ecosystem of Governance in India*, Bangalore: Centre for the Study of Culture & Society: 198–371.
Chaganti, S. (2013) 'The Measure of a Number', in Ashish Rajadhyaksha (ed.) *In the Wake of Aadhaar: Digital Ecosystem of Governance in India*, Bangalore: Centre for the Study of Culture & Society: 26–43.
Choi, J. H.-J. (2007) 'Approaching the Mobile Culture of East Asia', *M/C Journal: A Journal of Media and Culture*, 10 (1). Available at: journal.media-culture.org.au/0703/01-choi.php (Accessed on May 25, 2014).
Galbraith, P. W. (2010) 'Akihabara: Conditioning a Public "Otaku" Image', *Mechademia*, 5: 210–230.
Galbraith, P. W. and Lamarre, T. (2010) 'Otakulogy: A Dialogue', *Mechademia*, 5: 360–374.
Grace, H. (2014) *Culture, Aesthetics and Affect in Ubiquitous Media: The Prosaic Image*, Oxford and New York: Routledge.

Graham, S. (1998) 'The End of Geography or the Explosion of Space?: Conceptualizing Space, Place and Information Technology'. In P. K. Nayar (ed.) (2010) *The New Media and Cybercultures Anthology*, Sussex: Wiley-Blackwell: 90–108.

Hjorth, L. and Arnold, M. (2013) *Online@AsiaPacific: Mobile, Social and Locative Media in the AsiaPacific*, Oxford and New York: Routledge.

Hollan, D. (1992) 'Cross-Cultural Differences in the Self', *Journal of Anthropological Research*, 48 (4): 283–300.

Indian Digital Review Staff (2013) 'India has 554.8 mn mobile users; 143.2 mn Internet users: Study', *Indian Digital Review*. Available at: http://www.indiadigitalreview.com/news/india-has-5548-mn-mobile-users-1432-mn-internet-users-study/14350 (Accessed on July 11, 2014).

ITU Press Release (2014) 'ITU Releases 2014 ICT Figures'. Available at: http://www.itu.int/net/pressoffice/press_releases/2014/23.aspx#.U6rT9rFBl0y (Accessed on May 25, 2014).

ITU Statistics on ICT (2014) Available at: http://www.itu.int/en/ITU-D/Statistics/Pages/stat/default.aspx (Accessed on July 11, 2014).

Katz, J. E. and Aakhus, M. A. (2003) 'Making Meaning of Mobiles: A Theory of *Apparatgeist*'. In P. K. Nayar (ed.) (2010) *The New Media and Cybercultures Anthology*, Sussex: Wiley-Blackwell: 65–76.

Latour, B. (1996) 'On Actor-Network Theory: A Few Clarifications Plus More Than a Few Complications', *Soziale Welt*, vol. 47: 369-381.

Mitchell, W. (2003) 'Post-Sedentary Space'. In P. K. Nayar (ed.) (2010) *The New Media and Cybercultures Anthology*, Sussex: Wiley-Blackwell: 79–89.

Morley, D. and Roberts, K. (1992) 'Techno-Orientalism: Futures, Foreigners, and Phobias', *New Formations*, 16: 136–156.

Munro, R. (2009) 'Actor-Network Theory'. In S. Clegg and M. Haugaard (eds) *The Sage Handbook of Power*, London: Sage Publications: 125–139.

Murakami, T. (2001) 'Impotence Culture: Anime'. In J. Fleming (ed.) *My Reality: Contemporary Art and the Culture of Japanese Animation*, Iowa: Des Moines Art Centre: 58–66.

Rajadhyaksha, A. (2013) 'Digital Delivery of Services: The Indian Landscape'. In A. Rajadhyaksha (ed.) *In the Wake of Aadhaar*, Bangalore: Centre for the Study of Culture & Society: vii–l.

Rao, M. and Mendoza, L. (eds) (2005) *Asia Unplugged: The Wireless and Mobile Media Boom in the Asia-Pacific*, New Delhi and London: Response Books.

Rofel, L. (2007) *Desiring China: Experiments in Neoliberalism, Sexuality, and Public Culture*, Durham, NC: Duke University Press.

Staple, G. C. and Dixon, H. (1992) 'Telegeography: Mapping the New World Order', *Whole Earth Review*: 124–125.

Sundaram, R. (2010) *Pirate Modernity: Delhi's Media Urbanism*, Oxford: Oxford University Press.

Tewari, R. (2014) 'Aadhaar, DBT get a Lifeline, Modi to retain, push UPA schemes', *Indian Express* July 2007. Available at: http://indianexpress.com/article/india/india-others/aadhaar-dbt-get-a-lifeline-modi-to-retain-push-upa-schemes/ (Accessed on July 11, 2014).

Tikku, A. (2014) 'Tug of War over Aadhaar Slowing Down Its Progress', *Hindustan Times* July 3. Available at: www.hindustantimes.com/india-news/tug-of-war-over-aadhaar-slowing-its-progress/article1-1236114.aspx (Accessed on July 11, 2014).

Ueno, T. (1996) 'Japanimation and Techno-Orientalism'. Available at: www.t0.or.at/ueno/japan.htm (Accessed on July 1, 2014).

Voci, P. (2010) *China on Video: Smaller-Screen Realities*, Oxford and New York: Routledge.

Zhou, X. and Anand, S. (2014) 'In Conversation: Shaina Anand with Xin Zhou', *The Brooklyn Rail: Critical Perspectives on Art, Politics, and Culture*, June 5. Available at: http://www.brooklynrail.org/2014/06/film/shaina-anand-with-xin-zhou (Accessed on July 23, 2014).

3

Migrant youth and new media in Asia

Lina Tao and Stephanie Hemelryk Donald

This chapter offers an overview of key studies and issues regarding new media practices amongst migrant youth in the Asia-Pacific region. Children and young people are usually the most enthusiastic users of new Information and Communication Technologies (ICTs), and young migrants in the Asia-Pacific region are no exception. However, their identities as border-transgressors in the throes of maturation make the role of new media especially salient in their lives. Researchers in the fields of migration, media and childhood/youth are mutually involved in understanding how the nexus of growing up in Asia today as migrants and outsiders *and* growing up in a digitally enabled environment, impacts the lives of today's generation of young people. Their work explains how, using various digital media with a local, translocal, or transnational reach, Asian young migrants speak to global youth culture, and share commonalities with migrants in other territories. Their new media practices are globally familiar but also fascinatingly uncommon due to socio-cultural specificity and uneven development in the region.

In order to discover the depth and range of research in this area, we have organized the chapter into the following key four research themes. First, there is the issue of the digital divide. Young migrants are very often less well-off and less settled than local children and youths. As such, their status transforms them into the information have-less class, i.e., users of inexpensive, low-tech, mobility-limited ICTs. Second, there is the possibility of empowerment through mobile and social media use. New media facilitate and mediate the self-representation of young people, including migrants. This challenges the dominant stigmatizing narrative of migrants used by other social groups in mainstream media. Third, perhaps as a result of the challenge noted above, there are negative attitudes and punitive actions towards young migrants' engagement in new media. Such processes of censure and disempowerment take place in a broader context where moral panics over Internet-related youth problems are rampant. Fourth, the gender dimension is significant. Mobile media and the migratory experience enable young women to explore gender identities and negotiate intimate relationships. This occurs in a wider and longstanding context where conventional social norms of femininity continue to regulate their behavior and speech.

Introduction

Asia has been a theatre of large-scale, sustained, and diversified population movement since the 1970s. Due to uneven regional development and historical international relations, different Asian countries and territories have undergone different processes of migration. The newly industrialized countries or territories in East and Southeast Asia, such as Japan, Hong Kong, Taiwan, South Korea and Singapore, have witnessed massive labor recruitment since the 1980s (Asis and Piper 2008, 426). Other high-performing economies, including Malaysia and Thailand, have also drawn workers from the less developed countries in the region: Malaysia is a traditional source country of workers for Singapore; Thai workers take Taiwan as one of their major destinations; the Philippines represents the world's largest labor exporting country into and beyond the region; South Koreans have frequently moved across their immediate border to work and live in Japan during the post-colonial era; Australia regards India as the most important source of ICT workers; and Hong Kong has seen an influx of migrants from the mainland of China in the first decade of the twenty-first century (ibid; Ryang 2002, 895; Voigt-Graf and Khoo 2004,144; Wong 2008, 53).

Inside the mainland of China, transnational migration has been eclipsed by the much larger and more pressing issue of rural-to-urban migration, presently estimated at 260 million (China National Bureau of Statistics 2013). While intensive labor migration is the key characteristic of the Asia-Pacific region, various other types of population movement have emerged, such as international marriage migration, education migration, return migration, and even unauthorized migration. Overall, the diversified and complicated migration patterns indicate the increasing integration of regional labor markets and the burgeoning—albeit uneven and unstable—socioeconomic developments in Asia-Pacific (Asis and Piper 2008, 424).

The adoption of new media in the region is no less complicated and uneven than that of the population movement. In more developed countries such as Australia, Singapore, Japan and South Korea, the Internet has penetrated society, and mobile phones have become part of people's everyday life (Goggin 2010, 120; Lim 2010, 43; Matsuda 2010, 31; Yoon 2010, 108). However, the inequality of access to ICTs is also substantial in these countries, and the concept of the digital divide has dominated many analytical accounts, policy debates, and planning documents (Qiu et al. 2009, 1; also see Chapter 8 by Sun and Qiu in this book). When it comes to less developed countries in the region, such as China and India, the dichotomy between the information haves and the information have-nots is more prominent. Although India's ICT industry is burgeoning and has helped the country successfully carve out a niche in the global economy, the digital divide is notable: the rate of access to the Internet for the urban households is ten times that for rural ones (Mo, Swinnen, Zhang, Yi, Qu, Boswell and Rozelle 2013, 14). China hosts the world's largest national population of mobile phone users, and its Internet user population has overtaken that of the United States to become the largest in the world by 2008 (Qiu et al. 2009, 2). However, Internet penetration is four times higher in China's urban areas than in rural areas, and computer ownership is 14 times higher for urban children than the rural children (Mo et al. 2013, 14).

Both India and China have seen the formation of a new information class, i.e., the information have-less, who populate the vast gray area between the information haves and have-nots (Cartier, Castells and Qiu 2005, 9; Donner 2009, 93). Numerous rural-to-urban migrants, laid-off workers and small business owners in China tend to use inexpensive, low-end and mobility-limited ICT services, such as low-priced bandit-phones, unlicensed Internet cafés, or low-cost text messaging on the handset (Cartier et al. 2005, 14).

The information have-less who enjoy "immobile mobility"

Unequal access to the ICTs is substantial in Asia as well as other regions, but the binary model of the information-haves and have-nots, which remains the case in Western postindustrial societies, fails to address the particularities of digital divide in a few rapidly developing Asian countries (Qiu et al. 2009, 7). In particular, young rural-to-urban migrant workers in China have demonstrated some unique characteristics in their new media use, although these migrant youngsters are no different from their global peers in regard to enthusiasm towards new media.

In practice they have become heavy users of inexpensive and low-end ICTs: they pursue bandit-phones which copy or adapt brand originals and are sold at vastly decreased prices, such as Ciphone or Hiphone, instead of the more sophisticated and more expensive iPhone; they linger in unlicensed, smoky Internet cafés whose settings are not comparable to the comfortable home base enjoyed by the established urban population; they rely heavily on short message services and shun the more expensive voice call (Donald 2010). Although ICTs are typically associated with mobility and promise to keep everyone connected anytime anywhere, these low-end technologies and services offer more limited mobility with low functional choice, often constrained in a particular time and space (Cartier et al. 2005, 14).

Such low-cost and low-end ICTs nonetheless perform critical informational functions for young migrants. As Cara Wallis (2010, 58) aptly terms it, new media provide China's young migrant workers with "immobile mobility." Young rural-to-urban migrants are primarily employed in manual labor and service work, facing severe constraints on their control of space, time and mobility. They usually live 'isolated lives' due to their long work schedules, their socio-economic status as underclass outsiders, and the tendency for their lives to revolve around a very small geographic area (Wallis 2010, 61). It is common for them to work 10–14 hours a day, live with co-workers in tiny dorms; and many rarely venture beyond the few blocks where they live and work. Such "immobility" indicates that even although young rural migrants have moved to cities in seek of employment, their migration does not necessarily entail free-flowing physical mobility.

Whilst their autonomy in controlling the spatial arrangement of their existence is highly constrained by poverty and prejudice (Donald 2010, 4), the virtual mobility offered by mobile phones or the Internet enables them to imagine new identities, to explore modes of expression, and to maintain relationships despite physical distance. The notion "immobile mobility" refers to a socio-techno mode of being there virtually rather than physically. It acknowledges the ongoing spatial confinement of the migrant despite their great movement across geographical distance in the pursuit of work. It stresses the particular significance of new media for a socially and economically marginalized group, that is, new media function as a socio-techno means for China's young rural migrant workers to transcend myriad barriers of time, space, and class in the cities.

Professional use of innovative brand mobile phones is indicative of social wealth and higher-class status, so young migrant workers' use of bandit mobile phones or illegal Internet cafés may articulate rebellion against exclusion and marginalization (Donald 2010, 5). Their boundary-jumping forms of digital access signal a determination to be included, and a desire to participate in an informational society. Most rural-to-urban migrant youth in China have been driven to migrate by extreme financial need, expecting that the movement will entail an upward social mobility. However, being officially identified as rural residents, they are consistently denied access to the social welfare services in the cities, and are forced to live as second-class citizens (Goodburn 2009, 502).

Having been socially and economically marginalized, rural-to-urban migrants are further disadvantaged by constrained access to the ICTs and by their own digital competence, each problem reinforcing the other. While China is promoting the development of information technology for the national economy, the technologies and practices of rural-to-urban migrants are not reliably supported by the state. Nonetheless, young migrants find ways of making the ICTs to work to partially replace absent structures of support (Donald 2010, 10; Cartier et al. 2005, 10). As a social group located on the peripheries of China's success, they occupy spaces and pursue modes of access to the larger worlds of the Internet and other mobile communication technologies.

One distinctive feature of ICTs in Asia is that they are a kind of technological boundary jumper—providing a platform of accelerated development for the individual and the group, counteracting backwardness, boosting a sense of modernization and catching up with the West. Ideologically, ICTs are regarded as something good and necessary, particularly by nation states that are experiencing rapid urbanization and industrialization. Technology is constructed as a key strategic means for South Korea's "catch-up," and China's "linking tracks with the world" (Wallis 2013, 346; Choi 2010, 88). For individuals, it has become a means of personal transformation. Young migrants from underdeveloped villages tend to regard technology as a solution to their subjective problems, which may turn around their destiny as poor, un-modern, and low-quality (*di suzhi*) citizens (Wallis 2013, 349).

Yet, individual desires may contradict the state's development strategies, and are then ruthlessly cut then curtailed. In some cases, young and poor rural residents in China have been deliberately recruited and trained in computer skills, and then placed in data input companies, serving as low-tech laboring subjects with a low wage and little job security (Wallis 2013). They are merely allowed to use the computer for data input and are prohibited from accessing the Internet. These young migrants' desire for technological competence as a means for continuous self-improvement and social upward mobility (a desire which has been largely ignited by a national discourse of development, and media promotion) is eventually suppressed for the sake of the state's overall economic aims and the needs of the agents of informational capitalism.

The diffusion of ICTs has thereby contributed to extreme digital inequality in rapidly urbanizing and industrializing countries, transforming young migrant workers into either low-end, unreliable consumers or low-tech, exploitative laborers. In other words, a socio-economic underclass has now been transformed into a disadvantaged information class in the networked world. The rise of low-end ICTs has also been found in another fast developing Asian country, namely, India. As Jonathan Donner (2009) states, low-cost Short Message Service (SMS) is ubiquitous among small and informal business owners in urban India, but their use of many other functions on the mobile phone is very limited. The longterm connections between low-end ICTs and India's sizeable rural-to-urban migrants are yet to be investigated.

Compared to internal migrants, India's transnational ICT workers have received more research attention. Voigt-Graf and Khoo (2004, 148) find that two thirds of Indian temporary business arrivals in Australia work in the ICT industry; and that Indian ICT workers in Australia are very young, with over 60 percent aged 25 to 29. The emigration of Indian ICT workers is inextricably linked to the burgeoning ICT industry in India, particularly in the southern state of Karnataka. Nowadays Australia sees India as the most important source of ICT workers. With some caveats followed by attacks on Indian students and taxi drivers in 2010–2011, Australia is generally perceived by Indians as a clean country with a healthy environment. The shared history as Commonwealth nations provides a shared historical foundation and sense of continuity that supports migration. That is to say, the inequality of access to ICTs can foster the formation of low-end, low-tech information class, in which young migrants from underdeveloped areas often appear as a major force; but that ICTs may also contribute to skilled migration, in which young migrants act as well-regarded technology specialists. The contrast between this migration phenomenon and the low technological mobility recorded by Wallis in China, where aspirations may end in lifelong data entry, is worth further research.

Migrant youth self-representation versus the dominant stereotypes created by other social groups

New media have provided fundamental new opportunities for Asian youth to explore the world and negotiate their identities—much like rock music, travel and backpacking defined the 1950s–1970s for European and American school-leavers. This is especially meaningful for migrant youth, who have stepped across the borders that defined their geographical and social identities and consequently have become "Other" (Solinger 1999, 3). Previous studies find that the Internet fulfills three principal functions for young migrants:

1   A source of information about the new society, the homeland and various cultures;
2   A platform for online contacts with families and friends—both those left behind in the homeland and those in the new settlement context;
3   A tool for preserving one's native language (or dialect) and improving host language (or dialect) skills.

(Elias 2013, 339)

The Internet, together with mobile phones and other forms of mobile communication technology, enables young migrants to establish and maintain a "translocal network" (Cartier et al. 2005, 14). This network has a translocal reach and reflects migrants' attachments to multiple places resulting from their migratory life paths. In other words, migrants' mobility now has an informational dimension.

In countries with a long immigration history, such as Australia, digital media are increasingly recognized as an important resource for immigrant youth engagement. Digital media facilitate local expressions of identity and belonging (Gifford and Wilding 2013). One would add that this facilitation is local to the user but is enabled and meaningful because of the wide geo-spatial reach of the technology and communicative sphere that it creates. Even if a young person's identity (say on QQ) is only actually visible to 100–500 associates, the possibility that many more will know and recognize their efforts at self-expression brings depth to the identity project. More prosaically, digital literacy and opportunities are recommended as an essential component of youth settlement policies and services.

For young migrants from a disadvantaged socioeconomic background, such as young refugees, there is a particularly essential need to solve problems, support one another and seek a sense of belonging with the assistance of ICTs. In reality, the mobile phone has become a technology of everyday life for most refugee youth in Australia, and, when given the opportunity to access the Internet, they immediately become users of social media such as MySpace and Facebook in order to communicate with friends in their new settlement context as well as staying connected to those overseas (ibid.). For example, the films and photographs produced by Karen or Burmese youth in Australia illustrate how ICTs can open up possibilities for refugee youngsters to exercise different identities and explore different ways of "becoming." In some photos and clips, Karen youngsters present themselves in the center of the narrative, making fun on the iconic Australian beach while singing Karen songs. Another video clip shows Karen boys playing guitars, drinking beers, singing about love and love lost. This self-representation speaks to the trials of being young, refers to the global youth culture, and undermines the dominant trauma narrative about refugees (ibid.).

Such self-representation, or user-generated and distributed content, takes place in a context where the voice of migrant children and adolescents has long been neglected. Children and young people are often central actors in the process of migration, yet they are absent for the most part in the public and political debates (de Block and Buckingham 2007, ix). On the few occasions when they become visible, migrant children/youth tend to be typecast as either vulnerable victims or potential criminals. This stigmatization is located in a broader social context where children's subjectivity is overwhelmingly overlooked, as if they are unable to think, act, or speak in their own right (de Block and Buckingham 2007, 36). To give an example, a consistent discursive pattern has been perpetuated by the Chinese press: millions of rural migrant children are reduced to a few simplistic characteristics, namely, poor, passive, and school-aged (Luo 2011). Moreover, China's influential Twitter-like micro-blogging, which is renowned for neoliberal comments and diversified opinions, tends to reinforce the existing stereotypes against rural migrant children. Here new media come to serve as a new channel for messages of prejudice and discrimination against a marginalized social group (Tao 2014).

However, migrant children and youngsters have managed to appropriate new media to speak in their own terms. The emerging subculture "Shamate" in China is one of the many cases demonstrating migrant youth engagement in self-representation. "Shamate" is a virtual and informal group, consisting of Chinese rural-to-urban migrants who are in their late teens or early 20s (Lu 2013). They are usually distinguished by a spiky hairstyle, some body piercing, extremely heavy makeup, and cool-looking clothes from a street market. They use off-brand cell phones and inexpensive Internet cafés to take unconventional selfies, distribute their photos and comments, and interact with their mates online. The group is named after a deliberately nonsensical translation of the English word "smart," given that most "Shamate" members lack tertiary education and work low-paying jobs in the cities; a barber, security guard, deliveryman, or waitress (ibid.). While there is much to reflect on with regard to the socio-cultural meanings of the phenomenon, "Shamate" showcases how new media provide a space for migrant youth to represent themselves and have their own voices heard. This migrant-generated content often challenges the dominant stereotyping discourse which permeates the media platforms used by other population groups.

The perceived Internet-related youth problems and punitive approaches

Traditionally, children are expected to accommodate to adult cultural norms; but with new media, they are celebrated for their pioneering exploration (Livingstone 2013). Almost uniquely in relation to the Internet, children's knowledge is widely recognized as being more valuable than that of adults. That is to say, traditional inter-generational power relations seem to be challenged alongside the permeation of new media. In the digital world, the grandchild teaches the grandparent to Skype, the pupil challenges the teacher's knowledge, and even commerce tries to get down with the kids (ibid.). The largely unanticipated growth of peer-to-peer culture, user-generated content, social networking and remix culture, is stamping a youthful imprint on cultural domains hitherto dominated by adults.

At the same time, links have been drawn between child/adolescent problems and their Internet use. There are increasing moral panics about youth crimes that are mediated and facilitated by new media, such as violence, peer bully, pornography, or sexual assault (Spry 2010; Goggin 2010).

Digital media are perceived as a suspicious devil that may threaten young people's own or others' safety and wellbeing. In addition to motivating criminal behavior, youngsters' use of mobile media is also perceived to threaten culture by encouraging declines in standards of literacy, and a rise in poor communication skills, classroom disruption and cheating. As Damien Spry's (2010, 16) comparative study of Japan and Australia finds, attitudes towards children's media practices are often based on adult anxieties about putting children at risk, on adult aspirations for a new "Net Generation" of media-savvy creative types, or on the agendas of children's media producers who are driven by commercial imperatives. The political and public discourse on children/youth media use is overwhelmingly adult-centered, indicating a repressive regime of adult consensus. In the name of "protection," legislation by adults tends to control presumed media use excess by children and youngsters, rather than facilitate their use (Donald 2010, 9).

Among migrant families, children tend to adopt the new language and culture more rapidly than adults, which is often facilitated by new media, and parents tend to rely on their children's brokering for practical information about the new surroundings (de Block and Buckingham 2007, 336–338). However, young migrants' heavy use of new media is also vulnerable and easily stigmatized. Migrant youth's rapid adoption of new media and new surroundings is often seen as a potential factor in widening intergenerational cultural gaps, weakening parental authority and damaging family cohesion (ibid.). In some cases, young migrants' media use is even criminalized, as they have chosen low-priced copycat phones or unsupervised Internet cafés. China's Party-state once launched a four-month crackdown on unlicensed Internet cafés, with an especial focus on areas where young rural migrants are clustered (Donald 2010, 4). This action has drawn causal links between crime, migrant youth and the Internet, and has criminalized the notion of access to digital competency among young poor migrants. It reflects a punitive approach to managing contemporary youth culture and controlling population mobility.

Also, as discussed previously, the "Shamate" photos and films—i.e., young rural migrants' unconventional self-representation—have been ruthlessly mocked and criticized by the majority social groups. Many "Shamate" members have to retreat from public open social media, and turn to more private, stranger-blocked online spaces (Baidu baike 2008). A disadvantaged social group becomes more vulnerable due to the punitive attitudes and actions by local government and co-citizens. Migrant youth are often discouraged, if not excluded, from the possibility of self-taught digital literacy. Consequently, they are deprived of areas of competency which might allow access to even minimal social, political and cultural power.

The dimension of gender

One feature that comes to characterize labor migration in Asia is women's significant share in the process. In some countries, the feminization of migration has been notable. For example, women in the Philippines, Indonesia and Sri Lanka outnumber men among those legally deployed every year; 1:1 female and male Filipinos are equally likely to emigrate to other countries or territories (Asis and Piper 2008, 427). Female migration in Asia has thus become a main research topic, with a particular focus on women working as domestic workers (Asis and Piper 2008, 431). The peer-reviewed journal, *Asia Pacific Migration Journal,* which launched in 1992, has devoted several special issues to migrant women. In regard to the ICT industry, young male professionals tend to dominate the migration process, with females overwhelmingly appearing as secondary applicants for entrance to another country (Voigt-Graf and Khoo 2004, 148).

In recent years, young Asian women's international marriage has attracted increasing research attention, given that the numbers and the share of international marriages have been growing in Japan, Taiwan, and South Korea, etc. (see, for example, Takeda 2013; Bélanger, Lee and Wang

2010; Kim and Kim 2013). ICTs not only serve as a virtual intermediary for women to engage in a transnational relationship, but also continues to empower them after they successfully enter into marriage. For instance, Japanese women who emigrated to Australia following an international marriage often use web blogging to discuss the husband–wife relationship, daily childrearing experience, social exclusion and racial prejudice (Takeda 2013, 420). Such individual experiences are barely available in the conventional media, but online blogs allow the transnational wives to express themselves relatively freely.

Population movement, together with mobile communication technology, enables Asia's young women to explore gendered identities and negotiate their positions in the mesh of patriarchy. For China's young rural-to-urban migrant women, mobile phones offer them a new space to shape their gender identities and forge intimate relationships. They typically face "marriage dilemma" due to harsh work conditions and ubiquitous social exclusion (Wallis 2010). While mobile phones and the Internet are transforming the way in which people set up intimate relationships, such changes can be dramatic and turn into a significant life event for young rural migrant women. The stream of text messages and voice calls turns out to be crucial for these girls to get to know their (potential) partners, when face-to-face meetings are difficult or unaffordable (ibid.). Similar to the case of international marriage, technology here serves as the intermediary in rural migrant women's dating and marriage.

Migration may entail individual emancipation from patriarchal conditions, and ICTs may facilitate women's exploration of gender identity; but conventional socio-cultural norms that rule over gender differences can be perpetuated at the same time. This indicates the blending of technology and social culture, the mingling of traditional patriarchal norms and technological changes. As Wallis (2010, 62) finds in her fieldwork, many young migrant women in China believe that it is "inappropriate" or "unacceptable" for them to send out erotic messages, although it is "fine" for them to read it. Social norms of femininity continue to regulate their speech and behavior. While new communication technologies and migratory experiences have facilitated women to explore their identities and negotiate gendered relationships, traditional norms of power continue to regulate their speech and behavior.

Conclusion

In this chapter we have argued that Asian youth migratory experience and their fluid adult-becoming identity add multiple layers to their new media practices. In Asian countries that are undergoing rapid urbanization and industrialization, young migrants have typically moved from underdeveloped areas to burgeoning cities and developed states. In the first place, their migration has been driven by extreme financial need and by aspiration to upward socioeconomic mobility. However, they are often caught up in the inequality of information access in the host cities/ states, and are transformed into the informational underclass, i.e., users of inexpensive, low-end and low-tech ICTs. While global high-technology ICTs promise to keep everyone connected anytime anywhere, low-end technology and services offer more limited mobility with low functional choice, often constrained in a particular time and space. Nonetheless, migrant youth in Asia demonstrate zeal in appropriating new media and a desire to take part in an expressive informational society.

Existing migration and media studies have marked out the particular significance and especial meaning of new media for young migrant users. ICTs have provided them with a space to express their own views and concerns in their own terms. Such user-generated content often challenges, either intentionally or unintentionally, the dominant stigmatizing narrative which permeates the media used by other social groups. In other words, migrant children and youngsters, who used to be rendered invisible in the public discourse, are now empowered by ICTs to get their own voices heard if only by one another. Migrant youth's own expression via digital media is increasingly valued by migration/settlement policy-makers and practitioners in the field. Digital literacy and associated opportunities are gradually being recognized as an important component of youth settlement policies and services.

Despite the possible empowerment of migrant youth by new media, there are negative attitudes and punitive actions towards their media use. Young migrants' voices via new media continue to be overlooked or ignored in the cacophony of narratives on the Internet. Their own expression via new media can be ruthlessly mocked and be labeled as "problematic" by the majority social groups. This is illuminated by the unfavorable situation of Chinese "Shamate," i.e., the State's young and unruly rural-to-urban migrants. In some other cases, young migrants' engagement in new media has been stigmatized or even criminalized by local governors and citizens. Such processes of censure and disempowerment, led by the mainstream non-migrant social actors, are likely to deprive migrant youth of digital competency, rendering a socially and economically disadvantaged group more vulnerable.

Given women's notable share in the Asia-Pacific population movement, we have also examined the gender dimension in issues around youth, migration and new media. Again, ICTs are recognized as a tool empowering young migrant women in Asia. This situation is no different to that of global migrants. Mobile communication technologies have facilitated young female migrants to maintain translocal connections and express their own views which are rarely available in conventional media. More importantly, the new ICTs serve as an intermediary for young migrant women to explore gendered identities and forge intimate relationships. The particular significance of this has been spelled out considering their "border transgressor" status and dominant patriarchal social norms. Population migration may entail women's individual emancipation, and mobile communication technologies may enable them to negotiate gendered relationships and reclaim their positions in the mesh of patriarchy. Nonetheless, it should be noted that conventional socio-cultural norms of femininity continue to be perpetuated in the digital era, regulating young migrant women's expression and behavior. It implies the blending of technology and social culture with the fusion of conventional patriarchal norms and rapidly changing media.

References

Asis, M. and Piper, N. (2008) 'Researching international labor migration in Asia', *The Sociological Quarterly* 49(3): 423–444.

Baidu baike (Baidu Encyclopedia) (2008) *Shamate*. Available at: http://baike.baidu.com/view/1751808.htm (Accessed on July 2, 2014).

Bélanger, D., Lee, H.K. and Wang, H.Z. (2010) 'Ethnic diversity and statistics in East Asia: "Foreign brides" surveys in Taiwan and South Korea', *Ethnic and Racial Studies* 33(6): 1108–1130.

Cartier, C., Castells, M. and Qiu, J.L. (2005) 'The information have-less: Inequality, mobility, and translocal networks in Chinese cities', *Studies in Comparative International Development* 40(2): 9–34.

China National Bureau of Statistics (2013) *2012 nian quanguo nongmingong jiance diaocha baogao (The 2012 survey report of the state's peasant-turned workers)*. Available at: www.stats.gov.cn/tjsj/zxfb/201305/t20130527_12978.html (Accessed on July 2, 2014).

Choi, J.H.J. (2010) 'The city, self and connections: "transyouth" and urban social networking in Seoul'. In S.H. Donald, T.D. Anderson and D. Spry (eds) *Youth, society and mobile media in Asia*, New York: Routledge: 88–107.

de Block, L. and Buckingham, D. (2007) *Global children, global media: Migration, media and childhood*, New York: Palgrave Macmillan.

Donald, S.H. (2010) 'Why mobility matters: young people and media competency in the Asia-Pacific'. In S.H. Donald, T.D. Anderson and D. Spry (eds) *Youth, society and mobile media in Asia*, New York: Routledge: 3–12.

Donner, J. (2009) 'Mobile media on low-cost handsets: The resiliency of text messaging among small enterprises in India (and beyond)', *Mobile technologies: From telecommunications to media*: 93–104.

Elias, N. (2013) 'Immigrant children and media'. In Dafna Lemish (ed.) *The Routledge international handbook of children, adolescents and media*, New York: Routledge: 336–343.

Gifford, S.M., and Wilding, R. (2013) 'Digital escapes? ICTs, settlement and belonging among Karen youth in Melbourne, Australia', *Journal of Refugee Studies* 26(4): 558–575.

Goggin, G. (2010) 'Official and unofficial mobile media in Australia: youth, panics, innovation'. In S.H. Donald, T.D. Anderson and D. Spry (eds) *Youth, society and mobile media in Asia*, New York: Routledge: 120–134.

Goodburn, C. (2009) 'Learning from migrant education: A case study of the schooling of rural migrant children in Beijing', *International Journal of Educational Development* 29(5): 495–504.

Kim, H.S. and Kim, H. S. (2013) 'Depression in non-Korean women residing in South Korea following marriage to Korean men', *Archives of Psychiatric Nursing* 27(3): 148–155.

Lim, S. (2010) '"Your phone makes you, you": exploring the youth script in teen magazine representations of mobile media'. In S.H. Donald, T.D. Anderson and D. Spry (eds) *Youth, society and mobile media in Asia*, New York: Routledge: 43–56.

Livingstone, S. (2013) 'Children's Internet culture: power, change and vulnerability in twenty-first century childhood'. In D. Lemish (ed.) *The Routledge international handbook of children, adolescents and media*, New York: Routledge: 111–119.

Lu, R. (2013) Vanity fail: Look past their funky threads and outlandish hairdos; China's alienated young migrants are here to stay. Available at: www.foreignpolicy.com/articles/2013/12/02/meet_chinas_shamate_un_hip (Accessed on July 2, 2014).

Luo, A. (2011) *Meiti zai nongmingong zinü baodao zhong de zuowei yu fansi (The reflection on the press coverage of internal migrant children)*. Available at: www.naradafoundation.org/sys/html/lm_27/2011-08-26/172929.htm (Accessed on July 2, 2014).

Matsuda, M. (2010) 'Japanese mobile youth in the 2000s'. In S.H. Donald, T.D. Anderson and D. Spry (eds) *Youth, society and mobile media in Asia*, New York: Routledge: 31–42.

Mo, D., Swinnen, J., Zhang, L., Yi, H., Qu, Q., Boswell, M. and Rozelle, S. (2013) 'Can one-to-one computing narrow the digital divide and the educational gap in China? The case of Beijing migrant schools', *world development* 46: 14–29.

Qiu, J. L., Castells, M., and Cartier, C. (2009) *Working-class network society: Communication technology and the information have-less in urban China*, Cambridge, MA: MIT Press.

Ryang, S. (2002) 'A long loop: transmigration of Korean women in Japan', *International Migration Review* 36(3): 894–911.

Solinger, D.J. (1999) *Contesting citizenship in urban China: Peasant migrants, the state, and the logic of the market*, Oakland, CA: University of California Press.

Spry, D. (2010) 'Angels and devils: youth mobile media politics, fear, hope and policy in Japan and Australia'. In S.H. Donald, T.D. Anderson and D. Spry (eds) *Youth, society and mobile media in Asia*, New York: Routledge: 15–30.

Sun, P.S. and Qiu, J.L. (2016) 'New media cultures of Chinese migrant workers'. In L. Hjorth and O. Khoo (eds) *The Routledge handbook of new media in Asia*, London: Routledge: 93–104.

Takeda, A. (2013) 'Weblog narratives of Japanese migrant women in Australia: Consequences of international mobility and migration', *International Journal of Intercultural Relations* 37(4): 415–421.

Tao, L. (2014) 'The representation of internal migrant children in China's micro-blogsphere', paper presented at the 12th China Internet Research Conference, Hong Kong.

Voigt-Graf, C. and Khoo, S.E. (2004) 'Temporary migration of Indian ICT workers to Australia', *Asian and Pacific Migration Journal* 13(2): 137–154.

Wallis, C. (2010) 'The traditional meets the technological: mobile navigations of desire and intimacy'. In S.H. Donald, T.D. Anderson and D. Spry (eds) *Youth, society and mobile media in Asia*, New York: Routledge: 57–69.

Wallis, C. (2013) 'Technology and/as governmentality: the production of young rural women as low-tech laboring subjects in China', *Communication and Critical/Cultural Studies* 10(4): 341–358.

Wong, P. (2008) 'Without friends I will be very lonely—Migrant children in Hong Kong'. In E. Alerby and J. Brown (eds) *Voices from the margins: School experiences of refugee, migrant and indigenous children*, Rotterdam: Sense Publishers: 53–70.

Yoon, K. (2010) 'The representation of mobile youth in the post-colonial techno-nation of Korea'. In S.H. Donald, T.D. Anderson and D. Spry (eds) *Youth, society and mobile media in Asia*, New York: Routledge: 108–119.

4

Neo-regionalism and neoliberal Asia

Leo T.S. Ching

Asian regionalism has been predominantly a Japanese-led discourse, strategy, and ideology throughout the region's modern/colonial history. Asianism's condition of possibility is inseparable from the history of Western and Japanese imperialism and colonialism. To be more precise, Japan's evocation of regional solidarity is a response to the real and perceived threat of Western aggression and the justification of its own empire-building in Asia. Any discussion of regionalism cannot escape the West-Japan-Asia triad (Ching 2009). The relative lack of Japanese discourse on Asian regionalism today suggests two possible interpretations: that the West is no longer a threat and that the balance of power has shifted in the region.[1]

In this chapter, I argue that two regional developments under global capitalism—the rise of China and the Korean Wave—have radically transformed the Japan-centric model of an imagined regional integration. How do we apprehend this shift from a unipolar to a multipolar geo-cultural formation in the region? How new is this new regionalism? What is its relationship to the old one that the new one is purported surpassing? What is "new" about it? How do we assess its contradictory tendencies—is it progressive or regressive?

Borrowing Etienne Balibar's notion of the "neo," I call this new modality of Asian imaginary "neo-regionalism" (1991).[2] "Neo-racism" is Balibar's term to describe the shift in European racism from that of biological heredity to insurmountable cultural differences since the 1970s, or what he calls, "racism without races" (Balibar and Wallerstein 1991, 21). Neo-regionalism suggests that the concept of regionalism, real or imagined, will remain a spatial fix to buttress the contradiction between the nation-state and global capitalism as I have argued elsewhere (Ching 2000). Neo-regionalism describes the fundamental break that ushered in new conceptualizations of regionalism in Asia no longer dominated by Japan but articulated by other Asian countries as well. More importantly, this neo-regionalism is generated by, and is in turn generating, the process of neoliberal capitalism in Asia that began in the late 1970s and accelerated after the Asian financial crisis in the late 1990s. It signifies the incorporation of the Chinese economy and South Korean popular culture into world economy and global cultural industry. Neo-regionalism is also concomitant with the process of "dewesternization" that renders "Asia" as an option among other models of development and consumption, but does not challenge capitalism's underpinning assumptions.[3] The cultural logic of neo-regionalism consequently alerts us to the increased sense of precarity under neoliberal capitalism, especially among the region's youth.

China's rise

The so-called rise of China has profound implications as the provocative title of a recent book by Martin Jacques, *When China Rules the World*, foretells. Also, as the not so subtle subtitle, *The End of the Western World and the Birth of a New Global Order*, asserts, the ascent of China coincides with the decline of the West, especially American hegemony. While the day when Mandarin Chinese becomes the lingua franca is still far off (although it boasts the largest number of speakers in the world), many economic pundits are predicting China overtaking the US as the biggest economy in the world by 2021. Chinese expansionism to Africa and Latin America only signify the growing outreach of Chinese capital around the world and its imperial ambition (French 2014). The underside (or its darker side) of the rise of China has generated not only uneven development, increased gap between rich and poor, and associated social malaise, but also anti-Chinese sentiments in economic competitors such as Japan, the US and the EU.[4] The rise of China globally and regionally can be grasped in the larger development of the history of capitalism, not as a linear unfolding of a predetermined universalism, but as repetition (Karatani 2014).

In explicating the "stages" of global capitalism throughout history, Karatani Kojin observes that the different stages of global capitalism arise as "changes in the nature of the union between capital and the state and that these moreover unfold not as a linear development but as a cyclical process" (Karatani 2014, 272). In order to understand the cyclical nature of the modern world system (capital and state), Karatani insists on the repetition particular to capitalism and the state. He classifies the world-historical capitalism into five stages: Mercantilism (1750–1810), Liberalism (1810–1870), Imperialism (1870–1930), Late Capitalism (1930–1990), and Neoliberalism (1990–present). Each stage of global capitalism has its corresponding Hegemonic State (Britain in the era of Liberalism and the US in the era of Late Capitalism), Economic Policy (Imperialistic, Liberalism, Imperialistic, Liberalism, and Imperialistic), Capital (Merchant, Industrial, Finance, State-monopoly, and Multinational), World Commodity (Textiles, Light industry, Heavy industry, Durable consumer goods, and Information), and State (Absolute Monarchy, Nation-state, Imperialism, Welfare state, and Regionalism) (273).

What is instructive in Karatani's schematic for the purpose of my discussion is his characterization of the present state formation (from 1990 to present) as that of Regionalism—the desire to form supranational state to counter other regionalisms without relinquishing the sovereignty of the nation-state. Just as the Welfare state was the dominant state-form under Late Capitalism (1930–1990), regionalism emerges as the dominant state formation under Neoliberalism (1990–present). And this banding together of several states is conducted precisely under the pressure of global capitalism, but regionalism does not mean the abolition of the modern state. As Karatani reminds us, however, this supranational state is nothing new as its precursors can be seen in the Third Reich envisioned by Germany and the Greater East Asia Co-prosperity Sphere planned by Japan in the 1930s (283). He sees the reemergence of this tendency in other parts of the world as well. Karatani writes:

> We also need to note the emergence of Empire in other regions. The former world empires that were situated on the periphery of the modern world system—China, India, the Islamic world, Russia, and so on—have begun to reemerge. In each region, because the nation-state

emerged from the splitting up of former world empires, there is a still-raw past that includes not only a shared identity as a civilization but also a history of fragmentation and antagonism. That each state has as a nation bracketed off these memories of the past and formed a community that significantly restricts its own sovereignty show how keenly they feel the pressure of contemporary global capitalism.

(Karatani 2014, 283)

Despite the decline of American hegemony and the historical repetition of a new hegemon to take its place, Karatani does not see a new hegemonic state emerge out of the struggle among the regional empires. Recognizing the inevitability that China and India will emerge as economic powers, he is nonetheless cautious about anointing one of them as the next hegemon. In fact, Karatani argues that the development of China and India harbors the possibility of bringing global capitalism to an end due to the depletion of natural resources and accelerating environmental destruction and the exhaustion of China and India's agrarian population or what Marx calls "the reserve army of labor" (284). Leaving aside Karatani's messianic prognosis, it is important to note that he sees the post-1990 era of neoliberalism as more imperialistic than liberal. Much like the 1870s, with the previously hegemonic power in decline and without a clear successor, other countries have entered into a fierce struggle to become the next hegemonic power. Just as in the 1870s the old world empires (the Russian, Qing, Mughal, and Ottoman Empires) stubbornly held on from Western imperialism, since the 1990s, these old empires have revived to become new empires. In light of this historical repetition in global capitalism, the rise of China inaugurates significant changes in Asian regionalism, one that heretofore has been dominated by Japan in the modern/colonial period. Similarly, Jacques sees the region's realignment towards China bears some of the hallmarks of the tributary system, a Sinocentric hierarchical and concentric structure of relations that marked the Middle Kingdom's dominance in the era of world empires.[5]

If Karatani reconstructs the stages of global capitalism through the meta-narrative of repetition, the political scientists T.J. Pempel provides a more precise analysis of the rise of China and its implications to regionalism in East Asia (2008). Pempel's study also points to the dewesternizing tendency of Asian regionalism, which I will discuss in more detail later. Comparing to the end of the 1990s, Pempel argues that East Asian regionalism today has witnessed a few significant changes. First of all, the new regionalism is as much governmental and political as it is economic. Second, a bevy of new institutions have been created across Asia, particularly in the area of finance. Third, this new regionalism is more China-centric and exclusively "Asian" than it was before (Pempel 2008, 2). What prompted this shift to a more political (from economic-driven) and "Asian" (from an "open" and "inclusive") regionalism is the "Asian" economic crisis in the late 1990s. The Asian financial crisis has been instrumental in developing an Asian-centric regionalism, with China playing an increasingly important role. The financial meltdown has alarmed the governments of their vulnerability to global economic volatility and damaging effects of the US and IMF-imposed solutions.

In the wake of the crisis, many Asian governments wanted to construct a regional mechanism to mobilize Asia's extensive financial resources and to forge deeper financial ties across Asia despite (or precisely because of) Washington's rebuking of Tokyo's proposal to establish the Asian Monetary Fund, an Asian alternative to the IMF (5). East Asian regionalism has historically been more "open" and Asia-Pacific-centric, including Australia, the US and others. However, after the crisis, it has been predominantly the ASEAN Plus Three (China, Japan, and South Korea) countries that have been at the core of new regional ties.[6] Many Asian governments remained interested in finding a regional mechanism to forger deeper financial ties to buttress the instability of global capitalism.

How does China fit in this new regionalism? Pempel argues that with the economic crisis and China's accession to the WTO in 2002, China recognizes how much regional strength could enhance its influence. Citing Edward Friedman, Pempel locates China's embrace of regionalism in US blocking of Japan's effort to create an Asian financial mechanism to cushion such crisis although China was initially against the proposal as well. The Chinese Communist Party, according to Friedman, determined that regional financial cooperation could check American hegemony, as well as warding off the influence of Japan, the historically dominant power in the region (10). The growing influence of China in the region can be gleaned from the following statistics: more than half of China's total trade volume is within the East Asian region. It is the major recipient of intraregional Foreign Direct Investment while it is also increasingly becoming an exporter of FDI to the rest of the region. China undercut Japan's effort by proposing at the 2000 ASEAN Summit for an ASEAN-China Free Trade Agreement. In 2003, China surpassed the US and became South Korea's largest export market and was the number one destination for outgoing Korean FDI. China today buys about 40 percent of Taiwan's exports, and since 2002 more than half of Taiwan's FDI has been sunk into China (10–11).

Furthermore, there is a conspicuous shift of influence from Japan to China in inter-regional trades. Between 1980 and 2002, while China's share of East Asian exports increased from 6 percent to 25 percent Japan's fell from 50 percent to below 30 percent; similarly, while China's share of East Asian import over the same period increased from 8 percent to 21 percent, Japan's fell from 48 percent to 27 percent. (Jacques 2012, 354). China became Japan's largest export market in 2008, overtaking the United States, with the value of Japanese exports to China doubling between 2000 and 2003.

To borrow Raymond Williams's terms, what is *emergent* in the Asian regionalism is the process of de-Americanization (or dewesternization) by re-sinicization that began to challenge the postwar Cold War dominance of the US-Japan alliance in the region. In this regard, we are witnessing the re-emergence of China as world empire in what Karatani calls Regionalism. As China continues to manifest itself as the fulcrum of the regional economy, it is no longer inconceivable that China will soon achieve hegemony within the region in most respects—economic, political and cultural—other than military. Pempel argues, however, it is premature to anoint China as the next regional leader. For most of the postwar period, China had been skeptical of any approaches to "the region" as a collectivity, instead favoring advancement of Chinese interests through a combination of bilateral relations and global institutions (2008: 9–10). One might also add that historically, unlike Japan, China has not developed a systematic discourse or desire for regionalism. The Hua/Yi (Sinocentrism/Barbarism) worldview prevalent since the Ming dynasty was more a worldly concentric—rather than a regional-specific construction of Self and Others (Sun 2000). Furthermore, China's new ambition and desire for regional and world hegemony has fanned antagonism within the region especially with its assertive territorial claims in the South China Sea based on imperial/historical rather than postwar/international American supported claims. Regardless of China's intention in the region, the economic crisis of 1997 has precipitated a new regional formation that is less Japan-focused and US-driven. More importantly, this new regionalism is exposing the increasingly important fault line within the region: the exclusion or inclusion of the United States, with Japan always favoring inclusion, and China, tending to favor, though not always, exclusion.[7]

That ASEAN has become a model and lies at the core of new East Asian arrangements that provided them with templates of trade agreements only underscore the difficulty of integration in North East Asia. The question of Taiwan, the divided Korean peninsula and the enduring political antagonism between Japan and China, are just some of the geopolitical hurdles that have to be overcome in order to embark on a semblance of regional cooperation. As the Japan-centric (and US-dominant) regionalism gradually gives way to the rise of China, the politics of reconciliation between Japan and China becomes an urgent imperative.[8]

The Korean Wave

Beyond economic and geopolitical shifts in the region, another "challenge" to Japanese and American cultural hegemony in the region is the so-called Korean Wave. Similar to the desire for economic integration in the wake of Asian financial crisis, the condition of possibility for the Korean Wave likewise was spurt by South Korea's state and cultural industry's strategy to cope with regional crisis. The rapid surge of Korean Wave in the region is astounding given that as late as mid-1990s, Korean culture, especially popular culture, was not even on the regional and world map, so to speak (Shim 2006). Cho Hae-Joang (Cho 2005), writing on the competing discourses on the Korean Wave, dates the reporting of the news of Korean Wave in South Korean media around February 2001.

In the wake of the shock of the financial crisis in 1997 and the IMF bailout, the *hallyu* phenomenon became a sensation, and enabled Koreans to develop new senses of globalization, the culture industry, and a newly forming Asia in a short time span (Cho 2005, 149). This cultural phenomenon parallels the state-led economic development as the Korean government took the position that the Korean Wave must be the product of sheer competition in the global market and an export-oriented policy should be established to maximize economic profit (160). The initial role the Korean state has played in investing and promoting popular culture is an important aspect of its success.

Doobo Shim has argued that the Korean Wave is indebted to the media liberalization that swept across Asia in the 1990s: "Recent economic crisis in Asia brought about a situation where Asian buyers prefer the cheaper Korean programming; Korean television dramas were a quarter of the price of Japanese ones, and a tenth of the price of Hong Kong television drama as of 2000" (Shim 2006, 28). There are also attempts by the Korean big business making efforts to transform Korean Wave fans into consumers of Korean products and services (30).[9]

Another well-documented aspect of the Korean Wave besides state intervention that promotes cultural production as "national" policy is its "hybridization." Here, hybridization is understood as cultural forms that encompass both "universal" (or Western) and "particular" (with Korean branding) to appeal to, initially, Asian and subsequently, global, audiences.[10] Unlike Japanese popular culture, which is characterized by its "non-nation-specific" (mukokuseki) attributes, or their "culturally odorlessness" (Iwabuchi 2002), the Korean Wave attempts to strike a balance between "Western" and "Korean" in forms and contents. Pop music represents the most obvious process of this hybridization. Shim cites Seo Taiji and Boys' single "I Know" (1992), arguably the first rap track in Korea, as pioneering the mixing genres of rap, soul, rock and roll, techno, punk, hardcore and even *ppongjjak* that created a unique form of Korean pop along with dynamic dance movements (Shim 36).

Another aspect of the Korean Wave is to groom and prepare its stars for forays into regional and global markets. It is well known that Boa, one of the earlier Korean singers debuted in Japan, was learning Japanese and English rigorously when young and has since also mastered Chinese for the continental market. Korean Wave thus represents a synergy between the state and the culture industry, or the collapsing between economic and the cultural. With its stars produced through a rigorous and regimented industrializing system for regional and global consumption, the Korean Wave also reduces the bodies to commodities, humans as exports.[11]

The initial success of the Korean Wave in the region has generated a number of contending discourses in South Korea. Cho (2005) has identified three such positions: the cultural nationalist, the industrialist and neoliberal, and the postcolonial. The cultural nationalist position upholds family values with a Confucian sensibility that assumes a common "Asian culture." However, it is also anti-Japanese and anti-American. It espouses the notion of "co-evalness" among Asian nations and rejects the notion that Japanese culture was superior. The neoliberal position highlights the "industry" in cultural productions. It also demands state support and policies to sustain the Wave and to maximize economic profit. The neoliberals view the Korean Wave as an opportunity to increase the scale of production and to establish a distribution channel by making many commercially successful firms (Cho, 162). The more pertinent position for our discussion, the postcolonial, sees the Korean Wave as a result of several centuries of modernization, capitalist expansion, and the homogenization of global culture. Some critics in this camp equate popular culture with shallow and disposable culture of capitalism and wishes to promote the *"minjung"* (people's) culture stemming from the democratic movements in the 1980s instead. Others chastise the cultures of the Korean Wave as the "illicit union" of an export-oriented state and short-term capitalist logic that forces everything to either turning a quick profit or disappear from the marketplace (164).

A more nuanced approach, according to Cho, is that of Kim Hyun Mee, who proposes a two-pronged strategy of regionalism. Kim advocates the comprehension of the workings of secular capital and finding the site of intervention for building postcolonial communities in a "coeval" Asia. She emphasizes the "coevalness" of production and consumption shared by the people who have experienced the contemporaneous changes brought about by Asian modernity and who are seeking to solve its "problems." Furthermore, she emphasizes the diverse and different patterns of East Asian cultural consumption along class, race, and gender lines (Kim 2003, 166–167).

Not unlike what Fredric Jameson has argued for the reification and utopia of popular culture (Jameson 1979), Cho and Kim, while critical of the cultural nationalism and neoliberal condition of the Korean Wave, also see the potential of the Korean Wave in constructing a regional sphere of exchange and communication. The Cold War system has long prioritized and privileged the West (to a lesser extent, Japan) as the point of reference for peoples in the region. Cho and Kim believe that the Korean Wave can provide multiple points of "inter-referencing" (Chen 2010) in the region, as means of encountering and discovering "neighbors" who have long existed as "others."

Dewesternization and the Asian option

As we have seen, both China's new engagement with the region and the emergence of the Korean Wave owe their condition of possibility to the "Asian" financial crisis and the neoliberal turn. This neo-regionalism, as I have argued, is characterized by the rise of China as a major economic (and increasingly political) player and the Korean Wave as significant and viable option to the postwar Cold War American and Japanese cultural hegemony. It would be, however, a mistake to pronounce the demise of the US and Japan as dominant actors in the region. The US remains the only military superpower in the region (and the world). Despite two decades of economic downturn, Japan remains the third largest economy in the world.

In addition, it is not clear if this neo-regionalism will necessarily bring better cooperation and less antagonism within the region. What is certain, however, is that the postwar Cold War order is giving way to a multi-polar configuration whose regional design is still very much in question and in contention. While regional cultural formation and exchanges have proliferated in the last twenty years, first through Japanese, and now Korean, popular culture, it is questionable that popular culture can constitute some kind of a regional identity. It is perhaps more fruitful to analyze and interpret cultural texts popular in the region as sites of contestation where desire, fantasy and anxiety can be projected to cope with hardship and distress increasingly shared by young peoples in the region today under neoliberal capitalism.

Instead of apprehending the current state of "East Asian popular culture" (Chua 2004)[12] as an alternative to Americanization or "Western" cultures, or a celebrated hybridization between globalization and localization, it might be more useful to think its emergence as that of "dewesternization" and "the Asian option," two terms I borrow from Walter Mignolo (2011). Dewesternization is useful in this context because it embodies both the subversive potential *and* compliant logic that an East Asian cultural formation entails. This ambiguity has the benefit of not reducing regional cultural formation to uncritical triumphalism or universal globalism. As mentioned earlier, it is to understand East Asian popular culture as both reification and utopia in the circulation of regionalism. Dewesternization is also useful in characterizing the continuously shifting terrain of global capitalism, or what Karatani has called the neoliberalism/imperialism/regionalism stage, that characterizes the intensifying competition among capitalist nations and economies. "Asia" becomes another option of developmentalism and consumerism among other "options," but does not question or subvert the fundamental logic of the categories themselves. In this regard, dewesternization nicely captures the present mood and the shift of capitalist hegemony without a clear state power in the wake of Pax Americana.

The dissolution of the myth of westernization is underway according to what I call triumphant discourse of dewesternization. The rapid economic development has reinstated Asia back in the center stage of history where in the last two centuries it was dominated and monopolized by the West. The era of Western-centrism is over and it must confront and accept the rise of what Kishore Mahbubani has called the "new Asian hemisphere" (2008). The so-called decline of the West is neither controversial nor scandalous; the key here is how the event is analyzed and interpreted.

From a more critical perspective than Mahbubani's, Mignolo defines dewesternization as follows:

> Dewesternization is not a geographic but a political concept and refers to all states (corporate states) which are consolidating their economies without following the dictates of the US, the EU, the IMF or the World Bank. Delinking here does not mean delinking from "a type of economy" but from the instructions of the World Bank, the IMF and related institutions. The delinking is contained in the sphere of authority.
>
> *(Mignolo 2012)*

Put differently, dewesternization means "a political delinking from economic decisions" on the part of the BRICS (and others) in its refusal to follow the authority of the West. Dewesternization, in Mignolo's historicization, has its inception in the 1955 Bandung Conference. Dewesternization today, however, is coupled with the efforts of rewesternization such as the US's attempt at reclaiming its declining hegemony. Despite the positive tendency of dewesternization as it challenges the authority of the West, it does not delink from "a type of economy" such as the fantasy of development and growth at the expense of life.

As such, dewesternization is not, and cannot be, decolonial, a radical delinking from the colonial matrix of power that is the idea of development and growth. Dewesternization, however, does constitute an "option" other than the normalizing West. In its pursuit of neoliberal economics and commodified culture, neo-regionalism is dewesternizing but not anti-Westernization. Dewesternization, of course, did not come from nowhere. In the era of imperialism and colonialism, it took on the discourse of overcoming modernity in Japan, for example. Recent dewesternization has to do with the decentering of capitalism as a global abstraction (Dirlik

1994). More specifically, it has to do with the crisis unleashed by global financial capitalism. Both the Asian and global financial crises of 1997–8 and 2008 have dramatically sped up dewesternization and regionalization, at least in creating institutions that attempt at curbing future crises.

The Korean Wave, in this analysis, is not an incident centered in South Korea but part of the phenomenon of capitalism's rise in Asia, as a pop culture spectacle that appeared as part of the process of global capitalism, one that offers as an option to other forms of popular culture, Japanese or American. In the region, Korean entertainment industries have contributed greatly to forming a new subjectivity for a rapidly changing Asia by appealing to a certain middle and lower-middle class with upscale hyper-modern lifestyles.

More importantly, as Cho Hae-Joang has argued, "the Korean wave plays a significant role in accelerating the transformation of global residents into neoliberal subjects in an era where all types of communities are being disintegrated and atomized" (Cho 2005, 176). More specifically to the region, the Asian middle-class audience that was either antagonistic towards or bored with Western cultural hegemony played a significant role in promoting the Korean wave. Cho writes:

> The circulation of popular culture is narrowing the geographical, social, and psychological distance between Asians by providing many topics for conversations, stimulating tourism, and providing opportunity for diverse meetings. The non-Western people who have so far confirmed their existence only through the West are finding new opportunities to construct an alternate consciousness through the sharing of popular culture.
>
> *(2005, 177)*

It is an *alternate*, not *alternative* consciousness.

Boys Before Flowers and regional culture

As an example of dewesternization and the Asian option of popular culture, I would like to turn to the very popular *manga*/TV drama *Boys Before Flowers* (aka *Boys Over Flowers* or BBF). The choice of BBF is not arbitrary. BBF is arguably one of the most pan-Asian of all East Asian popular culture texts up to date. It is one of the few, if not the only text I am aware of, that has been remade into TV dramas in four countries and broadcast throughout East and Southeast Asia. The multi-sited circulation and success of the drama capture the fragmentation and unity of the structure of feeling that characterizes neo-regionalism. Originally a *shojo manga* by Kamio Yoko serialized in *Margaret Comics* from 1992 to 2004, with a film adaptation made only for the domestic market, it was the Taiwanese TV drama adaptation in 2001 that brought about its popularity in Southeast Asia, becoming the number one TV show in Indonesia and the Philippines. As an inverse importation, the popularity of the Taiwanese show prompted a Japanese version of the TV drama that aired in 2005. Subsequently, Korean and mainland Chinese versions were produced and aired in 2009.[13] The popularity of the drama was not limited to Asia. A kickstart project with strong fan support brought the show to the US in late 2012, but failed miserably.[14] How do we account for the success and successive remake of the shows in Asia and its whimpered failure in the US? The *manga* and dramas also generated conversations, gossips, memes, and opinions on the Internet throughout the region, making it a truly regional phenomenon.[15]

The popularity and circuity of BBF and its failure in the US offer an opportunity to think about neo-regionalism and its dewesternization impulses. I want to suggest that the fictionalized fantasy and romance in the *manga*/drama resonate with audiences in Asia and offer them, at least temporarily, a necessary "space off" (Robertson 1998) and reprieve from the rigid and oppressive education system and social relations. More specifically, I argue that the "pure" romance represented in the *manga*/drama offers a different option of enjoying "love" than the more open and direct "sex" proffered by American teen TV drama or Hollywood. Together, they represent symptoms of the neoliberal turn in the region since the early 1990s that has contributed to the profound sense of precarity, especially among the region's youth (Allison 2013).

Despite some variations and localizations, the four TV versions cohere with the *manga*'s basic premises: a romantic comedy about a lower-middle-class girl confronting F4 (Flower Four), four extremely wealthy, privileged, and handsome bullies at an exclusive elite high school. The popularity of the drama can be attributed to several basic formulae in what has been called the "idol drama": beautiful and handsome young protagonists, the exaggerated wealth and class difference between F4 and the female character, the inevitable romance that develops between the female lead and two of the F4s and its resolution. The drama's setting of a high school with the theme of bullying is quite familiar to viewers in the region. Dramas set in high schools (or junior high schools) have long been a staple in popular culture, mostly as ways for young people to cope with the stress and pressure of the examination system.

The concept of "seishun/qingchun" or youth has long functioned as an ideology in popular culture that exalted "freedom," "friendship," "love," etc., that provide the viewers a relief from the daily grind of schooling and its accompanied sociality. The dramatization of the school setting and its melodrama allow the audience to feel a sense of familiarity and experience the fantasy of possible transgression. This type of "campus drama" becomes more important as students are pressured to compete, to be disciplined and indoctrinated into masses suppressing individuality and creativity in the interest of national economic development and "social harmony." Despite uneven development in the region and unequal distribution of wealth within the nation-states, the pressure to succeed in school under intensifying competition for young people as a gateway to a prosperous future remain a dominant ideology despite the erosion of such myth under neoliberal globalization.

From a purely sociological perspective, the high school setting provides a time/space situation where budding love, friendship, teacher/student relations, aspirations, innocence together with hardship, failure, social hierarchy and other experiential and affective moments can be imagined, fantasized and played out before the characters (and viewers) move on to the harsh and demanding "real world." The female protagonist, Tsukushi,[16] from a lower-middle-class background, possesses strong sense of morality and justice, confronts the haughty yet handsome tormentors. Unlike other students who are in awe of F4 or are terrorized by them, Tsukushi, partly due to her gender and humbled class background, confronts F4 at every turn, despite being bullied by other students as well. In a sea of conformity, compliance under authority and privilege, Tsukushi is a maverick, the underdog who stands up for her friend, the weak and the common people. Tsukushi thus represents a possible struggle against the privileged class. The fascination and fantasy of class struggle in the collective political unconscious is highlighted, displayed, but at the end, has to be contained if not suppressed. The contrast between money/privilege and poverty/precarity is used as a narrative device to shift or change the plot line. Consequently, class difference becomes merely a prop to advance the up and down romantic relations between Tsukushi and Domyoji, the leader of F4, with Hanazawa, another member, constituting a possible love triangle.

The romantic tussle between the protagonists becomes the "real" intimacy that contains, if not displaces, the fantasy of class struggle. In the classical symptom of the so-called Cinderella Complex, Tsukushi, while reacting violently against F4's privilege and bullying, often has no choice but to acquiesce to or depend on their assistance, mostly due to her family's often abrupt and repeated descending into poverty. As a result, Tsukushi begins to understand Domyoji's kindness (that often erupts in violent ways) and the two get closer. However, as soon as their relationship grows, class differences erupt and their romance is disrupted, at least temporarily. Domyoji would frustratingly proclaim, "That's why I hate poor people," and Tsukushi would reflect fondly on her times in middle school when people were of more or less equal standing. This repetition between romance and class difference is only resolved when love trumps class. It is in the representation of "love" that I would suggest BBF offers some of the Asian readership/audience another option of imagining a hetero-normative relationship that alleviates the anxiety over fast-paced "modern" love.

As mentioned earlier, despite their unbridgeable class difference, Tsukushi and Domyoji gradually fall for each other. What ultimately enables the relationship to continue amidst all the twist and turns of the romantic comedy is their "true" love. Unlike the other playboys of the F4 team, Domyoji has no experience with women and Tsukushi is also a virgin. While the *manga/ drama*'s narrative brings the possibility of their sexual union on several occasions, they are always thwarted by comical accidents and continuously deferred to advance the storyline and grab the viewers'/readers' interest. The unconsummated desire, however, allows Tsukushi to discover Domyoji's thoughtfulness and his feelings for her. In one occasion, Domyoji actually rescues her from being sexually assaulted by a group of men who held grudges against Domyoji for bullying them before.[17]

The notion of a "pure" love and its allure is quite popular in dramas circulating in East Asia. *Winter's Sonata*, the Korean drama that arguably inaugurated the Korean Wave, for example, has "true" and "pure" love between the main protagonists as its fundamental motif. That drama was instrumental in making visible the middle-aged Japanese women, not only as consumers, but also as agents capable of reflecting (or at least beginning to reflect) on Japan's own colonial past (Mōri 2008). Their "nostalgia" for a "pure" love (which never existed in the first place) projects certain desire and fantasy that reawaken their feelings of romance and love. By positing the notion of "pure" love as what is attractive to East Asian audiences is not to essentialize it as an affect particular to East Asia. Rather, it is to suggest that a less erotic or sexualized manifestation of love provides the viewers another option of consumption and fantasy to other forms of amorous expressions seen in other Asian or non-Asian dramas. As William Reddy has argued, "romantic love" emerged in twelfth-century Europe as a way of coping, if not deflecting, the theological chastity on desire-as-appetite. The dichotomy between "true love" and "desire-as-appetite" undergirded the Western notion of "romantic love." Analyzing the South Asian and Japanese contexts in similar historical periods, Reddy found that the binarism between love and desire did not exist in the European counterparts (2012).

In contemporary East Asia, as with most of the modern world, the representations of love exist in multiple and overlapping ways. I am by no means arguing that the type of "pure" love expressed in *Winter's Sonata* or *Boys Over Flowers* are quintessentially "Asian." The popularity of Hollywood films such as the *Twilight* series also point to the increasing draw of young people towards hetero-normative relationship in its idealized and conservative tendencies in a real or perceived degenerating of traditional values such as love, family, friendship, etc. We might speculate that the growing attachment to innocence, friendship, romantic love and other affects is a worldwide symptom of the increased pressure young people are feeling under neoliberal global capitalism. Perhaps this transition is felt more severely in Asia under what Cho Hae-Joang has called "compressed modernity" or "turbo capitalism" (2001). Increased inequality, rising cost of living, insecure job prospect, intensifying competition, and urges for self-valorization, these neoliberal demands are thrust upon young people everywhere. Is it any wonder that fantasized class difference and pure love appeal to them?

Conclusion

As I write this, the "umbrella revolution"—the student-led occupied movement in Hong Kong that demands political reform—has come to a standstill without gaining concessions from the Beijing-backed Chief Executive. Despite its seemingly failure to enact political change, the democratic movement mobilized tens and thousands of young people to claim Hong Kong as their own and made their presence visible and voices heard. As many have argued, the political demands also stem from the growing sense of inequality and insecurity felt by many young people as a result of global neoliberalism and the collusion between Beijing's political center and Hong Kong's business elite (Dirlik 2014a). The increased sense of precarity is the fundamental source of young people's discontent. The protest echoes the so-called Sunflower Student Movement in Taiwan a few months before in demanding political transparency to protect local economy from the free trade agreement with China. The movement in Taiwan has, for the first time, moved beyond the traditional politics between that of the *waishengren* "mainlanders" and *bengshengren* "Taiwanese" binary. This radical new configuration, like that of Hong Kong's, is the assertion of what Arif Dirlik has called "placed-based politics" that rejects globalizing forces that is in service of capital and its political elites. Precarization under neoliberalism (as imperialism under globalization in Karatani's formulation) is no longer perceived as an exception, but becoming increasingly normalized in people's everyday lives.

Under the sway of neoliberalism and its discontent, the growing inequality also engenders growing conservatism among East Asian youth. Unlike the Umbrella or Sunflower movements that confront governments for political inclusion and economic justice, a wave of rising chauvinism and conservatism that targets not the status quo, but the marginalized and oppressed. The infamous website *Ilbe* in South Korea, for example, consists mostly of angry men spewing invectives against members of society who they feel are infringing on the traditional rights of Korean men.[18] Se-Woong Koo (2014), borrowing Park Seon-Yeong's analysis titled, "When the Weak Detest the Weak," comments on the current South Korean situation where "everyone is conditioned to see him- or herself as a 'have at all' cost, even going to the length of stepping on anyone perceived to have less power just to demonstrate one's own powerfulness." Malcontents like *Ilbe* are symptoms of the incessant pressure towards development for the younger generation. Koo writes:

> South Korea's young people are dealing with a miserable reality. They undergo onerous education for a promise that their future will amount to something. But when they graduate, landing a covetable job is fiercely competitive. Costs of living are high, and renting a place of your own, much less homeownership, is near impossible for a single person without the help of well-to-do parents. Everyone says one should get married and have children, but the expense of establishing a family is daunting. Consumption is endlessly encouraged. Debts pile up. There appears to be no hope on the horizon.
>
> *(Koo 2014)*

The situation sounds eerily similar in other parts of East Asia as well.

It is unlikely any popular culture will radically transform the status quo, although symbols, music, memes, social media, continue to produce narratives, images, affects, etc., to contest the notion that people's lives are nowadays dispensable and substitutable. Under increased precarity, nationalism has become the ideology to obfuscate present inequality and social ills among East Asians. The "official" attempts to resolve political issues, however, have not been popular among the fans with many finding them too didactic or boring. Under these conditions, popular culture such as *Boys Before Flowers* can potentially forge transnational alliances among young people in the region finding new opportunities to imagine alternative futures, albeit in limited ways.

Notes

1 Some examples of dominant regionalist imaginary in the last 50 years include: the flying geese model suggested by Akamatsu Kaname in the late 1960s and 1970s, the "Asian values" ideology of the 1990s and the spread of Japanese popular culture in the 2000s. Intellectual movements that involved scholars and activists in the region only earnestly began in the early 2000s and the center of gravity comes from the "periphery" network of scholars from Taiwan, South Korea, Singapore, and Hong Kong. They include *Inter-Asia Cultural Studies* and *ARENA* (Asian Regional Exchange for New Alternatives).

2 Of particular import here is Balibar's concern that through this *new* articulation of social practices and collective representations (neo-racism) constitute the development of what Gramsci calls hegemony. Similarly, questions of the long cycle of hegemonic shift has centered around the debate of whether Asia as a region (China and India in particular) constitutes the next hegemon.

3 In this regard, dewesternization entails some forms of rewesternization.

4 The growing display of China's "soft power" is beyond the scope of this chapter. For a concise and incisive critique of China's imperial reach in the field of knowledge production, see Dirlik 2014b.

5 Jacques cites present day China's "historic claims" to the various disputed islands and the "one country, two systems" principle informed Hong Kong's post-handover constitution as examples of China as a "civilization-state" (374–379).

6 Pempel lists the following examples as a more Asian-centric shift in the region: CMI (Chang-Mai Initiative), the EAS (East Asia Summit), the eleven countries in EMEAP (Executives' Meeting of East Asia-Pacific Central Banks) that drove the ABMI exclude any on the Eastern shores of the Pacific (e.g., the US, Canada, and other APEC members). CMI was also the mechanism that triggered the track-two Network of East Asian Think Tank (NEAT) forged in the wake of the financial crisis (9).

7 See Jacques 2012, 351. The growing cooperation and rivalry between China and the United States can be seen in the recent APEC meeting in Beijing. At the summit, Xi Jinping proposed a China-centered "Asia-Pacific Dream" and "two new Silk Roads" to counter the American-centric Transpacific Trade Partnership, which excludes China. See www.washingtonpost.com/world/asia_pacific/china-bypasses-american-new-silk-road-with-two-if-its-own/2013/10/14/49f9f60c-3284-11e3-ad00-ec4c6b31cbed_story.html (accessed on 11.13.2014).

8 For a recent study on questions of reconciliation within East Asia, see Tessa Morris-Suzuki et al. 2013.

9 In one of Shim's examples, LG Electronics provided Vietnamese television stations with several Korean television dramas for free, even covering the cost of dubbing (30).

10 It is important to note that the notion of "hybridization" employed by analysts of the Korean Wave tend to regard it as a descriptive category, and does not see hybridization as an analytical term that consists of subversive potential against dominant cultural forms theorized by postcolonialism. In this regard, hybridization in the Korean Wave is akin to multiculturalism in the global marketplace and does not imagine itself to be polyculturalism that challenges neoliberal capitalism (Prashad 2002).

11 For a critique of the Korean Wave and the differential obsession with the male and female bodies, see Epstein and Joo 2012.

12 Chua Beng-Huat has argued for a structural understanding of "East Asian popular culture" based on each locale's position in media production, distribution and consumption (Chua 2004). At the time of writing, Chua has rightly observed that in the circulation of East Asia (Japan, South Korea, Taiwan, and China) plus one (Singapore), Japan remains the locus of production, with China and Singapore relegated to sites of consumption and Taiwan and South Korea somewhere in between. The media landscape in recent years, however, has changed quite a bit. While Japan remains the hub of cultural production in the region, the popularity of the Korean Wave and the rapid media development in mainland China have muddled the strict divisions of labor in popular culture.

13 This does not mean the effects are the same across the region. For example, the popularity of the Taiwanese version in Southeast Asia has inspired young Filipina and Malay women to go to Taipei to work as domestic helpers partly because the modern and wealthy representation of Taipei in the drama.

14 The show went into hiatus on March 2014, completing only six out of the originally planned 16 episodes.

15 Some Internet conversations include: fans asking and ranking the most popular F4 in the series although limited to Taiwanese, South Korean and Japanese versions, images of all four dramas characters with fake

Vietnamese and Indian characters, fans seeking opinions on all four versions, and the misinformation that the Chinese version is pirated without copyright permission.

16 For matter of simplicity, I am using names of characters from the Japanese *manga*.

17 In the *manga*, Domyoji expresses his feelings to Tsukushi as follows: "I will chase you wherever you go," "I will follow you even to hell." In defiance to his mother's directive to find a more appropriate woman, he says, "I just love her and I won't love any other girl."

18 I thank Hyesong Lim for bringing this phenomenon to my attention.

References

Allison, A. (2013) *Precarious Japan*, Durham, NC: Duke University Press.

Balibar, E. and Wallerstein, I.M. (1991) *Race, Nation, Class: Ambiguous Identities*, New York: Verso.

Chen, K.H. (2010) *Asia as Method: Toward Deimperialization*, Durham, NC: Duke University Press.

Ching, L. (2000) 'Globalizing the Regional, Regionalizing the Global: Mass Culture and Asianism in the Age of Late Capital', *Public Culture*, 12(1), 233–257.

Ching, L. (2009) 'Japan in Asia'. In Tsutsui (ed.) *A Companion to Japanese History*, Malden, MA: Wiley-Blackwell: 407–423.

Cho, H.-J. (2001) '"You are entrapped in an imaginary well": The Formation of Subjectivity Within Compressed Development—A Feminist Critique of Modernity and Korean Culture', *Inter-Asia Cultural Studies*, 1(1): 49–69.

Cho, H.-J. (2005) 'Reading the Korean Wave as a Sign of Global Shift', *Korea Journal*, 45(4): 147–182.

Chua, B.H. (2004) 'Conceptualizing an East Asian Popular Culture', *Inter-Asia Cultural Studies*, 5(2), 200–221.

Dirlik, A. (1994) *After the Revolution: Waking to Global Capitalism*, Hanover, NH: Wesleyan University Press published by University Press of New England.

Dirlik, A. (2014a) *The Mouse that Roared: The Democratic Movement in Hong Kong.* Available at: www.agos.com.tr/tr/yazi/8181/the-mouse-that-roared-the-democratic-movement-in-hong-kong (Accessed on August 11, 2014).

Dirlik, A. (2014b) *Crisis and Criticism: The Predicament of Global Modernity.* Available at: http://boundary2.org/2014/09/16/crisis-and-criticism-the-predicament-of-global-modernity/ (Accessed on December 28, 2014).

Epstein, S. and Joo, R.M. (2012) 'Multiple Exposures: Korean Bodies and the Transnational Imagination', *The Asia-Pacific Journal*, 10 (33.1).

French, W.H. (2014) *China's Second Continent: How a Million Migrants Are Building a New Empire in Africa*, New York: Alfred A. Knopf.

Iwabuchi, K. (2002) *Recentering Globalization: Popular Culture and Japanese Transnationalism*, Durham, NC: Duke University Press.

Jacques, M. (2012) *When China Rules the World: The End of the Western World and the Birth of a New Global Order,* New York: Penguin Books.

Jameson, F. (1979) 'Reification and Utopia in Mass Culture', *Social Text*, 1(Winter): 130–148.

Karatani, K. (2014) *The Structure of World History: From Modes of Production to Modes of Exchange* (M.K. Bourdaghs, trans.), Durham, NC: Duke University Press.

Koo, S. (2014) *South Korea's Angry Young Men.* Available at: www.koreaexpose.com/voices/south-koreas-angry-young-men/ (Accessed on June 10, 2014).

Mahbubani, K. (2008) *The New Asian Hemisphere: The Irresistible Shift of Global Power to the East*, New York: Public Affairs.

Mee, K.H. (2003) "Daeman sok-ui hanguk daejung munhwa: munhwa 'beonyeok'-gwa 'honseonghwa'-ui munje-reul jungsim-euro" [Korean Pop Culture in Taiwan: On Cultural Translation and Hybridity]". In Hae-Joang, C. et al. (eds) *Hallyu-wa asia-ui daejung munhwa* [*Korean Wave and the Popular Culture in Asia*], Seoul: Yonsei University Press.

Mignolo, C. (2012) *Delinking, Decoloniality & Dewesternization: Interview with Walter Mignolo* (Part II). Interview by Christopher Mattison. Available at: http://criticallegalthinking.com/2012/05/02/delinking-decoloniality-dewesternization-interview-with-walter-mignolo-part-ii/ (Accessed on May 9, 2014).

Mignolo, W. (2011) *The Darker Side of Western Modernity: Global Futures, Decolonial Options*, Durham, NC: Duke University Press.

Mōri, Y. (2008) 'Winter Sonata and Cultural Practices of Active Fans in Japan: Considering Middle-Aged Women as Cultural Agents'. In B.H. Chua and K. Iwabuchi (eds) *East Asian Pop Culture: Analysing the Korean Wave*, Hong Kong: Hong Kong University Press: 127–141.

Morris-Suzuki, T., Low, M., Petrov, L., and Tsu, T. (2013) *East Asia Beyond the History Wars: Confronting the Ghosts of Violence*, Abingdon and New York: Routledge.

Pempel, T.J. (2008) *A China e o Emergente Regionalismo Asiático*. China Conferencia Nacionaal de politica Externa e Politica Internacional—III (Brazilia, Fundação Alexandre de Gusmão): 267–288 (the citations from this chapter are from a talk version of the published paper).

Prashad, V. (2002) *Everybody Was Kung Fu Fighting: Afro-Asian Connections and the Myth of Cultural Purity*, Boston: Beacon Press.

Reddy, W.M. (2012) *The Making of Romantic Love: Longing and Sexuality in Europe, South Asia, and Japan, 900–1200 CE*. Chicago, IL: University of Chicago Press.

Robertson, J.E. (1998) *Takarazuka: Sexual Politics and Popular Culture in Modern Japan*, Berkeley: University of California Press.

Shim, D. (2006) 'Hybridity and the Rise of Korean Popular Culture in Asia', *Media, Culture & Society*, 28(1): 25–44

Sun, S. (2000) 'How Does Asia Mean?' *Inter-Asia Cultural Studies*, 1(2): 319–341.

5

Mobilizing discontent: social media and networked activism since the Great East Japan Earthquake

Love Kindstrand, Keiko Nishimura and David H. Slater

The ways in which social media becomes recognized, legitimated and used as an effective tool of political activity—that is, framing issues, mobilizing members, logistical organizing of offline events and the subsequent re-representation of these events to a wider audience—depends upon a number of contingent factors. These factors differ quite widely with respect to time and place, media environment and social structure, cultural expectations and political context. In many cases, Japan included, social media is primarily used as a casual tool of social networking, a way for friends and families to stay in touch, a way for people to keep up with news and the flow of popular culture.

This situation changed in Japan during and since the events associated with the disasters of March 2011. In this chapter we describe this transformation through three key shifts which unfolded in chronological order from even before the tsunami reached shore, that moved from the instrumental to the constitutive and finally to the symbolic, communicative and social functions that enabled political potential heretofore undeveloped. Our argument is that through the instrumental use of these technologies, users established connections and flexible networks that then came to constitute a durable and effective post 3/11 politics.

A first shift leading to the realization of social media as more than a social networking tool was the use of social media to provide early and often exclusive information about the ongoing disaster and damage to property and life during the disaster. Social media was the first and primary way for most of us to experience the events, providing both up-to-date and visceral images of its unfolding. Often, this social media information was available when mainstream media was slower and less reliable, leading to a recognition of both the social and political potential of social media and the limitations, even intentional misrepresentations, of state generated or mainstream media broadcasts.

Second, we see the role social media played in the identification of life-threatening needs and of the resources to fill those needs in ways that engaged a much wider public in the collective effort of response and relief. It was primarily through social media, and in particular, through the crowd-sourcing of first disaster and radiation information and the subsequent digital consolidation of this information into bulletin boards and data bases, that need and resource were matched in timely and efficient ways. It was through social media that users fully contextualized the disaster as a political crisis and opportunity for wider, even democratic, participation.

Conversely, it was through these uses that social media were established as powerful and legitimate tools of social engagement and transformation. These two shifts were essential to the ways that social media was subsequently used to politically reframe the disaster in ways that pointed to the venal choices made by capital to put profit over citizens' safety, and the paltry efforts of the state to address these issues in ways that adhere to even the most rudimentary principles of social justice.

In our transition to the final section, we will suggest some general shifts that this significant increase in the production, consumption and general circulation of political information has had in the erasure of the "political" as a separate and often removed domain from the everyday. What we call the "politicization of the everyday" led directly to the renewed use of social media in the mobilization of what became the largest public demonstrations in Tokyo since the protests against the US-Japan Security Treaty (Ampo) in the 1960s. From the way that blogs and Facebook were used to frame issues and mobilize participants, to the role of Twitter micro-blogging in orchestrating public demonstrations, and of YouTube in disseminating these efforts to a global audience in visually arresting ways, we show how social media became the emblematic vehicles for many of the activities associated with traditional social movements and the generation of new sorts of activism.

Media environment

By 2011, Japan had one of the highest rates of penetration Internet use and Internet-ready mobile devices, most notably cell phones, in the world (Hashimoto 2011). According to a government white paper, the number of Internet users reached 94.62 million by the end of 2010, with an Internet penetration rate of 78.2 percent (Ministry of Internal Affairs and Communications [MIC] 2011), which means almost four in five Japanese use the Internet. Moreover, the ratio of mobile network devices is quite high: 96.3 percent of all Japanese households have mobile phones and 74.8 percent of the total Japanese population uses them, whereas computers are limited to 66.2 percent of the population (with these figures varying by age and geography; MIC 2010).

Thus, not only is the digital network already established, but also the dispersal of technology into the direct control of a significance portion of the population was already a fact of everyday life when the earthquake hit. The patterns of use were also distinctive in 2011 Japan. While voice communication is dominant in many countries, in Japan it is far more common to communication via text messaging (MIC 2011). Unlike voice, texts can be re-transmitted to other phones, a website or blog, and it thus can be circulated far wider and faster. The fact that most Japanese users often move among different types of social media, such as texting, posting, blogging (MIC 2011), and access them almost every day (MIC 2010), means that the possible range of dissemination of any text message is exponentially expanded. That is, the technological potential of social media as an instrumental communication was already quite wide. With the earthquake, tsunami and nuclear meltdown, this already robust network—of both technologies and patterns of use—became redirected to new political uses, previously unimagined by most.

This media environment greatly influenced the way people in Japan responded to the crisis. In the minutes just after the earthquake, many cell phone transmitters went down, but the mobile texting and social media functions were able to continue in many places at a more regular rate. Users turned to social media to find loved ones and get vital information by necessity. Even The National Research Institute for Earth Science and Disaster Prevention and the Japan Meteorological Agency began tweeting early alerts that were widely re-circulated automatically by "bots" (automated posting scripts). According to a study on post-quake Twitter usage, the number of posts (tweets) on the day of the quake increased to 1.8 times the average, reaching 330 million tweets in total (NEC Biglobe 2011).

Other social networking sites such as Mixi saw unprecedented spikes in use (IT Media 2011). Individual users started to redistribute the alerts, providing the first, and for a long time, only, images and up-to-date information of the disaster, often in real-time through visual reports from their own phones. As the trains stopped in Tokyo, stranding millions, news of overnight shelters were quickly circulated on Twitter. Microblogs and bulletin boards circulated information among strangers, while more commercial social networking platforms (Mixi and increasingly Facebook) were primarily used to confirm the safety of friends and relatives (Nikkei Business Publishing, 2011). Other bulletin board sites that are usually devoted to entertainment information, such as 2channel, saw a shift into disaster-related posts (NEC Biglobe 2011). Within days of the earthquake and tsunami, 64 percent of blog links, 32 percent of Twitter news links and the top 20 YouTube videos were all related to the crisis (Guskin 2011) and today, there are countless videos ranging from the picture of shaking of buildings to the tsunami waves rushing in to the scattered remains after the waters receded.

There were also important changes in public perception, creating an understanding if not a consensus among users and the public at large that social media was important because it allowed for faster information gathering than did mass media. About one third of those surveyed considered this necessary due to the lack of reliable information provided by the mass media and/or the government (Tomioka 2011). Many users explicitly framed their own use of social media as having a compensatory function—filling a gap left by the state and mass media.

Second, we see the taking up of social media content by the mass media outlets, often with explicit recognition that a particular content was user-generated. The use of user-generated content is widespread in many American news programs, but was not as significant in the Japanese mainstream until 2011. This served to legitimate a technology and patterns of use that had heretofore mainly been limited to social chatting or entertainment. Now, social media was understood as an important tool in life and death activity, indeed in a national project of response and recovery. Technologies and users who were once dismissed as "amateur," and thus unreliable hobbyists, were suddenly seen as providing information that was "authentic," in part because they were just ordinary people—just like the victims who happened to be on the spot, but also just like the viewers of mainstream media.

Making use of information networks: instrumental to constitutive

This physical network enabled the first and most necessary political act, that of making connection, the basis of networks of communication, the foundation for association, and in time, political mobilization. At this point, we can see the first practical realization of one of the primary characteristics of truly social media—the many-to-many communication that does not pass through single or unitary information manager. Of course, there are individuals who will "curate" their own sites, "uber-bloggers" with exceptional influence that shape the discourse on bulletin boards (Tsuda 2012), and direct newsfeeds with many followers. But we also see increased instances of individuals looking to communicate directly with others in ways that legitimated the efficacy and agency of social media as a many-to-many mode of communication.

As we have argued elsewhere (Slater, Nishimura and Kindstrand 2012), the role that social media played in the consolidation and redistribution of this user-generated information was also important, especially in ways that brought together the needs of the survivors and the available, if often unused or misused, resources. Survivors in trouble used texts and tweets to call out for help, or to alert others to those who needed help. But in the flood of messages, it was necessary to create some effective method of searching and linking. Twitter tweets are commonly linked or recontextualized through the use of "hashtags" that associate information with certain keywords. For example, one early 3/11 hashtag was "#j_j_helpme" (cf. Kobayashi 2011; MIC 2011) —where the # marks the string as a hashtag, the first "j" is for Japan and the second one for "*jishin*," meaning "earthquake" in Japanese. This was the primary method for providers, supporters or those with information of available resources to find messages of distress or identify needs. This practice began right away after the earthquake through user-generated activities in new or repurposed aggregation sites.

Facebook and Mixi, the two most popular commercial social networking services, brought together new constellations of users around requests for specific information. While existing networks rallied around relief causes, even strangers found and joined new groups in order to help. Meanwhile, special-purpose sites such as Google's People Finder, used all over the world to locate disaster victims, or other sites that "mashup" posts for needs and resources, often through sophisticated mapping functions, allow for the same many-to-many mode of communication (cf. Potts 2014). Thus we see, even from the beginning, that online communication led directly to offline action.

Reluctant social engagement through the emergence of connected digital civic spaces

The failure of established sources of information (mass media or the state) to provide timely, relevant and truthful information frustrates and disorients, panics and angers any public and especially one in a crisis situation. To provide this information is seen today by many as one of the primary roles, even responsibility, of a state to its citizens. Failure to provide this can result in a turning away from the state and mass media in ways that were often narrated as a deliberate and self-conscious one, usually with a negative evaluation of efficacy, and even the legitimacy, of the state and its efforts. Even among politically conservative populations, among those who are more used to unreflectively trusting their government and believing in mass media, this failure can create critical, even oppositional citizenry.

One of the first post-disaster examples of political engagement through social media was seen among farmers in Fukushima. In their attempt to gain reliable data on the danger they collectively faced, the usually fiercely independent farmers shared information, crowdsourcing radiation measurements, across wide swatches of farmland. These attempts produced measurements that were often dramatically at odds with official reports, and thus alerted many farmers to the scope of the problem. Just as importantly, the failure of city offices and representatives from the local or national government to respond to these discrepancies drove a wedge between government and local citizens. Explained a farming woman in Koriyama,

> "I guess it was then that we saw that [the government] was not going to be looking out for us; that we had to do it ourselves." She added, "This was a shock, since we never really thought like that. . . . If it was just our farm being high [in radiation], we probably would not have said anything, but when everyone was high, and we could see it all right there [in our blog], even people I did not know directly—well, there was no other way to think of it, right?[1]

Most of the non-farming population did not, of course, face such immediate and dire consequences. Nevertheless, in much the same way, social media provided important information that led to critical realization and engagement, and the means to highlight the ways in which this information contrasted with official accounts. One college student from Sendai explained her own movement into volunteerism and eventually activism.

> I was not sure at first if to trust information on the Internet, especially when the government or TV said that no one knew the truth. But for me, the key moment was when I read that everything was getting better in the newspaper, and then I saw a picture online, from Onagawa, I think, and it was complete destruction. I was shocked. I felt I could not trust the media, the regular media—TV and newspapers—anymore.

Another woman from Tokyo explained her progressive, if unintended, politicization explicitly with reference to simply being engaged in social media.

> I found that I could connect to so many people, of course, but also to get so many different points of view. If you follow the flow of information, you could get more views, and sort of figure out what you thought about things. . . . I was surprised that so much of what the government says might not be true.

An older mother explained her own "awakening" in this way:

> I am not a political person—I have never been interested in politics—but I found myself learning about [radiation], learning that in some cases, the government actually lied to us. Finally, I was actually debating things like energy policy or the "nuclear village" online.[2]

Political participation is an uneven phenomenon in the best of times, but the threat of Fukushima radiation has been an issue that provided common cause for a wide spectrum of society. It has led many old-time environmental activists and others self-identifying as 'political' (Avenell 2012) to become re-mobilized, in a rise of a sort of submerged politics in the waiting (cf. Cassegard 2014). Many more people unintentionally became political or felt forced to take a stand that had political implications while they were sorting out the more mundane issues of aid, survival and recovery. This resulted in the rise of many new people becoming involved, and even today, some 4 years after the crisis, most people who attend demonstrations are new or post-3.11 participants. Nevertheless, the vast majority are loath to identify themselves as "activists" or "political" at all, reflecting what others have called the "allergy to politics" (Mōri 2012) that plagues much of Japanese society.

The erasure of "politics" as a separate domain

While social media allowed both opportunity and motive for hundreds of thousands of people to link up to others in ways that had a direct effect in the provision of aid and support to those in need, exponentially more participated in the production, transmission and consumption of disaster and recovery information. In people's inboxes, newsfeeds or timelines, information on radiation levels in Fukushima, briefs to lawsuits, and directions to demonstrations circulated across the same networks as did family photos, TV personalities and club openings. We see a blurring of boundaries that once made distinct information sources, effectively removing the line that separated politics from the rest of people's lives. That is, what might once have been thought of a "political domain," removed from the mundane "everyday," is now far more integrated largely through social media, so much so that it is difficult, and for many, and meaningless to some, to even draw such distinctions. The political implications of this erasure are diverse.

This erasure can be seen as compromising the political potential of certain sorts of information through new associations (cf. Morozov 2014). When reports of radioactive coolant leaking into nearby ground water are wedged into one's newsfeeds around delicious desserts and bargain sales, what we see, in effect, is a collapse of distinctions that an older politics assumed to be important, even necessary; that politics is a sort of sacred domain that must be treated specially, seriously, differently. When this assumption is subverted, it can lead to a trivialization, even a commodification, of politics.

One local activist explains his view of this deterritorialization (cf. Savat and Poster 2009) like this: "I don't like using social media. I have to, but it makes everything the same." He continues, "When you read a story about the crackdown on media freedom, for example, what does it mean to 'Like' it? . . . It is as if we are all just consumers of entertainment and consumers of politics. [As if these two were] the same." Here, the assumption is that the everyday is organized around relatively empty consumption patterns—of things, of relationships, of information—and that this repositioning of politics precludes a more critical engagement, and compromises its transformation potential. This is a powerful argument, although it is not shared by everyone.

The other side of the argument is maybe more commonly expressed. Just as social media mix draws us into cheap entertainment and gossipy voyeurism, due to the way it engulfs users in new information-rich environments, it also exposed us to arguments and positions that we would never have been exposed to. We have shown this above. In this reading, the erasure of distinct political domain, its integration into the rest of our lives through social media, politics can claim a new potential. The absence of a clear, and maybe artificial line demarking a self-conscious, even fetishized realm of politics could move people to understand the immediacy, even the necessary intertwined nature of the political in the everyday. Explained one young man, a part-time worker today:

> I was a little bit ahead of my time [in adopting social media]. But it was all just to keep track of my friends and partying. After 3.11, [social media] was the only way to get information about volunteering, then about the safety of my food, and then about the different NPOs [working on food safety]. Even about study sessions and public meeting. Last week, I even went to a rally against war and Japan's Self Defense Forces. For me, each thing just led to another.

The conclusions he draws have been echoed elsewhere. Explained another older man from Fukushima:

> Today, I realize that these things—disaster, volunteering, radiation, politics and life (inochi)—these are completely linked. Just look at my newsfeed—it is all there. In the same way, I am linked to the others living in Fukushima or the real demo organizers here in Tokyo, just like I am linked to my friends and family.

This collapse of boundaries through social media into larger social media flow led many to recognize connections between the political implications of and in the everyday.

One organizer of local protest meetings in Tokyo explains how she exploits this possibility: "Before [3/11], I would have to always begin by explaining why this or that threat was 'relevant' to people's lives. Now, more people see how our activities are connected to their own lives." In reference to the passage of the State Secrets Law of December 2013 (see Repeta 2014), another organizer commented that "when you cannot fully separate the political [from the rest], it makes it that much harder to censor." She explains that the political is hidden, and thus safer from the government, in the continuous flow of everyday information (cf. Zuckerman 2007).

Mediations of post-disaster activism

In the wake of the 3/11 disaster, hundreds of thousands have joined antinuclear rallies across the country, resulting in some of the largest demonstrations in the post-war. While initially ignored by mass media, the protests soon captured the public imagination, prompting widespread endorsement, and declarations of a new era of citizen expressivity. The dominant mass media narrative surrounding this "age of demonstrations" (Karatani 2012), in the years since the 3/11 disaster, has been of spontaneous emergence: of youth, citizens or simply "ordinary people" finding new ways to express their discontent with political representation (cf. Oguma 2013). In ways similar to the wave of uprisings unfolding across the globe in the same period, social media quickly became an important symbol of this spontaneous coalescence. That is, from the so-called Arab Spring to the Indignados and Occupy movements, social media has become widely extolled as more than a mere organizational tool; hailed, often, as a universal catalyst for social change (Gerbaudo 2012).

These generalizations of spontaneous emergence inspired many to participate both online and offline, and as such should be taken seriously. But they also need to be unpacked in the context of local conditions. In this section, we argue that the successful mobilization of so many was also possible due to existing organizational skills and deployment of social capital through networks of dissent developed over the last decade, and even earlier. Interestingly, these networks were not directly those of a waning anti-nuclear movement (Broadbent 1999), nor always of the "invisible" connections forged between older cadres of the New Left (Ando 2013) but often by loosely organized assemblages of autonomous activists, diverse in terms of ideology and repertoire—almost all firmly participating in social media discourse.

In general, mobilization in the disaster aftermath unfolded in two parallel patterns: concentrated series of repeating events, well-organized and with participants numbering in the tens, even hundreds of thousands, and second, a simultaneous profusion of often ad-hoc anti-nuclear protest events, spearheaded by individuals with very little to no experience with public protest. In the first case, social media like Twitter was often talked about as a transparent tool and venue for communicating and coordinating popular discontent and mistrust of government policy. It is in the latter case that we first see the symbol of Twitter emphasized as embodying not only the technology that makes such connection possible, but as a driver or catalyst of such affective connections themselves (cf. Shirky 2008).

Individual expression among the many

The first post-disaster protest against nuclear energy had taken place a mere two weeks after the 3/11 disaster, organized by a high school student in Nagoya, of some 300 participants. But it was a monthly series of demonstrations that became the first symbol of a new age of citizen connectivity, agency and expressivity. On April 10, 2011, more than twenty thousand demonstrators marched exuberantly against nuclear power in Western Tokyo, accompanied by live performances and mobile sound systems; a dramatic contrast to the usually regimented and staid marches hosted by labor unions of much of the post-war period (cf. Manabe 2012; Hayashi and McKnight 2005).

A second demonstration the following month gathered similar numbers, and in June another twenty thousand dancing demonstrators peacefully occupied the square outside Shinjuku station in explicit solidarity with concurrent events in Cairo's Tahrir Square (Amamiya 2011). Social media was instrumental in achieving this kind of turnout. Announced on a blog less than two weeks in advance but widely disseminated across social networks, it became a widely known and awaited event. Yet organizers had little interest in glorifying social media's role as anything more than instrumental to such turnout, preferring a narrative of civil unrest generated by widespread, percolating discontent. As organizer Matsumoto Hajime of the group Amateur's Riot (Shiroto no Ran) explains, "It wasn't because our group tried to recruit many people . . . but because everyone was so angry that word got around on its own" (Manabe 2012). "Why did so many people turn up to the demonstration?" asks another organizer. "They wanted to express themselves, that's why."

At the same time, the instrumentality of social media was emphasized precisely because it symbolized a narrative of emergent citizen expressivity. In a web broadcast, Matsumoto explained his hope that "[even in] an atmosphere that constantly tells you to keep your worries to yourself, people can, even randomly, encounter this situation where it's suddenly possible to say something." Here Matsumoto is alluding to a spontaneously emerging discursive space that includes both exuberant protest crowds and digital publics—hashtags, video streams, imageboard threads, etc. The relationship between online and offline spheres of activity is described as at once instrumental and mutually constitutive: social media is both tool of organization and part of the party itself, situating the political into the everyday by translating an infected language of political participation into "something immanent to protesters' and spectators' own lives" (Hayashi and McKnight 2005, 90).

The campaign took place in a particular moment of post-disaster uncertainty, a lack of information and stifling atmosphere of mass-mediated, state directed, disaster commentary. Along with countless concerts, many popular television shows were cancelled in the first weeks. It was a moment when, much like after the Showa emperor's death in 1989 (Kohso 2006), state and mass media rallied around campaigns of national mourning, steeped in a narrative of pseudo-patriotic rhetoric. This time we saw calls of unity and cooperation, such as "Hang in there, Japan" (*Gambarō Nippon*) as well as more punitive messages that labeled non-official discourse as "dangerous rumor" (*fūhyō higai*) and calls for "self-restraint" (*jishuku*), read by many as "don't complain" and even "don't talk."

The early wave of antinuclear protests offered a space in which various concerns could be expressed simultaneously, in ways where social media proved particularly useful. In the past, and especially among the Japanese left, different groups often worked at cross-purposes, institutionally unable to come together even when they shared ideological positions. The failure was epitomized by the common situation of different groups organizing protest events at different parts of the city on the same day, in what often amounted to competitive, rather than supportive, practice.

On the other hand, in the post–3/11 era, social media figures simultaneously as both connection and environment association that does not coopt the distinctness of individual initiatives or distinct social identities (cf. Hardt and Negri 2004). It allowed different groups to work together to share information, cross tag each others' efforts, and even protest together without having any one group be the official sponsor of the event, thereby threatening the face of another group. This same dynamic, of allowing the many to cooperate without collapsing it into a unity or identity, is how organizers imagined an aggregate of people "showing their individuality while saying, 'We're against nuclear power'" (Manabe 2013).

Rather than a single institution (e.g., a church or labor union) framing a single position, social media encouraged a multitude of connections and contexts, demonstrating the many paths to and possible positions within a shared opposition to the restart of the reactors. In this case, the rallying around a common "adversary" was not so much radiation, nuclear energy or the nuclear industry, per se, as it was a broader, ideological complex of state complicity that many considered the cause of disaster itself, and certainly a complicity that retarded the response (see, for example, Hirose 2011).

Twitter demonstrations

Meanwhile, another group of organizers mobilized the symbolic power of social media in a more explicit direction. Much like the "Shabab-al-Facebook (Facebook Youth)" of the 2011 Egyptian revolution, the "TwitNoNukes" demonstrations elevated the Twitter platform itself into a symbol of active citizenship and dissent. While smaller and more conventional in style, these protest marches of a few thousand participants nevertheless presupposed and accounted for the role of social media in distinct ways. First, the enmeshment of actual and virtual protest spaces became very noticeable in the organizers' explicit endorsement of virtual protest participation as recognized and legitimate "participants." The "Twitter demonstrations" were broadcast live to online spectators vastly outnumbering physical participants. Here, social streaming interfaces like Ustream or Niconico produced a sense of effervescent participation for viewers, and successfully encouraged them to advertise and narrate real-time video feeds in ways that propagated across their own social network.

Secondly, TwitNoNukes organizers themselves derived their own celebrity status and legitimacy not from professional identities (as TV talents or academics) but from their authority as virtual content creators, curators and commentators in their respective subcultural communities. While most decisions were made by an established group of leaders, the public forum of Twitter hashtags implied an accessibility and accountability of individual organizers evocative of a liberal citizenship ideal (cf. Uesugi 2011; Coleman 2013). A TwitNoNukes flyer from early 2012 declares:

> Anyone opposed to nuclear power can participate in this demonstration, regardless of ideological convictions or beliefs or principles. "Radiation is scary!" "I'm worried about the health of my children!" "I want to abolish irradiated labor!" There are plenty of reasons for opposing nuclear power in our daily lives.

But while the "Twitter demonstrations" embodied an idea of individual expression organized collectively, it is a very different collectivity than the multitude imagined by early organizers. In the context of protest they framed their call to action as originating not from an organization or group, but from "individuals gathering on Twitter." Ideologically, these activists thus eschewed both the repertoires of traditional social movements as collective actors, as well as the exuberant performance and frivolity of earlier antinuclear demonstrations (cf. Futatsugi 2012, 144). Instead, they both espoused and embodied a radical individualism modeled on the very structure of the Twitter platform itself. One organizer explains that the campaign "begun after the disaster as a non-partisan, single-issue, simple way to 'lower the threshold' of protest."

In each of these instances, Twitter figures as a symbol embodying not only the technology that makes such connection possible, but also those social and affective connections themselves. Twitter was, in the first case, naturalized as a transparent medium in a cultural environment where spectacular street demonstrations, filled with a roster of artists performing from mobile sound system, was a legitimate venue of political expression. In the second example, Twitter emblematized a counterpublic (cf. Warner 2002) in which "ordinary people" coalesced around well-defined and above all legitimate political concerns.

The ubiquity of social media and the interpenetration of the political content into the everyday, as argued above, implicitly postulate an acting political subject who is simultaneously an "ordinary" person. In contrast, in pre-disaster Japan as elsewhere, recourse to the nomenclature of the "ordinary" or "regular" has been invoked to identify, secure or perform a non-political space and social identity, as we saw above among farmers. Yet, in the contemporary patterns of Twitter participation, a platform of everyday sociality, and the rhetoric of the movement organizers that explicitly included a wide range of participants, in effect re-politicized the "ordinary." As one organizer explains,

> When I march, it is not as an activist, but as just a regular person. To act is regular, and regular people have to act. It is nothing out of the ordinary, at all. . . . We are all regular people here.

A year after the disaster, these symbolic investments in social media returned in distilled form. Weekly antinuclear protests outside the prime minister's office (*Kantei-mae*) grew from a few dozen protesters to the hundreds of thousands. A survey asking participants at the weekly protests where they learned about the event revealed that Twitter was the primary source of information for 39.3 percent of the 491 respondents, while Facebook trumped television, newspapers and organizational newsletters at 6.7 percent (IPRSG 2012). Mass media attention to the weekly rallies seized on the connection between unprecedented turnout and the mobilizing role of social media in bold headlines. As the crowd grew toward the 200,000 mark, primetime television broadcasts announced a "surge" of protest "unfolding on Twitter" (Hōdō Station 2012). Commentators proclaimed the weekly assembly a new symbol of citizen expressivity and soon dubbed it the "Hydrangea Revolution," a nomenclature that was quickly inscribed in the weekly protests as part of their narratives of popular legitimacy.

At a July 2012 rally, sociologist Oguma Eiji declared that "if one person comes to the demonstration, it means another 100 agrees with her . . . and 100 to 200,000 participants equals one to two percent of Tokyo's population, times a hundred . . . that means the majority is on our side!" (Oguma 2012, 137). Similarly, former prime minister Hatoyama Yukio (one of many politicians who opportunistically sought to associate themselves with the protests) warned his fellow lawmakers "not to underestimate this people's power (*pīpuru pawā*); at last, the time has come for great changes caused by actions rather than words" (quoted in Iwakami 2012). At this point, we can see the way that social media has transgressed online and offline segmentation in order to constitute what is seen broadly within Japanese society as a legitimate and significant opposition to both the nuclear state and capital. On the fourth anniversary of 3/11 there are still weekly protests here, testifying to a tenacity and endurance few would have anticipated.

Ambivalent legacy

Social media have become appropriated instrumentally as tools of coordination and mobilization by countless social movements and political organizations worldwide. This chapter has focused on the ways in which social media functioned in liberatory ways, promoting generally progressive causes, local autonomy, environmental sustainability, human rights, representative due process and individual liberty. In any case, we have seen how social media has provided an alternative to both the narratives and expectations of a state and capital that captured popular attention and fostered protester turnout. But the potential to disseminate information in ways that mobilize a wide range of individuals to action are powerful tools that can be used by anyone for any cause.

A case in point in this phenomenon has been the increase in xenophobic demonstrations, primarily against ethnic Koreans, soon finding its locus in the 2011 campaign against private broadcaster Fuji TV and its alleged popularization of Korean soap operas among Japanese television viewers. Monthly demonstrations outside Fuji TV's Tokyo headquarters gathered up to 5,000 participants (with the number of Niconico spectators several times that), seemingly eager to emulate aspects of the "festive" tactics witnessed in the anti-nuclear rallies earlier that year. Coordinated through Twitter hashtags as well as 2-Channel threads and Niconico video feeds, these events branched out into boycotts and attempts at public "shaming" of the station's sponsors, generating considerable media attention before dissipating in a few months. Of particular interest here is not only how in the context of resurgent anti-nuclear protest, a completely different set of issues achieved such considerable organizational momentum, but how in both cases discontent with mass media fed into a similar discourse and use of social media technology as the locus and condition of possibility for an alternative political subjectivity.

The ideological struggle between rival social media constituencies gained new intensity in early 2013, as several antinuclear organizers used Twitter to declare their intent to join the burgeoning antiracist struggle; not as part of the "counter" assemblies but in direct street confrontation with racist groups. On February 9, 2013, live video feeds showed a group of 50 militant right-wingers chased out of Shin-Okubo shopping streets by a crowd of anti-racist activists. Here is a clear case of organizational experience and knowledge produced in socially mediated discourse, and reproduced and redirected horizontally to disparate, although clearly linked, struggles. Yet, even these dynamics contain their ironies. At a public forum at Waseda University in July 2013, invited speakers lamented the inability (of an unnamed collectivity) to "suffocate" the wave of anti-Korean sentiment in its digital cradle—before it "leaked out" onto the streets. This is an inversion of broader narratives of social media, one that subverts the function of social media as a tool for actualizing citizenship, and of the formative and ideological emphasis on liberation that has been at the heart of so much more of the social media politics of post-3/11 Japan.

In December, 2013, the Japanese government passed the State Secrets Law (see Repeta 2014), making it a crime to even inquire into matters that are stipulated to be of national interest. Exactly what information is classified as sensitive or even the criteria by which such classifications might be generated, let alone the process of determination, adjudication and punishment, are still left almost completely undefined. Ostensibly aimed at preventing military and industrial espionage, this law will probably further compromise the already tame, self-censoring mainstream news and TV in Japan. But in fact, the flow of possibly sensitive information is more likely to be found in the online publics of politically engaged, investigative work or critique that constitutes much of those parts of social media we have outlined above. Nevertheless, it is important to remember that other, much more ominous uses of both exclusion and repression are seemingly on the horizon in post-3/11 Japan.

Notes

1 Unless otherwise noted, all direct quotations are from the authors' original research.
2 For a discussion of the "nuclear village" see Kingston 2012.

References

Amamiya, K. (2011) *Occupy Tokyo!!!!!* Available at: http://ameblo.jp/amamiyakarin/entry–11049070440. html (Accessed on November 15, 2011).
Ando, T. (2013) *Japan's New Left Movements: Legacies for Civil Society*, New York: Routledge.
Avenell, S. (2012) 'From Fearsome Pollution to Fukushima: Environmental Activism and the Nuclear Blind Spot in Contemporary Japan', *Environmental History*, 17(2): 244–276.
Broadbent, J. (1999) *Environmental Politics in Japan: Networks of Power and Protest*, Cambridge: Cambridge University Press.

Cassegard, C. (2014) *Youth Movements, Trauma and Alternative Space in Contemporary Japan,* Leiden: Global Oriental.

Coleman, G. (2013) *Coding Freedom: The Ethics and Aesthetics of Hacking,* Princeton, NJ: Princeton University Press.

Futatsugi, S. (2012) 'Rensai: dokyumento han genpatsu demo 3: Twitter demo to Sayonara Atom', *Asahi Webronza.* Available at: http://astand.asahi.com/magazine/wrnational/special/2012030200020.html (Accessed on October 1, 2012).

Gerbaudo, P. (2012) *Tweets and the Streets: Social Media and Contemporary Activism,* London: Pluto.

Guskin, E. (2011) *In Social Media It's All About Japan: PEJ New Media Index March 14–18 (2011),* Pew Research Center. Available at: www.journalism.org/2011/03/24/social–media–its–all–about–japan/ (Accessed on February 8, 2015).

Hardt, M. and Negri, A. (2004) *Multitude: War and Democracy in the Age of Empire,* New York: Penguin.

Hashimoto, Y. (2011) *Media to Nihonjin: Kawariyuku Nichijō,* Tokyo: Iwanami Shoten.

Hayashi, S. and McKnight, A. (2005) 'Good-bye Kitty, Hello War: The Tactics of Spectacle and New Youth Movements in Urban Japan', *Positions: East Asia Cultures Critique,* 13(1): 87–113.

Hirose, T. (2011) *Fukushima Meltdown: The World's First Earthquake-Tsunami-Nuclear Disaster,* (Douglas Lummis, trans.), Charleston, SC: CreateSpace.

Hōdō Station (2012) Asahi Television.

Information Proliferation Rate Study Group (2012) '7.6 kantei-mae survey'. Available at: https://www.facebook.com/media/set/?set=a.436132629760698.100320.100000918939407&type=1&1=27bb2eb0e (Accessed on July 8, 2012).

IT Media (2011) 'Mikusi 2011 nen 3 gatsu ki wa zōshū zoueki', *Business Media Makoto.* Available at: http://bizmakoto.jp/makoto/articles/1105/10/news098.html (Accessed on February 8, 2015).

Iwakami, Y. (2012) *Hatoyama Yukio.* Available at: http://www.ustream.tv/recorded/24067190 (Accessed on July 18, 2012).

Karatani, K. (2012) 'Hito ga demo o suru shakai', *Sekai,* 834: 94–101.

Kingston, J. (2012) *Natural Disaster and Nuclear Crisis in Japan: Response and Recovery After Japan's 3/11,* New York: Routledge.

Kobayashi, A. (2011) *Disaster and Social Media: Confusion, and Connections Guiding Recovery [shinsai to sosharu media: konran, soshite saisei he michibiku hitobito no "tsunagari"],* Tokyo: Mainichi Communications.

Kohso, S. (2006) 'Angelus Novus in Millennial Japan'. In T. Yoda and H.D. Harootunian (eds) *Japan After Japan: Social and Cultural Life from the Recessionary 1990s to the Present,* Durham, NC: Duke University Press.

Manabe, N. (2012) 'The No Nukes 2012 Concert and the Role of Musicians in the Anti–nuclear Movement', *The Asia–Pacific Journal: Japan Focus,* 10(29): 2.

Manabe, N. (2013) 'Music in Japanese Antinuclear Demonstrations: The Evolution of a Contentious Performance Model', *The Asia–Pacific Journal: Japan Focus,* 11(42): 1.

Ministry of Internal Affairs and Communications (2010) *Information and Communications in Japan.* Available at: www.soumu.go.jp/johotsusintokei/whitepaper/ja/h22/pdf/index.html (Accessed on July 11, 2011).

Ministry of Internal Affairs and Communications (2011) *Result of Survey on Trend of Communication Uses of 2010.* Available at: www.soumu.go.jp/main_content/000114508.pdf (Accessed on July 7, 2011).

Mōri, Y. (2012) 'Demo no hōhōron'. In Twitnonukes (ed.) *Demo Iko! Koe wo agereba sekai ga kawaru; machi wo arukeba shakai ga mieru,* Tokyo: Kawade.

Morozov, E. (2014) *To Save Everything, Click Here: The Folly of Technological Solutionism,* New York: Public Affairs.

NEC Biglobe (2011) 'Biglobe ga 3 gatsu no tsuittaa riyō dōkō o happyō: Gekkan toppu 10 wa subete shinsai kanren, 3 gatsu 29 nichi no 1 i wa "kazu"', NEC Biglobe Press Release. Available at: http://trendy.nikkeibp.co.jp/article/pickup/20110427/1035385/?ST=life&P=4 (Accessed on February 8, 2015).

Nikkei Business Publishing (2011) 'Kokuen no naka demo, twitter no okage de panikku ni narazu: yaku 550 ken no koe de wakatta "shinsai to SNS"', *Nikkei Trendy Net.* Available at: http://trendy.nikkeibp.co.jp/article/pickup/20110427/1035385/?ST=life&P=4 (Accessed on February 8, 2015).

Oguma, E. (2012) 'Tokyo jinkō no 1%'. In Setouchi Jakucho, Satoshi Kamata, Yukito Krartain, et al. *Datsu-genpatsu to demo—soshite, minshushugi,* Tokyo: Chikuma.

Oguma, E. (2013) *Genpatsu o tomeru hitobito: 3.11 kara Kantei mae made,* Tokyo: Bungei Shunjū.

Potts, L. (2014) *Social Media in Disaster Response: How Experience Architects Can Build for Participation,* New York: Routledge.

Repeta, L. (2014) 'Japan's 2013 State Secrecy Act – The Abe Administration's Threat to News Reporting', *The Asia–Pacific Journal: Japan Focus,* 12(10): 1.

Savat, D. and Poster, M. (2009) *Deleuze and New Technology*, Edinburgh: Edinburgh University Press.

Shirky, C. (2008) *Here Comes Everybody: The Power of Organizing without Organizations*, New York: Penguin.

Slater, D.H., Nishimura, K. and Kindstrand, L. (2012) 'Social Media, Information and Political Activism in Japan's 3.11 Crisis', *The Asia–Pacific Journal: Japan Focus,* 10(24): 1.

Tomioka, A. (2011) *Jishin: Kigyō no sōsharu katsuyō, shinsaigo wa SNS to tsuittaa no tsukaiwake susum*, RBB Today. Available at: http://www.rbbtoday.com/article/2011/04/28/76606.html (Accessed on February 8, 2015).

Tsuda, D. (2012) *Web de eiji wo ugokasu!* Tokyo: Asahi Shinsho.

Uesugi, T. (2011) *Naze Twitter de tsubuyaku to Nihon ha kawaru no ka*, Tokyo: Shinyusha.

Warner, M. (2002) 'Publics and Counterpublics', *Public Culture*, 14(1): 49–90.

Zuckerman, E. (2007) *Cute Cat Theory: The China Corollary*. Available at: http://www.ethanzuckerman.com/blog/2007/12/03/cute–cat–theory–the–china–corollary/ (Accessed on November 12, 2014).

6

Bridging art, technology, and pop culture: some aspects of Japanese new media art today

Machiko Kusahara

In the 1930s, Walter Benjamin discussed how mechanical reproduction technology changed art in his seminal text "The Work of Art in the Age of Mechanical Reproduction." Today we live in an age of digital (re)production and communication technologies that allow a wider public to create, publish, and appreciate images and sounds. Uploading and downloading pictures or videos have become part of everyday life. Works by both professionals and hobbyists are listed side by side on the Net, making the border between them unclear. Digital media unleashed our desire to express and to be recognized, regardless of social or academic background. Actions have been taken to support and promote new forms of creativity. Creative Commons, the "Make" community, fab café, open source software such as "processing," are just some examples. The industry is interested in so-called user-generated content (UGC) as well. The remarkable success of the virtual singer Hatsune Miku in Japan since 2007 is an example of how people's creativity could burst out when appropriate tools and infrastructure are offered.[1] In short, a wide variety of creative activities are taking place outside the "art world" today, some reaching a professional level—there are plenty of stories of young talented people who were "discovered" on the Net and became professional artists.

What does this phenomenon mean to art and the "art world"? It seems there is still a clear divide between venues for these activities (YouTube, Vimeo, Instagram, Facebook, etc.) and the "authorized" exhibition spaces.[2] Should artists stay in the white cube, or should they try to reach a wider public outside museums and galleries? Can artists speak to the public without compromising artistic quality when there are so many "fun" things on the Net? And most importantly, what is art, and what is the role of an artist? There will not be a final answer to these questions.

These questions and concerns are more directly related to media artists. Using contemporary technology these artists question issues we face in media society. Like Mail art carried by Fluxus members they use everyday technology to create unusual artworks that challenge our understanding of the media. Or they use latest technologies that people have no access yet, giving us a glimpse of what is to come in the near future. In many ways media art inherits the experimental spirit of pre-war and post-war avant-garde art such as Dada, surrealism, futurism, Fluxus, and E.A.T. They often (mis)use popular media technologies of the time—such as film and television—not only to reveal or expand the medium itself but also to comment on the society and push the border of art itself.

Art and art history in Japan

Convergence of art, design, technology and entertainment has a long history in Japanese culture outside the academic art world.[3] It is important to remember what we understand as art is a paradigm that was established in the West as modern society formed itself. It is not a "natural" concept that would grow in any culture. Japanese art has a long history that was basically independent from that of the West until mid-nineteenth century.[4] As a result a unique aesthetics developed, which did not set a clear border between art and design. The distinction between Fine art and Applied art was not solid either, as can be seen from painted screens and sliding doors in old temples in Kyoto.

Even though art education in Japan is based on Western art history and Japanese contemporary artists have been internationally active, the border between art and its related fields remains more flexible compared to the West. Artists are invited to design commercial products, games and store facades, while designers create art works, installations, or curate art exhibitions.[5] In addition, widespread pop culture including *manga*, *anime*, character (*kyara*), and idol (*aidoru*) inevitably influence visual culture and inspire artists.[6] The composer Keiichiro Shibuya featured Hatsune Miku as the heroine and the only singer in his opera *The End* (2013). Conceived after the Great Earthquake of Tohoku, the virtual character (which is represented as a digital image) faces the fear of death as her 3D data starts to decay. A younger media artist, Daito Manabe, designs visual effects for the stage performances and the interactive website for the techno-pop band Perfume using the latest technology and with a distinctive style. It is a commercial work, but there is an unmistakable signature of the artist who is known for his experimental approach. Commercial projects do not conflict against his career as an artist. Rather, the feedback between artistic and commercial projects seems to be a driving force for his experiments.

Today there is a space where art, design, technology, entertainment and pop culture meet. Japanese cultural tradition and the power of pop culture help media artists to use the space to explore what media art could bring to us, pushing the border of art. In the following text, works and activities of artists who have played a major role in bridging these fields will be discussed. Behind the entertaining surface of their works there are serious thoughts on the nature of media art, the role of artists and our relationship to technology.

Media art and more: works by Toshio Iwai

For the media artist Toshio Iwai making his works more accessible to a wider public outside museums and galleries is an important part of his concept.[7] It is probably rooted in his childhood when his parents told him to design and create toys and gadgets himself instead of playing with off-the-shelf toys. Iwai gets ideas both from everyday life and from media history, surprising the audience often by a unique combination of already known technologies that produces magical results, as in case of his early installation *Time Stratem* (1985–1990), for which he used a TV monitor as a stroboscopic light source to create a sequence of 3D zoetrope effect. *Distorted House* (2005), developed in collaboration with NHK Science & Technology Research Laboratories, is a further development of sophisticated use of stroboscopic effects. Including his early series *Man-Machine-TV No. 1-8* (1989), many of Iwai's interactive pieces invite audience/visitors not only to enjoy the experience and feel the sense of awe but also to learn something about media and technology. Rather than keeping his creations on his own, he is interested in sharing them with others to help their creativity.

Figure 6.1   Toshio Iwai, *TENORI-ON* ©2007 Iwai/Yamaha

Such is the case with *TENORI-ON*, which Iwai co-developed with Yamaha in 2007. The electronic audiovisual instrument was meant for use by anyone from children to professional musicians.[8] The matrix of white LED lights functions both for input and output that produce sound and image simultaneously. The instrument is "the final version" of a series of works Iwai had developed over years on various platforms including cell phone and game machines, as well as physical setup with a transparent table and marbles. Translation and interaction between sound and image is the basic concept of these works. His works along this concept includes *Piano – As Image Media*, the piece he produced at ZKM in 1995, which was further developed in collaboration with the composer Ryuichi Sakamoto into *Music Plays Images x Images Play Music (MPIxIPM)*, winning the Golden Nica at Ars Electronica in 1997. In this piece, as Sakamoto played a MIDI piano, each sound turned into a pattern of light that arose from the piano and filled the space between the piano and the ceiling, before evaporating in the air. Then, images produced by movements of Sakamoto's hands turned into particles of light that would fall onto the piano keyboard, producing sounds while bouncing on it. Remote audiences on the Internet could send numbers representing the piano keys, which also turned into light patterns that would "hit" the keyboard and produced sound. It was truly a magical and beautiful performance. But his further goal was in making such conversations between sound and image accessible for anyone.

After working on a variety of platforms, from custom hardware to workstations, Iwai came to a conclusion that it is not an artist's job to maintain works by upgrading the operating system or transplanting to a new platform, which is a time consuming work without much creativity. He found it necessary and appropriate to collaborate with a reliable commercial company that produces, distributes and maintains such system. The idea was already realized with *ELECTRO-PLANKTON* (2005) for Nintendo's DS—the first "art" title for the game platform.[9] In traditional Western art history, art should not be "useful." Turning it into a commercial product will be even worse. But is it that simple? Do "products" such as Marcel Duchamp's *Rotorelief*, Nicolas Schoffer's *Lumino*, Olafur Eliasson's *Little Sun* have nothing to do with art? Interactive art already turned the audience into "users." Making one's artwork more widely accessible is a next logical step. Industrial reproduction technology does not provide Benjamin's aura, but it may help establish a new approach in art.

Iwai's involvement in pop culture is multiple. He made a major contribution to Japanese TV production with an experimental TV program for children titled *Ugo Ugo Lhuga* (1992–94). Besides designing the virtual set and characters he developed a low-cost system connecting Nintendo game controllers to personal computers and the high-end production system of the TV studio to enable real-time interaction between real and virtual characters.[10] He also invited young independent animators to include their low-resolution animation made with personal computers in the program.[11] The pop, speedy, and "surreal" (in fact, the main character Iwai created was a surrealist painter named *sur*) taste of the program was widely supported not only by children but also by adults. It was a rather shocking discovery in the TV industry that high quality image no longer had the highest priority for the audience, which is not surprising when many Japanese have grown up enjoying *manga* and playing games. Use of personal computers in TV production became commonplace since then.

Two very large three-dimensional zoetropes and several phenakistiscopes he created for the Ghibli Museum in suburban Tokyo, invited by the animation director Hayao Miyazaki, are other examples of Iwai's wide range of activity to bridge art and pop culture.[12] Children watch the zoetrope that features scenes from Miyazaki's popular animation film *Totoro* with their eyes and mouths wide open, truly excited to see the magical transition from static diorama to three-dimensional animation.[13]

The sense of playfulness so evident in all his works is closely related to the nature of interactive art. At the same time we can see traces of Japanese culture that allows flexible approach to art with appreciation of playfulness and curiosity to technology. With many works he created, Iwai led and made a major contribution to Japanese media art, encouraging younger artists as well as researchers and engineers to experiment across genres and categories, merging analog and digital technologies, pushing the border of art and beyond.

Imagination comes true: Kazuhiko Hachiya

Creative use of technology is essential in the works of Kazuhiko Hachiya. *Inter Dis-Communication Machine* (1993), which has been widely exhibited including at Ars Electronica 95, is a playful commentary to virtual reality. To experience this work two participants wear customary HMD-like helmets, each equipped with a CCD video camera and a microphone besides the screen and a headset. As in a normal VR setting, each participant can only see the screen in front of his/her eyes and hear the sound emitted from the headset. However, what he/she sees and hears are the images and sounds sent from the camera and the microphone attached to the other person's HMD. The two participants literally exchange their sight and sound, seeing the world from the other person's point of view. They have to communicate and collaborate in order to find their own locations in the real world.

The idea sounds simple, but the resulting experience is hilarious. Participants feel relieved when they finally meet and touch each other, hugging or shaking hands – which means finding and hugging oneself in the screen! Giving rise to a system for communication via an "inter-discommunication" system is the aim of this work. Behind Hachiya's approach toward communication is the notion of identity or self in Japanese cultural tradition. The sense of individuality has never been as strong as in the West, easily yielding to others' opinions rather than establishing one's own point of view.[14] Ironically, but playfully, *Dis-Communication Machine* shows what happens when one sees the world through someone else's vision.

Communication is one of Hachiya's major themes. *ThanksTail* (1996–2004) is a doggy-tail to be attached on the back of a car that the driver can use to express the sense of gratitude by remotely wagging it. Isn't it rather sad that cars are equipped only with communication tools for warning and alarming? He made a functioning prototype in 1996 as an artwork to be exhibited, but his goal was not in creating a museum piece but in making this attachment available for anyone, so that cars will get a device for a friendly communication and the automobile society we live in could be a little better. After the artist had uploaded a project proposal on his website calling for a business partner, a car accessory manufacturer, which happened to be a subsidiary of major toy company Takara, found it and showed an interest. As a result *ThanksTail* was distributed at major car accessory shops in 2004 as an interesting option for one's car, not as an artwork.[15]

PostPet (1997–2006) is another "product" by Hachiya based on his interest in designing more playful communication. *PostPet* is email software featuring a virtual pet that lives on the user's desktop and delivers email to his/her friends. A user could make a choice between one of the animals (dog, cat, turtle, rabbit) and robot characters to be one's "postman" while taking care of and enjoying conversation with his/her pet. The pet has its own life, moods and temperament.[16] As in the case of *Inter Dis-Communication Machine*, playful twists designed by the artist trigger more interaction among the users. *PostPet* became extremely successful and popular at the dawn of the Internet era in Japan on Sony Communication Network (SCN), one of the major Internet providers. Here again the artist conceived the idea and proposed it to a company to collaboratively realize the service.[17] Already practicing network art in the pre-Internet era in Japan, Hachiya saw a possibility in more creative and playful services on the Net for a wider audience, a vision that could not be realized without collaborating with a major provider that respects the artist's concept. It was a challenge for both the artist and the company, but the collaboration worked well.[18]

Realizing an imaginary vehicle is another theme of Hachiya. Since he saw the film *Back to the Future*, building an "air board" that would glide in the air without any wheels had become his dream. Hachiya took a special training session to learn to operate the world's smallest jet engine of the time and purchased one for his piece *AirBoard* (1997–2001). With his team of engineers and designers Hachiya built an "air board," which is about the same size as a surfboard but accommodates the jet engine. After several stages of development and trial the final test took place in 2001 in the courtyard of Tokyo's Museum of Contemporary Art on a heavily snowy day. The jet engine started and the *AirBoard* lifted itself above the water-soaked ground, gliding from the realm of imagination into reality, carrying Hachiya himself and then the lucky volunteers chosen from the audience. However, it didn't look very easy to stay balanced on the board—one would need to be experienced to keep riding it.

Figure 6.2   Kazuhiko Hachiya, *Open Sky Project: M-02J* (2014)

His next project using the jet engine was *Open Sky* (2003–present). The goal was to build a personal jet glider similar to the aircraft used by the heroine of Hayao Miyazaki's 1984 animation film *Nausicaa of The Valley of The Wind*. The seagull-shaped jet glider was designed by Hachiya and his collaborators using open source software. Design/development process and document videos were shared online, creating a community of supporters and making the project an arena for collaboration and discussion. After numerous test flights without the engine its gliding capability was proven. The jet engine was finally installed in 2013 and Hachiya has been test flying it.[19] According to Hachiya, the concept behind it is to show the possibility to "open the sky" to individuals.[20] Still, the initial motivation of the project seems to be similar to that of *AirBoard*—a genuine dream to realize the future machine shared in our imagination.[21]

The art of role playing: Maywa Denki

Maywa Denki is an art unit led by Novmichi Tosa.[22] It was originally co-founded with his elder brother Masamichi in 1993 as Novmichi's master thesis project. The brothers developed a series of electric and electronic "nonsense machines," named *Naki Series* and *Tsukuba Series* with more to follow.[23] Many of them are musical instruments of some kind they can use for performance besides exhibiting as art pieces. The duo became professional artists after winning the grand prize from Sony Music's Art Artist Audition in the same year.

The name of the unit means Maywa Electric company, and it is represented—or assimilated (as *mitate* in Japanese)—as a small-scale electric device manufacturing company led by a CEO (i.e., the artist), who invents strange products one after another in the struggle to survive the tough competition manipulated by mega-companies.[24] It is a fiction, but it is based on their family history. The name of the art unit was taken from the real electric device company their engineer father used to own and which went bankrupt when the brothers were young. The 1970s oil crisis smashed small industries that had supported the postwar rapid economic growth of the country. After Masamichi "retired because of age" in 2001 when he became 35, Novmichi took the position of CEO.

Maywa Denki creates a series of functional, stylish, yet funny and often satirical machines as "products" (i.e., art works), using both low-tech and high-tech, mixing mechanical, electric, and digital technologies. Many of them are robotic and function as musical instruments. Novmichi Tosa is a talented musician as well, who writes, composes and plays all the songs they sing including "Maywa Company Song," which are published as CDs.[25] Tosa and his "employees" (i.e., young artists and art students) perform on the stage wearing "company uniforms" (which is part of Japanese culture) singing and playing these "useless machines" one after another for their "product demonstration."[26] Usually the machines Tosa designs function amazingly properly, but if not, the trouble adds a comical element to the performance. Even at such moments the "employees" (who are called only by non-names such as Employee A, B, C, etc.) show no expression or emotion, but precisely do their tasks in a mechanical manner in silence, which makes the scene even more amusing. Everything is a sort of role-play.[27] Some of the instruments are available by order through their website. Smaller items, toys and gadgets are "mass-produced" at a factory in China and distributed by a small toy company named Cube through online and offline shops.[28]

Although Tosa calls his artworks "nonsense machines" and the performances are funny and enjoyable, there is an unmistakable irony toward the capitalistic nature of mass production/consumption society. Instead of criticizing it directly, he created an upside-down simulation of a small company, its products and workers who are inevitably part of the situation. Thus the world of Maywa Denki itself is a long-term and large-scale art project.[29] From this point of view an important element of Maywa Denki is "mass-produced" devices and gadgets that Tosa designs and makes commercially available.

In 1994 Tosa invented *Na-Cord NAKI-DX*, a fish-bone-shaped electric extension cable as a commercial product for home.[30] It was even officially registered as a product design. In the extremely funny video (in English) introducing *Naki Series*, Tosa explains *Na-Cord* visually reminds us that it connects and "go[es] between" the power station and home appliances.[31] He adds that the spikes may hurt the user's foot if stepped on barefoot by mistake (as shoes are not worn in Japanese houses). It reminds us of the nature of electricity we tend to forget—its possible harm to our body and life.[32] For those who could not afford *Na-Cord*, its mini-size version is easily available as a cell phone strap in various colors at a modest price. When attached to a cell phone, the strap may damage one's pocket with its spikes. The gadgets playfully reveal what is behind the "ubiquitous environment," not just about electricity or cell phones but also about our relationships to technology itself. In another "demonstration video" he explains in a matter-of-fact style how the product is "mass-produced," while on the screen ten or so middle-aged Japanese men and women assemble the parts in a small, rather dark old hall. The scene reminds us of Japan in 1960s, or it could be anywhere in Asia today under the impact of economic globalism. The video suggests there are multiple layers of meanings to be read behind *Na-Cord*.

A goal the industry and engineers pursue is a foolproof environment in which users do not have to think about technology. Technology becomes invisible in a black box or hidden behind walls. However, a media artist would rather visualize the true nature of technology. It can happen at users' homes, outside museums and galleries, if the artwork is designed to be safe (at least to certain extent) and maintenance-free. Mass-producing these gadgets in an anonymous factory in China is both a commentary to the consumer society today and a criticism to the "art world" that has nothing to do with the life of normal people using everyday commodity. But serious concepts are hidden beneath the playful top layer. Useful/useless, funny/ironical, pop and being a part of daily life, these products have appealed to those who are not necessarily regular museum-goers.[33] But once a user becomes interested in Maywa Denki through these funny gadgets or songs he publishes in J-pop style, one can approach the artist's more personal thoughts through his *Edelweiss Series* (2000–present) which represents a sci-fi like story in a futuristic imaginary world—or an artistic version of a role-playing game around sex, life and space. The series started with a story he wrote, followed by illustrations, storyboard, diorama, animation, jewels and books, as well as robotic instruments and sculptures he creates inspired by the story. Tosa felt he needed to launch the series as an output of his genuine artistic creativity without a pressure to be playful.[34] Yet it is still part of the Maywa Denki world. The robotic instruments and sculptures are used in the performances besides being shown at art exhibitions.

Wahha GoGo (2009) and *Otamatone* (2009) show how Tosa copes with an artwork and a commercial product simultaneously. Among many gadgets Maywa Denki has invented as commercial products, *Otamatone* became a smash hit that sold more than a million units. The tadpole-shaped handy musical instrument was developed after a series of human-size robotic instruments that simulate the function of human vocal cord. One of them is *Wahha GoGo* which laughs aloud when a human exerts enough energy to wind the robot up via the heavy rotating wheel. The artificial vocal cord controls the pitch, formant, and the volume of laughter with metal gears and cams, similar to the technique used by the nineteenth-century automata makers—everything is

Figure 6.3   Novmichi Tosa (Maywa Denki) plays the Otamatone Deluxe

analog. Deeply ironic, it is the human's sweat that makes the robot laugh, which in turn makes everyone start laughing.

Otamatone was developed using the same vocal cord idea. The artist's goal was to provide a musical instrument that anyone can play a melody without being able to read a musical score, which resonates to the idea behind Iwai's *TENORI-ON*. A user will play music by sliding fingers on the tadpole tail and pushing its *kawaii* (cute) face to get a vibration effect. However, it almost always gets slightly out of tune, which makes both the player and the audience laugh.[35] *Otamatone* immediately sold out during the Christmas season in 2009 and won the grand prize at the Toy Award in 2010 in its High Target Toy division. The artist has been adding different colors and models to the product line since then, including *Otamatone Melody* for children, *Otamatone Deluxe* for performance purposes, and *Otamatone Digital* with keyboard. Probably not many users of these instruments knew about Maywa Denki, but people liked the idea and the pop design of the product.[36] These commercial products and gadgets originate from his artistic concept, but are re-designed to meet various requirements.

There is not enough space to introduce the originality of the many artworks and gadgets Tosa has created since 1993.[37] All in all, Tosa's goal is making art accessible to a wider public either through art exhibitions and performances or as gadgets. Accepting the fact that we live in a mass consumption society, Tosa utilizes—or hacks—the "mass production" system, fully uses the net media for promotion, and distributes his "products" through Amazon. While the traditional system of art still values artworks based on its rarity in spite of Benjamin's discussion, Tosa believes in a different kind of value in art that penetrates people's lives, which is a logical development in the age of digital reproduction technology.

The culture of *mitate*

One of the early commercial products from Maywa Denki is a 64 pixel wearable display called *BITMAN* (1999), co-developed with a younger artist Ryota Kuwakubo. Kuwakubo also invented *Video Bulb* (2003-2004), a lipstick-like video memory that plays animation when plugged into the video jack of a TV monitor. Kuwakubo is known for interactive installations such as *PLX* (2001) and *LoopScape* (2003) that playfully and ironically change the language of shooting games, as well as for *Tenth Sentiment* (2010), a non-interactive installation in which an LED light from a miniature train casts shadows of daily commodities—mostly from 99 cent stores—placed on the floor, creating a dazzling visual magic. Like Maywa Denki, his works bridge analog and digital, machine and human body, with a sense of wonder but not without a connection to our daily life.[38] His latest commercialized work is Nikodama (earlier spelled Nicodama), which is a set of two "eyeballs" that wirelessly coordinate to blink together. By attaching them an object will instantly turn into a character with the effect of *mitate,* he explains. The concept is to help our environment by giving "life" to things people may easily throw away. The product made a great success as many users liked to create their own characters around them.[39]

Mitate is a term which often appears in explaining artworks as well as in daily life in Japan. It means a conscious act of showing/seeing a thing from a different viewpoint.[40] While it is based on universal human capability of imagination and association, *mitate* is a cultural phenomenon. It adds multiple layers of meanings to artworks and helps an artist to set a serious theme behind a playful and attractive surface. Maywa Denki's *Naki Series* is built on a series of *mitate*. Its basic concept is (according to Tosa) to understand oneself by assuming the artist were a fish in a tank. *Mitate* is involved in each piece as well. It is a way of using metaphors, associations, appropriation, simulation and double meanings often in a playful manner to (re)present and read/imagine alternative meanings behind real/physical (and often normal or unimportant) objects or scenes. Different to metaphor, *mitate* allows an interpretation very different from what is originally meant or actually visible. For this reason it was often used for satire. An important or sacred figure would be interpreted as figures such as a beggar, a prostitute or a daily utensil with a clever choice of words or images.

The origin of *mitate* goes back to medieval times. The word first appears in *Kojiki*—the book of history that is supposedly published in the early eighth century. The idea widely spread in Japanese culture including the tea ceremony, flower arrangement, bonsai, and gardens as well as religious ceremonies, and literature including *haiku*.[41] For example, at the stone garden of Ryoanji Temple, white sand will be seen as a representation of the ocean. The concept was defined in tea ceremony by its practical founder Rikyu as to see an object, not in the form that was originally intended for it, but as another thing. He found beauty in an everyday household article such as a gourd he appropriated into a flower base, or a Korean rice bowl as perfectly suitable to serve tea. The "found" object needs to be aesthetically interesting and fully functional, while the gap between its purported use and the newly discovered use brings an excitement.

The nature of *mitate* is in the fun of offering and discovering a surprisingly different meaning behind the presented reality. Clues are cleverly placed, while interpretation is open to each viewer as far as one could justify it. The term was often used in the Edo era (1600–1868) especially in kabuki and woodblock print titles. Part of the reason was the severe control on entertainment. Depicting contemporary and actual themes was strictly forbidden. To avoid legal conflicts, the art of *mitate* achieved its maximum complexity in the late Edo era, while its inventiveness and playfulness became an attraction by itself. The intellectual interplay was enjoyed among townspeople as well as with numerous books and prints.

The fun of "reading" images, the excitement in discovering something new, and multiple layers of meanings that invite a viewer to come back to a piece—these are the essence of appreciating art. With a more whimsical tone than metaphor, *mitate* creates a rich body of meaning that becomes an interface between an artist and a viewer.

Device Art

In the classic framework of art, an artwork is considered the final product of a maestro's talent, to be hung on the museum or gallery wall to be appreciated by the visitors behind the "Don't Touch" signs. The situation can be quite different with media art. Often a piece has no "final form" but keeps growing either autonomously or interactively. In interactive art the audience becomes participants, forming a part of the artwork. Instead of a paintbrush, a media artist may use invisible tools or industrial material, or invent the tool itself, which, in this case, becomes the "final" product for people for free use. Often "Please Touch!" would be more appropriate as a sticker on the wall. Although museums and galleries are still the most important venues for media artists to show their works (except for Internet art projects), the traditional paradigm of art based on Western art history no longer fully applies to media art. The participatory nature of media art indeed pre-empted and informed Nicolas Bourriaud's relational aesthetics (1998). Also, media art works are not meant for collectors but for a wider public who would enjoy and learn more about what media technology means to their life. Media arts expand the contexts for reaching people beyond museums and galleries.

Device Art is a project that started in Japan in 2004 as a proposal to the question what can be the specific features that characterize media art. Project members included Hachiya, Tosa and Kuwakubo among others. There were several reasons why the project was conceived and the artists gathered. First, a clear tendency in Japanese media art is the interest in designing the physical interface.[42] Not only artists but also young engineers and engineering students are eager to make art, or at least something enjoyable. Interest in technology and appreciation for the right tools and materials, a long tradition in Japanese culture, seems to be acting in media art as well.[43] Second, Japanese media art works have been often criticized that they tend to be playful rather than serious. Especially in interactive art, playfulness has an important role in inviting the audience to try the piece. Interestingly, statistically it is known that Japanese media artists are more interested in interactive art compared to other countries. As we have seen with works by artists, playfulness functions hand in hand with the system of *mitate*. In the current Japanese atmosphere, in which a too serious look is avoided by the general public, having a playful feature becomes an important strategy for artists to survive. But if the work is only playful, it will become a technological entertainment that would be soon forgotten. Third, the relationship between art and design seemed different from that in the West. An artist who produces "commercial products" for a good reason is respected. Analyzing these phenomena will bring a better understanding of what media art is and what it could be.

Device Art is defined as a type of media art that consists of a physical object such as a machine or an interface with certain mechanism—either analog or digital—as its core part to realize the artist's concept. We can imagine an interactive installation piece with an original interface and mechanism designed by the artist. According to Hiroo Iwata, an artist/engineer who conceived the project, "Device Art is a new form of art that displays the essence of technology through the use of new materials and mechatronic devices. This concept challenges the traditional paradigm of art by its convergence of technology, art and design."[44] While the first sentence seems to link technology with a functionalism akin engineering, Iwata's latter words highlight the importance of artists in revealing the "essence of technology."

More recently the role of play as essential to creative practice and industries has become conceptualized in the West (Sicart 2014) after a long legacy in Japan. Media art needs to be theorized for its own sake, not bound to traditional art history. Device Art started from an observation on Japanese media art, which eventually developed into more universal concepts such as the role of playfulness, use of metaphors and the relationship between art, design and commercial products. The flexibility in defining art in Japanese culture has certain advantage when compared to the Western art tradition that regards art as a privileged activity. On the other hand an artist needs to consciously maintain one's concept in a society in which the waves of pop culture wash the shore of art all the time. As in case of Hachiya's *AirBoard*, one may need to be experienced.

Notes

1 The users of the software can share their creativities on the Net without a concern on copyright restrictions. Miku phenomenon will be discussed in more detail later.

2 In the "multimedia" fever from mid 1990s to early 2000s, CD-ROM and the Net became popular platforms for digital artists. Museums and art festivals exhibited them. Walker Art Center's *Gallery 9* curated by Steve Dietz and the *Net Art Selection* for the 2002 Whitney Biennial curated by Christiane Paul are such examples. However, partly due to several practical reasons, offering computers to visitors to interact with artists' works has become a rather exceptional case in art exhibitions.

3 For more information and detailed analysis on Japanese media art in relation to design, technology and commercial product, see Kusahara (2006). Device Art is a concept derived from observation and analysis of Japanese media art today. It is also the name of a project carried by a group of artists, engineers and researchers including the author to seek for a new relationship between art, technology, science and design.

4 The influence came mostly from China.

5 In contemporary art, Takashi Murakami has been strategically breaking the borders. Yayoi Kusama, who was an active avant-garde artist in New York in the 1960s, designed the *iida* series of cell phones in 2009 with her famous red and white polka dots. Designers such as Masahiko Sato and Tokujin Yoshioka have been recognized by their artworks.

6 Already in 1920s Japanese Dada artists used *manga* as their medium. Masamu Yanase, a painter who co-founded a Dadaist group MAVO, was also a *manga* artist who contributed to a major newspaper. One of his MAVO colleagues Suiho Tagawa became extremely popular as a *manga* artist. In the 1960s *manga* became a medium of art again. Icons of pop culture have inspired artists such as Andy Warhol and Roy Lichtenstein, but Japanese artists may be more directly involved in contemporary culture.

7 Iwai graduated from the Plastic Art and Mixed Media graduate program of Tsukuba University where Katsuhiro Yamaguchi and other faculty members taught new media art. His works have been shown around the world, and he produced works as artist-in-residence at San Francisco's Exploratorium, ZKM in Karlsruhe, and IAMAS in Japan. More recently Iwai has been active and extremely successful as an author of children's books, which originated from materials he prepared for his own daughters. He also published a set of paper cut-out puppets for children to play with and make their own animation.

8 TENORI-ON instantly sold out on the Net when it was released. A professional VJ revealed he kept on tapping the keyboard to access Yamaha's website to get one for himself.

9 After he produced an interactive piece at Exploratorium for children, Iwai developed it into an "art-game" cartridge for the Nintendo Famicom console. It was never released by Nintendo, but later published as

SimTunes from Maxis. He also designed a "communication game" system for Sony's PlayStation 2, with which children can share the screen to draw together.

10 Two children interacted with the virtual characters. The real-time system was needed for efficient production of the daily program. All the sequences with the children for the week (5 days) could be recorded in one afternoon. The title of the program is the backward reading of "Go Go Girl."

11 Already with *Einstein TV* (1990–1991) Iwai used low resolution animation in "multimedia" aesthetics.

12 The two zoetropes are: *Totoro Pyon Pyon* (Totoro jumping) and *Josho Kiryu* (updraft air flow).

13 Iwai renovated the mechanisms of old toys such as flipbook, zoetrope and music box with electric and electronic technologies. Erkki Huhtamo discusses Iwai's works in detail from media archaeological viewpoint in a forthcoming book edited by Christiane Paul.

14 In Hachiya's earlier network project *Mega diary*, 100 participants on the net would exchange their diaries for 100 days to virtually share their lives without ever meeting in the real space. The project is meant to be repeated for 100 times with different members to reach the "mega" diary. In his interactive installation, *Seeing is believing,* which is based on *Mega diary,* visitors can read others' diaries through an optical coding/decoding system the artist developed.

15 As a commercial product it was not a great success due to technical limitations. (Bluetooth technology was not available then.)

16 *PostPet* is different in concept from having an agent for emailing or simulating real pets. The character design is pop and the conversation is often absurd. The fun is in giving up one's position as the master and allowing the pet to have its own life and character. Each pet has a temper of its own. A pet would not come home immediately if he/she meets a friend (i.e., another virtual pet) while delivering the message, which means the user cannot send another email using this software until it is back. The user would then call his/her friend and ask what his/her pet is doing there. A pet even starts writing messages if the user is not using the software often enough and the pet becomes bored. If the user still fails to care the pet, the frustrated pet would leave its room on the desktop and move to PostPet Park, where the community of ex-PostPets keeps on going. Users can visit PostPet Park to meet their former pets and become friends to other ex-users through their ex-pets, or enjoy online shopping at the stores. A wide variety of *PostPet* goods, events and related services were offered to users.

17 The software brought a great success to the company, selling 100,000 licenses in the first six months and increasing the number of young users. Later SCN users could choose between a standard web mail system or a *PostPet* mail service. The pink teddy bear Momo became the official mascot figure of SCN to be used for advertisement. It even appeared on the cover of a book written by an ex-CEO of Sony Group.

18 There were elements and technical issues he had to compromise or modify his ideas to meet requirements for a commercial product, he admits. But that was also an interesting challenge for him. After the service ended on SCN Hachiya continued the project as *PostPet Now.*

19 The original plan was to have a girl as a pilot true to the film, but eventually Hachiya decided to test-pilot the aircraft himself because of the possible risk of life. In fact the original engine from *AirBoard* burnt out at one point, and was replaced by a new engine. Questions and concerns about the relationship between our body and technology is an essential theme for Hachiya, who used to be a gymnast.

20 As can be guessed from the title of the project, which came from the book by Paul Virilio, Hachiya maintains a socio-political approach to media and media art since his early works.

21 Hachiya's other works can be visited at his website (partially bilingual): www.petworks.co.jp/~hachiya/works/shi_ting_jue_jiao_huanmashin.html (Accessed on February 1, 2015). PetWORKS is a company he co-founded to realize PostPet.

22 For the history, artworks (products) and Tosa's CV see the bilingual website: www.maywadenki.com/ (Accessed on February 1, 2015). His original name, Nobumichi, is often used in texts and websites.

23 There are 26 artworks in the *Naki Series* with a fish motif, each representing a piece of thought in Tosa's mind. *Tsukuba Series* is named after the name of the city and the university where he studied. Tosa and Kuwakubo studied at the same graduate program as Iwai.

24 The "corporate identity" was carefully designed by the artist and Sony Music's art director, Norio Nakamura.

25 Tosa composes in J-pop style. The techno-pop composer Satoru Wono helps with the musical arrange-ment and performs as "Mr. Ono, the Accountant" on the stage playing the role of a typical clerk of a small enterprise.

26 The uniform is a typical one used by electric engineers in "Maywa blue" color. The one for the "presi-dent" is specially designed by Agnes B.

27 Tosa jokes it's a *kosupure* (costume-play) as he wears the company uniform. Personal conversation.

28 Cube's website presents gadgets designed by Tosa and other independent artists/designers. See www.cube-works.co.jp/index_e.html (Accessed on February 1, 2015).

29 Behind "nonsense" and even crazy-looking works and products there is a systematic thinking and detailed plans for production and packaging. Maywa Denki was awarded the prestigious *Good Design Award* from Japan Industrial Design Promotion Organization in 2000, the first case the award was given to a human being, not a product.

30 When commercialized, the original spiky "bones" had to be rounded to a certain extent to meet the industrial standard. The head also became less aggressive. Compare the original *Na-Cord NAKI DX* and its commercialized version *Na-Cord* from following links: www.maywadenki.com/products/naki/na-cord/, www.maywadenki.com/products/goods/na-cord-series/ (Accessed on February 1, 2015).

31 *Na-Cord* is a homonym of a Japanese word meaning a go-between, or a matchmaker. Including *Na-Cord*, all the "products" in *Naki Series* involve *mitate*, a Japanese tradition of using metaphors and wordplays. The role of *mitate* will be discussed later.

32 It is a theme often featured in their early electric machines "using 100 volts" (100 volts is the Japanese standard). Electric wires were not insulated on purpose, producing blue sparks when played in the dark-ened auditorium as the artist risks the danger of being electrified.

33 In fact, Maywa Denki was chosen the most popular media artist according to a web-based voting carried by *Japan Media Arts Festival* in 2006.

34 Personal conversation. For detailed information on Edelweiss Series see www.maywadenki.com/products/edelweiss/ (Accessed on February 1, 2015).

35 It produces sound somewhat similar to Theremin.

36 About commercialization of artists' inventions see Kusahara "Device Art – Media Art Meets Mass Pro-duction" in *Digital by Design*, 275–279. The book introduces works by Tosa and other Japanese media artists.

37 There are many videos of performances and Tosa explaining products on YouTube.

38 Dunne and Raby (2013) call Kuwakubo an artist/designer.

39 According to Nikkei Trendy Net, Nikodama sold out the first lot of 3000 units in one month in July 2010. See http://trendy.nikkeibp.co.jp/article/column/20100826/1032760/ (Accessed on February 1, 2015).

40 *Mitate*, to be pronounced as mi-ta-té, is a genuine Japanese term concerning "the way one sees it." Needless to say it has no connection to the English word "imitate" as some people may speculate.

41 Masao Yamaguchi points out various examples of *mitate* in religious ceremonies (Yamaguchi and Takash-ina, 1996). About the use of *mitate* in literature see Amagasaki, 1988.

42 Today importance of interface design in media art seems to be more widely acknowledged. For example, the media art program at the University of Arts Linz is named Interface Culture.

43 Screech discusses how Japanese interacted with new technology in Edo Era in detail with a rich amount of examples.

44 www.deviceart.org/ (Accessed on October 31, 2014).

References

Amagasaki, A. (1988) *Nihon-no Retorikku* [*Rhetoric in Japan*], Tokyo: Chikuma Shobo.

Bourriaud, D. (1998) *Relational Aesthetics*, Paris: Les Press Du Reel.

Dunne, A., Raby, F. (2013) *Speculative Everything: Design, Fiction, and Social Dreaming*, Cambridge, MA/London: MIT Press.

Kusahara, M. (2006) 'Device Art: A New Approach in Understanding Japanese Contemporary Media Art'. In Grau, O. (ed.), *MediaArtHistories*, Cambridge, MA/London: MIT Press: 227–307.

Screech, T. (2002) *The Lens Within the Heart: The Western Scientific Gaze and Popular Imagery in Later Edo Japan*, Honolulu: University of Hawaii Press.

Sicart, M. (2014) *Play Matters*, Cambridge, MA/London: MIT Press.

Yamaguchi, M. and Takashina, S. (1996) '"Mitate" – to Nihon Bunka (*Mitate* and Japanese culture)', *Special issue on Symbolic Analogy, Substitution for a Superior, Dynamic Perspective, The Aesthetics of Japan No. 24*, Akiyama et al. (eds), Tokyo.

7

Struggling to stay relevant: the impact of the new media on Asia's cultural industries

Nissim Otmazgin

East Asia[1] over the last three decades has experienced a cultural renaissance rooted in the growth of its economies and booming urban consumerism, which is manifested in its massive circulation of contemporary popular culture and media-related commodities such as movies, pop music, animation, comics, television programs, and fashion magazines, as well as their derivative products such as games, food, toys, accessories, etc. The confluence of Chinese, Japanese, and Korean popular cultures, in particular, has intensified in recent decades reaching consumers of different national and linguistic boundaries, as well as inspiring a variety of transnational collaborations and co-productions involving creative personnel and companies from different parts of East Asia (Fung 2013; Lent and Fitzsimmons 2012; Otmazgin and Ben-Ari 2013). Some of these industries have formed alliances with international distributors and promoters and their products have sometimes circulated outside the East Asian region, particularly in Europe and North America (Jin and Otmazgin 2014, 47–48).

The growth in production, inner-regional trade and the consumption of popular and media culture in East Asia is related to several socio-cultural and technological changes. These include the emergence of a large pool of middle-class consumers who have time and money to spend, the advent of social media where cultural content is delivered and consumed almost instantly, the dissemination of accessible devices for consuming popular culture such as DVD players and smartphones, and the easing of political control over the importation of culture as part of the state's attempts to attain "soft power" (Chua 2000; Otmazgin and Ben-Ari 2012). These have all encouraged the cultural industries—as well as media entrepreneurs and promoters—to seek new expansion opportunities beyond their immediate domestic market. At the same time, changes in the distribution and consumption of cultural content, caused by the advent of new Internet-based media technologies, compel these industries to turn away from traditional production and marketing arrangements and explore new business models. This includes changing their attitude towards the role of social media as a means to both market and extract cultural creativity, thinking more creatively about how to approach consumers, and entering new media fields.

This chapter examines the strategies employed by media and cultural industries in Asia to cope with the changing nature of the market in which social media is swiftly replacing the old distribution and consumption channels. Drawing on in-depth interviews with professionals from different media-related companies—advertising, music, and games—the chapter analyzes the changing nature of their work, the challenges to their businesses, their responses to the damages inflicted by online piracy, and more broadly, the actions they have taken to reduce risks and remain profitable. The study describes a major shift toward a new stage, where companies and promoters are both responding and fearing the vast technological and social changes. This shift also entails developing new forms of production and marketing, which involve developing a much closer relationship between consumers and producers as part of corporate success.

The first part of this chapter elucidates the main changes in East Asia's media markets brought about by the new media and suggests a few analytical concepts to view these changes. The next three parts present insights from surveys as well as interviews with officials from companies engaged in advertising and cultural-event management (Dentsu), music (Sony Music Entertainment Japan) and games (Sega). The interviews were conducted in Japan and Singapore between 2010 and 2013. The interviews were semi-structured, e.g., the interviewees were asked a series of questions and follow-up questions but they were also encouraged to speak their mind on various issues concerning their work and the changing nature of the world's media and cultural industries. The conclusion outlines the main findings and presents a macro-picture of the transformation in the work of Asia's media industries.

Features of East Asia's media market

In the past two decades, East Asia has become a highly dynamic marketplace where commodities flow rapidly across national boundaries (Berry, Liscutin and Mackintosh 2009; Otmazgin 2013). At the same time, however, there have been major changes in the organization of cultural commodity production and consumption due to an increase in the utilization of alternative distribution channels brought about by information technology and social media, and resulting in a need for companies to revise their marketing strategies to accommodate these changes. Technological changes have enabled many consumers to access cultural content through various media forms, for example, by viewing television content online and not only via the conventional television set. The Internet, in particular, has provided a new marketing avenue for content, which in turn has weakened the control of the established industry over its marketing. These Internet-based technologies and behaviors present a new venue for swiftly delivering media culture across national boundaries, which are many times beyond the reach of state control.

More specifically, it is possible to recognize several key changes in East Asia's media market. First, there is an increasing usage of *networks* empowered by information technology in order to reduce cost, reach consumers more effectively, and consume cultural content. In order to overcome the economic heterogeneity and the diversification of the national economies of East Asia, regional production and marketing networks are key as they create a producer–consumer commodity, which reduces manufacturing and transaction costs, but at the same time reach consumers more effectively. A good example is the phenomenal success of pop single "Gangnam Style," which was based on the active promotion of both industry personnel and fans. The video clip topped two billion hits (as of June 2014) and served to publicize the artist Psy as well as generate huge indirect income for his production house YG Entertainment.

The reliance on networks is not unique to the cultural industries. It is part of a growing phenomenon in the world market where networks, rather than companies or institutions, are becoming increasingly important (Castells 2000). The usage of networks de facto creates a decentralized structure in the sense that the large corporations are internally de-centralized as networks and small- and medium-sized companies increasingly collaborate for specific business projects. These networks share information and link suppliers to consumers in order to meet demand. Assisted by new means of communication and information technology, networks help bridge some of the gaps between physical locations and deterritorize significant portions of the world economy (Hjorth 2009; Mosco 1999, 103–116).

Second, there is increasing *collaboration* between companies from different countries in order to market cultural content more efficiently or to invent a new hybrid popular culture and media-related commodities that can be marketed both inside and outside the East Asian region. A good example of this is the popularity of so-called "Asian movies," which mix and sometimes invent various "Asian" motifs and traditions for the sake of entertainment. Movies like *Crouching Tiger, Hidden Dragon, Initial D, Jan Dara, Musa,* and *2046* are multinational co-productions involving staff members and actors from China, Thailand, Malaysia, South Korea, and the Philippines, and are offered as "Asian" both within and outside East Asia (Otmazgin 2011, 260). These collaborations make good economic sense. Collaborations in popular culture, which involve a costly production and promotional campaigns, are a way of utilizing the know-how of different actors and sharing risks against bad decisions.

Collaborations with local companies have been an important component in the regional expansion of Japanese and South Korean cultural industries. Transnational collaborations have enabled Japanese and South Korean music and TV companies to approach potential consumers more efficiently as they utilize local knowledge with the market, as well as its distribution routes and the regulations issued by the local government. For the local cultural industries in places like Thailand, Indonesia, Singapore, and Hong Kong, working with Japanese and South Korean counterparts, which are more advanced in terms of popular culture production, has enabled them to access new technologies, formats, and know-how of popular culture production.

Third, there is a growing reliance on *social media* as a means to commercialize and consume popular culture, since people throughout the world, even in remote places, increasingly access popular culture content through accessible channels such as YouTube, and communicate with other fans using Facebook and other online platforms. The global success of Korean popular culture, known as "the Korean Wave" or "Hallyu," exemplifies the important role played by social media in spreading culture (Oh and Park 2012). In East Asia, Korean popular culture has reached fans outside of South Korea, in spite of the language differences, through clusters of dedicated fans relying heavily on social media to consume and sometimes translate Korean pop music, TV dramas, movies, and online games. In addition to consuming cultural content, Hallyu fans tend to participate in online forums and fan gatherings and communicate with each other, also using social media (Chua and Iwabuchi 2008; Jung 2011; Oh 2009).

Fourth, there is a growing tendency to synchronize different media formats and genres, a pattern that can be referred to as "mixed media" (MacWilliams 2008, 6). While this term was initially coined to describe the close synergy between *anime, manga,* and video games in Japan that creates a powerful synthesis of text, image, and sound, it is also useful for our purpose here to describe the increasing synchronization of various media forms in Asian markets, which are often promoted conjointly and popularize each other. One example is the production of Japanese and Korean pop idols, which are expected to be more than "just" music artist. For some of these idols, singing ability and extraordinary physical attributes are less important than that idols are expected to maintain close contact with their audiences and represent the notion that "anyone can be a star." Much of the fame (and income) of these idols is achieved through frequent appearances on television programs and commercials and their songs and music clips may also be used in commercials or as theme songs for TV programs (Ugaya 2005, 97–98). As we shall see later in this chapter, the companies I examine attempt to utilize and market different cultural commodities/genres rather than focusing on one certain product.

A last feature of East Asia's popular culture market, which, curiously, has had both a destructive and constructive impact on the spread of cultural content, is the abundance of *online piracy*.

Although illegal, online piracy provides accessible and cheap access to popular culture content while inflicting severe damage on the established cultural and media industries. According to the International Federation of the Phonographic Industry (IFPI), for every music track bought online, twenty are downloaded illegally. Many of the music albums appear online even before their formal release in shops or on the radio. New albums are sometimes available for illegal downloading even before being officially launched by their music label. In spite of governments' attempts to clamp down on piracy and the establishment of international organizations to fight it (such as the IFPI), piracy continues to be widespread.

The abundance of information technology makes the work of the industry and the police almost impossible. For example, tracing an online server that offers illegal downloading is extremely complicated and sometimes requires the cooperation of institutions and governments of different countries. As explained by the general manager of a music distribution company in Hong Kong: "We have almost given up fighting the online piracy of music because shutting down servers located in other countries requires a great amount of time and cooperation, which [is] not worth the effort."[2] At the same time, however, online piracy has played a constructive role in implanting imported popular culture across East Asia to a degree and intensity that would probably not have been achieved otherwise. Many people across East Asia and in other parts of the world would not have become familiar with pop music from Taiwan, an *anime* series from Japan, or a Korean TV drama if it hadn't been for piracy, which initially introduced them to these products.

The above developments indicate a region-wide change in East Asia's media market. They invoke both quantitative changes (e.g., a denser circulation of cultural content and more transnational collaborations in the production and marketing of commodified culture) and a qualitative shift toward a meta-system that is no longer based upon separate national economies or a certain product, but instead adjusts the location of production, distribution, and the consumption of goods according to transnational considerations.

Next, I would like to look closely at the way the media industries have responded to the above changes and have restructured their operations accordingly. The investigation is based on the experiences of three major companies in the fields of advertising, music, and games, and includes insights from interviews with professionals from these companies.

Dentsu Singapore: utilizing knowledge of the new media

Established in 1994, Dentsu Singapore is one of Singapore's biggest advertising agencies with over 80 employees. It is part of Dentsu, Japan's biggest advertising agency, which is deeply rooted in Japan's corporate structure and famous for producing innovative, pop-culture-like ad campaigns and multimedia-related events. Dentsu Singapore offers a wide range of media-related services including advertisements, events production, PR, market research, media planning, and various other communication services. According to Anthony Kang, then President of Dentsu Singapore,[3] Dentsu uses its know-how, proven record of creative advertising, and global connections to pursue business opportunities in the Asian market. It also mediates between companies interested in doing business in Asia and searches for new opportunities in the fields of media and advertising.

Dentsu Singapore's business model is based on two key components: First, to undertake ad and promotional campaigns for Japanese companies operating in overseas markets. Its domestic strong-hold and connections allows it to have business relations with Japanese companies that seem to trust Dentsu's judgment. Second, to utilize its advertising know-how gained within the Japanese domestic marketplace, in foreign markets. It is not much different from other

Japan-originated media companies like Amuse and Rojam, whose business model is based on initiating local production in Asia based on formats and knowledge acquired earlier in the Japanese market (Otmazgin 2013, 101–104).

Dentsu is a large and highly institutionalized company, but it still manages to maintain a strong entrepreneurial drive and to keep an eye out for new opportunities and markets. In this way, Dentsu adjusts very well to the changes described in the previous part of this chapter since it mediates between diverse actors and utilizes its know-how in various media formats, showing that even in an era of globalization where ideas and images travel freely, mediation and knowledge are still important.

One of Dentsu's most basic operations is conducting various market surveys in order to characterize potential consumers within detailed categories and in this way to effectively target specific groups of consumers. An integral part of this operation involves constant communication with young audiences through surveys and online discussions, while representatives of the company gauge their opinion on new products and recognize new fashion trends and new producible ideas. According to Hasegawa Yoshihiko, Chief Strategic Solution Director at Dentsu Asia Pacific,[4] these days it is not enough to only have some publicity for a certain product or service and hope that the consumers like it. Rather, you must reach out to the consumers, and communicate and discuss with them directly.

As for piracy, it seems that Dentsu has been trying to adjust to a situation where at least some of the Intellectual Property (IP) rights of the products it markets are infringed. According to Dentsu Singapore President Anthony Kang, eradicating piracy is a war the industry cannot win. According to him, the established industry can never accommodate and respond to the flexibility of pirated operations since no one can supervise countless online servers and consumers who download or deliver cultural content illegally. He gave the example of Singaporean *manga* (comic book) and *anime* distributor ODX, which attempted to prosecute individual cases of piracy but could not stop it. On the contrary—it made the fans angry and begin to hate the company. Now, even after ODX stopped prosecuting IP violations, it is still boycotted by the fans. Kang thinks that the media industry needs to have more creative ideas in regards to dealing with piracy, which could then become a powerful marketing device and not only a means for limiting illegal consumption. According to him, Dentsu has recently adjusted more to what he calls the "Chinese model"—generating revenue from live concerts and private events where you can control the people who enter (and charge them).

Dentsu uses its regional connections and knowledge to identify, produce, and market new culture-related initiatives and profit from them. In fact, Dentsu is one of the only Japanese companies which attempts to strategically market Japanese contemporary culture abroad on a wide scale based on a "pushing" campaign rather than only responding to local demands to emerge. Recognizing the limitation of the existing distribution channels of Japanese media culture to global markets, in 2010, Dentsu established Dentsu Entertainment USA in order to develop opportunities for Japanese *manga*, *anime*, fashion, and toy manufacturers.

The Anime Festival Asia (AFA) is an example of where Dentsu Singapore managed to maximize its capabilities and utilize the changing nature of the media market, which has a mixture of different cultural genres and where a large group of heterogeneous actors are involved. AFA is a yearly *anime* fair that Dentsu Singapore initiated and produces together with local companies. It started in Singapore in 2008, but since then has successfully taken place in Indonesia and Malaysia as well. The idea of AFA is to both cash in on the local popularity of *anime* and promote business opportunities and connections between the Japanese *anime* companies who are invited to the fair and local distributors.

Dentsu manages to mediate between the various companies involved in the event. These companies can be divided into five categories. First, big companies, such as Canon and Nestlé, which attempt to engage with new audiences through such gatherings by having their own booths, disseminating information, and sensing the market. Canon, for example, attempts to make the link between cosplay photography (costume play; a practice where fans of *anime* prepare and wear the costumes of their favorite *anime* figures) and Canon cameras and printing services. A second group includes medium-sized *anime* and *anime*-related companies, which aim to recognize new trends in the market. Since they operate in a highly dynamic environment where culture and fashion change swiftly, these companies need to keep their hand on the pulse for new trends and ideas. At these events, they sometimes meet other companies working in the field and also potential rivals. Even though the merchandise they sell at AFA does not always cover the cost of going to Singapore, their attendance has a wider research and marketing value. Third are small music, merchandise, *anime*, and game companies, especially from Japan, which are given space at the AFA venue (many of the venues are sponsored by the Japanese Ministry of Economy, Trade and Industry, which is interested in promoting the commercial value of Japanese culture and media products abroad). These companies, which mainly operate in the Japanese domestic market, hesitantly explore new marketing opportunities abroad. The fourth category encompasses local groups of amateurs involved in the small but creative industry of creating new *manga* or new *anime*-inspired designs and products, and they are given a space to display their innovations and perhaps meet interested representatives of the established industry. The final group is media- and *anime*-related companies and promoters from across Asia, many of whom are distributors of *anime* and *anime*-related accessories. For them, AFA offers an opportunity to advertise and market their products with the aim of establishing potential new business deals with other companies.

At AFA, Dentsu generates revenue from various elements: selling tickets and merchandise to visitors who come to the AFA event; collecting payment for the rental of booths from companies that come to present their merchandize and services; and receiving sponsorship from big companies. At this kind of event Dentsu also has high success in securing contracts with the Japanese government to produce Japanese culture-related events abroad. In fact, in addition to the "cool Singapore" campaign, designed to attract tourists to the city, Dentsu is responsible for engineering the "cool Japan" campaign in Asia, which was designed to increase the visibility of Japanese brand products in overseas markets and make better commercial use of Japan's pop culture success abroad. All of these endeavors depend on Dentsu's creative marketing and mediation.

Sony Music Entertainment Japan: hesitant response

Sony Music Entertainment Japan (SMEJ) is owned by Sony Corporation but operates independently from the US-based Sony Music Entertainment. It has a stronghold in the Japanese music market, which is the world's second biggest music market.[5] Like other Japanese music companies, SMEJ focused its attention almost entirely on the Japanese market, but from the end of the 1980s, it began following the demand in the local Asian markets, especially in Taiwan and Hong

Kong. These days, with the domestic market shrinking, SMEJ is thinking about expanding into foreign markets, especially in Asia, but so far the company has taken very little concrete action toward this goal.

Similar to other music companies worldwide, SMEJ has suffered from a decrease in sales and shrinking revenue due to the illegal downloading and reproduction of music. According to the Recording Industry Association of Japan (RIAJ), the value generated from the sales of recorded music in Japan has dropped from 452 billion yen in 2003 to 227 billion in 2012, whereas the sales of music CDs over the same period has fallen from 388 billion yen to 224 billion (Recording Industry Association of Japan 2013, 5). In Japan, CDs still result in about a third of sales, but this is declining. A decade ago, popular music albums used to sell about one million copies but these days, top albums hardly sell a tenth of this number.[6]

In order to respond to the changes and remain profitable, SMEJ is carefully examining four major advancement strategies. First, SMEJ is diversifying its income sources, attempting to generate profit not only by marketing recorded music in new forms other than CDs (like online sales), but increasingly by generating revenue from live concerts, music-related merchandise, and music-related royalties (commercials, movies, *anime*, and theme songs for TV programs). Another way is through creating better links between music and *anime*, which remains popular in Japan. According to Isayama Ken, Vice President of SMEJ and in charge of the company's international marketing, many of the *anime* movies and series in Japan use Sony music for their theme songs or in part of the movie/series, with the known examples being the Alchemist, Naruto, and Gintama. However, according to Isayama, this was "done way too late and now much of the momentum has gone."[7]

Second, SMEJ actively pursues a strategy of extracting talents from the wider public rather than "producing" music stars from scratch. According to Isayama, although the AKB48 model of an all-girl band that is engineered by an agency or a record company is successful and their albums have been on the Japanese top-selling music list in recent years, this model is difficult to follow and includes a lot of work and high risk. Instead, the music industry, including SMEJ, maintains close links with amateurs in order to recruit new talent. SMEJ has people going to live music venues in Tokyo, Osaka, and other cities to look for new talent, some of whom are then invited for an audition, followed by the production of a demo tape, a "brushing up" process, and, for a successful few, the production of single and an album. Recently, there has been more and more recruitment via the Internet and the company is keeping a constant eye on websites on which amateur music artists record themselves. Engineering artists, based on an idea of a producer, still takes place but it is becoming rarer. According to Isayama: "It's better to start where you already have something to work with."[8]

Third, SMJE is carefully reconsidering its stand toward piracy. According to Isayama, the problem with music piracy these days, especially in Asia, is not the price but the availability. It is easier to illegally access content online than purchase it legally. For example, it is not a problem for consumers in Hong Kong to pay one dollar for downloading a song, but it is easier and faster to do it illegally online. The industry needs to adjust but Isayama, however, admitted that they have not yet proceeded well in this direction due to formal and informal difficulties from both within and outside their company.

Lastly, SMEJ is slowly exploring new markets in East Asia, where it can potentially market Japanese music and Japanese know-how in music production. According to Isayama, Indonesia has recently been emerging as a promising market. Japanese pop music (J-pop) is increasingly popular there and has even overtaken Korean pop music (K-pop) in popularity. A local girl-band named JKT48 was created in Jakarta on the model of Japan's AKB48, and in November 2013 the Japanese recording association together with METI opened a J-pop café in Jakarta ("J-music

LAB") to promote J-music in the country. Indonesia has an expanding middle class, it maintains good diplomatic and economic relations with Japan, and historical tensions do not exist there as in other places in Asia, so Isayama remains optimistic.

SMEJ seems to understand that the changes in the world's music market do not work in its favor and it thus acknowledges the need to change. However, at the same time, SMEJ seems hesitant to leave its stronghold and proven success in the Japanese market, which still lays golden eggs. It tries to initiate new productions and to venture into new fields, but it remains hesitant and without a strong sense of urgency.

Sega: refocusing strategy

Sega is a multinational video game company headquartered in Tokyo, Japan, with multiple offices around the world. Sega developed and manufactured numerous home video game consoles from 1983 to 2001, before changing its strategy to focus on providing software as a third-party developer, exiting console manufacturing completely. The company has approximately 3,000 employees (10,000 in the whole conglomerate including its sister companies). It has been considered one of the world's leading companies for games, but since it began providing software it depends on hardware companies such as Nintendo and other computer manufacturers. Sega is known for its multi-million-selling game franchises including *Sonic the Hedgehog*, *Virtua Fighter*, *Phantasy Star*, *Yakuza*, and *Total War*. At present, Sega's operations are divided into two main categories: home games (for individual consumers) and amusement games (for commercial ventures like game centers). Many of the images in its games use animated features and there is a strong connection between the games, *anime*, animated characters, and music. In this sense, Sega is very much dependent on what we called earlier in the chapter "mixed media," referring to the synchronization of various media forms.

The work of Sega, like many others in the media industries, involves a heavy financial risk. Developing a new game takes about two years and there is no certainty that the game will prove successful. As Mukai Junichiro, Director of Licensing & Media Development at Sega, bluntly put it, "You don't know unless you try."[9] In the case of developing software, this seemingly carries less risk than hardware manufacturing but it still involves a lot of investment as well as long creative hours of work and market research.

However, in recent years, Sega has begun to employ a few strategies to reduce this risk of failure and remain profitable. First, it invests extensively in *audience targeting*. Sega attempts to develop games for specific groups of consumers in order to ensure a modicum consumer market for its products. For example, developing games with a special appeal for elementary school children; or games for the *Otaku* audience (ardent fans and heavy consumers of games), where, according to Mukai, images in the game should involve more *anime*-like sexy female characters, which is believed to be more appealing to this sector. Sega also tries to attract gamers with an interest in other forms of entertainment. For example, for older audiences who like sport, they develop specific games with emphasized sport content.

Secondly, Sega increasingly tries to utilize social media as a marketing tool as well as a medium to gauge new creative ideas for its games. According to Mukai, commercials on TV are less effective these days with the advent of the Internet and social media. They also cost much more and are sometimes not worth the investment. The Internet is also a good place to search for new ideas and new creative people. There are a few websites, which specialize in providing a stage for amateur illustrators to show their work and to possibly draw the attention of established companies. One such Internet forum is *pixiv*[10] which also ranks people who create animated characters. Some of the game and *anime* companies use these websites to announce job opportunities on new projects. Another example mentioned in the interview is the Japanese-made character MIKU, which is a game-embedded *anime*-like character that can also be made to sing. MIKU combines music, visual *anime*, and game software, and is based on the active participation of the audience who is expected to "feed" it with new songs.

As a means for recruitment, the games industry constantly uses social media to search for creative people with a certain talent rather than recruit promising workers who just graduated from art school. This is because, according to Nakamura Miho, a game designer at Sega, "It is impossible to cultivate genius and creative people in schools; we therefore need to search outside."[11] According to Mukai, unlike the "typical" Japanese working culture, at Sega and other game makers workers tend to move between jobs. For example, some start working at Sega, then move to another company, and then another one, and may finally return to Sega. This is because the creative structure in the game industry necessitates a more flexible working environment to accommodate the needs of people who are more artistic than the typical "salary man" employment system in Japan.

In spite of its attempts to adjust to the changing nature of the market, Sega has yet to pursue an active global strategy due to a general feeling that it does not know enough about foreign markets and because of piracy fears. In order to avoid piracy, Sega, as other game developers, attempts to build a strong connection between the software and the hardware. For example, Game Center produces software for a specific car-like machine, which is not easy to copy. Interestingly, there are not any major Chinese or Korean game companies emerging to present feasible competition to Sega (Korea specializes in online games), although they potentially have an advantage (cheaper labor) and it is easier to copy games than, for example, automobiles. According to Mukai, this is not because of lack of creativity or technology, but due to the need for specialized know-how. According to him, profiting in the game business involves long and complicated procedures and even then the risk is high and the profit relatively small.

As part of avoiding risky investments, Sega focuses almost entirely on the Japanese market and does not pursue its own active expansion strategy abroad. In addition to sales to global distributors, the globalization of Sega remains mainly in the form of outsourcing, especially to South Korea and China, which is seen as an effective way to reduce manufacturing costs and in some cases expand the product reach. According to Mukai, the global marketing of Sega only comes as a second step, if ever. The emphasis is very much on the domestic market and, unlike American companies, at the development stage, they do not think of global expansion potential. This is due to Sega's intimate knowledge of the market as a Japanese company (*boukoku*)—if they moved out of Japan they will "lose their advantage." However, this is also because Japan is still home to a large domestic market with many paying consumers. Interestingly, both Mukai and Nakamura did not provide the typical "cultural" explanations about not going abroad due to cultural differences, but rather emphasized the difficulty in logistics and marketing.

Conclusion

Media companies in Asia are going through a transformative stage brought about by intensified technological and social changes. These companies are expected to develop new strategies in order to adjust to the changing circumstances and remain profitable. As we have seen from the cases examined, these strategies include facilitating more accurate *audience targeting, diversifying activities, integrating different media fields* (rather than remaining a "music company" or an "advertising agency"), and *thinking creatively about piracy*.

One recurring point, which emerged from the interviews, was the need to facilitate closer reciprocity between the audience and the industry in order to achieve corporate success. The interaction between the established industry and the audience that consists of consumers and creative amateurs is viewed as beneficial for the marketing process as well as for gauging and extracting creativity from below. Unlike the so-called "Hollywood model,"[12] which typically depicts a small group of professionals creating media products for a wide global audience, this model advocates creative work carried out by a large group of people, both professional and amateur, who target specific groups of consumers and do not try to appeal to a wide "global audience" they know little about.

More specifically regarding Asia, as can be seen from two of the cases examined (Sega and SMEJ), there is a strong ambiguity towards expanding into Asian markets, which, on the one hand, is seen as an opportunity but, on the other, is viewed as unregulated and incomprehensible. These companies are still worried that they lack the knowledge of Asian markets, which is combined with their fears that such an adventure is too risky.

Notes

1 In this paper, "East Asia" refers to both Northeast Asia and Southeast Asia, especially to urban centers, which are the main sites for the reproduction and consumption of popular and media culture.
2 Keyman Luk, interview with the author, Hong Kong, June 22, 2010.
3 Interview, Singapore, November 13, 2011.
4 Interview, Singapore, November 13, 2011.
5 Japan is the world's second largest producer and consumer of commidified music following the US. In 2011, 25 percent of the world's total recorded music sales were in Japan compared to 26 percent in the US, of which 30 percent of the world's *physical* sales of music (CDs and DVDs) was in Japan (compared to 18 percent in the US) and 17 percent of *digital* sales (42 percent in the US). See Recording Industry Association of Japan 2013, 23.
6 Interview, Isayama Ken, Vice President of Sony Music Entertainment Japan, Tokyo, August 20, 2013.
7 Interview, Isayama Ken, Tokyo, August 20, 2013.
8 Interview, Isayama Ken, Tokyo, August 20, 2013.
9 Interview, Shinagawa, Tokyo, August 1, 2013.
10 See http://goods.pixiv.net/c84/
11 Interview, Shinagawa, Tokyo, August 1, 2013.
12 Although the so-called "Hollywood model" has changed over the years, gradually loosening the tight control the industry used to exert over the production of popular culture before the 1970s. See Storper 1994; Ryan 1992.

References

Berry, C., Liscutin, N. and Mackintosh, J.D. (eds) (2009) *Cultural Studies and Cultural Industries in Northeast Asia: What a Difference a Region Makes*, Hong Kong: University of Hong Kong Press.
Castells, M. (2000) 'Materials for an Exploratory Theory of the Network Society', *British Journal of Sociology*, 1(1): 5–24.
Chua, B.H. (2000) 'Consuming Asians: Ideas and Issues'. In B.H. Chua (ed.) *Consumption in Asia: Lifestyles and Identities*, London: Routledge.
Chua, B.H. and Iwabuchi, K. (2008) 'Introduction: East Asian TV Dramas: Identifications, Sentiments and Effects'. In B.H. Chua and K. Iwabuchi (eds) *East Asian Pop Culture: Analysing the Korean Wave*, Hong Kong: Hong Kong University Press.
Fung, A. (2013) *Asian Popular Culture: The Global (Dis)continuity*, London: Routledge.
Hjorth, L. (2009) 'Imaging Communities: Gendered Mobile Media in the Asia-Pacific', *The Asia-Pacific Journal*, 9(3). Available at: http://www.japanfocus.org/~Larissa-Hjorth/3064 (Accessed on August 6, 2014).
Jin, Y.D. and Otmazgin, N. (2014) 'East Asian Cultural Industries: Policies, Strategies, and Trajectories', *Pacific Affairs*, 87(1): 43–51.
Jung, S. (2011) 'K-pop, Indonesian Fandom, and Social Media'. In R.A. Reid and S. Gatson (eds) *Race and Ethnicity in Fandom*, Special issue, *Transformative Works and Cultures*, Vol. 8. Available at: http://www.journal.transformativeworks.com/index.php/twc/article/view/289/219 (Accessed on August 6, 2014).

Lent, J. and Fitzsimmons, L. (eds) (2012) *Asian Popular Culture in Transition*, London: Routledge.

MacWilliams, M. (2008) 'Introduction'. In M. MacWilliams (ed.) *Japanese Visual Culture: Explorations in the World of Manga and Anime*, New York: M.E. Sharpe.

Mosco, V. (1999) 'New York.Com: A Political Economy of the "Informational" City', *The Journal of Media Economics*, 12(2): 103–116.

Oh, I. (2009) 'Hallyu: The Rise of Transnational Cultural Consumers in China and Japan', *Korea Observer*, 40(3): 425–459.

Oh, I. and Park, G. (2012) 'From B2C to B2B: Selling Korean Pop Music in the Age of New Social Media', *Korea Observer*, 43(3) 365–397.

Otmazgin, N. (2011) 'Commodifying Asian-ness: Entrepreneurship and the Making of East Asian Popular Culture', *Media, Culture & Society*, 33(2): 259–274.

Otmazgin, N. (2013) *Regionalizing Culture: The Political Economy of Japanese Popular Culture in Asia*, Hawaii: University of Hawaii Press.

Otmazgin, N. and Ben-Ari, E. (2012) 'Cultural Industries and the State in East and Southeast Asia'. In N. Otmazgin and E. Ben-Ari (eds) *Popular Culture and the State in East and Southeast Asia*, London: Routledge.

Otmazgin, N. and Ben-Ari, E. (2013) 'Introduction: History and Theory in the Study of Cultural Collaborations'. In N. Otmazgin and E. Ben-Ari (eds) *Popular Culture Co-productions and Collaborations in East and Southeast Asia*, Singapore: National University of Singapore Press and Kyoto University Press.

Recording Industry Association of Japan (2013) RIAJ Yearbook 2013: Statistics Trends. Tokyo: RIAJ. Available at: http://www.riaj.or.jp/issue/industry/pdf/RIAJ2013E.pdf (Accessed on July 22, 2014).

Ryan, B. (1992) *Making Capital from Culture: The Corporate Form of Capitalist Cultural Production*, De Gruyter Studies in Organization, Vol. 35, Berlin and New York: Walter de Gruyter.

Storper, M. (1994) 'The Transition to Flexible Specialisation in the US Film Industry: External Economies, the Division of Labour and the Crossing of Industrial Divides'. In A. Amin (ed.) *Post-Fordism: A Reader*, Oxford: Blackwell.

Ugaya, H. (2005) *J-Poppu toha Nanika Kyodaika suru Ongaku Sangyō* [What Is J-Pop? The Expanding Music Industry], Tokyo: Iwanami Shinsho.

Part II

New media cultures, politics and literacies

8

The new media cultures of Chinese migrant workers

Sophie Ping Sun and Jack Linchuan Qiu

The intersection between new media and migrant workers is a scholarly domain that deserves special attention in Asian contexts, particularly in China. In recent years, Internet and mobile communication in Asia have become notable research topics in the region and globally (Lo and Wei 2010; Qiu 2010a). However, as Qiu and Bu (2013) discovered from a comprehensive review of China ICT studies in both Chinese and English languages, only a small proportion of academic publications deal with issues related to less privileged users such as migrant workers.

Yet, compared to other parts of the world, a most important reality about new media in Asia is the region's increasingly leading position in ICT production, from hardware manufacture to software programming to the provision of services. While the rise of Samsung and Huawei follows earlier Japanese electronics manufacture brands such as Sony and Panasonic, the consolidation of the world's new media production prowess in countries like China and India is, in many ways, unprecedented (Smil 2013). As the "world's factory" at the beginning of the twenty-first century, China and its massive workforce play an important role in global media transformations. Its 260 million migrant workers not only produce most of the world's new media gadgets, they also form the bedrock of a new media consumption market and the new cultural formations therein.

We cannot get a comprehensive understanding of new media cultures in China, let alone in Asia, by focusing merely on elite consumption patterns. Arguably, more important is to grasp the productive processes and cultural practices of the ordinary working population when Internet and mobile phones diffuse into their everyday work and life. According to official China Internet Network Information Center (CNNIC), 79.1 percent of Chinese Internet users only have high school or lower education attainment by the end of 2013. In other words, working-class populations such as migrant workers have become the overwhelming majority of new media users in the country.

How should we approach Chinese workers and their increasing role in developing new media cultures? Much of the labor in China's industrialization process, especially in its export-oriented industries, results from massive rural-to-urban migration. Like in other developing countries of the Asia Pacific (Doron and Jeffrey 2013), these migrant workers not only provide labor power in the production and circulation processes indispensable to new media industries, they have also become essential to the formation of new consumer markets and new cultures at the grassroots (Qiu 2009; Wallis 2013).

Since the 2008 global financial crisis, there have been many studies—in Chinese and in English—of Chinese migrant workers and their new media cultures. They have examined such a broad range of issues as social class, occupational variation, media literacy, and collective action. Compared to earlier studies, what are the questions and findings in these studies? What are the major debates? Is there an emerging consensus? Why are the debates so, in China and in the global context of research on new media cultures? This chapter poses these questions while starting to identify recent research trends in studies, published in English and Chinese, on China's new media industry and its population of migrant workers.

Approaches to class and new media cultures

"Communication", wrote Yuezhi Zhao in 2008, the year of Beijing Olympics, "seems to have never been so central to the processes of political legitimation, capital accumulation, social relations restructuring, and cultural transformation" (2008, 339). There has indeed been a fundamental cultural transformation when a new material culture of electronic gadgets, especially mobile devices, becomes widespread among Chinese migrant workers. It is not just the multiplication of objects but also the formation of new social and organizational networks, as small as a QQ Cluster (a popular online discussion space among small groups of Chinese workers), and as large as Tencent corporation, which owns QQ and is China's largest Internet company worth more than US$148 billion in September 2014 on the Hong Kong Stock Exchange.

Beneath the ICT material culture and the organizational units of online networks as well as corporate entities, lies the deeper cultural transformation of values and value systems, for example, when traditional Chinese collectivistic culture is eroded by the growth of individualistic consumerism online. Here the new media cultures of migrant workers are not abstract. Nor are they invisible. Given the diversity of working-class occupations (Qiu 2009; Ding 2014), their internal variation in gender (Wallis 2013; Liu 2013; He 2010) as well as ethnic and regional identity (Sun and Yang 2012; Zang 2012), it is not feasible to exhaust, in one chapter, all the variations and their dynamics in Chinese cyberspace.

However, it is still possible to discern overall trends. Ten years ago, when the majority of Chinese Internet users were college-educated, China's new media cultures used to be rather elite-dominated, looking down upon migrant workers. However one of the most notable changes in recent years is the rise of *diaosi* (屌丝) also known as "diaosi culture" (Li and Li 2013). *Diaosi* in Chinese refers to people, especially males, who are from the lower classes, with low income and social status. Yet they refer to themselves as *diaosi* in an ironic but increasingly self-confident manner, while ridiculing those who are called *gaodashang* (高大上), i.e., people who are "tall, grand, and from higher classes". Active members of *diaosi* culture include mostly migrant workers in China's expanding industrial, services, and low-end IT sectors, who use new media outlets to express their class identities, psychological conditions and life expectancies.

Broadly speaking, we see three interrelated research trends in the literature since 2008 on new media and migrant cultures: (a) class and identity construction; (b) new media use and social capital; and (c) new media empowerment and collective action. Rather than entirely new, all these topics include classic concerns in sociological and cultural analysis, but they also contain novel elements for the examination of China's emerging new media cultures, whose relevance is both regional in the Asia Pacific and global. This chapter shall discuss the main findings, debates, trends and questions concerning new media and migrant workers, which researchers in and outside China have worked on in recent years. Our aim is to at least partially discuss questions concerning class analysis from various sociological approaches, be they Marxian, Weberian, or Durkheimian, including the possibility of a working-class network society, and the extent to which new media empowers migrant workers.

Even though China is under the rule of the CCP (Chinese Communist Party), which proclaims Marxism as its guiding ideology, when it comes to analyzing issues related to migrant workers, most researchers tend to employ Weberian and Durkheimian approaches. This may have resulted from a backlash against Maoist class struggle that has dominated the country for three decades until the end of 1970s. Hence Weber and Durkheim became much more attractive to scholars when China entered its post-Mao era. This is especially so after the opening up policy and the great change in social structure it has brought to Chinese society (Li et al. 2004; Sun 2003; Lu 2002; Sun et al. 1994). Under such circumstances, researchers tend to understand social class mainly based on occupation, while also taking economic status, education, and organizational resources into consideration (Zhao and Fu 2010).

For instance, Li (2008) develops ten criteria in defining social class in China: means of production, income, market status, occupation, political rights, cultural capital, social capital, reputation, civil rights, and human resources. Different researchers have different orientations, some being more Weberian (e.g., Sun 2003; Sun et al. 1994) while focusing on the significance of cultural factors in forming social class, as well as the risk of stratum solidification. Others are more Durkheimian (e.g., Li et al. 1992, 2004), concerned more with the increasing anomie during China's social transformation, and how to deal with anomie and reduce risk.

There has been, however, a notable resurgence of Marxian approaches across the disciplines from sociology, literature and film studies, to cultural analysis (Pun and Chan 2013; Pun and Lu 2010; Guo et al. 2011; Shen 2006). These researchers emphasize the remaking and (semi-)proletarianization of China's new working class (Pun and Lu 2010), with special attention paid to workers' collective action and social activism.

A consensus that has emerged from researchers across the disciplines is the remarkable difference between the so-called "second-generation migrant workers" (AKA *xinshengdao nongmingong*) and their parents' generation (Zheng and Yi 2014; Chan and Pu 2010; Pun and Chan 2013; Wallis 2013; Li and Tian 2011). The first generation of migrant workers refers to people who were born in 1960s or 1970s, who moved from countryside to industrializing urban areas in the 1980s and 1990s (Pun and Lu 2010). The pioneers are females who worked in Shenzhen, China's first Special Economic Zone. The second generation includes those born in the 1970s or 1980s, employed as workers since the 2000s. Many of these young workers grew up in urban areas with their parents without ever working in farmlands. Or they were brought up in the countryside by their grandparents, who sometimes spoiled the kids, almost always encouraging them to pursue a better life "outside." Both routes lead to higher expectations among second-generation migrant workers as compared to their parents for salaries, working conditions, and life-time planning in the city, while corporate profit margins start to decline with increasing global and regional competition especially since the 2008–2009 global financial crisis.

The demarcation between first- and second-generation migrant workers is of course relative, but there has been initial evidence showing that the two groups have begun to see themselves as from distinct "class positions' (Pun and Lu 2010). Raised up in the post-Mao reform period, many young migrant workers have developed their own political claims while getting involved in collective action more quickly than their parents, thanks at least in part to the widespread of low-end "working-class ICTs" such as Internet cafés and mobile phones (Qiu 2009; Wang 2011). Based on a nationwide probability sample (CCSS or China Comprehensive Social Survey), Li and Tian (2011, 8) discovered in 2011 that 56.1 percent of second-generation migrant workers have used the Internet; 43.9 percent of them send text messages everyday. On the contrary, among first-generation migrant workers, 90.1 percent have never gone online and only 2.9 percent of them use text message on daily basis. It is therefore unsurprising that young migrant workers have become the bedrock of China's new working class especially when it comes to the formation of their new media cultures.

Class and identity

Discussion on class and class-consciousness is a key issue in studies on migrant workers in contemporary China (Carrilo and Goodman 2012). While most studies on new-generation migrant workers have paid insufficient attention to new media cultures, this is too important a dimension of the class-making dynamics to be neglected. Its impact is not limited to the grassroots level. By giving rise to entire new markets such as QQ, new corporations such as Tencent, and new cultures such as diaosi, young migrant workers have shaped China's new media cultures as a whole beyond its earlier elite class confines (Qiu 2009).

On the one hand, millions of migrant workers have joined the electronics manufacture industry as China becomes the "world's factory" for ICT hardware. On the other hand, they have become the bulk of new media users in China. These are fundamental changes in China's industrialization and digitalization processes that result in the emergence of a new stratum between the "haves" and the "have-nots", i.e., the "information have-less" using a full spectrum of "working-class ICTs" from Internet cafés to SMS to *shanzhai* mobile phones. This is the techno-social basis for the rise of China's "network labor" (Qiu 2013).

But such a "new ICT-based working class" needs to be understood in a larger context beyond industrialization and the spread of digital new media. One crucial factor is the role of mainstream mass media, which usually stereotype migrant workers as incapable, poor, and helpless. It is therefore very rare for mass media to provide meaningful service to migrant workers, who have to turn to new media due to their strong existential needs: seeking jobs in a new city, finding residence, healthcare, and ways to keep in touch, for example, by using Mobile QQ, the most popular instant-messenger service among Chinese migrant workers (Koch et al. 2009; Hjorth et al. 2014). The majority of Mobile QQ users are migrant workers, who have used the affordable yet convenient online service to form community, express their opinions, and organize collective action (Ding 2011; Wang 2011).

As previously stated, many researchers turned away from Marxian traditions during the 1980s and 1990s to employ Weberian or Durkheimian approaches in their study of Chinese class/strata. Even though CCP claims Marxism as its guiding philosophy, this has looked increasingly like a pretension (Chan 2012; Yang 2012). Therefore, debates arise on whether "class" is still a necessary concept. In other words, is it still suitable to describe the conditions in China today, especially for migrant workers? By employing participant observation and interview among migrant workers, Chris Chan (2012) notes that the protests of migrant workers "are rooted in the production regime of capitalism and are a significant part of emerging class conflict" (309). For him, "class" and class-consciousness still exist among workers, and the consciousness of the new working class exists not only in language and self expression, it also has a solid material basis in Chinese society.

According to Leung and So (2012), first-generation migrant workers maintain a muted class-consciousness while regarding themselves as "peasants" (*nongmin*), "peasant workers" (*nongmingong*) or "non-state workers" (*mingong*). However, second-generation migrant workers see themselves as real workers. They call themselves "the working class" (*gongren jieji*) or "workers" (*gongren*). This kind of class-consciousness is heightened especially when they get involved in collective action. Pun and Lu also point out that young migrant workers have quite different life experience from their parents. They are less concerned about economic goals, more determined in personal development and freedom. Thus, the new working class "has gradually become aware of its class position and has participated in a series of collective actions" (Pun and Lu 2010, 512).

Some scholars are concerned about the dynamics between new media and the process of class formation. Facilitated by Internet and social media, the formation of the new working class is no longer limited within traditional parameters of the political parties or occupation-based industrial work. Rather, the locale of class making is diffused beyond the confines of old politics and institutions (Qiu 2013). This continues the historical trend of "membership unlimited"(Thompson 1996) in working-class formation, which can also be deemed as a new development in China's previously elite-dominated new media cultures. According to Qiu (2013), through the help of social media and other ICTs, a networking working class is forming. However, old challenges to class formation persist such as gender, race, ethnicity, nationality and religious belief.

For researchers such as Zhou (2012), the adoption of new media among the migrant workers has affected their class identity, especially people's subjective class identification. For migrant workers, new media adoption becomes a significant predictor to confirm their class identities. Others also take notes that for migrant workers, the mobile phone gets special meaning far beyond a communication tool—it is also a symbol helping them to establish their identity as a urban resident (Jiang 2013; Liu et al. 2014). However, new media also brings problems. Using a Durkheimian approach, Dong and Liu (2012) argue that many migrant workers tend to marginalize themselves in forming isolated groups using new media, while identifying themselves as belonging to the lower social strata only. For example, QQ Cluster, a popular online group chat service, often consists of closed communities that are not open to "outsiders."

Another strand of studies focuses on the discursive power brought by new media. Xu (2012) maintains that the development of ICTs makes social stratification more acute in China because uneven distribution of new media resources leads to unequal distribution of discursive power among different social strata. Zhao and Fu (2010) concur with Xu based on findings from their content analysis of posts in the Public Opinion Channel of People.com.cn (*renminwang yuqing pindao*), the online discussion platform hosted by the official *People's Daily*. Against the hype about new media's democratizing effect, they find out that the chances are slim for lower-strata netizens such as workers and farmers to voice their opinions. Meanwhile, those from the middle strata such as professionals, small business owners, and service-sector employees have the most say in this Internet forum, even more than officials, managers, and other members of the upper strata.

Are migrant workers today forming their own class-consciousness or class identity? This has been an ongoing debate. Scholars such as Leung and So (2012) as well as Chan (2012) maintain that there is a potential for the formation of class-consciousness in modern China, especially among second-generation migrant workers. They have begun to identify themselves as members of the working class while raising their own claims (Pun and Lu 2010). In the first decade of the twenty-first century, notable evidence for a maturing working class fighting for their rights and political claims includes the passing of the Labor Contract Law, the Honda Strike, public outcry (including workers' collective action) in the aftermath of suicides at Foxconn, the world's largest electronics manufacturer.

However, this optimism is not always shared. Chan and Siu, for instance, argue that Chinese migrant workers are "still waging isolated and uncoordinated rights-based protests and strikes" (2012, 82). They conclude that it is difficult to form class-consciousness because workers elsewhere, e.g., in Europe, also spent a long time to achieve this goal. Pun and Lu (2010) also note the new working class is undergoing the process of proletarianization, but it is "unfinished." While the result of this process remains uncertain, it will continue to be constrained by such objective conditions as the factory regime and the *hukou* household registration system. Equally important for Pun and Lu, the challenge comes from the difficulty in making the social and political subject (*zhuti*) of this new working class.

It is important to point out that, for both the optimists and those with reservations, new media culture is seldom the center of their scholarly scrutiny. Although these researchers have also taken note of workers' Internet and especially mobile phone communication patterns, the new cultural formations through working-class ICTs often remain of secondary importance, for example, as an intervening factor between working conditions and class formation, but not as a decisive factor given the political economy constraints.

We, however, think one should not underestimate the significant role of new media cultures in the making of China's new working class. Class consciousness is, after all, a cultural formation. It cannot exist without migrant workers discovering their collective identities, constructing social belonging and sharing across the strata, sectoral boundaries, gender, and political constraint. Class consciousness is also a historical phenomenon, whose coming into being is contingent upon the specific contexts and time frames conceived by members of the working class at a given time (Chan and Siu 2012; Yang 2012). For Chinese migrant workers today, new media cultures are where the collective takes place, where the sharing gets networked, where the historical contexts become substantiated.

New media and social capital

Like in many other parts of the world, China's profound transformation can be seen in its greatly enhanced "mobility of people, products, occupations and information" (Castells 2000, 52). For most of the new working class, they leave home and come to an unfamiliar place. Compared with those growing up in the city, migrant workers usually have less resources and social capital (Palmer et al. 2011). Therefore developing new social networks is of vital significance for them simply to survive, which becomes more important as commercial mass media in general ignore workers' existential needs. It is against this background that new media starts to play an unprecedented role in networking among migrant workers and beyond (Liu et al. 2014), which has become the social basis for new digital cultures. In the following, we shall discuss these changes brought by new media to individual migrant workers and the social class as a whole.

New media have created major impact on the life of individuals belonging to the new working class. Working-class ICTs such as mobile phones are quite popular among migrant workers (Liu et al. 2014). Researchers in recent years have concentrated on three main functions of new media, which are essential to migrant workers: (a) interpersonal communication (Zhou and Lu 2011), (b) leisure and entertainment (Liu et al. 2014), and (c) information seeking (Liu et al. 2014; Zheng and Wang 2014; Zhou and Lu 2011). In a survey conducted by Zhou and Lu (2011), migrant workers rank "solving loneliness" and "making new friends and keeping in touch" as the top one and two goals when they adopt new media tools. Most frequently they use QQ, the popular instant-messenger, and Baidu, the biggest search engine in China. QQ is probably the most essential part of migrant workers' online life. Through QQ they build virtual community and keep in touch with their friends. Meanwhile, the Qzone (QQ *kongjian*) blog service, also offered by Tencent, is attached to QQ and often used for information and entertainment purposes among second-generation migrant workers, as well as some members of their parents' generation. Compared to an average English-language blog, Qzone blogs are often more colorful, full of avatars, jingles, and latest popular songs. This is where a plethora of new media cultures flourish among members of the new working class, which most members of China's rising middle class are unaware of.

Unlike in most countries where Google dominates, in China netizens across the social strata use Baidu to search for information. Migrant workers use this service when they encounter problems in everyday life and when they look for jobs. But they also have their own preferred search engines such as 3G Portal or 3G Menhu (http://xuan.3g.cn/) which has been optimized for low-end mobile Internet users. Ding and Song (2010) conducted a study in Shuangfeng, West China, and found that mobile phones contribute greatly to migrant workers seeking a better life. When they have mobile phones, they can communicate with their friends and search for information faster, which gives them advantage in the labor market since they can act more quickly than before. Ngan and Ma (2012) had similar observations in Dongguan where mobile phones and SMS equip migrant workers with quick, reliable, and essential information about job opportunities.

Other researchers are more concerned with the relationship between new media and social capital. Although systematic inequality persists in China, migrant workers deal with the hardships differently. They used to have little options other than enduring the hardship passively. But with the spread of working-class ICTs, researchers discover that new media plays an important role in migrant workers' social capital bonding and bridging (Liu et al. 2014; Chen 2011). With the help of new media, especially QQ, they form their own groups, informing, comforting and helping each other. Even though most of the groups are loosely organized, there are also well-organized virtual groups, which maintain clear objectives and have developed routines for their online and offline activities, thus providing fertile ground for the formation of new media cultures.

There are, however, challenges with the spread of working-class ICTs. Certain factories in South China also attempt to control migrant workers in their mobile phone usage by, for example, prohibiting mobile phones on the assembly line (Peng and Choi 2013). Other employers try to put a limit on workers' mobile phone usage even when they are off duty, claiming this would make them more efficient at work (Qiu 2009). A dynamic of control and resistance is integral to the process of production and factory management when it comes to new media use. According to these studies, the ways migrant workers use new media are also influenced by a host of other factors such as education, occupation, economic condition, marital status, and working hours.

Another key issue is to what extent new media helps migrant workers with their social capital bonding and bridging. Researchers have reached the consensus that working-class ICTs, especially mobile phones, help migrant workers to increase their bonding social capital (Zheng and Wang 2014; Dong and Liu 2012; Yang 2012; Chen 2011; Palmer et al. 2011; Zhou and Lu 2011). Most migrant workers tend to relocate to a certain destination and find a job there based on their fellow villager relationship. They keep in touch by using QQ or SMS, and usually these groups they have built are based on regional or blood ties.

However, Yang (2012) argues that new media usage does not increase migrant workers' bridging social capital. When they form their own groups, this tends to isolate them from other social groups and decrease their communication with the outside world (Dong and Liu 2012; Yang 2012). Government regulations including often at times discriminatory measures in the destination city put migrant workers on the defense, feeling being abandoned. As time passes, as the online bonding among migrants may lead to "self-marginalization" (Dong and Liu 2012) because these "new relationships" based on new media can be quite homogeneous, relying for example still on traditional regional affiliations and blood ties rather than broadening their social networks, as Ding (2014) found in her study of Hunan taxi drivers in Shenzhen. This increase in bonding social capital, juxtaposed with decreasing bridging social capital, reminds us of Robert Park's classic text *The Immigrant Press and Its Control* (1922).

There are, however, important variations among Chinese migrant workers especially with regard to the different occupations. Not all groups are like taxi drivers in Shenzhen, who tend to organize themselves on the basis of shared regional identity. It would be much less likely for workers in manufacturing industries and other service sector employees, for example in restaurants or retail, to form similar online communities of such high internal homogeneity.

From a macro perspective, the diffusion of new media changes not only individual lives but also the entire working class. This technology diffusion occurred at a time when, for the first time, China's working class is truly intergraded into the capitalist world system, not only at its margin or semi-peripheries but also forming a core production and consumption army. Therefore, it is timely to ponder the possibility for a working-class network society, its transformative potentials for media cultures in China and the world over (Qiu 2009).

The remarkable spread of working-class ICTs poses serious challenge to traditional hierarchies of information inequality in China. Yet, we also have to acknowledge that the change has just begun and barriers persist to achieving more equality in the long run (Zheng and Wang 2014). Can this trend toward working-class network society continue in the future? Will it empower the information have-less? Can this kind of information society narrow the digital divide? These are fundamental questions for the future of new media cultures in China and for Chinese migrant workers as well.

Collective action and empowerment

New media contributed to the Arab Spring, which shocked the world, but they are only one of the factors along with other, arguably more important, forces such as political power. Nevertheless the role of new media is notable in places where civil society is suppressed, democratic culture absent, economy controlled, income and literacy level low (Khondker 2011; Bellin 2004). Facebook, Twitter, YouTube, and mobile phones together facilitated mobilization in ways that would have been impossible in the Arab countries. News about protests in Tunisia diffused throughout the Arab world more quickly than before, resulting in a global movement (Bruns et al. 2013). It is a good reference point for China because the country is undergoing a tremendous social transition as well.

As discussed earlier, contemporary China is characterized by growing social inequalities, problematic public policies, and insufficient channels for public opinion expression. These all add to the special importance of working-class ICTs as instrument for the lower classes. Facilitated by the new media platforms such as online forums, the collective action of migrant workers managed to breach the blockade of mainstream media to reach the society at large, even internationally. There is a long line of such practices. Back in 2004, more than six years before the Arab Spring, there were already landmark events of workers using online forums successfully in mobilization and agenda setting for nationwide discussion, for example, the strike at Chongqing No. 3403 Factory in 2004 (Zhao 2008, 309–315). Although participants in this strike were mostly old-generation workers in state-owned enterprises, they also worked with young migrants, some of whom risked jail sentences to use the Internet for purposes of collective action. Since then, local state authorities and corporate censors have both stepped up their efforts in preventing workers from using working-class ICTs for political and cultural expression. However, the pattern persists, as second-generation migrant workers become the most important driving force for the formation of new media cultures at the grassroots level.

Why has contentious politics become a key component of migrant workers' new media cultures in recent years? Pun and Lu (2010) argue that the transition of generations is the main cause. On one hand, the new working class has different aims, values, and life expectations from their parents. On the other hand, the new working class are more conscious of their proletariat identity while also having their own political articulations. The Report on Second-Generation Migrant Workers (2010) also finds that young workers are more aware of their working-class identity and political rights than previous generations. Among the young workers, 52.4 percent are willing to take part in collective action when it has to do with their rights. According to Gallagher (2011) this is in part due to China's "one child policy," which has led to increasing labor shortage, thereby making the working class more powerful and more prominent. Increased power and media attention then feeds back to more frequent collective action among ICT-equipped young migrant workers as has been observed in recent years.

There is of course a time-honored tradition for Chinese workers to engage in collective action, long before the establishment of the People's Republic in 1949. What then is new when workers start to use the Internet? Working with workers at the Honda factory, which had a major industrial action in 2010, Wang (2011) discovered the important role of Internet in promoting workers' causes and communicating internally and externally for the collective action. By using QQ and other tools online, workers were able to establish cross-regional connections, discuss strategies, share experiences, carry out timely mobilization, which would have been much less effective without working-class ICTs.

Another prominent example is workers' mobilization following the "suicide express" at Foxconn, the world's largest electronics manufacturer. Between January and May 2010, 13 young Foxconn workers attempted to commit suicide. The tragedies provoked many worker-poets, worker-musicians, even worker-directors to produce and release a considerable amount of poetry, songs, videos, and blogs to memorize and reflect on those passed away (Qiu 2014). BBS, blogs, and microblogging were among the most frequently used, creating a large pool of what Qiu calls WGC (short for "worker-generated content"). This is echoed by Liu (2011) who regards microblogging as a new way to empower migrant workers especially when things are related to their rights, work, and life, even though this trend is only starting to materialize and remains relatively marginal at the fringe of Chinese cyberspace.

Going back to the questions at the beginning of this chapter, an emerging consensus in the literature is that migrant workers have begun to use new media for collective organizing. For them, new media is not only a tool for sharing and communication but also an important weapon to fight against unfair treatment and struggle for more workers' rights. However, it remains debatable to what extent Internet and mobile communication really empower migrant workers (Xu 2012). Also important to note is that, in recent years, research on collective action is scarce probably because the powers that be have made data collection more difficult, as well as because it is a relatively new field of scholarly inquiry, at least in China, today.

Conclusion

As previously stated, different scholars employ different definitions of "class" in analyzing Chinese migrant workers including their new media cultures, using such diversified terminologies as "class analysis," "strata analysis" and "stratification analysis." One interesting phenomenon is that many scholars choose to combine classic traditions in class analysis. For instance, Yang (2012) uses Marxian-Weberian terminology in analyzing class as located in a single, non-resolvable source of conflict, while scholars such as Chan (2012) and Chan and Siu (2012) also pay attention to the cultural dimension of power, knowledge, and prestige. Still others like Xu (2012) and Zhao and Fu (2010) combine Weber and Durkheim by seeing class in a paired relationship of domination and subordination, whose conflict may still be reconciliatory, as they maintain all strata in society function together to achieve harmony and solidity. There are also researchers following just one approach, be it Marxian (Pun and Lu 2010) or Weberian (Zhou and Lu 2011). It will be intriguing to explore why this happens in the context of China's social transformation, economic development, and political change. As Yang (2012) points out, analysis of social class in China today is often more political-ideological than sociological. Although the CCP is more concerned about economic development and social stability, it also has to pay lip service to Marxism. Class analysis therefore often becomes a confluence of interests, taking in multiple approaches at a time.

We have also observed limitations in the literature. First is the quantity of publications. Even though China has 260 million migrant workers and the number is still growing, the number of publications on this topic remains minimal. There was a tidal wave of Chinese-language publications from 2003 to 2008 when the previous leadership of Hu Jintao and Wen Jiabao prioritized the construction of a "harmonious society" and made social equality for migrant workers one of its most important policy goals. However, few publications before 2008 mentioned new media at all. Since 2008, the total number of studies on migrant workers has declined, although relatively speaking there have been more discussions on migrant workers and their new media cultures. But this is far from enough given the huge number of Chinese migrant workers and their increasing predominance as the backbone of China's network society.

Second, in terms of research methodology, it is clear that English-language publications on Chinese migrants and their new media cultures tend to rely on qualitative data such as ethnography, interview, and focus groups. But research in Chinese does not follow a single methodological path. Many of them are opinion essays with little empirical evidence, which is a consistent pattern in China ICT studies overall (Qiu and Bu 2013). Yet, among the Chinese-language studies there is also a notable trend of increasing utilization of systematic quantitative data such as survey and content analysis, although it is not uncommon to see research based on ethnography and participant observation. In this sense, it is probably fair to say that Chinese-language publications on the new media cultures of migrant workers tend to be eclectic in their modes of data collection and analysis.

Third, "Marx is back." After widespread usage of Weberian and/or Durkheimian approaches, we have seen a return to Marxian approaches among both Chinese- and English-language publications. This has led to more attention to China's new working class, especially regarding the means of production, labor relationships, political economy, and related power structures. Even though terminologies such as "stratification" and "identity" remain more popular than "class" and "class-consciousness" in this academic field, the notable revival of Marxian approaches has to be understood as part of a profound reality change with second-generation migrant workers becoming the backbone of China's emerging working-class network society. It is also part and parcel of a profound cultural change when Chinese migrant workers become more assertive with their rights, and more outspoken online, using an enlarged toolkit of working-class ICTs, including some of the latest social media as well.

Bibliography

Bellin, E. (2004) 'The robustness of authoritarianism in the Middle East: Exceptionalism in comparative perspective', *Comparative Politics*, 36(2): 139–157.

Bruns, A., Highfield, T. and Burgess, J. (2013) 'The Arab Spring and social media audiences. English and Arabic Twitter users and their networks', *American Behavioral Scientist*, 57(7): 871–898.

Carrillo, B. and Goodman, D.S.G. (eds) (2012) *Peasants and Workers in the Transformation of Urban China*, Cheltenham: Edward Elgar.

Castells, M. (2000) 'Information technology and global capitalism'. In W. Hutton and A. Giddens (eds) *On the Edge: Living with Global Capitalism*, New York: The New Press.

Chan, A. and Siu, K. (2012) 'Chinese migrant workers: factors constraining the emergence of class consciousness', in B. Carrillo and D.S.G. Goodman (eds) *Peasants and Workers in the Transformation of Urban China*, Cheltenham: Edward Elgar.

Chan, C.K.C. (2012) 'Class or citizenship? Debating workplace conflict in China', *Journal of Contemporary Asia*, 42(2): 308–327.

Doron, A. and Jeffrey, R. (2013) *The Great Indian Phone Book: How the Cheap Cell Phone Changes Business, Politics, and Daily Life*, Cambridge, MA: Harvard University Press.

Gallagher, M. (2011) 'Changes in the world's workshop: the demographic, social, and political factors behind China's movement' paper presented at Labor Relationship and Development Conference in China, Beijing.

He, M. J. (2010) 'Labor and divisions between sisters: a case study of the He Ji restaurant production regime', *Social Sciences in China*, 31(2): 165–178.

Hjorth, L., Qiu, L., Zhou, B. and Ding, W. (2014) 'The social in the mobile: QQ as cross-generational media in China'. In G. Goggin and L. Hjorth (eds) *The Routledge Companion to Mobile Media*, Oxford: Routledge.

Khondker, H.H. (2011) 'Role of the new media in the Arab Spring', *Globalizations*, 8(5): 675–679.

Koch, P.T., Koch, B.J., Huang, K. and Chen, W. (2009) 'Beauty is in the eye of the QQ user: Instant messaging in China'. In G. Gerard and M. Mark (eds) *Internationalizing Internet Studies: Beyond Anglophone Paradigms*, London: Routledge: 265–284.

Leung, P. and So, A.Y. (2012) 'The making and re-making of the working class in South China'. In B. Carrillo and S.G. Goodman (eds) *China's Peasants and Workers: Changing Class Identities*, Cheltenham: Edward Elgar: 62–78.

Liu, J., Boden, A., Randall, D. W., and Wulf, V. (2014) 'Enriching the distressing reality: social media use by Chinese migrant workers', paper presented at The 17th ACM conference on Computer Supported Cooperative Work and Social Computing, ACM: 710–721.

Lo, V.-H. and Wei, R. (2010) 'New media and political communication in Asia', *Asian Journal of Communication*, 20(2): 264–275.

Ngai, P. and Huilin, L. (2010) 'A culture of violence: the labor subcontracting system and collective action by construction workers in post-Socialist China', *The China Journal*, 143–158.

Ngan, R. and Ma, S.K. (2012) 'Mobile phones and the empowerment of migrant workers in job search in China's Pearl River Delta', *New Connectivities in China*, 105–119.

Palmer, N.A., Perkins, D.D. and Xu, Q. (2011) 'Social capital and community participation among migrant workers in China', *Journal of Community Psychology*, 39(1): 89–105.

Park, R. (1922) *The Immigrant Press and Its Control*, New York: Harper & Brothers.

Peng, Y. and Choi, S. Y. (2013) 'Mobile phone use among migrant factory workers in south China: technologies of power and resistance', *The China Quarterly*, 215: 553–571.

Pun, N. and Chan, J. (2013) 'The spatial politics of labor in China: life, labor, and a new generation of migrant workers', *South Atlantic Quarterly*, 112(1): 179–190.

Pun, N. and Lu, H. (2010) 'Unfinished proletarianization: self, anger, and class action among the second generation of peasant-workers in present-day China', *Modern China*, 36(5): 493–519.

Qiu, J.L. (2009) *Working-class Network Society: Communication Technology and the Information Have-less in Urban China*, Cambridge, MA: MIT Press.

Qiu, J.L. (2010) 'Mobile communication research in Asia', *Asian Journal of Communication*, 20(2): 213–229.

Qiu, J.L. (2013) 'Network societies and internet studies: rethinking time, space, and class'. In W. H. Dutton (ed.) *The Oxford Handbook of Internet Studies*, Oxford: Oxford University Press: 109–128.

Qiu, J.L. and Bu, W. (2013) 'China ICT studies: A review of the field, 1989–2014', *The China Review*, 13(2): 123–152.

Smil, V. (2013) *Made in the USA: The Rise and Retreat of American Manufacturing*, Cambridge, MA: MIT Press.

Thompson, N. W. (1996) *Political Economy and the Labour Party: The Economics of Democratic Socialism, 1884–1995*, London: Ucl Press Ltd.

Wallis, C. (2013) *Technomobility in China: Young Migrant Women and Mobile Phones*, New York: New York University Press.

Yang, G. (2012) 'Classes without class consciousness and class consciousness without classes: the meaning of class in the People's Republic of China', *Journal of Contemporary China*, 21(77): 723–739.

Zang, X. (2012) 'Scaling the Socioeconomic Ladder: Uyghur perceptions of class status', *Journal of Contemporary China*, 21(78): 1029–1043.

Zhao, Y. (2008) *Communication in China: Political Economy, Power, and Conflict*, Lanham, MD: Rowman and Littlefield.

丁未 (2011) 新媒體賦權： 理論建構與個案分析—以中國稀有血型群體網路自組織為例. 開放時代, (001): 124–145.

关于新生代农民工的研究报告，2010年6月。全国总工会新生代农民工问题课题组。

刘晓旋 (2011) 微博场， 离农民工权益话语的救赎有多远?—以新浪微博为例的实证研究. 第二届华中地区新闻与传播学科研究生学术论坛获奖论文.

刘鸿谕 (2013) 80 后女性农民工城市适应性研究 (Master's thesis, 贵州财经大学).

周葆華 & 呂舒寧 (2011) 上海市新生代農民工新媒體使用與評價的實證研究. 新聞大學, 2: 145–150.

邱林川 (2014) 告别 i 奴: 富士康，数字资本主义与网络劳工抵抗. 社会, 34(4): 119–137.

姜兰花 (2013) 流动空间里的空间人—新生代农民工手机媒体使用初探. 长沙大学学报, 27(6): 121–123.

孙信茹, & 楊星星 (2012) 媒介化社會中的少數民族村民傳播實踐與賦權—雲南大羊普米族村的研究個案. 現代傳播: 中國傳媒大學學報, 34(3): 23–28.

許燕 (2012) 以近年熱點事件及其應對為例看中國社會各階層媒介話語重構 (上) 新聞大學, (6): 115–119.

陳韻博 (2011) 新媒體賦權: 新生代農民工對 QQ 的使用與滿足研究. 當代青年研究, (8): 22–25.

董延芳, & 劉傳江 (2012) 農民工市民化中的被邊緣化與自邊緣化: 以湖北省為例. 武漢大學學報: 哲學社會科學版, 65(1): 122–125.

趙雲澤, & 付冰清 (2010) 當下中國網路話語權的社會階層結構分析. 國際新聞界, (5): 63–70.

孙立平 (2003) 断裂: 20 世纪 90 年代以来的中国社会. 社会科学文献出版社.

孙立平, 王汉生, 王思斌, 林彬, & 杨善华 (1994) 改革以来中国社会结构的变迁. 中国社会科学, 2: 47–62.

李培林, 李强, & 孙立平 (2004) 中国社会分层. 社会科学文献出版社.

陆学艺 (ed.) (2002) 当代中国社会阶层研究报告/中国社会阶层研究丛书. 社会科学文献出版社.

李强 (2008) 社会分层十讲. 社会科学文献出版社.

李培林 (1992) 另一只看不见的手: 社会结构转型. 中国社会科学, 5(3).

沈原 (2006) 社会转型与工人阶级的再形成. 社会学研究, (2): 13–36.

郭于华, 沈原, 潘毅, & 卢晖临 (2011) 当代农民工的抗争与中国劳资关系转型. (香港) 二十一世纪, (124): 4–14.

丁未 (2014) 流动的家园: "攸县的哥村" 社区传播与身份共同体研究. 北京: 社会科学文献出版社.

李超民, & 李礼 (2013) "屌丝" 现象的后现代话语检视. 中国青年研究, (1): 13–16.

丁未, & 宋晨 (2010) 在路上: 手机与农民工自主性的获得—以西部双峰村农民工求职经历为个案. 现代传播: 中国传媒大学学报, (9), 95–100.

李培林, 田丰 (2011) 中国新生代农民工: 社会态度和行为选择. 社会, 3(1).

刘磊, 朱红根 and 康兰媛 (2014) 农民工留城意愿影响因素分析—基于上海, 广州, 深圳 724 份调查数据. 湖南农业大学学报: 社会科学版, 15(2), 41–46.

汪建华 (2011) 互联网动员与代工厂工人集体抗争. 开放时代, 11, 114–128.

郑欣 and 王悦 (2014) 新媒体赋权: 新生代农民工就业信息获取研究. 当代传播, 2, 51–52.

郑欣 and 衣旭峰 (2014) 风险适应与媒介赋权: 新生代农民工学习充电研究. 西南民族大学学报: 人文社会科学版, 35(5), 134–139.

周葆华 (2012) 从同一效果到差异效果: 对新媒体与主观阶层认同关系的多层分析. 新闻大学, (6), 54–62.

9

Young people, new media and citizenship in Asia

Shobha Vadrevu

Against a backdrop of rising income inequality on a global scale and the political upheavals this has led to around the world (Piketty 2014), the role of new media as an agent of change has been interrogated and explained in various and nuanced ways: in some cases, it has been credited with playing a part in enabling political change (Rheingold 2002; Shirky 2011); in others it has been too easily co-opted as a tool of surveillance and control by governments, rendering citizen attempts muted, if not impotent (Rodan 1998; Morozov 2011). With the increasing participation of young people in online political activity around the world, as well as the increasingly pervasive use of digital technologies by young people, a conceptual field linking youth, citizenship and new media has emerged that arguably calls for new understandings of citizenship.

The youth–citizenship–new media intersection has also taken on more intense and complex meanings as it intersects with discourses linking new media technologies with new types of agency. Additionally, these technologies and their pervasive use are associated with an entire generation. Terms such as "digital natives" (Prensky 2001), and "cyberkids" (Holloway and Valentine 2003) point to the conceptualization of young people's identities as being inseparable from the technologies that they use, and research has delved into their relationships with and through these technologies (Ito 2010; boyd 2014). These technologically enmeshed identities have given rise to both expectations as well as apprehensions. Expectations have centered on better educational outcomes via learning technologies (Squire 2011; Beetham and Sharpe 2013), increased civic participation via democratic platforms (Loader 2007; Bennett et al. 2011; Dahlgren 2013), and greater economic opportunities (Plomp 2013). Apprehensions have been directed at antisocial tendencies via addiction to devices and immersion in virtual environments (Ko et al. 2012), risky behaviors via sexual experimentation online (Baumgartner et al. 2010) and cyberbullying (Kowalski et al. 2012). These expectations and apprehensions have led to numerous attempts to shape the behavior and aspirations of young citizens around the world, through such means as the introduction of media literacy curricula in schools and youth outreach initiatives by various groups (Fisherkeller 2011).

What is often missing from scholarly attempts to understand the intersection of youth, new media and citizenship writ large, however, is a contextual grounding in the cultural and political history of specific regions and countries. The forces of globalization have led to some homogenization of structures and institutions worldwide, but there are regional and national differences, with varying levels of resistance and acceptance (Castells 2010). Furthermore, globalization has resulted in the intensification of inequalities—not just between North and South, but within each region as well (Sreekumar 2013).

In this chapter, the intersection between youth, new media and citizenship will be discussed in the particular context of Asia, with a focus on how the intersection has taken shape. Starting with a brief description of the region's political diversity, the chapter traces some continuities and discontinuities across two case studies—one a full democracy and the other a hybrid regime—suggesting that regardless of the formal level of democracy, the use of new media by civil society activists involves certain challenges and negotiations which are rooted in the sociopolitical context and have spillover effects into discourses about technology and youth. The chapter concludes with a reflection on the Asian technological citizen, and the possibilities for conceptualizing youthful agency in this context.

The politics of Asia

Asia is a politically diverse region, ranging from the self-reliant socialism of North Korea (Park 2002) to the "authoritarian leviathans" of Southeast Asia (Slater 2010) and India's massive and complex democracy (Kohli 2014). It is also economically diverse, with the East Asian sub-region having a history of outperforming many of the other states (Hamashita 2013).

According to the Economist Intelligence Unit's (EIU's) Democracy Index 2013,[1] from the Asian region,[2] only Japan and South Korea are included under the category of *full democracies*. India, Taiwan, Timor Leste, Indonesia, Malaysia, Hong Kong, the Philippines and Thailand are listed under *flawed democracies*. Singapore, Bangladesh, Sri Lanka, Bhutan, Nepal, Pakistan and Cambodia are named *hybrid regimes*. Vietnam, China, Myanmar, Laos and North Korea are listed as *authoritarian regimes*.

The Asian region also encompasses multiple ethnic and religious groups. Duara (2010) offers an interesting problematization of the notion of an Asian region, by hypothesizing that it is the result of a number of phases of regionalization—that is, projects through which the region was conceptualized. He starts with imperial regionalization, by which the colonial powers (most notably Britain) "created significant regional interdependencies in Asia" which "had the effect of intensifying some of the old relationships and generating new linkages between the cities" (964). Following this, he describes the work of three Asian intellectuals, analyzing it through the lens of "the anti-imperialist regionalization project in Asia" (Duara 2010, 969). In this way, Duara argues, it is possible to see emerging the conception of the unity of Asia founded on different principles, based on a common historical and religious culture. However, he points out that this was an abstract project which was appropriated and converted by various nationalistic movements, as well as being unreflective of the realities of regional dynamics. After World War II, Cold War imperatives led to the encouragement of regional and intraregional associations. According to Duara, in a global situation of increasing political and financial complexity, the economic ties facilitated by these associations have continued the regionalization project.

Against this backdrop, integration is deepened by flows of people within the region, although the interplay of nationalization and globalization results in severe inequalities between citizens with transnational mobility and those to whom such mobility is denied. Furthermore, individual states cope with rhetorics of nationalism even as global and regional interdependencies deepen, resulting in the impossibility of imagining any sort of homogenized or essentialised Asian culture.

Duara notes that even the rise of waves of popular culture consumption that spread across the region does not necessarily lead to cultural homogenization.

This historical and cultural perspective is an important one for the consideration of youth citizenship in Asia, and for the study of its mediation by digital technologies. The understanding that the Asian region has been constructed through imperialisms and imaginings informs not only modern conceptualizations of citizenship, but also youth and new media in Asia as three separate as well as intersecting constructs. As noted by Duara, citizenship is a deeply divided experience across the region. The introduction of new media into this context has various consequences. In some cases it enables citizens to mobilize and collectively assert their rights—for example in Malaysia, the organizers of the massive "Bersih 2.0" rally calling for clean and fair elections were able to use social media to unite diverse groups of people, resulting in 50,000 Malaysians taking to the streets (Weiss 2012). In other cases new media creates new exclusions—for example in India, the installation of cyberkiosks in some villages, rather than closing digital divides, sometimes ended up creating new ones (Sreekumar 2011). This chapter will explain how, in addition to these consequences, new media also affords states the ability to exert more control over their citizens, paradoxically constructing youths as both the bright future of the nation and its moral burden at the same time.

In the following sections, two country-based case studies will be presented that show various combinations of these consequences and their implications for the political efficacy and socialization of young people. South Korea and Singapore have been chosen because they have much in common in terms of current trends concerning youth and new media. Both part of the East Asian sub-region, their economic performance outstrips that of states in other parts of Asia. As a result, their Internet and mobile penetration rates are high, supported by well-developed infrastructure and educational policy geared towards developing young people's technological skills to prepare them for an advanced workforce (Lin et al. 2010). In terms of the political landscape, however, they are very different, resulting in different dynamics at the intersection of youth, new media and citizenship. At the same time, as new media is integrated into all levels of society and use becomes more pervasive, it can be seen that state surveillance and policing in both countries become more sophisticated. This has implications for conceptualizing the agency of the young Asian technological citizen.

Full democracy: the case of South Korea

South Korea's recent political history covers alternating cycles of liberal and authoritarian government, with its current democratic system being in place since 1988. Divided from its northern portion by the United States and the then Soviet Union in 1948, South Korea's colonial influence was from Japan, rather than the West, unlike a large part of Asia. Historically, four factors have had a shaping influence on the political culture of South Korea:

> the tradition of its own people, reaching back into the Siberian steppes of five thousand or more years ago; the power and culture of neighboring China; the impact of Japan, particularly since the late nineteenth century; [and] the economic and cultural inroads of the West.
>
> *(Macdonald and Clark 1996, 26)*

According to Macdonald and Clark (1996), as of 1996, Korean understanding of democracy was in a state of flux, with old beliefs in the value of hierarchies, principles, and family privacy overlaid by Western institutional forms. The sense of citizen participation was growing, although the sense of abstract justice and universal human rights as a matter of rights and obligations were "weak in comparison to group loyalties and duties" (119). As South Korea developed economically, political participation became more intense and widespread in response to the emergence of more complex needs. Politically important groups such as the armed forces, the bureaucracy, businesspeople, internal security forces, politicians and political parties, mass media, intellectuals, church groups, students, labor, and farmers/fishermen were engaged in a variety of political acts (139).

Student groups in particular have been very active, and the government's response was to attempt to suppress this activism through surveillance, although campus culture picked up again in the 1990s. In fact by the 1990s, after the institution of the Sixth Republic through structural political change, the Internet was being widely used for "progressive and oppositional civic actions and political campaigns" (Lee 2013, 123). Lee notes, however, that in the Korean context, where political groups have been very active for a long time, the Internet is not being used as a tool to intensify extant practices of engagement. Rather, it has led to new forms of engagement by citizens who do not always position themselves within traditional political groups. This "netizen movement," Lee argues, maintains independence from institutionalized political groups, and has "reshaped the political and social landscape of Korea" (124). Lee also points out that the term "netizen" should be defined according to cultural context, noting that while it had positive connotations in its origin (Hauben and Hauben 1998), in Korea it sometimes has more negative connotations such as "radical" or "irresponsible."

Lee places the origins of the netizen movement in a community that was set up to "solve the problems of cyberspace by proposing democratic alternatives and solutions" (128). A key political game changer was the flattening of hierarchies (normally associated with traditional political groups) through the use of standardized honorifics. Progressive social reform and online freedom of speech were common goals of early actors within the netizen movement. As more pre-existing social movements adopted new media technologies as a tool, the netizen movement developed a separate identity from them. Significantly, young people were engaged when the netizen movement took on less overtly political causes—notably the mobilization of fan support for sports. An Internet-based fan club known as the "Red Devils" managed to coordinate street cheering for the national football team by more than 22 million young people, mostly in their teens and twenties. This age demographic had been seen as apathetic till this moment. The evolution of the netizens as a movement separate from mainstream politics was taken forward with online discussion of a contentious event in 2002 that the press did not cover, resulting in nationwide demonstrations. When established social movement organizations got involved with these demonstrations, their hierarchical organizational structures were seen as out of sync with the flatter and more rhizomatic nature of the netizens, and the two groups eventually ended up taking different political positions as well.

As the netizen movement established itself, it emerged as one that was constituted by younger citizens who were more Internet-savvy. In the 2002 Presidential Election, the sort of sports fandom that had been established online and the sense of a youthful and passionate collective took new shape as an online fan base for the new candidate who stood against the more conservative and institutionally backed one. The fresh face was voted in, and this was seen as a generational phenomenon, with young citizens asserting themselves over an older order. As the political scene developed and new media was integrated more deeply into the politics of the country, more groups did start using it to gain power, including conservative right wing groups and more established political organizations. This was seen as possibly having a deleterious impact on the progressive ethos of the netizen movement. A contentious event in 2008 involving the decision to import

US beef, however, once again brought the movement and its young members to the forefront, as they mobilized support and organized vigils. Online discussions became more vibrant and even groups that had previously been non-political or non-partisan joined in the fray.

Importantly for a discussion on youth, new media and citizenship, from this 2008 event emerged young female netizens who played significant roles online and offline, thereby changing the face of South Korean politics. Furthermore, netizen involvement in the event also lent an organic quality to the protests, which allowed them to grow beyond the beef issue and coalesce into a critique of the prevailing leadership. Youthful involvement and lack of traditional hierarchical leadership also led to the use of satire and playful responses to state provocations. The traditional organizations could not gain a foothold. Their role in mediating political action was taken over by new media and the young people who had discovered their ability to connect through it.

This emergence of the young netizen as politically powerful yet selective about causes (Lee 2006), uninterested in traditional political collectives and issues, and even prone to turning on fellow netizens in what Epstein and Jung (2011) refer to as "cyber witch-hunts" as they form sometimes oppressive cultural tribes, coincides with a growing discourse about young South Koreans as avid gamers and intensive mobile phone users who are part of a powerful cultural and economic shift (Fung 2013; Lie 2014; Taylor 2012; Kuwahara 2014), leading to a large body of research into their gaming habits (Seok and DaCosta 2012[3]), Internet and mobile phone addiction (Heo et al. 2014; Kim et al. 2014) and digital literacy (Park et al. 2014). Yoon's (2006) exploration of how young people are represented in popular discourses of mobile phone technology reveals that "the different streams of discourse . . . appear to reflect widespread anxieties in Korea about becoming involved in 'global' material culture and seek to counter this tendency through rearticulating hegemonic social relations" (753). Thus in a context where frugality was widely advocated to counter globalizing forces, young people were seen as over-consuming with regard to mobile phone technology, and engaging in trivial (as opposed to economically productive) activities. Their use of the individualizing technology of the mobile phone was also seen as damaging to the traditional culture of collective harmony. Yoon argues that the moral regulation of the student-consumer who emerged out of these panics constituted the young South Korean as a "neo-Confucian cyberkid" who was a consumer of the technology but within the framework of the neo-Confucian habitus.

Even as the political fervor of young people in South Korea is seen as being diverted into subjectivities and activities of consumption and transgression, new media has been integrated into the political culture of the country at higher levels. Thus Lee (2015) describes how the South Korean government successfully utilized new media to promote participation among citizens for hosting the G20 Summit in Seoul in 2010. Lee concludes that "shared norms and ideologies can be mobilized to work against narratives of dissent and to produce hegemonic consent from citizens," and that nationalism, nationalistic citizenship, and geopolitical ideologies played a role in producing counternarratives against the anti-G20 protests that were conducted both online and offline. Lee's argument is ultimately that new media allows for more sophisticated policing of citizens by the state. At the same time, direct policing and surveillance appear to be on the rise in South Korea (The Economist 2014), an affordance of new media technology that is increasingly being used around the world by governments on their own citizens.

Hybrid regime: the case of Singapore

Singapore achieved independence from its British colonial masters in 1963, as part of Malaysia. However, its current status as an independent and sovereign nation-state was the result of its expulsion from the federation in 1965 (Turnbull 1989). Its independence was thus a reluctant one (Chua 1995). Helmed since 1959 by the People's Action Party (PAP), Singapore has been lauded as an economic success story (Lim 1983; James et al. 1989; Leipziger 2001). Its colonial past, paucity of natural resources, geographic location in the midst of a region that does not completely share its secular and capitalist ethos (Mutalib 1996) and small size have been held up as potentially insurmountable hurdles that were yet overcome on the road to economic prosperity (Huff 1995). The state seems to have been built on democratic principles but there are grey areas in the definition of Singapore's political system (Mutalib 2000; Diamond 2002; Zolo 2004).

Chua (1995) theorizes that consensus among citizens for the massive transformations in cultural attitudes and values that were needed to meet the demands of capitalist industrialization was achieved through ideological processes that fit conceptually into a neo-Marxist framework. The result, in terms of political system, is communitarianism without competitive politics (Chua 2004), and a depoliticized citizenry that has traded its political power in exchange for economic growth (Chua 1995). Hong and Huang (2008), in their examination of how Singapore's history was carefully constructed to endorse the power of the state in the form of the ruling party, also highlight the preoccupation of Singaporeans with economic development and their intimidation by "complicated and sensitive" issues (150). They observe that many topics had been ruled out of bounds for public discussion, such that by the time the post-independence generation had reached adulthood, the government felt that there was a disconnect between these citizens and their political leaders. This disconnect translated into a lack of involvement of young people in politics, which was seen by the government as a problem for self-renewal of leadership. State efforts to repoliticize young people by "[creating] more space for young Singaporeans to express ideas and to promote political awareness among young people" (Hong and Huang 2008, 157) are described by Hong and Huang as being unsystematic and spasmodic, with some forums being opened up with government permission—notably in the universities—and then being curtailed because they were becoming too politically active.

In a context of lack of press freedom (George 2012), suppression of opposition parties (Gomez 2006), and manipulation of legislation and public discourse (Rajah 2012), the Internet presented possibilities for surmounting these obstacles to democracy, and was quickly adopted by civil society. With the advent of social media, there has been the perception that the thus-far quiescent citizenry has been repoliticized:

> The social media revolution gave voice to and amplified the dissatisfaction and opposition views. Singaporeans are now more vocal, more demanding of their rights and they want their views heard. They have lost their fear for speaking up and voting for the opposition. Politics has become competitive again. The political culture has transformed. Singaporeans have been repoliticised.
>
> *(Chan 2013, 15)*

More critical voices however have noted that while new media has had some impact on the political landscape, it has stopped short of enabling action seeking substantive systemic change. Thus while new media allows civil society to connect with international bodies for support (Gomez 2005), and provides a platform for citizens to participate in documenting their heritage (Liew et al. 2014), overcoming the constraints imposed by the political system proves difficult. For example, Sreekumar and Vadrevu (2013a) show how even influential actors who use satire to pave the way for questioning the dominant narratives of the ruling party, thereby shaping the quality of democratic discourse in Singapore, do not go beyond the limits of the country's non-Western liberal democratic framework. In a study of young activists in Singapore, Zhang (2013) found that their perceptions of activism were framed by the possibilities afforded to them by new media technologies within the narratives of the state.

The tenuousness with which young people approach political engagement has its roots in offi-cial discourse by the state and state-controlled media that seeks to subsume their identity into the nation-building project. Thus Kong (2006) suggests that there is a political and ideological basis to the engineering of moral panics such that moral policing is seen as necessary for the successful development of a national identity. Tarulevicz (2010) casts a critical gaze on policies directed at young people, and notes that policies towards young offenders highlight the state's anxiety about non-conformity, while the compulsory National Service that all male citizens perform by serv-ing in the army for two years may be seen as a mechanism for masculinized nation building. In addition, discourses around young people that label them in various ways reflect the prevailing tension between nationalism and political apathy. Through these policies and discourses, Taru-levicz comes to the conclusion that youth in Singapore cannot really be seen as agents of change, despite rhetoric about the liberalizing effect of new media, affluence, and globalization.

Indeed, even as social media is perceived as opening up space for democratic discourse in Singapore, there is a distinct silence with regard to discursive indicators of a significant youth presence in this space. One example of this is demonstrated by the phenomenon of online politi-cal memes, whereby political actors share memes on social media that satirize politicians. This is a deceptively banal act, but in reality quite significant. Political cartoons have not been permitted in Singapore (Chua 2014), and as recently as 2013, a cartoonist was arrested for alleged sedition (Loh 2013). The memes however have become standard fare on social media. A study of young people's perception of the political value of these memes however revealed a deep ambivalence towards them (Sreekumar and Vadrevu 2013b). While the memes potentially lower barriers to access in terms of political participation—a sort of "silly citizenship" (Hartley 2010)—the young people in the study discounted them as political artefacts in favor of longer and more serious blog posts. Yet they were not writing these posts either, cautious about not being knowledgeable enough.

Through its education system, Singapore aims to construct young people as skilled users of technology who are compliant with the social order. Lim et al.'s (2011) case study of a state-sponsored media production competition that focuses on National Education (an aspect of citizenship education in Singapore) demonstrates this objective in action. Their analysis shows that while the students' media products are of high quality—aided by media professionals—the videos themselves are didactic in their approach, exhorting viewers to align themselves to a par-ticular aspect of the national narrative. While elsewhere, media production has been associated with youthful imaginaries (Asthana 2011) and the critical examination of social realities (Lemish 2011), in Singapore no such scope seems to exist. Indeed, as young people become more active on social media, campaigns to regulate their behavior online have become more intensive. The "Safer Internet Day 2015" campaign mounted by the Media Literacy Council includes a video (hosted on YouTube) reminding viewers to be kind and thoughtful online, because "your next online post can hurt or heal" (a tagline that appeared on the Media Literacy Council's Facebook page when the video link was shared there).

Over and above these direct messages that urge compliance to social order, technological mediation of citizenship in Singapore also takes the form of intensive surveillance. Sophisticated and extensive surveillance mechanisms have been put in place, as described by Harris (2014), who notes that "Singapore is testing whether mass surveillance and big data can not only protect national security, but actually engineer a more harmonious society." Lee (2013) notes that despite news about Singapore being an advanced surveillance state, the citizens seem unconcerned. The phenomenon of "open networks, closed regimes" (Kalathil and Boas 2010) takes on new forms in this context, and a mark of Singapore's success in deepening this phenomenon may be seen in China's efforts to emulate aspects of Singapore's "authoritarian modernity" (Ortmann and Thompson 2014).

Discussion and conclusion

A comparison of the two country cases reveals that the political socialization and sense of efficacy that young people gain via new media is rooted in their cultural context. When the Asian region is considered as a whole, there is often an expectation of some cultural homogeneity. This expectation is the result of the very regionalization projects that Duara identifies. Yet these projects were superimposed onto pre-existing social relations. In South Korea, the presence of an already vibrant civil society provided an environment in which young people could see new media as affording new possibilities for intervention and engagement. In Singapore, on the other hand, new media emerged in a context of tight regulation of public spaces and citizen action. Young people were not socialized to challenge the status quo at any level, and there was no perception of efficacy. While new media was quickly adopted by an oft-suppressed civil society to advance their causes, and online activity by political actors substantively shaped the quality of democratic discourse, young people as a demographic have not been associated with these trends. This explains why, even with access to the same infrastructure and penetration rates, the intersection of youth, new media and citizenship took shape in very different ways in both cases.

After a point, however, it is possible to view the two cases as growing closer together in what may be seen as a new project of regionalization centered on the young Asian technological citizen. In the South Korean case, new media did allow young citizens to develop a sense of efficacy. This efficacy was, however, selectively applied, drawing them away from traditionally vibrant civil society groups and leaving them vulnerable to state discourses positioning them in the center of moral panics. The new subjectivity that they had developed was further mediated through pathologizing discourses and consumptive priorities. In Singapore, young people have been subjected to similar modes of state socialization via state-sponsored media initiatives and pointed discourses about the need for responsibility and kindness online. These patterns can be seen in other countries in Asia as well. Sreekumar (2014) shows how cyber cafés in small and medium towns in six Asian countries became sites of moral policing by state and civil society, producing new narratives of ethics, morality, progress and modernity. If there is a new imagining of a culturally homogeneous Asia, it may very well be one where narratives of empowerment via new media are laid over pre-existing norms relating to the place of young people in society. Whether the totem of traditional morality is Confucius or Gandhi, the perception of new media as a gateway to modernity, while initially embraced because of economic aspirations, appears to take on more intense connotations of risk because of its central location in the lived realities of the young.

As the state becomes more sophisticated in its use of new media to create hegemonic narratives, and as the capacity of the state to engage in extensive surveillance grows, the sustainability of youthful political engagement through new media comes into question. The intersection of youth, new media and citizenship in Asia needs to be understood in terms of its cultural and political history, as well as its new hegemonic narratives and practices. There are vast differences within the region, and the sheer number of ways in which youth citizenship has been shaped by new media is perhaps unsurprising. At the same time, however, whether in the context of Japan's plummeting birth rate (BBC News Asia 2015) or India's youth bulge (NYT 2014), youth is "the discursive screen onto which a society's fears and hopes are projected" (Smaill 2008, 3). As states become enmeshed in geopolitical and technological networks (Castells 2010), their need and power to control their citizens through the very new media that held hopes for empowerment increase (Morozov 2011). Whether in democratic or non-democratic contexts, the juxtaposition of discourses concerning youth and new media with increasingly sophisticated state intervention on multiple fronts results in what is arguably a new type of citizenship.

This begs the question of space for agency for the young citizen who is immersed in technosocial situations (Ito and Okabe 2005) and interpellated as a technosocial subject (Shah 2007) in Asia's emerging technological society. The term "technological society" was first brought into prominence by the book of the same name by Jacques Ellul (Ellul and Merton 1964). Ellul argued that such a society was one in which the human was subsumed by the technological, such that the logic of technology came to exert a force of its own with a totalizing effect. Other critical scholars have attempted to theorize this technological phenomenon that is so closely intertwined with the logics of capitalism, seeking ways of understanding power in modern societies. For Foucault, governmentality[4] is characterized by an attempt to articulate the manner in which the members of the technological society work upon themselves even as they are disciplined into particular modes of thought and action.

In this interaction of forces from different directions, argues Barry (2001), lie spaces for resistance. Using a sociotechnical framework, Barry (2001, 6) posits that "even the most apparently anti-technological of protests has a certain technical dimension. Moreover, even the most bureaucratic institutions may contain practices and activities which are politically inventive." Thus the technological society may be seen not as one in which technological forces subsume humanity, but as one in which human and non-human actors form a network of what Barry refers to as "political machines." This lens allows us to revisit the issue of citizenship in the technological society, with a view to understanding not just how agency may be demonstrated and utilized, but under what conditions it develops in the first place.

Specifically in the Asian context, where technology from the West has been the springboard for forward movement along the developmental trajectory (Arrighi et al. 2003), and where discourses of Asian exceptionalism have been heavily debated (Kinnvall and Jönsson 2002), the technological society as one in which technology both mediates and constitutes citizenship opens up the scope for exploring how technological relationships operate at global and local levels, and how young people speak back to the shaping of their identity at the point where media technologies and citizenship converge. As the South Korean and Singapore cases show, cultural and political histories interact with technological regimes in Asia to shape a new type of citizen. As young people in Asia deepen their technological relationships and subjectivities, the new project of regionalization should be one that seeks to understand this new citizenship, and to find spaces for youthful agency in the relational interstices of political machines.

Notes

1 The index is compiled based on electoral processes, functioning of government, political participation, political culture and civil liberties.
2 For the purposes of this chapter, only South Asian, East Asian, North Asian and Southeast Asian countries are included. Central Asian states are excluded from the current review because of their historical connection with Europe rather than Asia.

3 Interestingly in view of the arguments that fall under the heading of moral panics, the authors suggest that even in an intense gaming culture like South Korea's, addiction rates may not be as high as generally believed.
4 See, for example, Burchell et al. (1991) and Foucault and Lemke (1999).

References

Arrighi, G., Hamashita, T. and Selden, M. (2003) *The resurgence of East Asia: 500, 150 and 50 year perspectives*, London; New York: Psychology Press.

Asthana, S. (2011) 'Youth media imaginaries in the Arab world: A narrative and discourse analysis'. In J. Fisherkeller (ed.) *International perspectives on youth media: Cultures of production and education*, New York: Peter Lang.

Barry, A. (2001) *Political machines: Governing a technological society*, London; New York: Athlone Press.

Baumgartner, S.E., Valkenburg, P.M. and Peter, J. (2010) 'Assessing causality in the relationship between adolescents' risky sexual online behavior and their perceptions of this behavior', *Journal of Youth and Adolescence*, 39(10): 1226–1239.

BBC News Asia (2015) *Concern as Japan's 2014 birth rate falls to record low*. Available at: www.bbc.co.uk/news/world-asia-30653825 (Accessed on January 15, 2015).

Beetham, H. and Sharpe, R. (eds.) (2013) *Rethinking pedagogy for a digital age: Designing for 21st century learning*, New York: Routledge.

Bennett, W.L., Wells, C. and Freelon, D. (2011) 'Communicating civic engagement: Contrasting models of citizenship in the youth web sphere', *Journal of Communication*, 61: 835–856.

boyd, d. (2014) *It's complicated: The social lives of networked teens*, New Haven: Yale University Press.

Burchell, G., Gordon, C. and Miller, P. (eds.) (1991) *The Foucault effect: Studies in governmentality*, Chicago: University of Chicago Press.

Castells, M. (2010) *The power of identity* (2nd edn), Malden, MA: Wiley-Blackwell.

Chan, H.C. (2013) 'Governance in Singapore: History and legacy'. Chapter 1 in *Singapore Perspectives* 2013: 7–16.

Chua, B.H. (1995) *Communitarian ideology and democracy in Singapore*, Oxford: Routledge.

Chua, B.H. (2004) 'Communitarianism without competitive politics'. In B.H. Chua (ed.) *Communitarian politics in Asia*, London: RoutledgeCurzon.

Chua, M. (2014) *LKY: Political cartoons*, Singapore: Epigram Books.

Dahlgren, P. (ed.) (2013) *Young citizens and new media: Learning for democratic participation*, New York: Routledge.

Diamond, L. (2002), 'Elections without democracy: Thinking about hybrid regimes', *Journal of Democracy*, 13(2): 21–35.

Duara, P. (2010) 'Asia redux: Conceptualizing a region for our times', *The Journal of Asian Studies*, 69: 963–983.

Economist Intelligence Unit (2013) *Democracy Index 2013: Democracy in limbo*. Available at: www.eiu.com/Handlers/WhitepaperHandler.ashx?fi=Democracy_Index_2013_WEB-2.pdf&mode=wp&campaignid=Democracy0814 (Accessed on January 15, 2015).

Ellul, J. and Merton, R.K. (1964) *The technological society*, New York: Vintage.

Epstein, S. and Jung, S. (2011) 'Korean youth netizenship and its discontents', *Media International Australia, Incorporating Culture & Policy*, 141: 78–86.

Fisherkeller, J. (ed.) (2011) *International perspectives on youth media: Cultures of production and education*, New York: Peter Lang.

Foucault, G. and Lemke, T. (1999) 'Governmentality and the risk society', *Economy and Society*, 28(1): 138–148.

Fung, A.Y. (ed.) (2013) *Asian popular culture: the global (dis)continuity*, London: Routledge.

George, C. (2012) *Freedom from the press: Journalism and state power in Singapore*, Singapore: NUS Press.

Gomez, J. (2005) 'International NGOs: Filling the "gap" in Singapore's civil society', *Sojourn: Journal of Social Issues in Southeast Asia*, 20(2): 177–207.

Gomez, J. (2006) 'Restricting free speech: the impact of opposition parties in Singapore', *The Copenhagen Journal of Asian Studies*, 23: 105–131.

Hamashita, T. (2013) *China, East Asia and the global economy: Regional and historical perspectives*, Abingdon, Oxon; New York: Routledge.

Harris, S. (2014) 'The social laboratory', *Foreign Policy*. Available at: www.foreignpolicy.com/articles/2014/07/29/the_social_laboratory_singapore_surveillance_state?utm_content=buffer722d9&utm_medium=social&utm_source=facebook.com&utm_campaign=buffer (Accessed on July 29, 2014).

Hartley, J. (2010) 'Silly citizenship', *Critical Discourse Studies*, 7(4): 233–248.

Hauben, M. and Hauben, R. (1998) 'Netizens: On the history and impact of Usenet and the Internet', *First Monday*, 3(7).

Heo, J., Oh, J., Subramanian, S.V., Kim, Y. and Kawachi, I. (2014) 'Addictive internet use among Korean adolescents: A national survey', *PloS one*, 9(2), e87819.

Holloway, S.L. and Valentine, G. (2003) *Cyberkids: Children in the information age*, London: Routledge.

Hong, L., and Huang, J. (2008) *The scripting of a national history: Singapore and its pasts*, Singapore: NUS Press.

Huff, W. (1995) 'What is the Singapore model of economic development?' *Cambridge Journal of Economics*, 19: 735–759.

Ito, M. (2010) *Hanging out, messing around, and geeking out: Kids living and learning with new media*, Cambridge, MA: MIT Press.

Ito, M. and Okabe, D. (2005) 'Technosocial situations: Emergent structurings of mobile email use'. In M. Ito, D. Okabe and M. Matsuda (eds.) *Personal, portable, pedestrian: Mobile phones in Japanese life*, Cambridge, MA: MIT Press.

James, W.E., Naya, S. and Meier, G.M. (1989) *Asian development: Economic success and policy lessons*, University of Wisconsin Press.

Kalathil, S. and Boas, T.C. (2010) *Open networks, closed regimes: The impact of the Internet on authoritarian rule*, Washington, DC: Carnegie Endowment.

Kim, D., Lee, Y., Lee, J., Nam, J.K. and Chung, Y. (2014) 'Development of Korean smartphone addiction proneness scale for youth', *PloS one*, 9(5), e97920.

Kinnvall, C. and Jönsson, K. (2002) *Globalization and democratization in Asia: The construction of identity*, New York: Routledge.

Ko, C.H., Yen, J.Y., Yen, C.F., Chen, C.S. and Chen, C.C. (2012) 'The association between Internet addiction and psychiatric disorder: a review of the literature', *European Psychiatry*, 27(1): 1–8.

Kohli, A. (ed.) (2014) *India's democracy: An analysis of changing state–society relations*, Princeton: Princeton University Press.

Kong, L. (2006) 'Music and moral geographies: Constructions of "nation" and identity in Singapore', *Geo-Journal*, 65(1–2): 103–111.

Kowalski, R.M., Limber, S., Limber, S.P. and Agatston, P.W. (2012) *Cyberbullying: Bullying in the digital age*, Malden, MA: Wiley-Blackwell.

Kuwahara, Y. (ed.) (2014) *The Korean wave: Korean popular culture in global context*, Palgrave Macmillan.

Lee, J. (2013) 'The netizen movement: A new wave in the social movements of Korea'. Chapter 10 in H.Y. Cho, L. Surendra and H.J. Cho (eds.) *Contemporary South Korean society: A critical perspective*, USA and Canada: Routledge.

Lee, K. (2015) 'When Big Brother uses Twitter, too: Productive forms of policing and the role of media in the Seoul G20 protests in South Korea', *Communication, Culture & Critique*, 1–19.

Lee, S.J. (2006) 'The assertive nationalism of South Korean youth: Cultural dynamism and political activism', *SAIS Review*, 26(2): 123–132.

Lee, T. (2013) 'Singapore an advanced surveillance state, but citizens don't mind', Tech in Asia. Available at: http://www.techinasia.com/singapore-advanced-surveillance-state-citizens-mind/ (Accessed on July 23, 2014).

Leipziger, D.M. (2001) *Lessons from East Asia* (reprint), Ann Arbor: University of Michigan Press.

Lemish, P. (2011) Facilitating the Social Reality Challenge with youth filmmakers. In J. Fisherkeller (ed.) *International perspectives on youth media: Cultures of production and education*, New York: Peter Lang.

Lie, J. (2014) *K-pop: Popular music, cultural amnesia, and economic innovation in South Korea*, Oakland, CA: University of California Press.

Liew, K.K., Pang, N. and Chan, B. (2014) 'Industrial railroad to digital memory routes: Remembering the last railway in Singapore', *Media, Culture & Society*, 36(6): 761–775.

Lim, L.Y.C. (1983) 'Singapore's success: The myth of the free market economy', *Asian Survey*, 23(6): 752–764.

Lim, S.S., Nekmat, E. and Vadrevu, S. (2011) 'Singapore's experience in fostering youth media production: The implications of state-led school and public education initiatives'. In J. Fisherkeller (ed.) *International perspectives on youth media: Cultures of production and education*, New York: Peter Lang.

Lin, W.Y., Cheong, P.H., Kim, Y.C. and Jung, J.Y. (2010) 'Becoming citizens: Youths' civic uses of new media in five digital cities in East Asia', *Journal of Adolescent Research*, 25(6): 839–857.

Loader, B. (2007) *Young citizens in the digital age: Political engagement, young people and new media*, New York: Routledge.

Loh, A. (2013) 'Singapore cartoonist arrested for alleged sedition'. *Yahoo News Singapore*, Available at: https://sg.news.yahoo.com/blogs/singaporescene/pore-cartoonist-arrested-alleged-sedition-143415161.html (Accessed on January 15, 2015).

Macdonald, D.S. and Clark, D.N. (1996) *The Koreans: Contemporary politics and society*, Boulder, CO: Westview Press.

Media Literacy Council (2015) *Safer Internet Day 2015: Let's create a better internet together*. Video. Available at: https://www.youtube.com/watch?v=dIS4qndqZQM (Accessed on February 10, 2015).

Morozov, E. (2011) *The net delusion: The dark side of Internet freedom*, New York: PublicAffairs.

Mutalib, H. (1996) 'Islamic education in Singapore: Present trends and challenges for the future', *Journal of Muslim Minority Affairs*, 16(2): 233–240.

Mutalib, H. (2000) 'Illiberal democracy and the future of opposition in Singapore', *Third World Quarterly*, 21(2): 313–342.

Ortmann, S. and Thompson, M.R. (2014) 'China's obsession with Singapore: Learning authoritarian modernity', *The Pacific Review*, 27(3): 433–455.

Park, H.S. (2002) *North Korea: The politics of unconventional wisdom*, Boulder, CO: Lynne Rienner Publishers.

Park, S., Kim, E.M. and Na, E.Y. (2014) 'Online activities, digital media literacy, and networked individualism of Korean youth', *Youth & Society*, 1–21.

Piketty, T. (2014) *Capital in the twenty-first century*, Cambridge, MA: The Belknap Press of Harvard University Press.

Plomp, T. (2013) 'Preparing education for the information society: The need for new knowledge and skills', *International Journal of Social Media and Interactive Learning Environments*, 1(1): 3–18.

Prensky, M. (2001) 'Digital natives, digital immigrants', *On the Horizon*, 9(5): 1–6.

Rajah, J. (2012) *Authoritarian rule of law*, New York: Cambridge University Press.

Rheingold, H. (2002) *Smart mobs: The next social revolution*, Cambridge, MA: Perseus.

Rodan, G. (1998) 'The Internet and political control in Singapore', *Political Science Quarterly*, 113(1): 63–89.

Seok, S. and DaCosta, B. (2012) 'The world's most intense online gaming culture: Addiction and high-engagement prevalence rates among South Korean adolescents and young adults', *Computers in Human Behavior*, 28(6): 2143–2151.

Shah, N. (2007) 'Subject to technology: Internet pornography, cyber-terrorism and the Indian state', *Inter-Asia Cultural Studies*, 8(3): 349–366.

Shirky, C. (2011) 'The political power of social media', *Foreign Affairs*, 90(1): 28–41.

Slater, D. (2010) *Ordering power: Contentious politics and authoritarian leviathans in Southeast Asia*, Cambridge; New York: Cambridge University Press.

Smaill, B. (2008) 'Asia Pacific modernities: Thinking through youth media locales'. In U.M. Rodrigues and B. Smaill (eds.) *Youth, media and culture in the Asia Pacific region*, Newcastle: Cambridge Scholars Publishing.

Squire, K. (2011) *Video games and learning: Teaching and participatory culture in the digital age. Technology, Education–Connections (the TEC Series)*, New York: Teachers College Press.

Sreekumar, T.T. (2011) *ICTs and development in India: Perspectives on the rural network society*, London: Anthem Press.

Sreekumar, T.T. (2013) 'Global South perspectives on youth culture and gender imaginations in the technological society', *Journal of Creative Communications*, 8(2–3): 77–88.

Sreekumar, T.T. (2014) 'New media, space and marginality: A comparative perspective on cyber café use in small and medium towns in Asia'. Paper presented at the *International Association for Media and Communication Research* (IAMCR) Annual Conference, Hyderabad, India, July 15–19, 2014.

Sreekumar, T.T. and Vadrevu, S. (2013a) 'Subpolitics and democracy: The role of new media in the 2011 General Elections in Singapore', *Science Technology & Society*, 18(2): 231–249.

Sreekumar, T.T. and Vadrevu, S. (2013b) 'Online political memes and youth political engagement in Singapore'. *Selected Papers of Internet Research, 3*. Association of Internet Researchers conference, Denver, Colorado, USA, October 23rd to 26th 2013.

Tarulevicz, N. (2010) 'Singaporean youths must have wings and yet know where their nest is', *IJAPS*, 6(2): 23–48.

Taylor, T.L. (2012) *Raising the stakes: E-sports and the professionalization of computer gaming*, Cambridge, MA: MIT Press

The Economist (2014) *Why South Korea is really an Internet dinosaur.* Available at: http://www.economist. com/blogs/economist-explains/2014/02/economist-explains-3 (Accessed on January 15, 2015).

The New York Times (2014) 'India's youth challenge'. *The Opinion Pages.* Available at: http://www.nytimes. com/2014/04/18/opinion/indias-youth-challenge.html?_r=0 (Accessed on January 15, 2015).

Turnbull, C. (1989) *A history of Singapore, 1819–1988*, Kuala Lumpur; New York: Oxford University Press.

Weiss, M.L. (2012) *Politics in cyberspace: New media in Malaysia*, Singapore: Friedrich-Ebert-Stiftung.

Yoon, K. (2006) 'The making of neo-Confucian cyberkids: Representations of young mobile phone users in South Korea', *New Media & Society*, 8(5): 753–771.

Zhang, W.Y. (2013) 'Refining youth activism through digital technology in Singapore', *The International Communication Gazette*, 75(3): 253–270.

Zolo, D. (2004) 'The "Singapore model": Democracy, communication, and globalization'. In K. Nash and A. Scott (eds.) *The Blackwell Companion to Political Sociology*, Hoboken, NJ: John Wiley and Sons.

10

New media, censorship and gender: using obscenity law to restrict online self-expression in Japan and China

Mark McLelland

The widespread take-up of Internet technologies from the mid-1990s has proven challenging to nation states that seek to limit access to ideas, information or images that the political class considers dangerous or inappropriate for the general population. As a largely deterritorialized technology, the Internet allows access to material that circumvents national legislatures and ignores local ratings systems and in so doing facilitates all kinds of inter-cultural and transnational flows of communication. Different countries have different sensitivities regarding the kinds of material that should not be freely available to their citizens and although the entry of such material is closely scrutinized at land borders, maintaining virtual barriers is much more difficult.

In many Asian societies forms of political speech are subject to suppression, but what kinds of speech are deemed problematic differs with the society. *Lèse majesté*, for example, which involves speech that impugns the integrity of the ruling family, is a serious offense in Thailand, but in Japan where the monarchy is similarly revered, it is not a matter for the Criminal Code. In Japan, where freedom of expression is guaranteed by Article 21 of the country's constitution, criticism of the imperial family is not sanctioned by law, but is regulated via media etiquette. Whereas Thai authorities do monitor the Internet to suppress speech criticizing the monarchy (Kummetha 2014), Japanese Internet sites are famous for a level of critical inquiry and free expression that is not always evident in the nation's press (McNeill 2014, 72–73). This is evidenced in the Princess Mako scandal when in 2008 a cute animated version of the emperor's then seventeen-year-old daughter became a hit on Nico Nico Dōga, Japan's top video sharing site, but was condemned by the imperial household agency (Condry 2011, 275–276). In contrast, Japan's neighbor China, while also guaranteeing freedom of expression in Article 35 of its constitution, is particularly vigilant about monitoring the Internet for criticisms of the government or other forms of political speech that are considered destabilizing.

Another form of speech that is closely monitored by most Asian nations is obscenity, including but not limited to forms of visual pornography. Both Japan and China have legal provisions that forbid the production and dissemination of "obscene materials" but the legislation in neither country offers a clear description of what constitutes obscenity. In Japan since the 1970s pornography has been considered legal so long as it is clearly marked as adult-only and no genitalia or pubic hair are clearly visible (McLelland 2015, 247; Allison 2000, 160). These restrictions apply equally to depictions of real people or imaginary *manga*-style characterizations.

In China on the other hand, a much wider swathe of materials is likely to be deemed obscene and regulated by the police. Unlike Japan, specific kinds of actions are highlighted as potentially obscene, including depictions of "abnormal" activities involving homosexuality, incest, minors, or any kind of violence or sado-masochism (Yan 2015, 389). Also, unlike Japan which has not recently prosecuted any text-based articles for obscenity, the Chinese authorities are vigilant against written as well as visual depictions of material that gives "too much detail" (Yan 2015, 389).

In this chapter, I look at recent developments in obscenity prosecution in Japan and China from a gendered and youth perspective. Although much anti-pornography discourse operates from the standpoint that pornography is a male enterprise that demeans and degrades women and is thereby dangerous to youth, in recent years in both Japan and China, women, specifically young women, have been caught up in pornography debates and anti-obscenity prosecutions that have led to censorship and even the deprivation of liberty. Although the conditions under which these women's actions have been condemned are different, it is worth considering why women's media have been targeted and whose interests are served by criticizing them. The purpose of the chapter is to challenge the ideas that there are universal standards or agreement over the meaning of contentious terms such as "pornography" or "obscenity," and that engaging in sexual communication online is necessarily a danger to young people (see also McLelland in press). Indeed, pornography and obscenity are political terms that can be used by various groups, or by the State itself, to forward specific agendas that sometimes include restricting or closing down women's speech.

As Anne Allison has pointed out, anglophone discussions of pornography have largely overlooked standards and practices concerning the regulation of sexual expression in non-Western countries; or, when they are attended to, as in the case of Japan, "practices and texts involving the representation, alteration and aestheticization of bodies have been judged by Western (or universalist) standards" (2000, 54). Allison calls for the need to "foreground the local context" when analyzing the ways in which certain forms of speech or illustration are deemed unacceptable. This is particularly important in the Internet age when all manner of representations are available for download and where new media technologies have generated new kinds of transnational media flows, influences and audiences. "Obscenity" has notoriously always been in the eye of the beholder, but as new media technologies lead to audience fragmentation and increasingly heterogeneous consumption patterns within societies, understanding how obscenity is used as a mechanism to close down speech, in what circumstances and in whose interests, can help us understand the increasingly complex and unmanageable ways in which new media are impacting the lives of diverse populations within and outside Asia.

Legislating against obscenity in Japan

As noted above, Japan constitutionally guarantees freedom of expression (Banerjee and Logan 2008, 247). The main limitation to this freedom is the prohibition of "obscenity" dating back to the Criminal Code of 1880 and maintained today in paragraph 175 of the current code which sanctions a person who distributes or sells "an obscene writing, picture or other object or who publicly displays the same." Since the 1970s, the obscenity legislation has been applied very specifically to prohibit representations of genitalia and pubic hair. Overall sexual scenarios that can include violence, group sex and even rape are not captured by the legislation, so long as the offending organs are blurred or blanked out and an appropriate age rating is published on the cover. Both real and fictional representations are covered by the legislation. In Japan all officially marketed pornographic representations whether online or in stores and whether involving actual models or purely fictional *manga* or *anime* characters must have genitalia pixelated or be otherwise masked.

The age of consent for sex mentioned in the Criminal Code is 13 in Japan but the Child Welfare Law prohibits persons under the age of 18 from appearing in pornographic material or engaging in sex work (Lunsing 2004, 59). In addition a series of local ordinances further regulate the sexual behaviors of those under 18 as well as the manner in which fictional representations of such behavior may be depicted (McLelland 2015, 247; Nagaoka 2009). However, unlike many Western jurisdictions, there is no outright prohibition of fictional characters who may "appear to be" under the age of 18 in sexual scenarios. This means many Japanese *manga* and *anime* that deal in sexual themes can fall foul of "child-abuse publications" legislation when imported or downloaded in some Western countries including Canada, the UK and Australia, which have all seen successful prosecutions for possession of such material in recent years.

In Japan although the production and distribution of child pornography depicting real people was outlawed in 1999, until recently "simple possession" of these materials remained a grey area, largely to do with ambiguity about what, exactly, constitutes "child pornography" (Nagaoka 2009). Japan, for instance, supports a large "junior idol" industry consisting of print and digital reproductions of Japanese and Caucasian child models in skimpy swimsuits in poses that could be deemed erotic. This material is not covered by obscenity legislation since there are no sex acts or visible genitalia.

In June 2014 the upper house of the Diet, Japan's parliament, finally voted to outlaw the possession of child pornography. Much was made in the anglophone press about the lateness of this move by Japan and these reports also expressed consternation over the fact that fictional *manga* and animation representations of under-age characters in sexual scenarios had been excluded from the new regulations (Fletcher 2015; Fackler 2014). However, nowhere in these overseas' commentaries was it mentioned that Japan's constitution guarantees freedom of expression and that any kind of blanket censorship is therefore difficult to introduce. This is in fact a similar situation as pertains in the United States and is unsurprising given that the current Japanese constitution was drafted by the US authorities during their occupation of the country from 1945 to 1952. Unlike in many countries, including Canada, the UK and Australia, where legislation bans outright all purely fictional representations of under-age sex, including in cartoon form, that is considered "offensive" (Byberg 2012; Eiland 2009), there is no such blanket ban in place in the US where "not all VCP [virtual child porn] is *technically* prohibited" (Byberg 2012, 13; emphasis in the original). Hence, Japan is in no sense unusual or a pariah in its failure to legislate against representations of under-age sexual activity in fictional formats. Like in the US, there are constitutional reasons why such a blanket prohibition would be unlikely to succeed.

Despite the fact that definitions of child pornography and penalties for its production, circulation and possession differ widely across jurisdictions, English-language reporting on the recent legal developments in Japan, including an article in the *New York Times* (Fackler 2014), have assumed a unified developed world that Japan was somehow lagging behind. The decision of legislators to exclude fictional images in *manga* and *anime* was explained as simply "a concession to the nation's powerful publishing and entertainment industries" (Fackler 2014). In addition the Japanese nation as a whole was pictured as somewhat blasé about the legislative reform, it being reported that "the passage of the law barely merited a mention on the nightly news" (Fackler 2014), the reason for this being, in the opinion of the journalist, "Japan's more casual social attitudes when it comes to the sexual objectification of women of all ages" (Fackler 2014).

Although the Western press posits Japan's reluctance to prohibit fictional depictions of under-age sex as a symptom of male bias against women and children, there has been no mention of the role that Japanese women play in producing, consuming and disseminating erotic materials, as artists, authors and fans. Two well-known genres are the highly erotic "ladies comics" (Jones 2005), authored by and targeted at adult women, and the more youth-oriented "Boys Love" *manga* (see also Chapter 32 by Katrien Jacobs in this volume). "Under-age" representations mostly occur in "Boys Love" (BL) *manga*, novels, games and online fiction which feature roman-tic and sexual liaisons between "beautiful boys" and adult men. BL was originally pioneered in the early 1970s by a group of female *manga* artists known as the "Year 24 Group," due to all members being born in or around the twenty-fourth year of Emperor Showa's reign, that is, 1949 (McLelland and Welker 2015, 9). Although early examples of the genre in the 1970s were fairly demure, as Nagaike notes, BL has developed into "an example of narrative pornography directed at female readers" and "BL narratives include all kinds of sexual acts, such as hand jobs, fellatio, digital penetration of the anus and S/M" (2003, 80). Indeed because most BL narratives are structured around a dominant "*seme*" (attacker) and "*uke*" (receiver) in a variety of "pairings," it is not unusual to see coercive sex and even rape depicted (McLelland and Welker 2015, 10).

As Allison argues, *manga* have deliberately developed a visual style "intended not to mimic reality but tweak it" so as to create "a space that distances the reader from her or his everyday world" (2000, 57). Indeed it is precisely the two-dimensionality of these characters and lack of reference to any physically existing persons, which many *manga* fans find so attractive (Galbraith 2015a, 215). With this in mind, it is significant that a number of feminist academics and female writers, including Keiko Takemiya (a member of the Year 24 group), whose 1976 *manga Song of the Wind and the Trees* was a foundational text for what was later to develop into the BL genre, have spoken out in opposition to introduce censorship of *manga*. In 2011, Takemiya published an article where she expressed fears that her own iconic work would be targeted by police who might deem the exploration of themes such as sexual abuse within the family and homosexual love to be "harmful to youth." She pointed out that it was ironic that *Song of the Wind and the Trees*, a very popular *manga* which many of today's mothers have grown up reading, was now in danger of being removed from general circulation because it could be deemed "harmful" to their children.

BL is popular with girls and women of all ages in Japan (McLelland and Welker 2015, 3). Since the 1990s the genre has diversified and includes not only officially produced *manga*, but a large market of amateur *manga* (*dōjinshi* or self-published zines) (Thorn 2004), as well as animations, art work, computer games and "light novels" (Welker 2015). These items are for sale online, at general as well as specialist book stores, at fan conventions and are held by some libraries. In addition to the considerable market for hard-copy BL media, whether in official or amateur form, there are also a variety of online forums for the discussion and dissemination of BL materials, including cell phone novels, online games and fan fiction sites. In this regard it is similar in many ways to Western women's "slash fiction" which also pairs "beautiful boys" with other boys and adult men, as in the Harry Potter slash fandom (Tosenberger 2008). Although BL is barely acknowledged by Western journalists who focus instead on criticizing the sexualized depictions of girls enjoyed by male *manga* and *anime* fans, "Boys Love" is frequently discussed in the Japanese press and is the subject of academic inquiry by Japanese and Western feminist and queer studies academics (Nagaike and Aoyama 2015).

Given that fans of the genre realize that their interest in male-male fantasy sex is looked down upon by others in society, many self-identify with the term *fujoshi*, a Sino-Japanese compound, the original characters of which signify "women and girls" (Hester 2015, 169). However, by switching out the character "*fu*" meaning "woman" with the homophonous character "*fu*" meaning "fermented" or "rotten," the fans identify themselves as "rotten girls." As Galbraith's ethnography of a group of female *fujoshi* shows, many fans are happy to differentiate themselves from "normals"—persons whose fantasy lives are preoccupied with conventional relationships. BL fans on the contrary identify themselves as having an "abundant imagination" that allows them to "fantasize about anything" (2015b, 155). These rotten girls have been the subject of light-hearted treatment in a series of novels, TV shows and *manga* (Hester 2015) but more recently have been subject to negative media scrutiny and Internet attacks by those who see their interests as pathological and liable to harm the wider society, especially young people.

Scrutinizing Japan's "rotten girls"

Japan's rotten girls first gained mainstream media attention around 2004–2005 when a series of journalistic exposés of their consumption practices was published in the general media. In 2008 a new controversy erupted when a genre of "light novels" dedicated to the theme of "boys love" was the target of an Internet campaign calling for their removal from the shelves of libraries in Sakai City, part of the Osaka metropolitan district. In August 2008 in response to these complaints, the Sakai library had made the unilateral decisions to remove all BL novels from the shelves and place them in a storage facility, to only lend them out on request to mature-age readers and to refrain from purchasing any further BL titles. The national press picked up the dispute and began running articles about this "troubling" genre, remarking on the sheer volume of BL titles in library collections. The total number of BL novels in Sakai public libraries was reported to be 5,500. Other media reports also made much of the fact that these sexual stories featuring male–male romance were requested by women known as "rotten girls" (*fujoshi*), thus drawing attention to the self-consciously subversive nature of the works' readership.

The library's actions generated considerable debate on Japan's social networking website *mixi* and on BBS sites set up to "scrutinize" so-called "FemiNazi" attacks on traditional gender roles, with BL's detractors launching a range of critiques. The main points reiterated by BL opponents were that BL is a pornographic genre and as such should be treated akin to male-oriented pornography and kept away from minors because of its "bad effects." Furthermore, having defined the genre as pornographic, the use of tax-payers' money to acquire BL was "inappropriate." Also, the fact that the genre dealt in male–male sexual relations could be construed as a form of "sexual harassment" toward heterosexual readers. However, the argument of most interest was that the popularity of BL among female youth was a sign that young women were confused about appropriate gender roles, thus highlighting the difference between the *fujoshi* and so-called "normals."

After an Internet campaign in support of returning the BL items to the shelves, the intervention of a number of women councilors, and the involvement of high-profile feminist academic Chizuko Ueno, the sequestered items were eventually returned to general circulation. However, the lack of transparency over how the decision to remove the BL books was made and the lack of explanation as to why only BL titles were targeted caused concern among feminist critics of the library. Feminist commentators such as Ueno were quick to identify the anti-BL campaign as part of a more general "backlash" by conservative groups against feminist measures critiquing traditional gender roles with which BL's supposed "promotion" of homosexuality seems to have become confused (Atsuta 2012; Ueno 2009).

Japan's obscenity legislation is often criticized by overseas journalists who believe that its specific emphasis on the visibility of the acts depicted (as opposed to their nature) allows depiction of scenes of underage sex, bestiality, and violence which tacitly support male exploitation of women and children. However, the Sakai library incident shows that the narrow manner in which the legislation is interpreted actually allows a great deal of freedom of expression, a freedom which is fiercely defended by feminist artists and academics in Japan. Attempts to have BL titles removed from libraries could not be based on the "obscenity" of their contents but instead relied on arguments over the appropriateness of the use of public money to make available this kind of material.

The particularity of Japanese obscenity law has, however, recently been successfully deployed to prosecute and detain at least one female artist in Japan. Although not herself a *fujoshi*, artist Megumi Igarashi exhibits under the name "Rokudenashiko," which translates along the lines of "Good-for-nothing-girl" and clearly positions her as opposed to accepted notions of feminine propriety. In March 2014 the artist made a digital scan of her vagina and then used a 3D printer to manufacture various objects in its guise.

The various vagina objects included a kayak which the artist financed via a crowdsourcing venture on her website and then paddled up and down the Tama River between Tokyo and Kanagawa. The artist's purpose was to de-stigmatize talking about female parts. As she pointed out there are many affectionate diminutive ways of referencing the penis in Japanese, but relatively few words referring to the vagina, all of which can be considered obscene. The bright yellow kayak itself was later exhibited in a Tokyo gallery and it was not the production of the boat itself that led to the artist's prosecution. Rather she was originally arrested in July 2014 for sending the *code* from the original scan of her vagina to her supporters via the Internet. Although the code itself was just a series of zeros and ones, had her supporters had access to a 3D printer then they could have produced an anatomically correct representation of her vagina. In October 2014, Rokudenashiko was arrested once more, this time along with Minori Watanabe, the owner of feminist sex store Love Piece Club, for the display of miniature figurines modeled on the artist's vagina. However, as Watanabe pointed out, the police seemed to have no problem with the penis-shaped dildos also on display in the store (items that could actually be used for sexual acts unlike the artist's decorative figurines). At the time of writing, Igarashi has been indicted on charges of obscenity, and it remains to be seen how this prosecution will play out in the courts (*Asahi Shimbun* 2014).

The above cases, both featuring sexualized media by female fans and artists, show how the particularity of Japan's obscenity legislation has both benefits and pitfalls for female sexual expression. While the BL fan network is largely unhindered by censorship so long as the technical limits on depiction of genitalia are respected, depictions of actual genitalia, even when represented in an "artistic" context, are liable to be surveilled and prosecuted by the police. Rather than being "victims" of Japan's somewhat nebulous obscenity legislation as Western journalistic accounts suggest, the limited framing of obscenity in Japan means that Japanese women are often able to express themselves with considerable freedom, especially in comparison with their Chinese neighbors.

Legislating against obscenity in China

Like Japan, the People's Republic of China has constitutional guarantees to freedom of expression but these guarantees are largely ineffective in the face of government censorship which covers all kinds of political speech as well as representations of obscenity. Provisions against obscenity, on paper at least, focus on "profit-making acts" as designated in Article 363(1) of the constitution, prohibiting "producing, duplicating, publishing, selling or disseminating obscene articles" (Yan 2015, 388). Unlike Japan, the Chinese authorities have exerted a great deal of effort aimed at limiting the general population's exposure to pornographic content on the Internet. Overseas pornography websites are of course banned but this has not limited the spread of what Jacobs (2012) terms "people's pornography," that is, user-generated sexual content outside of the commercial media (see also Chapter 32 in this volume).

Although Japan has been criticized for the tardiness of its legislation to prevent the production and dissemination of child pornography, which was not enacted till 1999, little has been written concerning Chinese legislation on this matter. Child pornography is not specifically mentioned as a prohibited item in Chinese legislation but since 2004 the production, dissemination or display of sexual conduct by those under the age of 18 has been stipulated as unlawful in a Judicial Interpretation. This is significant because "never before had the dissemination of child pornography been specifically dealt with and punished" (Yan 2015, 397). However, as Yan notes, the Interpretation is focused on production and dissemination, "implying that the mere possession of online child pornography is not a crime"—a situation that pertained also in Japan until 2014. A further Judicial Interpretation in 2010 increased the criminal liabilities for those dealing in child pornography material but did not clearly specify whether such materials are those derived "from real minors or are only computer-generated" (Yan 2015, 398). Hence it is not clear whether child pornography measures can be used to capture BL materials as they can be in some Western jurisdictions.

Since April 2014 authorities in China have been conducting a "Cleaning the Web" campaign aimed at removing "pornographic and vulgar information" that "severely harms the physical and mental health of minors, and seriously corrupts social ethos" (Ni 2014). The 2014 campaign is but the latest phase of ongoing attempts by the authorities to restrict access to sexually explicit material. This includes new regulations in 2013 that placed enhanced limitations on Western and Japanese movies and TV dramas that could be legally streamed. Programs featuring "one-night stands, adultery, supernatural occurrences and gambling" were signaled out in a circular released by the State Administration of Press, Publication, Radio, Film and Television (*Shanghaiist* 2014). The Chinese authorities are not simply anxious about the negative impact that foreign sexual mores may have upon the population but have also been pursuing a crackdown on local content. For instance, since 2007, rewards have been offered for those who report persons who circulate pornographic images via mobile phones. It is also since 2007 that Chinese BL fans have come under increased state and media scrutiny, accused of "selling pornography, promoting incest and 'poisoning' young minds" (Feng 2009, 4).

Scrutinizing China's "rotten girls"

In recent years female producers of user-generated sexual content similar to and inspired by Japanese BL culture have become targets of state surveillance and suppression. The BL subculture is a lively part of *manga* and *anime* fandom throughout the Chinese-speaking world including mainland China (Liu 2009), Hong Kong (Jacobs 2011) and Taiwan (Martin 2012). As Jacobs points out, "Most BL fans in China and Hong Kong are happy to adopt the identity of a 'rotten girl' based on the Japanese label of *fujoshi*" (2011, 161). Although the term BL is widely known and used throughout the fandom in China, *danmei* is a more frequently used Chinese term. *Danmei* is the Mandarin pronunciation of the Japanese word *tanbi* (McLelland and Welker 2015, 11; Feng 2009, 4), which refers to decadent, highly aestheticized literary forms and often applied to literature dealing with male homosexuality. Chinese *danmei* stories "celebrate explicit homoerotic relationships between boys or men—fictional characters taken from mainstream media, real-life celebrities, and male personifications of day-to-day objects and animals, as well as original characters" (Yi 2013). Like online versions of BL, *danmei* is a form of user-generated pornography that is created and disseminated by "relatively young women" who "appear receptive to unconventional sexual relationships and graphic sex in *danmei* novels, as compared to more strictly censored heterosexual romance fiction" (Feng 2009, 4).

Drawing on typical BL tropes, *danmei* stories often feature a power differential between older and younger males, exploring the dynamic between "active" and "passive" partners that can include coerced sex and even rape. These fictions are particularly prone to being labelled obscene, since, as mentioned, Chinese legislation specifically signals out homosexuality, incest and sado-masochism as problem categories. As Xu and Yang point out, incest is a common narrative trope in *danmei* and represents "a feminine attempt to reorder the power structure within the family," but since the family is conflated with the state in Chinese social organization, these narrative attempts at displacement have significant political implications (2013, 31).

Danmei can also include real-life characters such as the members of the boy band TF Boys (all of whom were under age 14 when they first debuted in 2013). These *fictional* stories (even when dealing with real individuals) attest to the popularity of stories about romantic interactions between the very young which is by no means limited to Japan. In the Chinese context, Yang and Xu (2014) suggest that the romantic and sexual scenarios imagined as taking place among youthful characters is related to the literary trope of *qingmei zhuma* or "green plum and bamboo horse" first recorded by the Tang poet Li Bai (701–762) who described how the innocent friendship of childhood can later turn into romance. As Yang and Xu note "for a thousand years, green plum and bamboo horse [has been] considered the most romantic and valuable human relationship, more romantic than love at first sight" (2014).

However, unlike in the West, where condemnation of depictions of youthful-looking characters in imaginary sexual scenarios is becoming hegemonic, it is not the age of the characters depicted in *danmei* fiction which causes the most concern in China but rather their homosexual content. Women's *danmei* sites have been discussed negatively in the Chinese media since 2007 when they first came under state scrutiny and began to be closed down. Liu notes how the "scribble wall" at a 2007 government-sponsored animation convention in Shanghai was used by *danmei* fans to criticize the government's actions in taking down one of their favorite sites. She argues that fans used the board "to counteract the compulsively-moralistic government propaganda concerning 'the harmonious family' and its concurrent need to repress deviance and uphold virtue" (2009).

During another crack-down on Internet pornography in 2010 *danmei* fans were again subjected to critique in the mainstream media. An August 2010 article in the *Guangzhou Daily* suggested that these fan girls needed "psychiatric help" whereas other editorials surmised that the fans "might cause societal harm because of the anti-mainstream, rebellious nature of their practice" (Yi 2013). The websites that hosted this kind of fan fiction were not simply served with take-down orders for the offensive content, but in 2011 the police arrested a number of fan authors. According to Yi (2013), in March 2011, police in Zhengzhou Province arrested 32 fan writers, all of them women, for posting stories with homoerotic content to a website. This resulted in the posting of satirical comics to the microblogging site Sina Weibo, joking that there was insufficient space in all China's prisons to house all the women who participated in the exchange of these kinds of stories.

The material effect of this sustained scrutiny has been a heightened self-censorship on many of the China-based websites on which *danmei* fiction is made available. In response to the 2010 Internet crackdown Shanda Literature, for instance, which supports a number of websites on which all kinds of user-generated fiction is hosted, established a comprehensive self-censorship system for all of its subsidiary websites, "including a bank of sensitive words to automatically filter and block harmful content" (Yang and Xu 2014). During the 2014 campaign, one of its subsidiaries Jinjiang, "acted specifically on BL and closed its BL and fanfic subsite for a whole week" (Yang and Xu 2014). These sites have also acted to remove search terms such as BL and *danmei* from users' contents descriptions so as to lessen the risk of illicit material being brought to the authorities' attention. Chinese fan fiction websites hosted overseas, however, have largely ignored the cleaning the net campaigns, since the mainland authorities can only block access to the site but cannot compel material to be taken down or altered (Yang and Xu 2014). *Danmei* writers resident in China, however, are still vulnerable to police action.

Conclusion

As can be seen from the preceding discussion, the context surrounding the controversies generated by BL and *danmei* are rather different in Japan and China from that in many Western societies, where depictions of characters who may "appear to be" under age in sexual scenarios are potentially caught up in child pornography legislation. The widespread credulity and disbelief expressed in the Western press over Japan's supposed "refusal" to include fantasy representations of under-age sex in the legislation is indicative of the widespread ignorance of the different purposes to which sexual fantasy might be deployed in the Internet age.

Most journalistic commentaries have focused on how violent and sexist representations of women and girls are symptomatic of Japan's patriarchal culture, without any consideration that women themselves are speaking back to this sexist system via their own fantasy narratives—narratives in which the bodies of boys and young men are deployed as vehicles for female self-expression and gender critique. This movement is by no means limited to Japan and China, or even to East Asia. Similar arguments have been made for the popularity of BL among young women in the Philippines (Santos Fermin 2013), Indonesia (Abraham 2010) and throughout Western countries (Pagliassotti 2010). As Thorn notes, these kinds of narratives find favor among a certain demographic of women in many industrialized nations since "what these fans share in common is discontent with the standards of femininity to which they are expected to adhere and a social environment and historical moment that does not validate or sympathize with that discontent" (2004, 180).

In Japan, where fantasy material is concerned, the fact that current interpretations of obscenity legislation attend only to the degree of visibility of sexual organs and not to the nature of the sexual acts, nor the ages or genders of the participants, has enabled the widespread growth of the BL phenomenon. The media may well criticize the "rotten girls" who make up the BL fandom, but legislators have very little control over the rotten girls' imaginations and the police are unable to become involved in their online or offline self-expression.

However, the fact that the Japanese police are willing to move against female sexual self-expression is illustrated by the arrest and detention of vagina-artist Rokudenashiko. Although her transmission via the Internet of digital data (not even an actual image) of her vagina was not in itself a sexual act, the fact that the data could, on the receiver's end, be reassembled into a realistic depiction of the actual thing was sufficient for the police to act against her. As far as works of the imagination are concerned, however, so long as the rather technical limits of the obscenity legislation are respected, there are no limits on content. This has enabled BL to develop into a vibrant commercial genre as well as support a range of fan activities that take place online. If Japan were to extend its child pornography laws to capture purely fictional representations of under-age sex, then this would have a negative impact on women's BL fandom and endanger many female artists and readers who could potentially be subject to police harassment and arrest, as has happened to Rokudenashiko.

In China, however, obscenity legislation is being interpreted much more broadly. Although so far BL and *danmei* fiction is not being classed as a type of child pornography as is potentially a problem in the West, the fact that it deals with homosexual content and incestuous relations is highlighted as reason for its suppression. It is, however, precisely the homosexual, "taboo" nature of the love stories that makes them so popular with fans since these same-sex romances are the perfect vehicle to launch critiques of the normative, familial rhetoric purveyed by the authorities—a characteristic that typifies the BL fandom internationally. It is the fact the *danmei* fiction focuses on "anti-social" sex that has caused *danmei* fandom to be signaled out by the authorities as a form of unwholesome and destabilizing activity—and the scrutiny has even eventuated in a number of arrests.

The activities of Japan's and China's "rotten girls," although the source of some concern and consternation in their respective societies, have largely been unmentioned in recent Western debates around the dangers of Internet pornography, particularly child pornography. However, the spread of BL from Japan to China and the manner in which BL's protest against the prevalent sex and gender system have been indigenized in China to reflect local gendered and political concerns, is a fascinating case study of how the Internet enables transnational forms of community building among women. It also encourages us to rethink the various forms of political action engendered by new media technologies and the important role that "obscene" depictions can play as a form of cultural critique as well as the ways in which obscenity legislation is constantly repurposed for different ends across the digital domain.

References

Abraham, Y. (2010) 'Boys Love Thrives in Conservative Indonesia'. In A. Levi, M. McHarry and D. Pagliassotti, *Boys Love Manga: Essays on the Sexual Ambiguity and Cross-Cultural Fandom of the Genre*, Jefferson, NC: McFarland, 44–57.

Allison, A. (2000) *Permitted and Prohibited Desires: Mothers, Comics and Censorship in Japan*, Berkeley: University of California Press.

Asahi Shimbun (2014) 'Detained *manga* artist denies work modeled on her vagina is obscene'. Available at: http://ajw.asahi.com/article/behind_news/social_affairs/AJ201412230021 (Accessed January 14, 2015).

Atsuta, K. (2012) '"BL" haijo kara mieta sabetsu to sei no kyōju no ishuku [Discrimination and the decline of enjoyment of sex from the perspective of the removal of 'BL']', *Yuriika*, December: 184–191.

Banerjee, I. and Logan, S. (2008) 'Japan'. In Indrajit Banerjee and Stephen Logan (eds) *Asian Communication Handbook 2008*, Singapore: Asian Media Information and Communication Centre: 237–256.

Byberg, J. (2012) 'Childless Porn: A Victimless Crime?' *Social Science Research Network*. Available at: http://papers.ssrn.com/sol3/papers.cfm?abstract_id=2114564 (Accessed December 13, 2014).

Condry, I. (2011) 'Love Revolution: Anime, Masculinity and the Future'. In S. Fruhstuck and A. Walthall (eds) *Recreating Japanese Men*, Berkeley: University of California Press: 262–283.

Eiland, M. (2009) 'From Cartoon Art to Child Pornography', *International Journal of Comic Art*, 11(2): 396–409.

Fackler, M. (2014) 'Japan Outlaws Possession of Child Pornography'. Available at: www.nytimes.com/2014/06/19/world/asia/japan-bans-possession-of-child-pornography-after-years-of-pressure.html?_r=0 (Accessed January 14, 2015).

Feng, J. (2009) '"Addicted to Beauty": Consuming and Producing Web-Based Chinese *Danmei* Fiction at Jinjiiang', *Modern Chinese Literature and Culture*, 21(2): 1–41.

Fermin, S. T. A. (2013) 'Appropriating Yaoi and Boys Love in the Philippines: Conflict, Resistance and Imaginations Through and Beyond Japan', *Electronic Journal of Contemporary Japanese Studies*, 13(3). Available at: http://japanesestudies.org.uk/ejcjs/vol13/iss3/fermin.html (Accessed January 14, 2015).

Fletcher, J. (2015) 'Why Hasn't Japan Banned Child-porn Comics?' *BBC News*. Available at: www.bbc.com/news/magazine-30698640 (Accessed January 14, 2015).

Galbraith, P. (2015a) 'Otaku Sexuality in Japan'. In M. McLelland and V. Mackie (eds) *The Routledge Handbook of Sexuality Studies in East Asia*, Oxon: Routledge: 205–216.

Galbraith, P. (2015b) 'Moe Talk: Affective Communication among Female Fans of Yaoi in Japan'. In M. McLelland, K. Nagaike, K. Suganuma and J. Welker (eds) *Boys Love Manga and Beyond: History, Culture and Community in Japan*, Jackson: University of Mississippi Press: 153–168.

Hester, J. (2015) 'Fujoshi Emergent: Shifting Popular Representations of *Yaoi*/BL fandom in Japan'. In M. McLelland, K. Nagaike, K. Suganuma and J. Welker (eds) *Boys Love Manga and Beyond: History, Culture and Community in Japan*, Jackson: University of Mississippi Press: 169–188.

Jacobs, K. (2012) *People's Pornography: Sex and Surveillance on the Chinese Internet*, Chicago: Intellect Books.

Jones, G. (2005) 'Bad Girls Like to Watch: Writing and Reading Ladies' Comics'. In L. Miller and J. Bardsley (eds) *Bad Girls of Japan*, New York: Palgrave: 97–109.

Kummetha, T. (2014) 'Thai Authorities Reportedly to Conduct Mass Surveillance of Thai Internet Users, Targeting Lèse Majesté', *Prachatai English*, September 10. Available at: http://www.prachatai.com/english/node/4331 (Accessed January 14, 2015).

Liu, T. (2009) 'Conflicting Discourses on Boys' Love and Subcultural Tactics in Mainland China and Hong Kong', *Intersections: Gender and Sexuality in Asia and the Pacific*, 20. Available at: http://intersections.anu.edu.au/issue20/liu.htm (Accessed January 14, 2015).

Lunsing, W. (2004) 'Japanese Sex Workers: Between Choice and Coercion'. In E. Micollier (ed.) *Sexual Cultures in East Asia*, London: RoutledgeCurzon: 54–75.

Martin, F. (2012) 'Girls who Love Boys' Love: Japanese Homoerotic Manga as Trans-National Taiwan Culture', *Inter-Asia Cultural Studies*, 13(2): 365–383.

McLelland, M. (2015) '"How to Sex?": The Contested Nature of Sexuality in Japan'. In J. Baab (ed.) *The Sage Handbook of Modern Japanese Studies*, Thousand Oaks: Sage, 246–267.

McLelland, M. (in press), 'Not In Front of the Parents! Young People, Sexual Literacies and Intimate Citizenship in the Internet Age', *Sexualities*.

McLelland, M. and Welker, J. (2015) 'An Introduction to Boys Love in Japan'. In M. McLelland, K. Nagaike, K. Suganuma and J. Welker (eds) *Boys Love Manga and Beyond: History, Culture and Community in Japan*, Jackson: University of Mississippi Press: 3–20.

McNeill, D. (2014) 'Japan's Contemporary Media'. In Jeff Kingston (ed.) *Critical Issues in Contemporary Japan*, Oxon: Routledge: 64–75.

Nagaike, K. (2003) 'Perverse Sexualities, Perverse Desires: Representations of Female Fantasies and Yaoi Manga as Pornography Directed at Women', *U.S.-Japan Women's Journal*, 25: 76–103.

Nagaike, K. and Aoyama, T. (2015) 'What Is Japanese "BL Studies"? A Historical and Critical Overview'. In M. McLelland, K. Nagaike, K. Suganuma and J. Welker (eds) *Boys Love Manga and Beyond: History, Culture and Community in Japan*, Jackson: University of Mississippi Press: 119–140.

Nagaoka, Y. (2009) 'Manga no sei hyōgen kisei o nerata tōjōrei kaitei meguru kōbō [Concerning the pros and cons of pursuing reform of local ordinances regulating sexual expression in *manga*]', *Tsukuru*, 40(5): 64–71.

Ni, Y. (2014) 'Cleaning Up the Web: China Cracks Down on Pornographic and other Unsavory Content to Protect Young Internet Surfers', *Beijing Review*. Available at: http://www.bjreview.com.cn/print/txt/2014-07/07/content_628014.htm (Accessed January 14, 2015).

Pagliassotti, D. (2010) 'Better than Romance? Japanese BL Manga and the Subgenre of Male/Male Romantic Fiction'. In A. Levi, M. McHarry and D. Pagliassotti (eds), *Boys Love Manga: Essays on the Sexual Ambiguity and Cross-Cultural Fandom of the Genre*, Jefferson, NC: McFarland: 59–82.

Shanghaiist (2014) 'Scenes of One-Night Stands, Adultery, to Be Cut from Chinese TV'. Available at: http://shanghaiist.com/2014/11/13/streaming_sites_to_cut.php (Accessed January 14, 2015).

Takemiya, K. (2011) 'Kaze to ki no uta' wa auto! Aidentiti o mamoru tameni [Song of the Wind and Trees is Out! For the Sake of Protecting Identity]', *Popyuraa karuchaa kenkyū*, 5(1): 8–18.

Thorn, M. (2004) 'Girls and Women Getting Out of Hand: The Pleasure and Politics of Japan's Amateur Comics Community'. In W.W. Kelly (ed.) *Fanning the Flames: Fans and Consumer Culture in Contemporary Japan*, Albany: State University of New York Press: 169–186.

Tosenberger, C. (2008) 'Homosexuality at the Online Hogwarts: Harry Potter Slash Fanfiction', *Children's Literature*, 36: 185–207.

Ueno C. (2009) 'Sakai-shi toshokan, BL hon haijo sodo tenmatsu [The Circumstances Surrounding the Controversial Exclusion of BL Books at Sakai Municipal Library]' *Tsukuru*, 39(5): 106–112.

Welker, J. (2015) 'A Brief History of *Shōnen'ai*, *Yaoi* and Boys Love'. In M. McLelland, K. Nagaike, K. Suganuma and J. Welker (eds) *Boys Love Manga and Beyond: History, Culture and Community in Japan*, Jackson: University of Mississippi Press: 42–74.

Xu, Y. and L. Yang (2013) 'Forbidden Love: Incest, Generational Conflict and the Erotics of Power in Chinese BL Fiction', *Journal of Graphic Novels and Comics*, 4(1): 30–43.

Yan, M.N. (2015) 'Regulating Online Pornography in Mainland China and Hong Kong'. In M. McLelland and V. Mackie (eds) *The Routledge Handbook of Sexuality Studies in East Asia*, Oxon: Routledge: 387–401.

Yang, L. and Xu, Y. (2014) 'A Love that Dare Not Speak its Name Aloud: Chinese Boys Love Fandom in the 2014 "Cleaning the Web" Campaign'. Paper given at the *Manga Futures Conference*, University of Wollongong, October 31–November 3, 2014.

Yi, E. J. (2013) 'Reflection on Chinese Boys Love Fans: An Insider's View', *Transformative Works and Cultures* 12. Available at: http://journal.transformativeworks.org/index.php/twc/rt/printerFriendly/424/390 (Accessed January 14, 2015).

11

Materiality of an online community: everyday life of global sport fans in South Korea

Younghan Cho

Introduction: new technology and sportscapes

Labels associated with the Internet evoke futuristic images (e.g., virtuality, novelty, and new frontier). However, the term "virtual" often cloaks varying or even contradictory cultural practices on the Internet; furthermore, some of its central characteristics are not drastically different from those of other technologies. In addition, deeply ingrained media habits prevented people from changing their uses of media and even new media like the Internet may repeat similar issues such as digital divide, fragmentation, and polarization based on their incomes, ideologies, languages, and gender (Croteau and Hoynes 1997; Wilson and Peterson 2002). However, the Internet readily supplies the sense of virtual space and the ways that people use online spaces indicate a recursive relationship between online and offline. Nowadays, so many people (particularly the young) "live" both offline and online so that even the phrase "real life" can seem questionable.

The Internet is crucial to Asian sportscapes because it enables sport as a commodity to be globalized with tremendous rapidity. In particular, the global circulation of US sports raises concerns about cultural homogenization and economic imbalances caused by their unidirectional flow from the United States to the rest of the world. At the same time, Internet space is also crucial to sport fans in Asia because access to such spaces enables fans to rapidly consume, enjoy, and appropriate globally circulated sporting commodities without regard to physical location. Online spaces also allow local fans to become acquainted with other fans and to communicate instantaneously with them. These activities render the Internet critical to the construction of sports fandom in Asia. In South Korea (hereafter Korea), as elsewhere, Major League Baseball (hereafter MLB) fans utilize online spaces to obtain information about numerous subjects associated with baseball, as well as about baseball itself, and to communicate with each other through greetings and discussions.

This study explores the ways that Korean MLB fans participate in a particular online community and interact with others there. It suggests that these fans' uses of time and space online add complexity or duality to their community, which I refer to as its materiality. The duality stems mainly from two notions about online time and space: first that these are intersected by people's offline lives and their views on local and national issues; and second that they are embedded in the ambivalence that local posters express about global sports. In so doing, Korean sports fans' usages of time and space online contribute to constructing multiple senses of temporality and spatiality rather than substituting virtuality for time and space.

For this study I chose one of the most popular and active Web sites for Korean MLB fans, MLBPARK (www.mlbpark.com), which enjoys an excellent reputation as an information source. To explore the complex relationships of global sports and local fans on the Internet, this study employs Internet ethnography, which includes my participatory observation of its bulletin boards and face-to-face interviews with Korean fans (Cho 2007).[1] I argue that the fans' articulations of time and space on the Internet demonstrate the possibility of living in multiple senses of temporality and spatiality that fluctuate between virtual and real, online and offline, and among the local, national, and global.

Global sports and local fans on the Internet

Unlike other American cultural exports, sport occupies an ambiguous position in this global era (Andrews and Cole 2002; Cho, Leary and Jackson 2012). On the one hand, sports as a commodity seems to replace the role once played by Hollywood films, popular music and American TV shows in expanding US cultural dominance. The globalization of sports has been made possible by the ability of satellite TV and the Internet to cross borders and convey massive amounts of information. One well-known example of the use of sports as a marketing tool is Rupert Murdoch's News Corporation (Andrews 2004, 99; Robertson 2004, 293). On the other hand, unlike other popular genres, global sports are often closely related to local and national sentiments. Global sports may not bear the weight of "the project of globalization in its fullest sense" although as mega-media events sports are effective harbingers of globalization (Rowe 2003: 281). Not only has the recent globalization of US sports not severed the inherent connection between sports and their national or local roots, it contributes to the formation of many types of global-local nexus.

One of the most illustrative examples of a global-local nexus is MLB fandom in Korea (Cho 2009). Around the world, MLB expands its markets through diversifying the ways sports fans can enjoy baseball. An important contribution is made, of course, by the Internet, which has connected billions of people in most of the world's developed nations (Westerbeek and Smith 2003, 158). Accordingly, in the late 1990s MLB launched its Internet division (MLBAM, Major League Baseball Advanced Media). Since 2003, MLB has broadcast almost every game on its own website, www.mlb.com. That year, MLBAM became profitable and by 2005 its annual gross was $220 million; during that two-year period, the initial 550,000 subscribers grew to 1,300,000 (Klein 2006: 249).

As the Internet infrastructure in Korea continues to provide a wide variety of ways for Korean fans to enjoy MLB, independently of satellite or cable TV, Internet use and MLB fandom are growing mutually dependent. Of course the Internet functions as a major source of information and news about MLB and players, but it also allows the creation and development of online communities comprised of Korean MLB fans. Such communities, many of which are created out of enthusiasm for a specific athlete or team, contribute to nurturing local fanhood and also indicate the activity level of sports fans (Boyle and Haynes 2004).

The popularity of MLB in Korea began suddenly in the late 1990s when Chan-ho Park, the first Korean MLB player to pitch for the L.A. Dodgers, began to play extremely well. During his best seasons, 1997 to 2001, Korean mass media spotlighted him as a national hero (Cho 2008). Media attention to MLB waned after these peak years, however, so Korean MLB fans have had to rely on the Internet as a way of obtaining information and developing social relationships with other fans. Online, fans share MLB news and their own thoughts, which supplement the limited information available from mainstream media. Their activities also attract new fans to MLB, some of whom have discovered it through online communities. As old and new fans satiate their interest in MLB and form social relationships, they assume a distinct collective identity in their online communities. Korean MLB fans, as citizens of one of the world's most wired countries, are particularly active users of such spaces to nurture their interests, contribute and obtain news and information, and share gossip. Online communities have performed a particularly life-giving function within MLB fandom since 2002, when Park was in a slump and the national networks were broadcasting fewer MLB games.

Online communities of MLB fans in South Korea developed concurrently with the popularity of MLB. In 1997, what was arguably the first Korean MLB fan site (www.yagoo.co.kr) was created; next came MYMLB (www.mymlb.co.kr) and iccsports (www.iccsports.com). These early communities were not stable, either in terms of membership or longevity; however, after use of the World Wide Web became ubiquitous, new communities such as MLBPARK (www.mlbpark. com), MLBBADA (www.mlbbada.com), MLBKOREA (www.mlbkorea.com), and MLBMAX (www.mlbmax.co.kr) were formed in the mid 2000s. As of 2015, MLBPARK continues to enjoy popularity while a couple of communities such as MLBKOREA and MLBMAX have been closed.

One unique aspect of Korean MLB fan communities is that they began as personal homepages, not for-profit groups, or subsidiaries of newspaper companies. A couple of communities are even operated by only one person (MLBBADA by Peabada and MLBKOREA by semi-Chanho). Depending on who is in charge, each community has its own culture and rules; this individuality enables most of them to remain autonomous and minimally commercial. Despite the efforts of owners/administrators, it is impossible for them to provide all the information and news upon which the activities and vitality of these communities are based. That the survival of these online communities depends upon the heavy participation of numerous MLB fans implies that these fans are also heavy Internet users. MLBPARK is one of the oldest and biggest online communities among numerous MLB websites founded and populated by Koreans. The majority of MLBPARK's population consists of people who are MLB fans, Koreans, native speakers of Korean, and Korean MLB fans residing in South Korea, although some live in other countries (Cho 2007). Compared to the generally short life cycles of online communities of sports fans, this one is venerable (it was launched on February 20, 2001).

To explore which Korean fans utilize the Internet space, I employ Internet ethnography as my methodology, in which I undertook participatory observation on an online community (www. mlbpark.com) between 2005 and 2006.[2] I found an ethnographic approach "useful for observing concrete, diverse, and even contradictory responses of Korean MLB fans, who are no longer limited to a geographical place but rather connect with each other on the Internet" (Cho 2014, 5). In addition, I also interviewed 14 Korean MLB fans; all of them are male and resided in Korea. All were between 20 and 30 years old, and all but three were college students. Unlike a traditional ethnographer, I treat my observations of the community as my major data, including analysis of the bulletin boards, and the interviews as supplementary.

In MLBPARK, fans express a full range of opinions about Park and his contribution to the popularity of MLB in South Korea; some still share significant memories of watching him during the IMF intervention. The community includes all types of fans, from novices who follow only Korean players in MLB to maniacs who can enumerate the records of their favorite teams and players in detail. Perhaps most significantly, many members of MLBPARK regard this online space as a community in which they can not only exchange opinions and obtain information about MLB but also share personal stories and details of their daily lives. Fans often conduct political and nationalistic discussions and are usually very quick to post information about current events and controversies. Their online etiquette is also intriguing: even when they are simply adding replies to others' comments, their interactions read like conversations. Comments and reactions may be posted while games are being watched, whereas other postings may be spontaneous or the result of long deliberations.

Furthermore, in MLBPARK, behavioral patterns and cultural practices such as posting, adding replies and exchanging messages become social norms and cultural artifacts in the community. Rituals are also established, for example when lurkers reveal themselves or the community bids farewell to departing members. Ritualized messages usually elicit relevant comment; as such reciprocal interactions are routinized, they become normative traditions in the community. Online communities also have codes of conduct, so disciplinary actions are occasionally taken by their administrators (Bird 2003), who can delete posting, suspend users' IDs temporarily or permanently, and block users' IP addresses. For instance, a code, which was announced in May 2005 includes details about the maximum numbers of posts per day and a rule that sexual images may be posted only at night. The social aspects of fans' activities online contribute to the construction of both individual and collective identities, which are essential for making their virtual space into a community.

An online space is both a displaced and a rooted community, whose existence relies more upon common interests and shared practices than on physical boundaries (Hine 2000). The duality of MLBPARK stems not only from the difference between where they are living (Korea) and where MLB as their hobby plays (the US) but also from the interconnectedness between their online and offline lives.

Materiality of online community

As technology makes the routine compression of time and space possible, the Internet lifts social interaction out of spatial and temporal contexts. At the same time, technological breakthroughs have provided people with numerous options for interacting in cyberspace, such as e-newsgroups, IRC (Internet Relay Chat), MUDs (Multi-User Dungeons), and blogs (web logs). Accordingly, people can communicate either simultaneously or asynchronously no matter where they stay geographically. Korean MLB fans in online community are neither always only virtual beings, however, nor do they conduct their online lives in isolation from their offline lives. Despite their common interest in MLB, their conversations frequently evoke and intersect with the national, for example Korean players in MLB or the role of nationalism in baseball fanhood. Fans also habitually mention their personal memories about MLB and mention various aspects of the community's history.

Such uses of time and space online indicate that fans construct multiple senses of temporality and spatiality. These are promulgated not only by the intersection between online and offline existence, but also by the ambivalence that local fans express about global sports. Virtual time does not replace chronological time in online community but rather coexists with it and provides alternative ways of structuring social relations. Castells finds two features of virtual time from its simultaneity and timelessness, in which the latter indicates "the mixing of times in the media" or a "non-sequential time of cultural product" (1996, 492). In this process, spatiality becomes a way to think through the mutual availability and shared coherence of situated practices, interpretations, and accounts. As Castells noted, "space of flows and timeless time are the material foundations of a new culture" (1996, 406). In light of these conclusions, I suggest that fans' articulations of multiple temporalities and spatialities are the basis of the materiality of online community.

Community time: uneven but simultaneous

Time does not exist in a unitary way on the Internet; instead, temporality becomes disordered and a traditional sense of time is often erased. Nonetheless, the multiple temporalities of the Internet are portrayed as both highly ordered and highly meaningful by participants. Fans in online community must constantly construct, navigate, and adjust uneven temporalities that may be virtual, national, global, or a combination of all three. I describe online time as a set of uneven but simultaneous temporalities that can be summarized as the promise of anytime, national time patterns, and convergence between the past and the present.

The primary dimension of online temporality is characterized by the Internet's promise of connectivity whenever a user wishes. This description manifests as a timeless, virtual, or even cosmopolitan temporality in the community; fans connect whenever they want and from wherever they are. However, "anytime" does not literally mean that fans are always connected to or reside in the community. Therefore, the promise of eternal access and connectivity may be more important than actual connection at any given moment.

The promise of anytime also signals that the community is always open and welcoming. For fans, this notion supplies a sense of belonging as well as emotional attachment to the community itself. Through the promise of access whenever they desire it to a community that never closes, many MLB fans find solace in the virtual world. In fact, the MLBPARK banner on its homepage announces that it is "the only paradise constructed by Internet people."[3]

Crav: Here, I can feel a tie with others who have similar emotions, sentiments, and thoughts. I am really thrilled to experience such commonality. . . . I dare to say that I will leave [post] my feelings here today even if this place is going to disappear tomorrow.

The promise of anytime, however, is not always kept; nor is its impact on fans always positive. When connections are temporarily unavailable due to technical problems, fans quickly become irritated and unsettled and a "connection error" message during periods of heavy traffic always elicits huge complaints.

The combination of belongingness and a guarantee of eternal accessibility cause some fans to develop a kind of addiction which, as a modern pathology, is closely related to such issues as security, separation, and the desire for communication. Some fans, who find community participation therapeutic, openly discuss their obsession.

Keric: This community has become a place in which I can fully express my feelings. As I recall, I have connected to the community every day since July 2005. Well . . . I have to say that it is time for me to say good-bye to the community and others because I am going to prepare for a big exam which might determine my future career. Nonetheless, I am not sure whether I really can stop visiting here because this place is so addictive.

Other fans regret spending time and energy in MLBPARK.

Gorald: We are simply wandering here. I find myself turning on the computer and logging in to this community every night. Such routines seem to be really meaningless and wastes of time. It is so shameful to imagine that someone else studies hard while I randomly spend time here.

The temporality of anytime can be regarded as an empty signifier. It might epitomize virtual or timeless time, but its actualization is more indicative of members' emotional attachment to their community. The second temporality in online community is national time, one of several locally-linked time patterns that co-exist with the timeless temporality that generally characterizes Korean MLB fans' overall perception of online time. One national time pattern is seen in the increased and idiosyncratic community participation on the game days of Korean MLB players. Because of the time difference between the US and Korea, fans stay awake for the start of these games, which for them is either late at night or early in the morning. While they wait, they interact with other fans by chatting, and during the games they post progress reports to the bulletin boards. Although the broadcasting times force most fans to watch the games alone, on TV, many are able to simultaneously reside in the community as they watch on the Internet. The latter group can post spontaneous reactions and opinions to the community in real time, a specific use of time that demonstrates Korean fans' nationalistic attachments to MLB.

Another national time pattern is late-night usage. MLBPARK is most densely populated at this time, when fans are relaxing at home. Another attraction of this time slot is that members can only post images with sexual content between midnight and dawn. These must contain warnings in their titles, such as "No [viewer] under 19 [years old]." This pattern is questioned when a fan who lives in the US asked whether he could post adult content during the night in his time zone, which is 12 hours later than Korea's. Rather than stirring controversy, this question was simply regarded as odd by most members, who assume that the community is on local time (in the Tokyo time zone).

The inquiry does generate critical questions regarding time, however, such as whether any specific time zone is necessary for online community, and if so, what the criteria should be for choosing one (locations of the majority of participants or the location of the server, which stores and distributes the content of the community). Responses to the fan's question posted from the US show that members in Korea assume the community functions in one common time zone, which they regard as a "national" time zone. Although temporal consistency is decided by the community, their sense of local or regional time remains important.

The third characteristic is the convergence between the past, as expressed by fans' personal memories and recollections of community history, and their present discussions. Remembering "the old days," either individually or on behalf of the virtual community is not only a practice of reconstruction but is also situated in the present. As Storey (2003) succinctly described this nexus, memories bring the past into the present.

Since its founding in February 2001, the growth of MLBPARK's membership has caused unexpected problems. For example, a sudden influx of new members makes it difficult to maintain a comfortable atmosphere. Some temporary participants, who do not develop an attachment to the community but only leave contentious posts and attempt to cause flame wars, are also a source of serious disruption. In response to such troubles, old members often try to mediate disputes and minimize the negative results of heated discussions. More generally, members try to forge a collective narrative through shared nostalgia for the community's "old days," including its early stages and prolific posters who may have departed, and by regularly comparing the community's past and present. These journeys down memory lane become more salient when the community encounters conflicts between old and new fans or is subjected to flame wars instigated by temporary visitors. By suggesting that what the community was is always better than what it is, some fans attempt to romanticize its history.

Sack: In the beginning, MLBPARK was regarded as a "paradise" although now it has become hard to believe [that such a past existed]. Despite [claims of] "paradise," it seems that the term "addiction" encapsulates the current condition of this community.

Moha: Recently, I came to remember the old days when I shared mundane stories with other members. It was just two years ago: this place was filled with crude but very sincere humor and lots of smiles among intimates. However, nowadays, I observe that dryness or fastidiousness has become a dominant pattern here.

The ways that fans bring their personal memories into present discussions indicate that past and present cannot be completely separated, even in online space. This sense of unified time suggests that both evaluating and evoking the past contribute productively to interpreting the present community as well as in grounding its members in the community's present. Collective efforts to remember are at the very core of these fans' identity, because memory is as much collective as individual.

The online activities of fans in MLBPARK online demonstrate that online community performs time, but in a way that is neither free-floating nor traditional. Online temporalities are complicated, uneven, and simultaneous; they are social constructs as well as concrete outcomes of the fans' practices. Fans are capable of orienting themselves within multiple temporalities such as virtual and real, global and national, past and present, and also of managing this array. In practice, their management of online time indicates that they are not only required to but are capable of maintaining equilibrium between past and present, self and community, and offline and online.

Community space: asymmetric but synchronous

In the Internet's space of flows, spatiality refers to more than physical proximity and distance: emphasis is on connection rather than location. In MLBPARK, most fans who reside in Korea experience baseball vicariously, by watching games on TV or the Internet and sharing their thoughts with others in online community. Such Internet use clearly helps to break the connection between physical place and social place. Although fans occasionally construct virtual territory that is neither essential nor linked with real places, and although they clearly recognize the gaps between global and local, virtual and offline, their basic sense of space is still rooted in their local places.

In spite of these disparities, fans are able to participate joyfully in online community with multiple senses of space that do not disrupt their connections to their actual localities. This multiplicity can be described as a set of asymmetric but synchronous spatialities that fall into three categories of location: the US (literally, the field of dreams); Korea (specifically South Korea, to which fans have geographical proximity); and the online community (which has virtual borders and boundaries).

First, Korean MLB fans perceive the significance of the gap between where they are (Korea) and where MLB plays (the US). This perception does not imply that their sense of space is merely removed or disembedded from where they are located; rather, it epitomizes asymmetric relations between two places in terms of both geographical distance and unequal positioning. In online community, the US, home of Major League Baseball, is viewed not as a neutral place but as the object of fans' desires: their field of dreams. Many interviewees expressed a strong wish to travel to America in order to visit MLB team stadiums and attend live games.

This asymmetric spatiality was clearly revealed by the postings of Korean fans living in the US during the first World Baseball Classic in March, 2006. When the South Korean national team won several games in a row, members of MLBPARK swarmed the community. Several posted that they were in the stadium during various games; exchanges aroused tremendous envy from fans who could only watch in Korea.

Octo: Dear Sami, I am sorry for not meeting you during the game. I sat in the first-base corner, and felt [as if I was] in Seoul Stadium because the Anaheim stadium was filled with Korean fans. This game was the greatest one.

Dodger: Oops. Yesterday, I was also in the stadium. My seat was F133.

Sami: Really . . . *Dodger*!!! I was in F134. We were so close.

Sack Artist: It is Mr. Octo [and *Dodger*] who I think [are] the happiest fans in the community because you were in the stadium twice. It would be the experience of a lifetime to watch such a game on the spot.

Fans in Korea tend to make much of any information provided by fans in the US, which they call "news on the spot," and to lavish attention on the lucky ones who provide it. Translations of English newspaper articles about baseball and personally taken photos of MLB players and stadiums are particularly welcomed. This was my experience when I updated news about the Chicago Cubs; community members knew that I lived in the US so they thanked me. Ironically, however, they celebrated my residency in the country without realizing that I actually lived in North Carolina—hundreds of miles from Chicago. Other prolific posters are subject to similar misunderstandings; for example, *ledeo* lives in Korea but updates news about the Texas Rangers from Dallas newspapers so often that he is assumed to live in Texas. This sort of confusion symbolizes a shared fantasy of place—in this case, the US, home of their dream league, MLB. In online community, links to physical/geographic location are not universally erased but are expressed in specific contexts, which in turn results in highly differentiated senses of space.

These examples show a multilevel concept of space among Korean MLB fans, whose geographical location may become less significant as they enjoy MLB via TV and the Internet. The US, however, is still perceived as the location of their desire.

The second feature is the significance borne by fans' locality and geographical proximity. Although the community exists in virtual space, within it great emphasis is placed upon on sharing ordinary life offline as well as online. Fans in the community are connected to each other through MLB, an American sports league, but are still rooted in their local places. For example, some of them seem to have as much interest in KBO (Korean Professional Baseball League) as in MLB.

I noticed during my face-to-face interviews with South Korean fans that talking about their favorite local teams was an efficient ice-breaker. In addition, the interviewees were eager to converse about the latest local news—a tendency shared by other savvy Internet users in MLBPARK. Whether or not it is the direct subject of face-to-face conversation, Internet community works behind the scenes via the local interests of fans who "draw back cyberspace into offline processes and practices" (Wilson and Peterson 2002, 455).

The significance of fans' localities is influenced by their geographical proximity in South Korea, where almost every fan can meet any other fan in less than a one-day trip. I myself traveled from Seoul to Busan in three hours by train while another fan drove for three hours from a different province; MLBPARK's official offline meeting, held in Seoul semi-annually, attracts fans from many provinces. Several interviewees also told me that they attend regular, private gatherings besides the official ones. All of these factors (close geographical proximity, easy accessibility, and the frequent possibility of face-to-face meetings) help fans generate a stable, if varied, sense of locality.

Fisher: What if we have a chance of meeting everyone offline? Can we shake hands and develop a harmonious mood?

South Korean MLB fans' online community interactions indicate a recursive relationship between virtual and offline existence. This reciprocal relationship helps fans hold to older senses of self and place as they constitute new, complex senses of place and locality. Thus, as a result of their geographical proximity, fans with a common attraction to a global sport (MLB) also show strong attachments to local and national issues and a shared sense of confinement. These communally held significances of locality and geographical proximity form the core of the community's space.

Third, spatialities are formed through the construction of a virtual boundary around the online community. MLBPARK members' delineation of this boundary expresses their desire to preserve MLBPARK as the largest and longest-running online MLB fan community in Korea.

As discussed above, remembering the community's "old days" contributes to constructing its boundary vis-à-vis other MLB fan Web sites. As with other kinds of Internet communities, MLB fans in South Korea often develop an exclusive loyalty to a particular community and a sense of competition with other sites. One example is the rivalry between MLBPARK and MLBKOREA, whose members tend to show hostility to each other. Even though no rule prohibits MLBPARK members from visiting MLBKOREA, mentioning its name is not recommended at MLBPARK except in the context of criticism. By making much of these differences and disagreements, fans set up "our" territory against "theirs."

Some fans openly exhort others to put their commitment into practice, especially by respecting the originality of posts. Because copying and pasting is so easy and routine in online spaces, many posts on MLBPARK are taken from other sites. One fan eloquently protests this practice:

Rock & Roll: I don't like the idea of copying and pasting posts from other Korean MLB fan sites into our community. Such a trend hurts my pride as a member of this community, because it shows me that our community is late to report the latest MLB news compared to other sites. It is a shame just to copy other sites' contents into our community.

The large number of responses this post received, regardless of how many were in agreement, shows that boundary issues are highly relevant to online fans. However, to call an online community a "virtual territory" might seem oxymoronic, because boundaries in the Internet are easily blurred and information and issues at specialty websites usually overlap. Most South Korean MLB fans, as prolific Internet users, visit and participate in several South Korean MLB sites. Also, a community's desire to constitute its own territory is undermined by the unpredictable duration of membership.

On the one hand, any online community can disappear in a moment; on the other, prolific posters are as likely as temporary visitors to leave an established community. While it is also true that fans, as members of a particular community, constitute that community's boundary, community territory ironically becomes a space of denizens, both unidentified and temporary, who continuously leave and are replaced by newcomers. As a result, the territory of any online community inherently comprises so much ambiguity and ambivalence, that are so relentlessly and constantly constructed by fans, that it may evaporate into anonymity, i.e., no one's territory.

On the Internet, as Castells suggested, "localities become disembedded from their cultural, historical, and geographical meaning and reintegrated into functional networks, or into image collages" (Castells 1996, 375). Such a transformation of spatiality does not necessarily mean that a space of flows can always be substituted for the space of places, however. Instead, Korean MLB fans in online community constantly reconstruct their notions of space, which are inevitably bound by their local places, their perceptions of the gaps between places, and their desire to build their own territory. Therefore, the space of online community can be constituted as a set of symmetric spatialities that fans perform synchronously.

Conclusion

Korean MLB fans construct online community by sharing information about MLB and by interacting with other fans. How fans use time and space in the community demonstrates that the Internet's virtuality does not replace traditional concepts of time and space, but rather that this virtuality contributes to constructing multiple senses of temporality and spatiality. This multiplicity is promulgated not only by the intersection between online and offline, but also by the ambivalence that local fans feel about global sports. Online interactions among members of MLBPARK allow them to develop alternative ways of managing diverse or even contradictory temporalities and spatialities on the Internet by fluctuating between anytime and national time, and between global and local (which they equate with national). These dualities continuously constitute the multiplicity and complexity of online time and space, adding uneven and asymmetric dimensions to them in online community. The multiple temporalities and spatialities that fans construct through their participation form the source of the community's materiality.

In turn, the materiality of the community allows fans to develop a multiplicity of identities. Participants in MLBPARK constitute their identities not only as MLB fans but also as fans of their local baseball teams and as community members, as well as nationalistically as (South) Koreans. The terms "we," "fans," "members," and "Koreans" are used constantly and interchangeably. At the same time, because technological innovations are influencing the creation of new social and cultural sensibilities in cyberspace, these fans are able to express themselves in personal, intimate ways. This multiplicity enables community members to imagine and inhabit flexible or even fragmented selves, and also indicates relatedness among diverse identities as well as the interconnectedness of fans' offline identities and social conditions. Certain dualities inherent within the community, as explicated above, highlight the interaction between online and offline via the online identities of fans. In turn, both online and offline interactions help negotiate, reproduce, and index these identities in a variety of ways. Despite the temptation of anytime access, most fans regulate their visits to online community harmoniously with their offline activities.

South Korean MLB fans do not passively receive cultural elements but instead actively produce, distribute, and consume MLB as a way of pursuing pleasure. Of course, the ways that fans utilize online community as a source of leisure and consumption are complex and ever-changing. Undeniably, the national has emerged as a fluid, relational space wherein local fans constantly negotiate between global products and local/national roots. Online communities evince the same characteristics as members experience them and, in the case of MLBPARK, enjoy MLB within the larger continuum of their offline lives.

As Miller and Slater (2001) suggested, it would be misleading to assume that experiences of South Korean MLB fans online lead either to nationalism or to cosmopolitanism. Suffice to say that nationalist sensibilities are deeply embedded in the fans' ways of enjoying MLB and participating in online community. Their articulations of time and space on the Internet demonstrates the possibility of living in temporalities and spatialities that fluctuate not only between online and offline, but also among local, national, and global. In addition, the presence of alternativeness, interconnectedness, and multiplicity within the community suggest that "closer attention be given to deconstructing dichotomies of offline and online, real and virtual, and individual and collective" (Wilson and Peterson 2002, 456).

Finally, these fluctuations in online community can be assessed in terms of glocalization. The implications of the US sports fandom in South Korea can be more usefully assessed through the theoretical frame of glocalization as continuum, which involves glocalization from above and glocalization from below; the latter refers to the diverse ways that local fans consume and enjoy MLB. South Korean MLB fandom epitomizes on type of glocalization from below.

The online community of MLBPARK, in which multiple temporalities and spatialities are traversed, does not require its participants to remove themselves from their own places and time zones. In this sense, South Korean MLB fans are more than long-distance partisans; they also use their interest in a global sport to extend their local relationships and facilitate their local affiliation. Through enjoying US sports and interacting with fellow enthusiasts in online community, these fans have developed their understanding of the national and have constructed a complex sense of locality, shared time patterns, and a unique history.

Online community as established and enacted by South Korean MLB fans demonstrates that the globalization of US sports not only relies upon local responses but is also utilized to rearticulate local and national identity. In global sports, the local is not the other of the global; in Korea particularly, both the local and the national have actively, enthusiastically responded to the arrival of US sports.

Notes

1 This study is a part of the larger project that examines transnational fandom among Korean MLB fans.
2 For more details on the online methodology that I utilize, see Cho (2014).
3 All quotations are from my ethnographic data on the online community (www.mlbpark.com). To protect the identities of fans in the community, I identify them by their pseudo names. I have also translated their posts, which were originally written in Korean, into English.

References

Andrews, D. (2004) 'Speaking the "universal language of entertainment": News Corporation, culture and the global sport media economy', in D. Rowe (ed.) *Critical Readings: Sport, Culture and the Media*, Maidenhead: Open University Press.

Andrews, D. and Cole, C.L. (2002) 'The Nation reconsidered', *Journal of Sport & Social Issues*, 26(2): 123–242.

Bird, S.E. (2003) *The Audience in Everyday Life: Living in a Media World*, New York: Routledge.

Boyle, R. and Haynes, R. (2004) *Football in the New Media Age*, New York: Routledge.

Castells, M. (1996) *The Rise of the Network Society*, Cambridge, MA: Blackwell.

Cho, Y. (2007) 'The emergence of individuated nationalism among major league baseball fans in South Korea', Unpublished doctoral dissertation, University of North Carolina, Chapel Hill.

Cho, Y. (2008) 'The national crisis and de/reconstructing nationalism in South Korea during the IMF intervention', *Inter-Asia Cultural Studies*, 9(1): 82–95.

Cho, Y. (2009) 'The glocalization of U.S. sports in South Korea', *Sociology of Sport Journal*, 26(2): 320–334.

Cho, Y. (2014) 'Toward the post-Westernization of baseball?: The national-regional-global nexus of Korean Major League Baseball fans during the 2006 World Baseball Classic', *International Review for Sociology of Sport*, 1–18. doi: 10.1177/1012690214552658.

Cho, Y., Leary, C. and Jackson, S. (2012) 'Glocalization of sports in Asia', *Sociology of Sport Journal*, 29(4): 421–432.

Croteau, D. and Hoynes, W. (1997) *Media/Society: Industries, Images and Audiences*, Thousand Oaks, London and New Delhi: Pine Forge Press.

Hine, C. (2000) *Virtual Ethnography*, London, Thousand Oaks and New Delhi: Sage Publications.

Klein, A.K. (2006) *Growing the Game: The Globalization of Major League Baseball*, New Haven and London: Yale University Press.

Miller, D. and Slater, D. (2001) *The Internet: An Ethnographic Approach*, Oxford and New York: Berg.

Robertson, C. (2004) 'A Sporting Gesture?: BSkyB, Manchester United, global media and sport', *Television & New Media*, 5(4): 291–314.

Rowe, D. (2003) 'Sport and the repudiation of the global', *International Review for the Sociology of Sport*, 38(3): 281–294.

Storey, J. (2003) *Inventing Popular Culture: From Folklore to Globalization*, Malden, MA: Blackwell.

Westerbeek, H. and Smith, A. (2003) *Sport Business in the Global Marketplace*, New York: Palgrave Macmillan.

Wilson, S.M. and Peterson, L.C. (2002) 'The anthropology of online communities', *Annual Review of Anthropology*, 31: 449–467.

12

A new media movement and a new praxis @passiontimes.hk

Pui-lam Law

This chapter attempts to argue that new media is not just a platform for providing a new mode of communication. Indeed, as evidenced by the Iran presidential election in 2009 and the political movement of Arab Spring in 2010, the power of new media can facilitate political action. In these movements, however, the strong anti-government attitude had already been there and what was needed was an efficacious means for calling upon the people to come out. The role new media played in this series of political action was an alternative means supplementary to the traditional modes of communication.

In this chapter, I shall use the case of *Passion Times*,[1] a new media platform in Hong Kong, run by Civic Passion, a politically radical group, to argue that new media is more than a means of communication; new media can trigger a new political movement, leading to a critique of ideology and turning the virtual political movement into actual political action. I shall first introduce the strained political situation in Hong Kong and how the traditional mainstream there is co-constructing the political reality with the dominant political groups. I shall then turn to introduce the *Passion Times* and Civic Passion, explaining how they operate their new media platform and what their critical stance is towards the Hong Kong politics. Finally I shall use the case study of a June 4 memorial rally organized by *Passion Times* to illustrate how they are turning their critique into action.

A brief introduction to the political situation in Hong Kong

In the early years after 1997 when the PRC exercised sovereignty over Hong Kong, most people in Hong Kong were hardly aware of the fact that the political and social situation of Hong Kong was changing as compared to the colonial period under the British administration. In recent years, as the Chinese government has been increasingly exercising its influence on Hong Kong, more and more people have started experiencing that the Chinese government is extensively maneuvering Hong Kong local policy. They have begun to fear that the high degree of autonomy of self-governance guaranteed by the one-country-two-systems principle would accordingly come to an end. Consequently, the idea of localism has been growing fast in response to the swift and sweeping political change in recent years.

Two examples illustrate this development. In 2013, 74 percent of the 54 million tourists to Hong Kong were from Mainland China. This represents a growth of 500 percent since the implementation in 2003 of the Individual Visit Scheme, a scheme which allows individuals from the PRC to visit Hong Kong.[2] The Individual Visit Scheme has led to a series of social problems in Hong Kong. As the health care service and food safety in Hong Kong are much better and more reliable than in Mainland China, many pregnant Chinese women made use of the Hong Kong health care scheme to give birth in Hong Kong public or the private hospitals, resulting in a shortage of both manpower and resources for the obstetrics and gynecology wards. This has seriously affected the availability of services for local expectant mothers. In addition, a great many mainland Chinese individual visitors also bought the infant milk formula in bulk and brought these back to China, leading to a shortage of supply in Hong Kong.

As the number of individual visitors has sharply increased, businesses targeting mainland tourists such as jewelry and cosmetics shops, as well as those selling luxury goods, have extended to the shopping malls of local communities in the new territories. This has fuelled the discontent of local communities.

The influence has been tremendous on the local economy as well as various kinds of business and services developed for or by the local Hongkongers. For instance, some restaurants famous for selling local food have been forced to close down as they could no longer afford the increase of rent resulting from the titanic expansion of businesses for Mainland visitors. The huge number of tourists from China has created an enormous disembedding power in uprooting the local culture and economy of Hong Kong.

These factors have set in motion conflict between the Hongkongers and the Mainland Chinese. Consequently, localism has developed rapidly in recent years. In addition, the Hongkongers have been urging the Hong Kong Special Administrative Government to revise the Individual Visitor Scheme so as to limit the number of mainland visitors. Their urge was in vain, however, as the government repeatedly pointed out that the Individual Visitor Scheme was endorsed by the Central Government and it was profitable to the Hong Kong economy. The discontent against the local and the Chinese communist government has therefore been increasing.

A second example regards political reform, which has always been a controversial issue in Hong Kong. Under the one-country-two-systems principle, Hong Kong has been promised to have her Chief Executive and the members of Legislative Council ultimately elected by universal suffrage. Hong Kong was to have had universal suffrage in 2007 but the Standing Committee of the National People's Congress (NPCSC) of the PRC unilaterally interpreted Article 7 of Annex 1 and Article III of Annex II in 2004 as suggesting that the conditions did not exist for universal suffrage in 2007. The speed of moving towards universal suffrage has been deliberately slowed down by the Chinese Communist government.

The hope that both the Chief Executive and Legislative Councillor could be elected by universal suffrage was again destroyed in the 2012 electoral reform. The 2012 election fell short of expectations despite the fact that the number of Chief Executive Election Committee was increased from 800 to 1200 and the number of seats of both the functional and geographic constituencies of the Legislative Council election was increased.

Despite the fact that the Standing Committee of the Tenth National People's Congress ruled in 2007 that Hong Kong might implement the universal suffrage in 2017 in electing the Chief Executive, the NPCSC decided on August 31, 2014 that the candidates should be nominated by a nominating committee. In addition, the Chinese government also maintained that the candidates should be patriotic to the PRC and Hong Kong.

Most of the politically active groups believed that these two criteria were developed for screening candidates whose political views should be in alignment with the Chinese government. Thus some political active groups proposed public nomination so as to avoid Beijing's screening. Some proposed the idea of occupying Central, the finance and economic center in Hong Kong, if a genuine universal suffrage could not be attained in the 2017 Chief Executive election; those who espouse the localist idea advanced a more radical proposal that the Basic Law should be re-written so that Hongkongers could decide on their own the election method.

Simply put, these groups of people do not believe that Chinese government will really grant high degree of autonomy to Hong Kong; on the contrary, they have found that the degree of autonomy was substantially decreasing and that Hong Kong has been simply treated as a colony of China. Indeed, the decision made by the NPCSC led to the outbreak of Umbrella Revolution by the end of September 2014, a revolution fighting for a genuine universal suffrage in Hong Kong.

Hong Kong traditional mainstream media

With regards to political communication, Gurevitch, Coleman and Blumler (2009, 166) point out that mainstream media such as television has moved from the role of reporting political events to the role of constructing the political reality with the politicians. The case of Hong Kong is indeed barely different from cases in the Western societies. The traditional mainstream media, the plutocrats, and the politicians have not only dominated the political discourse but they have also co-constructed the political reality of Hong Kong. The co-construction process has not only distorted the political communication but also stifled the critical opinions.

The traditional mainstream media in Hong Kong could be briefly classified into three categories. The first one is pro-communist media, which consists mostly of print media. This has long been funded by the Communist government and supported the communist regime since the British colonial period. In this media, any issues related to communist China are given a positive stance; for instance, convincing the public that the Individual Visitor Scheme had contributed to the economic development of Hong Kong despite the fact that the scheme had already induced enormous negative social consequences. Pro-communist media has very limited influence as it is among the most unpopular media in Hong Kong.

The second type of traditional mainstream media is that having strong economic connections either in China or with the most influential local businesses. In order for their businesses to survive, this group of mainstream media would practice self-censorship when reporting or discussing sensitive political issues. They would sometimes proactively co-construct the political reality with the government or the pro-establishment politician. For instance, they would tone down the problem of the shortage of infant formula and the post specious argument that the shortage is a sheer market issue and has nothing to do with the flood of individual Chinese visitors.

The third type of traditional mainstream media supports a more genuine democratic reform. While this media is very critical of the Hong Kong and Communist governments, it also adheres to sino-centric ideology. Briefly put, this media prefers Confucian harmony over conflict and nationalism over localism. When reporting on conflict between the Hongkongers and individual Chinese visitors, this media scarcely included the localist viewpoint. As this group of media had been constructing a political reality of a unified China, the voice of localism was silenced in news reports and discussion.

As shown in the above examples, communist China has been exercising tightening control on Hong Kong local policy, and due to the growing conflict between Chinese visitors and the

Hongkongers, the localist consciousness has been developing rapidly and extensively in recent years. Despite this, any news related to the localist movements or ideas have either been suppressed or mediated in a very negative way in these three categories of traditional mainstream media.

While the traditional mainstream media had been blacking out the localist's news and stifling their voices, new media has emerged as a possible way out for the localist to break through the suppression and to communicate their political ideas and action to the public.

New media and new modes of communication

With the fast and ubiquitous development of Information and Communication Technologies (ICTs) such as the Internet, mobile phone, iPad, and notebook computer in the past two decades, people have more options for communicating information. In addition, these ICTs, particularly with the inception of Web 2.0 technology, form new ways and a new platform for receiving and disseminating information. For instance, thanks to the mobile Internet, television audiences can watch their favorite serials at any time and any place they like. Receiving information can be free from any spatial and temporal constraints. Audiences can also generate their news content and post them on the Internet. Audiences can now become actors. Simply put, the ICTs have radically changed the traditional forms of communication. As such, ICTs are not merely digital media, they are new media (Dewdney and Ride 2006, 21).

With the inception of new media, news or discussion which had been blacked out by the traditional mainstream media can now be disseminated on the Internet through the viral power of social network sites (Shah et al. 2005). People can also actively scrutinize and criticize the credibility of news content. The new media has gradually evolved to become the fifth estate (Dutton 2009; Cooper 2006), opening a brand new way of enhancing the accountability of the mainstream media and government.

Indeed, new media can also be a platform for promoting new ideas and facilitating political movements. An example from Facebook: Wan Chin,[3] a Facebook blogger who used to be a famous columnist writing articles on Hong Kong local culture, is one of the prominent advocates of localism on the Internet. In recent years, as his articles have strong localist elements and were therefore scarcely accepted for publishing in newspapers, he has turned to posting his localist ideas online. He has become famous through this forum and has attracted tens of thousands of followers on social media. As he is renowned for providing discussion of localist ideas online, his print books which are collections of his online posts have been bestsellers in recent years. In addition, his ideas have also had substantial influence on several localist movements that have taken place in the past two years. The case of Wan Chin not only shows that new media can function as the fifth estate but also demonstrates that the successful use of new media can be conducive to online and offline political movements, or a new kind of praxis. In what follows, I shall use the case of *Passion Times* to illustrate thoroughly the relationship between new media movement and a new form of political movement.

Passion Times and Civic Passion

Passion Times was established in September 2012 by Yeung-tat Wong and his supporters, the members of Civil Passion. Civic Passion was formed for the purpose of supporting their leader Yeung-tat Wong and his wife Sau-wai Chan, who were running in the 2012 Hong

Kong Legislative Election. Though Wong and Chan had received 36,608 votes, this was still 1,938 less than required in order for them to be elected. They learnt from the election campaign that the influence of traditional mainstream media remained enormous. Although some mainstream media support a genuine democratic reform, they have their own agenda in constructing the political reality of Hong Kong. As aforementioned, these media support the sino-centric ideology and stifle the voices of the localist. The voice of Civic Passion, as a political group with the mission to fight for the democracy and political autonomy of Hong Kong against the Chinese Communist government's domination on local politics, would certainly have been suppressed by the mainstream media. In order to break through the suppression of the traditional mainstream media and to communicate their political ideas to the public, they therefore set up *Passion Times*.[4]

Passion Times is primarily a new media platform, consisting of online news, online blog columns covering various topics such as comments on Hong Kong's political or social issues, cultural analysis, academic articles, and lifestyle stories. The blog columns consist of a great wide variety of topics, hoping to attract as broad a range as possible of online readers.

In addition to blog columns and news on their webpage, *Passion Times* also has Internet video programs. During its first year of establishment, there were three programs a night starting from 9 p.m. to 12 midnight during the weekdays, and one or two programs during the weekends. Starting from December 2013, they launched a new program entitled *Passion Politics*, running from Monday to Friday from 8 p.m. to 9 p.m. in the evening. From March 2014 onwards, working together with another Internet media *MyRadio*, they launched another morning program called *Good Morning Our Hong Kong*, also running from Monday to Friday, from 8 a.m. to 10 a.m. in the morning. All the programs are broadcast in video, while audiences can choose either video or just audio mode. Most of the programs are live but audiences can download archived programs from the website or through smart phone apps such as Podcast or the one developed by *Passion Times* specifically for the iOS and Android systems.

Before launching *Passion Politics* and *Good Morning Our Hong Kong*, *Humour and King*, anchored by Yeung-tat Wong and his wife Sau-wai Chan, was the most popular program in their platform. *Humour and King* uses humor to provide commentary on the social, cultural, as well as political issues in Hong Kong. Usually, live online audiences are over 4,000 and sometimes up to 6,000; the download or replay rate for program is at the average of 100,000 times from unique IPs, and the highest hit at around 160,000 from unique IPs.

Passion Politics and *Good Morning Our Hong Kong* are also equally popular as compared with *Humour and King*. *Passion Politics* is anchored by Yeung-tat Wong and three to four core members of Civic Passion. This program is primarily designed to provide serious and in-depth analysis of political issues in Hong Kong, particularly the issues centering on 2016 and 2017 political reform. The program became popular very quickly and live online audiences were usually over 5,000.

As compared with *Passion Politics*, *Good Morning Our Hong Kong* is a more comprehensive program on daily social and political issues; it sometimes covers stories on local lifestyles and cultures. The main anchors are Yeung-tat Wong and Yuk-man Wong, a renowned radical legislative councilor who established *MyRadio* and shares almost the same political ideals with Wong and Civic Passion. This is also a very popular program with over 5,000 online live audiences each day. The average downloads or replay rates for each of these two programs are also at the average of 100,000 times from unique IPs.

Figure 12.1   The anchors of *Good Morning Our Hong Kong*: Tom Leung, Yeung-tat Wong, Yuk-man Wong, Christine Wong, Lok-hang Tam (from left to right)

(Courtesy of *Passion Times*)

Another very popular program on online gaming is called *Otaku of Cultural Studies*. Its online live audiences have peaked at over 40,000, when one of the most popular Japanese online games, *Puzzle and Dragons*, had a special event in August 2013. Other popular programs include *Mysterious Studies & Research, Passion Civic Education, Animal Panic, Girls' Hotline, Call Number, Sex and Taboo, The House Wife Foundation Classes, Movie Club, Christian Religion*, and *Martial Arts and Combat Skills*. The wide variety of programs is designed to attract different kind of the Internet users so that their political ideas would not only communicate to those politically like-minded audiences.

Up to August 2014, the total number of unique IPs visiting the *Passion Times* webpage was 1,631,602.[5] Among these IPs, 79 percent were local. Before the launch of *Passion Politics* in December 2013, the total number of unique IPs visiting the *Passion Times* webpage was 433,987; and before the launch of *Good Morning Our Hong Kong* in March 2014, the number of IPs was 699,764. Apparently, the two flagship programs, which focused centrally on local political and social issues, had considerable attraction for the online public.

The number of online and offline audiences had been increasing fast since the launch of the two new programs, but it has been increased enormously since the outbreak of the Umbrella Revolution. The Umbrella Revolution, which took place in the fall of 2014, was an unprecedented and huge occupying movement aimed at fighting for a genuine universal suffrage in 2017. The *Passion Times* reporters had been incessantly providing update news with photos and videos since the first day of occupation despite facing baton, pepper spray, and tear gas in the occupied areas. In addition, *Passion Times* had also been doing the live broadcasting of the two flagship programs in the occupied areas, mostly in Mongkok in order to communicate political ideas of Civic Passion to the protesters and public face to face.

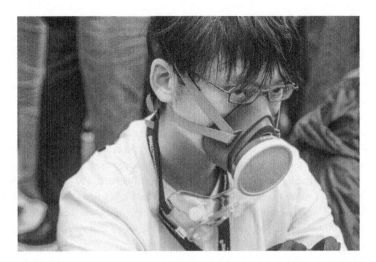

Figure 12.2 Passion Times reporter Ca Ru Choi (Facebook name) wearing tear gas mask in the occupied area

(Courtesy of Ca Ru Choi)

Figure 12.3 Humour and King doing a live broadcast in the occupied area, Nathan Road in MongKok

(Courtesy of *Passion Times*)

Since the Umbrella Revolution, the live online audiences of *Passion Politics* and *Good Morning Our Hong Kong* have increased from the average 5,000 to over 15,000. The average download rate is ranged from 170,000 to 210,000 from unique IPs. The total number of unique IPs visiting *Passion Times* webpage has gone up to 1,824,603.[6]

The web page of *Passion Times* is also closely connected to the *Passion Times* Facebook page. This is tremendously important in making use of the viral power of social media in effectively spreading their political ideals to the online public. The connection is established in two ways. First, they set up a *Passion Times* Facebook page account and invite their audiences to "like" the page. When audiences "like" their page, they would receive notifications whenever *Passion Times* posts news, articles, or their political actions on the page. Since the launch of the account in October 2012, the Facebook page of *Passion Times* had earned 19,000 "likes" by September 2013 (Law 2014), and more than 60,000 by September 2014.[7] During the Umbrella Revolution, as *Passion Times* had unremittingly provided first-hand update news, the number of "likes" has already reached 296,000.[8] That means 296,000 Facebook users will receive posting notifications from *Passion Times*.

Second, when audiences go to watch a live program, by clicking the "connect" button on the web page, their Facebook account connects to the chat room of the program and allows instant commentary on either the program or other audience members' comments. This strengthens the communications between the anchor and the audience and among audiences themselves. Each of the Internet video programs forms their own group on Facebook and the program anchor encourages their audiences to join the group for communicating the news and information of the program concerned. Most of these groups are also open for the online users to join. In order to cultivate group participation, the anchor, for example Yeung-tat Wong, would post some interesting post-program information to the group for discussion. This is particularly important for *Passion Times*, as when they have important online news, social or political comments, they will post them in all these online groups in order to extend their reach into the Internet more broadly (Bakker and de Vreese 2011).

Indeed, *Passion Times* has relied heavily on their webpage, the Internet program, and the viral power of Facebook to communicate their political ideals to the public. As the establishment of *Passion Times* is to break through the traditional mainstream media's suppression of the political ideals of Civic Passion, *Passion Times* is undoubtedly a platform for Civic Passion to disseminate their localist position of political reform. Accordingly, *Passion Times* is not a politically neutral media platform providing the pros and cons discussion of the 2017 political reform. Their editorial policy is threefold. First, as many new media have already been providing online news, *Passion Times* would place a high priority on publishing the news concerning localist issues or political reform. This is meant to provide the online viewers an apparent image of what their concern is. Second, they themselves would proactively post articles stating, explaining, or arguing their political stance whenever there are issues concerning the political reform or localist-sinophiliac disputes. Third, whenever they post news or blog articles, they would try their best to make the titles, the brief description, and more importantly the photographs strikingly arresting. This is of utmost importance in attracting the attention of the online users as the information online is flooding every day.

The second platform for disseminating their political ideals is the Internet video program. Before launching *Passion Politics* and *Good Morning Our Hong Kong*, *Humour and King* was the major program for communicating their political ideals to the public. While this program has had a very high rate of live online audience and high download rate, this program runs only once a week and cannot follow closely and comment at the first instance the daily political issues, particularly when the consultation of the 2017 political reform commenced in December 2013 and will make inroads into a solid framework by the end of 2014. They therefore found it necessary to launch *Good Morning Our Hong Kong* and *Passion Politics* which run from Monday to Friday each morning and evening respectively so that they can in the first instance follow the news and debate of the political reform, respond critically to the specious arguments advanced by the establishments, and spell out their localist stance on political reform amid the rapid development and changes of the political ecology since the commencement of the consultation. In addition to the video program, they would sometimes also transcribe into words the significant ideas presented in the program and post it as post-program articles. These flagship programs have shouldered the mission of arousing the consciousness of the public that the importance of defending the high degree of autonomy of self-governance and striving for a genuine universal suffrage.

All the webpage links with brief description of the news, blog column articles, program, and program articles are also posted on the *Passion Times* Facebook page and all the Passion program Facebook groups. Those who "liked" their page will receive notification once the link is posted. Within the first 24 hours of the Umbrella Revolution, more than 100,000 Facebook users liked the *Passion Times* Facebook page; apparently, they wanted to get news notification from their page. By the end of the Revolution, just less than 3 months, they had earned more than 230,000 "likes" more, almost 5 times of what they had in the past 2 years. Simply put, the more "likes" they have earned, the more influence they will have. As the number of "like" has been increasing steadily for the past two years and astoundingly fast during the Revolution, the share rate of the news, articles, and programs have been increasing accordingly.

In addition, those shared in the Facebook program groups can make use of the viral power of social networking to reach a broader online public. Many news and blog articles have exceeded 10,000 likes or shares. The highest share rate has hit 20,000. The number of online readers had also been considerably increasing since the inception of two flagship programs. The unique IPs viewing blog articles and news had exceeded 1,400,000 and page view 5,500,000 in August 2014.[9] The page view has even reached 8,400,000 since the outbreak of the Revolution.[10]

Wong and Civic Passion have not limited their political communication to the new media as they learnt from their election campaign in 2012 that the influence of print newspaper remained enormous. Wong and his Civil Passion have also published print newspaper and delivered it to the public free of charge monthly. They have also developed *Passion Teens*, a weekly comic magazine. They hope that the magazine could attract the attention of the teenagers on the one hand and that their print publication could be visible on the newspaper stall on the other. Both the newspaper and comic magazine have the *Passion Times* quick response code for readers to use their smart phone to reach their website conveniently. Recognizing the importance of face-to-face communication, *Passion Times* has also organized drama performances. In 2013, the idea of Occupying Central so as to negotiate with Communist China the launch of a genuine universal suffrage gained enormous attention and discussion in Hong Kong. *Passion Times* was very critical of this idea and its planning and therefore staged their arguments through drama performance.

New media movement: from virtual to actual

Since *Passion Times* launched their new media platform, they have always initiated online political movements against the pro-establishment online propaganda or the pundit or sinophiliac's online articles embedded with strong sino-centric values so as to pursue a universal suffrage with a localist stance. The simplest way is to encourage the online supporters to post their critical arguments as comments to the "comment" column of all these kind of articles. This is not only to flood these pro-establishment or sino-centric ideas but also to demonstrate to the online public the alternative arguments for their consideration. While *Passion Times* does not limit the communication of political ideals to the online public, their political action is not confined to the virtual world as well. They have also extended their online critique to actual political actions.

Indeed, *Passion Times* and Civic Passion organized several political actions. In 2013, right after the first of July demonstration, an annual anti-government demonstration since 1997, *Passion Times* and Civic Passion gathered almost a thousand supporters and organized a burning Basic Law event. The event was a symbolic gesture showing that they refused to accept Basic Law which had been unilaterally written and revised by the Communist China. They have also proposed that Hongkongers should revise by themselves the Basic Law ensuring that Hong Kong could really enjoy a high degree of autonomy in self-governance. They also joined the protest called on by the online localists against the Individual Visit Scheme.

In 2014, *Passion Times* together with Yuk-man Wong, the most radical legislative councilor and the founder of *MyRadio*, had organized another large-scale event on the fourth of June at square of Freedom Fighter of Cultural Centre in Tsimshatsui, Kowloon Peninsula. This event was considered as a more militant protest as compared with the annual candlelight vigil in memory of the June 4 Tiananmen Square massacre held in Victoria Park in Hong Kong Island.[11]

While hundreds of thousands of Hongkongers have attended the Victoria Park June 4 evening candlelight vigil for more than two decades since the massacre in 1989, a great many of the participants, particularly the localists, have been very unhappy both of the organizer, a group called the "Hong Kong Alliance in Support of Patriotic Democratic Movement" (the Alliance),[12] and of the nature of the gathering. First, many people think that the Alliance, particularly the pan-democratic politicians in that group, have been using the June 4 massacre and the candlelight vigil as a means to achieve their political glory and interests. As such, they have done nothing but merely tried their very effort to expose themselves to the limelight of mainstream media in the vigil. The candlelight vigil had then turned into a kind of memorial ritual. Second, nearly all the members of the Alliance are sinophiliac and believe that fighting for the democracy of China is of paramount importance since they believe that only a democratic China would grant Hong Kong genuine universal suffrage. Thus the localists have felt that the slogans chanted, the songs sung, and the speeches they delivered in the vigil have been spreading a sino-centric ideology which would undoubtedly tame the steely determination of Hongkongers both in defending the high degree of local autonomy and asking for Hongkongers rule Hong Kong.

Passion Times and Civic Passion are indeed not against holding an annual memorial gathering. But as a political group defending local value, culture, and political autonomy against the Communist manipulation, they are highly critical of the members of the Alliance as well as the way they have organized the vigil. As they agreed to the above criticism, they believed that they had to deconstruct the dominant sino-centric discourse and advanced their localist value by organizing another June 4 vigil in Tsimshatsui. They called upon the people to attend their Tsimshatsui June 4 meeting by explaining their position and their ideas as to why they were against the Victoria Park vigil in their *Passion Politics* and *Good Morning Our Hong Kong* programs. Wong and some active members also posted their critical ideas on their new media platform; and in addition, they also called upon the audiences and online public to submit their critical viewpoints to their platform explaining why they have to say farewell to the Victoria Park candlelight vigil.

They edited all these articles into a June 4 online collection which consists of fifty-seven pieces of work. As they understood that the online articles could hardly reach to the offline public, they therefore chose the best six articles and printed them off in the form of a booklet. They prepared a hundred thousand copies and delivered them together with the monthly newspaper to the public in order to have their ideas on June 4 vigil reach a broader offline public.

Despite the fact that the mainstream media had silenced the localist voice in general and this alternative June 4 meeting in particular, on the fourth of June 2014 evening in Tsimshatsui, they had successfully attracted 7,000 people to the June 4 memorial rally.

During this rally, they first delivered the message to the public that Hongkongers should not only just mourn the dead but also stand up to defend their land, their ways of life, and their political autonomy against the totalitarian regime which perpetrated the brutal massacre in 1989. Second, instead of conducting candlelight mourning, Wong and his ally Yuk-man Wong together burnt the Communist flag on the stage as a gesture of fighting valorously against the Communist China's increasing on local polity, and simultaneously the attendees were holding their smartphone up playing back video of burning the communist flag. More importantly, they pronounced that they would occupy the Hong Kong Legislative Council if the government did not grant a genuine 2017 political reform. When the rally was over, thousands of attendees were marching in the Canton Road, protesting against the Individual Visitor Scheme and Communist China in this very popular shopping street with many internationally famous brand shops for the rich Chinese visitors.

Figure 12.4   Burning the Communist flag at the rally

(Courtesy of *Passion Times*)

Figure 12.5 The rally attendees were holding their smartphones up, playing back the video of burning the Communist flag

(Courtesy of *Passion Times*)

Although the voice of the localist was expressed strongly in the rally, as usual, almost all the local mainstream media did not report anything about this alternative June 4 meeting, and even those that reported it did so in a very small column. Despite this, the works that have been done by *Passion Times* and Civic Passion have demonstrated that they are relentless in pursuing their localist mission.

In the past two years, the programs of *Passion Times*, the protest or political gatherings, particularly the June 4 memorial rally, organized by Civic Passion, had embarrassed both the Hong Kong and the Chinese Communist governments, the *Passion Times* website had always been under severe distributed denial of service (DDoS) attack. Indeed the most devastating DDoS attack that *Passion Times* experienced was during the Umbrella Revolution. As the attack was violent, which severely affected the routine operation of the service providers, the local as well as many overseas Internet service providers from many different countries were reluctant to provide service for them. CloudFlare, a very famous company for Internet security, was also unable to protect them because the highest attack *Passion Times* had had was 500 Gbit/s, which is similar to over 250 million of enquiries in each second. They therefore had to shop around for other Internet security companies but were unsuccessful. For instance, ClouDNS had provided them service for only two hours and found that they could not handle the volume of attack. Eventually with the support of Google, *Passion Times'* website has returned to normal since mid-November, 2014.[13] *Passion Times*, which has been promoting a new media movement and a new political praxis, has also introduced an unprecedented scale of cyber-attack.

Conclusion: new media movement and the critique of ideology

Passion Times has exhibited a new media movement followed by a new praxis. Undoubtedly, new media has been conducive to a number of revolutionary waves of demonstrations and protests. This can be witnessed by the aforementioned Iran presidential election and political movement in Arab Spring which took place in 2009 and 2010 respectively. It would be difficult to deny the fact that new media can facilitate political communication as well as political participation (Ward et al. 2003; Hardy and Scheufele 2005; Shah et al. 2005; Bakker and de Vreese 2011). But the case of *Passion Times* and Civic Passion is about more than facilitating political communication and online and offline participation. I would argue that the case of *Passion Times* and Civic Passion has demonstrated that a new media movement can be a critique of ideology which is conducive to new praxis.

Passion Times is more than a platform for political communication; it is also a platform for the critique of ideology. As mentioned above, the Hong Kong mainstream media has co-constructed a political reality with the politicians, opinion leaders, and the pundits. Ordinary people, particularly the grassroots, can hardly have the opportunity to voice out their critique in the mainstream media and deconstruct mediated political reality.

Thanks to the development of ICTs, the Internet with Web 2.0 technology provides a new mode of communication. The function of user-generated content indeed opens up the possibility of bottom-up communication and the viral power of social networking can then efficaciously disseminate the voice of the suppressed. New media has contributed to the possible reconfiguration of the balance of communicative power which had long been dominated by the mainstream media. New media therefore serves the function of communicating the pluralistic voices to the public.

Passion Times and Civic Passion have successfully made use of these communicative technologies to break through the suppression and communicate their localist position of political reform to the online public. The aim of their communication is twofold. First, they have attempted to launch critique on the Chinese communist-cum-sino-centric domination on the Hong Kong polity in general and political reform in particular. Through video programs, particularly the two flagship programs on Hong Kong politics, and the blog articles, they try to communicate their localist critical viewpoints to the public so as to arouse the public's consciousness that Communist China is tightening her control on Hong Kong and that the sino-centric value is merely an ideology to tame our determination in defending the localist value, culture, social life, and political autonomy.

Second, the communication is also aimed at consolidating the public for political action. Those program groups on Facebook are central for broadening their political communication as the program audiences are not only receiving information as in the case of traditional mainstream media; the audiences are also actors as well. Through the dozens of program groups on Facebook (each with more than 1,000 members), they can virally extend their critical message to cover a wide variety of the online public. The 2014 Tsimshatsui June 4 rally witnessed their success in consolidating thousands of people for political action. Thus *Passion Times* is not just a platform for communication but a platform for political movement, for turning the critical voice of the virtual into the action of the actual.

Notes

1 I am highly indebted to Yeung-Tat Wong for providing me his ideas, information, and materials on *Passion Times*. Thanks also go to David Chang for giving me the figures related to the online popularity of *Passion Times*.

2 For more details, see *Assessment Report on Hong Kong's Capacity to Receive Tourists* (Commerce and Economic Development Bureau 2013), www.tourism.gov.hk/resources/english/paperreport_doc/misc/2014-01-17/Assessment_Report_eng.pdf

3 For more about Wan Chin, please visit his Facebook page, www.facebook.com/wan.chin.75?fref=ts
4 For more details about the establishment of *Passion Times*, please see P-l. Law 2014.
5 Data obtained from the *Passion Times* administrative team on August 11, 2014.
6 Data obtained from the *Passion Times* administrative team on January 26, 2015.
7 www.facebook.com/passiontimes (Accessed on September 20, 2014).
8 www.facebook.com/passiontimes (Accessed on January 28, 2015).
9 Data obtained from the *Passion Times* administrative team on August 11, 2014.
10 Data obtained from the *Passion Times* administrative team on January 26, 2015.
11 http://sinosphere.blogs.nytimes.com/2014/06/05/a-more-militant-protest-demands-reforms-from-beijing/?_php=true&_type=blogs&_r=0 (Accessed on August 1, 2014).
12 For more details about this group, see www.alliance.org.hk/english/index.html
13 For more information on *Passion Times* under the DDoS attack, please refer to the following links: www.passiontimes.hk/article/10-09-2014/19156; www.passiontimes.hk/article/11-16-2014/19657

References

Bakker, T.P. and de Vreese, C.H. (2011) 'Good News for the Future? Young People, Internet Use, and Political Participation', *Communication Research*, 20(10): 1–20.

Commerce and Economic Development Bureau (2013) *Assessment Report on Hong Kong's Capacity to Receive Tourists*, Hong Kong: HKSAR Publications.

Cooper, S.D. (2006) *Watching the Watchdog: Bloggers as the Fifth Estate*, Washington: Marquette Books.

Dewdney, A. and Ride, P. (2006) *The New Media Handbook*, London: Routledge.

Dutton, W.H. (2009) 'The fifth estate emerging through the network of networks', *Prometheus*, 27(1): 1–15.

Gurevitch, M., Coleman, S. and Blumler, J.G. (2009) 'Political communication—old and new media relationship', *The Annals of the American Academy of Political and Social Science*, 625: 164–181.

Hardy, B.W. and Scheufele, D.A. (2005) 'Examining Differential Gains from Internet Use: Comparing the Moderating Role of Talk and Online Interactions', *Journal of Communication* 55(1), 71–84.

P.-I. Law (2014) 'Political communication, the Internet, and mobile media: the case of *Passion Times* in Hong Kong', in G. Goggin and L. Hjorth (eds) *Routledge Companion to Mobile Media*, New York: Routledge.

Shah, D., Cho, J., Eveland, W. and Kwak, N. (2005) 'Information and expression in a digital age: Modeling Internet effects on civic participation', *Communication Research* 32(5): 531–565.

Ward, S., Gibson, R. and Lusoli, W. (2003) 'Online Participation and Mobilisation in Britain: Hype, Hope and Reality', *Parliamentary Affairs* 56, 652–668.

13

A right and not a privilege: freedom of expression and new media in Malaysia

Susan Leong

On October 30, 2013, the Appeals Court of Malaysia upheld the High Court ruling that the Home Minister cannot refuse online news portal, Malaysiakini's, application for a permit to print without cause (2013c). In so doing, the court reconfirmed Judge Abang Iskandar Abang Hashim's earlier judgment that the Home Ministry's rejection of Malaysiakini's application was not only "improper and irrational" but had also failed to grant the plaintiff "a fundamental liberty enshrined in the Constitution"—the right to freedom of expression (Mayberry 2012). Primarily a subscription-based online news portal with 400,000 unique daily visitors (2014e), Malaysiakini originally lodged the application for a press permit in April 2010 to print 40,000 copies of their content for distribution in the Klang Valley. When the application was summarily refused consideration five months later, Malaysiakini filed for judicial review with the High Court, which delivered a decision two years later (Mageswari 2013). The Malaysian government then appealed the ruling, subsequently upheld by the Appeals Court. To-date the news portal has yet to go to print.

To follow the application's progression from mere application for a press permit to a matter brought before the High, and then Appeals Courts, is to comprehend the twists and turns in the ongoing debate over new media's position in Malaysia and the national aspirations tethering new media to development that underpinned and drove the dispute over the years. New media is at once an instrument of, and space for, alternative discourses that receives little airing in an otherwise hobbled media space. In other words, the interstitial space that new media occupy in Malaysia today owes a lot to their juxtaposition against encumbered traditional broadcast media, for as Weiss puts it, "[w]ere discursive space not at such a premium, new media would be more likely simply to amplify those discourses found elsewhere (2013, 609). I use the terms traditional and broadcasting media interchangeably here to include television, radio, print, press and film, and new media to denote the range of technologies enabled by the Internet, which includes but is not limited to the World Wide Web (www), social media, instant messaging and Internet telephony.

The emergence of new media as an alternative discursive space is also an outcome of the state's 1998 undertaking not to censor the Internet in Malaysia. Contained in the package known as the Bill of Guarantees,[1] the initial promise was made in the interest of attracting "foreign high-tech information industries" investments to the Multimedia Super Corridor (MSC) technology zone.

Such latitude was considered a necessary compromise if the MSC was to replicate the creative, playful setting instrumental to Silicon Valley-style innovation (Leong 2014, 80). Still, it is important to note that, unlike freedom of speech, the undertaking not to censor the Internet is not enshrined in the Constitution or any of the laws of Malaysia, and thus is open to reneging. What stops the government from doing so is unclear. Weiss contends it is for want of a way "to suppress new technologies of voice without tilting towards autocracy" (2014, 869); I would argue it is beyond an issue of a graceful exit. Indeed, I see it as a result of how the entangled historical understandings of how nation, media and technology relate to each other within Malaysia's social imaginary are in dispute with their contemporary interpretations. Hence, whilst Malaysiakini's pursuit of the elusive permission to print is the departure point for this chapter, the primary purpose here is to lay bare the roots of Malaysia's distinct stance on new media as opposed to those of its Southeast Asian neighbors.

Prosperity before voice

According to Atkins, it is because nation formation and technological advancements were "cross-cutting" each other in the 1950s and 1960s that the then new nation-states of Malaysia, Singapore, Indonesia and the Philippines put in place broadcast media systems that were "highly state-centric" (Atkins 2013, 38). Established in the expedient days of nation formation immediately following on from British devolution, Malaysia's broadcasting systems framework made no provisions for the notion of the media as the fourth estate. Instead, as a new state in the grip of nation-building, the founding government of Malaysia placed the need for prosperity above that of an independent, reflexive and inquiring media that might act as the voice of a nation's people. Historically, then, the allotted role of the media in Malaysia is subordinate: to complement government policies and operate under the supervision of the state.

Writing specifically of Malaysiakini, Pang defines developmental journalism as a model whereby "the media openly practise pro-government policy to aid in nation building" (2006, 72). That the press should be controlled by the government "in the name of mobilizing economic growth" is a position that goes back to the 1970s (Sussman, 1976), which the United Nations declared as "the decade of development" (Wallerstein 2005, 1264). Hence, the antecedents of developmental journalism are deeply entwined with the post WWII concept of the developmental state whose "ideology and legitimacy rests on an ability to get out of the traditional poverty gap and promote sustained economic development" wherein, the "ability to improve the economic conditions of its inhabitants is both the goal of the ruling elite and a means to keep power" (Reinert 2010, 5). Though since overshadowed by globalisation and neo-liberalism, as an ideology developmentalism still holds great sway in many of the nations formed post WWII in Asia and Africa.

Nonetheless, as the contrasting public service broadcasting model put in place in Europe as well as Australia and Canada testify, prosperity before voice was not inevitable (Atkins 2013, 48). Unlike the state broadcasters of the three nations named above, Malaysia's state broadcaster came under direct government supervision right from the start. Rather than inquiry and reflection, the Malaysian state broadcaster's responsibility was to complement the government policy goals of "development, national unity and economic growth" (Atkins 2013, 48). The distinction attributed to Malaysia then was the perception of a fragile balance of sensitivities surrounding issues of race and religion in early nationhood. As the logic goes, a strong hand is required to govern an unruly, heterogeneous population.[2] The violence of the 1969 riots that saw well over a 100 fatalities is still routinely issued as a cautionary reminder against open dissent and upsetting the equilibrium achieved between ethno-religious groups (2011c). The prioritization of development over other national objectives has received "very little conceptual adjustment" (Atkins 2013, 38) and remains applicable to all traditional media in Malaysia today.

Three factors must be valid for the developmental media model to function. The first has to do with how media production is organized. Centralized and professionalized media production technologies such as television, print, film and radio lend themselves readily to the one-to-many diffusion model of mass communication and thus, top-down control fundamental to the model. The developmental media model also makes sense only if the populace's preferred channel for gathering news and information is mainstream media. When the majority of news and information gathering is no longer funneled through state-sanctioned channels, the developmental media model loses its stranglehold on public opinion. Finally, the general populace's view of what nation building constitutes and the reasons for it must coincide with that of the state.

Over more than five decades of independence, there have been many occasions where the three factors conducive to the developmental media model did not coincide. Hence, the rationale privileging development over voice has had to be buttressed with a combination of punitive laws, legal action and control exerted via direct and indirect media ownership by the prevalent powers (Sani 2009, 52–56; Whiting and Majoribanks 2013, 91–92). The measures that restrain traditional media from fuller expression and greater inquiry of the status quo include laws that pertain specifically to media as well as those aimed at broadly suppressing sedition and curbing access to information related to the public interest such as the Internal Security Act (ISA) and Official Secrets Act (OSA) respectively (Sani 2010). Although the conditions leading to the enactments of these laws have since altered, their full rescindment has not taken place. Rather, older laws have been repealed and new ones shaped to perform the same job in the name of counter-terrorism. The ISA, for example, has been replaced with two laws: the *Peaceful Assembly Act* (2011b), which as Whiting points out is more aptly named the prevention of assembly act (2011); and the *Security Offences (Special Measures) Act* (2012c).

The specific legislation that governs Malaysiakini's application for a press permit is known as the PPPA (*Printing Presses and Publication Act 1984*). Originally the *Printing Presses Ordinance* (1948), the PPPA was revised in 1971 after the 1969 riots to give government the power to shut down newspapers that treaded on "national sensitivities" or "were detrimental to national development goals." Up until its 2012 amendments, the Act stipulated that all media licenses held were subject to annual renewal at the "absolute discretion" of the Home Minister without judicial review and provided a jail term or heavy fine for all those found guilty of "publishing false news" (Sani 2009, 62–63). While the 2012 amendments mean that once granted media permits no longer need to be renewed annually and their issue does come within judicial oversight, the Home Minister retains the right to revoke permits.

As the indefinite suspension of news weekly, *The Heat,* shows,[3] the suspicions and uncertainty created by decades of poor transparency are far from dispelled. *The Heat* was launched in September 2013, in print and online, with a view to bring a politics and socio-economic focus to local issues (2013a). It was suspended indefinitely in December 2013, allegedly for not informing the Home Ministry of a change in ownership and not responding to two "show cause" letters (Ng 2014). That the suspension came after the weekly published an article highlighting the large sums spent on travel and consultants by Prime Minister, Najib Razak and his wife, did not escape the comment of observers (Boo 2013; Gangopadhyay and Ng 2013). Although reinstated after a month, *The Heat* has since rebadged itself as *The Heat Online*, a "current affairs site focused on investigative journalism" of "affairs relating to Malaysia and Asia" and is now only available online (2014c). Though less authoritarian after the 2012 amendments, the PPPA still hands the government immense power to wield over the fate of mainstream media corporations.

The market for independent news media in Malaysia today is highly competitive and increasingly precarious. Fellow online news site, *The Nut Graph*, closed its metaphorical doors at the end of July 2014 after six years of "making sense of politics and popular culture" (Surin 2014). Additionally, competitor news portal *FZ Daily*'s print permit was approved, deferred and revoked within a few months despite winning the right to judicial review like Malaysiakini (2014b). At the same time even the most established mastheads like the *New York Times* are contemplating an end to their print versions and retreating behind pay-walls (O'Dell 2010). The Malaysian press industry is also far from thriving with the circulation of flagship papers across Malay, English, Chinese and Tamil falling consistently from year to year (2014f, 2012b). All of which makes Malaysiakini's intention to add print to its digital editions a remarkable step.

Started in 1999, Malaysiakini remains staunchly independent in a country where mainstream news sources have been co-opted (George 2006). It first applied for press accreditation in 2000 in order to gain entry to government press briefings, ministerial and official functions (Pang 2006, 87). The news portal's continued viability as a source of autonomous views despite the lack of press accreditation is an eloquent rebuttal to the imagined dangers of veering from the developmental media model. As an example of how independent media can operate, Malaysiakini's endurance is not lost on others. The rejection of developmental media is palpable in journalist Eric Loo's clarion call to fellow activists at the Red Pencil protests for media freedom (cited in Palatino 2014):

> Let's refuse to buy their interpretation of political realities, their version of history. It's time we tell our own stories and circulate online what we know to be true, stories that reflect today's political realities than those framed by the mainstream media.

Malaysiakini's application for a print permit spans the PPPA's pre- and post-2012 updates and its success at judicial review marks an important point in media legislation. Unlike with *FZ Daily*, there has been no final revocation. It is not difficult to understand there is more at stake. Due to Malaysiakini's status as a flagship of alternative media its challenges, triumphs and defeats are matters of significance to those concerned at the nation's record of media freedom, which in 2013 was 64 out of 100 (2014d). Should the current developmental media model continue into future or can *budaya selasa* (the culture of comfort) (Khoo 2010, 145) be sufficiently and peacefully disrupted for Malaysia to embrace a different vision? Beyond its narrow fate, Malaysiakini's fight is a much-awaited sign for Malaysians who are keen to see if the founders, Gan and Chandran, were indeed right when they declared Malaysia to be "entering a new era of nation-building" (George 2006, 172).

Who writes the nation-state?

It is important to understand that by the time the idea of nation formation came about the two other significations of race and religion had already come to dominate how Malaysian society understood itself. As a center of trade in the region, people of various faiths and creeds ranging from animism, Hinduism, Islam, Buddhism and Christianity had already made their way to Malaysia (Andaya and Andaya 2001, 18). Hence religion as a means of distinguishing between groups of people predated the nineteenth-century colonial period. The same might be said of the idea of race, which had, amongst others, nebulous thirteenth-century indigenous origins (Winstedt 1966, 16). According to Reid (2009), for example, the earliest known usage of the term *Melayu* (Malay) was to identify a line of kings, style of language and manners originating in Malacca. The Chinese, who arrived in waves to seek employment and trade, were also used to identifying, arranging and offering support to their compatriots based on regional and linguistic distinctions (Pan 1999, 172–173). Victorian understandings filtered through into Malaysian society and hardened race and religion into categories of enumerative and administrative organization in the interest of "racialised capitalism" (Noor 2009, 83).

The Malays were singled out as a community whose ways of being were under threat from the encroachment of the more aggressive races such as the Chinese and, therefore, in need of protection (Harper 1999, 228). Laws such as the *Malay Reservation Land Act 1913* reified this understanding, enacted as they were, to "protect the sovereign rights and interests of the Malays, particularly from disposing their lands to non-Malays" in Pahang, Perak, Negeri Sembilan and Selangor (Ariffin 2013, 1). This belief in the vulnerability of the Malays became further embedded when the Yang di-Pertuan Agong (King) was entrusted with the responsibility to protect the rights of the Malays alongside those of natives of Sabah and Sarawak in Article 152 of the Constitution of Malaysia (2006, 145). Defined in the Constitution as persons who profess "the religion of Islam, habitually speak the Malay language and conform to Malay custom among other things" (2006, 153), the special position of the Malays separates them from the rest of the population to this day.

It was to a social imaginary preformed of ethno-religious communities that the Westphalian model of the nation was brought into Malaysia and the broader Southeast Asian region (Turner 2007, 408). At about the time of Malaysia gaining independence from Britain to become a nation in its own right not only was broadcasting technology in its infancy, the realities of life in the peninsula were also rather grim. In the period of 1957–1958 the overall Gini coefficient for Peninsular Malaysia was 0.412 and conditions were worse in the urban rather than rural areas (Snodgrass, cited in 1998a, 6). Collectively, the Malays had the lowest household income at 134 Ringgit Malaysia (RM) compared to 288RM for the Chinese and 228RM for the Indians (ibid). Practiced in running along lines established during the colonial era, Malaysia's foundational narrative came to be as a nation consisting of multiple ethno-religious groups with competing interests whose tensions the state must contain. In time this view extended to the order of life in Malaysia from the everyday matters of education to the issue of political affiliations.

The narrative of a composite nation on the edge of fragmentation received emphatic confirmation in 1969 when riots arose out of frustrations over socio-economic disparities (Heng 1997). The income disparity ratio between the Malay and Chinese communities in 1970 was 2.3, having worsened from 2.1 in 1957 (Hashim 1998, 6). The National Economic Plan (NEP) formulated in response to the 1969 tensions was framed as restoration of national unity through the expansion of "Malay participation in the modern commercial and industrial sectors" but it also did much to ingrain the need to pacify and safeguard the interests of the Malay majority into the social imaginary (Anand 1983, 9). Faced with the extant socio-political frictions and dominant view of Malaysia as "a society precariously balanced on the razor's edge, where one false or even true word can lead to calamity" (Mahathir, cited in Atkins 2013, 50), it is small wonder that nation-building in the form of maintaining the status quo and downplaying dissent became a major part of the mainstream media's agenda. Conversely, to express an alternative point-of-view of the nation or question the position of the government on issues of race and religion was provocative and tantamount to incitement.

Even so, it is as well to remember that viewpoints contesting those broadcasted over mainstream media were never entirely silenced and did exist before the introduction of the Internet. Stalwarts of Malaysian civil society like *Aliran* (short for *Aliran Kesedaran Negara*, National Consciousness Movement) started in 1977 and SUARAM (*Suara Rakyat Malaysia*, Voice of the Malaysian People), have been espousing such for decades through small-run print publications like *Aliran Monthly* and annual ones like the *Malaysian Human Rights Report* (2012a; 2010). Others include the *Harakah Daily* (owned by the Pan-Islamic Malaysia Party, PAS) and *The Rocket*, owned by the DAP or Democratic Action Party (Sani 2009, 63). What these alternate voices did not enjoy, due to the mix of a lack of funds and mainstream media structure and costs, were the mass exposure, multiplicity of voices and popular support now facilitated by new media.

The foment around the 1998 ousting from office and wrongful imprisonment of then Deputy Prime Minister, Anwar Ibrahim, is usually credited as the catalyst of online dissent in Malaysia (Vee 2011, 43). It is certainly the case that witnessing the dramatic unfolding of *Reformasi* that ensued, helped Malaysiakini co-founders to appreciate the potential of new media for the expression of independent views (George 2006, 161). In recent times, there have been instances where the incongruity between what was imagined of Malaysia as a nation in the 1960s to 1970s failed to accord with contemporary experiences of Malaysia. The plight of Lina Joy who tried and failed to get the authorities to recognize her conversion from Islam to Christianity is one of those cases that inadvertently asked what a re-imagining of Malaysia as a nation might be (Kortteinen 2008). Other occasions include the 2008 General Elections that denied the ruling *Barisan Nasional* (BN, National Front) coalition its accustomed two-third parliamentary majority and the mass repeat rallies organized under the banner of *Bersih* (clean) in the pursuit of electoral reform in 2007, 2011, 2012 and 2013 (Weiss 2014, 875–6). Due to their historical enmeshment, there remains great difficulty untangling talk of race from religion and discussions on what makes Malaysia a nation. Nonetheless, a vibrant civil society that enjoys an "intimate and multifaceted relationship" with a censorship-free Internet (Vee, 2011, 50) has allowed the freedom of expression ideal to gain a foothold in Malaysian society. This has gradually shifted Malaysians' conditioned reluctance to freely and openly discussing matters that concern these intertwined significations in public and privately. Other developments within and surrounding the nation have contributed to this change.

Malaysia today has an overwhelming young population, with over 73 percent between the ages of 15–39 years in 2013 (2013d). Of these the band between the ages of 20 to 24 years are not only the heaviest users of new media at 21.4 percent (2014a, 12), they also form the largest group of mobile phone owners (2012d, 10). In 2012, 18.6 million or 63.8 percent of the population were Internet users (2013b, 8). Household Internet usage is predominantly urban (75.8 percent in 2012) and broadband penetration moderate at 23.5 percent. Two-thirds of Malaysia's Internet users access the Internet via laptops and more do so from their homes than anywhere else (2013b, 19). Malaysians are also avid users of social media, sending no less than 14 million tweets by February 2014 via its 760,000 active Twitter users (2014h). Over 84 percent of Malaysian Internet users also have a Facebook account (2013b, 19).

The young, tech-attuned population of new media users is also an important, vocal and influential voter base. The resultant diversity of voices given freedom of expression online has resulted in local satire programs like *That Effing Show*, news portals like *The Malaysian Insider*[4] and a thriving blogsphere that includes blogs hypercritical of the government like Raja Petra Kamaruddin's Free Malaysia Today and dozens by politicians such as Tony Pua[5] and Anwar Ibrahim.[6] Individual citizens can now also offer their opinion on all kinds of matters via sections like 'Letters to the Editors' and comments on blogs, online news portals and articles. Though the quality and tone of these individual views are not always cordial or constructive, the fact that they are shared and open to public view online is important for it illustrates that the ideology that puts prosperity before voice, of development before democracy, no longer dominates. The decentralized, distributed and open nature of new media production is one reason for that rearrangement of priorities. The availability and volume of divergent views is another. Media forms facilitated by the Internet brought in an era of many-to-many communication that displaces two out of the three factors that need to be in place for the developmental media model to continue its functioning.

Equally, as Vee (2011) observes, the government has been working to build its new media competencies. This is especially since the ruling BN coalition deems the opposition's gains in the 2008 election to be in large part due to their proficiency in and voice through new media (2008). Deprived of proper access to mainstream media, the opposition coalition PR (*Pakatan Rakyat*, People's Alliance) had compensated with a reported 7,500 online websites and blogs (2011a, 325), a factor that seemingly worked in their favor. Additionally, the government is employing more sophisticated tactics in the online battle for public opinion, switching from the linear, unidirectional and top-down forms of control used in the past such as DNS (domain name system) blocking and non-linear "counterinformation strategies where the state is an active player competing for online reader attention" (Vee 2011, 56). Prime Minister Najib Razak's Twitter account, for example, is by far the most popular in the nation with 1.93 million followers (2014g). In 2012, he even started a Facebook account using the name 'Ah Jib Gor' (Brother Najib) to reach out to the Malaysian Chinese (2012e). This is a marked improvement on early failures to understand the basic differences between multifaceted and multichannel new media and streamlined broadcast media that saw the Information Minister in 1995 announce an official Malaysia page on the Internet in the mistaken belief that that would suffice as a single conduit of information about the nation (Atkins 2013, 326). Still, old habits die hard and the temptation to use tried and tested methods to silence unwanted criticism won through when Prime Minister Najib Razak filed suit against Malaysiakini for defamation (2014e).

There is one obvious answer to why Malaysiakini seeks a press permit. Accreditation and access to official and/or government briefings is the privilege of licensed media holders. Without the permit, Malaysiakini is denied official recognition as a media outlet by the government. This hampers the news portal's day-to-day function but it is, as I have argued, not the only reason for the repeated and tenacious applications for a press permit. The fact that a full quarter of Malaysia's 29.3 million population are not Internet users (2013b) and three-quarters of mobile phone owners still use feature rather than smart phones (2012d, 17) means there is also a sizeable readership who might be reached via mainstream media. There are also broader issues and consequences to do with who writes the nation-state here. Before the recent developments described above, there would have been little doubt that it is the government of the day with the help of an acquiescent mainstream media who does so. Now, with Malaysians fast acquiring and practicing the "habits of critique, engagement and mobilization" (Leong 2014, 126), the answers to this question are now far less certain, more flexible and irredeemably contestable.

Conclusion

Implemented in the Mahathir era, Vision (*Wawasan*) 2020 is among the most ambitious of national development policies that Malaysia has seen (Mahathir 1991). First aired in 1991, it was the platform from which Malaysia's longest serving Prime Minister, Mohamad Mahathir, breathed life into many aspirations that still resonate with the nation today. One such notion is that of *Bangsa Malaysia* (Malaysian race)[7] who make up "a united Malaysian nation with a sense of common and shared destiny . . . [one] at peace with itself, territorially, and ethnically integrated, living in harmony and full and fair partnership" which was but briefly mentioned and has yet become amongst the most powerful and enduring parts of the grand vision (Mahathir 1991). Others, such as the liberalization of the Malaysian economy and the Multimedia Super Corridor (MSC), were acted upon and came to spawn unintended outcomes.

The one unintended consequence that has preoccupied this chapter is the space for alternative views on nation-building that new media has opened up. There are those who read the current media situation in Malaysia as one where there is "a hardening of a ruling power intent on surviving as an electoral authoritarian regime, rather than pursuing a swift transition to democracy through an acceptance of media liberation" (Tapsell 2013, 631). I am with Khoo (2014), who sees it as the evidence of a dialogue within the populace as well as between the citizenry and government, whereby Malaysians are enacting "constitutional patriotism" after their own lights on the way to becoming truly *Bangsa Malaysia*.

Notes

1 See http://www.mscmalaysia.my/blogs
2 Singapore also approached early nationhood with a multiethnic makeup and has made much the same argument with regards to media regulation and control with different levels of success (Lee 2010).
3 Originally published at http://www.theheat.com.my, the publication is now available at http://theheatonline.asia/
4 http://www.themalaysianinsider.com and http://www.popteevee.net/that-effing-show/
5 http://tonypua.blogspot.com.au/
6 http://anwaribrahimblog.com/
7 As Gabriel (2011) explains, there is no direct and clear English expression for the term, which is why it remains controversial and deeply contested. Malaysian race is one translation.

References

(1996) 'Bill to ensure best deal for investors'. Available at: http://global.factiva.com.dbgw.lis.curtin.edu.au/ha/default.aspx (Accessed November 29, 2012).

(2006) 'Laws of Malaysia: Federal Constitution'. Available at: http://www.agc.gov.my/images/Personalisation/Buss/pdf/Federal%20Consti%20(BI%20text).pdf (Accessed August 26, 2014).

(2008) 'How BN lost the media war'. Available at: http://global.factiva.com.dbgw.lis.curtin.edu.au/ha/default.aspx (Accessed June 21, 2008).

(2010) 'Suaram 20 years'. Available at: http://www.youtube.com/watch?v=KO4RwDEUwz4&feature=plcp (Accessed September 11, 2012).

(2011a) 'Country profile: Malaysia', in Deibert, R., Palfrey, J., Rohozinski, R. and Zittrain, J. (eds) *Access Contested: Security, Identity, and Resistance in Asian Cyberspace*. Available at: http://access.opennet.net/contested/country-profiles/ (Accessed August 12, 2014).

(2011b) 'Najib announces repeal of ISA'. Available at: http://www.malaysiakini.com/news/175949 (Accessed September 21, 2011).

(2011c) 'Nazri uses May 13 riots to justify street protest ban'. Available at: http://www.malaysiakini.com/news/183222 (Accessed December 5, 2011).

(2012a) 'About us'. Available at: http://aliran.com/about-us (Accessed December 9, 2012).

(2012b) 'Circulation figures, newspapers – West Malaysia publications'. Available at: http://abcm.org.my/reports/2011/ABC-Circulation-Returns-Jul-to-Dec-2011-PENINSULAR.pdf (Accessed August 26, 2014).

(2012c) 'End to Malaysia's ISA'. Available at: http://news.asiaone.com/News/AsiaOne%2BNews/Malaysia/Story/A1Story20120422-341230.html (Accessed December 12, 2012).

(2012d) 'Hand phone users survey 2012'. Available at: http://www.skmm.gov.my/skmmgovmy/media/General/pdf/130717_HPUS2012.pdf (Accessed August 12, 2014).

(2012e) 'Now, Najib has Chinese Facebook "Ah Jib Gor"'. Available at: http://www.1malaysia.com.my/news_archive/now-najib-has-chinese-facebook-ah-jib-gor/ (Accessed August 21, 2014).

(2013a) 'Heat-ing up the Malaysian media scene'. Available at: http://www.theantdaily.com/Main/Heat-ing-up-the-Malaysian-media-scene (Accessed January 21, 2015).

(2013b) *Internet Users Survey 2012*'. Available at: http://www.skmm.gov.my/skmmgovmy/media/General/pdf/InternetUsersSurvey2012.pdf (Accessed August 15, 2014).

(2013c) 'Malaysia court rules critical news portal can go to print'. Available at: http://news.asiaone.com/news/malaysia/malaysia-court-rules-critical-news-portal-can-go-print (Accessed December 9, 2013).

(2013d) 'Table 8.1.4n: Population by age group, sex and ethnic group, 2013, Malaysia'. Available at: http://mysidc.statistics.gov.my/index.php?lang=en# (Accessed August 15, 2014).

(2014a) 'Communications & multimedia: pocket book of statistics Q1 2014'. Available at: http://www.skmm.gov.my/skmmgovmy/media/General/pdf/Q1_2014C-MPocket.pdf (Accessed August 15, 2014).

(2014b) 'Home Ministry makes about-turn on publishing permit for FZ Daily'. Available at: http://www.themalaysianinsider.com/malaysia/article/home-ministry-makes-about-turn-on-publishing-permit-for-fz-daily (Accessed August 20, 2014).

(2014c) 'Introducing our Alliance'. Available at: http://igarworldwide.com/ (Accessed January 21, 2015).

(2014d) 'Malaysia: Freedom of the press 2013'. Available at: http://www.freedomhouse.org/report/freedom-press/2013/malaysia - .U_Vwt8e-GFw (Accessed August 21, 2014).

(2014e) 'Malaysia: Premier threatens outspoken website'. Available at: http://www.hrw.org/news/2014/05/28/malaysia-premier-threatens-outspoken-website (Accessed August 12, 2014).

(2014f) 'NSTP papers see massive plunge in circulation after GE13'. Available at: http://www.themalaysianinsider.com/malaysia/article/nstp-papers-see-massive-plunge-in-circulation-after-ge13 (Accessed August 12, 2014).

(2014g) 'Twitter users trend in Malaysia 2014'. Available at: http://blog.zocialinc.com/en/twitter-trend-malaysia-2014/ (Accessed August 19, 2014).

Anand, S. (1983) *Inequality and Poverty in Malaysia: Measurement and Decomposition*, Washington: The World Bank.

Andaya, B.W. and Andaya, L.Y. (2001) *A History of Malaysia*, Basingstoke: Palgrave.

Ariffin, S.M. (2013) 'Malay reservation land—unleashing a century of trust', *International Surveying Research Journal*, 3: 1–28.

Atkins, W. (2013) *The Politics of Southeast Asia's New Media*, Hoboken: Taylor and Francis.

Boo, S.-L. (2013) 'After The Heat freeze, Malaysian bar calls for PPPA repeal'. Available at: http://www.themalaymailonline.com/malaysia/article/after-the-heat-freeze-malaysian-bar-calls-for-pppa-repeal-sthash.V1qudpkW.dpuf (Accessed August 19, 2014).

Gabriel, S.P. (2011) 'Translating Bangsa Malaysia', *Critical Asian Studies*, 43: 349–372.

Gangopadhyay, A. and Ng, J. (2013) 'Newspaper suspended after report on Malaysian leader's spending'. Available at: http://online.wsj.com/news/articles/SB10001424052702304773104579270223088723530 (Accessed August 19, 2014).

George, C. (2006) *Contentious Journalism and the Internet*, Singapore: Singapore University Press.

Harper, T.N. (1999) *The End of Empire and the Making of Malaya*, New York: Cambridge University Press.

Hashim, S.M. (1998) *Income Inequality and Poverty in Malaysia*, Lanham: Rowman and Littlefield.

Heng, P.H. (1997) 'The new economic policy and the Chinese community in peninsular Malaysia', *The Developing Economics*, XXXV: 262–292.

Khoo, G.C. (2010) 'Through our own eyes'. In Yeoh, G.S. (ed.) *Media, Culture and Society in Malaysia*, Abingdon: Routledge.

Khoo, G.C. (2014) 'The rise of constitutional patriotism in Malaysian civil society', *Asian Studies Review*, 38: 325–344.

Kortteinen, T. (2008) 'Islamic resurgence and the ethnicization of the Malaysian state: the case of Lina Joy', *Sojourn: Journal of Social Issues in Southeast Asia*, 23: 216–233.

Lee, T. (2010) *The Media, Cultural Control and Government in Singapore*, Abingdon: Routledge.

Leong, S. (2014) *New Media and the Nation in Malaysia: Malaysianet*, London: Routledge.

Mageswari, M. (2013) 'Malaysiakini to apply for newspaper permit again, says lawyer'. Available at: http://www.thestar.com.my/News/Nation/2013/12/03/Malaysiakini-to-push-for-paper-permit.aspx (Accessed December 9, 2013).

Mahahtir, M. (1991) 'Vision 2020: the way forward'. Available at: http://unpan1.un.org/intradoc/groups/public/documents/APCITY/UNPAN003223.pdf (Accessed April 17, 2007).

Mayberry, K. (2012) 'Malaysian website tests press freedom limits'. Available at: http://www.aljazeera.com/indepth/features/2012/10/2012102912444985435.html (Accessed August 12, 2014).

Ng, E. (2014) 'Putrajaya lifts suspension on the Heat'. Available at: http://www.themalaysianinsider.com/malaysia/article/putrajaya-lifts-suspension-on-the-heat (Accessed August 19, 2014).

Noor, F.A. (2009). *What Your Teacher Didn't Tell You: The Annexe Lectures*, Petaling Jaya: Matahari.

O'Dell, J. (2010) 'New York Times will go out of "print" sometime in the future'. Available at: http://mashable.com/2010/09/08/nytimes-print/ (Accessed December 9, 2013).

Palatino, M. (2014) '"Red pencil protest" demands media freedom in Malaysia'. Available at: http://advocacy.globalvoicesonline.org/2014/01/14/red-pencil-protest-demands-media-freedom-in-malaysia/ (Accessed August 13, 2014).

Pan, L. (1999) *The Encyclopedia of the Chinese Overseas*, Cambridge, MA: Harvard University Press.

Pang, A. (2006) 'Managing news in a managed media: mediating the message in Malaysianini', *Asia Pacific Media Educator*: 71–95.

Reid, A. (2009) *Imperial Alchemy: Nationalism and Political Identity in Southeast Asia,* Leiden: Cambridge University Press.

Reinert, E.S. (2010) 'Developmentalism', *Working Papers in Technology Governance and Economic Dynamics,* Tallinn: The Other Canon Foundation.

Sani, M.A.M. (2009) *The Public Sphere and Media Politics in Malaysia,* Newcastle upon Tyne: Cambridge Scholars.

Sani, M.A.M. (2010) 'Constitutional and legislation practices in protecting ethnic relations in Malaysia: restrict hate speech, not legitimate political speech', in Sani, M.A.M., Nakamura, R. and Shamsuddin, T.L. (eds) *Dynamic of Ethnic Relations in Southeast Asia,* Newcastle upon Tyne: Cambridge Scholars.

Surin, J.A. (2014) 'The Nut Graph stops publication'. Available at: http://www.thenutgraph.com/the-nut-graph-stops-publication/comment-26967 (Accessed August 20, 2014).

Sussman, L.R. (1976) 'Developmental journalism', *Quadrant,* November edn.

Tapsell, R. (2013) 'The media freedom movement in Malaysia and the electoral authoritarian regime', *Journal of Contemporary Asia,* 43: 613–635.

Turner, B.S. (2007) 'Islam, religious revival and the sovereign state', *The Muslim World,* 97: 405–418.

Vee, V.T. (2011) 'The struggle for digital freedom of speech: the Malaysian sociopolitical blogsphere's experience', in Deibert, R., Palfrey, J., Rohozinski, R. and Zittrain, J. (eds) *Access Contested: Security, Identity, and Resistance in Asian Cyberspace.* Available at: http://access.opennet.net/wp-content/uploads/2011/12/accesscontested-chapter-03.pdf (Accessed August 12, 2014).

Wallerstein, I. (2005) 'After developmentalism and gloablization, what?', *Social Forces,* 83: 1263–1278.

Weiss, M.L. (2013) 'Parsing the Power of "New Media" in Malaysia', *Journal of Contemporary Asia,* 43: 591–612.

Weiss, M.L. (2014) 'Of inequality and irritation: new agendas and activism in Malaysia and Singapore', *Democratization,* 21: 867–887.

Whiting, A. (2011) 'Malaysia – Assembling the Peaceful Assembly Act'. Available at: http://asiapacific.anu.edu.au/newmandala/2011/12/06/malaysia-assembling-the-peaceful-assembly-act/ (Accessed December 13, 2012).

Whiting, A. and Majoribanks, T. (2013) 'Media professionals' perceptions of defamation and other constraints upon news reporting in Malaysia and Singapore'. In Kenyon, A.T., Majoribanks, T. and Whiting, A. (eds) *Democracy, Media and Law in Malaysia and Singapore,* Abingdon: Taylor and Francis.

Winstedt, R. (1966) *Malaya and its History,* London: Hutchinson University Library.

Part III
Intimate publics, screen and haptic cultures

Part III

14

Chinese social media, "publicness" and one-party rule

Gloria Davies

How should we understand the changes brought to China by digital technology and online communications? In what ways does the spectacle of Chinese "netizens" speaking back to "the Party" on social media distract us from seeing the Party's increasing mastery and command of the mainland cybersphere? Can public culture flourish under one-party rule? These are questions that have and continue to frame a significant debate in the media and scholarship (e.g., Davies 2012; Sullivan 2014; Xiao 2011; Yang 2013).

There is no doubt that the Internet and social media are powerful tools of change. Examples abound of Chinese "netizens" (*wangmin*) using the technology, first of bulletin board systems (since 1999), then blogs (from 2002) and later microblogs (especially after 2009), to defy state censorship, expose corruption, organize civic action and protest for a wide range of causes. The state organization China Internet Network Information Center (CNNIC) reported in January 2014 that Internet penetration in China at the end of 2013 had reached a whopping 45.8 percent, with a total of 618 million Internet users, of which at least 500 million were mobile users. With rapidly increasing participation levels, public culture in China has grown more diverse and contentious. But censorship and propaganda have also become more methodical and sophisticated to match.

The Chinese Communist Party (CCP) remains firmly in power. With the exception of Xinjiang and Tibet where independence movements have been brutally purged, in China today, and despite an abundance of everyday complaints online, there is little serious opposition to party-state rule. People who actively campaign for human rights are very few, numbering in the few hundreds, while those who actually call for democracy, such as the 2010 Nobel Peace Laureate Liu Xiaobo currently serving an eleven-year jail sentence, are even rarer. Nonetheless this tiny minority of individuals are subjected to constant policing and frequent episodes of harassment and detention (Pils 2014). In stark contrast, Party membership has risen rapidly in recent decades. Official sources report that Party membership stood at 85.13 million at the end of 2012 and, of this number, 3.23 million were new members admitted as late as 2012 (Xinhua News 2013).

As an opening gambit, let me suggest that as people's lives become increasingly mediated by screen-based and keyboard actions, "the threshold between *here* (*analogue, carbon-based, off-line*) and *there* (*digital, silicon-based, online*)" will continue to fade (Floridi 2010, 16). This blurring both reflects and affects how humans conduct themselves and relate to one another in an increasingly cyber-mediated world. The only certainty is that, for good or ill, this change will accelerate and precisely because it is unprecedented, its consequences will only rarely be anticipated, if at all.

Freedom and affordance

To properly understand the history and uses of social media in China, we must first consider the interdependence of freedom and technology. In a democracy characterized by the rule of law, people assume freedom as their natural right. They assume the right to act, speak, think, write and associate with others as they choose—that the state's right to intervene must be confined to situations that pose a serious risk of harm or constitute a threat to public safety and national security. Consequently, any perceived expansion of the state's right to intervene is controversial, receives extensive coverage and generates heated public debate as happened in the United States in the months following Edward Snowden's June 2013 revelations of the National Security Agency (NSA) collecting private information via emails, Skype and other chat platforms and social networking sites without a warrant.

However, in China, where the Communist government conceives and describes itself as a centralized democracy, the state accords itself the right to intervene into the lives of citizens and to suppress the media and public debate on their behalf as it sees fit. Hence while under Article 35 of China's Constitution, citizens are granted "freedom of speech, publication, assembly, association, procession and demonstration," and under Article 41, the "right to criticize and make suggestions regarding any state organ or functionary," these provisions are firmly checked by Article 105 which gives the government extremely broad powers to monitor, detain, and jail persons suspected of "incit[ing] others by spreading rumours or slanders or any other means to subvert the State power or overthrow the socialist system" (HRIC 2010).

In the pre-Internet era, the Chinese government's censorship capabilities were indeed formidable. Since then however, and notwithstanding hefty investments in censorship tools and an extensive dedicated Internet police force, it has yet to become able to bring online communications effectively, let alone fully, under its control. A particular source of state anxiety has been the organization of street protests and crowd support for local causes (called "collective strolls" in Chinese) via mobile and social media technology. The street march in Xiamen on June 1, 2007 against the construction of a chemical plant, which news reports estimated as involving between 8,000 and 10,000 protestors, is commonly cited as the first online-facilitated massive demonstration of this kind. Organized via mobile SMS, BBS and blog posts, the Xiamen march attracted international media attention and inspired similar protests across China in subsequent years. These protests, mostly confined to a specific local cause, do not develop into broader demands for political reform. The prominent activist-scholar Yu Jianrong observed that rural and urban protestors are concerned primarily with protecting their livelihoods and financial interests, "not about starting a revolution" (Yu 2009).

Because Chinese citizens voice their concerns in unprecedented numbers on social media, the state has sought to assure them that it is, of course, only looking after their interests:

> Increasingly, officials at all levels are making a conspicuous show of their receptiveness to online public opinion. They publicize their chats with Netizens. Government agencies have opened up Web sites for citizens' petitions. Law enforcement officers have started inviting Netizens to provide information for their criminal investigations.
>
> *(Shirk 2011, 18–19)*

Freedom is contingent on affordance—the range of applications and uses to which a technology can be put. Affordance cuts both ways: the technology that facilitates free speech and popular contention is continually matched by technology that strengthens the state's capacity for policing and surveillance. As the well-known blogger and journalist Michael Anti observed in 2012:

> You can't use Weibo [microblogging] to organize a social movement because as soon as you use the word "gather," the keyword would get picked up and the warning would be sent to the local police station. So even before you gather at the restaurant, you'll already have the police there. I call it Censorship 2.0.
>
> *(Magistad 2012)*

Moreover, it is not simply that technology "frees" and "unfrees" depending on how it is used. More fundamentally, affordance redefines freedom. If we extend freedom to include one's right to privacy—freedom from unwanted publicity and effective control over access to one's personal information—the findings of media scholars indicate a growing acceptance of the intrusions enabled by technology. Sherry Turkle writes:

> If you relinquish your privacy on MySpace or Facebook about everything from your musical preferences to your sexual hang-ups, you are less likely to be troubled by an anonymous government agency knowing whom you call or what websites you frequent. Some are even gratified by a certain public exposure; it feels like validation, not violation.
>
> *(2011: 263)*

In China where government intrusions are a fact of life, citizens are less concerned about defending their privacy than the public's right to know. In democratic societies, there is significant public interest in the "right to be forgotten," a proposition covering situations from the evident right to demand suppression of false information about oneself to the problematic claim that one should have the right to block true information about one's past that may damage one's reputation in the present. The "right to be forgotten" can work against the "right to know." In China, the "right to be forgotten" has yet to gain traction. Chinese Internet users remain far more interested in advancing freedom of information.

The demand for information in China is mostly uncontroversial as most people use the Internet, mobile and social media technology to shop, chat and socialize, to follow their favourite celebrities and to access information ranging from the daily news, entertainment and sports, through market and stock market information, to tabloid and technology news. Official figures for 2012 indicate that 242 million people in China bought goods online. By 2013, the number had increased to 302 million, with retail sales totaling 1.85 trillion yuan (US$296.57 billion) (People's Daily Online 2014). Social media play an increasingly important role in China's e-commerce and in facilitating consumer freedom and the consumer's right to know. 2013 statistics indicate that "forty percent of China's online shoppers read and post reviews about products—more than double the number in the US" (cited in KPMG 2014).

Since 2013, China's policy makers have highlighted the need to develop the nation's big data capabilities across state and non-state sectors. On this point, the impressive array of open data on Internet usage in China attests to improved public access to information. For instance, CNNIC's November 2013 report on China's two leading social media vehicles, Weibo and WeChat (Weixin), reveals that of Weibo's 129 million active users, 64.6 percent accessed the platform after meals, 61.8 percent before sleep, 39.2 percent at work or study, and 38.4 percent while commuting. For the even more popular WeChat (with active users at 355 million in late 2013), the top activities were: texting (91.8 percent); voice messaging (90.4 percent); use of "moments" (74.5 percent); and group chatting (62.4 percent).

Official open data of this kind forms an important part of the market intelligence that meta-data media consultancies (Chinese and foreign) provide to their clients. CNNIC also uses its data to formulate policies and procedures for Internet use in China. However, CNNIC's relatively benign data work is complemented by the secret operations of various other state agencies involved in controlling, surveilling and producing propaganda for the Internet. Estimates of state-employed online commentators who post in support of the official position on any given topic place them in the hundreds of thousands. They first attracted international notice in the mid- to late 2000s, coinciding with the growth of microblogging, when Chinese netizens began disparaging them as the "Fifty-cent Party" on the rumor that the government (in 2004) paid fifty-cents per comment. The state's censors and commentators are now joined by "Internet public opinion analysts," officially recognized as a profession in China since 2013 because of state-accredited training programs. A widely-relayed article in the *Beijing News*—well-known for its investigative journalism—described the work of these analysts as that of "gathering and studying the views and attitudes of netizens to produce reports for decision-makers" (2013). The article stated that across China's state and non-state sectors, there were already some two million "Internet public opinion analysts."

On data gathering and analysis, we should also note the unusual abundance of "top ten" lists of buzzwords and topics on the Chinese Internet. These lists are the work of Chinese technology companies (in particular of Hudong, which hosts China's largest wiki-site) and they far exceed in number and variety similar types of lists that other countries have compiled of their national online trends. These lists reflect something of a Chinese preoccupation with identifying "national characteristics."

Censorship, however, consistently skews any attempt at identifying national characteristics. One notable instance occurred in February 2011 when the anonymous organizers of China's still-born "Jasmine Movement" called online for weekly street rallies in major Chinese cities to protest against the abuse of state power. In their open letter, posted on websites hosted outside China, they explained they merely sought to express public concern and had no intention of challenging CCP rule. Nonetheless, the Party leadership was so alarmed by this show of disobedience that it launched a nationwide crackdown on dissidence and imposed a blanket ban on all online content containing the word "jasmine." One noted casualty of this punitive search was a video of then Party General Secretary and China's President, Hu Jintao, singing the well-known Chinese folk song "Lovely Jasmine Flower" (Davies 2012, 124).

These tensions between increased openness and tightened control make China's social media environment less predictable than counterpart environments in democratic societies. Moreover, as China's tourism industry grows, online travel tips now frequently include information about blocked access to Facebook, Twitter and YouTube, with visitors being inducted into China's complexly segregated social media environment: luxury hotels in the major cities often provide virtual private networks (VPNs) allowing hotel guests to access a wide range of otherwise blocked websites; people travelling more cheaply must purchase their own portable VPNs.

There are two classes of Internet users in China: a minority who surf the global Internet with relative ease; and the hindered majority who encounter the restricted mainland Internet. The highly mobile nature of digital information ensures that members of the hindered majority can always find new ways of circumventing censorship. Knowing or "following" people on social media with VPN access is important in this regard.

The nexus between freedom and affordance depends on what lengths Internet users will go to access blocked information. It also depends on the ever-shifting balance between the state's encouragement of market freedom (to boost the economy) and the restrictions it imposes on public discussion (to safeguard the party-state system). Rebecca MacKinnon writes that the willingness of Internet companies in China to comply with state censorship has produced a form of "networked authoritarianism." This is a situation where "companies can be used as an opaque extension of state power" because of an onerous legal responsibility for all data posted and relayed on their Internet services.

> If private companies fail to censor and monitor their users to the government's satisfaction, they will lose their business licences and be forced to shut down. All large Internet companies operating in China have entire departments of employees with hundreds of people whose sole job is to police users and censor content around the clock.
>
> *(MacKinnon 2011, 197–198)*

Accordingly, even though "the average person with Internet or mobile access has a much greater sense of freedom—and may even feel like he or she has the ability to speak and be heard," the mainland Internet itself remains customized to the state's requirements.

Blogs and the new "publicness"

What crucially distinguishes authoritarianism from "networked authoritarianism" is that the latter, operating in the digital age, must contend with the volatile forces that the new "publicness" can unleash. Media consultants and scholars use the term "publicness" (e.g. Hjorth and Arnold 2013, 125; Tierny 2013, 37) to highlight the hyper-enhanced nature of social experience in a networked world. This is a world where more and more information about people's (offline) lives finds its way online to become accessible to complete strangers and exploitable by individuals, groups, commercial and state agencies and criminal organizations, where serendipitous remarks and images randomly captured on camera phones can elicit sudden and massive interest, and where (as the global population of Internet users continues to grow) "massive" is now measured in the hundreds of millions or even a billion views.

Every technological improvement in data search, storage and retrieval advances "publicness." Jeff Jarvis, author of the bestselling *What Would Google Do?*, argues that since "publicness" is inevitable, people should seek to maximize their online presence: "The more public you are, the easier you can be found, the more opportunities you have" (Jarvis 2009, 45). But solicited entrepreneurial publicity and unsolicited volatile consequences go together on the Internet. Indeed, the participatory effect of social media is what makes "publicness" unpredictable, and for that reason, compelling.

Social media and China's netizenry appeared and developed together. Two events of August 2002 are frequently noted as inaugurating the use of social media in China: the launch by Internet entrepreneur Isaac Mao of his weblog site, isaac.mao.com; and the founding of BlogChina.com (which became Bokee in 2005) by another entrepreneur, Fang Xingdong. Other blog platforms soon appeared. Initially, blogging attracted limited interest and was pursued mostly by people with advanced Internet literacy. In June 2003, however, one account kept at BlogChina.com—that of then Guangzhou-based journalist Li Li—turned blogging into an overnight sensation (Goldkorn 2013, 327–331). Writing under the moniker Muzi Mei, Li regaled readers of her blog with details of her sexual encounters with different men. Visits to her site soared when she posted on 26 July that her one-night stand with the rock musician Wang Lei was "not so hot." (Zhou 2003).

Muzi Mei showed that with a blog account and a newsworthy story, fame was within anyone's reach. She also showed how easy it was to subject others to unsolicited publicity. This latter facility of social media acquired many uses in subsequent years: from civic-minded exposés of injustice and wrongdoing, through the cyber vigilantism of China's self-styled "human flesh search engines," to defamatory revelations against persons and companies, and opportunistic postings of celebrities, officials and even ordinary people caught *in flagrante delicto*.

A key reason for Muzi Mei's extraordinary publicity was that she did not attract censorship for some five months after first achieving notoriety in June 2003. When the authorities finally denounced her in an editorial published in the influential state-run *Beijing Evening News* on 16 November, her blog had become China's most-visited website. Sina.com, which bought the rights to serialize Muzi Mei's then forthcoming book, credited her with boosting visits to its home page (which had begun featuring interviews with and articles by the author) from twenty to thirty million over a ten-day period in early November 2003. The *Beijing Evening News* editorial thus accused Sina.com of attempting to profit from her immoral conduct. A week later, the government banned her book. Muzi Mei promptly closed down her blog to avoid further state censure (Yardley 2003).

From 2003 to 2007, publicness expanded: China's celebrities set up blogs to maintain and grow their fan base, intellectuals and writers used theirs to publicize their insights and musings while journalists and editors, frustrated by media restrictions in the workplace, wrote the news they preferred as blog posts. Of the last group, Jeremy Goldkorn observes:

> Sometimes their stories would be wiped from the Internet almost as soon as they were published (even then small blog companies had to self-censor if they wanted to stay in business), but there was at least some chance that readers would see and circulate the texts before they disappeared.

> *(2013, 331)*

Blogs also became part of the publicity machine of commercial companies and state organizations and an effective way for NGOs to relay information and receive feedback. For millions of Chinese Internet users, blogging became an everyday activity through which to share personal news and interests and to socialize with friends near and far. A levelling of both high and low, the serious and the trivial gathered pace on the Chinese Internet as the blogging population grew exponentially. In December 2007, William Ding, CEO of NetEase (a leading Internet company established in 1997), noted that registered blog accounts in China had reached 39 million by 2006, representing a 333 percent increase over the number in 2005.

In May 2008, the catastrophic earthquake in Sichuan (with official figures of 69,197 killed, 374,176 injured, and 18,222 missing) highlighted the importance of the Internet for independent media coverage and crowd organization and mobilization. In the earthquake's aftermath, the state-controlled media lagged far behind the depth and range of coverage provided by commercial news websites (of which *Caijing* and *Southern Weekly* were leaders that year), Web portals (of which Sina, NetEase and Sohu were at the fore), together with the posts and live coverage of citizen journalists and cyber-investigators (whose blog accounts were hosted at these and other Web portals). NGO websites, community blogs and online forums played a key part in the coordination of disaster relief efforts and the collection of public donations that reportedly quickly exceeded the state's relief work funds.

Optimism about the impact of social media on government accountability ran high, especially among liberal-minded intellectuals. In May 2009, Li Datong (the eminent Beijing-based journalist whose critical candor cost him his job in 2006 as editor-in-chief of *Freezing Point*, an influential Party publication), declared "Today the state media follow every step of the Internet":

> Traditional media, under stringent control from propaganda officers, are afraid of making mistakes. They have lost the nose for news and can only pick up after the Net. Because of the Net, the Chinese people have never been more active or effective in identifying news and participating in public opinions.
>
> *(Li 2009)*

But anti-foreign fervor in the lead-up to the 2008 Beijing Olympics also revealed the efficiency of social media for spreading hate speech online and offline. The Anti-CNN.com blog founded in March 2008 attracted particular notice with its violent tirades against Western media bias. Its founder Rao Jin, then a Beijing-based graduate student, claimed that the website drew ten million visitors at the peak of its popularity.

By the late 2000s, the immense popularity of Chinese celebrity blogs (in particular that of bestselling author and cultural entrepreneur Han Han) had become a focus of global media interest. December 2009 saw Han Han named as Person of the Year by *Asia Week* magazine. From 2006 to 2009, his blog account, which used bawdy wit to satirize life under party-state rule, drew more than 300 million visitors. Consequently, in *Time* magazine's 2010 poll of the world's 100 most influential people, Han was ranked second (with 873,230 votes), behind the Iranian opposition politician Mir-Hossein Mousavi (at 1,492,879 votes).

Media interest in Han also brought the rhetorical tactics of Chinese public discourse to international notice. Among Chinese netizens, the term "edge ball" refers to the use of coded or oblique language to allude to censored topics. Evan Osnos (2011) wrote that the celebrity author "excelled at 'edge ball'" but that his posts were admired not so much for their originality but because they expressed "what so many others only thought."

Microblogs and the politics of publicness

International publicity for Han Han's blog came at a time when he and other Chinese celebrities were fast migrating to microblogs, in particular to Sina Weibo.[1] In September 2010, Sina Corporation's "White Paper on the Chinese market for Weibo in its inaugural year" showed Sina Weibo as the market leader at 60.9 percent, followed in descending order by rivals NetEase (42.3 percent), Tencent (34.1 percent) and Sohu (23.3 percent) and other companies with even lower stakes. Sina coined the term "Weibo" (hence justifying 2010 as the product's inaugural year) but microblogs had begun in China in 2006 with the Twitter accounts of a cosmopolitan minority. In 2007, several Chinese microblog services were established, of which Fanfou was the most popular. On July 6, 2009, the government shut down all microblogging services in China and blocked Internet access in Urumqi, the capital of Xinjiang, after violent ethnic clashes there between Han Chinese and Uighurs resulted in 156 deaths and more than 1500 arrests. Dru Gladney (July 9, 2009), a specialist on China's Muslim minorities, described the Urumqi riots as "perhaps the world's first 'ethnic pandemic'" spread by social media. As a result Facebook, Twitter and YouTube were blocked in China from this point onwards.

Sina Weibo's successful launch in August 2009 at a time of heightened censorship indicated the company had given the state ample assurances of self-monitoring. By the time other companies set up their Weibo services in January 2010, Sina Weibo was already a household name. As Gady Epstein has observed, Sina Weibo's success owed to it being a "government-trusted sandbox for cynics, celebrities, influential bloggers and media elites" yet also "China's most potent incubator for subversive Internet memes, much to the consternation of bungling local officials across the country" (Epstein 2011).

The 140-character Unicode format of the microblog proved a huge advantage for the Chinese language. As most Chinese characters are meaningful words, significantly more semantic content can appear in a 140-character Chinese post than in its 140-character English counterpart (Benney 2011). Moreover, Weibo's media-rich platform offers a range of functions (such as conversation threading, polling and tracking as well as the inclusion of emoticons, images and videos in posts) that are absent from Twitter. These linguistic and technological advantages enabled Weibo users to post not just "Tweets" but something closer to blog posts. As the artist-activist Ai Weiwei famously wrote on Twitter: "In the Chinese language, 140 characters is a novella" (quoted in Sullivan 2014, 28).

Weibo grew quickly. By December 2011, CNNIC reported 250 million registered users across the different Weibo providers—a 296 percent rise over 2010 figures. CNNIC's December 2012 report drew a distinction between *active* registered users at 309 million and the *total* number of (active and inactive) registered users at more than 500 million. From 2010 through early 2013, Weibo served as the preferred news and social networking source of Chinese Internet users. When Kaiser Kuo, Director of International Communications for China's leading search engine Baidu, was interviewed in August 2012, he remarked that Weibo showed itself capable at times of "driving . . . the entire national dialogue" (quoted in Magistad 2012).

There were indeed times when Weibo enabled a given economic, environmental or social problem to attract massive publicity. Prominent microbloggers known as "big Vs," individuals with verified (V) real-name Weibo accounts with more than a million followers, have played an important role as opinion moulders in this regard. For instance, when Beijing-based real-estate billionaire Pan Shiyi (whose Sina Weibo account had some eight million followers in 2011) called for accurate official data for PM 2.5 (fine particulate matter) pollution readings in several posts in October and November 2011, air quality monitoring (a topic already under discussion) received an enormous boost. When the government announced in January 2012 that Beijing would start releasing PM 2.5 data, Pan's Weibo posts were singled out in media reports as a catalyst for this reform.

Nonetheless, of the tens of millions of Weibo comments posted daily, those expressing public concern (or anger) over the abuse of power, air and food safety, or that discuss hazards, accidents and incidents, make up only a small fraction. Celebrity gossip and scandal posts are far more prevalent. Moreover, since its delayed reaction to the "Muzi Mei phenomenon" in 2003, the government has become significantly more adept at preventive censorship, rewarding companies that exercise "self-discipline" with actual "Awards for Contributions to Self-Discipline in China's Internet Industry" whilst punishing the non-compliant with steep fines and the suspension of commercial licences.

When Liu Xiaobo reflected in 2003 on "the year of Muzi Mei," he noted that because sex sold well and did not threaten the party-state system, an "erotic carnival" flourished on the Chinese Internet and became confused with the idea of freedom. The result was the eclipse and displacement of "ideas about political freedom" by a decadent harking back to "traditions of sexual abandon in China's imperial times" (2012, 173). Liu's point is worth noting when we consider how, as Chinese technology companies have competed to increase revenue and market share, online sexual content has flourished on the mainland Internet.

Sex ads are a prominent feature of mainland Chinese websites, including sites carrying official news and propaganda. The government periodically conducts campaigns against pornography and lewdness but these have been weak and ineffectual in comparison with its extreme crackdowns on political dissent. In April 2014, the government announced a new "Clean the Web" campaign of which Sina became a casualty in May.

The company received hefty penalties for hosting "pornographic and obscene" content: an offence other Internet companies were also guilty but of which Sina was singled out. Commentators speculated that the company was really being punished for its failure to rein in Sina Weibo. These penalties, coinciding with a mass migration of users from Weibo to Tencent's WeChat service starting in mid-2013, contributed to volatile fluctuations in Sina's share price (Clover and Song 2013).

Reflecting on the difficulties of operating in China's Internet market, Kaiser Kuo remarked that companies which succeed did so by being adept at "serving two masters" (Kuo in Magistad 2012). They "need to keep users happy and none of them labours under the illusion that people prefer censored search results." Accordingly, "we are obliged to obey the law in China. And we are also compelled to explore the elasticity of our boundaries" (Kuo in Magistad 2012).

Sina has been keen to comply. In March 2012, the government mandated real-name registration for all Weibo accounts. In May 2012, Sina introduced a points-based system for its Weibo account holders, whereby those found guilty of offences, in particular of spreading false information, would be publicly shamed as having a "low credit" rating. It dutifully implemented the system even as its own Weibo account holders derided the company for cowardice.

"Big V" accounts have been a mixed blessing for China's Weibo providers because the publicity they attract has political consequences. On the one hand, the Weibo accounts of the rich, famous and influential enhance the brand of a given provider. On the other hand, "big Vs" which attract the disapproval of the authorities also implicate the websites on which their posts appear. The party-state's vigilance against the threat of any powerful counter-voice owes not only to its authoritarian rule but also to its awareness of the authority that revered exemplars can command in Chinese society. In the Maoist period, people worshipped Mao and strove to learn from nominated exemplars such as Lei Feng. In the post-Mao decades, Party leaders have sought, without success, to make the Party an object of popular reverence. Instead, under market conditions, it was "successful personages" (*chenggong renshi*) who became the new exemplars. An entire industry of "successology" (*chenggongxue*) has flourished since the 1980s in the form of books, courses, magazines, radio and TV shows and other cultural products (Davies 2010).

Blogs (since 2003) and microblogs (since 2009) that project an aura of direct connection between "big Vs" and their followers further enhances the affective power of these celebrated individuals. Because the government understands public discourse in terms of achieving a "unified calibre" (*tongyi koujing*), it sees "big Vs" who defend intellectual independence as ultimately undermining its authority. The fact that Weibo users so visibly parodied the official discourse from 2010 to 2013 has only increased the government's unease.

In August 2013, the new administration under President Xi Jinping launched a nationwide crackdown on Weibo "rumor-mongering." Numerous arrests were made, of which two attracted particular notice because they were "big Vs": liberal-minded venture capitalists Charles Xue and Wang Gongquan who had used their Weibo accounts to encourage public participation in social causes. Their subsequent humiliation through public confessions proved effective in intimidating other celebrity microbloggers into cautious silence.

In September 2013, the Supreme People's Court and the Supreme People's Procuratorate issued a judicial statement that extended crimes of defamation, creating disturbances, illegal business operations and extortion to include online communications. The state's targets were posts that attracted significant public notice: any communication judged unseemly, and which has been viewed more than 5,000 times or relayed more than 500 times, was now open to prosecution as a criminal act.

These developments, defended as an all-out war on "false information," resulted in departures from Weibo and migrations to Tencent's WeChat platform. CNNIC's January 2014 report (2014, 7) indicated that the total number of registered Weibo users (across different providers) had decreased by almost 28 million, representing a 9 percent decline over the previous year's figures. But the loss to mainland public discourse of its most powerful vehicle to date—an open communication channel—is far greater than 9 percent. Unlike Weibo, WeChat is a messaging system designed primarily for private group communication, with chatrooms normally limited to 40 people. Although WeChat allows the creation of public accounts, it limits them to one post per day (Creemers 2014: 21). These restrictions forestalled the massive followings that "big V" accounts had attracted on Weibo, while enabling discourse on WeChat to be far more easily contained. Nonetheless, as WeChat has grown, censorship has increased, with the government announcing on May 27, 2014, a crackdown to "eliminate malpractice" on the new platform, focused on those "spreading rumours and information relating to violence, terrorism and pornography, as well as those using instant messaging for fraud" (Xinhua News 2014).

Consumerism and entertainment are the beneficiaries of these ongoing forms of state control. The most popular Sina Weibo post on record was set on March 31, 2014 when Beijing actor Wen Zhang (with 52 plus million followers at the time) apologized to his then pregnant actress wife Ma Yili (with 31 plus million followers) for his affair with co-star Yao Di. Figures of "2.5 million comments and 1 million shares in just 10 hours" were soon relayed in media reports. Within only 24 hours Wen's post had been viewed a staggering 180 million times. And Ma's gracious reply which appeared only three minutes after Wen's post: "Cherish what you have at the moment. Being in love is easy, being married is not" attracted 100 million views over the same 24 hour period together with millions of applausive comments and became an instant meme. On April 17, 2014, a post featuring screen shots of Wen's and Ma's Weibo accounts showed their followers had increased by over a million each to 53,192,964 and 33,944,662 respectively in that short time (Sabrina 2014). Publicness, as voyeuristic publicity, enjoys few restrictions on the Mainland.

Note

1 In 2010, Sina ranked Han's Weibo account as the second most popular. The top ranking went to actress Yao Chen, the still reigning "queen of Weibo" whose account began with two million followers and grew to more than 54 million in 2013.

References

Beijing News [Xin jing bao] (2013) 'Wangluo yuqing fenxishi: yao zuode bushi ceshan [Internet public opinion analysts: their work is not to censor]', *Xin jing bao*. Available at: http://epaper.bjnews.com.cn/html/2013-10/03/content_469152.htm?div=-1 (Accessed June 1, 2014).

Benney, J. (2011) 'Editorial Twitter and Legal Activism in China', *Communication, Politics and Culture*, 44(1): 5–20.

Clover, C. and Song, J. (2013) 'China Tightens Censorship on Mobile Messaging Apps', *Financial Times*. Available at: http://www.ft.com/intl/cms/s/0/81075e92-1e00-11e4-ab52-00144feabdc0.html#axzz 3B7AdzyX3 (Accessed October 31, 2013).

CNNIC (2014) 'CNNIC Released the 33rd Statistical Report on Internet Development in China', *CNNIC*. Available at: http://www1.cnnic.cn/AU/MediaC/rdxw/hotnews/201401/t20140117_43849.htm (Accessed June 1, 2014).

Creemers, R. (2014) 'The Privilege of Speech and New Media: Conceptualizing China's Communications Law in the Internet Age', paper presented at the conference *New Media, the Internet and a Changing China*, University of Pennsylvannia, 34 pp.

Davies, D.J. (2010) 'China's Celebrity Entrepreneurs: Business Models for "Success"', in L. Edwards and E. Jeffreys (eds) *Celebrity in China*, Hong Kong: Hong Kong University Press.

Davies, G. (2012) 'Discontent in Digital China', in G.R. Barmé et al. *China Story Yearbook 2012: Red Rising, Red Eclipse*, Canberra: ANU.

Epstein, G. (2011) 'Sina Weibo', *Forbes*. Available at: http://www.forbes.com/global/2011/0314/features-charles-chao-twitter-fanfou-china-sina-weibo.html (Accessed January 1, 2014).

Floridi, L. (2010) *Information: A Very Short Introduction*, Oxford: Oxford University Press.

Goldkorn, J. (2013) 'China's Internet: A Civilising Process'. In G.R. Barmé and J. Goldkorn (eds) *China Story Yearbook 2013: Civilising China*, Canberra: ANU.

Hjorth, L. and Arnold, M. (2013) *Online @AsiaPacific: Mobile, Social and Locative in the Asia–Pacific Region*, Abingdon: Routledge.

HRIC (2010) 'Relevant Chinese Law', *Human Rights in China*. Available at: http://www.hrichina.org/en/content/3204 (Accessed on January 1, 2014).

Jarvis, J. (2009) *What Would Google Do?* New York: HarperCollins.

KPMG (2014) 'E-commerce in China: Driving a New Consumer Culture'. Available at: http://www.kpmg.com/CN/en/IssuesAndInsights/ArticlesPublications/Newsletters/China-360/Documents/China-360-Issue15-201401-E-commerce-in-China.pdf (Accessed June 1, 2014).

Li, D. (2009) 'A Modern End to Media Suppression', *The Guardian*. Available at: http://www.guardian.co.uk/world/2009/may/19/china-new-media (Accessed January 1, 2014).

Liu, X. (2012) *No Enemies, No Hatred*. Cambridge, MA: Harvard University Press.

MacKinnon, R. (2011) 'Corporate Accountability in Networked Asia'. In R. Deibert, et al., *Access Contested: Security, Identity, and Resistance in Asian Cyberspace by the Open Net Initiative*, Cambridge, MA: MIT Press.

Magistad, K. (2012) 'How Weibo Is Changing China', *Yale Global Online*. Available at: http://www.yaleglobal.yale.edu/content/how-weibo-changing-china?utm_source=YaleGlobal+Newsletter&utm_campaign=c2a720c18b-Newsletter9_14_2010&utm_medium=email (Accessed January 1, 2014).

Osnos, E. (2011) 'The Han Dynasty', *The New Yorker*, July issue. Available at: http://www.newyorker.com/magazine/2011/07/04/the-han-dynasty (Accessed 1 January 2014).

People's Daily Online (2014) 'China Now World's Largest Online Retail Market'. Available at: http://english.peopledaily.com.cn/98649/8561698.html (Accessed June 1, 2014).

Pils, E. (2014) *China's Human Rights Lawyers and Contemporary Chinese Law*, Abingdon: Routledge.

Sabrina (2014) 'Weibo Trending Topic Attracted Massive User Discussion', *China Internet Watch*. Available at: http://www.chinainternetwatch.com/7132/weibo-trending-topic-attracted-massive-user-discussion/ (Accessed June 1, 2014).

Shirk, S. (2011) 'Changing Media, Changing China'. In S. Shirk (ed.) *Changing Media, Changing China*, New York: Oxford University Press.

Sullivan, J. (2014) 'China's Weibo: Is Faster Different?' *New Media and Society*, 16(1): 24–37.

Tierny, T. (2013) *The Public Space of Social Media: Connected Cultures of the Network Society*, New York: Routledge.

Turkle, S. (2011) *Alone Together: Why We Expect More from Technology and Less from Each Other*, New York: Basic Books.

Xiao, Q. (2011) 'The Rise of Online Public Opinion and Its Impact'. In S. Shirk (ed.) *Changing Media, Changing China*, New York: Oxford University Press.

Xinhua News (2013) 'China's Communist Party Membership Exceeds 85 Million'. Available at: http://english.cpc.people.com.cn/206972/206974/8305636.html (Accessed January 1, 2014).

Xinhua News (2014) 'China to Clean Up Instant Messaging Services'. Available at: http://news.xinhuanet.com/english/china/2014-05/27/c_133366093.htm (Accessed June 1, 2014).

Yang, G. (2013) *The Power of the Internet in China: Citizen Activism Online*, New York: Columbia University Press.

Yardley, J. (2003) 'Internet Column Thrills and Inflames China,' *New York Times*. Available at: http://www.nytimes.com/2003/11/30/world/internet-sex-column-thrills-and-inflames-china.html (Accessed January 1, 2014).

Yu, J. (2009) 'Maintaining a Baseline of Social Stability', translated transcript. Available at: http://chinastudygroup.net/2010/4/yu-jianrong-on-maintaining-a-baseline-of-social-stability/ (Accessed January 1, 2014).

Zhou, Y. (2003) 'Muzi Mei "yi qing shu" hongdong wangluo shijie" [Muzi Mei's "Ashes of Love" makes waves in the online world]', *Xinhua Net.* Available at: http://news.xinhuanet.com/book/2003-11/14/content_1178974.htm (Accessed January 1, 2014).

15

Complicating connectivity: women's negotiations with smartphones in an Indian slum

Jo Tacchi and Tripta Chandola

The transformational possibilities of smartphones are particularly emphasized in places where there are development needs. Whether framed by international or national development agendas, the link between smart technologies and progress is hard to challenge. Yet we still know little about the actual uses of new technologies by non-elite "invisible users," and their "changing sense of the wider world and their place within it" formulated through their engagement with new technologies (Burrell 2012, 4). The frames and theories through which we place people and their uses can blind us to what is happening in particular contexts with particular people. Slater (2013) describes the "holy trinity" of "new media," "development" and "globalization" as irrefutable organizing frames for our thinking about the future, and yet he shows how they are in fact just one (albeit dominant) story about the future. He urges us to consider such terms and frameworks as "part of the fields we study and act within, to render them as topics rather than resources" (2013, 2). They represent "northern cosmologies" and the beliefs around and classifications of these same terms (or elements within them) from the point of view and experience of "invisible users" often looks different.

Buskens (2010, 19) is similarly concerned with our lack of critical attention to the frameworks we use for constructing knowledge in the field of ICT for development. She suggests that while it is appropriate to focus on recognizing and working to increase the agency of the beneficiaries of development, the agency of those who set the agendas is largely ignored:

> Although their [donors, practitioners, researchers, scholars] agency may be less visible, and definitely under less scrutiny, their frames of mind impact directly the way meaning is made of Southern women's experiences, dreams, and perspectives in the context of human development, poverty, and ICTs.

Tenhunen's (2008, 517) ethnographic study in a village in West Bengal demonstrates how mobile phone users' agency is of interest but this is not the only kind of agency at play, and of importance to our understanding of the place of mobile phones, in this village. The state and multinational companies "play central roles in shaping the mobile market's recent expansion into new regions."

This chapter aims to complicate ideas about the relationship of smartphones to notions of progress and development by describing some of the things that smartphones are to women living in a Delhi slum. Through this description, the broader social, cultural and political contingencies of these women's lives are made visible, as are some dominant public discourses that otherwise crassly represent or conceal them. The media regularly report the expansion of new technologies, subscribers, use and growth of related businesses. On the one hand, new media are linked to the notion of India as a modern, global and influential country; on the other hand, there is also a concern to monitor and restrict new media use by certain groups.

The chapter draws upon ethnographic research in the slum spanning over a decade, from early 2004. It situates the penetration and use of smartphones in the slum within the broader context of the marginalized position that slums represent within the materiality of the city, as well as slum-dwellers' marginalized position as citizens of the city as negotiated through everyday life. Here we present accounts of smartphone use by women to describe how they navigate the dual displacement and violence of gender and marginalization. They are doubly marginalized—first as slum-dwellers and secondly as women. Examining their uses of smartphones goes some way towards making this marginalization visible but also shows their agency within cultural and social structures.

Background

Having located both the site of this research, and the people within it as "marginalized," it is important to state that this is a relative categorization and is itself part of what is under study. In our approach to the ethnographic research reported on here, our site and the people within it are both central and privileged. That is to say, their experience, practices, world views, meaning making, knowledge and beliefs are the focus of our fieldwork and analysis. Rather than attempting to interpret and understand them through frameworks or theories of marginalization or development, we have attempted to use the research to rethink and challenge those theories. The same applies to ideas of new media and technologies, which we aim to decenter in an effort to achieve what Slater (2013, 9) calls "ethical symmetry." This means that the starting point for this discussion of smartphones and what they mean for some women in this slum cluster is an open question regarding what smartphones are and what they mean here in Govindpuri, Delhi.

The slums of Govindpuri in Delhi have been the site of a series of ethnographic studies[1] that we have conducted together and separately since 2004. The slums are made up of three "camps," Nehru, Navjeevan and Bhumhiheen. They were first established in the late 1970s (Basu 1988, 118). The slums of Govindpuri are not a notified slum area, and are therefore, despite their long history, considered to be illegal.[2] Despite this, many of the residents are recognized as citizens of Delhi, and provided with "ration cards." These cards serve to validate their identities, allow access to subsidized food and other household items, and, importantly, establish their claims to "resettlement" when the Govindpuri slums are demolished.

The initial settlers of the camps mostly comprised of migrant groups and laborers from different parts of the country, seeking to improve their opportunities in the city. The lack of infrastructural support and access to basic facilities left "squatting" in unoccupied, barren land as the only available option. Since then multiple generations of some families have grown up in the slums. Even though in the last decades the income levels of the residents have significantly improved, the opportunities available to them to "move out" of the slums remain limited. Living in the slums allows them a certain "standard of living," however limited, which they would not be able to maintain if they shifted into legal settlements, because of the costs of property, rents and other expenses. Moreover, the entitlement to a resettled plot of land in a legal settlement in case of demolition is a very compelling motivation for the residents to continue living in the slums; in fact, for most the promise of this entitlement is the only available recourse towards a "legal, respectable" identity in the city. Alongside the permanent residents of the slums, the camps continue to host a burgeoning, fluid population of migrant laborers arriving in the city to better their opportunities.

In our long-term engagement with Govindpuri, the slums and their technological landscape have undergone significant transformations. We have observed dynamic, constantly evolving technological cultures and practices within the slums. Whilst we focus here on women and smartphones, this is not to "render technical" (Li 2007) the complexity of the social, cultural and political processes in the space. We complicate this by considering smartphones as "active agent[s] in evolving gendered relationships that must be understood within their culturally embedded everyday uses and settings" (Tacchi, Kitner and Crawford 2012, 529).

Growing penetration of mobile phones in India

The combined factors of the *New Economic Policy* (1991) and the subsequent *New Telecoms Policies* (1994, 1997 and *Broadband Policy*, 2004) unleashed unprecedented growth in the telecommunications sector in India (Singhal and Rogers 2001). The government considers the sector "an important tool for socio-economic development for a nation."[3] Prior to 1991 the sector was controlled by government monopoly. The opening up to competition in service provision, and the de-licensing of the manufacturing of telecoms equipment, has led to widespread uptake of mobile connections and the local production of handsets at competitive prices. By 2004, when we began our research, the impacts of these policies were evident. The number of commercial service providers was increasing, more competitive service plans were available, and mobile handsets were becoming more affordable, at least for middle-class, urban Indians. At that time these services still had limited penetration amongst the lower-middle classes and urban poor, including in the slums in Govindpuri.

Today, however, to not have a mobile connection in Govindpuri is regarded as a severe social and economic hindrance. Mobile penetration in India stands at 73 percent, while mobile-internet penetration is 11 percent, but shifting quickly with the availability of low-cost smartphones (Adwitiya 2014). This reflects the availability of increasingly "affordable smart-phones (Rs3,000– Rs10,000/US$50–US$165) designed for the Indian user from indigenous manufacturers such as Micromax, Karbonn, etc., as well as increasingly low-cost data connectivity options more people are shifting to smartphones and mobile Internet" (Adwitiya 2014). Most households in Govindpuri have at least one mobile handset and it is common practice for a handset to have more than one connection (multiple SIM cards).

Indeed it is difficult to visit Govindpuri and not have a conversation about smartphones. The brand, the model and its capabilities are often discussed at length, and considered a status symbol. Once, when Chandola visited after spending a few months in Australia, she was asked to "show" her mobile phone to the group of men, women and children who were inquiring after her trip. When they discovered that she was not using a smartphone, but a very basic mobile phone model, the group was dismayed. They questioned whether she could be "doing well for herself?" Smartphones are increasingly popular amongst the youth finding less favor amongst older people who continue to use standard feature mobile handsets.

Service providers have introduced schemes targeted to the lower-middle classes, urban poor and a growing section of the migrant population. There are options to top-up credit starting from as low as Rs5, usually bundled with other incentives such as free text messages to connections on the same service. Most of the residents of Govindpuri have pre-paid connections, which is not a purely economic decision. Security checks (usually involving submission of identification and residential proof) are easier to circumvent in the case of a pre-paid connection. The thriving extra-legal mobile phone markets in Govindpuri allow residents to acquire pre-paid connections without necessarily providing their details. A significant section of the population in Govindpuri, including migrant workers, does not have these documents to produce. The latest handsets circulate at lower cost through these extra-legal mobile markets along with second-hand phones and Chinese-made imitations of popular brands that cost a quarter of the cost of the original.

For the many people working as daily wage earners, including for example plumbers, construction site workers, masons and maids, the mobile phone has provided a convenient, cost-effective and time-saving means to connect to employers and employment opportunities. Phones also keep residents in touch with family members living elsewhere, helping with the circulation of news and the provision of assistance when required, within local social networks and remote kinship networks. These kinds of uses can be understood as "social logistics" (Tenhunen 2008) that can be observed in a range of places where mobile phone penetration is reaching into lower socioeconomic groups. "[M]obile technology amplifies ongoing processes of cultural change but does so selectively, so that it brings about the homogenization of 'social logistics'" (ibid., 515).

This "homogenization" of social logistics brings about new social constellations but these must be related to culture and cultural change in order to be understood locally, "[t]he new communication systems are influencing and drawing from local social, cultural, and political processes" (ibid.). Mobile phone use is related to ongoing local processes of transformation, and must be understood in relation to them. Tenhunen's study of a village in West Bengal demonstrates the need to understand this relationship, since "the appropriation of phones draws from culture and, conversely, contributes to changes in culture and society" (2008, 517).

Jeffrey and Dorron (2013) approach mobile phones in India rather differently to Tenhunen. The subtitle of their book, *The Great Indian Phonebook: how cheap mobile phones change business, politics and daily life* pre-warns an approach that is looking at mobile phones as transformational technologies that change the social and cultural. Tenhunen's argument is very different:

> Telephony shapes social logistics, at the same time intensifying the ongoing contest of meanings. Instead of homogenizing cultures, mobile technology reinforces these cultural patterns and processes that can be reconciled with emerging social logistics.
>
> *(2008, 531)*

For Tenhunen an appropriate research agenda explores how emerging social logistics relate to local meanings. Local existing and enduring meaning structures cannot be ignored by the villagers she studied, and cannot be overlooked when interpreting their lives. These structures "exist in motion" (2008, 517), and are subject to contestation and change, and mobile phones can extend and magnify villagers' relationships and add diversity of connections.

However, Jeffrey and Dorron give it far more "disruptive potential," so that amongst its affordances in India is the power to escape existing structures, as long as "people, of course, must already have the imagination to want to do things differently" (2013, 14). Such a statement ignores the weight, social and cultural importance, and the politics of existing structures, as if they can be simply replaced. Our research aligns with Tenhunen's approach to mobiles regarding the importance of locating our understandings in local cultures and politics. Alternatives such as represented by Jeffrey and Dorron miss the crucial place of appropriation and local cultures and meanings, promulgate hyperbole, and credit the technology itself with the power to transform.

The moral landscape for mobile phones

How the penetration of mobile phones is understood in some official reports and media coverage contrasts with an approach that locates such understandings in local cultures and politics. In the 2011 Indian census, information was captured for the first time on a range of new measures including internet access and mobile phone ownership. Mobile phones in India have effectively "leapfrogged" older communication and information technologies (Tenhunen 2008; Jeffrey and Dorrin 2013) that required costly physical infrastructures that are largely considered to be the responsibility of governments. Mobiles, on the other hand, are proliferating and reaching into previously technologically unconnected areas through a mixture of public and commercial initiative. Rather than a social good, with universal service agendas pressuring governments to act, commercial operators are tapping into new markets with "affordable" devices and connections. Discussions of universal service provision are replaced with discussions of consumerism. There are moral judgements at play here, and in media reports of the census findings, mobile phone uptake in slums is compared to spending on sanitation. Gupta, in the *Hindustan Times,* reports that "India's first-ever census of household amenities and assets in slums has revealed that slum dwellers are . . . spending more on TV sets, computers and mobile phones *rather* than sanitation" (2013, our emphasis). Jeffrey and Dorron (2013, 6), calling the mobile phone "the most widely shared item of luxury and indulgence the country had ever seen," also make uncritical reference to the census data and to journalists' fascination with the statistics that show that across the country there are more mobile phones than toilets.

The inclusion in the census of a range of media technologies is used to determine living standards in the slums and contrasted with "non slums." In such reportage basic sanitation—conventionally considered as the state's responsibility—is represented as a consumer option that loses out because slum dwellers spend their money on mobile phones. This shows a shifting imagination in which the urban poor are now identified as proactive, engaged consumers with the agency to exercise choice, and in such reportage that choice is questioned with moralistic undertones. This construction of the urban poor permits the state to distance itself from responsibilities towards disenfranchised citizens and their rights, subsidies and entitlements. This instance of juxtaposing the use of mobile phones with sanitation is a particularly exaggerated example of collapsing the discourse of "cleanliness" and "consumption" that emphasizes a loss of citizenship rights and the rise of the privileges and responsibilities of consumers (Chandola 2013).

This moralistic tone is extended to the use of mobile phones by women. The highly demarcated gendered ownership and use of technologies is undergoing significant change in Govindpuri; however, it would be a gross misrepresentation to suggest anything close to gendered neutrality in technological use. In our initial years of research here (2004–2005) we were witness to a woman being beaten up publicly for watching television (in effect for indulging in leisure when she should have been attending to her household duties), and in another instance a young girl, who was observed publicly talking on her mobile phone—a rarity at that time—was compelled by social pressures to abandon her higher studies. The parents of the girl were keen for her to pursue her education, but neighbors considered the "uninhibited" freedoms she exercised by attending college unescorted, and using her mobile phone, as immoral. The parents responded to the threat of social ostracization and potential damage to their daughter's reputation.

In the last decade the overall situation in Govindpuri has changed significantly. The post-liberalized context allowed opportunities formerly unavailable to most residents and has led to improved living standards, most evident in the transformation of many houses from *kaccha* (temporary constructions made from materials such as bamboo and plastic) to *pucca* (permanent brick and mortar constructions). Increased exposure to the "outside" world, in which access to technologies has played a significant role, has increased the premium on education for boys and girls. The number of women completing secondary school and entering into higher education has increased as well as the number of women seeking regular employment as white-collar workers. The implications of these changes are significant in that women are extended sanctions and permissions that were earlier prohibited, including venturing outside of the neighborhood for work and for leisure unescorted, wearing Western clothes such as jeans, and ownership and use of mobile technologies. However, gendered negotiations are not dissolved of their politics of control and subjugation.

For example, Payal was a 17-year-old resident of Bhumhiheen camp. She was appointed as a local research assistant for an early study in 2004. An ambitious young woman with "dreams," she felt that her mother, a local politician, and her two elder brothers were restrictive and controlling. She often voiced these concerns and expressed her helplessness in not being able to take charge of the situation. She expressly articulated this as a form of "violence." She was not allowed to venture out on her own, pursue higher education, seek a job and own a mobile. She is now a married woman of 27 with a young son. Her marital home is outside the slums in a legal settlement. She is able to travel with relative freedom, and owns a mobile phone. She is very proud of the fact that she is no longer a slum-dweller, but she still spends a significant amount of time in her maternal home. Her position in the maternal family has significantly changed, especially since the arrival of her elder brother's wife. Within the complex gendered hierarchy of the family as a unit, the daughter-in-law position is generally the least autonomous or favorable. With Babli's arrival, Payal could shift the burden of the gendered "violence" she encountered by exercising control over the former. And thus Babli, even after six years of marriage, is not allowed to venture outside the neighborhood on her own, there is no consideration of her seeking employment, and she is not permitted a mobile phone.

While Payal considered the restrictions placed on her as a form of violence, there is widespread concern across India about physical violence against women, including rape and murder cases. The Indian media captures the excitement about new technologies and its possibilities, but it is also a window into a darker side of life, where gendered oppression and violence lurk. Headlines capture views on the use of mobile phones by young women (or "girls" as they are more regularly called in such reporting), which is often directly linked to a current public concern with regularly reported violence and rape.[4] One response is in the form of regular calls by high profile politicians and others to restrict young women's mobile phone use.[5] Such views do invite public outrage and protests[6] and are countered by alternative discourses asserting the rights of women. However, an anxiousness about women using mobiles and having unrestricted access to the internet is palpable in such reportage; either the use of mobiles is celebrated for educational and empowering capacities, or denounced for corrupting influences. The reckoning of women as informed and assured consumers who employ these technologies to assert their identities and explore the opportunities it allows is conspicuous by its absence in these reports, especially when the women in question belong to the category of "non elite" users.

Complicating connectivity: Rani and Monica

It is clear then that Govindpuri slums are highly gendered spaces where the mobility of women is changing but remains restricted spatially, morally, socially and culturally (Chandola 2010, 2012a, 2012b), within local structures of meanings. Tenhunen (2008, 517) shows how for the villagers in her study, "Such symbolic fields as kinship and rituals represent dominant practices and enduring meaning structures which cannot be ignored." That is to say, phones increased and intensified already existing social networks. Nevertheless, phones add a diversity of connectedness, and are in some cases used to "maintain defiant and secret contacts" (2008, 524). Mobile phones "help women extend their sphere unobtrusively without overtly moving out of the domestic sphere," and "extend social possibilities beyond what culture dictates as proper" (2008, 527). For women in the West Bengal village, this might mean regular contact with the natal village, and challenges to ideas of appropriate distance between marriage family and natal family, which in turn impacts on issues of honor. We can explore ways in which women are able to extend social possibilities, while remaining firmly located within local structures of meanings, through the example of two young women in Govindpuri.

Rani is 26, Monica is 21. They are neighbors in a Muslim-dominated area of Navjeevan camp. Their respective households are dominated by women. Rani's household decisions are essentially determined by her. In Monica's case, it is her mother who controls the household and their grocery shop business with an iron-fist. Both Rani and Monica are highly aspirational, constantly "scheming" to improve their situations. But this is where the similarities end. Rani is illiterate. In the past she has worked regularly as a sex-worker, and still does so occasionally, though this is not common knowledge amongst the members of the community. Monica is a college graduate who has a diploma in fashion design and merchandising. She is the most educated member of her family, and this is proudly announced both by her and other family members to visitors and members of the community. She has been working since 2011, when she completed her diploma course. She fluently converses in English, a capability which is rare amongst the residents of the slum camps.

Both Rani and Monica own smartphones. Rani has a Nokia Asha 501. Monica uses a Micromax Canvas 2. Rani is quick to mention that hers is a "first-hand, new phone, costing Rs5,000" which she bought from a "proper" shop and which has a one-year warranty. Monica admits to "loving" her present phone, but adds with a hint of deeply-felt loss, that her "dream phone" was a Nokia N8, a high-end model which she bought in 2011 for Rs24,000, after saving money from her first job. Her younger brother had borrowed her phone to attend a wedding and somehow managed to lose it. Unable to immediately afford a phone of similar specifications she settled for her current second-hand model which cost her Rs6000.

Rani and Monica are both expert users of their smartphones and the various functionalities. However, the difference in which they can articulate their usage reveals their differing sensibilities. Whilst Monica's articulation of her choice of the model she uses is premised around its technical specifications—3G enabled, memory, RAM capacity, battery life, the quality of picture the camera allows, pixel size, and so on, Rani's appreciation is more haptic, where the size of the screen, ease of using the touch screen, camera and listening to music are discussed. However, Rani is known for her expertise with electronics, and took Chandola on a tour of her smartphone. She showed how she clicked pictures from her camera, its quality, the set in her gallery, the music collection, and played some songs to establish the quality of the speakers on her phone. Rani claims she needs to spend just half-an-hour, at most, with any smartphone, of any technical specifications and with as complex functionalities as possible for her to "master" it.

She is proficient at setting up (and resolving issues) with audio and video players. She fixes electrical connections, and often has to be curtailed in her enthusiasm to take apart mobile handsets. It is a common sight for neighbors to come to Rani to learn the functionalities of their newly acquired phones. And with the Chinese-made smartphones cheaply available, Rani has become quite an expert and much in demand. She exploited these capabilities and her extended social networks to enter the second-hand and extra-legal "mobile markets," making money by facilitating mobile handset sales. Even though she is illiterate she sends and receives several text messages in a day. Some of them are conversational, but most of them are forwarded poetries and words of affections, which her brother or one of her educated neighbors read to her.

Monica has a post-paid connection, uncommon in the slums. She pays Rs99 per month for the connection, which allows her 200 minutes of free local and STD calls and 1000 free text messages. She also has a data package costing Rs250 per month to access the internet. Monica categorically identifies the smartphone as having played a significant role in her professional growth, for example by helping her to improve her English (through things such as spell checking and language learning), and allowing her to constantly update her résumé on a job site, www.naukri. com. She found her present job through this site. Rani also exploits her smartphone's functionalities to further her prospects, using its dual-sim capacity to maintain contact with her sex work clients. The two connections can be active at the same time, but only one of them is in her name. When she has to negotiate and engage with her clients, she is careful not to use that one.

Rani and Monica's experiences with smartphones are complicated by their social positions. Rani, unlike most women in Govindpuri, enjoys relatively uninhibited spatial, social and cultural mobility. She has been the *de facto* head of the household since she returned at the age of 18 from an abusive marriage. Her father died of alcohol-related disease. She has managed to support herself, her young daughter, her mother, brothers and her sisters. When she first returned she tried working as a maid in a nearby middle-class neighborhood but found her treatment to be dehumanizing. She found she could retain far more control and earn significantly more money through sex work. She has earned enough money to improve the condition of her family, but also fears the implications for them of the kind of work she does if it becomes known. While she is aware that some do know her line of work, she has made useful connections to local crime figures and wealthy men, and so neither her family nor neighbors condemn her openly since her family depend on her earnings, and her neighbors occasionally need to seek her help when they have local issues.

> My family is so hypocritical; of course they know where the money is coming from and had no issue about taking it when they needed but if there is the slightest issue, they call me a [whore], and say I bring shame to the family. Earlier I used to get affected by what they said, but now I retort back and say, who is worse a [whore] or those who eat of her living.

Rani's particular position has allowed her a rarely available economic, social and spatial mobility, and yet it is also highly precarious (Tacchi 2014).

Monica's experience of spatial and social mobilities in the same context are dramatically different from Rani's. Her first job involved an hour commute each way, but she loved her job, and the experience and exposure that it brought. However, only five months into it she left.

> Amma [mother] made it impossible. She would call me every half hour to inquire what I was doing, and if I did not answer the phone, she would start calling the land line. It was most embarrassing. If I said I would reach home by seven, and was delayed on account of traffic or some work, she would get hysterical. The limit was when one-day she landed up at my work, because the previous night my boss—a Man—had called about some work. I just could not take it.

Her mother considers this strict control over her daughter's movements as her "duty"; these days, "young girls need to be protected. There are so many distractions, and we cannot allow her to go astray." She fears Monica might marry outside her religion, or get into a "love marriage." Monica finds this control difficult to negotiate, and said that if she did not have the connections her smartphone allowed she would go mad. She is constantly online accessing social media sites. She has mild flirtations on Facebook and boasts almost 400 friends, not all of them known to her offline. She does not have a boyfriend, and thinks that she will get married to a groom of her parents' choice, but she thinks that in the meantime her online relationships are harmless. We were intrigued by these liberties available to Monica, which are surprisingly unrestricted. Monica explained, and not without mischief,

> of course Amma does not know what I am up to on the phone. She thinks I am texting, and gets annoyed at times but that is it. She does not know internet, or Facebook. And not that I am doing something really *wrong,* just a bit of fun on the side.

Conclusion

Rani and Monica are both, in different ways, using their mobiles to defy social controls and extend social possibilities, but they are doing so within a set of meaning structures that while they are changing over time, remain strong enough to require them to act secretively. We can see how the social logistics provided by the phones are important to them, how they increase their economic possibilities, help them manage social and familial relationships, but the actual form and function of these employment opportunities and social relationships are only understood when explored within the particular local situations they live within.

These examples highlight the limitations of available techno-developmental discourses which are inclined towards drawing linear and direct links between access to technologies of connectedness and increased mobilities (social, geographic, economic, or political). We can complicate notions of mobility through the examples of Rani and Monica. Marriage, for example, plays an important role in framing their opportunities. Rani is illiterate, left her marriage after one year with her baby daughter due to abuse, and as such she was socially, culturally and economically highly vulnerable. Her family could not afford to support her and her baby, so she took things into her own hands, and whilst what she chose[7] to do to earn money (sex work) makes her vulnerable on a number of counts, it also allows her to not only support herself but also her extended family. The relationships, drivers and tensions at play in Rani's situation are of course far more complex than we are able to describe here. Meanwhile, Monica is well educated and has worked in office jobs since graduation. While closely observed and monitored by her mother, she finds her smartphone to be a way to circumvent the social restrictions placed upon her. Her mother will be seeking out marriage partners very soon, and when married Monica will once again have to negotiate and manage the expectations and restrictions of her new family and new role. This goes some way to help us understand how technologies of connectedness, though non-hierarchical within their operational capacity, unfold within existing social, cultural and moral landscapes. The practices of, and around, these technologies both embody the hierarchies and particularities of these landscapes, and extend social possibilities, sometimes defiantly and secretly (Tenhunen 2008).

Our central argument is that the inherent potential (and alternatively, threat) of mobile technologies to re-calibrate the social order needs to be treated with caution. There is a danger of either situating these technologies in an overly deterministic projection of the future, or to highlight the static-ness of social order and its traditions. Between Rani and Monica we can see two very distinctly gendered but also very different experiences of life in the slum, and their particular encounters with mobile phones. The examples discussed in this chapter should complicate broader narratives of new media and its transformational potential. What we gain from complicating this is a range of different perspectives on everyday lives and the varied implications of devices such as smartphones. This complicates what being connected means for these women. The currency of connection plays out within broader structures and gendered negotiations in this marginalized site in a global city. The imaginations, aspirations and agencies of these women that are afforded by new media (Appadurai 1996) are crucially tied into their social, cultural, political and gendered positions.

Notes

1 Tacchi and Chandola's ethnographic research in Govindpuri began in 2004, funded by the Department for International Development, and lasted for 18 months. Between 2006 and 2009, Chandola undertook further ethnographic work for her doctorate under the supervision of Tacchi. Subsequently Chandola has continued through post-doctoral work, both with Tacchi and on her own.
2 http://delhishelterboard.in/main/?page_id=128 (accessed September 14, 2014).
3 http://www.dot.gov.in/about-us/telecom-glance (accessed September 14, 2014).
4 http://www.telegraphindia.com/1140715/jsp/frontpage/story_18615353.jsp#.VAQiObtGVv4
5 http://timesofindia.indiatimes.com/india/Karnataka-house-panel-blames-mobiles-for-rise-in-rape-and-molestation-cases/articleshow/38228687.cms (accessed September 14, 2014).
6 See, http://www.theglobeandmail.com/news/world/protesters-outraged-after-indian-guru-says-gang-rape-victim-not-blameless/article7097073/; http://timesofindia.indiatimes.com/city/varanasi/Rural-women-learn-alphabets-through-mobile-phones/articleshow/11341893.cms; and, http://www.zdnet.com/in/iball-launches-safety-phone-for-women-in-india-7000024421/ (all accessed September 1, 2014).
7 It is worth noting that her "choice" was made in the face of the options available to her and the urgent need for her to support her family. She prefers us to understand her "choice" to be a sex worker as an assertive act, a means to maintain control over her life and, indeed, her body. However, this does need to be understood within the options available to her, her experience of violence through marriage, and many other factors.

References

Adwitiya, A. (2014) 'India: The Meteoric Rise of Smartphones' Unitus Seed Fund website'. Available at: http://usf.vc/updates/india-meteoric-rise-smartphones/ (Accessed August 31, 2014).

Appadurai, A. (1996) *Modernity at Large: Cultural Dimensions of Globalization*, Minneapolis: University of Minnesota Press.

Basu, A.R. (1988) *Urban Squatter Housing in Third World*, Mittal Publications.

Burrell, J. (2012) *Invisible Users: Youth in the Internet Cafés of Urban Ghana*, Cambridge, MA: MIT Press.

Buskens, I. (2010) 'Agency and Reflexivity in ICT4D research: questioning women's options, poverty, and human development', *Information Technologies & International Development*, 6, Special Edition: 19–24.

Chandola, T. (2010) 'Listening into others: In-between noise and silence'. Unpublished PhD thesis, Queensland University of Technology, Brisbane.

Chandola, T. (2012a) 'Listening into others: moralising the soundscapes in Delhi', *International Development Planning Review*, 34(4): 391–408.

Chandola, T. (2012b) 'Listening in to water routes: soundscapes as cultural systems', *International Journal of Cultural Studies*, 16(1): 55–69.

Chandola, T. (2013) 'Dumped through technology: a policymaker's guide to disenfranchising slum dwellers', *Journal of Creative Communications*, 8(2-3): 265–275.

Gupta, M.D. (2013) 'Amenities in slums match up to urban homes', *Hindustan Times*. Available at: www.hindustantimes.com/India-news/NewDelhi/Amenities-in-slums-match-up-to-urban-homes/Article1-1030205.aspx (Accessed August 30, 2014).

Jeffrey, R. and Dorron, A. (2013) *The Great Indian Phone Book: How Cheap Mobile Phones Change Business, Politics and Daily Life*, London: Hurst and Company.

Li, T. M. (2007) *The Will to Improve: Governmentatlity, Developments, and the Practice of Politics*, Durham, NC: Duke University Press.

Singhal, A. and Rogers, E.M. (2001) *India's Communication Revolution: From Bullock Carts to Cyber Marts*, New Delhi: Sage.

Slater, D. (2013) *New Media, Development and Globalization: Making Connections in the Global South*, Hoboken, NJ: John Wiley & Sons.

Tacchi, J. (2014) 'Being meaningfully mobile: mobile phones and development'. In J. Servaes (ed.) *Technological Determinism and Communication for Sustainable Social Change*, Lanham, MD: Lexington Books.

Tacchi, J., Kitner, K.R. and Crawford, K. (2012) 'Meaningful mobility: gender, development and mobile phones', *Feminist Media Studies*, 12(4): 528–537.

Tenhunen, S. (2008) 'Mobile technology in the village: ICTs, culture, and social logistics in India', *The Journal of the Royal Anthropological Institute*, 14(3): 515–534.

16

The blended lives of young Chinese online

David Kurt Herold

Like their peers around the world, Chinese youth—here defined as people between the late teens and the late twenties (i.e., final years in school and settling down in full-time employment)—spend much of their lives online using a variety of devices to do so. While their basic behaviour is similar to youth elsewhere, though, the encounter young people in China have with the Internet is quite different and influenced by both the socio-political setting of the Internet in China, as well as particularly Chinese economic forces.

If one travels on public transport in China, one is surrounded by young people accessing the Internet or chatting with friends online using their mobile phones—just as in much of the rest of the world. One difference to Europe and North America that is very noticeable is that most of the phones in use are either very cheap Chinese-made Android devices or even non-smart phones using a text-based browser to access web sites or built-in applications to chat online, which is one of the reasons Chinese websites feature more text content than equivalent sites outside China (Thibault 2010).

A further difference that is easily noticeable is that the variety of online tools in use by people appears to be greater. While Chinese Internet users do use equivalents to Facebook (e.g., Renren) or Twitter (e.g., Sina Weibo) and while WeChat is currently the most popular Internet application in China, many older tools are still in use. It is not uncommon for Chinese Internet users to still access Bulletin Board Systems (BBS) or online forums, or chat with friends using the QQ messaging system.

Additionally, Chinese Internet users appear to be more multi-task oriented than non-Chinese, as studies into the behaviour of Chinese consumers show (e.g., Crampton 2011; Spelich 2014; Wang 2010) as well as visits to Internet cafés or other public access points (Zhang 2015). A Chinese Internet user will typically use a number of different applications concurrently, i.e., watch a movie or TV series online, while playing an online game in another window and chatting with friends using QQ, as well as staying logged in to Weibo and WeChat to keep track of messages that might interest them.

The ever increasing capabilities of mobile phones and tablets also support this engagement with their affordance of near ubiquity of access to the Internet and its integration into the offline lives of young Chinese. The technological affordances have made it possible for the lives of young

Chinese to turn into *blended lives* that consist of both online and offline elements that interact with and complement each other in uniquely Chinese ways based on their framing.

The Chinese Internet and its framing

The Chinese Internet's socio-political framing

One of the biggest differences between the Internet in China and the Internet elsewhere is that the former is run on hardware and controlled by state-owned entities, which gives Chinese government authorities a greater level of control over and access to Internet data than elsewhere (Herold 2011c). Individual Internet users are aware of the level of control possible for Chinese government authorities and thus adjust their own behavior so as to meet or evade imagined censorship rules.

James Fallows provided a detailed look at the control of the Chinese government over the Internet and why it was (and still is) so effective, despite its many technical flaws (Fallows 2008). He explained that the Chinese authorities use a variety of IP-blocking, service-blocking and content-censoring technologies not primarily to make access to the non-Chinese Internet impossible, but rather to render it inconvenient and slow, and therefore not interesting to the majority of Internet users. Despite the age of the article and the fast changing nature of the Internet, his analysis is still as valid now as it was then.

Roberts, Larochelle, Faris and Palfrey (2011) showed that very few Chinese Internet users access contents on servers outside China, as frequent time-outs and slow speeds make them undesirable (see also M.W.L. Fong 2009). Taneja and Wu (2014) additionally demonstrate that Chinese Internet users are also restricted in their access of the worldwide Internet by their own cultural restrictions and language abilities, which leads them to conclude that cultural proximity is an even more influential factor restraining Chinese Internet users than government censorship. The average Chinese Internet user is not interested in the Internet outside China because it does not talk about the local China experienced by the Internet user, and because it is not in Chinese.

The artificially created but largely user-accepted separation of the Chinese Internet from the Internet outside China is further strengthened by Chinese cultural tendencies that favour isolation rooted in a feeling of cultural superiority combined with the belief that most non-Chinese wish to hurt China and hinder its development (Herold 2010, 2012), as "core elements of Chinese culture are reinforced via ICTs" (Chu, 2008, see also Chu and Cheng 2011). Chinese Internet users are not only hindered from accessing the worldwide Internet—the majority is also not interested in accessing *foreign* websites that only criticize China. Instead they access the *Chinese* Internet to interact with friends connected to their offline lives.

Within China, Chinese Internet users tend to be more communicative than the average Internet user accessing the non-Chinese Internet. While both access information online and might leave comments on websites, Chinese users tend to forward interesting stories to people in their network more often than non-Chinese users (see, e.g., Li et al. 2012; Yu, Asur and Huberman 2012; Zhang and Pentina 2012) and news stories often become famous more because they are forwarded between Internet users online, rather than because many people for example watched a TV broadcast. In one example, during the recent scandal about the selling of out-of-date meat by Fast-Food restaurants in China, China's Central TV (CCTV) broadcast a report on practices at McDonald's that only became widely known after being referred to on CCTV's micro-blog and the subsequent re-posting of the entry by over 180,000 micro-blog users whose network of connections also re-posted it to their connections (CCTV 2013).

Even the Chinese government's White Paper on *The Internet in China* (Information Office of the State Council of the People's Republic of China 2010) emphasizes its communicative nature and that Internet users wish to communicate and exchange information with other Internet users, including government authorities, rather than merely consuming new information by themselves (see the discussion in Herold 2011b, 203–207). The White Paper encourages this behaviour of Chinese Internet users but advises government officials to become active in these interactions online with the goal of guiding public discussions in directions agreeable to the government.

A second feature of online China that is based on the socio-political framing of "the Internet," meaning the web as accessed through a web browser, or virtual worlds such as online games – is its virtuality, in the sense that many Internet users in China separate their online activities from their offline identities while also believing that the Internet is not entirely *real*, nor its effects measurable in the offline world (Barboza 2007, 2010). Simultaneously, however, youth employ different online tools as a part of their offline, *blended* lives in Christine Hine's sense of "the internet . . . embedded in our daily lives" (2015, Blurb). While the internet (small i), has become "an unremarkable way of carrying out our interactions with one another" (Hine 2015, Blurb), the Internet (capital I) is seen as a *virtual* playground in which to engage in activities that people would not dare to try offline or as a training field for eventual offline duties such as, e.g., marriage (Wu, Fore, Wang and Ho 2007; Wu and Wang 2011).

> [F]or Chinese youth the virtual world provides a venue for expressing autonomy that is not available to them in the real world. In the virtual world, Chinese youth can do as they choose without concern about the impact of their behavior on others.
>
> *(Jackson et al. 2008, 285)*

Within this *virtual* playground Chinese Internet users prefer to connect with other Internet users using *online* labels that are not easily connected to an *offline* person (Farrall 2008; Farrall and Herold 2011). Studies on the preferences of Chinese Internet users have repeatedly shown that they regard the "disclosure of personal privacy the most disgusting online experience" (Kong 2007, 159; see also Wang 2002, 559–563; Yao-Huai 2005).

Despite rapidly growing numbers of households that own computers and near universal possession of mobile phones capable of accessing the Internet, over 30 percent of Chinese Internet users still access the Internet from Internet cafés or similar public access points (China Internet Network Information Center (CNNIC) 2014, 18). Government regulations requiring the real-name registration of Internet users and frequent campaigns to enforce them have not changed the fact that many of these Internet cafés still allow their users to access the Internet anonymously (see, e.g., Liang and Lu 2010)—both as a marketing tool, as well as a tax-avoidance measure by the owners of the Internet cafés.

Online identities are further hidden through the use of strings of numbers instead of personal names to express a sentiment based on the homophones of the Chinese words for numbers, e.g., the number combination 59188 stands for 'I just want to become rich', while the combination 52 . . . can be used to express 'I love . . .' (Beam 2014). Messaging services such as QQ also allow users to adopt a changeable label to stand in for their actual user name, again to express a sentiment, as, e.g., in nationalistic outpourings of support for China's international actions expressed in the adoption of the user label 'I heart China' (Yu 2010). Similarly, Bulletin Board Services (BBS) and online forums allow users to create site-specific nicknames adding another layer of anonymity to a Chinese person's engagement with the Internet.

While it is possible to penetrate the layers of anonymity, especially for government authorities employing the resources of a modern state or the determined efforts of the infamous online manhunts called *Human Flesh Search Engine* (Cheung 2009; Herold 2011a; B. Wang et al. 2010; F.Y. Wang et al. 2010), individual Chinese Internet users are able to safeguard their (illusion of) anonymity in their everyday use of the Internet unless they specifically wish to disclose it (Farrall and Herold 2011).

A final consequence of the Internet's socio-political framing that also has an impact on the economic framing of the Internet in China worth mentioning here is the relative youth of its users. Largely as the result of the perception of the Internet as a virtual playground many Chinese believe that the Internet is a place for young people and not for adults who are too busy with *real* life. Close to 60 percent of Internet users in China are under the age of 30 (China Internet Network Information Center (CNNIC) 2014, 14) and the percentage of Internet users with only a High School education or worse stands at almost 80 percent (China Internet Network Information Center (CNNIC) 2014, 15), while in China's Guangdong province "80 percent of the 1,000 primary and high school students polled started surfing the Internet before they turned 10" (*China Daily* 2010).

The Chinese Internet is geared towards younger users and their interests, and is thus entertainment-heavy with numerous sites offering the easy download of movies, music, books, etc., as well as a wide variety of online gaming on offer from massively multiplayer online role-playing games (MMORPGs) to sites offering large collections of browser-based mini-games. The Chinese government's spotty enforcement of copyright rules serves to support the wide selection on offer to young Internet users in China, which is further bolstered by the generally shared assumption that the Chinese authorities prefer Internet users to entertain rather than inform or organize themselves politically online.

As a result of this socio-political framing, the Internet in China thus presents itself as a particularly gossipy and rather remote village of masked and mostly young individuals having fun on the Chinese Internet, which is only loosely connected to the rest of the world.

Economic drivers of difference

In Europe and in North America most Internet users have a credit card or bank account linked to at least a part of their online presence, e.g., through an account at Amazon or EBay, or via their smartphone's application marketplace, most Chinese Internet users do not. As the most recent report of the CNNIC points out 50 percent of Chinese Internet users have an income of less than 2000 RMB (roughly US$ 230) per month (2014, 17). This is due in part to China's status as a developing country (notwithstanding its recent meteoric rise in economic world-rankings), but also a consequence of the youth and low educational level of most of the Chinese Internet users.

The relative poverty of Chinese Internet users has a number of consequences as it means for example that most Internet sites in China have to operate as free or advertising supported sites that are accessible to non-smart (cheap) mobile phones; that is, phones that are largely text-based (see also Li 2012). Additionally, e-commerce sites have to offer their users payment options that allow them to pay offline and in cash, e.g., Taobao, China's largest online auction site, has opened kiosks in many supermarkets where buyers can pay for their purchases in cash.

Many of China's young and poor Internet users see the Internet mainly as a cheap source of entertainment as other venues are too expensive for them (Barboza 2010). As the costs of cinema tickets or entrance fees for discos and night clubs have soared in China, the Internet has become the last affordable place for people to turn to, if they wish to listen to music, watch movies, play games, or interact with friends and families living far away (C. Fong 2009)—in particular as many Internet cafés still only charge their users less than 5 RMB per hour with special offers for overnight package-deals.

The combination of low disposable incomes with negligent law enforcement has contributed to a flourishing market in copied hardware, known as *shanzhai* products (Hennessey 2011), and pirated software (Chan, Ma and Wong 2013), which make it almost impossible for computer companies to monetize their product ideas. Ironically, this has meant that many Chinese Internet users are highly skilled in the use of (outside China) expensive software packages such as Adobe Photoshop or 3D modelling and video-editing software suites, despite the often decried dearth of creative products developed by Chinese companies.

China's young Internet users are (in)famous for their Photoshop (PS) and their video skills both of which enrich the Chinese Internet in general and the postings of many individual Chinese Internet users in particular. For example, when making fun of Chinese officials (Fauna 2011), institutions (Fauna 2009), or individuals (Menning 2009) the PS skills of Chinese Internet users are employed to great effect. China's online village is thus populated by poor but relatively skilled people looking for entertainment and an outlet for their creativity.

Blended lives

Two examples shall serve to illustrate how the framing of the Internet in China affects its usage by young Chinese. Although they will not be able to showcase *all* the effects of China's context, they will demonstrate how young Chinese combine the ubiquity of access to the Internet in everyday life with a high degree of interactivity in accessed contents and low tech requirements (e.g., non-smart mobile phones) to live blended lives incorporating the online and the offline. While much in these examples is similar to the behavior elsewhere, the level of interactivity, and the interdependence of online and offline components is worth noting, in particular when alongside the sources referenced in the introduction.

First example: making purchases at Taobao

The auction site Taobao successfully managed to fend off EBay's entry into the Chinese market (Chen, Zhang, Yuan and Huang 2007; Li, Li and Lin 2008) and has by now become many people's first choice for purchases of any kind, no matter how odd (The Economist 2013), "because it really understood Chinese customers" (Wang 2010). The buying and selling of items on Taobao is an interesting example of how Chinese Internet users combine different access routes as well as offline tools to complete a transaction on the auction site thus turning it into a combination of online and offline activity, i.e., a *blended* interaction, where "online and offline are interwoven in everyday experience" (Hine 2015, Blurb; see also Spelich 2014).

On Taobao, the purchasing process begins with a search for a specific item or brand the buyer wishes to purchase. The buyer typically chooses the item and particularly the brand based on online postings by other Internet users, either discussions, or recommendations or other pieces of information posted on different sites. Often, some of these recommendations will be on the screen of a mobile phone, or displayed in a window on a computer screen while the Taobao site is displayed on another screen (computer, mobile phone, or tablet) or another window.

Search results on Taobao present the buyer with a wide range of prices for the item depending on the level of genuineness of the article, e.g., a search for winter coats of the *Canada Goose* brand returns coats priced between 100 and 14,000 RMB for the same coats. Additionally, the listing provides information on how many people have purchased each item from the seller on the site, as well as the location of the seller. To narrow down their choice, potential buyers then turn to their friends and family, talking to people around them directly, while also consulting others via SMS, the QQ or WeChat messaging services, etc.

Each item's own page provides additional information about the item, as well as about the seller, as well as comments left by previous buyers—similar to EBay's information on items. Where the two sites differ is that on Taobao sellers are available for online chats via a built-in chat client. Sellers who are offline lose buyers. Buyers usually begin chatting with the seller via the built-in client, but later switch to QQ or WeChat to continue their conversation, often using their mobile phone to do so. If the two parties manage to agree on a deal outside of Taobao, they can avoid the auction sites fees. The chat will touch upon the genuineness of the article and—to stay with *Canada Goose*—whether or not the article will meet the needs of the buyer, e.g., a winter vacation in Northern Europe with expected temperatures below minus twenty degrees Celsius. If necessary, the seller will suggest the buyer switch to a slightly less fake item meeting the buyer's needs.

During their chat, buyers and sellers will turn to other devices or screens to check on shipping possibilities, to compare the seller's offer with those of other sellers and with the brand's own web site listing currently available models and their features, to talk with friends and family again, etc. Once a purchase is agreed, buyer and seller usually exchange mobile phone numbers and addresses and the seller arranges for the delivery of the item. Buyers only pay for their purchases after receiving and approving of the goods—either via online banking, or paying in cash at a Taobao kiosk, or sending money via money order, etc.

From start to finish, the purchase is a highly interactive process in which offline and multiple forms of online communication are integrated to meet the needs of buyers and sellers. This becomes especially obvious if one compares the process to the much simpler one on EBay that requires almost no direct contact between buyers and sellers. While an EBay purchase is more like ordering from an online catalogue, Taobao works more like a series of stalls at an offline market in China. Both sellers and buyers on Taobao switch between communication technologies seamlessly thus turning the purchase into a *blended* rather than either an *online* or an *offline* experience.

The auction site itself often only serves as a convenient initial meeting place for buyers and sellers, while the purchasing process encompasses multiple online and offline elements to make it more *real* and to protect both sellers and buyers from fraud. Trust between the buyers and sellers is established and supported by the blending of online with offline contact points that together serve to guarantee the identities of buyers and sellers. They become *real* to each other based on a mix of online and offline elements, i.e. their identities are composites of the online and offline, *blended* identities that are more meaningful than either the one or the other.

Second example: going for dinner

Going for dinner at a fancy restaurant in China has also increasingly become a blended experience during recent years. From the choice of restaurants to the conversations around the dinner table, different Information and Communication Technologies (ICTs) are an integral part of the experience. Rather than being seen as an interruption or hindrance, mobile phones in particular have become an essential ingredient of a successful evening.

In choosing a restaurant for an evening out with family and/or friends, many Chinese—like their peers outside China—now turn to online sources to choose a restaurant. They check reviews and photos of dishes posted by previous patrons of the restaurants under considerations, and they try to locate discount coupons for restaurants online. Throughout the process, they consult friends and family to compare and narrow down the choices employing a variety of tools and applications to do so.

Once a restaurant has been chosen and the required number of tables been booked—either online or via the mobile phone, invitations are sent out and participants confirmed via SMS, QQ,

WeChat or by phone. The guests themselves use their smart phone maps to get to the dinner (or the taxi drivers consult their own smartphones or navigation systems when trying to find the restaurant). The entire planning for and organization of the dinner has thus become a blended event consisting of many online and offline interactions that combine to make the dinner possible.

Upon arrival at the restaurant and while waiting for others to arrive, guests can jointly surf online for free on computers provided by many of the better restaurants and/or watch TV on the almost ubiquitous screens on the walls and check on their friends and family using their phones or tablets. At the same time, they can already begin consuming drinks or snacks, thus starting the dinner officially, which is important for keeping reserved tables in the restaurant if the rest of the party arrives late.

Conversations during dinner consist of online and offline elements as most people have their phone on the table next to their food and interact with their network of friends on QQ, WeChat, etc., while also taking and posting photos of the food served as their own commentary on the quality of the restaurant. Topics of conversation at the table manage to include elements from the TV screens on the wall, from QQ, WeChat or Weibo microblog messages appearing on the screens of phones and tablets, as well as offline events reported by the people around the table.

During dinners the author experienced in July 2014 it was remarkable how many of the conversations made reference to WeChat messages about China's president Xi Jinping from speculations about the next targets of his anti-corruption campaign to admonishments that *XiDaDa* (roughly translatable as *Big Man Xi*) encourages people not to waste food and to finish all the dishes ordered in restaurants. Conversations incorporated elements from the screens individuals were interacting with, and offline comments were fed back into the screens by people around the table. Much of the conversations also incorporate references to vocabulary currently fashionable on online platforms in a curious appropriation of an almost national "online vernacular" in local and often in-dialect, offline conversations (de Seta 2015). Dinners thus have to be understood as blended events with large networks of people participating in the interactions either directly or indirectly. To ignore the online components of a dinner would mean misrepresenting the event and its participating actors.

Enjoyment of a dinner party is shared by offline and online actors in multiple, connected and interacting ways in a back and forth in which the online is not intruding on the offline gathering but has become an integral part of the blended experience of a shared dinner, thus contributing to the increasingly blended lives of young Chinese.

Living blended lives . . . in China

Young people in China experience similar lives as their counterparts elsewhere regarding the use of ICTs in everyday life. While these similarities exist, though, both the intensity of ICT use, as well as both the socio-political, as well as the economic contexts of ICT use create marked differences. These differences are important for an understanding of young Chinese in today's China as they no longer live offline lives with some online components, but instead spend their lives switching between the two.

Rather than being mere users of ICTs or integrating ICTs into their lives, young Chinese live *blended* lives switching between online and offline interactions within a conversation or transaction to the point that a research focus on just one of the two raises questions about the validity of the research. Online and offline complement each other in the lives of young Chinese, whose lives can only be researched in their own context if both elements are investigated and the *blend* is presented in the results.

It makes little sense to study 'what Chinese people do online' without considering the offline contexts of their online activities. Similarly, studies of young Chinese people that ignore the Internet cannot accurately describe the lives of young Chinese anymore. It is the sum of the *blended* practices of individual Chinese Internet users and their networks *in their online and offline settings* that make up the lives of young Chinese.

References

Barboza, D. (2007) *Internet Boom in China Is Built on Virtual Fun*. Available at: http://www.nytimes.com/2007/02/05/world/asia/05virtual.html (Accessed on July 28, 2014).

Barboza, D. (2010) *For Chinese, Web Is Way to Entertainment*. Available at: http://www.nytimes.com/2010/04/19/technology/19chinaweb.html (Accessed on July 28, 2014).

Beam, C. (2014) *Chinese Number Websites: The Secret Meaning of URLs*. Available at: http://www.newrepublic.com/article/117608/chinese-number-websites-secret-meaning-urls (Accessed on July 28, 2014).

CCTV (2013) *Kungfu, KFC and McDonald's Not Hygienic*. Available at: http://www.weibo.com/2656274875/A0W8LiyD4#_rnd1406549780690 (Accessed on July 28, 2014).

Chan, R.Y.K., Ma, K.H.Y. and Wong, Y.H. (2013) 'The Software Piracy Decision-Making Process of Chinese Computer Users', *The Information Society*, 29: 203–218.

Chen, J., Zhang, C., Yuan, Y.F. and Huang, L.H. (2007) 'Understanding the emerging C2C electronic market in China: An experience seeking social marketplace', *Electronic Markets*, 17: 86–100.

Cheung, A.S.Y. (2009) 'China Internet going wild: Cyber-hunting versus privacy protection', *Computer Law & Security Review*, 25: 275–279.

China Daily (2010) *In Internet Age, Age No Bar for Surfers*. Available at: http://english.people.com.cn/90001/90776/90882/7056967.html (Accessed on July 28, 2014).

China Internet Network Information Center (CNNIC) (2014) *The 34th Statistical Survey Report on the Internet Development in China*, Beijing, CNNIC.

Chu, W.-C.R. (2008) 'The dynamics of cyber China: The characteristics of Chinese ICT use', *Knowledge, Technology, and Policy*, 21: 29–35.

Chu, W.-C.R. and Cheng, C.-T. (2011) 'Cultural convulsions: Examining the Chineseness of cyber China'. In Herold, D.K. and Marolt, P. (eds) *Online Society in China: Creating, Celebrating, and Instrumentalising the Online Carnival*, London and New York: Routledge.

Crampton, T. (2011) *Social Media in China: The Same, but Different*. Available at: http://www.chinabusinessreview.com/social-media-in-china-the-same-but-different/ (Accessed January 30, 2015).

de Seta, G. (2015) *Networked Carnival, Heavenly Kingdom Digital Folklore and User Practices in China's National Internet*. Unpublished PhD thesis. HK Polytechnic University.

Fallows, J. (2008) *'The Connection Has Been Reset'*. Available at: http://www.theatlantic.com/magazine/archive/2008/03/-ldquo-the-connection-has-been-reset-rdquo/6650/ (Accessed July 26, 2014).

Farrall, K.N. (2008) 'Global privacy in flux: Illuminating privacy across cultures in China and the US', *Journal of Communication*, 2: 993–1030.

Farrall, K.N. and Herold, D.K. (2011) 'Identity vs. anonymity: Chinese netizens and questions of identifiability'. In Herold, D.K. and Marolt, P. (eds) *Online Society in China: Creating, Celebrating, and Instrumentalising the Online Carnival*, London and New York: Routledge.

Fauna 2009. *CCTV Fire: Funny Photoshops By Chinese Netizens*. Available at: http://www.chinasmack.com/2009/pictures/cctv-fire-funny-photoshops-by-chinese-netizens.html (Accessed July 29, 2014).

Fauna 2011. *Floating Chinese Government Officials Inspect New Road*. Available at: http://www.chinasmack.com/2011/pictures/floating-chinese-government-officials-stun-netizens.html (Accessed July 29, 2014).

Fong, C. (2009) *'Sea turtles' Powering China's Internet Growth*. Available at: http://edition.cnn.com/2009/TECH/09/30/digitalbiz.redwired/index.html (Accessed July 29, 2014).

Fong, M.W.L. (2009) 'Digital divide between urban and rural regions in China', *The Electronic Journal on Information Systems in Developing Countries*, 36: 1–12.

Hennessey, W. (2011) 'Deconstructing Shanzhai – China's copycat counterculture: Catch me if you can', *Campbell Law Review*, 34: 609–660.

Herold, D.K. (2010) 'Nationalism vs. democracy – China's bloggers and the Western media'. In Yao, S., Bin, W., Morgan, S. and Sutherland, D. (eds) *Sustainable Reform and Development in Post-Olympic China*, London and New York: Routledge.

Herold, D.K. (2011a) 'Human flesh search engines: Carnivalesque riots as components of a "Chinese democracy"'. In Herold, D.K. and Marolt, P. (eds) *Online Society in China: Creating, Celebrating, and Instrumentalising the Online Carnival*, London and New York: Routledge.

Herold, D.K. (2011b) 'Netizens and citizens, cyberspace and modern China'. In Herold, D.K. and Marolt, P. (eds) *Online Society in China: Creating, celebrating, and instrumentalising the online carnival*, London and New York: Routledge.

Herold, D.K. (2011c) 'Noise, spectacle, politics: Carnival in Chinese cyberspace'. In Herold, D.K. and Marolt, P. (eds) *Online Society in China: Creating, Celebrating, and Instrumentalising the Online Carnival*, London and New York: Routledge.

Herold, D.K. (2012) 'Rage and reflection – Chinese nationalism online between emotional venting and measured opinion'. In Law, P.-L. (ed.) *New Connectivities in China: Virtual, Actual, and Local Interactions*, Berlin, Amsterdam and New York: Springer.

Hine, C. (2015) *Ethnography for the Internet: Embedded, Embodied, and Everyday*, London and New York: Bloomsbury.

Information Office of the State Council of the People's Republic of China. 2010. *The Internet in China*. Available at: http://www.china.org.cn/government/whitepaper/node_7093508.htm (Accessed July 29, 2014).

Jackson, L.A., Zhao, Y., Qiu, W., Kolenic, A. III, Fitzgerald, H.E., Harold, R. and Von Eye, A. (2008) 'Cultural differences in morality in the real and virtual worlds: A comparison of Chinese and US youth', *CyberPsychology & Behavior*, 11: 279–286.

Kong, L. (2007) 'Online privacy in China: A survey on information practices of Chinese websites', *Chinese Journal of International Law*, 6: 157–183.

Li, C.-W. (2012) *Difference between Chinese and Western Websites*. Available at: http://www.pluscreativity.com/blog/difference-between-chinese-and-western-websites/ (Accessed July 28, 2014).

Li, D., Li, J. and Lin, Z. (2008) 'Online consumer-to-consumer market in China – A comparative study of Taobao and eBay', *Electronic Commerce Research and Applications*, 7: 55–67.

Li, D., Zhang, J., Sun, G.G., Tang, J., Ding, Y. and Luo, Z. (2012) 'What is the nature of Chinese microblogging: Unveiling the unique features of Tencent Weibo', *arXiv Preprint*, 1211.2197. Available at: http://arxiv.org/abs/1211.2197 (Accessed July 29, 2014).

Liang, B. and Lu, H. (2010) 'Internet development, censorship, and cyber crimes in China', *Journal of Contemporary Criminal Justice*, 26: 103–120.

Menning, C. (2009) *Little Fatty*. Available at: http://knowyourmeme.com/memes/little-fatty (Accessed July 29, 2014).

Roberts, H., Larochelle, D., Faris, R. and Palfrey, J. (2011) *Mapping Local Internet Control*, Berkman Center for Internet & Society at Harvard University.

Spelich, J.W. (2014) *7 Key Differences Between Chinese and Western Consumers*. Available at: http://multichannelmerchant.com/blog/7-key-differences-chinese-western-consumers-28102014/ (Accessed January 30, 2015).

Taneja, H. and Wu, A.X. (2014) 'Does the Great Firewall really isolate the Chinese? Integrating access blockage with cultural factors to explain web user behavior', *The Information Society*, 30: 297–309.

The Economist (2013) *Available Online: Dead but Not Buried*. Available at: http://www.economist.com/news/china/21591890-there-little-you-cannot-buy-chinese-internet-dead-not-buried (Accessed on July 28, 2014).

Thibault (2010) *Comparison of Web Design: Global vs. Chinese Version*. Available at: http://www.them.pro/Comparison-web-design-global-vs-Chinese-version (Accessed January 30, 2015).

Wang, B., Yao, Y., Hou, B., Liao, D. and Chen, D. (2010) 'Knowledge aggregation in human flesh search', *2010 IEEE/ACM Int'l Conference on Green Computing and Communications & Int'l Conference on Cyber, Physical and Social Computing*: 825–830.

Wang, F.Y., Zeng, D., Hendler, J.A., Zhang, Q., Feng, Z., Gao, Y., Wang, H. and Lai, G. (2010) 'A study of the human flesh search engine: Crowd-powered expansion of online knowledge', *Computer*: 45–53.

Wang, H.H. (2010) *How EBay Failed In China*. Available at: http://www.forbes.com/sites/china/2010/09/12/how-ebay-failed-in-china/ (Accessed on July 28, 2014).

Wang, R.R. (2002) 'Globalizing the heart of the dragon: The impact of technology on Confucian ethical values', *Journal of Chinese Philosophy*, 29: 553–569.

Wu, W. and Wang, X. (2011) 'Lost in virtual carnival and masquerade: In-game marriage on the Chinese Internet'. In Herold, D.K. and Marolt, P. (eds) *Online Society in China: Creating, Celebrating, and Instrumentalising the Online Carnival*, London and New York: Routledge.

Wu, W., Fore, S., Wang, X. and Ho, P.S.Y. (2007) 'Beyond virtual carnival and masquerade: In-game marriage on the Chinese Internet', *Games and Culture*, 2: 59–89.

Yao-Huai, L. (2005) 'Privacy and data privacy issues in contemporary China', *Ethics and Information Technology*, 7: 7–15.

Yu, L.L., Asur, S. and Huberman, B.A. (2012) 'Artificial inflation: The real story of trends and trend-setters in Sina Weibo', *Privacy, Security, Risk and Trust (PASSAT), 2012 International Conference on and 2012 International Conference on Social Computing (SocialCom)*: 514–519.

Yu, Y. (2010) 'Olympic aspirations: Reconstructed images, national identity and international integration', *The International Journal of the History of Sport*, 27: 2821–2841.

Zhang, G. (2015) *'There is no escape the daily grind': Everyday Lore of Chinese Gamers*. Unpublished MPhil thesis. HK Polytechnic University.

Zhang, L. and Pentina, I. (2012) 'Motivations and usage patterns of Weibo', *Cyberpsychology, Behavior, and Social Networking*, 15: 312–317.

17

Lines for connectedness: a study of social media practices in Japanese families

Kana Ohashi and Fumitoshi Kato

Uses of mobile media technologies have been changing various aspects of our day-to-day activities. Especially, with the advent of smartphones, the feel of connectedness may have changed through social media services (e.g., LINE, Facebook, and Twitter). How do social media contribute to shape and reshape our conventional communication behavior? What are the characteristics of our communication via social media? The present study aims to understand the ways in which social media practices may influence the relationships among family members. To anchor our discussion, we will refer to an on-going research project in Japan in which we focus primarily on daughter–mother relationships.

Changes in family forms and lifestyles in Japan

High economic growth in Japan has resulted in the population being densely concentrated in urban areas and has led to the formation of nuclear families consisting only of "a couple and child/ren," which is now regarded as an exemplary family model (Nonoyama 2009). However, in recent years, family forms are becoming more diverse because of the decrease in the number of people getting married, the tendency to marry later, and the decline in the number of children. The number of couples that got married in 2012 was 670,000, which is 60 percent or 430,000 less than the level in 1972, when the number was 1.1 million (Ministry of Health, Labour and Welfare 2013). On the other hand, the average age at first marriage in Japan was 30.8 years old (male), and 29.2 years old (female) in 2012, which is a rise of 3.0 years (male) and 4.0 years (female) over the last three decades (Ministry of Health, Labour and Welfare 2013). The total fertility rate (TFR) also fell to a record-low of 1.26 in 2005, while it reached 4.3 in the age of the first baby boom (1947-49) (Cabinet Office 2013). Despite the slow increase in TFR in 2011, when it was 1.39, the number still remains low compared with European countries and the United States.

Furthermore, trends in percentage distribution of households by structure of household show that the percentages of one-person households and couple-only households have been increasing in recent years (Statistics and Information Department, Ministry of Health, Labour and Welfare 2012). As of 2010, 25.5 percent of all households are one-person households and 22.6 percent of which is couple-only. The factors for the diversification of family structures after the age of high economic growth in Japan include the rise of self-actualization as a result of the spread of higher education, increase in female labor force participation rate based on the need for supplementary income especially after the era of low growth, and growing awareness of diverse lifestyles in both Japan and other countries, stimulated by the advent of information society (Nonoyama 2009).

Hisaya Nonoyama, an advocate of "family lifestyle approach," proposed that the various types of family structures are selected by individuals based on their own lifestyle-orientation, and that it has become an increasingly important consideration for individuals. Within the context of "family," which is selected and formed as a lifestyle, individuals have to actively make efforts to build and maintain "close/intimate relationships" in order to enter the circle of a certain family, otherwise s/he cannot enter or s/he falls out of the family circle (Nonoyama 2009). This overlaps with the idea of "intimacy," which puts forward the idea that "communication is the means of establishing a good relationship in the first place, and it is the chief rationale for its continuation" (Giddens 2009, 330). It is pointed out that the diversification of family structures and the spread of various types of media are highly interrelated (Amagasa 2012).

Family and the use of *keitai*

One type of media that has a significant association with families in Japan is "*keitai*" (Amagasa 2012). *Keitai* is an everyday word for mobile phones and personal handyphones (PHS). Like Matsuda we chose to use this word "to make clear our position on mobile phones and PHS: they are not new technologies/media introduced from the outside but rather technologies/media that come to be embedded in society" (2006, 20).

In Japan, *keitai* started to spread in 1990s and the youth was the driving force behind widespread *keitai* adoption despite the fact that the device was first introduced in companies as a business tool (Dobashi 2006). When *keitai* was becoming popular, especially among the youth, children started to stay in their own rooms, becoming absorbed in text messaging and using the Internet. This caused conversation between parents and children to become less frequent, inciting discussions around the negative impacts of *keitai* (Amagasa 2012).

On the other hand, there has been an accumulation of research that has questioned such a deterministic approach to technology and instead aimed to elucidate how *keitai* are incorporated into the context of family relationships through specific usage of *keitai*. Through questionnaire study conducted with high school students, Tsuji (2003) found that calls and text message communication via *keitai* enabled a relaxed connection between the parents and a child, where a long enough distance was maintained so that the child does not feel constrained and yet the relationship was not completely cut off. Dobashi (2006) demonstrated through interviews conducted on housewives' *keitai* usages that housewives introduced *keitai* into their day-to-day activities by appraising *keitai* from the perspective of sustaining family relationship, in particular the parent–child/ren relationship. Based on the existing research by Japanese scholars on *keitai* and family relationships, Amagasa (2012) stated that *keitai* have become an indispensable tool in "being a family" in today's society where families cannot be sustained without making an effort to build a "close relationship."

Smartphones and social media use

Previous research on *keitai* and family relationships focused primarily on communication via phone calls, e-mails and SMS. However, the use of social media associated with the recent spread of smartphones has not been explored extensively. In Japan, the popularization of smartphones began in the late 2000s when the first iPhone arrived. According to a survey conducted by the

Institute for Information and Communications Policy (IICP) in 2013, the utilization rate of smartphones was 52.8 percent, which was twenty points up from the previous poll (IICP 2014). The age group that uses smartphones most frequently was people in their 20s (87.9 percent), followed by those in their 30s (78.7 percent), teens (63.3 percent), 40s (58.8 percent), 50s (32.4 percent), and 60s (8.7 percent). With the growing popularity of smartphones, people started to call them *"sumaho"* in distinction from *keitai*. Now for many people the word *keitai* means feature phones (conventional mobile phones). Given these circumstances, in this chapter, we use *"keitai"* for feature phones and *"sumaho"* for smartphones.

The spread of *sumaho* also resulted in a rapid increase in social media use, especially among the younger generation. The current utilization rate of social media is 57.1 percent overall, with 91 percent in the 20s age group, 80.8 percent in 30s, 76.3 percent in teens, 60.5 percent in 40s, 36.7 percent in 50s, and 14.3 percent in 60s (IICP 2014). The following shows the usage of the three most frequently used social media services among each age group (IICP 2014).

- Teens: LINE is most popular (70.5 percent), followed by Twitter (39.6 percent) and Google+ (30.9 percent).
- 20s: LINE (80.3 percent), Facebook (57.0 percent), and Twitter (47.1 percent).
- 30s: LINE (65.4 percent), Facebook (42.0 percent), and Google+ (37.8 percent).
- 40s: LINE (42.6 percent), Google+ (27.4 percent), and Facebook (20.3 percent).
- 50s: LINE (22.3 percent), Google+ (20.7 percent), and Facebook (15.2 percent).
- 60s: Google+ (7.7 percent), Facebook (5.0 percent), and LINE (4.3 percent).

Compared with the previous year, the social media service in which the utilization rate grew the most was LINE. Moreover, the utilization rate of LINE grew more than thirty points in all generations under the 40s. The utilization rate of Facebook increased to 57.0 percent in the 20s, while it remained unchanged in teens (20 percent). It increased ten to 20 points in other age groups. Based on such circumstances, one can presume that the usage of social media via *sumaho* will become incorporated in the context of family relationships in the future, in place of phone calls and text messaging through *keitai*. With this in the background, this study aims to elucidate how people use social media to form, sustain, block, sever, and regenerate relationships as a family.

Understanding the use of social media in family contexts

The objective of the present study was neither to illustrate the image of an average social media user nor to demonstrate the common usage of social media. The objective, instead, is to elucidate the specific and varied practices of how people use social media in their relationships with their family, in particular the child–parent relationship. An effective method used for this type of nascent research study is to focus on "extreme users" (Dobashi 2013). This study has also made references to this approach. Matsuda (2014) elucidated in her study on gender difference in the usage of *keitai* that young women have a strong orientation toward communication. They therefore use social media and write blogs more actively. For this study, we decided to employ in-depth interviews with young women, as the study's subjects, who actively use social media with their parent/s.

The interview participants were recruited through various channels, including students from the university that the authors belonged to, as well as from friends and acquaintances. In the period between December 2013 and May 2014, eight women aged between the 20s and the early 30s agreed to participate in this study. The interviews were conducted at locations the participants were familiar with, on a one-to-one basis between one of the authors and the participants, spanning from one to two hours. Attention was focused on having a cooperative process during this interview. The participants were asked to discuss within their interview that took a conversation format how they came to own their first *keitai* and their social media usage with their parent/s after purchasing a *sumaho*. The participants themselves determined who is included in their "family." The participants were asked to bring their *sumaho* during the interview and to provide screen shots, to a feasible extent, of interactions between family members using social media. The interview was recorded with consent by the participants.

After the end of the interview, the recorded data were transcribed. The transcribed data were organized in the following manner. First, the content of the data was read by the authors. Areas where similar contents were repeatedly made were summarized to an extent that the context was not lost. Thereafter, the speech style was changed to everyday dialogue form. Nouns that can be used to specify individuals were converted into symbols or aliases. Coding was performed for sections where the participants discuss practices with parent/s via social media. Then, we generated headings (sub-headings) to summarize the nature of such practices. Finally, the data was organized using a "case example-code matrix" (Sato 2011). By using tabulation software, each participant was allocated in the column section as case examples. Headings generated through the process of coding were placed in the row section. Excerpts from the responses that pertain to each cell were added (Figure 17.1). Sato (2011) postulated that developing such a data matrix during a qualitative analysis sufficiently pays attention to the individuality and specificity of each case. At the same time, he also suggested that data matrices could be an effective process for detecting general patterns or certain regularities that exceed the particularity of the case.

| | 母とビデオ通話 | 母とメッセージ交換 | 父とメッセージ交換 | グループ内メッセージ交換 | | 父と相互に閲覧 | 母と相互に閲覧 |
				家族全員	家族内の個別グループ		
ゆうこ		春から父が単身赴任、母が働きをはじめた。父は離れててふだん会わないので、前程ひんばんには3人のラインは使わなくなり、かわりに母と二人のやりとりが増えた。母が帰ってくるまでに家事をできるところまでやろうにしていて、お米何合といて、っていう連絡をしたりだとか、なんにに帰るよっていう連絡が主。私はものすごく方向音痴、母は、ものすごく方向感覚が鋭くて、地図も読める。たとえば、私が朝用事があって、途中で合流して、一緒にお茶したり買い物にいくときは、母がラインの位置情報を送ってくれて、それを見ながら行く。	父が単身赴任する前は、父が帰るときたまた。まれ私のバイトが終わると、車で乗せて帰ってくれるので、それの連絡をたまにしていた。		お父さんとお母さんと私の家族ラインを使っている(兄はスマホに変えたばかりでこれまで使っていなかった)、ごはんできたよ、とか、明日ある何時に起こしてほしいとか、週末にどこいきたい?とかっていうやりとりをする。みんなが家にいてもいる部屋がちがう場合はラインする。		
たかえ				ファミリーには、家族全員入ってる。基本は、母が犬の写真を投げまくる。	姉と私と母のグループは、3人で出かけたときの写真をどんどん共有する。姉と父がけんかしたのがきっかけで、父をのぞいたグループができた。それで、今度いつでかける?という会話も生まれて、どんどん3人だけのコミュニティが形成されている。		facebookは、母は、私が大学から家に帰ると、今日投稿したの見た?ってすごい言う。自分の作った料理をうまく写真とれたんだけど、今日の写真上手だったしよとか、母は友達とご飯行ったとか、飲み行ったりしたときも、写真をけっこうアップする。写真見た?ちょっと顔みんに映ってたでしょ上顔みんとその

Figure 17.1 Case example—code matrix

Results

Profile of the participants

The participants' name (pseudonym), age, occupation, scope of "family" assumed by the participant, household structure, resident area, social media currently in use, social media used with their
parent/s, are summarized below (Figure 17.2).

Adopting the first keitai

Parent/s of six participants out of eight bought them their first *keitai* when they were in elementary or secondary school so that the parent/s can contact them on the way to and from private
tutoring schools (cram schools). The role of the private tutoring school in Japan is so significant
that people say, "Japan's education is not explained without referring to private tutoring schools"
(Kuroishi and Takahashi 2009). According to the Cabinet Office, the percentage of pupils going
to private tutoring schools has increased in the last two decades (Cabinet Office 2007). In 1990s,
when most of the participants spent their childhood, private tutoring schools became a trillion
yen industry (Kuroishi and Takahashi 2009). During these days, a lifestyle of going to private
tutoring school after (formal) school and going home late at night prevailed among pupils. On
the other hand, *keitai* has just started to become popular around the same time. Participants reflect
upon the days as follows:

> When I was in fourth or fifth grade, kids-*keitai* started to become trendy and all of my friends
> wanted one. I persuaded my mom to buy one so she can keep track of my safety when I go

Name	Age	Occupation	Family members (age)	Household structure	Resident area	Social media currently in use	Social media used with parent/s
Satomi	31	housewife	father (73) mother (70) husband (33) daughter (4) father-in-law (59) mother-in-law (59) sister-in-law (29) sister-in-law's husband (30)	live in the same two-family house with in-laws	the Greater Tokyo Area	LINE Facebook	Facebook
Rika	32	flight attendant	mother (72)	live alone	the Greater Tokyo Area	LINE Facebook	LINE Facebook
Maki	32	company employee	mother (57)	live with her mother	the Greater Tokyo Area	LINE Facebook	LINE Facebook
Yuko	23	university student	father (53) mother (51) big brother (24)	live with her mother and big brother	the Greater Tokyo Area	LINE Facebook Twitter Instagram	LINE
Takae	21	university student	father (52) mother (52) big sister (23) pet dog (7)	live with her family	the Greater Tokyo Area	LINE Facebook Twitter	LINE Facebook
Haruko	22	university student	father (53) mother (48) little brother (19)	live with her parents	the Greater Tokyo Area	LINE Facebook Twitter Instagram	LINE Facebook
Aya	20	university student	father (N.D.) mother (N.D.)	live alone	the Greater Tokyo Area	LINE Facebook Twitter	LINE
Shizuka	20	university student	father (52) mother (48) little sister (18)	live with her family	the Greater Tokyo Area	LINE Facebook Twitter Instagram	LINE

Figure 17.2 Profile of the participants

to the private tutoring school. I got one when I was in fifth grade. However, she set parental control on it so I couldn't access the Internet.

(Aya)

My mom bought me a *keitai* when I was in the ninth grade for the sake of safety when I come home from the private tutoring school at night. But for me, it was just for contacting my friends.

(Rika)

My parents bought me my first *keitai* when I was in sixth grade because I go home late from the private tutoring school. It was a folding-type and was set inaccessible to the Internet by my parents. I decorated it with rhinestones. I used it to contact my parents and my friends. My parents were very strict, and I was scolded when I use it late at night. I was told not to bring my *keitai* to my room so I had to leave it in the living room.

(Shizuka)

As described, many parents bought *keitai* for their daughters (participants) for the sake of security, who began to commute alone in the wake of private tutoring schools. The daughter, however, assimilated *keitai* into everyday life, and was motivated to contact not only her parent/s but also her friends and to access to the Internet. The parent tried to monitor and/or control their daughter's *keitai* use accordingly by setting up rules for using her *keitai* or by limiting the use of the Internet.

From keitai *to* sumaho

All the participants renewed their *keitai* to *sumaho* within the past five years. Furthermore, all the participants in their 20s purchased a *sumaho* when they enrolled at university. There was a transition in their lifestyle of being protected/monitored by their parent/s to that of making their own decisions. At the same time, they also transitioned from conventional *keitai* bought by their parent/s to *sumaho* selected and bought by themselves. Many of the participants used *keitai* under their parents' surveillance and control when they were teenagers. However, they are now free from any rule or control by their parent/s. During the conventional *keitai* era, the main purpose was to confirm where they were and what time they will arrive home by calling or sending e-mail (SMS) to their parent/s. After purchasing a *sumaho*, social media replaced calling or sending e-mail and SMS.

Social media practices between daughter and parent/s

In this section, a series of social media practices between daughter and parent/s focusing on LINE, Facebook, and Twitter will be described, using a "case example-code matrix" based on interview data carried out by the authors.

LINE

Seven out of eight participants use LINE most often among other social media in communicating with their parent/s. On top of that, four out of these seven participants have a "family" group on LINE and send messages back and forth with their parent/s and sibling/s as follows:

In the family group, all my family members are included. Usually, it's my mom who sends massive amounts of photos of our dog.

(Takae)

My family writes about how they are doing in the family group. My younger brother tells us when he is coming home from his year abroad and my parents send us photos when they go travelling. It's handy to share photos and videos with everyone in the family. When my younger brother graduated from university, he sent a graduation photo and a message to us to thank our parents. I was deeply moved because at that time we all lived separately. I also sent my future plans to them when I was studying abroad. I felt I was saved at that moment. Before using LINE we didn't share photos when we were travelling. I think we started to use LINE in this way because we started to live separately. Until now we could have sent e-mails simultaneously to everyone, but we didn't. I like LINE because we can communicate like having a chat.

(Haruko)

Shizuka explains why she started to use LINE to communicate with her family as follows:

My family has a LINE group. We usually contact each other using LINE. On LINE, it's not really anything private, but they can't see other posts like Twitter or Facebook. Like e-mail or chat, my family can't see the contents that are not made public. Because my friends and I fool around on Twitter and Facebook, it feels more private on LINE. A big reason is because my parents monitored my *keitai* when I was in secondary school, that's why I don't want to be controlled any more.

There are also intimate communication between daughter and mother on LINE, as follows:

I use free video calls to talk to my mom when I'm abroad. Even if I'm not at home, I can show her my face and the scenery of where I am. (Rika)

I usually get in touch with my mom more than my dad. I send her anything, like when I make dinner. I would send a photo to my mom. (Aya)

I use stamps with my mom, like those that show a short message like "thanks."

(Haruko, Figure 17.3)

On LINE, only simple communication was found between daughter–father relationships, such as setting the time to meet. Emotional and expressive communication mentioned above could not be found within daughter–father dyads.

Facebook

Five out of eight participants use Facebook to communicate with their parent/s. They make good use of the check-in and photo uploading functions on Facebook.

My father told me to check-in on Facebook at all the places that I go to when I travel. He gets angry if I don't. He said that I don't have to call him, he can make sure that I am safe when I check-in. That's why I check-in at least once a day at the hotel or at the station when I travel.

(Haruko)

My mom checks whether or not I'm safe through Facebook when I am on holiday. Especially when I'm overseas, she can see whether I'm travelling according to the schedule without having to e-mail her all the time.

(Maki)

Figure 17.3   Example of messages and stamps on LINE

Because I don't live with my parents anymore, I want to show them roughly how I am doing by uploading photos. I want to show them how their grandchild is doing too. When my dad upload a photo I can also make sure that he looks fine. If it's e-mail, there is a burden to reply each message, but on Facebook it's convenient that we can easily see how each other is doing.

(Satomi)

When I get home from university, my mom would ask me, "Did you see my post on Facebook? I took a really good photo of the food I made. The photo is really nice, right?" I would say, "Yeah, it is."

(Takae)

Additionally, there are three participants who blocked their father on Facebook:

I blocked my dad. I feel that I would be monitored if I add him. For example, what I did at the school society, and I am scared that he will find out where I am if I am tagged in my friends' posts.

(Shizuka)

I became Facebook friends with my dad once, but his friends started to like my photos and I didn't like that, so I blocked my dad.

(Takae)

I feel embarrassed when my dad looks at my timeline. There are times when I go travelling without telling my family so I don't want them to see my photos.

(Aya)

Twitter

Six out of eight participants use Twitter; however, no one used it to communicate with their parent/s. Rather, they are trying not to make any point of contact with their parent/s by not teaching their parent/s how to use it, blocking them, and/or making another hidden private account.

My mom asked me to teach her how to use Twitter, but I try to avoid it.

(Aya)

When I got into a fight with my mom, I posted something like "People in menopause are annoying." My mom doesn't use Twitter, but my dad found my tweet and got really angry at me, so I blocked him.

(Haruko)

I have two Twitter accounts. Once I posted something like "I am teaching my mom how to use the computer because she is clueless about it." My friend saw it and told her mom, and her mom told my mom about it. She got angry and said "Why did you say something bad about me on the Internet?" So I made another private account that only my friends can browse. I only post what I really think on that account.

(Takae)

Discussion

As shown, most of the interviewees were using more than one social media service. In other words, they are actively selecting and combining different modes of communication depending on their own understandings about the nature of the relationship, as well as the situation therein. Overall, they seem to be highly skilled in terms of handling information on *sumaho*. Among their options, currently LINE is the most favored social media service for maintaining and reinforcing mother–daughter relationships. Combined with the use of "stamps," the use of LINE may complement their face-to-face interactions. Seemingly intricate and delicate issues were handled by their careful use of the social media services.

Through the interviews, we recognized that the relationships between parents and children are gradually changing as they begin to adopt new mobile media technologies. During the age of *keitai*, children were the ones monitored by their parents. In contrast, children became the ones who monitor the use of technologies by their parents. Growing up with *keitai*, the interviewees' generation, in their 20s and 30s, can be understood as an early adopter of new technologies and services. And thus children are now in the position to introduce, teach, and facilitate the use of social media services for their parents, rather than being introduced and taught by them. As specimens of interview data indicated, children can refuse to teach their parents how to use new services whenever they decide to do so. Or, they can always refuse or modify the status of linkage between their parents.

When we reflect upon the nature of our social relationships, being with someone or being on-site (at the time of the event) is becoming more and more important. Social media services may enable us to promote a sense of belonging and connectedness among family members.

Acknowledgement

This study draws from an Australian Research Council Linkage Grant with Intel entitled "Locating the Mobile" (LP130100848). We thank all of the participants in the study. We also thank Joyce Lam for her assistance in proofreading and translating this paper.

References

Amagasa, K. (2012) 'Keitai to Kazoku (Keitai and Family)'. In T. Okada and M. Matsuda (eds) *Keitai shakai-ron (Keitai Society)*, Tokyo: Yuhikaku.

Cabinet Office (2007) *Kokumin seikatsu hakusho (White Paper on National Life 2007)*. Available at: http://www5.cao.go.jp/seikatsu/whitepaper/h19/10_pdf/01_honpen/pdf/07sh_0101_3.pdf (Accessed August 26, 2014).

Cabinet Office (2013) *Shoushika shakai taisaku hakusho (White Paper on Countermeasures to the Falling Birth Rate Society 2013)*. Available at: http://www8.cao.go.jp/shoushi/shoushika/whitepaper/measures/w-2013/25webhonpen/html/b1_s1-1.html (Accessed August 26, 2014).

Dobashi, S. (2006) 'The Gendered Use of *keitai* in Domestic Contexts'. In M. Ito, D. Okabe and M. Matsuda (eds) *Personal, Portable, Pedestrian*, Cambridge, MA: MIT Press.

Dobashi, S. (2013) '*Keitai de toshi ni kakawaru (Getting Involved in the City by Using Keitai)*'. In S. Dobashi, K. Minamida and I. Tsuji (eds) *Digital media no shakaigaku (Digital Sociology)*, Tokyo: Hokuju shuppan.

Giddens, A. (2009) *Sociology* (6th edn), Cambridge: Polity Press.

Institute for Information and Communications Policy (2014) *Heisei 25 nen jouhou tsushin media no riyou jikan to jouhou koudou ni kansuru chousa sokuhou (The Results of a Survey of the Utilization Time of Telecommunication Media and Information Behavior)*. Available at: http://www.soumu.go.jp/iicp/chousakenkyu/data/research/survey/telecom/2014/h25mediariyou_1sokuhou.pdf (Accessed June 30, 2014).

Kuroishi, N. and Takahashi, M. (2009) 'A Study on Collaborations between the Cram-school Industry and Public Education: From Present Circumstances to Future Proposals', *Publications of Japan Professional School of Education*, 3: 1–14.

Matsuda, M. (2006) 'Discourses of *Keitai* in Japan'. In M. Ito, D. Okabe and M. Matsuda (eds) *Personal, Portable, Pedestrian*, Cambridge, MA: MIT Press.

Matsuda, M. (2014) '*Gender ni yoru Keitai riyou no sai (The Gendered Use of Keitai)*'. In M. Matsuda, S. Dobashi and I. Tsuji (eds) *Keitai no 2000 nendai (The 2000s of Keitai)*, Tokyo: Tokyo daigaku shuppankai.

Ministry of Health, Labour and Welfare (2013) *Heisei 25 nendoban kouseiroudou hakusho (White Paper on Health, Labour and Welfare 2013)*. Available at: http://www.mhlw.go.jp/wp/hakusyo/kousei/13/dl/1-02-2.pdf (Accessed August 26, 2014).

Nonoyama, H. (2009) *Ronten Handbook Kazoku shakaigaku (Handbook of Family Sociology)*, Kyoto: Sekaishi-sosha.

Sato, I. (2011) *Shitsuteki data bunsekihou (Methods of Qualitative Data Analysis)*, Tokyo: Shinyosha.

Statistics and Information Department, Ministry of Health, Labour and Welfare (2012) *Graph de miru setai no joukyou (Graphical Review of Japanese Household)*. Available at: http://www.mhlw.go.jp/toukei/list/dl/20-21-01.pdf (Accessed June 30, 2014).

Tsuji, D. (2003) 'Wakamono ni okeru idoutai tsushin media no riyou to kazoku kankei no henyou (The Mobile Telecommunication Media Usage Among Young People and the Transformation of Family Relationship)'. In *21 seiki koudo jouhouka, globalka shakai ni okeru ningen, shakaikankei (Twentieth Century Advanced Informatization, Human and Social Relationship in Globalized Society)*, Osaka: Institute of Economic and Political Studies, Kansai University.

18

E/motion: mobility and intimacy

Helen Grace

More smiles? More money. Nothing will be so powerful in destroying the healing virtues of a smile.

(Federici 1975, 1)

In an astutely perceptive move in late 2012, timed to coincide with the Christmas and New Year rush, Hong Kong-based Cathay Pacific cabin crew threatened to withhold smiles as part of a work-to-rule campaign for higher wages (South China Morning Post 2012). The gesture effectively pinpointed a particular quality expected of employees in global service industries today. The corporate appropriation of the bodily performance of hospitality assumes the free flow of affect as natural resource, like air or water, requiring no effort to produce, and the widely reported gesture underlines a specific biopolitical dimension of work: the very corporeal action of a person, expropriated, abstracted and generalized as corporate image. New information and communication technologies (ICTs) have been at the forefront of this refiguring of public/private relations, blurring the lines between labor and love within and beyond the domestic sphere as these "charismatic technologies" (Fortunati 2001) shift identity and mutate in their passage from work to play and beyond.

If an image of Asian hospitality—as gift freely given—has been commodified as a precise selling point consistently used by Asian airlines[1] to appeal especially to business travelers (Lo 2014), this very increase of business travel is itself a measure of increased global capital flows and major shifts in everyday life. Accompanying the receptivity and attention given to the comfort of business travelers in their separation from their own private lives is an even larger layer of mobility catering to the more widespread provision of labor and service for the global business class and Western consumers generally. The UN estimates that there are 232 million migrant workers in the world today,[2] 87.5 percent of whom are older than 24 and 48 percent of whom are women (UN 2013).

For this population of migrant workers, mobile media provides a key means of balancing labor demands and family maintenance, and while the international development literature concerns itself with macro-economic questions, the lived experience of mobility for those who enable development, especially through their immaterial labor, is marked by highly emotional questions of economics and intimacy.

Fortunati, Pertierra and Vincent argue that the appropriation of new media by these migrant workers—enabled by globalization and broadband advances—changes the way people migrate today and that these developments have become one of the leading forces driving contemporary political, cultural and economic transformation (2011, 1). The same changes that have transformed the lives of this population have also transformed everyday life more generally—in greater mobility, in whatever passenger class or form of transport travelers find themselves.

The everyday creative uses of mobile communications and ubiquitous media in Asia are a relatively understudied aspect of technological change and while considerable attention is given to the proliferation of images and other forms of expression as a mass phenomenon, close attention to the banal details of quotidian creativity (user created content or UCC) is overshadowed by much greater attention to the role of new media in political expression—in "mass media" and social media. In part this emphasis relates to an emphasis on *public* expression in media studies as a sphere of importance, rather than to the much more widespread and typical *private* and intimate forms of expression—a divide that has a clear gendered dimension.

Harootunian notes that the everyday appears as "a spectral precinct of time/space" (2004, 194) containing the shadows of other possible lives and temporalities and Hjorth, in discussing camera phone pictures, observes how the banal and "familiar" tropes of amateur photography are naturalized into emerging networked power relations, suggesting the role that the use of ubiquitous media might play in predicting the emergence of larger emerging popular forces (2009b, 159).[3]

Questions of intimacy and labor, emotion and affect have thus become a major focus of Western research (Hochschild 1983; Giddens 1992; Hochschild 2003; Ehrenreich and Hochschild 2004; Zelizer 2005; Illouz 2007; Luhmann 2010) and an affective turn has been identified (Sedgwick and Frank 1995; Hardt 1999; Negri 1999; Brennan 2004; Clough and Halley 2007; Seigworth and Gregg 2010). The threads and skeins of intimacy crisscrossing countries and continents are also mapped in a range of work, registering the general contours of expression and/or new media in specific locations (Tadiar 2004, 2009; Ong 2006; Rofel 2007; Hjorth 2009a; Constable 2010; Fortunati, Pertierra and Vincent 2011; Madianou and Miller 2012; Wallis 2013; Grace 2014).

In initial attention to new technologies and their domestication, research emphasis focused on consumption practices (Silverstone and Hirsch 1994, 32–47; Silverstone and Haddon 1996), whereas in many Asian countries, the luxury of a separation between production and consumption does not exist. Domestic space is less likely to be a refuge from work, but rather an extension of production space—or the factory itself. This means that consumption, production and social reproduction form a circuit within which mobility and intimacy circulate as the specific kind of "metamorphosis of space and time" (Fortunati, 2002) that mobile media enables (see also Berry, Kim and Spigel 2010).

This manifests itself in widely diverse low level innovations using new media technologies in both public and domestic space and is seen perhaps most starkly in the way in which the mobile phone is used to manage family life (Uy-Tioco 2007; Madionou and Miller 2011, 2012; Cabanes and Acadera 2012). In mapping the intensely emotional landscape of mobility and intimacy, some key methodological issues and themes emerge. In their introduction to *Electronic Emotion* (2009), Vincent and Fortunati note that studies of emotions and ICTs are still in their infancy, and, in a similar way it is fair to say that such studies in Asia are still in embryonic form. The problem with this trope of immaturity and underdevelopment is that it takes for granted the power of "mature" disciplines, in which established "authorities"—the "adults" in "grown-up" places—can then step in and speak generally and authoritatively for those "children" whose language stumbles and stutters. This impacts above all on regional research itself.

Sun Sun Lim and Gerard Goggin recently identified a notable "paradox" in observing how closely associated with Asia the *mobile* face of new mediated communication actually is, and yet how little this registers in "the communications research enterprise and its fundamental under-pinnings" (Lim and Goggin 2014). In response it should be recalled that the very formation of knowledge regimes and the consolidation of professional associations in the postwar period has been inflected by particular knowledge protocols and a specific discourse of academic freedom established during the Cold War. The shadow of this history is still very much alive and inti-mately lived throughout Asia today, in the very forms of subjectivity that earlier servitude to imperial expansion and geopolitical force has demanded.

In communication studies, this history is markedly played out in the dominance of quan-titative research and in an overall emphasis on empiricism and pragmatism (for discussion of communications research in Asia see Qiu 2010 and So 2010), reflecting the impact of American influence, especially in Japan, Korea, Taiwan, Hong Kong and the Philippines in the post-war period and the opportunities for education in US universities afforded many students, either by family support or foreign aid programs.

So, in identifying an "emerging research agenda," there remains the question of where this agenda-setting is still located. "Asia" has been a zone of occidental exploration since the begin-nings of European expansion and a vast literature of oriental/ist expertise is already well estab-lished globally—and even in the communications field, there are now many journals focusing on Asia or on China, Japan, India, or Southeast Asia. Anyone who lives *in* Asia is especially conscious of the regular sweep of Western researchers, carrying out projects, establishing research contacts or networks and generally marking out the territory in new disciplinary fields—as has been done for several hundred years now.

There is already substantial critical literature in cultural studies, providing excellent systemic analysis of this state of play and it is beyond the scope of this chapter to do more than refer to some of this (see, in particular, Sakai and Solomon 2006; Chen 2010; Ross 2010 and *Inter Asia Cultural Studies* Special Issue 2009). Additionally, important alternative research/publication proj-ects, such as the West Heavens initiative,[4] or the Traces series,[5] provide an Inter-Asian intellectual circuit, shifting and decentering established networks.

Emotions run high in considering these questions of knowledge inequalities that impact directly on people's careers and futures, raising more general questions of emotion, intimacy and affective labor, taking us to the core of what matters - and motivates, both personally and politi-cally. The social impact of ICTs is noted in some of the earliest texts (Katz and Aakhus 2002), but Asia is initially marginal in these studies and more technical HCI studies and the "uses and gratifications" model of social research cannot easily accommodate questions of intimacy. At first, the seemingly pointless and meaningless everyday personalization activities of users—especially in Japan, Korea and Hong Kong—seem unworthy of research by technologists keen to develop devices to sell to people, and it takes some time to understand that the very ordinariness of banal use underpins the forms of innovation that characterize the originality of creative expression in ubiquitous media.

The value of everyday use has long been understood by technology companies in the hiring of ethnographers and anthropologists and in the work they do (Bell 2006; Bell and Dourish 2007; Enderle 2010; Dourish and Bell 2011). In the Asia-Pacific, Hjorth's work in particular consistently emphasizes the intimate aspects of new media use regionally (Hjorth 2003, 2005, 2008a, 2008b, 2009a, 2009b, 2011) and Fortunati's foundational work on affective labor (1981) substantially impacts on contemporary research.

The increasing association of the mobile phone with intimacy and embodiment is seen in the evolution of naming: in the United States, as Ito notes, the device is called the *cellular phone*—defined by its technical infrastructure; in the United Kingdom it is called the *mobile*, a definition that refers to being untethered from a fixed location, but in Japan it is known as the more affective *keitai*, meaning "something you carry with you" (Ito Okabe and Matsuda 2006, 1). This shift in focus to the more embodied, personalized and intimate uses of the device coincides with closer studies of mobile media in Japan, surveyed in *Personal, Portable, Pedestrian* (Ito, Okabe and Matsuda 2006), the first book-length collection that focuses on the transformations of everyday life in Asia, effected by "intimate" technologies.

The term *keitai* (see also Hjorth 2003) captures the very *mentality* of embodied new media and in its sense of the mobility of the person who carries it, the term refers to a more dynamic and socially-engaged subjectivity in contrast to the figure of the stationary, more isolated and anti-social *otaku* (Azuma 2009; Eiji 2010)—although the experiential reality of mobile communications and online sociality is that *location* itself becomes relative (Hjorth and Kim 2005). In any case, it is in the observations of new media cultures and imaginaries, especially in Japan (around *anime* and *manga*, games and gaming and mobile media), that the cultural value of user-created content begins to be taken seriously.

If Japan is an early focus for critical studies of globalization (Iwabuchi, 2002), South Korea emerges as a particular site of innovative new media use (Kim 2003). The most innovative uses of new media are found in the modes of personalization of technologies (Kim 2002; Yoon 2003) and detailed and highly subtle readings of these practices have been undertaken by Hjorth in particular and Lee (2005, 2013). The emotional intensities of new media use in Korea directly influence the studies of intimacy in, for example, text messaging in Hong Kong (Lin 2005) and inspire closer focus on camera phone practices and affectivity (Grace 2014).

The global capital of affective text messaging and mobile intimacy is however the Philippines, where transnational life is highly reliant on mobile media and intensities of mediated experience take especially radical forms (Pertierra 2005, 2006; Solis 2007; Uy-Tioco 2007; Cabanes and Acadera 2012; Madianou and Miller 2011, 2012; McKay 2012; Tsujimotoa 2014). Some studies of intimacy and mobility in Singapore (Kitiarsa 2008; Yeoh and Huang 2010) focus especially on migrant workers, although there is acknowledgment of uneven distribution of access (Zainudeen, Iqbal and Samarajiva 2010) and some research looks at the perceived threats of mobile phones to the integrity of the household in India for example (Doron 2012).

The unprecedented scale of internal migration in China has had a huge impact on social and emotional life and while there are key texts that consider aspects of personal expression, intimacy and creativity (Qiu 2009; Wallis 2013; Chu, Fortunati, Law and Young 2012; Law 2012), questions of where the borderlines between public, private and personal are still being debated. The distinction between these terms is especially well discussed in Yang's (2012) elaboration of mobile phone use in urban contexts, introducing a further bifurcation of the somewhat Habermasian model of "public/private." The "personal"—as an extra dimension between public and private— appears then, not as a form of individualism, but as a means of customization (of technologies, spaces, emotions), in the context of a widespread commercialization of emotional/affective labor.

This commercialization has been a feature of the post-war/Cold War period regionally, in which the intimate service skills of large sections of the population have been widely drawn upon, well before a discourse of "economic miracle" produced by widespread foreign direct investment transformed economies by mobilizing affective labor and transforming everyday life. In the transformed space of collective intersubjectivities, of working and not working and dreaming of other forms of life, the game of life itself has generated a complex interplay between love and technological intimacy.

On intimacy

The word "intimacy" is widely used in the literature on new media, and when attempts are made to define it, these range from the very loose ("a certain type of privacy that we refer to as intimacy and this intimacy has led to a change in the perception of personal space and increased freedom" (Watkins, Kitner and Mehta 2012, 690)) to the more technical ("practices of co-present engagement" (Watkins, Hjorth and Koskinen 2012, 665)) to the more conceptual ("the migration of intimacy from a space between people to a space of technological mediation" (Hjorth 2011, 55)) amidst the recognition of a decided commercialization of emotional labor (Fortunati and Taipale 2012).

If in Western conceptions of immaterial and affective labor the emphasis has been on new forms of work (Lazzarato 1996; Hardt 1999), on professional and creative labor (Terranova 2000; Gregg 2013) and "playbor", (Kücklich 2005), this emphasis is generally disengaged from the domestic sphere (what Fortunati (1981) refers to as "the secret workshop") and the highly gendered work of intimacy—except when it spills into paid work. The immateriality of this work, so often considered beyond measure, becomes highly visible on Sundays and holidays in cities like Hong Kong and Taipei, when domestic "helpers" pour into the streets and public areas surrounding major buildings (sharing food, caring for each other in public manifestations of the usually invisible care that enables social life in these cities)—or when airline cabin crew refuse to smile.

Hjorth (2009a), in response to Giddens' (1992) idealized view of intimacy and consumption, discusses intimacy as a localized practice in the Asia-Pacific, and this is materialized in the research surveyed here. In general, the concept of biopower and its links to affective and immaterial labor in the work of Hardt, Negri and the Italian autonomists is generous in its acknowledgement of the central influence of Foucault. There seems to be more reluctance to acknowledge the centrality of the experimental thought of Lotta Femminista (Fortunati 2007, 2013) in giving rise to the very *potentiality* of immaterial labor, in its encounter with the work that men especially refuse to do. In any case, much of the labor that is refused in the West's "post-workerist" imaginary has not disappeared at all but has largely moved to Asia, enabling the kind of "migration of intimacy from a space between people to a space of technological mediation" that Hjorth's very useful description precisely captures.

The subject's demise

Various models of subjectivity are activated in attempts to understand new media use and behavior in Asia. These are aimed at dealing with the problem of cultural difference, although they tend to reveal their source in established Western knowledge regimes and the influence of powerful professional associations consolidated in the postwar period, determining the shape of disciplinary knowledge. So the dominance of social psychology, social constructionism and symbolic interactionism is evident in the reliance on, for example, the model of the bicultural self (Ye, Sarrica and Fortunati 2014) or the model of co-presence and the relational self (Gergen 1973, 2002, 2009).

Although a notion of the bicultural self has been adopted and linked to specific Chinese experience (Lu and Yang 2006; Lu et al. 2008), the model is imported via US-based experimental psychology. In general, in attempting to shortcut the complexities of intercultural engagement, there is a tendency in such theories of subjectivity to make comparisons between a Western "standard" and an ethnographic subject—but the real transformations of subjectivity that new media reflect now exist in a greater porosity of individuation required by mobility. In this context it is the model of Western individualism that is proving to be too inflexible in adapting to the demands of contemporary life. The challenge of explaining one culture from within another remains, however. As Rey Chow puts it, "We are left with the problem of how cultural difference can be imagined without being collapsed into the neutrality of a globalist technocracy . . . and without being frozen into the lifeless 'image' of the other" (Chow 1993, 48).

Notes

1 Beginning in 1972 with Singapore Airline's use of the 'Singapore Girl' advertising campaign, featuring cabin crew, dressed in the traditional sarong kebaya, freshly tweaked by Parisian haute couture designer, Pierre Balmain.
2 Ten times the entire population of Australia.
3 This is played out in the participation of many ostensibly non-political people, spontaneously mobilized by, for example the Sunflower Movement in Taiwan in 2013 and the Umbrella Movement in Hong Kong in 2014, whose social engagement begins in the sharing of ubiquitous media, as our research has shown.
4 http://westheavens.net/en (Accessed August 15, 2014)—translating the work of major South Asian thinkers into Chinese.
5 http://www.hkupress.org/Common/Reader/Channel/ShowPage.jsp?Cid=14&Pid=4&Version=0&Charset=iso-8859-1&page=0&cat=18 (Accessed August 15, 2014)—translating work between Chinese, English, Japanese and Korean.

References

Azuma, H. (2009) *Otaku: Japan's Database Animals*, Minneapolis: University of Minnesota Press.
Bell, G. (2006) 'The Age of the Thumb: A Cultural Reading of Mobile Technologies from Asia', *Knowledge, Technology, & Policy*, 19(2): 41–57.
Bell, G. and Dourish, P. (2007) 'Yesterday's Tomorrows: Notes on Ubiquitous Computing's Dominant Vision', *Personal and Ubiquitous Computing*, 11(2): 133–143.
Berry, C., Kim, S. and Spigel, L. (eds) (2010) *Electronic Elsewheres: Media, Technology, and the Experience of Social Space*, Minneapolis: University of Minnesota Press.
Brennan, T. (2004) *The Transmission of Affect*, Ithaca: Cornell University Press.
Cabanes, J.V.A. and Acadera, K.A.F. (2012) 'Of Mobile Phones and Mother-fathers: Calls, Text Messages, and Conjugal Power Relations in Mother-away Filipino Families', *New Media Society*, 14(6): 916–993.
Chen, K.H. (2010) *Asia as Method: Toward Deimperialization*, Durham, NC: Duke University Press.
Chow, R. (1993) 'Where Have All the Natives Gone?' In R. Chow *Writing Diaspora: Tactics of Intervention in Contemporary Cultural Studies*, Bloomington: Indiana University Press: 27–54.
Chu, R.W.-C., Fortunati L., Law P.-L. and Yang, S. (eds) (2012) *Mobile Communication and Greater China*, Abingdon: Routledge.
Clough, P.T. and Halley, J. (eds) (2007) *The Affective Turn: Theorizing the Social*, Durham, NC: Duke University Press.
Constable, N. (ed.) (2010) *Migrant Workers in Asia: Distant Divides, Intimate Connections*, Abingdon: Routledge.
Doron, A. (2012) 'Mobile Persons: Cell Phones, Gender and the Self in North India', *The Asia Pacific Journal of Anthropology*, 13(5): 414–443
Dourish, P. and Bell, G. (2011) *Divining a Digital Future: Mess and Mythology in Ubiquitous Computing*, Cambridge, MA: MIT Press.

Ehrenreich, B. and Hochschild, A.R. (2004) *Global Woman: Nannies, Maids, and Sex Workers in the New Economy*, New York: Holt Paperbacks.

Eiji, O. (2010) 'World and Variation: The Reproduction and Consumption of Narrative', *Mechademia*, 5: 99–116.

Enderle, R. (2010) 'Genevieve Bell: Intel's Secret Weapon', *TG Daily*. Available at: http://www.tgdaily. com/hardware-opinion/50438-genevieve-bell-intel's-secret-weapon (Accessed on April 21, 2014).

Federici, S. (1975) *Wages Against Housework*, Bristol: Power of Women Collective/Falling Wall Press.

Fortunati, L. (1995) *The Arcane of Reproduction: Housework, Prostitution, Labor and Capital*, New York: Autonomedia (originally published as *L'Arcano della Reproduzione: Casalinghe, Prostitute, Operai e Capitale*, Venezia: Marsilio Editori, 1981)

Fortunati, L. (2001) 'The Mobile Phone: An Identity on the Move', *Personal and Ubiquitous Computing*, 5(2): 85–98.

Fortunati, L. (2002) 'The Mobile Phone: Towards New Categories and Social Relations', *Information, Communication & Society*, 5(4): 513–528, DOI: 10.1080/13691180208538803.

Fortunati, L. (2007) 'Immaterial Labor and Its Machinization', *Ephemera: Theory and Politics in Organization*, 7(1): 139–157.

Fortunati, L. (2013) 'Learning to struggle: my story between workerism and feminism', *Viewpoint Magazine*. Availableat:http://viewpointmag.com/2013/09/15/learning-to-struggle-my-story-between-workerism-and-feminism/ (Accessed on July 23, 2014).

Fortunati, L. and Taipale, S. (2012) 'Women's Emotions towards the Mobile Phone', *Feminist Media Studies*, 12(4): 538–549.

Fortunati, L., Pertierra, R. and Vincent, J. (2011) *Migration, Diaspora and Information Technology in Global Societies*, London: Routledge.

Gergen, K. (1973) 'Social Psychology as History', *Journal of Personality and Social Psychology*, 26(2): 309–320.

Gergen, K. (2002) 'Cell Phone Technology and the Challenge of Absent Presence'. In J. Katz and M. Aarhus (eds) *Perpetual Contact: Mobile Communication, Private Talk, Public Performance*, Cambridge: Cambridge University Press.

Gergen, K. (2009) *Relational Being: Beyond Self and Community*, New York: Oxford University Press.

Giddens, A. (1992) *The Transformation of Intimacy: Sexuality, Love, and Eroticism in Modern Societies*, Stanford: Stanford University Press.

Grace, H. (2014) *Culture, Aesthetics and Affect in Ubiquitous Media: The Prosaic Image*, London: Routledge.

Gregg, M. (2013) *Work's Intimacy*, Oxford: Polity Press.

Hardt, M. (1999) 'Affective Labor', *boundary 2*, 26(2): 89–100.

Harootunian, H. (2004) 'Shadowing History: National Narratives and the Persistence of the Everyday', *Cultural Studies*, 18(2–3): 181–200.

Hjorth, L. (2003) 'Kawaii@keitai'. In N. Gottlieb and M. McLelland *Japanese Cybercultures*, New York: Routledge: 50–59.

Hjorth, L. (2008a) 'Cybercute Politics: The Internet Cyworld and Gender Performativity in Korea'. In Y. Kim (ed.) *Media Consumption and Everyday Life in Asia*, London: Routledge: 203–216.

Hjorth, L. (2008b) 'Waiting for Immediacy: The Convergent Inertia of Mobility and Immobility'. In K. Nyíri (ed.) *Integration and Ubiquity: Towards a Philosophy of Telecommunications Convergence*, Vienna: Passagen Verlag: 189–196.

Hjorth, L. (2009a) *Mobile Media in the Asia Pacific: Gender and the Art of Being Mobile*, Abingdon: Routledge.

Hjorth, L. (2009b) 'Photo Shopping: A snapshot on camera phone practices', *Knowledge, Technology & Policy*, 22(3): 157–159.

Hjorth, L. (2011) 'It's Complicated: A Case Study of Personalisation in an Age of Social and Mobile Media', *Communication, Politics & Culture*, 44(1): 45–59.

Hjorth, L. and Kim, H.-W. (2005) 'Being There and Being Here: Gendered Customising of Mobile 3G Practices Through a Case Study in Seoul', *Convergence*, 11: 49–55.

Hochschild, A.R. (1983) *The Managed Heart: Commercialization of Human Feeling*, Oakland: University of California Press.

Hochschild, A.R. (2003) *The Commercialization of Intimate Life: Notes from Home and Work*, Oakland: University of California Press.

Illouz, E. (2007) *Cold Intimacies: The Making of Emotional Capitalism*, Cambridge: Polity.

Inter Asia Cultural Studies (2009) Special Issue, Neoliberal conditions of knowledge, 10(2).

Ito, M., Okabe, D. and Matsuda, M. (2006) *Personal, Portable, Pedestrian: Mobile Phones in Japanese Life*, Cambridge, MA: MIT Press.

Iwabuchi, K. (2002) *Recentering Globalization: Popular Culture and Japanese Transnationalism*, Durham, NC: Duke University Press.

Katz, J.E. and Aakhus, M.A. (eds) (2002) *Perpetual Contact: Mobile Communication, Private Talk, Public Performance*, Cambridge: Cambridge University Press.

Kim, S.-D. (2002) 'Korea: Personal Meanings'. In J.E. Katz and M.A. Aakhus (eds) *Perpetual Contact: Mobile Communication, Private Talk, Public Performance*, Cambridge: Cambridge University Press: 63–79.

Kim S.-D. (2003) 'The Shaping of New Politics in the Era of Mobile and Cyber Communication: The Internet, Mobile Phone and Political Participation in Korea'. In K. Nyíri (ed.) *Mobile Democracy: Essays on Society, Self and Politics*, Vienna: Passager Verlag: 317–326.

Kitiarsa, P. (2008) 'Thai Migrants in Singapore: State, Intimacy and Desire', *Gender, Place & Culture: A Journal of Feminist Geography*, 15(6): 595–610.

Kücklich, J. (2005) 'Precarious Playbor: Modders and the Digital Games Industry', *The Fibreculture Journal*, 5. Available at: http://www.journal.fibreculture.org/issue5/kucklich.html (Accessed on September 15, 2014).

Law, P-L. (ed.) (2012) *New Connectivities in China: Virtual, Actual and Local Interactions*, Dordrecht: Springer.

Lazzarato, M. (1996) 'Immaterial Labor'. In P. Virno and M. Hardt (eds) *Radical Thought in Italy: A Potential Politics*, Minneapolis: University of Minnesota Press: 133–147.

Lee, D.-H. (2005) 'Women's Creation of Camera Phone Culture', *The Fibreculture Journal*, 6. Available at: http://six.fibreculturejournal.org/fcj-038-womens-creation-of-camera-phone-culture/ (Accessed on July 22, 2014).

Lee, D.-H. (2013) 'Smartphones, Mobile Social Space, and New Sociality in Korea', *Mobile Media & Communication*, 1(3): 269–284.

Lim, S.S. and Goggin, G. (2014) 'Mobile Communication in Asia: Issues and Imperatives – Introduction to the Special Section', *Journal of Computer-Mediated Communication*, 19: 663–666.

Lin, A.M.Y. (2005) 'New Youth Digital Literacies and Mobile Connectivity: Text Messaging among Hong Kong College Students', *Fibreculture*, 6. Available at: http://journal.fibreculture.org/issue6/index.html (Accessed on July 22, 2014).

Lo, A. (2014) 'More Respect All Round Would Help Cathay Pacific's Harassed Attendants', *South China Morning Post*.

Lu, L. and Yang, K.S. (2006) 'Emergence and Composition of the Traditional–Modern Bicultural Self of People in Contemporary Taiwanese Societies', *Asian Journal of Social Psychology*, 9: 167–175.

Lu, L., Kao, S.F., Chang, T.T., Wu, H.P. and Jin, Z. (2008) 'The Individual- and Social-oriented Chinese Bicultural Self: A Subcultural Analysis Contrasting Mainland Chinese and Taiwanese', *Social Behavior and Personality: An International Journal*, 36: 337–346.

Luhmann, N. (2010) *Love: A Sketch* (A. Kieserling ed. and K. Cross trans.), Cambridge: Polity.

McKay, D. (2012) *Global Filipinos*, Bloomington: Indiana University Press.

Madianou, M. and Miller, D. (2011) 'Mobile Phone Parenting: Reconfiguring Relationships between Filipina Migrant Mothers and their Left-behind Children', *New Media Society*, 13(3): 457–470.

Madianou, M. and Miller, D. (2012) *Migration and New Media: Transnational Families and Polymedia*, Abingdon, Routledge.

Negri, A. (1999) 'Value and Affect', *boundary 2*, 26(2): 77–88.

Ong, A. (2006) *Neoliberalism as Exception: Mutations in Citizenship and Sovereignty*, Durham, NC: Duke University Press.

Pertierra, R. (2005) 'Mobile Phones, Identity and Discursive Intimacy', *Human Technology: An Interdisciplinary Journal on Humans in ICT Environments*, 1(1): 23–44.

Pertierra, R. (2006) *Transforming Technologies: Altered Selves – Mobile Phones and Internet Use in the Philippines*, Manila: De Salle University Press.

Qiu, J.L.-C. (2009) *Mobile, Working-Class Network Society: Communication Technology and the Information Have-Less in Urban China*, Cambridge MA: MIT Press.

Qiu, J.L.-C. (2010) Mobile Communication Research in Asia: Changing Technological and Intellectual Geopolitics? *Asian Journal of Communication*, 20(2): 213–229.

Rofel, L. (2007) *Desiring China: Experiments in Neoliberalism, Sexuality, and Public Culture*, Durham, NC: Duke University Press.

Ross, A. (2010) 'The Rise of the Global University'. In A. Ross *Nice Work If You Can Get It: Life and Labor in Precarious Times*, New York: NYU Press: 189–206.

Sakai, N. and Solomon, J. (eds) (2006) *Translation, Biopolitics, Colonial Difference*, Traces Series (published in English, Chinese, Japanese and Korean), Hong Kong: Hong Kong University Press.

Sedgwick, E. and Frank, A. (eds) (1995) *Shame and its Sisters: A Silvan Tomkins Reader*, Durham, NC: Duke University Press.

Seigworth, G. and Gregg, M. (eds) (2010) *The Affect Reader*, Durham, NC: Duke University Press.

Silverstone, R. and Haddon, L. (1996) 'Design and the Domestication of Information and Communication Technologies: Technical Change and Everyday Life'. In R. Silverstone and R. Mansell (eds) *Communication by Design. The Politics of Information and Communication Technologies*, Oxford: Oxford University Press: 44–74.

Silverstone, R. and Hirsch, E. (eds) (1994) *Consuming Technologies: Media and Information in Domestic Spaces*, London: Routledge, 32–47.

So, C.Y.-K. (2010) 'The Rise of Asian Communication Research: A Citation Study of SSCI Journals', *Asian Journal of Communication*, 20(2): 230–247.

Solis, R.J.C. (2007) 'Texting Love: An Exploration of Text Messaging as a Medium for Romance in the Philippines', *M/C Journal*, 10(1). Available at: http://journal.media-culture.org.au/0703/05-solis.php (Accessed on July 22, 2014).

South China Morning Post (2012) 'Cathay attendants threaten no smiles, meals or alcohol on flights', December 13. Available at: http://www.scmp.com/news/hong-kong/article/1104487/cathay-attendants-threaten-no-smiles-meals-or-alcohol-flights (Accessed on June 26, 2015).

Tadiar, N.X.N. (2004) *Fantasy Production: Sexual Economies and Other Philippine Consequences for the New World Order*, Hong Kong: Hong Kong University Press.

Tadiar, N.X.N. (2009) *Things Fall Away: Philippine Historical Experience and the Makings of Globalization*, Durham, NC: Duke University Press.

Terranova, T. (2000) 'Free Labor: Producing Culture for the Digital Economy', *Social Text*, 18(2): 33–58.

Ticineto, C.P. and Halley, J. (eds) (2007) *The Affective Turn: Theorizing the Social*, Durham, NC: Duke University Press.

Tsujimoto, T. (2014) 'Negotiating Gender Dynamics in Heteronormativity: Extramarital Intimacy among migrant Filipino Workers in South Korea', *Gender, Place & Culture: A Journal of Feminist Geography*, 21(6): 750–767.

UN (2013) 'Migrants by Origin and Destination', *Population Facts* No. 2013/3, United Nations Department of Economic and Social Affairs, Population Division. Available at: http://www.un.org/en/ga/68/meetings/migration/pdf/International%20Migration%202013_Migrants%20by%20origin%20and%20destination.pdf (Accessed July 26, 2014).

Uy-Tioco, C. (2007) 'Overseas Filipino Workers and Text Messaging: Reinventing Transnational Mothering', *Continuum: Journal of Media & Cultural Studies*, 21(2): 253–265.

Vincent, J. and Fortunati, L. (2009) 'Electronic Emotion: The Mediation of Emotion via Information and Communication Technologies', *Interdisciplinary Communication Studies*, 3, Bern, Switzerland: Peter Lang.

Wallis, C., (2013) *Technomobility in China: Young Migrant Women and Mobile Phones*, New York: NYU Press.

Watkins, J., Hjorth, L. and Koskinen, I. (2012) 'Wising Up: Revising Mobile Media in an Age of Smartphones', *Continuum: Journal of Media & Cultural Studies*, 26(5): 665–668.

Watkins, J., Kitner, K.R. and Mehta, D. (2012) 'Mobile and Smartphone Use in Urban and Rural India', *Continuum: Journal of Media & Cultural Studies*, 26(5): 685–697.

Yang, B.-X. (2012) 'Social Networks and Individualism: Some Issues on the Role of Mobile Phones in Urban China'. In R.W.-C. Chu, L. Fortunati, P.-L. Law, and S.-H. Yang (eds) *Mobile Communication and Greater China*, London: Routledge: 128–142.

Ye, W.M., Sarrica, M. and Fortunati, L. (2014), 'Two Selves and Online Forums in China', *Asian Journal of Social Psychology*, 17: 1–11.

Yeoh, B.S-A. and Huang, S. (2010) 'Transnational Domestic Workers and the Negotiation of Mobility and Work Practices in Singapore's Home', *Spaces, Mobilities*, 5(2): 219–236.

Yoon, K.-W. (2003) 'Retraditionalizing the Mobile: Young People's Sociality and Mobile Phone Use in Seoul, South Korea', *European Journal of Cultural Studies*, 6(3): 327–343.

Zainudeen, A., Iqbal, T. and Samarajiva, R. (2010) 'Who's Got the Phone? Gender and the Use of the Telephone at the Bottom of the Pyramid', *New Media Society*, 12(4): 549–566.

Zelizer, V. (2005) *The Purchase of Intimacy*, Princeton, NJ: Princeton University Press.

19

Locative social media engagement and intergenerational relationships in China

Baohua Zhou and Miao Xiao

Mobile Internet is enjoying a rapid penetration period in China with the popularization of smartphones. According to the latest survey report from China Internet Network Information Center (CNNIC 2015), up until the end of 2014 there were 557 million mobile Internet users, accounting for 85.8 percent of the 649 million Internet users and 41.1 percent of the whole population, surpassing PC Internet users. Accompanying this process is the emergence of location-based services in Chinese mobile and social media practice. Jiepang, also known as China's Foursquare, is one of the first generation locative media to have attracted a lot of urban youth users (Hjorth and Gu 2012). Since then, people have also used various integrative social media for locative information sharing, like Weibo (microblog service similar to Twitter), Renren (popular SNS among students like Facebook), and especially WeChat (mobile messaging app service similar to WhatsApp).

With these locative social media, people can easily share their locations with others directly through the "check-in" tools or indirectly by posting the instant status or pictures. Locative social media has changed not only communication modes amongst friends but also amongst family members, particularly intergenerational relationships. Aged parents have in the past been considered Internet "have-nots" or inactive "have-less" given the difficulty of learning how to use new computer technologies. However, with the emergence of more convenient mobile Internet services, it is easier for them to get online. WeChat, an easy-to-use messaging mobile app, has attracted 600 million users, including many middle aged and elderly people. For the first time young people are "meeting" their parents on locative social media in a large scale.

What arises is an interesting communication and social phenomenon in contemporary China. Since the one-child policy widely carried out in China from the early 1980s, intergenerational communication within the family has attracted much academic interest (e.g., Liu 2008; Lei 2013). Yet few studies have been conducted on this topic in the era of digital media, especially when parents and their children become online "friends" for the first time. How does this happen? How do they interact with each other on locative social media? Do they like these new interactions? What does this mean for intergenerational relationships?

One approach in exploring these questions is the recent theoretical discussion of "bottom-up" technology transmission phenomenon within families (Correa et al. 2013; Correa 2014). This approach argues that different from the traditional "top-down" socialization pattern where parents guide the media usage of their children, it is the children who are early-adopters of new media technologies and more skilled users who are now teaching their parents how to use digital media. The children actually play the role of "brokers" in families and facilitate their parents' connections to the new communication technologies as well as the richer social resources (Katz, 2010). The studies also find that the extent to which youth influence their parents' learning of new information technologies are influenced by structural factors (youths' age, gender roles, and family socioeconomic status) and family structure (parental authority and child–parent interactions). Since locative media is a new communication technology emerging in Chinese society and novel for aged parents, we will analyze if the "bottom-up" technology transmission pattern happens in the family intergenerational communication process.

Other studies further analyze the impacts of digital media usage on family relationships. There are two main streams of view: negative (pessimistic) and positive (optimistic). The negative approaches focus on the increasing likelihood of family conflicts over the Internet (Kiesler et al. 2000; Mesch 2006) and the "distracting" effect of the Internet that challenges "family time" and "family boundaries" (Mesch 2006). With the domestication of new media technologies in families, parents and children may have conflicting perceptions and attitudes towards new media, which increases arguments over new media technologies among family members, especially between adolescents and parents. For example, parents always expect children to use the Internet for educational purposes, so when youth use the Internet for social and entertainment purposes, parental expectations presumably contradict that kind of use, thus probably arising in conflict. For locative media use, we may also explore whether parents and children have conflicting expectations concerning ways of using new media. New media use is also seen as an activity that reduces the time that parents and children spend together in common activities according to the "time displacement" hypothesis (Nie et al. 2002), which is argued as a threat to family cohesion. The argument is that family members need to have time to stay together to facilitate family communication and closeness and protect the "boundaries" between family members and the external world, while unfortunately the new media technologies distract them by blurring the boundaries between work and home (Salaff 2002) and decreasing the sharing time. Therefore, high frequency of Internet use might be negatively associated with family time and also family cohesion.

Another set of scholars argue that new media has positive impacts on family cohesion and intergenerational communication. An important explanation is that the new media technologies actually offer more opportunities for family members to stay together and feel closeness. First, new media provide opportunities for parents and children to collaborate and discuss over the new technologies. For example, they can play games together or collaborate on software installation (Kiesler et al. 2000; Orleans and Laney 2000). Secondly and more importantly, the new technologies help separated family members to feel the "virtual co-presence" or "connected presence" to overcome long-distance to some extent (Baldassar 2007, 2008; Horst 2006). New technology increases overall communication frequency of transnational families (Wilding 2006). For many families whose members live geographically apart, Skype meetings have become a family routine. Aguila (2011) vividly describes how one father feels togetherness with his daughter when he watches her cooking in her kitchen through Skype and they feel their home is extended through the "virtual co-presence." Focusing on the context of Chinese migrants in London and their ageing parents in China, Kang (2012) analyzes how young migrants maintain their "long-distance intimacy" with parents through Internet tools. Her study also revealed the gender inequality in this digital kinship process by identifying that mothers who are traditionally the care-giving persons in families have been marginalized as they lack digital capacity. The role of care and intimacy is now increasingly reassigned to male family members such as fathers. Lam's (2013) study is among the few ones that explore the translocal context in contemporary China. She finds that the new ICTs have supplemented traditional face-to-face interaction to help family members living apart connect, get social and mental support, and exchange social and cultural knowledge, thus maintaining and strengthening family solidarity in the virtual space.

Based on the above literature review, this chapter presents some preliminary research on the interaction between locative social media and intergenerational relationship in Chinese families. We will illustrate how the locative media engagement is practiced as a "bottom-up" technology transmission and how it interacts with the "virtual co-presence" and "long-distance intimacy" shared among parents and children, especially for those who are geographically apart. Also, we will explore if parents and children have any conflicts regarding use of locative media. The data comes from six in-depth family interviews conducted in Shanghai in 2013. Among all the children, five are college students and one is from middle school; four are girls and two are boys. Four children live apart from their parents as they are studying in Shanghai and their ageing parents live in their hometown. All children and at least one parent from each family use locative social media. The most popular and frequently-used one is WeChat. At the same time some children also use Weibo, Renren, or other location-based social media sometimes. Only one boy uses Jiepang.

Bottom-up technology transmission

The "bottom-up" technology transmission phenomenon is observed in the practice of inter-generational family communication in China. In five families out of six, parents' WeChat apps were installed by their children. The exception is the middle school boy (R), as his parents are younger than those of college-level children and thus more familiar with new technology. Some parents ask for their children's help to install WeChat because they want to "keep up with the social trend" as their friends are also using it, while others do so only in order to "keep up with their children," to stay in touch, and learn what their children do in their daily lives. Especially for those translocal families, maintaining intimacy and taking up the responsibility of care has become a crucial motivation for the parents to adopt WeChat. At the same time, young people also think it is a convenient, cheap and fashionable way to communicate with their parents via WeChat so they are pleased to install it for their parents and teach them how to use it. The social need of intergenerational communication is thus an important force to promote the bottom-up technology transmission phenomenon in China.

By adopting and using WeChat, parents and children can share each others' location either by communicating directly or by tracking the uploads of "moments," which can show locative information. In terms of direct communication, grouping a "family chat room" is a popular practice, complementary to one-to-one online chatting. In our interview, three families have their own WeChat "family group," composed of only three persons—dad, mom and child. Comparatively, the tracking of the moments is more indirect and hidden. The transfer between these two channels is also flexible: the parents may turn to their "family group" to ask their children for details when they find out something about which they want to learn more from their children's posts.

With the help of young people, the parents have become skilled at using WeChat. They keep track of their children's posts, asking them about details, but rarely post, except for the youngest parents. The parents are eager to know what the young people do and where they go via WeChat, while the young people seem not so interested about their parents' daily lives. They teach parents to use new media mainly to meet their parents' needs, not in order to know more about them. The children are more excited about their ambient environment, such as updates from their classmates and peers. Comparatively, the lives of their parents considered boring and unchanging to them, as two interviewees describe, "nothing new besides their workplace and colleagues, and they rarely go touring" (K), and "their life is just like that. Never changes" (Y). The lurking of the parents on WeChat further enhances this unbalanced care-giving between parents and children.

Previous studies reveal that gender imbalance occurs in this bottom-up technology transmission process, which has also been confirmed in the current empirical analysis. As Ti's mother doesn't have a smartphone, she depends on Ti's father for news about their daughter. In the past, Ti talked more to her mother about her life; with the intervention of new technology, her father is now more informed about Ti's movements than her mother. "He can get a word in about what I have posted on WeChat when we talk or when I talk with my mother, for which I'm surprised," Ti said.

Watching quietly, chatting occasionally

Most of the time, parents only watch their children's WeChat updates quietly. In this way, they feel they are updated about what their children do and where they go. They do not ask their children everything in order to avoid interruption and conflict, especially when they feel their children are reluctant to share with them too much about their daily lives, for which we will elaborate more in the subsequent section. R is such a case. He is a heavy user of locative social media, from Qzone at primary school, and Renren at high school, to Weibo, Douban, Jiepang and WeChat in university. His mother keeps following him quietly as he switches from one platform to another. R has known that for a long time, and they actually form a tacit agreement that R's mother follows him on social media without asking him questions. R's mother tells us in the interview, "R is not a boy who likes to share his life with us. So I just want to know what he is doing and what his interests are recently." R also admits that he doesn't talk much with his parents as "it's not necessary." Though his home is located in Shanghai and he also studies in Shanghai, he goes back home only once a month to pick up seasonal clothes and calls his parents only when he feels it is necessary to discuss with them "key issues," such as living expenses and his future plans of studying abroad. In this situation, watching R's locative social media accounts quietly has become a key channel for his parents to know about their son.

Nevertheless, an important strength of social media like WeChat is that they can facilitate parents to start a conversation with their children naturally and smoothly. Observing their children's locative social media contents has prepared rich resources for the parents to trigger a conversation or to give "essential cares or suggestions" (R's mother). For example, one day when R's mother noticed that R frequently updated "nike+" records, she recognized that her son was running. When R went home, his mother naturally mentioned his running experience and reminded him not to run late at night. "He wouldn't tell us if I didn't notice it," R's mother is proud of this conversation. Another chance to trigger conversation occurs usually when the young people leave the current locations to travel. The locative changes on social media can be tracked by their careful parents, which will lead a new conversation between them. When R was a sophomore, he joined a trip to Nanjing, just two hours away from Shanghai by train. During the journey, he posted some messages on his social media accounts without clearly claiming where he was going. To his surprise, as soon as he arrived at the hotel, he received his mother's phone call. "They saw a photo of my train tickets in my Weibo." His mother asked about who he went there with and where they stayed. "After all, he left Shanghai and went to a new place, so I felt a bit worried," R's mother explained the importance that the locative information meant to her. She paid close attention to R's online updates during that period to ensure her son was safe when he was staying in different places.

The flexibility between quiet watching and occasional talking is also important to those families whose parents and children keep in frequent contact via other channels like phone calls. To them the traditional phone calling and new locative social media can meet different needs in their long-distance intergenerational communication and supplement each other. Specifically, they tend to talk about "big issues" like job hunting and personal development on the telephone, while locative sharing on social media helps the parents to know more life trivia of their children, or things that both of them don't feel necessary to be discussed on the phone. Even the simplest message on locative media—such as an instant status updating on WeChat, "on my way to school, good weather!"—can show the parents where their children are, what they are doing, and how they are feeling. These clues can also become triggers to start a conversation on the phone.

As Kang (2012) observes in her empirical study on Chinese migrants in London whose ageing parents in China, some young people have to spend long hours working or studying, so for them phone calls are not allowed but Internet use is less restricted in terms of time and access. That is why Y's mother recognizes that WeChat is very useful for her to communicate with Y. She likes to speak to Y, but when Y is in school, she doesn't know whether Y is in class or busy and when Y is available to receive her phone call. In the past, she can only wait or send SMS via cellphone, which she thinks will turn into a pressure to Y. Now, with locative social media, she can easily leave messages to ask, or just tell her daughter what she is doing and feeling. Y can easily respond to her on WeChat even though she cannot speak to her mother on the phone. WeChat has thus given parents and children more opportunities to communicate when they cannot find proper time to make a phone call.

Gender also matters in this process. Although fathers tend to have higher capacity to handle the new technology, mothers show more care about their children. Ti's father, fluent in using WeChat, admits that he only checks Ti's posts occasionally, when he is free. He doesn't pay special attention to Ti's life details. "I care about 'big issues' like her job hunting, finding a boyfriend, or scholarship," he explains to the researchers.

Virtual co-presence and long-distance intimacy

As noted earlier, scholars have used the concept of virtual co-presence or connected presence to theorize the feeling of togetherness that ICTs brings about to overcome distance (Baldassar 2007, 2008; Horst 2006; Wilding 2006). In our interviews, all the parents agreed that the locative social media and information sharing promote intimacy with their children by helping them to know more life trivia, and to feel a sense of co-presence, as well as offering more opportunities for care-giving. This is a common feeling for parents, no matter what their intergenerational communication status is.

These findings need to be understood in the context of China's social realities of the rural-urban divide, the educational gap and the translocal experience shared among parents and children. Since the economic reform started in the early 1980s, social mobility has been fast growing and many family members are living apart in different locations seeking upward mobility as reciprocal aspirations (Lam 2013). As quality universities concentrate in large cities like Beijing and Shanghai, young people across the nation come to big cities to pursue their academic goals, leaving parents in hometowns. As most parents do not have the experience of studying in cities, they know little about it. They tend to imagine the cities as places full of opportunities while also filled with threats, thus they worry about their children's safety. While phone calls or short messages are usually events oriented, locative sharing messages on SNS provide them more opportunities to give care to their children.

C's mother is very careful about C's safety. In her definition, the "safety area" for C is the university campus. If C leaves campus, she would like to know where C goes and if C is fine. C's mother tells researchers that she feels much closer to C since using WeChat:

> I want to know about her living, her mood and where she goes and with whom. I worry about her safety. WeChat is a convenient way. I think I know more about her than before. Previously, we usually send messages which cost money. Now I can know what she is doing at the moment. I see where she is. I see her photos. I feel we're closer. It's just like I'm with her.

K's mother does not show as much concern as C's mother. Her definition for K's safe area is the city; that is, she will not feel too worried as long as K doesn't leave Shanghai. But she still relies on WeChat to chat with K. She thinks K's life in Shanghai is interesting and she wants to know as much as she can via WeChat. When she sees K's pictures of instant locations, she feels like sharing the same feeling with K, keeping up with the pace, and getting "a sense of participation in her life." Ti's father is also curious about Ti's life in Shanghai. He wants Ti to share with him the pictures she takes—"Really great pictures. I just want to know where she is and I feel we are closer with that." Sometimes when the parents find no updates from their children, they miss them. Ti's mother asks her son to show photos if he doesn't upload photos on WeChat. "I hope to see more pictures of him, which makes me to feel staying with him," she explains.

From the above interviews, we find that parents all agree that locative sharing facilitates their long-distance intimacy with their children. The feeling is also shared by the young people. R admits that the locative social media like WeChat bring some benefits to his relationship with his mother.

> I'm not the kind of child who likes to share daily life with parents, while mom cares much about it. By keeping close attention to my social network and locative social media, she can find a way knowing my daily life and thus understand me better. As a result, we can generate a harmonious relationship.

K feels that she sometimes enjoys communication with her parents on WeChat. "By WeChat I don't need to explain to them particularly. For example, when I joined a chorus competition, I told them it was a competition among schools of my university, but they were not familiar with that. I posted some photos and told them 'see my photos', then they knew immediately." Especially when she is doing something good, she is more than happy to show them to her parents.

> There are more things I would like to share with them, especially those showing that I'm a daughter whom they are proud of, for example, I'm participating in school activities, I'm getting some prize, or just I'm cute . . . We are happy to enjoy these moments.

Y also thinks that locative media help her parents to know more about her daily life. "My life in university is colorful, and my parents don't know much about how university life can be. They can know my life through my updates on WeChat, no matter small or big issues, that's good." Y says that she wouldn't tell her parents everything on the phone, but through WeChat updates, her parents can vividly see how her life is, which makes them feel closer.

As noted earlier, though some parents themselves also share locative information, their children don't show as much caring as they give to them. The young people think their parents' lives are not so interesting. But when sometimes they click "like" under those photos, their parents will feel quite happy about that. As Y's mother puts, "Y sometimes clicks 'like' for my pictures that show my travelling with friends. I am happy to see that." Parents feel more intimacy with their children once they get the interactions and co-presence from their children, even if which are "ritual."

Pressure of over-care and "worry about worries"

When parents emphasize how they benefit from knowing about their children's immediate status and detailed daily lives via the WeChat, children seem to be caught in a dilemma of both the advantages and disadvantages of adding parents as "friends" on social media, thus they hold conflicting attitudes toward locative sharing. On the one hand, the young people agree that the locative social media and information sharing facilitate their communication and intimacy with their parents; on the other hand, the monitoring from the parents becomes a pressure of "over-care" for the children.

C is such a typical case. She describes her mother as crazily concerning about her safety. Her mother keeps tracking her "footprint" on WeChat. "My mom wants to know every motion of mine," C complains. Every time she updates new moments or pictures, her parents will ask for details about them. Several days ago C went to a friend's house and posted some photos on her WeChat. Her mother immediately asked her on their WeChat family chatting group, "Where did you go? Where is the place in the photos? Did you go there alone?" C has to respond to her parents with details. If she doesn't report her activities in time, her mother will ask her on WeChat or even call her. While it should be noticed that it is not the locative media brings "over-care" to C, as her mother has kept this kind of "over-care" since C was a little girl. The difference is the media. In the past, her mother called her at night almost every day to check if she was staying at her dormitory, the "safe area." C remembers her mother even called the police when C got back to campus half an hour later than usual and her mobile phone was unfortunately powered-off. To some extent C has been used to this situation, "I have to report my 'doing list' to my parents if I don't use WeChat." Over-care on WeChat is an extension of existing daily over-care from the parents.

Ti has a different story. Ti says that she is a quite independent girl. She has stayed in Beijing for four years before she began her masters study in Shanghai. She has get used to managing her personal life by herself and don't want to explain the details to her parents, as she argues, "My parents only need to know that I'm healthy and happy." Luckily in the past her parents have no channels to monitor her mobility and life trivia. But now she finds that things have been changing. When Ti uploads a photo, her father often comments and asks, "Where are you? Where is it?" She feels bothered—"What's the use of that! They don't know much about my school things; they don't understand and can't help." Ti says that she would like to share with her parents if she goes somewhere interesting, but she doesn't want to be questioned.

Unlike C's mother, K's parents encourage her to go out. So K doesn't care if her parents see her location on locative social media. However, she also has things that she doesn't want to be seen or asked about by her parents. Sometimes she complains on SNS and her parents then ask her what has happened; sometimes she posts photos late at night and her mother is garrulous about how this is detrimental to her health. In these situations, K also feels the over-care from her parents. To her, they are just "negative emotions that everybody can have" and "I don't want them to worry about that," so she blocked her parents a few times on WeChat for this kind of reason.

This case illustrates another common phenomenon shared by young people in their communication with their parents: "worry about worries." That is, the "over-care" from the parents makes their children recognize the worries of their parents, which reversely becomes the worries of the children.

"I don't want them to worry about me too much, since it's not good for their health"—Y can feel the worries from her parents. Sometimes her unconscious message may cause worries from parents. Once she posted a message saying, "There is no hope for short persons in this era" as self-mockery. Immediately her father replied to her in one-to-one chatting: "Don't be sad. Great people are always short. See Deng Xiaoping and Napoleon!" Y thought this was quite funny, since she showed this message to her friends. She realizes that her parents are worried about whether she feels self-abasement because of the height.

Strategic management

With the pressure of "over-care" and "worry about worries," some young people have considered whether to refuse to add parents as friends on locative social media. In our interviews, K, Y, and R all had the experience of blocking their parents on WeChat, but finally they added them back again. The main reason behind this process is the "protests" from the parents. When R once blocked his mother, he received a phone call from his mother immediately. "There must be some problem with my WeChat," said his mother. "I cannot see your photos at all." He could do nothing but "re-friend" his mother. K and Y's parents also called them to explain when they found they were blocked on WeChat. "We don't want to intervene in our children's lives. We don't want control them. We are supportive. We just want to be informed and can give some suggestions." Normally the young people don't want to make their parents unhappy so they compromise. Another reason is that the young people do need to communicate with their parents and share good news with them. As a result, they all agree that fully blocking parents on locative media is not a good choice and it will be better to strategically manage the postings on locative social media.

The most common strategy is "selective posting to please parents." As noted earlier, there are stories that children are eager to inform parents while also private matters that they would like to hide. To avoid "over-care," young people will consider their parents as a "special audience" and assume their possible responses before posting locations on the social media. If they are doing something beyond their parents' expectations or at some place beyond the "safe area" perceived by parents, they will not post these photos or check-in. They will carefully manage the posts and locative information since they don't want their parents to worry about them.

C told us her experience when she was in Europe as an exchange student. Though she went out travelling frequently, she only occasionally updated her status about travelling, as she knew every time she went out her parents would worry. At the same time she had to post some pictures and check in sometimes otherwise her parents wouldn't believe in her. R knows clearly that his parents are happy to see him busy studying and working, so every time when he wants to post something on his social media, he will think about whether what he is posting is suitable for his parents to read. "Negative emotions, jokes only for the youth, and hanging out with friends are not good content for them." He is now used to this kind of self-censorship on locative social media. Besides the content, the time of posting is also a subject to be strategically managed. Y sometimes updated her status late at night, which was disapproved of by her mother. She has changed her strategy by deleting the night posts before her parents see them the next morning.

The second popular strategy is "flexible mobility among different platforms." Multiple SNS platforms usage offers children a way to resolve the dilemma between showing themselves and avoiding parents' over-worries. All the interviewed parents have WeChat accounts but few have Weibo or Renren. So some children choose to post things that may raise the concerns of their parents on Weibo or Renren. K is such a case. She stops displaying "negative feelings" on WeChat and expresses them on Weibo. If she wants to say something late at night, she also chooses to post on Weibo where her parents cannot see her posts.

The third strategy is "tentative blocking and adding back after deletion," which means that the young people will tentatively block their parents when they want to post something which may possibly make their parents unhappy or confused and then add them back after they delete the sensitive information. Y has done so frequently. Sometimes she wants to share some interesting stories or "bad emotions" with her friends, but she doesn't want her parents to worry about her, so she chooses to block her parents for a while. When she deletes those updates, she adds her parents back.

The above strategies had been widely taken by the young people when the interviews were done in 2013. With the updating of WeChat in 2014 comes more convenient strategies for them. The latest version of WeChat allows users to post for a "niche audience" by setting different groups. Now more young people group their parents and relatives into a specific group and selectively post to them.

Conclusion

Locative social media, especially WeChat, have become the main online communication tool for parents and children to connect and interact with each other in contemporary China. This chapter explores how locative social media are adopted and used by Chinese families, and how the embedment of locative media into family impacts intergenerational relationships. Based on interviews with six families, we make some preliminary findings on this topic. First, the "bottom-up" technology transmission phenomenon is observed in parents' adoption of locative social media in the Chinese context. It should also be noted that an important force in facilitating this process is the social need of intergenerational communication within families. That is, the parents learn to use locative social media with the help of the young people mainly in order to keep updated about their children's information and mobility.

Second, with the assistance of locative social media, parents have more opportunities to give care to their children. Especially for the translocal families in China, locative social media have become the main channel for both parents and children to feel the "co-presence" or "connected-presence" to overcome the distance. Normally the parents watch the updates of their children's locative media quietly, which then can then trigger conversations between them. At the same time, the young people also have the need to use locative social media to show the good aspects of their lives and moods to their parents. Locative social media therefore does have the potential to promote family cohesion as well as intergenerational relationships in the Chinese context.

Third, an interesting concept arising from the empirical study is the "safe area," which especially shows the importance of "locative" social media. Parents care if their children are staying in the "safe area" defined by them, whether in school or in the city. The locative sharing on social media could help the parents to keep tracking of their children's mobility and give care to them. The forming of the idea of a "safe area" deserves more explorations in the further analyses.

Fourth, as discussed in the literature review, the locative social media not only facilitates intergenerational relationships within families, but also gives rise to potential conflicts and problems. Unlike the factors of attitudinal difference or boundary blurring revealed in previous studies, the main conflicts over the locative social media found in this study are the "over-care" from the parents and the "worry about worries" of the children. The over-care from the parents drives them to monitor the locative social media of their children intensively, which turns into the pressure of "worry about worries" for them. Responding to this situation, young people are also learning how to manage their locative sharing on the social media carefully, to please their parents and to maintain a harmonious intergenerational relationship. Locative social media are thus crucial sites for researchers to further observe the dynamics of intergenerational relationships in digital China, for which the current chapter is just a starting point.

Acknowledgment

This chapter is supported by the Australian Research Council Linkage Project, "Locating the Mobile" (#LP130100848), the Chinese National Social Science Foundation Project, "The Influence of Social Media on Public Opinion in Transitional China" (#13CXW021), and Shanghai Social Science Foundation Project "New Media Empowerment" (#2012BXW004).

References

Aguila, A. (2011) 'Time and space on Skype: Families experience togetherness while apart', *Explorations in Media Ecology*, 10(3–4): 303–312.

Baldassar, L. (2007) 'Transnational families and aged care: the mobility of care and the migracy of aging', *Journal of Ethnic and Migration Studies*, 33(2): 275–297.

Baldassar, L. (2008) 'Missing kin and longing to be together: emotions and the construction of copresence in transnational relationships', *Journal of Intercultural Studies*, 29(3): 247–266.

CNNIC (2015) Statistical survey report on the Internet development in China. Available at: http://www.cnnic.cn/hlwfzyj/hlwxzbg/201502/P020150203551802054676.pdf (Accessed on February 3, 2015). (In Chinese)

Correa, T. (2014) 'Bottom-up technology transmission within families: Exploring how youths influence their parents' digital media use with dyadic data', *Journal of Communication*, 64: 103–124.

Correa, T., Straubhaar, J., Spence, J. and Chen, W. (2013) 'Brokering new technologies: The role of children in their parents' usage of the Internet', *New Media and Society*. Epub ahead of print October 15, DOI: 10.1177/1461444813506975.

Hjorth, L. and Gu, K. (2012) 'The place of emplaced visualities: A case study of smartphone visuality and location-based social media in Shanghai, China', *Journal of Media & Cultural Studies*, 26(5): 699–713.

Horst, H. (2006) 'The blessings and burdens of communication: cell phones in Jamaican transnational social fields', *Global Networks*, 6(2): 143–159.

Kang, T. (2012) 'Gendered media, changing intimacy: Internet-mediated transnational communication in the family sphere', *Media Culture Society*, 34: 146.

Katz, V. (2010) 'How children of immigrants use media to connect their families to the community', *Journal of Children and Media*, 4(3): 298–315.

Kiesler, S., Zdaniuk, B., Lundmark, V. and Kraut, R. (2000) 'Troubles with the Internet: The dynamics of help at home', *Human–Computer Interaction*, 15: 322–351.

Lam, S. (2013) 'ICT's impact on family solidarity and upward mobility in translocal China', *Asian Journal of Communication*, 23(3): 322–340.

Lei, L. (2013) 'Sons, daughters, and intergenerational support in China', *Chinese Sociological Review*, 45(3): 26–52.

Liu, F. (2008) 'Negotiating the filial self—Young-adult only—children and intergenerational relationships in China', *Young*, 16(4): 409–430.

Mesch, G.S. (2006) 'Family relations and the Internet: Exploring a family boundaries approach', *The Journal of Family Communication*, 6(2): 119–138.

Nie, N.H., Hillygus, D.S. and Erbing, L. (2002) 'Internet use, interpersonal relationships, and sociability: A time diary study'. In B. Wellman and C. Haythornthwaite (eds) *The Internet in everyday life*, Oxford: Blackwell: 215–244.

Orleans, M. and Laney, M.C. (2000) 'Early adolescent social networks and computer use', *Social Science Computer Review*, 18: 56–72.

Salaff, J.W. (2002) 'Where home is the office: The new form of flexible work'. In B. Wellman and C. Haythornthwaite (eds) *The Internet in everyday life*, Oxford: Blackwell: 464–495.

Wilding, R. (2006) 'Virtual intimacies? Families communicating across transnational contexts', *Global Networks*, 6(2): 125–142.

20

Short circuits of Southeast Asian cinema: Viddsee and the project of online social viewing

Olivia Khoo

Short films are the new movies of the social web age

Ho Jia Jian

Referred to alternately as "micro-cinema" (Baumgärtel 2011), "mini" films (Foo 2002), and "light" movies (Voci 2012), the short format film has been integral to the development of Southeast Asian cinema's increasingly prominent international profile in the last two decades. While the exhibition of short films from Southeast Asia has grown on the major international film festival circuit, what is far less examined is the formation of a regional viewing community that is growing in parallel, online. This chapter examines the role played by Singapore start-up company Viddsee, which promotes itself as an "online social watching" platform, in growing this community. Co-founded by engineer/filmmakers Ho Jia Jian and Derek Tan in September 2012, Viddsee was built when Ho and Tan struggled to find distribution for their own short film productions.

The chapter evaluates how online distribution and exhibition sites like Viddsee are responding to, and in turn precipitating, different audience consumption practices as filmmakers in Southeast Asia continue to seek ways of making and marketing films that have relevance beyond local audiences while at the same time building an active (online) community in the region.

Online film distribution in Asia has tended to be associated with piracy—that is, the illegal download of film and television programs through the Internet in tandem with the physical circulation of pirated DVDs and VCDs. This chapter focuses on the more productive (and legal) aspects of online film distribution and exhibition to consider how online viewing forms part of the sociality of everyday life in Southeast Asia and how independent filmmakers from the region are actively participating in the creation of an online community and network. Before introducing the example of Viddsee, it is worthwhile briefly outlining the development of independent cinema in Southeast Asia, particularly through the short format film.

Short films in Southeast Asia

The profile of Southeast Asian cinema, in particular its independent cinema, has grown significantly in the last two decades. Part of this growth can be attributed to the success of Southeast

Asian films on the international film festival circuit, which has led to the exposure of filmmakers, stories and styles from the region. While there have been a few high profile feature film examples that have been successful on the festival circuit, such as Apichatpong Weerasethakul's *Uncle Boonmee Who Can Recall His Past Lives* (2010, Thailand), which won the Palme d'Or at the Cannes Film Festival, and Anthony Chen's *Ilo Ilo* (2013, Singapore), which won the Camera d'Or at Cannes, it is predominantly short films (films under 60 minutes running time) that have achieved widespread success, with many winning awards internationally.

This increasing recognition of cinema from the region is in line with significant changes in the film industries of Southeast Asian nations. Producer Juan Foo (2002) refers to short films as "mini cinema," stressing the importance of this form to many of the smaller film industries in Southeast Asia. Foo posits that a nation's cinema begins with its short films. In Singapore, for example, short film production has grown since 2000 as part of Singapore's film renaissance of the late 1990s. This has been a direct result of government financial support through the Singapore Film Commission and by allowing short films to feature in a competitive category at the Singapore International Film Festival, which in turn has paved the way for the success of Singapore shorts at other major international film festivals, including Cannes and Rotterdam. Whereas in some national film industries it is difficult to obtain funding for short films because of low prospects for a return, in Singapore short films are seen as a "stepping stone" to success in the feature film industry, as nurturing local talent to achieve success internationally, and therefore culturally significant in their own right. For this reason, short films have been well supported through state funding.[2] The short form has been embraced by filmmakers in the region for other reasons. As Jan and Yvonne Uhde note, "As the short is not a format used for general commercial release, it is less subject to censorship control and therefore allows for greater artistic freedom and experimentation, an advantage especially important in tightly controlled Singapore" (2004, 20).

Writing on the contemporary short film movement in the Philippines, Nick Deocampo (1985) suggests that short films are a "new" form of Filipino cinema—marking a period distinct from the 1970s commercial and independent cinema in the country. Deocampo notes that the short film format has been taken up fervently by the youth in the Philippines since the 1980s as a way of telling their own politicized stories. Deocampo characterizes the short film in the Philippines as a "submerged cinema" that has always existed, but as the "other" to the commercial cinema, with "its own history, aesthetics, ideology, and practicing filmmakers" (1985, viii). Deocampo argues, "a counter-culture results from this tenacity to survive despite prevailing hindrances like rising costs, absence of a 'professional system' to sustain film production and distribution, competition from commercial films and video, and an audience that has yet to be tapped" (1985, viii). This tendency towards the development of a film counter-culture is echoed in the independent short film cultures of Malaysia, Thailand, and Indonesia.[3]

Alongside these industrial and cultural developments are technological developments that have also impacted on the way films are made and how they are distributed and screened. Empowered by easy and cheap access to digital video (DV) technology, digital filmmaking has had a major impact on film cultures in Asia, in terms of democratizing the "art" of filmmaking to those not professionally trained, and providing a greater range of potential distribution channels, including the Internet and mobile phones (Baumgärtel 2011, 62; Marchetti 2008, 414). The production of short films using smartphones has been an exciting area of development in the field of mobile media creative practice, and recent work has reflected on the new forms, practices and formats of mobile media making that are enabled in an age of smartphones (see Berkeley 2014; Schleser 2014). Although outside the scope of this chapter, much of the aesthetic and formal concerns of mobile media making, for example their pedestrian quality, their personal nature, and their portability (see Ito et al. 2005 in the case of Japan), are reflected in other forms of DV short film culture in Asia.

Writing specifically in the context of China, where issues of censorship and state control are ever-present, Voci (2012) suggests that "smaller screens such as the DV camera, the computer monitor—and, within it, the Internet window—and the cell phone display screen have created new public spaces where many long-standing divisions between high-brow and low-brow, mainstream and counterculture, conventional and experimental are dissolving and being reinvented" (xx). Voci notes that movies made by and for smaller screens are marked by a "lightness"; "light" movies are characterized by "small production costs, distribution ambitions, economic impact, limited audiences [and] quick and volatile circulation" (xx).[4]

These factors outlined by Voci foster the development of new publics, including an emerging online public. Although smaller-screen practices tend to be personal and individual (it is difficult to share a mobile phone or laptop screen with another viewer or viewers), the viewing practices associated with smaller screens also tend to be collectively shared, even though the actual watching experience may be individually experienced (Voci 2012, 12). This is because short format films, many of which are downloadable or streamed through the Internet, are more "portable" in the sense of being able to be shared online, through Facebook, Twitter and blogs, as well as emailed or sent via SMS messaging. Their portability (and digital nature) means that they can also be edited or remade by other viewers. That is, the "lightness" of short films, which in digital form are often made to accommodate smaller screens, defines both their production *and* distribution contexts.

While Voci refers to small-screen practices as marking a form of individualized or personal viewing ("viewers *appropriate* smaller-screen movies [download, save, carry and transfer, gift them] at a very personal level" (2012, xxi; original emphasis)), and indeed many viewers take individual control and ownership of the films outside of major institutions and industries, I suggest that the online distribution of short format films within Southeast Asia opens up another kind of sociality tied to the increasing interactivity of the cinematic form. The films that are shown on Viddsee are not necessarily *public*, in the sense of being widely consumed, but the viewing practices associated with watching these films can be described as social. To reconceive of this kind of individualized viewing experience as social and interactive, it is useful to consider the strategies through which Viddsee seeks to engender or foster a sense of "social viewing" online, and the extent to which it has been successful after being in business for just over two years.

Viddsee: curating Southeast Asia through its short films

Rated as one of the top 50 start-up companies at Asia's largest technology conference, Echelon 2013, Viddsee is a video content hosting site launched in February 2013. It sits below much larger Euro-American dominated video services like YouTube and Vimeo, and other national and regional services showing predominantly Asian content. For example, China has its own video-sharing websites, including the largest, Youku Tudou, which targets mainly local Chinese audiences, with content ranging from South Korean TV dramas, Japanese animation and music videos to user generated content in the form of original videos and videoblogging. Viki, a video streaming website based in Singapore and founded by Razmig Hovaghimian, Changseong Ho and Jiwon Moon in 2007, and AsiaPacificFilms.com, run by members of the Network for the Promotion of Asian Cinema (NETPAC), are two other examples based in Asia that offer on-demand streaming of movies, TV shows and music videos.[4] The landscape of online content hosting and distribution sites on the Internet is diverse and constantly proliferating. Two things set Viddsee apart. The first is its focus on short format films, and the second is the element of curation, with films on Viddsee being vetted and organized into channels by the founders Ho Jia Jian and Derek Tan. The question is: to what extent is the "social engineering" of an online community of viewers possible, or even desirable, and through what means might it be achievable?

While the content on sites such as YouTube and Youku Tudou is not necessarily "short," Viddsee, in contrast, hosts films usually under 30 minutes (and on average between 6 and 10 minutes long), with a focus on Southeast Asian short films.[5] Dedicated channels stream films from Singapore, Indonesia, Malaysia, the Philippines, Cambodia and Thailand, with a range of films from other Southeast Asian nations, such as Myanmar, scattered throughout other channels. Viddsee does host films from across East Asia, including Japan (through its Node Japan channel), Hong Kong (through the Freshwave channel), and India (through the Humara Cinema channel), but the main focus is on short films from Singapore and Southeast Asia. Not all of the channels are organized according to country of origin; several are compiled according to regional or subregional groupings. Viddsee's "Asian Short Films" channel features on Yahoo's entertainment portals for Singapore, Malaysia, and the Philippines, and Viddsee has also partnered with the ASEAN International Film Festival and Awards, the Singapore Short Film Awards, the Asian Film Archive, and Tropfest Southeast Asia to create dedicated channels.

Being a "niche content platform" (Wong 2013) filmmakers are more easily able to reach their target audience and audiences do not have to surf through large amounts of content to find what they are looking for. Viddsee's founders have said in an interview, "While content is readily available over the Internet today, it's still hard to find culturally contextual content from Singapore and around Southeast Asia" ('Singapore startup' 2013). Ho explains, "I explored the option of putting my film on Vimeo and YouTube, but the problem for filmmakers is that just getting their work online doesn't guarantee that it'll be watched by a large audience. Good short films get drowned among Gangnam Style parodies on YouTube, and discovery of Asian films is hard on Vimeo" (Russell 2013). As a site focused on short films from Asia, Viddsee is unique.

The second element that distinguishes Viddsee from other content hosting sites is the fact that material on the site is curated. Viddsee has been described as a "targeted platform [that] . . . curate[s] an audience for short films" ('Singapore startup' 2013), and as "a socially-equipped site with a light touch of curation" (Millward 2013). Each film is vetted by Ho and Tan for quality and suitability with no cost charged for putting videos on the site and, at this stage, no advertising either (the company has been funded by a Startup Grant from Singapore's "Action Community for Entrepreneurship").[6] With other video hosting sites, there is no content curation, or any effort made to build a community for either audiences or filmmakers. It is this aspect of curation that is perhaps the most distinguishing feature of the site.

In just over two years Viddsee has grown a large community of viewers, with over 500 short films in its archive. Over five million people have watched at least one short film on Viddsee, with roughly a third being active (repeat) users from over 98 different countries (Bischoff 2014; Racoma 2013). Seventy percent of Viddsee's viewers are from Asia, but English subtitles on most of the films means that they are also readily accessible by US, Australian, and UK-based viewers (Bischoff 2014).

A sense of community emerging from the use of this site is integral to the company's ethos, which describes itself as an "online social watching service" (*Viddsee*). Viddsee's founders have a motto—"short films are the new movies of the social web age"—and the company's logo is a video screen within a chat bubble, encapsulating the site's desire to provide social interaction about Southeast Asian short films. Viddsee's model is heavily reliant on interaction between viewers and the site actively encourages ongoing discussion, engagement and exchange about each film posted, for example by providing colorful editorial descriptions and synopses of films, or by occasionally posing questions on Facebook as provocations for viewers to respond to. Indeed, the company's distribution strategy is closely integrated with social networking sites like Facebook and Twitter, with users given the option of logging in via their Facebook account to provide comments and ratings.[7] Viddsee refers to these ratings as micro-ratings, relating to elements such as story, acting, camera and sound production, thus providing feedback on technical aspects also benefiting the filmmakers.[8]

In this way, Viddsee genuinely seeks to include filmmakers in the community it seeks to build. While the dominant model for Southeast Asian films is to try to be shown at prestigious international film festivals and then to receive DVD distribution, Viddsee provides an alternative avenue with a very different kind of community based audience.[9] The site includes not only films by emerging filmmakers that would otherwise receive little or no distribution by other means, but also films by well-known, successful festival filmmakers, including Anthony Chen, Royston Tan and Tan Pin Pin, in support of this model.[10] These elements together create a model that actively seeks to foster the creation of a social community of viewers (and filmmakers) in Southeast Asia.

Although there is some content curation on Viddsee, because films are vetted and also because they are organized according to tags and channels, viewers also have freedom to choose what they want to watch and are able to discover films based on shared parameters such as country, genre, or topic, or to follow "trending" films (a "Viddsee Buzz" link, described as a "discovery guide," features highlighted films under the tagline "Your daily dose of Asian stories"). This sense of "discovery" is important to creating ownership and a sense of individuality, as well as fostering the social aspect of the site—wanting to share and discuss short films found with those sharing similar interests and tastes. Through this model, Viddsee has "transferred the power of discovery from film buyers and distributors to audiences" (Tan 2013).

Engineering social viewing through social message films

Viddsee's unique features—a focus on Southeast Asian short films (which are more portable, sharable)—and the element of curation combined with an encouragement of social interaction), have seen it grow rapidly in a short space of time. After two years, how successful has Viddsee's model been in fostering "online social watching" in Southeast Asia? While the site may have a community of viewers that are "connected" through Facebook and Twitter, this is not necessarily a community in conversation or dialogue. While a small number of films on Viddsee have a high amount of "likes" on Facebook, some in the hundreds or even thousands, only a very small percentage of individual films have any comments, and if they do it is usually only one or two comments at most. How do we gauge participation or measure community building: through "likes," comments, or shares on social media? Perhaps a better frame of analysis for what the site seeks to do is to contemplate how it imagines Southeast Asia, and Asia more broadly, as a regionally connected community of viewers.

Viddsee's project of fostering a regional community through a shared visual archive can be regarded as a means of getting viewers within Asia (and Southeast Asia in particular) to talk to one another, aligning it to some extent with Kuan-Hsing Chen's notion of Asia as method. Chen writes in his book *Asia as Method: Toward Deimperialisation*,

> the implication of Asia as method is that using Asia as an imaginary anchoring point can allow societies in Asia to become one another's reference points, so that the understanding of the self can be transformed, and subjectivity rebuilt. Pushing the project one step further, it becomes possible to imagine that historical experiences and practise in Asia can

be developed as an alternative horizon, perspective, or method for posing a different set of questions about world history.

(2010, xv)

To think about Asia as method is to rethink how we might conceive of Asia not as an object deduced from the understandings, perceptions and articulations of either the Euro-American West or imperialist Japan, but as its own reference point. On perhaps a smaller scale of ambition, the founders of Viddsee pose similar questions about the value of regional integration, in this case through local communities of viewing. Arguably, watching, sharing and curating digital short films from Asia online foster the formation of a new kind of sociality and the possibility of new pedagogical practices tied to "social watching" of films from across the region. One way that Viddsee has sought to engender community formation and interest has been through the use of the site to promote a relationship between "social viewing" and "social message" films. For Viddsee, social viewing also carries some responsibility towards conveying a social message.

Kamil Haque, an actor and festival consultant for the ASEAN International Film Festival and Awards (AIFFA), which has collaborated with Viddsee to host a channel, says, "I see distribution platforms like Viddsee as great big soapboxes for the ASEAN community-at-large to collaborate, to create, to share, to entertain and most importantly to educate" (Viddsee 2013). In terms of this "educational" function, the site foregrounds "social message" films as part of the act of social viewing and community building. A short film added to the site in June 2014, *Purple Light* (directed by Javior Chew, Cecilia Ang and Charlene Yiu), is based on a true story about a gay army recruit to the National Singapore Army and his exploration of his sexuality with one of his fellow cadets and best friend. It is one of four films on Viddsee tagged with the topic "LGBT" (Lesbian, Gay, Bisexual, Transgender). Viddsee also hosts a channel called "Our Better World," an initiative of the Singapore International Foundation, which aims to share stories "to inspire good."[11] The channel includes films such as *They Should Be at the World Cup* (directed by Anshul Tiwari) on Singapore's cerebral palsy football team, *Deaf, Loud and Proud* (also directed by Anshul Tiwari), on the deaf percussion band, ExtraOrdinary Horizons, and *Paraplegic's Dream Bike Ride* (directed by Peter Wall), a short film about a woman left paralyzed after a motorcycle accident who rides again in a modified motorcycle that accommodates her wheelchair in a trip from Jakarta to Bali. Viddsee also hosts short films about street kids in Mumbai and South Asian migrant workers to Singapore, amidst comedies and animation and, most recently, original web series.

Perhaps it is these "social message" films that allow viewers to engage more actively in what Carter and Arroyo call "participatory pedagogy" (2011, 291). The forms of participation that the site offers are not necessarily those of political action or activism, but rather operate on a more subtle level of persuasion by exposing viewers to alternative forms of identities, stories and experiences, opening up the potential for a slow changing of attitudes. In brokering potential forms of interaction between viewers, Viddsee is promoting the value of dialogue between Southeast Asian neighbors through a shared contemporary cinema.

Conclusion

In this chapter I have been interested in how the act of curation and the forms of social interaction engendered by Viddsee allow us to contemplate the use of digital media, in this case digital short films, in the building of an online community of viewers in Southeast Asia. Through social interaction and participation, filmmakers and audiences engaging through Viddsee provide a critique of the individualized act of viewing on "small screens." Combined with the site's elements of curation and audio-visual archiving, Viddsee also structures our viewing choices to produce certain pedagogical and emotional outcomes. Viddsee's social watching platform facilitates, in however limited a way, the coming together of Southeast Asia as a region that is constituted both on- and offline by local viewing communities that are not reliant upon an external perspective or source of "curation" for their existence or validation but participates in a form of sociality that more closely resembles the forms of inter-Asia referencing that are called for in the Asia as method project.

New digital distribution practices and models like Viddsee are a way for the industry to respond to and in turn precipitate different audience consumption practices (including online streaming) as filmmakers continue to seek ways of making films that will cross national markets and audiences seek new avenues of content discovery and ways of being social, without leaving their homes, computers, or mobile phones.

Notes

1 The Singapore Film Commission's now defunct Short Film Grant supported over 70 short films in 2006, compared with only 11 short films in 1998. The definition of a short film for the purposes of the grant was any film under 30 minutes. In September 2011, Singapore's Media Development Authority overhauled its Grants Schemes, replacing them with five new schemes covering development, production, marketing, and talent assistance. Short films will now be funded under one of these schemes.

2 See for example Lim 2014, 520.

3 The name Viki is a combination of video and wiki since, like Wikipedia, the site also relies on volunteers, including subtitlers, for content management.

4 The site does stream a limited number of feature films (the first feature, *S11* (directed by Gilbert Chan and Joshua Chiang, 2001) was posted on 25 May 2013). The company quotes that 40 percent of Viddsee's audiences view their films on mobile phones (Racoma 2013), and Viddsee launched a mobile app in June 2013. The short format film is particularly suited to these users accessing through their mobile phones using internet connections, and caters to bandwidth requirements, shorter attention spans, and distracted viewing contexts.

5 ACE usually provides S$50,000 for each grant, supporting approximately 500 startups as part of this scheme.

6 As of February 2015, Viddsee has over 100,000 "Likes" on Facebook and 15,000 followers on Twitter.

7 Jean Burgess and Joshua Green (2009) have commented on the generative nature of video sharing, suggesting that participation is crucial to YouTube's structure. Being "literate" on YouTube is about how to navigate it "as a social network" (72). The comments attached to videos are a "crucial part of YouTube participation and social interaction" (Lange 2010, para 28); users come to expect a sense of reciprocity with other participants in the shared online video culture.

8 In October 2013 Viddsee organised with Singapore's 15th DigiCon6 for viewers to watch and vote for the top 18 finalist animations on their DigiCon6 channel. Viddsee was the official digital partner of the ASEAN International Film Festival and Awards 2013, which expanded its inaugural short film festival beyond Malaysia to audiences around ASEAN countries online. Thus, Viddsee is not just a place for the discovery of new films, but also participates in the archiving of these short films. It does not completely disregard the desire of filmmakers to find success on the film festival circuit, partnering with film festivals in order to improve the visibility of both the site itself and the films on it.

9 Kelvin Sng, director of *The Gang*, says, "Viddsee is a new platform for short films, and having my film on it is also a way of showing my support to it. . . . I was actually planning to release *The Gang* on DVD together with another mid-length film that I executive-produced called *Steadfast* (2010). But, I decided to share it through Viddsee to thank everyone with *The Gang* made available for viewing free of charge to all" ('Singapore startup' 2013).

10 The Singapore International Foundation (previously called Singapore Volunteer Overseas) is a not-for-profit organization established on August 1, 1991. Its Vision is described as "Making Friends for a Better

World" (http://www.sif.org.sg/vision_mission): "We build enduring relationships between Singaporeans and world communities, and harness these friendships to enrich lives and effect positive change across the world" (http://www.sif.org.sg/what_we_do#sthash.85l7DIRF.dpuf).

References

Baumgärtel, T. (2011) 'Imagined Communities, Imagined Worlds: Independent Film from South East Asia in the Global Mediascape', *Transnational Cinemas*, 2(1): 57–71.

Berkeley, L. (2014) 'Tram Travels: Smartphone Video Production and the Essay Film'. In M. Berry and Max S. (eds) *Mobile Media Making in an Age of Smartphones*, London: Palgrave Pivot.

Bischoff, P. (2014) 'Viddsee Brands Itself as a Launchpad for Asian Short Films, Adds Web Series to Boot', *Tech in Asia*. Available at: http://www.techinasia.com/viddsee-brands-launchpad-asian-short-films-adds-web-series-boot/ (Accessed on April 22, 2015).

Burgess, J. and J. Green (2009) *YouTube: Online Video and Participatory Culture*, Cambridge: Polity Press.

Carter, G. V. and S. J. Arroyo (2011) 'Tubing the Future: Participatory Pedagogy and YouTube U in 2020', *Computers and Composition*, 28: 292–302.

Chen K.-H. (2010) *Asia as Method: Toward Deimperialisation*, Durham, NC: Duke University Press.

Deocampo, N. (1985) *Short Film: Emergence of a New Philippine Cinema*, Manila: Communication Foundation for Asia.

Foo, J. (2002) 'Mini Cinema', *FilmsAsia*. Available at: http://www.filmsasia.net/gpage77.html (Accessed on April 22, 2015).

Htun, L. M. (2013) 'Viddsee Provides Launchpad for Young Filmmakers', *Myanmar Times*. Available at: http://www.mmtimes.com/index.php/lifestyle/7534-creating-web-space-for-local-talent.html (Accessed on April 22, 2015).

Ito, M., Misa M. and Daisuke O. (2005) *Personal, Pedestrian and Portable: Mobile Phones in Japanese Life*, Cambridge, MA: MIT Press.

Lange, P. M. (2010) 'Achieving Creative Integrity on YouTube, Reciprocities and Tensions'. Available at: http://enculturation.camden.rutgers.edu/achieving-creative-integrity (Accessed on April 22, 2015).

Lim, J. B.Y. (2014) 'Rhizomatic Behaviours in Social Media: V-logging and the Independent Film Industry in Malaysia', *International Journal of Cultural Studies*, 17(5): 517–535.

Marchetti, G. (2008) 'Asian Film and Digital Culture'. In Robert Kolker (ed) *The Oxford Handbook of Film and Media Studies*, London: Oxford University Press: 414–421.

Millward, S. (2013) 'New Startup Makes Southeast Asian Short Films More Social and Accessible', *Techniasia*. Available at: http://www.techinasia.com/new-viddsee-for-southeast-asian-short-films/ (Accessed on April 22, 2015).

Racoma, J. A. (2013) 'Viddsee Launches Mobile Web App, Looks to Grow Community', *Floost*. Available at: http://e27.co/viddsee-launches-mobile-web-app-looks-to-grow-community/ (Accessed on April 22, 2015).

Russell, J. (2013) 'Viddsee Is a Place for Southeast Asia's Top Short Filmmakers to Showcase Their Work', *The Next Web*. Available at: http://thenextweb.com/asia/2013/02/06/viddsee-southeast-short-films/ (Accessed on June 18, 2015).

Schleser, M. (2014) 'Connecting through Mobile Autobiographies: Self-reflexive Mobile Filmmaking, Self-representation and Selfies'. In Marsha Berry and Max Schleser (eds) *Mobile Media Making in an Age of Smartphones*, London: Palgrave Pivot.

'Singapore Startup Viddsee Streams Regional Short Films for the Social Web' (2013) *The Online Citizen*. Available at: http://citizen1120.rssing.com/chan-12672527/all_p1.html (Accessed on April 22, 2015).

Tan, E. (2013) 'Watch the Best of Singapore's Short Films on Viddsee and Hear from Their Co-founder', *Singapore News*. Available at: http://sg.news.yahoo.com/watch-best-singapore-short-films-viddsee-hear-co-050730745.html (Accessed on April 22, 2015).

Uhde, J. and Y. Ng Uhde (2004) 'Singapore Cinema: Spotlight on Short Film Production', *Spectator*, 24(2): 18–26.

Viddsee. Available at: http://www.viddsee.com (Accessed on April 22, 2015).

Viddsee (2013) 'Viddsee Showcases Selected Nominated Regional Short Films from ASEAN International Film Festival & Awards (AIFFA) 2013', press release. Available at: http://www.hcac.sg/press/Viddsee%20 Press%20Release.pdf (Accessed on April 22, 2015).

Voci, P. (2012) *China on Video: Smaller-Screen Realities*, London: Routledge.

Wong, K. (2013) 'Watching Southeast Asian Short Films with Viddsee', *Pop Culture Online*, 34. Available at: http://www.popcultureonline.net/pop-corn/watching-southeast-asian-short-films-viddsee (Accessed on April 22, 2015).

Part IV
Mapping mobile, diasporic and queer Asia

Part IV

Mapping mobile, diasporic
and queer Asia

21

At the crossroads of change: new media and migration in Asia

Sun Sun Lim, Becky Pham and Kakit Cheong

A region of dramatic growth and transformation, Asia is witnessing an ever accelerating flow of capital, goods, and people, both within and beyond its geographical boundaries. Accordingly, domestic and international migration has also intensified in this thriving continent. Underlying this ceaseless flow of people is a rich technological landscape that enables communication links between migrants and their left-behind families, albeit with uneven levels of access to technology that translate into variations in the quality and nature of communication. Such long-distance communication has been revolutionized by new media, including various Internet- and mobile phone-based platforms. This chapter charts key trends in migration within Asia through a systematic review of key literature, and explains the critical role that new media platforms play in the process of migration, from the establishment and sustenance of emotional bonds to the generation of capital that can contribute to improved job opportunities and an enhanced quality of life.

Waves of migration in Asia

Migration within, into, and out of Asia has been occurring for centuries, albeit not at the blistering pace that we see today (Castles and Miller 2009). According to the United Nations, it is estimated that in 2013, Asia hosted 71 out of 232 million international migrants, making it the second largest migration area in the world (Skeldon 2013). Furthermore, the continent remains the world's largest migration corridor, with 54 million international migrants residing in a different Asian country from where they were born (Skeldon 2013). These staggering figures underscore the importance of examining migration in Asia.

In the early twentieth century, outward migration from Asia was relatively low due to the legislative and restrictive policies of the Western colonial powers. However, as foreign trade and investment increased in the 1960s, Western countries such as the United States and Canada acted to repeal discriminatory rules against Asians, thus allowing more international migrants to work overseas (Castles and Miller 2009). Notably, not all migrations during this period were undertaken voluntarily. For example, during the Vietnam War, more than 3 million 'boat people' from Vietnam, Laos, and Cambodia were forced to relocate to countries such as Australia, the United States, and Canada. These migrants often served as a first link in migratory chains, facilitating the relocation of future generations of friends and relatives. Right up to the 1970s, international migration in Asia was still relatively limited in scale and significance, and population reviews such as the Second Asian Population Conference of 1972 failed to even mention the topic (Hugo 2005).

It was during the 1970s oil boom in the Middle East that migration in Asia increased sharply. Massive construction projects in the Gulf States led to a surge in demand for both skilled and unskilled workers, sparking a significant flow of Filipino migrant workers (Madianou and Miller 2011). By 1985, there were more than 3.2 million Asians in the Gulf States (Abella and Ducanes 2009) and with the exception of the Gulf War, international migrants have continued to work in the Middle East in large numbers, to the extent that they now form the majority of the total population in countries such as Qatar (85 percent), United Arab Emirates (70 percent), and Kuwait (69 percent) (Henning 2011). Similarly, other fast-growing economies with declining population growth rates, such as Singapore and Hong Kong, have increasingly relied on importing both skilled and unskilled workers to sustain their economic momentum.

In recent decades, Asia has witnessed an intensification of inward and outward migration. Factors such as higher levels of educational achievement, introduction of new information and communication technologies, improved transportation, and the internationalization of business and labor markets, have greatly influenced the number of Asians moving between countries, and created new migration patterns as well. For example, given the demands of the construction industry, migrant workers were initially predominantly male. However, with increased demands for domestic or healthcare services in more economically developed Asian countries, a feminization of migration has occurred, with women comprising 48 percent of all international migrants worldwide as of 2013 (Skeldon 2013). Furthermore, migration in Asia is no longer dominated by low wage workers as new migrant groups have emerged, including professionals (Gupta et al. 2014; Sidhu et al. 2014), students (Ge and Ho 2014; Hutchison 2014), self-employed migrants (Dutta et al. 2014), migrant brides (Ullah 2014), and undocumented or illegal migrants (Samson 2014).

Regardless of the socio-economic status of the migrant, researchers have voiced concerns about the challenges such individuals face in their lives. Organizations such as the International Labour Organization (ILO) find that international migrants, and unskilled workers in particular, face discrimination and work safety issues as listed on its website. As the ILO explains, such workers are typically recruited to perform risky and unpleasant jobs that nationals are unwilling or unable to do, and are often abused or exploited in the process. More egregiously, migrants are often made to pay high fees to the intermediaries who help them secure jobs, resulting in a 'debt-bondage' situation where they are heavily indebted to employment agencies or employers, thus binding them for long periods. Apart from the challenges in their working environments, international migrants typically face many systemic challenges which may affect their mental health and well-being. These include the absence of integration policies (Simich et al. 2005), language barriers, racism, discrimination, and alienation (Chung et al. 2008), all of which impose considerable stress on migrants.

Evolution of technologies of mediation

As migrants move to new host countries with unfamiliar cultures and few or no relatives or friends, communication with their home countries and their left-behind families remains a priority during the adaptation process. Many studies have shown how Asian migrants have actively utilized different channels over time to keep in contact with their home countries—from earlier, simpler methods (letters, written cards, cassette tapes, pictures) to more recent technological devices (landline phones, mobile phones, computers, laptops) and Internet-based services (online chatting, online calling, social media).

Before the prevalence of telephones, communication between Asian migrants and their left-behind families was through channels that required minimal or no media competency. For Filipinos, who constitute one of Asia's largest and earliest migrant groups, phone booths and long-distance calls were not available in the Philippines until the late 1980s, and even then, were expensive and rarely used (Paragas 2010). Contact between Filipino migrants and their left-behind families during the 1980s was through letters, written cards, cassette tapes, and pictures sent by post or via family friends who were returning home. Such communication options could only be accessed occasionally, and the messages took a long time to reach their destinations (Bonini 2011; Paragas 2010). Similarly, Nepalese migrants also wrote letters home before telephones were available (Gartaula et al. 2012). Besides communicating familial love and kinship through messages and photographs, migrant workers in Asia have also used remittances to fulfil that purpose, sending money home through friends and bank account transfers, or via agencies such as Western Union. Sending remittances is not merely a financial transaction but amounts to 'intimacy established across borders' (Parreñas 2005, 324), especially when migrants could ask their children or spouse to co-manage the remittance with them (Gartaula et al. 2012; Parreñas 2005). In effect, these remittances serve as compensation for the migrants' physical absence since they are used to pay for the children's education or general household needs (Fresnoza-Flot 2009; Gartaula et al. 2012; Lan 2003).

Landlines and mobile phones gradually became more common and affordable across Asia in the 1990s and throughout the 2000s. In the Philippines, mobile calling prices decreased significantly in 1996 (Paragas 2010). Similarly, in the past 25 years, regulatory reforms in South Asia have led to a reduction in mobile call charges and a corresponding rise in the number of mobile phone subscribers (Gunawardene 2014). As of 2013, India had 867.80 million unique mobile subscribers (Telecomtiger 2013) while China had 630 million (GSMA Intelligence 2014); in Vietnam there are 145 mobile phones for every 100 people (Do 2012).

Superseding relatively inefficient letters, cards, cassette tapes and pictures sent through the postal service, phone calls made through landlines or mobile phones provide Asian migrants with a reliable and synchronous communication platform. These technologies help migrants throughout Asia to bridge the geographical distance with their loved ones, as in the case of migrant workers in China (Lang et al. 2010; Law and Peng 2007; Law and Peng 2008; Oreglia 2010; Xia 2011; Yang 2008), Bangladesh (Chib et al. 2013), the Philippines (Barber 2008; Bonini 2011; Chib et al. 2014; Chib et al. 2013; Fresnoza-Flot 2009; Lan 2003; Madianou 2012; Madianou and Miller 2011; Paragas 2010; Thomas and Lim 2011; Uy-Tioco 2007; Yao 2009), India (Seshan 2012; Thomas and Lim 2011), Indonesia (Chib et al. 2014), Nepal (Gartaula et al. 2012), Sri Lanka (Hugo and Ukwatta 2010), and Vietnam (Hoang and Yeoh 2012). Phone calls allow for instant interactions and reduced uncertainty between migrants and their home countries. The synchronicity of phone calls is even more acutely appreciated in times of emergency when migrants want to check on the well-being of their left-behind families. For example, after the 8.0 magnitude earthquake in Sichuan, China in 2008, mobile phone calls from Guangdong province to Sichuan increased by 1,000 times because of the millions of Sichuan migrant workers staying in Guangdong at the time (Xia 2011).

Since their emergence, mobile phones have been embraced by migrant workers in Asia because they offer significantly more affordances and benefits than landlines (Law and Peng 2007, 2008; Paragas 2010). Compared with shared landlines, mobile phones can be privately owned and personally used and are avidly deployed by migrant workers to maintain affective ties with their significant others. For example, mobile phones give Chinese migrant workers the convenience of calling home to send greetings and wishes, without having to queue for public phone booths during important holidays and festivals (Law and Peng 2007). Mobile phones also allow migrants to engage in highly affordable text messaging with family back home, enhanced with a variety of emoticons, animations and ringtones (Barber 2008; Bonini 2011; Law and Peng 2007; Thomas and Lim 2011; Uy-Tioco 2007). Text messages are also used as a prelude to voice calls, to check if their families are available and vice versa (Bonini 2011; Law and Peng 2007), thereby preventing the disruption of ongoing activities for both sides: 'text messages are used as a lubricant, while the telephone, chats and the webcam are the fuel that keeps the family intimacy alive at a distance' (Bonini 2011, 879).

Alongside telephones, the Internet penetrated Asia in the late 1990s and has diffused rapidly throughout the region since. As of 2012, 1.03 billion Internet users are from Asia, constituting 45 percent of the global online population (We Are Social Singapore 2012). With this proliferation of online connections, Asian migrants enjoy even more communication options, and have gravitated towards new channels such as computers, laptops, emails, online calls, online chats, microblogs and online social networks such as Facebook and Google+ (Bonini 2011; Chib et al. 2014; Hoang and Yeoh 2012; Francisco 2013; Liu et al. 2014; Yao 2009). To illustrate this shift, whereas Internet usage was rare among Chinese female migrants in Beijing in 2007, by 2009, many of them owned laptops and frequently used online instant messaging services such as QQ and MSN, or social networking sites such as 51.com and kaixin001.com (Oreglia 2010). Some also take photos or record videos on their mobile phones and then send them electronically to their families (Paragas 2010). However, Fresnoza-Flot (2009) noted that among Filipino migrants, mobile phones still seemed to be more widely used than the Internet because they may not be computer literate or they simply preferred mobile phones over the Internet. That being said, the growing ubiquity of Internet-enabled smartphones and the emergence of communication apps have blurred the lines between mobile phones and the Internet, and mobile phone usage among migrants is taking on a higher level of complexity.

Building bonds

While migration is undeniably a physical process of relocation, it is most certainly an emotional undertaking as well. Separated from family and friends, migrants go through the disorientating exercise of navigating an unfamiliar land, finding their feet and fostering new friendships, while sustaining ties with kin back home. Confronted with the challenges of an alien landscape, the migrants' home countries assume even greater significance, serving as the roots that anchor them as individuals, and imbuing them with a greater sense of self.

In such a context, communication platforms of all sorts play a critical role in helping migrants sustain connections with their left-behind families, fulfil familial duties from afar, and to seek emotional support from people in both home and host countries. As Asian migrants are often considered outsiders in the host countries (Law and Peng 2007), or encounter hostility from locals (Law and Peng 2008; Liu et al. 2014), their identities as parents or spouses to their left-behind families and friends of their left-behind peers remain important to them since support for their families is among the reasons they migrate in the first place. They often call home or chat online to stay updated on the conditions of their family members (Barber 2008; Bonini 2011; Law and Peng 2007; Liu et al. 2014; Madianou and Miller 2011; Thomas and Lim 2011), to fulfil their familial responsibilities (Barber 2008, Chib et al. 2014; Francisco 2013; Fresnoza-Flot 2009; Gartaula et al. 2012; Hoang and Yeoh 2012; Hugo and Ukwatta 2010; Lan 2003; Madianou 2012; Madianou and Miller 2011; Parreñas 2005; Thomas and Lim 2011; Uy-Tioco 2007) or to preserve their identities as friends to left-behind peers (Law and Peng 2007; Peng 2008; Thomas and Lim 2011).

Specifically, extensive research has delved into how Asian migrant workers continue to parent their left-behind children. In particular, many studies have explored how Asian values shape the familial obligations of female migrant workers as wives and mothers (Barber 2008), having to perform the roles of both breadwinner and mother at the same time (Fresnoza-Flot 2009). These migrant mothers actively use mobile phones and/or the Internet to keep abreast of their children's lives and monitor them from afar as in the case of female migrant workers from the Philippines (Barber 2008; Chib et al. 2014; Francisco 2013; Fresnoza-Flot 2009; Lan 2003; Madianou 2012; Madianou and Miller 2011; Parreñas 2005; Thomas and Lim 2011; Uy-Tioco 2007), Indonesia (Chib et al. 2014), and Sri Lanka (Hugo and Ukwatta 2010). These digital connections enable migrant mothers to maintain a high level of involvement in their children's lives, to the point of helping them with homework (Parreñas 2005), monitoring their children's Facebook posts (Chib et al. 2014), even having access to passwords that allow them to check their children's email and Facebook accounts (Madianou 2012). Some Filipino migrant mothers used Skype to 'watch' their children grow up, but also as a means of surveillance. Through webcam enabled video chats, they scrutinized their homes to ensure that their hard-earned money was not squandered on luxurious items, while also maintaining the mother–child hierarchy (Francisco 2013).

While research on male migrant workers has not paid as much attention to the affective dimensions of their overseas stints, this hardly indicates their absence. One study found that Vietnamese male migrant workers in Korea used the Internet and webcam every night to talk to their families while their children would in turn tell them stories or sing them songs (Hoang and Yeoh 2012). Such acts create a comforting 'absent presence' (Pertierra 2005, 26) of these migrant parents during their children's formative years. Migrant mothers consider these connections to their families so crucial that they ensure that their remittances can cover the cost of communication devices and telecommunication service subscriptions for their children (Fresnoza-Flot 2009). Apart from parenting at a distance, Asian migrants also use the media to fulfil their responsibilities to their left-behind spouses. For example, Nepalese male migrants use mobile phones to call their wives at home to discuss matters relating to finances and their children, as well as to express their love, thus alleviating the geographical and emotional distance between them (Gartaula et al. 2012).

Unfortunately, not all mediated communication leads to the successful maintenance of family ties. The costs of mediated connection, even if significantly reduced over the years, can still be prohibitive for many. Resource inequalities and poor infrastructure result in significant disparities in the infocomm service access enjoyed by overseas migrants and their left-behind families. For example, international calls can be exorbitant in Vietnam, and the left-behind families refrain from calling their migrant relatives often, making a concerted effort to shorten their phone calls and to focus only on important matters (Hoang and Yeoh 2012). Other Vietnamese migrants in the same study were farm workers who worked in deep forests with no access to mediated communication channels, and could only call home as rarely as once per month. As a result, the migrant fathers and mothers were unable to keep track of their children's upbringing, causing the children to refuse to talk to them on the phone, or to become shy and uncomfortable when their parents finally came back to visit them. Other adverse consequences of the separation between migrant workers and their left-behind children include the children's disobedience or emotional problems (Hugo and Ukwatta 2010), or their failure to empathize with their parents (Lan 2003). Migrant workers also experience stress and psychological burdens when their families contact them with requests for money or advice during family emergencies (Barber 2008; Lan 2003; Thomas and Lim 2011). Usage of various communication services can also translate into onerous financial commitments for migrants, especially those in low wage jobs. For example, the purchase of mobile phones and the monthly subscription costs have been found to put a significant strain on the limited savings of migrant workers (Law and Peng 2007; Thomas and Lim 2011).

Apart from communication with their home countries, communication with the social networks that migrants foster in their host countries is also significant for the migrants' sense of identity and well-being. Migrants use mediated communication both to ease their assimilation to their host country and also to 'hold on to their native cultural identity' (Lee et al. 2012, 73), as a study of Asian students in the US found. Similarly, Filipino migrants in the UK blog about British weather, culture, and sports, while also reminiscing about the Philippines, its food, music and humor (Yao 2009). They also wrote these blog posts as a 'therapeutic release' way to seek more friends and support in their adopted homes (Yao 2009). Indeed, connections with fellow migrants from the same country of origin are a definite salve for loneliness and alienation. One study revealed how traditional South Asian recipes shared online serve as a 'social glue' that binds together South Asian migrants all over the world. Through the sharing of ethnic recipes, the migrants draw solace from mingling with fellow nationals, resulting in them feeling less isolated and alienated (Hegde 2014). These mediated connections can be further developed to organise face-to-face gatherings, as seen in studies of migrant workers in China (Lang et al. 2010; Law and Peng 2007), and from India and the Philippines (Thomas and Lim 2011). By meeting other migrants from the same hometown, they can share in a sense of belonging and pride in their origins (Peng 2008). Chinese migrant workers were also found to use the Internet to interact with strangers online and to open up about aspects of their lives that they would not reveal in normal contexts (Law and Peng 2007; Peng 2008), or to create virtual communities comprising migrants from the same hometown to share about their emotional lives (Peng 2008). Interestingly, a study by Liu et al. (2014) found that rural–urban Chinese migrant workers used online social media to create for themselves a better, more educated online identity as a respite from the harsh realities of their tough working conditions and low status.

Creating capital

Besides building and sustaining affective ties with their family and acquaintances, migrants also make use of mediated communication for practical and instrumental purposes, fundamentally seeking to improve their employment prospects and lived existence in their host countries.

As better working conditions or higher wages remain key pull factors for individuals to migrate (Castles and Miller 2009; Hugo 2005), both skilled and unskilled migrants exploit mediated communication channels in their quest for better opportunities in their host countries. Among skilled migrants in particular, prior studies have revealed how they avail of migrant networks to build economic capital (Gupta et al. 2014; Raghuram 2008; Saxenian 1999). Such economic capital is built on the foundations of social capital, as illustrated by a study of immigrant entrepreneurs in Silicon Valley. It found that the proliferation of ethnic professional associations in Silicon Valley correspond to the growing success of numerous Chinese and Indian-run businesses because immigrant entrepreneurs rely on formal and informal ethnic networks to forge partnerships and facilitate the flows of capital, skills and technology (Saxenian 2002).

New immigrant entrepreneurs in particular greatly benefit from such transnational networks as they are able to secure financing or seek business advice from more experienced associates (Saxenian et al. 2002). In addition, these migrant networks have increasingly made use of ICTs to create and maintain local and global connections. For example in India, business media sites such as 'Siliconindia' actively promote the entrepreneurial success of professionals in India and abroad to encourage more professionals to follow suit (Biswas 2014). Immigrant entrepreneurs hoping to create start-ups back in their native country also often utilize mediated communication technologies such as email and Skype to consult with government officials to address financial or regulatory concerns (Saxenian et al. 2002). Finally, as numerous studies show, ICTs remain a key determinant for entrepreneurial success (Barba-Sánchez et al. 2007; Wolcott et al. 2008; White et al. 2014). For example, ICT applications allow for the improvement of productivity and efficiency of production processes, while at the same time, contribute to the information and knowledge management of the company. Furthermore, technologies such as social media have also allowed for companies to manage their external relationships with suppliers and customers with ease (Barba-Sánchez et al. 2007).

In the same vein, low-wage migrant workers utilize mediated communication platforms to connect with other migrants, and even to rally together for better working conditions. For example in 2012, a migrant factory worker posted a picture on the microblogging site Weibo to protest a decision by the factory's management to slash performance bonuses. Within the hour, the story was picked up by local labor activists and the media, which in turn, resulted in the management agreeing to restore more than half of the bonus the next day (Kidd 2014). Similarly, migrant factory workers employed by Foxconn, the world's largest electronic manufacturer, chose to use their mobile phones to capture audio and images of their working conditions after eighteen workers jumped to their death (Qiu 2014). In addition, low wage migrant workers also rely on community networks to learn about informal job opportunities which can help them improve their employment prospects. A case in point is female migrant workers in Singapore who depend heavily on their mobile phones to contact employment agencies and former employers to build an extended network of support and opportunity. Through these networks, the women were able to gain access to critical information such as job openings, remittance methods and cost-saving strategies (Thomas and Lim 2010).

Mindful of their marginalized status and motivated by their desire for self-betterment, many migrant workers avidly adopt ICTs in pursuit of personal development and self-improvement. One study of Indonesian domestic helpers in Singapore showed how they learnt to use ICTs so as to enrol in various distance learning courses conducted by the Open University including accountancy, management, public management and communication studies (Wardoyo and Mahmud 2013). These women used their laptop computers to download learning materials, participate in online discussions with peers, search for information, and complete assignments. These women viewed the pursuit of an education as a way to seek better employment and to attain a greater sense of self-respect.

While the specific acquisition of new skills and healthier job prospects is crucial to migrants, so too is the overall ability to adapt to the host country. International migrants typically face myriad social and cultural challenges while learning to live in a foreign country. As a result, they often experience 'acculturative stresses' (Lueck and Wilson 2010, 48) or culture shocks which may lead to health problems such as lack of appetite or sleep, low energy levels, headaches, and depression. In response, migrants have been found to rely on mediated communication to cope with such obstacles. Research has shown that to ease their process of assimilation, migrants often rely on their networks of contacts to learn new languages and acquire cultural skills. For example, a study of East Asian students studying in the US found a positive correlation between the use of English-language mass media and English proficiency (Lee et al. 2012). Interestingly, it uncovered how migrant students use mass media in their host country to lower their 'levels of social difficulty' (Lee et al. 2012, 69), and rely on 'weak online ties' as information sources pertaining to the host country's culture or customs. Similarly, a study of international students engaged in study abroad programs, including Asian students in the US, found that these youths enhance their overseas experiences through their use of social media networks such as Facebook to develop necessary socio-cultural skills and gain self-confidence, which in turn contributed to an improved sense of mental well-being (Sandel 2014). In addition, these students often relied on similar technologies to create and maintain a network of local and international friends whom they could approach to learn more about the host country's values and customs.

Conclusion

While the passage of migrants around the world is already supported by transportation linkages, immigration procedures, housing provisions, remittance structures, medical amenities, and migrant training, it is imperative that media and communication platforms be regarded as a fundamental constituent of migration infrastructure. The socio-emotional bonds that communication helps to foster between migrants and their networks in both home and host countries are critical for boosting their sense of well-being, and enhancing their psychological resilience for facing the challenges of a foreign environment. The social capital that migrants can build and sustain through mediated communications can also help to enrich their employment prospects and build a positive career trajectory. Our historical sweep of the evolution of technologies of mediation has demonstrated that with each new communication affordance, migrants in Asia have derived greater support for the migration process, thus opening the door to more opportunities, and paving the way for stronger affective ties with their significant others. Migration is increasingly a reality for many in Asia as the countries in the region become more densely interconnected and more tightly linked to the global economy. States cannot seek to reap the gains of migration flows while ignoring their associated costs. Instead, they must actively collaborate with NGOs and civic organizations to bridge access and skills divides that prevent migrants from leveraging the benefits of the most economical and efficient communication platforms that link them to their communities, both immediate and extended.

References

Abella, M. and Ducanes, G. (2009) 'The Effect of the Global Economic Crisis on Asian Migrant Workers and Governments' Responses', Bangkok: International Labour Office Regional Office.

Barba-Sánchez, V., M.D.P. Martínez-Ruiz and A. Jiménez-Zarco (2007) 'Drivers, benefits and challenges of ICT adoption by small and medium sized enterprises (SMEs): a literature review', *Problems and Perspectives in Management*, 5(1): 104–115.

Barber, P.G. (2008) 'Cell phones, complicity, and class politics in the Philippine labor diaspora', *Focaal*, 2008(51): 28–42.

Biswas, R.R. (2014) 'Reverse migrant entrepreneurs in India: motivations, trajectories and realities', *Indian Skilled Migration and Development*, Springer: 285–307.

Bonini, T. (2011) 'The media as "home-making" tools: life story of a Filipino migrant in Milan', *Media, Culture & Society*, 33(6): 869–883.

Castles, S. and M.J. Miller (2009) 'Migration in the Asia-Pacific region', *Migration Information Source*.

Chib, A., H.A Wilkin and S.R.M. Hua (2013) 'International migrant workers' use of mobile phones to seek social support in Singapore', *Information Technologies & International Development*, 9(4).

Chib, A., S. Malik, R. G. Aricat, and S.Z. Kadir (2014) 'Migrant mothering and mobile phones: Negotiations of transnational identity', *Mobile Media & Communication*, 2(1): 73–93.

Chung, R.C.Y., F. Bemak, D.P. Ortiz and P.A. Sandoval-Perez (2008) 'Promoting the mental health of immigrants: A multicultural/social justice perspective', *Journal of Counseling & Development*, 86(3): 310–317.

Do, A. (2012) 'In Vietnam, for every 100 people there are 145 mobile phones'. Available at: http://www.techinasia.com/vietnam–100-people-145-mobile-phones/ (Accessed on July 22, 2014).

Dutta, N., S. Kar and S. Roy (2014) *Education and Self-employment: South Asian Immigrants in the US Labor Market* (No. 8152), Institute for the Study of Labor (IZA).

Francisco, V. (2013) 'The Internet is magic: Technology, intimacy and transnational families', *Critical Sociology*, 1–18.

Fresnoza-Flot, A. (2009) 'Migration status and transnational mothering: The case of Filipino migrants in France', *Global Networks*, 9(2): 252–270.

Gartaula, H.N., L. Visser and A. Niehof (2012) 'Socio-cultural dispositions and wellbeing of the women left behind: A case of migrant households in Nepal', *Social Indicators Research*, 108(3): 401–420.

Ge, Y. and K. Ho (2014) 'Researching international student migration in Asia: research design and project management issues', *Journal of Population Research*: 1–21.

GSMA Intelligence (2014) 'Half a billion Chinese citizens have subscribed to the mobile internet'. Available at: https://gsmaintelligence.com/files/analysis/?file=2014-06-09-half-a-billion-chinese-citizens-have-subscribed-to-the-mobile-internet.pdf (Accessed on July 22, 2014).

Gunawardene, N. (2014) 'South Asia analysis: Cell phone empowers South Asia's poor'. Available at: http://www.scidev.net/south-asia/communication/analysis-blog/sa-analysis-cell-phones-empower-south-asia-s-poor.html (Accessed on July 22, 2014).

Gupta, T.D., G. Man, K. Mirchandani and R. Ng (2014) 'Class borders: Chinese and South Asian Canadian professional women navigating the labor market', *Asian and Pacific Migration Journal*, 23(1): 55.

Hegde, R.S. (2014) 'Food blogs and the digital reimagination of South Asian diasporic publics', *South Asian Diaspora*, 6(1): 89–103.

Henning, S. (2011) International Migration and Development in Asia and the Pacific: Key Issues and Recommendations for Action. Lecture presented at Strengthening Dialogue between ESCWA and ESCAP Countries on International Migration and Development in Beirut, Lebanon.

Hoang, L.A. and B.S. Yeoh (2012) 'Sustaining families across transnational spaces: Vietnamese migrant parents and their left-behind children', *Asian Studies Review*, 36(3): 307–325.

Hugo, G. (2005) 'The new international migration in Asia: Challenges for population research,' *Asian Population Studies*, 1(1): 93–120.

Hugo, G. and S. Ukwatta (2010) 'Sri Lankan female domestic workers overseas—The impact on their children', *Asian and Pacific Migration Journal*, 19(2): 237–263.

Hutchison, C. (2014) 'Internationally inclusive science education: Addressing the needs of migrants and international students in the era of globalization'. In M.M. Atwater, M. Russell and M.B. Butler (eds) *Multicultural Science Education*, Dordrecht: Springer: 137–158.

Kidd, D. (2014) '10 young Chinese workers, contentious politics, and cyberactivism in the global factory.' *Cyberactivism on the Participatory Web*: 208.

Lan, P.C. (2003) 'Maid or madam? Filipina migrant workers and the continuity of domestic labor', *Gender & Society*, 17(2): 187–208.

Lang, X., E. Oreglia and S. Thomas (2010) 'Social practices and mobile phone use of young migrant workers'. In *Proceedings of the 12th International Conference on Human–Computer Interaction with Mobile Devices and Services*, ACM.

Law, P. and Y. Peng (2007) 'Cellphones and the social lives of migrant workers in Southern China'. In R. Pertierra (ed.) *The Social Construction and Usage of Communication Technologies: Asian and European Experiences*, Quezon City: The University of the Philippines Press.

Law, P.L. and Y. Peng (2008) 'Mobile networks: migrant workers in southern China'. In J. E. Katz (ed.) *Handbook of Mobile Communication Studies*, Cambridge, MA: MIT Press.

Lee, J.W.Y., B. Kim, T. Lee and M.S. Kim (2012) 'Uncovering the use of Facebook during an exchange program', *China Media Research*, 8(4): 62–76.

Liu, J., A. Boden, D.W. Randall and V. Wulf (2014) 'Enriching the distressing reality: social media use by Chinese migrant workers', in *Proceedings of the 17th ACM Conference on Computer Supported Cooperative Work & Social Computing*, ACM.

Lueck, K. and M. Wilson (2010) 'Acculturative stress in Asian immigrants: The impact of social and linguistic factors', *International Journal of Intercultural Relations*, 34(1): 47–57.

Madianou, M. (2012) 'Migration and the accentuated ambivalence of motherhood: The role of ICTs in Filipino transnational families', *Global Networks*, 12(3): 277–295.

Madianou, M. and D. Miller (2011) 'Mobile phone parenting: Reconfiguring relationships between Filipina migrant mothers and their left-behind children', *New Media & Society*, 13(3): 457–470.

Oreglia, E. (2010) 'Creating community, rejecting community: Migrant women in Beijing', *The Journal of Community Informatics*, 5(3–4).

Paragas, F. (2010) 'Migrant workers and mobile phones: Technological, temporal, and spatial simultaneity'. In R. Ling and S.W. Campbell (ed.) *The Reconstruction of Space and Time: Mobile Communication Practices*, New Brunswick: Transaction Publishers.

Parreñas, R. (2005) 'Long distance intimacy: class, gender and intergenerational relations between mothers and children in Filipino transnational families', *Global Networks*, 5(4): 317–336.

Peng, Y. (2008) 'Internet use of migrant workers in the Pearl River Delta', *Knowledge, Technology & Policy*, 21(2): 47–54.

Pertierra, R. (2005) 'Mobile phones, identity and discursive intimacy', *Human Technology: An Interdisciplinary Journal on Humans in ICT Environments*, 1(1): 23–44.

Qiu, J.L. (2014) 'Communication & global power shifts | "Power to the people!": Mobiles, migrants, and social movements in Asia', *International Journal of Communication*, 8: 16.

Raghuram, P. (2008) 'Migrant women in male-dominated sectors of the labour market: a research agenda', *Population, Space and Place*, 14(1): 43–57.

Samson, F.L. (2014) 'Asian American attitudes towards a US citizenship path for illegal immigrants: Immigration reform as racialised politics', *Journal of Ethnic and Migration Studies*, (ahead-of-print): 1–21.

Sandel, T.L. (2014) '"Oh, I'm here!": Social media's impact on the cross-cultural adaptation of students studying abroad', *Journal of Intercultural Communication Research*, 43(1): 1–29.

Saxenian, A. (1999) *Silicon Valley's New Immigrant Entrepreneurs*, San Francisco: Public Policy Institute of California.

Saxenian, A. (2002) 'Silicon Valley's new immigrant high-growth entrepreneurs', *Economic Development Quarterly*, 16(1): 20–31.

Saxenian, A., Y. Motoyama and X. Quan (2002) *Local and Global Networks of Immigrant Professionals in Silicon Valley*, San Francisco: Public Policy Institute of California.

Seshan, G. (2012) 'Migrants in Qatar: A socio-economic profile', *Journal of Arabian Studies*, 2(2): 157–171.

Sidhu, R., Yeoh, B. and Chang, S. (2015). 'A situated analysis of global knowledge networks: capital accumulation strategies of transnationally mobile scientists in Singapore', *Higher Education*, 69(1), 79–101.

Simich, L., M. Beiser, M. Stewart and E. Mwakarimba (2005) 'Providing social support for immigrants and refugees in Canada: Challenges and directions', *Journal of Immigrant and Minority Health*, 7(4): 259–268.

Skeldon, R. (2013) *Global Migration: Demographics Aspects and Its Relevance for Development*, P. Division, United Nations Department of Economic and Social Affairs.

Telecomtiger (2013) 'India now has 867.80 million mobile users'. Available at: http://www.telecomtiger.com/PolicyNRegulation_fullstory.aspx?passfrom=PolicyNRegulation&storyid=17660&section=S174 (Accessed on July 22, 2014).

Thomas, M. and S.S. Lim (2011) 'On maids and mobile phones: ICT use by female migrant workers in Singapore and its policy implications'. In J. E. Katz (ed.) *Mobile Communication: Dimensions of Social Policy*, New Brunswick: Transaction Publishers.

Ullah, A.K.M.A. (2014) 'How International is international: A study on international marriage migration in Asia'. In J. Zhang and H. Duncan (eds) *Migration in China and Asia*, Dordrecht: Springer: 113–130.

Uy-Tioco, C. (2007) 'Overseas Filipino workers and text messaging: Reinventing transnational mothering', *Continuum: Journal of Media & Cultural Studies*, 21(2): 253–265.

Wardoyo, R. J. and Mahmud, N. (2013) 'Benefits and barriers of learning and using ICTs at open university: a case study of Indonesian domestic workers in Singapore'. In *Proceedings of the Sixth International Conference on Information and Communication Technologies and Development: Full Papers-Volume 1* (pp. 215–226). ACM.

We Are Social Singapore (2012) 'Social, digital and mobile in Asia, October 2012'. Available at: http://www.slideshare.net/wearesocialsg/we-are-socials-guide-to-social-digital-mobile-in-asia-oct-2012 (Accessed on July 22, 2014).

White, G. R., A. Afolayan and E. Plant (2014) 'Challenges to the adoption of e-commerce technology for supply chain management in a developing economy: A focus on Nigerian SMEs', *E-commerce Platform Acceptance*, Springer: 23–39.

Wolcott, P., M. Kamal and S. Qureshi (2008) 'Meeting the challenges of ICT adoption by micro-enterprises', *Journal of Enterprise Information Management*, 21(6): 616–632.

Xia, Y. (2011) 'Mobile phones' roles following China's 2008 earthquake'. In J.E. Katz (ed.) *Mobile Communication: Dimensions of Social Policy*, New Brunswick: Transaction Publishers.

Yang, K. (2008) 'A preliminary study on the use of mobile phones amongst migrant workers in Beijing', *Knowledge, Technology & Policy*, 21(2): 65–72.

Yao, A. (2009) 'Enriching the migrant experience: Blogging motivations, privacy and offline lives of Filipino women in Britain', *First Monday*, 14(3).

22

Digital kinships: intergenerational locative media in Tokyo, Shanghai and Melbourne

Larissa Hjorth, Heather Horst, Sarah Pink,
Baohua Zhou, Fumitoshi Kato, Genevieve Bell,
Kana Ohashi, Chris Marmo and Miao Xiao

New media location-based services like Google Maps and practices like geo-tagging have become an integral part of everyday life, entangling movements across relationships, lifestyles, places and spaces. Existing research has shown that the growth of locative media is impacting upon how people experience place, time and mobility, in ways that are uneven across cultural, generational and temporal scales (Gazzard 2011; Farman 2011; de Souza e Silva and Frith 2012). Few studies have tried to understand how different generations are using locative media for everyday "friendly" surveillance—to stay in touch, to keep children "safe" and to monitor the activities of children, partners and parents (Sengupta 2012; Clark 2012). Understanding the cultural and intergenerational dimensions of people's locative media use can provide new insights into culturally nuanced notions of new media. In particular, mapping the digital practices through and around the family can help us to comprehend the tension between the tenacity of kinship ties and their transformation through digital entanglements.

This chapter presents new research into how locative media are shaping, and being shaped by, practices of intimacy and privacy in intergenerational families. While debates around lifestyle and consumer culture in Asia have focused upon individualization and the idea of a "break" with traditional values, especially as a result of new media (McVeigh 2003; Chua 2010; Robison and Goodman 1996), we argue for a middle ground approach that focuses on the reproduction of kinship through media rituals. These quotidian media practices both re-enact older familial rituals and give birth to new ones.

Drawing on three vignettes developed as short-term ethnographies (Pink and Morgan 2013) with families in Tokyo, Shanghai and Melbourne in November 2013, this chapter outlines a framework for conceptualizing the mundane ways in which locative media are used. In all three locations, we conducted in-depth interviews involving scenarios of use and solicited a-day-in-your-life narratives from family members. As we illustrate, the comparison of three different cultural contexts enables an exploration of multiple configurations in the adoption of locative media–including the uneven development of locative media, their uses and their intergenerational uptake.

Tokyo, Shanghai and Melbourne provide three contrasting sites through which to understand locative media practices. Residents of Tokyo have been using locative media for over a decade.

Shanghai is an example of rapid and large-scale uptake of locative media by the youth—generations born post-1980 such as the *ba ling hou* and *jiu ling hou* (literally, the post-1980 and post-1990 generations) (CNNIC 2013; Pink and Hjorth 2013; Hjorth et al. 2014). In comparison with Tokyo and Shanghai, Melbourne has a more recent uptake locative media through high rates of smartphone penetration over the past two years (ABS 2013; Our Mobile Planet 2012). By contrasting these three divergent technocultures and the genealogies of their emergence, this chapter seeks to understand the emerging and existing practices, motivations, and perceptions around intergeneration uses of locative media in mundane settings in everyday life. We then consider these practices in terms of four underlying themes—*digital kinship, intimate co-presence, affective ambience,* and *the intimate mundane.*

These four concepts underscore the ways in which intimacy, family and place are being transformed in an age of locative media. *Digital kinship* is a central tenet of the project, which embeds the study into broader debates about the changing (or residual) nature of what it means to be a "family" in an age of networked media (Clark 2012; Horst 2010, 2011). Kinship has always been important to ethnographic understandings of culture. With the added dimension of the digital, we see how kinship moves in and out of online and offline spaces and, in turn, how these spaces have come to develop their own histories, connections and memories. Our attention to digital kinship also accounts for the changing family structure associated with contemporary Asian cities such as Shanghai and Tokyo, including the increasing trend towards nuclear families. It also acknowledges changing definitions of family in multicultural urban areas like Melbourne, such as the growth in GLBT families, single parents and families without children. These new forms of families are, in turn, shaping emergent meanings and forms of kinship and relatedness.

Throughout this chapter we focus upon the ways that families, in all their specificity, use social media to create and maintain connection as well as disconnection. While the concept of digital kinship enables us to understand the new formations of families, we have been particularly interested in understanding the mechanisms through which kinship and relatedness are made and maintained. One concept that emerged during the initial phases of the study is *intimate co-presence.* Intimate co-presence is both a practice and a quality, even a sensibility, through which family members maintain their relationships. Co-presence has been viewed as a productive way for rethinking traditional binaries such as online versus offline that are no longer adequate to everyday life (Licoppe 2004). The rubric of co-presence provides a broader conceptual framework for understanding intimacy and mediation as something that has always been an integral part of being human.

As we have noted elsewhere, intimacy has always been mediated, if not by technologies then by memories, language and gestures (Hjorth 2009; Horst and Miller 2012). The concept of intimate co-presence allows us to connect the contemporary with the historical by considering the evolution of mediated intimacies. Intimacy can be understood on various levels from individual and personal to social and cultural (Hertzeld 1997). Our usage of intimacy engages with personal, cultural and social notions of intimacy as always mediated.

Just as mobile media amplify debates around intimacy and degrees of co-presence, it is also embedded in the everyday through its relationship with the creation of ambience. *Affective ambience* plays to the idea that media often drop into the background of everyday life. Its particular affects and textures become embedded in the everyday. Mimi Ito's notion of the "full-time intimate community" captures this definition of ambience. As Okabe (2004) argues, "The visual information shared between intimates also represents a similar social practice, of sharing ambient awareness with close friends, family and loved ones who are not physically co-present" (n.p.). Ambience is often used to describe sound, music and lighting but has also been used in computing and science (especially human–computer interaction) to evoke information and music to provide feeling. In short, ambience is about the *texture* of *context, emotion,* and *affect.* In this study we noted a type of ambience we define as affective ambience, whereby one's use or non-use of locative media shapes and affects the production of ambience around people, media and contexts.

Lastly, the concept of the *intimate mundane* provides a lens through which to understand how locative media practices are embedded in the ordinary and mundane detail of everyday life—the often not explicitly thought about or spoken about tasks that we perform, sometimes with family members, as we go about our everyday routines. Attention to the mundane means attention to the essential activities that underpin the more enchanting manifestations of the everyday (Pink et al. 2013). Attention to the digital in this context is no less important (e.g., see Coleman 2010), particularly since uses of digital media are very often dispersed throughout other everyday practical activities such as laundry, showering, getting up in the morning and going to bed (see Pink and Leder Mackley 2012). Through the vignettes below, we explore how these four concepts play out across and through locative media in relation to digital kinship. As we argue digital kinship involves entanglements between older-style kinship relations, rituals and new modes of understanding within digital spaces.

Genealogies of locative media in Shanghai

While not everyone in the world owns a computer, the ubiquity of mobile phones has allowed many people access to online media, and globally, the mobile phone is becoming a dominant platform for accessing online content. In China, the total number of mobile phones in 2012 was 1.04 billion (CNNIC 2013). The significant role played by mobile phones as the dominant portal for social and online media is highlighted by the China Internet Network Information Center (CNNIC) 2013 report, which noted that mobile Web users now total just over 463 million.

In China, mobile phones have made online content accessible across the urban/rural divide. With over 200 million smartphone subscribers,[1] increasingly mobile social media like QQ and Weibo are an important part of China's media space (Hjorth et al. 2014, 291). A Chinese family with only one child per couple in the youngest generation(s) exemplifies the impact of three and a half decades of government policy. Many in the *ba ling hou* and *jiu ling hou* single-child generations are experiencing a type of economic and geographic mobility their parents could never have imagined. In the midst of this mobility, mobile media feature as a way in which to maintain familial rituals and belonging.

A key part of this mobile media space involves the convergence of locative, social, and mobile media. While mobile media provide a bridge for cross-generational intimacy, it is location-based service (LBS) that is a distinctive practice of China's younger generations. Through smartphones equipped with cameras and GPS (Geographic Positioning Systems), young people are able to document, illustrate, and narrate a sense of identity, sociality, and place in new ways. Through LBS, they are providing new visualities of their journey as they experience emergent forms of geographic and socioeconomic mobility (Hjorth and Gu 2012).

Locative media have burgeoned with the expansion of the mobile Internet in China. There are not only LBS-focused apps like Jiepang (similar to Foursquare), but also SNS apps that integrate LBS functions like Weibo (Microblog) and WeChat (a media rich messenger-like app). In fact, apps like Jiepang with its relatively simple LBS function are losing popularity to SNS apps that not only include an LBS function but also build in more ways to show location besides "check-in," like photo-sharing.

In 2013, we interviewed six families in which at least two of the younger generations (grandparents sometimes, plus always parents and children) used locative media. All families were translocal, meaning that the young people were studying and living in Shanghai, while their parents and grandparents lived far away, in the family's hometown. The main interview questions covered how they used LBS and how such usage influenced intergenerational communication. In all of the six families, WeChat was the main online communication tool connecting parents and children. As a result, they received each other's locative information mainly through posts that marked the location, or clues to the location in photos. In five families out of six, the parents' WeChat apps had been installed by their children. Both parents and children described WeChat as a convenient, money-saving and fashionable way to communicate.

This led us to ask: how do parents and their children think about the influence of WeChat on inter-generational communication? We found that while children noted both the advantages and the disadvantages of adding parents as "friends" on locative media, all parents emphasized the benefits of knowing about their children's immediate status and detailed daily lives from WeChat (especially since they were not living with their children). Here we see friendly surveillance (what Matsuda (2009) calls "mom in the pocket") at work whereby the locative media capabilities of geotagging afford parents with ways in which to monitor their child's mundane movements in a manner that is intimate and yet not invasive. Parents all felt relieved to know more about their children's daily lives in such an efficient way without appearing like they were interfering.

Through indirect snooping on WeChat, parents could gain an ambient sense of their children's movements. To add their children as friends on WeChat provided parents with a sense of intimate co-presence with their children and engagement in their children's lives. For example, one mother noted that by checking her daughter's "moments" (social network uploads), "I can know what she is doing at the moment. I feel we're closer. I see where she is and see her photos, so it's just like I'm staying with her." This is an example of how locative media can afford an overlay between intimate co-presence and affective ambience to create digital kinships. That is, the (online) co-presence is both intimate and ambient, reflecting and expanding upon existing kinships through digital analogies.

Another advantage is that family members have more topics to talk about as they weave the online with offline. This weaving between different forms of intimate co-presence across physical, electronic and psychological realms is further enhanced by the nature of WeChat. For example, incidental details about the everyday might not warrant direct discussion. When parents asked about mundane matters, children would often answer "nothing much [happened]." However, with locative media interweaving the social with the geographic, stories on the move were made present to both parties. Shared camera phone pictures could offer a site for discussion. One schoolboy interviewed noted that he was aware of his mother stealthily following all his social and locative media accounts, yet he accepted this friendly surveillance because it allows his mother an ambient sense of his life that makes her content. The boy stated,

> I'm not the kind of child who likes to share my daily life with my parents, but mom cares a lot about it. . . . Sometimes she pretends to casually mention something she saw on my posts, for example, "You went to Suzhou last week?" and we'll talk about that.

Locative media usage was most significant when the geographic distance was greatest. When the children were still in middle school, they lived with their parents and the parents knew a great deal about their daily lives. In this situation, the impact of location sharing is not obvious. When the children enroll in university, however, their lives become more varied and parents know less about that, so parents have a stronger desire to follow their children's lives. It is at this stage in the cross-generational relationship that the affective ambience extended across distance by social and locative media becomes more important.

The disadvantages perceived by children are mostly about monitoring from their parents. Children are aware that certain movements and moments might worry their parents, and hence choose to negotiate this in various ways, such as "self-censorship" before posting messages, selective exposure to their parents, and strategic blocking of their parents for a while and then adding them back. Generally speaking, many felt there was little worth hiding from their parents. Moreover, parents deployed emotional means to dissuade their children from blocking them, as was illustrated in two interviews. When mothers found they couldn't see their daughters' uploads, they questioned their daughters as to why they had blocked them and requested them to "add them back." Both mothers phoned their daughters to express how they cared about them and their disappointment and unhappiness about being blocked. The daughters then unblocked them and have since had to self-edit more systematically.

Patterns of family interaction manifest in particular ways through locative media. For those "democratic" families in which parents and children enjoy relatively independent spaces, parents won't ask much about children's daily activities because they know that their children wouldn't like it. They just watch *quietly*. Other parents have more power and want to know almost everything about their children. The media literacies of parents can also influence how they use locative media to interact with their children. In families whose parents are both adept at new technology, mothers seem to be more active than fathers in social media use, and communicate more with their children.

In a counter-example, however, in Tintin's family, her mother is not proficient with mobile apps, so she has to live vicariously through her husband's media usage with Tintin. Tintin used to be closer to her mother, but she admits that now that she interacts with her father more frequently on social media, their relationship has become more intimate. Tintin's media usage such as geotagged photos with her parents shows how digital kinship can be recast through the intimate, ambient and mundane gestures of media co-presence.

Genealogies of locative media in Tokyo

In Japan, since the mid-1970s, a nuclear family consisting only of "a couple and child(ren)" has come to be regarded as an exemplary model of the family (Nonoyama 2009). However, in recent years, the composition of the typical family has diversified due to the decrease in the number of people getting married, tendency to marry later, and the decline in the number of children. The number of couples married in 2012 was 670,000, which was 60 percent less than the level in 1972, when the number was 1.1 million (Ministry of Health, Labour and Welfare 2013).

In light of these familial and lifestyle shifts, Hisaya Nonoyama, an advocate of the "family lifestyle approach," argues that today, the notion of "family" indicates various forms of family selected by individuals' lifestyles, and family has become an important object of choice for individuals. Thus, within a context of "family"—which is selected and formed *as* a lifestyle—individuals have to exert active effort to build and maintain "familiar relationships," otherwise they cannot enter or they fall out of the family circle. Nonoyama's research leads us to ask: how do family members communicate with each other to form or maintain lifestyle-based "families of choice" in Japan today?

In Japan, mobile phones, which started to become common in the mid-1990s, are used as a tool to connect family members in these families of choice (Ito et al. 2005). From the late 2000s, smartphones started to become an integral communication tool among family members, not only through their provision of e-mail, SMS, and telephone services, but also as a portal to social media. According to a survey conducted by the Institute for Information and Communications Policy (IICP) in 2013, the utilization rate of smartphones was 52.8 percent, which was twenty points up from the previous poll (IICP 2014). The age group that uses smartphones most frequently was people in their 20s (87.9 percent), followed by those in their 30s (78.7 percent), teens (63.3

percent), 40s (58.8 percent), 50s (32.4 percent), and 60s (8.7 percent). These statistics are echoed in our fieldwork with families. In the following section we discuss some of our key findings in terms of media practices, lifestyles and digital kinship.

Rika is a 32-year-old female flight attendant who lives in a bedsit about an hour by train from Tokyo. Just a stone's throw away from her apartment, Rika's only family, her 72-year-old mother, lives alone. Rika often leaves home for work early in the morning and returns home late. Reflecting the "family-as-chosen-lifestyle" trend noted above, she and her mother respect each other's daily rhythms by living separately. Rika's first mobile phone was the one that her mother bought her when she was in junior high school, for personal security purposes on her way home from after-school cram school. Since then, she has been using her mobile phone for communicating with her mother on a daily basis. After graduating from university, the mobile phone became even more important in maintaining Rika's relationship with her mother as Rika started to fly all around the world as a flight attendant. Overseas flights occasionally cause unexpected delays. "I couldn't come back to Japan when there was a flood in Thailand and a volcanic explosion in Iceland. In these situations, if it wasn't for mobile phones, my mother would not have been able to find out if I was OK," she says. In her airline, the family of employees is not allowed to make calls directly to the airline if a hijacking occurs. This makes the mobile phone indispensable in allowing Rika to communicate with her mother especially when she is abroad.

Until two years ago, Rika used to use SMS when she was abroad—which cost one dollar (per message) anywhere in the world—to communicate with her mother. After she bought a Samsung GALAXY smartphone and tablet PC two years ago, and a tablet PC for her mother, they started to use Facebook and LINE instead of SMS. When she was in junior high, her mother bought a mobile phone for her. Now the roles are reversed with Rika buying her mother the communication devices. Rather than buying a smartphone, Rika bought an easy-to-use tablet PC with a large screen, given her mother's age. Rika always gives a fully charged tablet PC to her mother before she leaves Japan.

Rika often does a "check-in" on Facebook when she visits abroad on business. One reason is to let her mother know where she is. Her mother does not have her own Facebook account. So Rika keeps her own Facebook account logged-on on the tablet PC, and gives it to her mother so that she can check Rika's timeline without it being bothersome. In the past, she used to give a paper-based hotel list to her mother, but now Facebook "check-ins" suffice. LINE also has a key role in connecting the pair when they are away from each other. They can talk or chat for free by using LINE–now the most used social media app in Japan–when they have a WiFi connection, regardless of their location (80.3 percent of 20s, 70.5 percent of teens and 65.4 percent of 30s use LINE (Institute for Information and Communications Policy, hereinafter IICP 2014)).

For example, Rika communicated with her mother using LINE video call while she was travelling in Sedona, Arizona. "We can talk face-to-face using LINE video call. And it's free. When I was in Sedona, I wanted to tell my mother that 'I am in *this* kind of place!' by showing the scenery and my face." Rika's mother says about being able to communicate easily with her daughter using Facebook and LINE that, "It's nice. I can feel safe." There are few people who use social media in her generation. In the 60s age group, only 5 percent use Facebook and 4.3 percent use LINE (IICP 2014). Rika's mother does not know much about how to use Facebook and LINE yet, but she is thinking of taking a tablet course to master these technologies in the near future.

Through this interview, we recognized that the relationship between mother and daughter was gradually changing as they begin to adopt new mobile media technologies. During the age of the *keitai* (mobile phone), children were the ones monitored by their parents. In contrast, children now became the ones who monitor the use of technologies by their parents. Growing up with *keitai*, the interviewees' generation (30s) can be understood as one that tends to be an early adopter of new technologies and services. And thus children are now in the position to introduce, teach, and facilitate the use of social media services for their parents, rather than being introduced and taught by them. These participants suggest how social and locative media can contribute to our understandings of the notion of "family." Interestingly enough, we found that a definition of "family" may derive from the function of the media themselves. Like the phenomenon of "friends" in social network sites (boyd 2008), users understand and define their "family" by applying the classifier of "friends/family members" provided by the app. By doing so, users are beginning to generate new forms of digital kinship.

Our interviewees also illustrated situations in which they felt togetherness or connectedness with their family members, while they are physically apart. Smartphones and tablet PCs are utilized to create and maintain their intimacy. The "stamp" function (cartoon emoticons) of LINE and other messenger services is becoming an integral part of social and locative media, providing users with emotional, non-verbal aspects of communication. Another key concept, the intimate mundane, also resonated with our Japan interviews. Given the historical entrenchment of *keitai* culture in Japan, smartphones and tablet PCs are inextricably embedded in day-to-day activities. Daily "check-ins" to Facebook timelines and exchanges of stamps via LINE are no longer "new" events for the users. Rather, they seem to play a key role in organizing their mundane practices, providing a template for tempo-spatial micro-coordinations around differing schedules.

Genealogies of locative media in Melbourne

Melbourne provides a compelling site for studying a relatively recent locative media uptake. Here as in Shanghai and Tokyo, smartphones play a key role in mediating and representing lifestyle. Smartphones with locative technologies are relatively pervasive in Australia, and this rate of pervasiveness is increasing rapidly. Smartphone penetration is Australia was 37 percent at the beginning of 2011; two years later, at the beginning of 2013, that figure had risen to 65 percent (Our Mobile Planet 2013; ACMA 2013). But unlike Tokyo, which has already a decade of mobile Internet, Melbourne is relatively new to the phenomenon. Other recent research has indicated that the number of people who own either a smartphone or a tablet has risen to over 70 percent in this Australian city (Deepend 2014). Device penetration is relatively high across most age demographics. Within certain age brackets, such as the 25–29 demographic, ownership of smart devices is over 90 percent; however, even older demographics, such as the over-60s, report smartphone ownership of 55 percent (ibid.).

In June 2012, there were an estimated 6.4 million families living in Australia consisting of a total of 19.4 million family members. The vast majority of families were couple families (83 percent) with about half of the couple families having dependents living with them (43 percent). The next largest group was one-parent families (15 percent), and two out of every three one-parent families had dependents living with them (67 percent). Of the 961,000 one-parent families, 81 percent were single mothers (ABS 2013).

Unlike Shanghai and Tokyo, which are characterized by a relatively monocultural permanent population with a steady tide of international visitors, in Melbourne multiculturalism is a key feature of the permanent population, with 42 percent of its residents born overseas and the most commonly spoken language after English being Mandarin (10 percent) (City of Melbourne 2013). In a City of Melbourne report, a total of 207 ancestries were identified for residents, along with 138 overseas countries of birth and 121 languages other than English spoken at home (2013). It is clearly important to engage with this multicultural aspect of Melbourne's social tapestry. In a preliminary study conducted in October and November of 2013, we conducted some initial probing into relationships with, and through, locative media within families. We sought to recruit participants whose backgrounds reflected cultural diversity and diaspora. We initially conducted a survey via Survey Monkey recruited via Twitter, Facebook ads, and AirTasker. The majority of respondents fell between the ages of 2 and 39 (60 percent); 70 percent used locative media and the Internet to keep in touch with family "very often" or "extremely often"; 90 percent had a smartphone; and attitudes to locative media were mostly positive, although 40 percent stated privacy as a concern. From these 40 surveys we then recruited two families to conduct preliminary home visits, diary studies and interviews.

The first family was made up of Japanese migrants, a self-described "nuclear" family of four: mother (Nina, 63), father (Tony, 68), son (Phil, 34), daughter (Kate, 31) and daughter-in-law (Phil's wife, Yin, 31). The family was originally from Yokohama, and had lived in Australia for 25 years, with the children being 8 and 10 years old when they moved. Both parents are now retired, both children are married, and Phil's wife was present for the interviews. Kate uses her work iPad to check her Facebook feed at home. She is not "friends" with her parents on Facebook, although her husband is "friends" with her dad, and he sees most of her pictures through his profile. Kate checks her social media profiles in and around her workday as a Japanese teacher. After work is when she will often call her brother, and comment on his Facebook posts. Her checking reflects Kate's daily rhythms through a type of affective ambience that is located in the intimate mundane. Mundane thoughts and images are posted to give her friends and family an intimate co-present sense of her everyday life. In this way, locative media move in and out of the background of everyday life to help Kate navigate social and spatial assemblages, and entanglements between her Japanese and Australian self.

This family's media use showed how locative media are important in navigating transnational relationships by giving users the ability to gain a sense of place through online maps. In maintaining relationships with friends and family overseas, social and locative media become pivotal for both parents and children to maintain digital kinship through intimate co-presence. Tony, the father, used Facebook to keep in touch with people in Japan, posting comments about weather and traffic, and sometimes photos. Nina, the mother, said early on that she was "not good at technical things," but later on Tony showed us her desk, with her own computer housing social media pages.

The second family was a Chinese Australian family consisting of husband (Jack, 32), wife (Laura, 30) and wife's mother (CiCi, 60). Jack and Laura were in their early 30s and recently married. CiCi had recently moved in with them, beginning a year-long stay. Jack and Laura had been in Australia for seven and three years respectively; both are from Shandong province and work as professionals in the IT sector. Jack's mother still lives in Shandong, and doesn't visit Australia often. He is more likely to go back to China, as he likes visiting his friends there as well as seeing his mother (and cousin). He emails her once a week and they talk about how life is going. His mother wants to know if he works too much. They don't use anything other than email to communicate.

Jacks uses Weibo and WeChat to keep in touch with his Chinese friends, both in China and in Australia. He and his wife are connected on a number of social networks, including both "Aussie" and "Chinese" ones. They don't communicate on them very often, however. Jack thinks that Laura posts more than him. Laura complains that he only posts sports and car news, although he will sometimes post pictures of Laura in Melbourne parks and other beautiful locations so that her friends can see. Laura uses Weibo, WeChat, QQ, Facebook and Twitter. Much like Jack, she uses these for different purposes and different sets of friends and family. She accesses these on her iPhone (when out) and her iPad (when home). She mainly uses the "Chinese" services to update her friends in China on her life in Melbourne. She also likes to check what her friends in China are doing, and how they are. She leaves messages for them on Weibo and WeChat so that they can see them at their convenience: the time difference is important, especially during the working week when they would struggle to have free-time that overlaps.

Figure 22.1   Laura's iPad and the affective ambience of a traditional lotus flower as screensaver

CiCi primarily uses QQ on her mobile phone (an iPhone). When she's in Australia, CiCi enjoys going on walks in the neighborhood and taking photos on her phone. Social and locative media provide CiCi with the ability to map her experiences in Australia in an ambient manner that is both intimate and co-present with contacts in China. She can share images and experiences with friends and family in China and have discussions with them in real-time. This affordance for digital kinship that transcends geographic distance is important for CiCi as a visitor. In contrast, for both Laura and Jack, as they try to settle in Melbourne, the social and locative media they use have been compartmentalized according to geographic location and social relation. Media like QQ is overtly for digital kinship (that is, communication with family members). Weibo and WeChat are for intimate co-presence with friends back in China. Facebook is for Melbourne friends.

Conclusion

In this chapter, through paralleling three very different cultural, linguistic and technological contexts, we have explored how similarities and differences in cross-generational media literacy and intimacy are emerging. By examining familial media practices, we have tried to show how we can gain insight into both emergent and residual-traditional cultural practices. We have deployed the notion of digital kinship to understand digital media practices within familial lives as both re-enacting older rituals and providing new ways of imagining the contemporary family. Our initial research with families' use of locative media technologies suggests that the concepts of *intimate co-presence*, *affective ambience* and the *intimate mundane* enable the understanding of the relationships and atmospheres that are being generated across our three focus cities.

We have seen how locative media are being interwoven into the development of new norms of what we are terming digital kinship. From Rika and her mother in Japan to Kate and her Japanese family in Melbourne, locative media are being used to mediate the intimate mundane. From blocking familial friend requests, to developing a stronger relationship with one's father due to frequent social media connection, contemporary families are using these media to negotiate the knowing and unknowing, tacit and spoken. Providing affective ambience to "fill in" the gaps of cross-generational contact and affording new ways to provide constant comfort for family members separated by geographic distance, locative media entangle with everyday lives to provide a lens onto contemporary negotiations of family, place and intimacy.

As mobile apps are domesticated into the everyday routines of our participants, we can see how people shape the media, just as the media shape them. Mobile apps like LINE in Japan and DayMap in Australia are allowing parents and children to monitor and survey each other's practices while also affording new modes of negotiating co-presence in an increasingly mobile world. Parents have always watched children and children have always edited their behavior in the presence of their parents, but as the locative media apps become a more integral part of everyday life, we have a new opportunity to understand emergent and enduring forms of kinship and intimate co-presence (Matsuda 2009).

When kinship becomes a digitally inflected phenomenon, digital kinship can be understood as entangled within the three concepts of *intimate co-presence, affective ambience* and the *intimate mundane*. As we have demonstrated, living with digital media in families is differently experienced in different places. However, these three concepts effectively pull together the common threads of residual and emergent meanings and practices of family in the three research localities we have considered.

Acknowledgements

This research is funded by an Australian Research Council Linkage grant with Intel (LP130100848). This chapter is a revised version of Larissa Hjorth, Heather Horst, Sarah Pink, Baohua Zhou, Fumitoshi Kato, Genevieve Bell, Kana Ohashi, Chris Marmo, and Miao Xiao 'Locating the Mobile: Intergenerational Locative Media in Tokyo, Shanghai and Melbourne', in the forthcoming F. Martin, T. Lewis and W. Sun (eds) *Lifestyle Media in Asia,* New York: Routledge.

Note

1   This is the official rate. However, unofficial rates are believed to be higher with countless millions of *shanzhai* (or pirate) hardware versions linked to prepaid subscriptions.

References

ABS (2013) *Family Statistics 6224.0.55.001—Labour Force, Australia: Labour Force Status and Other Characteristics of Families.* Available at: http://www.abs.gov.au/ausstats/abs@.nsf/Products/6224.0.55.001~Jun%20 2012~Chapter~Australian%20Families (Accessed on January 5, 2015).
ACMA (2013) *Communications Report 2011–12 series. Report 3 – Smartphones and Tablets. Take-up and Use in Australia. Summary Report.* Available at: http://www.acma.gov.au/theACMA/Library/Corporate-library/Corporate-publications/australia-mobile-digital-economy (Accessed on January 5, 2015).
boyd, d. (2008) 'Facebook's Privacy Trainwreck: Exposure, Invasion, and Social Convergence', *Convergence*, 14(1).
China Internet Network Information Center (CNNIC) (2013) *Statistical Report on Internet in China.* Available at: http://www1.cnnic.cn/IDR/ReportDownloads/201302/P020130221391269963814.pdf (Accessed on January 5, 2015).
Chua, B. H. (2010) 'Disrupting Hegemonic Liberalism in East Asia', *boundary 2*, 37(2). Available at: http://boundary2.dukejournals.org/content/37/2/199.full.pdf (Accessed on January 5, 2015).

City of Melbourne (2013) *Multicultural Community Demographic Profile*. Available at: www.melbourne.vic.gov. au (Accessed on January 5, 2015).

Clark, L. S. (2012) *The Parent App: Understanding Families in a Digital Age*, Oxford: Oxford University Press.

Coleman, G. (2010) 'Ethnographic Approaches to Digital Media', *Annual Review of Anthropology*, 39: 487–505.

Deepend (2014) *MAKING DIGITAL WORK HARDER: Australian Mobile Device Ownership and Home Usage Report 2014*. Available at: http://www.deepend.com.au/download-white-paper-device-usage-in-the-home (Accessed on January 5, 2015).

de Souza e Silva, A. and Frith, J. (2012) *Mobile Interfaces in Public Spaces*, New York: Routledge.

Farman, J. (2011) *Mobile Interface Theory*, London: Routledge.

Gazzard, A. (2011) 'Location, Location, Location: Collecting Space and Place in Mobile Media', *Convergence*, 17(4): 405–417.

Hertzeld, M. (1997) *Cultural Intimacy: Social Poetics in the Nation-State*, New York: Routledge.

Hjorth, L. (2009) *Mobile Media in the Asia-Pacific*, London: Routledge.

Hjorth, L. and Gu, K. (2012) 'The Place of Emplaced Visualities: A Case Study of Smartphone Visuality and Location-Based Social Media in Shanghai, China', *Continuum: Journal of Media & Cultural Studies*, 26(5): 699–713.

Hjorth, L., Qui, J. L., Zhou, B. and Wei, D. (2014) 'The Social in the Mobile: QQ as cross-generational media in China'. In G. Goggin and L. Hjorth (eds) *The Routledge Companion to Mobile Media*, New York: Routledge: 291–299.

Horst, H. A. (2011) 'Grandmothers, Girlfriends and Big Men: The Gendered Geographies of Jamaican Transnational Communication'. In L. Fortunati, R. Pertierra and J. Vincent (eds) *Migration, Diaspora and Information Technology in Global Societies*, London: Routledge.

Horst, H. A. (2010) 'Families'. In M. Ito et al. *Hanging Out, Messing Around, and Geeking Out: Kids Living and Learning with New Media*, Cambridge, MA: MIT Press.

Horst, H. and Miller D. (eds) (2012) *Digital Anthropology*, London: Sage.

Institute for Information and Communications Policy (IICP) (2014) 'Heisei 25 nen jouhou tsushin media no riyou jikan to jouhou koudou ni kansuru chousa sokuhou [The results of a survey of the utilization time of telecommunication media and information behaviour]'. Available at: http://www.soumu.go.jp/iicp/chou-sakenkyu/data/research/survey/telecom/2014/h25mediariyou_1sokuhou.pdf (Accessed on June 30, 2014).

Ito, M., Okabe, D. and Matsuda, M. (2005) (eds) *Pedestrian, Portable and Personal*, Cambridge, MA: MIT Press.

Licoppe, C. (2004) '"Connected" Presence: The Emergence of a New Repertoire for Managing Social Relationships in a Changing Communication Technoscape', *Environment and Planning Design: Society and Space*, 22(1): 135–156.

Matsuda, M. (2009) 'Mobile Media and the Transformation of the Family'. In G. Goggin and L. Hjorth (eds) *Mobile Technologies*, New York: Routledge: 68–72.

McVeigh, B. (2003) 'Individualization, Individuality, Interiority, and the Internet'. In N. Gottlieb and M. McLelland (eds) *Japanese Cybercultures*, London: Routledge: 19–33.

Ministry of Health, Labour and Welfare (2013) 'Heisei 25 nendoban kouseiroudou hakusho [White Paper on Health, Labour and Welfare 2013]'. Available at: http://www.mhlw.go.jp/wp/hakusyo/kousei/13/dl/1-02-2.pdf (Accessed on August 26, 2014).

Nonoyama, H. (2009) *Ronten Handbook Kazoku shakaigaku [Handbook of Family Sociology]*, Kyoto: Sekaishi-sosha.

Okabe, D. (2004) *Emergent Social Practices, Situations and Relations through Everyday Camera Phone Use*, 2004 International Conference on Mobile Communication in Seoul, Korea, October 18–19, 2004. Available at: http://www.itofisher.com/mito/archives/okabe_seoul.pdf (Accessed on January 5, 2015).

Our Mobile Planet (2013) Available at: http://www.slideshare.net/tessierv/google-our-mobile-planet-feb-2012 (Accessed June 2, 2015)

Pink, S. and Hjorth, L. (2013) 'Emplaced Cartographies: Reconceptualising Camera Phone Practices in an Age of Locative Media', *Media International Australia*, 145: 145–156.

Pink, S. and Leder Mackley, K. (2012) 'Video and a Sense of the Invisible: Approaching Domestic Energy Consumption Through the Sensory Home', *Sociological Research Online*, 17(1): 3. Available at: http://www.socresonline.org.uk/17/1/3.html (Accessed on January 5, 2015).

Pink, S. and Morgan, J. (2013) 'Short-Term Ethnography: Intense Routes to Knowing', *Symbolic Interaction*, 36(3): 351–361.

Pink, S., Leder Mackley, K., Mitchell, V. Escobar-Tello, C., Hanratty, M., Bhamra, T. and Morosanu, R. (2013) 'Applying the Lens of Sensory Ethnography to Sustainable HCI', *Transactions on Computer–Human Interaction* 20(4): article no. 25.

Robison, R. and Goodman, D.S.G. (eds) (1996) *The New Rich in Asia*, London: Routledge.

Sengupta, S. (2012) '"Big Brother?" No, It's Parents', *New York Times*. Available at: http://tinyurl.com/aysm5ud (Accessed on January 5, 2015).

23

Essential labels? Gender identity politics on Hong Kong lesbian mobile phone application *Butterfly*

Denise Tse-Shang Tang

In her mid-40s, Kar Yin logs on to the Hong Kong *les* application *Butterfly* every other day. She posts photos of her daily meals and everyday objects she finds fascinating on the mobile phone application. She checks the discussion boards and briefly browses through them so as to get a sense of what are the most popular topics and the most debated issues in Hong Kong *les* communities. Topic threads of ordinary objects and seemingly mundane everyday life are also intriguing to her. The app itself has also contributed to building novel excitement in Kar Yin's relationship with her partner of 15 years. Her partner who works long hours also goes on the application whenever she can to check in on Kar Yin's daily activities via the photos uploaded.

This daily practice of "mobile intimacy," a concept introduced by Hjorth and Arnold (2013), is enacted by Kar Yin in her communication with her long-time partner in both online and offline social worlds. Online topics continue its course by developing into offline conversation subjects when they see each other in the evenings. Kar Yin's style of mobile intimacy was fashioned both by the accessibility of mobile media and the public performance of intimacy as Kar Yin's photos were not exclusively targeted just for her partner but rather, posted on a discussion board for other *Butterfly* members to view and to comment on. Yet it was precisely this form of mobile intimacy that provided Kar Yin and her partner stability and continuity of their lesbian relationship. The existence of a *les*-specific mobile application does not only introduce a new social world to a marginalized community, it also enables existing social relations to further develop and maintain their vibrancy as in the case of Kar Yin and her partner.

Women with same-sex desires or *les*, as commonly known in Hong Kong, have long been meeting up through regular channels such as social gatherings organized by lesbian community organizations, private parties known through insiders or venturing into the few karaoke bars and cafés catering for *les* (Tang 2011). The onset of the Internet in the 1990s has enabled individuals to set up bulletin boards, chat rooms, websites to distribute information ranging from global lesbian, gay, bisexual, transgender and queer news to local social events. Bulletin boards were popular sites where users posed questions ranging from coming out to family and love woes to shopping for chestbinders to pet care. *Blur-F*, a popular website which ran from 2000 to 2011, has been widely cited by *les* as a useful platform to obtain and exchange information in the community prior to the arrival of *Facebook* and other websites.

Whereas online bulletin boards and chat rooms facilitated news exchange and increased social interactions in more than a decade, mobile communication has increased the scale and speed of sharing information and social participation. Hong Kong has one of the highest penetration rates in the world estimating at 238.6 percent with 17.22 million mobile service subscribers as of February 2014. 12.37 million out of these 17.22 million subscribers were 3G/4G service customers, which pointed to the potential number of users downloading and uploading large files at high speed via the Internet.[1] It also indicated that Hong Kong users could regularly stream videos, browse the Internet, and at the same time participate on complicated and sophisticated mobile phone applications. High penetration rates also saw Facebook opening its second Asia office in Hong Kong in 2011 after Singapore.[2] Goggin, by exploring the iPhone beyond its pioneering communication technologies, urges us to acknowledge "the heightened role of the senses, emotions and affects activated in new ways by the iPhone" (Goggin 2012, 21). Although the iPhone is not the major means of mobile communication and the sole communication device for this study, its symbolism as a choice smartphone cannot be denied among general users. Returning to the opening narrative of Kar Yin, she had never found the need to replace her out-dated Nokia mobile phone until her partner strongly suggested that she purchase a smartphone for better communication. Kar Yin also takes her partner's suggestion as an indication for her desire to be closer through the help of a mobile application.

In this chapter, I aim to primarily investigate the social meanings of gender identities in Hong Kong lesbian mobile media culture through a case study of a lesbian-specific mobile phone application *Butterfly*. A user on *Butterfly* was obliged to select among four gender identities, as in tomboy (*tb*), tomboy's girl (*tbg*), pure and no label, in order to gain successful registration for further participation. These terms were commonly used by Hong Kong *les* to determine one's gender role within a relationship and were based on both physical appearances as well as social characteristics of masculinity and femininity. Through participant observation on *Butterfly* and ethnographic interviews with nine participants and three core members of the software development team, this study attempts to examine how gender identity politics and gender roles are manifested and negotiated among female same-sex relations on mobile media.

Presenting the first Hong Kong *les* mobile app: *Butterfly*

Launched on March 29, 2013, *Butterfly* is a mobile phone application targeted towards Hong Kong *les* communities. The application developers took only two to three months to build up the mobile platform, as one of the core members was a senior software developer at one of the global Internet companies. I came into contact with the software developers through a Hong Kong queer women and trans community group, Women Coalition of Hong Kong SAR. Similar to other *les* businesses, *Butterfly*'s team members all have full-time employment in various occupational fields.

The maintenance of the app was conducted in between working hours with board moderators often managing different discussion boards and their relevant threads during lunch hours, work breaks and late evenings. When I posed the question of what motivated the creation of *Butterfly*, one of the core team members Ah Chung gave an earnest laugh and proclaimed, "It is my own hobby, my happiness in gathering people together." Ah Chung envisioned the app to continue the mission of another *les*-specific website Blur-F but in a mobile phone application format. *Blur-F* was consistently mentioned by interview participants of this study as the most accessible social media platform to obtain information pertaining to *les* communities.

Butterfly collected 3,000 users in its first three months and it has grown exponentially in six months reaching one million users. There were three million users registered for the application as of July 2014. Promotional activities for the app began immediately after its inception by coordinating announcements with two local queer women community-based organizations and a queer women karaoke bar. Seventy percent of the users were registered in Hong Kong with the rest of the users based in Taiwan, Malaysia, Singapore, various Australian and North American cities. Two core members with an initial investment of approximately two hundred thousand Hong Kong dollars solely financed the application. Subsequent monthly charges ranged from six thousand to ten thousand Hong Kong dollars depending on bandwidth resulting from web traffic. Peak seasons included the months of July and August where students frequently utilized the app as a result of summer holidays. At the same time, fraudulent postings by imposters such as sales persons or men looking for lesbians were also more common during these months.

LGBT and social media

Lesbian, gay, bisexual and transgender (LGBT) individuals have long used social media to articulate the processes of constructing genders and sexual identities (Alexander 2002; Berry et al. 2003; O'Riordan and Phillips 2007). The Internet as a precursory social media platform enabled LGBT individuals to establish social relations with others across time and space constraints. Accessibility is an issue as is the affordability of computers, laptops, tablets and mobile phones. Being online means being able to represent oneself as a social being in a particular context or online community.

In the case of LGBT individuals, self-representation is crucial to the usage of social media. In a study on the management of sexual identities in coming out videos on YouTube, Alexander and Losh (2010) point out the accumulation of online coming out narratives as potentially transformative for LGBT persons yet also attracting homophobes to voice out their discontents by vlogging. Coming out videos and their subsequent vlogging entries can be battlegrounds for authenticity, racial politics, power, sexual morality and identities. A study on transgender personal ads on Craigslist showed the specificity of terms used by trans-persons and observed that further elaborations were often necessary in addition to a first identity marker. For example, the term FTM was accompanied by a statement "transitioning/-ed from female to male" or in another personal ad, "a guy with a pie . . . not a chick with a dick" (Farr 2010, 93). Farr argued that the accompanying language to explain the term itself was a form of resistance to negative stereotypes and a way of educating readers of the personal ads. Personal identity is not only constructed through one's continuous effort to post messages online, to write blog entries, to check-in at places or to post photographs or videos. Rather, a person's identity can be influenced by comments made by others in the process of blogging or vlogging.

In a study on the influence of social media institutions on intimate story-telling practices of Swedish youth, De Ridder (2013) investigated the software design of social networking site *Netlog* in constructing self-representations of youth intimate identities. The software design of *Netlog* required users to choose between male or female, heterosexual, non-heterosexual or not defined. De Ridder observed that a significant portion of boys aged 13 to 18 years old in the study who were looking for relationships, clearly defined their sexuality status. He argued that software platforms could easily become "strong fixing tools" in keeping sexuality stable rather than coming up with multiple choices for users (De Ridder 2013, 13).

Drushel (2010) concluded in a study of lesbian, gay, bisexual and queer-identified *MySpace* users that social capital in the form of establishing supportive networks is often accumulated through accepting "friend" requests of people who live in close geographical proximity. Offline social relationships were continued after online social interactions were established on *MySpace*. In another study on identity construction involving queer religious youth on *Facebook*, Taylor,

Falconer and Snowden pointed out that some queer religious youth came out online to deliberately avoid challenging "visceral, embodied encounters" and instead to view this way of coming out as "temporal, controlled encounters" (Taylor et al. 2014, 11). The recent addition of gender categories on *Facebook* might have changed the way we show our online identities but its effect remains to be examined in the long run. These studies aim to demonstrate the agency exercised by LGBT individuals in using and maneuvering social networking sites.

Mobile communication

In mobile communication studies, Cumiskey and Hjorth (2013) highlighted the social and cultural perspectives in mobile media studies by applying the notion of seamlessness in mobile media practices. Understanding seamlessness as an inevitable descriptor in mobile media practices, Cumiskey and Hjorth reinstate the key topics of place and intimacy into the bourgeoning field of mobile media studies. Place remains a key concept where mobile media users were charted on geographical locations. Being in place and being present is the promise of mobile media technologies. Intimate practices on mobile media, as "mediated interactions and connected relationships," can be both reliable and unreliable at the same time (Cumiskey and Hjorth 2013, 3). A connection lost or a message misread is commonplace.

Cumiskey and Hjorth steer the debate to illustrate our attendance to seamlessness as our need "to aspire to be seamless," hence drawing us to face the possibility of failure in everyday moments of connecting and reconnecting (Cumiskey and Hjorth 2013, 4). The aspiration to be technologically seamless can be translated into an expectant form of seamless sociability, meaning that we assume our technological devices can offer immediate connections as much as our immediate responses to social encounters on mobile media. The common occurrence of missing a text or a slow response from an intimate partner can face consequences of doubt, disbelief and frustration.

Drawing on earlier scholarship on intimacies and as mentioned in the introduction of this chapter, Hjorth and Arnold suggest the term "mobile intimacy," referring to intimacies generated by the speed, movement, fluidity, and porous nature afforded by social media practices (Hjorth and Arnold 2013, 6). Mobile intimacies point to the practice of intimacies as moving "across technological, geographic, psychological, physical and temporal differences" between online and offline social worlds (Hjorth and Arnold 2013, 7). Popularized by China's *ba ling hou* (post-80s generation), location-based social media *Jie Pang* users keep up their presence within social networks by posting regularly their geographical locations and performing excellence in "geographical or locational knowledge" by checking-in on exclusive places (Hjorth et al. 2012, 57).

Meng Di (2013), in her study of microblogging practices among mainland immigrant women in Hong Kong, observed that the women's self-representations through text and images were continuously revised after social interactions with online mobile audiences. The aforementioned brief literature review demonstrated the intricate linkages between intimacies, speed, place, performativity, identity formations and agency that are facilitated by mobile media technologies. This research study on *Butterfly* aims to explore how *les* intimacies mediated through mobile media and consumed by women who were 35 years old and above can further contribute to our understanding of *les* sexualities, social relationships and social media.

Research methodology

For this qualitative research study, a non-probability snowball sampling method was used to collect data. I posted recruitment messages on three discussion boards including community news and events, a general board, and a forty year old plus group. I also contacted a local queer women non-profit organization for referral to *Butterfly*'s app developers. Three members aged 35 to 40 years old from the app development team were interviewed. A snowballing approach was also used during fieldwork when interview participants referred other informants to me. I have conducted participant observation on the app since I registered on *Butterfly* in August 2013. Specific attention was focused on discussion threads with topics that were explicitly titled for users 30 years old and above, as well as 40 years old and above. Content analysis was based on comment exchanges within specific topic threads situated in various boards.

For this pilot study, nine in-depth interviews were conducted with participants who were 35 or older and who were regular *Butterfly* users. Nine participants differed in their amount of usage ranging from logging onto *Butterfly* five times a day to logging in twice a week, but all participants went through a period of logging in every day and participating by either reading other people's posts or commenting on them. Data collection began in August of 2013 and ended in July of the following year. All interviewees identified as female and ranged from 35 to 48 years of age. Four out of nine participants have had heterosexual marriages with one participant still in a marriage. All participants had significant romantic and sexual relationships with women. The scope of occupations included health-related, sales and marketing, service industry, art, business and finance. I understand that my sample of interview participants is not representative of the diversity of lesbian, bisexual and transgender social media users. By limiting the recruitment of interview participants to *Butterfly*, I have excluded users on other social media platforms popular among LGBT communities such as *Weibo* and *WeChat*. *Butterfly* was selected as a research online site because of its specific target audience of women who identified as having sexual and romantic desires with other women. Transgender persons, both female-to-male and male-to-female, might have used the application for the same purposes but transgender participation might be limited due to the marketing of the app as a *les* app.

During the semi-structured interviews, open-ended questions based on social media, online experience, relationships, community participation and generational differences were asked. Interviews were conducted in Cantonese, taped and recorded with consent forms signed. Confidentiality of participants was ensured using pseudonyms. This study uses a grounded theory approach to code data as themes emerged with each round of coding (Strauss and Corbin 1990). I took up the task of coding data into themes and comparing emergent themes.

Local identity, local communities

A distinguishing factor for *Butterfly* is the app's usage of Cantonese Chinese as the language for broad communication. Minor differences between a Cantonese usage of Chinese and another Chinese dialect such as a Taiwanese usage of Chinese can be found from the titling of discussion boards to the postings among users themselves. One clear example is the use of Cantonese slang in a discussion board literally translated as "Blowing Water (吹水) Board." In Cantonese Chinese, the title of the discussion board denoted a general chatting space, thereby allowing users to post any topic onto the board. The colloquial term "blowing water" pronounced as "ceoi seoi" can also mean talking nonsense or bragging. For the purpose of this research, I shall refer the board as "Talking Nonsense Board." The board title was only legible among Cantonese Chinese users therefore limiting a majority of users for the application as local Hongkongers. As a result, simplified Chinese characters were seldom seen on *Butterfly* as most registered users communicate through traditional Chinese characters. The insistence of developing a local app is not unanticipated given the postcolonial history of the city. English language tends to symbolize a language of authority, superiority and class status whereas Cantonese Chinese remains a commoner's language.

In Hong Kong, the dual use of English and Cantonese Chinese language in everyday life poses complications for app development. Upon surveying existing social media, *Butterfly* developers chose to develop a Cantonese Chinese specific app for local *les* communities. Although there are still thirty percent of all registered users from outside of Hong Kong, these users often identify themselves as overseas Hong Kong students or from neighbouring countries such as Singapore, Taiwan and occasionally from the Southern Chinese city of Guangzhou.

Thirty-seven years old Sophia concluded that an app distinguished from the Singaporean social networking site *Fridae* and the location-based mobile phone app *Brenda* is essential for Hong Kong users. Most informants from this study concurred with the importance of using Cantonese Chinese in social media. Both *Fridae* and *Brenda* have been mentioned by informants as English or foreign apps that cater to expatriates or English-speaking locals in Hong Kong. In the last decade, the rise of the Hong Kong democracy movement has posited language politics as a pertinent and at times, a divisive issue. The use of Cantonese or Mandarin in specific contexts has stirred up both positive and negative emotions among Hongkongers of different social classes. This is not to say that Hong Kong *les* do not go on apps that were popular among *nutongzhi* in Taiwan or Mainland China such as *Loh Do* and *the L*. But as most informants in this study suggested, an app with users living in Hong Kong could offer more opportunities for socializing in everyday life.

On the other hand, English has been historically recognized as a preferred language as recognized by its dominance within secondary school public examinations for university admissions. In this study, two informants who have graduated from secondary schools during the 1970s have continued their education in secretary diploma courses which emphasized English training as the pathway to career success. One informant, 48 years old Catherine, stated that she did not know how to input Chinese on computers and has only recently picked up the skills to use handwriting software for inputting Chinese characters. The process of replying to messages on *Butterfly* became more tedious and time-consuming. Yet she felt that she had no choice but to use the app due to its widespread popularity for making friends or for meeting potential lovers.

Gender roles, gender identities

When I asked app developer Ah Chung about the reasons for asking users to declare their gender roles during registration, she explained:

> Roles are important to us, like the terms *tb* and *tbg*. Actually, the process in defining roles was disastrous. I felt like I'm not comprehensive enough. We know the roles need to be localized. Selecting the role categories was so difficult, it was as if we could never end the list. We also kept asking ourselves what did we mean by *no label* and *pure*. I know we did not include bisexual or transgender. . . . I think we feel we don't really understand transgender identities. To us, if a user says she is a female, then she is female.

When we further discussed the omission of transgender as a category to choose one's online identity, Ah Chung focused on the app developer's understanding of transgender as a generational issue. Recently, transgender visibility gained prominence through the activism of community leaders based in non-government organizations such as Gender Concerns, Transgender Equality & Acceptance Movement-Hong Kong, Transgender Resource Centre and Rainbow of Hong Kong (Cheung 2012). In her late 30s, Ah Chung might have perceived gender identity terms such as transgender, FTM or MTF as not of common usage among the target audience of *Butterfly*, in particular since these terms were not available or popularized for one's description of gender identity when she was growing up in Hong Kong. The exclusion of bisexuality as a sexual identification, on the other hand, was simply assumed into *les* identification.

As I have observed on *Butterfly*, there were often postings about being bisexual and a need to connect with other bisexuals on the app. Responses to such postings have ranged from inquisitive, accusatory to affirmative statements. Inquisitive responses included questions on why a woman becomes a bisexual, whereas accusatory replies were often biphobic to the extent of questioning why a bisexual woman is on *Butterfly*. Positive statements were more affirmative of bisexuality and often follow after fervent discussion on the reasons for being bisexual.

Whereas gender identities such as *tb*, *tbg* and *pure* gained common usage among Hong Kong *les* communities, it has often been associated with a younger *les* population. Different from gay men's digital culture, lesbian digital culture seldom uses photos of body parts to depict one's sexual desirability. Gay male cyber culture tends to celebrate the use of body images within the parameters of gay pornography (Mowlabocus 2010, 210). The "Talking Nonsense Board" on *Butterfly* contained many topic threads with contentious debates on the categorizing issues of *tb*, *tbg* and *pure*. Each user's chosen user name and gender identity choice was displayed whenever a post was made. If a user decided to input her age and place of residence for an online profile, then the information would be publicly displayed on each post as well. But why is selecting a label still considered necessary for a user to register for a *les* mobile phone application? What are the social implications of selecting a label?

Fifty year old Ho Yan was one of the two persons who made contact with me on *Butterfly* after I posted recruitment notices of my research project. After we had sent several private messages to each other, we finally met up for an interview in a restaurant located in one of the redeveloped new towns, Tsuen Wan. Tsuen Wan has recently seen an influx of mainland Chinese daily shoppers to its newly built shopping malls. During the interview, we could hear speakers of various Chinese dialects inhabiting the same space as we were. It has been a living reality for Hongkongers to learn to live with mainland Chinese immigrants as well as the daily visitors crossing the border to shop for necessities. Ho Yan finished secondary school and attended a vocational college for secretarial studies. Secretarial studies as a career option was most popular for young women graduating from secondary school during the nineteen sixties and nineteen seventies in Hong Kong. Ho Yan has since worked as a clerk in various companies ranging from trading to logistics. She has begun to use *Butterfly* through learning about the app from a community event hosted by a local lesbian organization. When I asked her about her choice of gender roles on the app, she stated,

> Actually, I didn't like to separate into categories. I don't really like labels. But I can see why a *tb* needs to be separated out or known. But personally, I like the label *pure*. The label *pure* sounds very innocent to me. Being *les* to me is very innocent. You know in our generation, being *les* is really a taboo. You couldn't even hold hands.

Ho Yan's story partially resonated with the story of Catherine. Still being in a marriage with a man, she survived a tumultuous breakup with a woman and a sudden job loss. Catherine recalled that she "reached a person's lowest point in life." She realized that she needed to "pick herself up again" and started seeing friends again. A friend she has met online through a Taiwanese *nutongzhi* chat room *2GetHer* a decade ago let her know about *Butterfly*.[3] Without hesitation, Catherine registered as a user and chose her gender role as *no label*. Browsing through group titles on various discussion boards such as "Making Friends," "Looking for Love" and "Talking Nonsense," she joined a group chat titled "40 Years Plus." In describing her choice of a *no label* category, she explained that she has never liked labels and it was very odd to pick one just for joining the app. But surprisingly, she received a number of personal messages asking her about her choice of *no label*. One of the people who sent her a message asking for her label choice eventually became her girlfriend. Catherine alluded to her label choice of *no label* as an opening chapter to the beginning of her relationship. Similar to Ho Yan, she also attended secretarial studies after secondary school graduation.

Another informant, Grace has long become familiar with *les* websites and bulletin boards such as *Blur-F*, *Queer Sisters*, *Nutongxueshe*, *Fridae* and Taiwanese Internet forums. Being divorced, Grace sought social support in *les* communities by actively searching for online information and attending local community events. Grace also came to know of *Butterfly* through one of the community events. When she first downloaded *Butterfly*, the app crashed with her phone's software and she did not proceed to use it. But after her friends mentioned *Butterfly* again a couple of months later, she solved the software issue and became a frequent participant on *Butterfly*.

> I have always posted real information on Butterfly. I have never thought of putting fake information on it. I just picked *tbg*. I don't think there is a need to change this piece of information. I think labels are based on appearances. If I choose *tb* as the label, I would look too feminine and people might think I'm lying.

In my earlier ethnographic work with Hong Kong women with same-sex desires, physical appearances appear to be the primary determining factor for one's choice of gender identities as *tb*, *tbg* or *pure*. But the categories do not simply point at physical appearances, rather they are fluid signifiers of sexual desires and are often destabilized in processes of sexual identification. In other words, one can choose to be a *tb* but prefer to date another *tb*, rather than being assumed to be only interested in *tbg*. Choosing *tb* as a label on the app might be perceived as limiting to the *tb* user. Indeed, one can assume that a *tb* user can also look at the profile of another *tb* user if there is romantic interest in *tb–tb* relationships. But the familiar usage of these terms in the community and the reinforced label selection on using the app might have curbed imaginative connections. A discussion topic "Everybody has their own definition of gender roles" was posted by pencil on January 19, 2014 and it began with a brief summary of gender roles.

> pencil, PURE, 25
>
> 19/1/14 11:12 p.m.
>
> TB, TBG, PURE, No Label. . .. . .
>
> If you ask ten persons the same question, you will get ten different answers.
>
> After all, the tongzhi community is built up by all of us, everybody has their own right to define. Why don't each one of us talk a bit about our own definition~
>
> Let me be the first one to throw out something~
>
> TB: masculine appearance, loves girls with feminine appearances.
>
> TBG: feminine appearance, loves girls with masculine appearances.
>
> PURE: considers themselves as not fitting in the above two categories.
>
> No Label: considers themselves as not fitting in the above three categories or as not necessary to fit into any category. (9 thumbs up)

> Peony, NO LABEL
>
> 19/1/14 12:20 a.m.
>
> My categories are les, gay, straight, bi, trans.

CoCo, NO LABEL, 22

19/1/14 12:32 a.m.

Basically there is no need to have any labels (screen displaying an emoticon with a sarcastic look)

Jay, PURE, 33

19/1/14 1:38 a.m.

About pure, what I want to say is . . .

Pure refers to those lesbians who are in between B and G and who likes girls.

Pure does not have any specific dress style, not like a B who is masculine or a G who only likes a B. . . . If you don't need to find another G and you don't think of yourself as a boy, then you might be a Pure. (16 thumbs up)

Under this thread, the label *pure* appears to be a neutral identity fitting for those who are not declaring loyalty to being tomboyish or being feminine. Identifying as a *tb* or a *b*, a *tbg* or a *g* seems to gain immediate understanding among *les* online communities. In another thread titled "Marketing Yourself on *Butterfly*," Tracy identifying as a *pure* puts out a lamenting call on behalf of women who take on the *pure* identity. The entire thread garnered 91 responses from its inception at December 15, 2013 with the latest comment dated April 28, 2014.

Tracy, NO LABEL

15/12/13 8:30 p.m.

Among lesbians, I realized everyone likes to categorize herself using labels. TB la, TBG la, even for those PURE, they have to classify as PURE leaning towards B, PURE leaning towards G. . . . Somehow I feel that I'm in-between, really in the middle, the PURE kind. This kind of person has no market, I'm not like those B who can be cool and have lots of girlfriends, and I'm not like those G who likes to dress up super feminine and attract Bs, how can an in-between person like me find partners? Please help. Is there anyone out there who is as sad as I am . . . (81 thumbs up)

Among the twenty-four users who responded to the post on the same night, Mandy who was a *pure*, responded to Tracy's post after 36 minutes,

Basically, a PURE will not want to be with a B, and will want to be with a G, but a G will not care about us PUREs. It is also hard to meet other PURES who want to be with PURES, therefore we can only eat ourselves! (37 thumbs up)

The term "eat ourselves" can be taken to mean being alone, without friends or any other form of social support. Here Mandy laid out a dating path for a *pure* and Tracy responded six minutes later,

Eat ourselves! . . . so sad but true (screen display of emoticons with shocking faces) Want to be with G but G doesn't care about me is exactly what I am going through. High five! (screen display of emoticon featuring a hand and another emoticon with a cat snuffling) (17 thumbs up)

Winnie who identified as a Pure responded at 11:04 p.m. on the same night.

I think being styling, being cool, being attractive / sexy is not only for TB or TBG. Whether you are attractive or not depends on your partner's view. Actually it is most important to be yourself. But having a heart, being polite and being ambitious / wanting to better oneself always sell! (6 thumbs up)

Winnie's emphasis on being true to oneself was also echoed by other users in ensuing posts. She downplayed the significance of attaching a gender role to one's profile and redirected the conversation to personal characteristics. But in an hour later, pencil put up the following post:

pencil, PURE, 25

16/12/13 12:35 p.m.

There are actually a lot of Pure/no labels. But because of the ambiguity in these positions, usually it's useless (sad emoticon). At the end of the day, the most easiest pairing is still the most obvious a B with a G . . . (3 thumbs up)

In reviewing other threads along the same topic, pencil's comment forms a common sentiment among Hong Kong *les* who still subscribe to the pairing of a *B* with a *G*. These pairings might have appeared to be more visible in public spaces but queer scholarship has continued to focus on the fluidity of sexualities and gender identities. The suggested pairing of a tomboy with a tomboy's girl has even been regarded as guilty of being old-fashioned. Yet, online conversations of these gender categories continued to assert influence on perceptions of lesbian dating practices. One of my informants Leslie chose *tb* without hesitation when she registered for *Butterfly*, "Occasionally, I tried to be a *pure*. (Laughter) I think it is good to have categories. It makes it much easier to find partners. A much easier search!" Leslie was living in Taiwan when she went online and found the app; she was trying to make friends "within the same circle" rather than looking for potential partners.

Labelling oneself presumes the formation of one-directional relationships like a *tb–tbg* relationship yet the category of *pure* is perpetually puzzling to categorize in a relationship formula. Since the label itself is shown right underneath a profile pic, one can quickly browse the label and determine whether to pursue a potential lover. Kar Yin agreed with Leslie's assertion of gender roles as a useful tool to meet others for dating or relationships, she stated,

It is true that some people specifically choose others to talk to as a result of their appearances. That's why it is good to have categories. It makes life simpler and easier. There is almost no need to ask so many questions. It is just *tb* or *tbg*, plain and easy.

Being target-oriented in seeking partners was also brought up in my interview with Ching Fung. "Labels may not be the most important to me but where they live is." Referring to the neighborhoods listed on users' profiles, Ching Fung elaborated, "I don't mind going to Tsim Sha Tsui or Yau Ma Tei but travelling all the way to Tuen Mun or Yuen Long is another matter." The central areas of Tsim Sha Tsui and Yau Ma Tei would take Ching Fung approximately 20 minutes from the subway station close to her home. But Tuen Mun or Yuen Long would take at least an hour travelling on public transportation. The concern for geographical close proximity in a city known for high density, tight living spaces, overcrowding and ease of transportation seems to be a paradoxical truth. But here time was of the essence for Ching Fung and even *potential* dating opportunities were governed by time.

Conclusion

In conclusion, mobile media applications for social networking will continue to be popularized among women with same-sex desires. *Butterfly*, as the first app to be commonly utilized by Hong Kong *les* demonstrated the critical importance of having an app with local sensibilities.

By using colloquial terms for discussion board titles and gender identity categories, *Butterfly* invited users to debate on the purpose of using gender identity categories. As pointed out by scholarship on mobile media studies, it is not only the brevity of messages but the communicative practices associated with chatting that enable mobile conversations to be effective in areas of intimacy. By conducting initial research on gender identity politics and the negotiation processes of gender roles among Hong Kong *les* who used mobile media as one of the key platforms for social networking, I aim to demonstrate the complexity in defining gender identity terms and its continued relevance among Hong Kong *les* in both online and offline communities.

Notes

1 Information from Office of the Communications Authority, the Hong Kong Government. Available at: http://www.gov.hk/en/about/abouthk/factsheets/docs/telecommunications.pdf (Accessed June 1, 2014).
2 South China Morning Post (2013) 'Facebook to spur more digital advertising in Hong Kong'. Available at: http://www.scmp.com/business/companies/article/1306489/facebook-spur-more-digital-advertising-hong-kong (Accessed May 1, 2014).
3 The Mandarin Chinese term *nutongzhi* is commonly used in Taiwan to denote women with same-sex desires.

References

Alexander, J. (2002) 'Queer webs: Representations of LGBT people and communities on the world wide web', *International Journal of Sexuality and Gender Studies*, 7(2&3): 77–84.

Alexander, J. and Losh, E. (2010) '"A YouTube of One's Own?": "Coming Out" Videos as Rhetorical Action'. In C. Pullen and M. Cooper (eds) (2010) *LGBT Identity and Online New Media*, New York and Oxford: Routledge: 27–50.

Berry, C., Martin F. and Yue, A. (eds) (2003) *Mobile Cultures: New Media in Queer Asia*, Durham, NC: Duke University Press.

Cheung, E.P.K. (2012) 'Transgenders in Hong Kong: From Shame to Pride'. In H. Chiang (ed) *Transgender China*, New York: Palgrave Macmillan: 263–285.

Cumiskey, K.M. and Hjorth, L. (2013) 'Between the Seams: Mobile Media Practice, Presence and Politics'. In K.M. Cumiskey and L. Hjorth (eds) *Mobile Media Practices, Presence and Politics: The Challenge of Being Seamlessly Mobile*, New York and Oxford: Routledge: 1–11.

De Ridder, S. (2013) 'Are digital media institutions shaping youth's intimate stories? Strategies and tactics in the social networking site Netlog', *New Media & Society*, 0(0): 1–19.

Di, M. (2013) 'Wandering Between Self-Expression and Recognition: A Case Study of the Mobile Micro-blogging Practices of Young Chinese Women in Hong Kong', in K.M. Cumiskey and L. Hjorth (eds) *Mobile Media Practices, Presence and Politics: The Challenge of Being Seamlessly Mobile*, New York and Oxford: Routledge: 116–134.

Drushel, B.E. (2010) 'Virtually Supportive: Self-Disclosure of Minority Sexualities through Online Social Networking Sites'. In C. Pullen and M. Cooper (eds) (2010) *LGBT Identity and Online New Media*, New York and Oxford: Routledge: 62–72.

Farr, D. (2010) 'A Very Personal World: Advertisement and Identity of Trans-persons on Craigslist'. In C. Pullen and M. Cooper (eds) (2010) *LGBT Identity and Online New Media*, New York and Oxford: Routledge: 87–99.

Goggin, G. (2012) 'The iPhone and Communication'. In L. Hjorth, J. Burgess and I. Richardson (eds) *Studying Mobile Media: Cultural Technologies, Mobile Communication, and the iPhone*, New York and Oxford: Routledge: 11–27.

Hjorth, L. and Arnold, M. (2013) *Online@AsiaPacific: Mobile, Social and Locative Media in the Asia-Pacific*, New York and Oxford: Routledge.

Hjorth, L. Wilken, R. and Gu, K. (2012) 'Ambient Intimacy: A Case Study of the iPhone, Presence, and Location-based Social Networking in Shanghai, China'. In L. Hjorth, J. Burgess and I. Richardson (eds)

Studying Mobile Media: Cultural Technologies, Mobile Communication, and the iPhone, New York and Oxford: Routledge: 43–62.

Mowlabocus, S. (2010) 'Look at Me! Images, Validation, and Cultural Currency on Gaydar'. In C. Pullen and M. Cooper (eds) *LGBT Identity and Online New Media*, New York and Oxford: Routledge: 201–214.

O'Riordan, K. and Phillips, D.J. (2007) *Queer Online: Media, Technology & Sexuality*, New York: Peter Lang Publishers.

Strauss, A. and Corbin, J. (1990) *Basics of Qualitative Research: Grounded Theory Procedures and Techniques.* Newbury Park, CA: Sage.

Tang, D. (2011) *Conditional Spaces: Hong Kong Lesbian Desires and Everyday Life*, Hong Kong: Hong Kong University Press.

Taylor, Y., Falconer, E. and Snowden, R. (2014) 'Queer youth, Facebook and faith: Facebook methodologies and online identities', *New Media & Society*, DOI: 10.1177/1461444814544000 (Accessed on July 24, 2014).

24

Queer mobiles and mobile queers: intersections, vectors, and movements in India

Nishant Shah

The economic and cultural neo-liberalization that India has embraced over the last two decades, fueled by its development dreams of becoming a technological capital and the radical infrastructure building to support the burgeoning Information and Communication Technology (ICT) industries, has been marked by two persistent questions: the question of technology and the question of sexuality. These are both discrete but also deeply intertwined questions because at the heart of both these are anxieties about modernity, identity, bodies, and regulation. The anxieties emerge from a series of paradoxes that have become characteristic of postcolonial societies in several parts of the world.

The technological shift produces the "Digital Divide" (Ragneddo and Muschert 2013) that intersects with all earlier axes of inequality, like caste, class, religion, gender and sexuality, and amplifies and weaves these in an alarming tapestry of discrimination and exclusion. Inequality, in access to resources, standards of living, claims to bodies, and recourse to protection from violence, is evident in the ways in which the digital technological policy and policing operate in the country. Indeed, the question of technology comprises two interrelated questions of technology: the first wonders what the technological can do to transform the social, cultural, political and economic landscape of the country and create a global presence for an India which is to "shine" (Radhakrishnan 2011). The second question examines, with anxiety, the ways in which the technological revolution is transforming the country, into unexpected, unknowing and unknowable forms producing new challenges for the state (Nilekani 2010) as it transitions from being a welfare state into a neoliberal developmental state.

At the heart of these questions is the growing recognition that while the Internet might save lives, provide jobs, and swing political movements, it is also the playground of the dirty, the forbidden, and the smutty. With mobile computing and communication devices in the country now far exceeding the number of adults in it,[1] there is an unprecedented number of people accessing porn,[2] sexting and hooking up (Poonam 2012), and forming queer collectives that are ungoverned and often untraceable (Doron and Jeffrey 2013). Especially, as one of the youngest countries in the world,[3] where technology is creating "single cities" filled with young people who are far away from traditional family and society structures, there is a growing and uncontrollable pattern of unconventional gender and sexual partnerships that are becoming more visible.

This paradox that the technological embodies is paralleled by a similar anxiety around questions of sexual identities and desires. On the one hand, there is a growing public discourse around sexual permissiveness and acceptance in the country. Gender and sexuality have never been as visible as they have been in this technologically shifting India. From eroticized representations in Bollywood and TV advertisements to media report on gruesome tales of violence and death; from queer pride marches to having the first transgender elected political leader; from an explosion of the pink economy (Binnie 2005) to systemic discrimination and protests against sexual identities and choices that question the status quo (Bose and Bhattacharyya 2008) we have never been this vocal about these questions.

Even as the Internet debates rage on, advocating for acceptance or eradication of queer identities, there is a growing concern on the other hand that the digital leads to a gentrification of politics, privileging an elite queer who become the central focus of the activism and discourse. A new fringe of queerness emerges that remains doubly invisible (Narrain 2004).

This is not an echoing of the early worries that the Internet, in its connected anonymity, might become a large "digital closet" (Görkemli 2014) that becomes inescapable. Instead, it points out that the technosexual queer carries with it particular codes of the global queer, that excludes anybody who does not fall in the narrow demography of the English speaking, urban, educated, middle or upper class, single and mobile body who gets to occupy the privileged position of sculpting the perfect queer body and identity that connects, not with other nodes in the country but in the global pink network of fabulousness (Kavi 2009).

The entwining of the technological and the sexual leads to two "prewired responses" (Achuthan 2011) in an attempt to find a resolution. The first response is to imagine the technological as invasive, rendering the human body frail, creating new bodies of exclusion, and thus to be resisted, by empowering the humanist agenda (Muñoz 2009). This manifests itself in the strong invocations of a mythical glorious history where we were always queer-friendly, always tolerant, and thus calling for a nativist return to religious, cultural roots as a resistance to these global, "Western" technologies (Roy 1998) that come and destroy the habits and habitus of the *homo mobilus*.

The second response is to imagine the bodies as already fragile, robbed of dignity and desire, and in need of a rescue that the technologies will offer. This is evident in the "technology as panacea" (Bagga et al. 2005) shaped programs like ICT4D (Information and Communication Technologies For Development) or new media and cultural studies analyses that concentrate on access, usage, inclusion and infrastructure as the key indicators of a successful resolution of these questions (Berry et al. 2003). The intentions and questions from the two approaches are extremely important, and appear diametrically opposite. However, they betray a foundational paradox: they both reinforce a separation between the sexual and the technological, even though they find their critical momentum in the entwining of the two.

Thus, questions of privacy and data security, catalyzed by the building of a biometric identity census in the country (Rajadhyaksha 2013), remain questions of technology—concentrating on architecture, regulation, protocols, policies, and the rights to be safe, secure, and forgotten. The problem of "sexuality" is quickly "resolved" by introducing a field that allows people to identify themselves as "Male, Female or Other" (Shaikh 2012). The anxiety of how such a database might enable more homophobia, targeted discrimination by social and economic structures (like health care, for instance), and emphasize a fixity of gender and sexuality on the biological metrics of the body, remains outside the "digital dilemmas" (Franklin 2013).

Similarly, sexuality—its visibility, building of political and social communities, rights and responsibilities, protection and safety—gets identified as a particular condition of the social and the cultural. Its interactions with the technological are limited to building apps and mobilizing people for protests. The forced separation between being queer and being digital is implied in both the claims of looking at technologies as queer, examining the perversions and possibilities of sexual exploration that the digital anonymous spaces enable, or in arguments about thinking of queer as a technology, building on the Foucaultian sense of technologies of constructing the self.

I, thus, seek to move away from these relationships between queerness and mobility which work through a contradictory move where on the one hand, it is presumed that both of these "concepts" are known and understood, and on the other, they are posited as unknowable and unknown, both in themselves and their relationship with each other. Instead, I offer three inter-related but different entry-points to think the mobile queer, drawing from cyberculture theory and everyday queer practices in India. These cases are symptomatic of a larger landscape of mobility and queerness that is changing, and offers a new framework to understand and map the lived reality of sexuality and digital technology not only in India but in other such rapidly changing spaces across the uneven spectrum of globalization.

The queer and the mobile

There is an element of surreptitious pleasure, of illicit connections, of anonymous and hidden subcultures that accompanies the associations of queerness and mobile phones in India. There is an unquestionable emergence of a queer subculture that is attributed to the digital technologies of computing and communication. The emergence of the World Wide Web, with more than 43 million users in the country, accompanied by the mobile explosion, means that for the first time, without the fear of discrimination and harassment, queer men and women have been able to form connections of physical and emotional intimacy which were unavailable in an India before the digital. The proliferation of websites like PlanetRomeo or location based applications (like Grindr, for instance) on smart phones, has resulted in at least younger users forming a queer sextopia which gives them access to spaces, places, locations and bodies that can escape the radar of authoritarian moral vigilantism.

The emergence of these spaces of connection is not merely about people finding a safe space for sexual encounters—though that is one of the promises that bring people to the queer Internet. These dating platforms also foster a sense of community, allowing the users to imagine themselves as a part of a larger collective, thus enabling a social and political imagination that has empowered the queer rights movement in the country. Political protests, the orchestration of Queer Pride festivals, the public presence of queer love and intimacy, at least in the more urban nodes of the country, have created a network of queer traffic that is both assuring and joyful.

The new visibility of the queer bodies and spaces has inspired significant scholarship where discourse and practice in the field map how queer people use these different digital and mobile technologies to facilitate their different activities (Ganesh and Bhattacharjya 2011), or concentrate on how the presence of the digital technologies have created a queer public which challenges the status quo of sexual authoritarianism in the country (Narrain and Bhan 2005). While both these focus areas are important to understand and support the growing queer rights based activism, they operate through a separation of the queer and the mobile. The queer body and these mobile technologies are presumed to have nothing to do with each other, and efforts are directed at mapping and tracking these emergent relationships. The pre-technological queer is seen to evolve on the digital. The technologies are presumed neutral and their deployment in queerness keeps it as an externality to the form and formulation of queerness.

I propose that we need to think of the queer and the mobile, not as these discrete categories, but as intrinsically and inextricably linked together—that they are simultaneously produced by, produced through, and produced with each other. The simultaneity (Heidegger 1982) of the queer identity, body, sexuality and politics with the digital proliferation, emergence, regulation and control, is perhaps best embedded in the landmark legal case that came to been known as "The Lucknow Incident" (Gupta 2006). At a surface level, it is a straightforward enough case. On January 3, 2006, policemen in the city of Lucknow, in Central India, after masquerading as gay men on the popular dating website guys4men.com, invited several men they met through the website to meet IRL (in real life), at a local cruising site that was frequented by gay men.

When one of the persons showed up, undercover police entrapped and intimidated him, and forced him to call others that he had regular contact with. They used him to arrange a meeting with three other men from his queer contact list and arrested them as well. The First Information Report (FIR) that the police put forward, suggesting that these four men were found in "obscene conditions in a public space" was later refuted and disproved by an independent fact finding mission including gender and sexuality activists, as well as lawyers and political actors.[4] The media had a field day, where sensational headlines of "Gay sex ring on the Internet busted" in a "brave homosexual coup" arresting those who are attacking Indian values and society, were splattered all across major news channels and newspapers.[5] The sensational element was as much about the queerness of these men, as it was about the social web (Internet and cell phones) which allows for these kinds of "immoral" activities and connections to happen.

While much has been written about the morally reprehensible and legally questionable actions of the judicial apparatus and the policing actors involved, there is something else that is of interest for this particular chapter—it is the entwining of the queer and the mobile in ways that are not just about a queer person using the mobile phone. Instead, there is a strange production of the relationships between queerness and the digital, of which the mobile is a growing component, which this incident betrays. The most startling thing in this case has been the question of evidence. The initial police reports fabricated physical evidence of "obscene behavior in public" which was cited as the key reason for the arrest of these four men. However, once this report was debunked, the only evidence that was present, to ascribe queerness to these four, closeted men, was digital traces. In fact, things got more confounding because at least two of the men were married to women and had biological children—surely affirming their straightness rather than their queerness. And yet, their presence on the gay dating website, their knowing each other and their coming to meet based on fantasies scripted online, enabled the police to paint them as queer.

Ironically, in order to entrap these men, the policemen who created "false" profiles on the website had also entered into exactly same processes—they had created fantasy avatars of themselves, they scripted narratives of their queer desires, they contacted men on the pretext of having sex, and then met them in offline public spaces. However, the cops, whose queer performances were sanctioned, were not made accountable for their actions as queer. The punishment that was levelled at the four men was premised on performance and intention, on desire and fantasy, rather than a physical action. What was being punished was an action or transaction which had not occurred. The queerness, in the absence of material evidence or witnesses, got constructed because of access to, presence on, use of, and connecting through the digital technologies.

The queer and the digital were no longer separable in this case. The digital has brought with it the notions of danger and dirtiness which get coupled with similar ideas of immoral, unnatural, and pathology that get invoked in the construction of queerness in India. In the conflation of digital avatars and the physical identities, the Lucknow Incident brings to the fore a different way of looking at the mobile and the queer—as ontologically bound together, each one produced by the other: where the digital and its ability to transcend, transgress, circumvent and resist patriarchal and authoritarian codes of the society, is understood as queer.

Queer bodies thus get constructed not in their sexual practices but in their engagement with the digital devices and networks that they travel through. They are both, mobile, adaptable, dislocated and untethered, that constructs them as suspicious and surreptitious. Obscenity is in the traffic surplus of the digital network as it is in the sexuality of our queer bodies. Bodies are queer only as they become mobile in the pervert-to-pervert networks, and the technologies are queer in how they proliferate, leak and insinuate themselves in our everyday lives. Both of them are also subject to regulation, containment, chastisement and punishment, which bind them in their origin and definition.

The queer mobile

The mobile, as I am unpacking it, plays manifold roles. It is a witness to the queer encounters, archiving them in the relentlessly unforgetting folds of the digital. It is evidence for things that leak out of the digital. It is an instrument of perversion, queer in its transgressions and possibilities of subversion. The mobile, with its ubiquitous presence, has become the thing that produces queer objects, bodies and spaces, not because it facilitates connections and exchanges between queer subjects. Instead, I propose that the mobile, in its very quantification and documentation of our traces and actions, renders us queer, producing queerness as a condition which can be activated rather than being queer as a static process.

The ambiguity of queerness—when it does not take the bold declarative defiant form of "coming out" (Martin et al. 2008)—is captured well in the mobile, because as it records, documents and shares, it produces a space that allows for queerness to emerge.

An illustration of this argument is in user generated videos labelled as "*kand* videos" or "*masti* videos" from India, shared on platforms like YouTube. Shot in university dorms and shared apartments, *Kand* videos, unlike the Western frat-videos that celebrate straight men's sexual conquests, remain in the space of "innocent fun." They invoke a space of "male bonding" showing young adult men, in several states of undress, drunk, touching each other, simulating sexual intimacy as a joke, hazing and stripping one another, dancing in drag or just "horsing around."

These videos, uploaded as an example of just "young men having fun" are explicitly straight. Like the #NoHomo hashtag on Twitter, when they share, they go out of their way to confirm how there is no "gayness" in these videos. And yet, as we see the comments on YouTube we quickly realize that this is being consumed as gay porn by many users, for whom this remains the only "authentic" representation of a homoerotic space within the Indian milieu. The comment wars between those who fantasize about the semi-naked male bodies in the video and those who condemn these commenters as "fag" or "pervert" take on predictable shapes.

However, what is interesting is how the presence of the mobile recording devices, sometimes surreptitious, but more often than not as the witness to these revelries, offers the possibility of reading these videos as queer, despite their avowed distance from any homosexual intention or purport. The bodies that appear in these videos are not queer identified. And yet, the presence of the mobile, the ability to record these moments of illicit intimacies, and the digital touching that happens as they travel on social media networks, renders these videos and the bodies in them, available for queer consumption. The queerness, in this instance, is not located in the act or the body, but in the technologies that penetrate the intimate sociality, leaking and betraying these acts, to an audience which consumes it for queer fantasies.

I want to posit that the presence of the mobile as both the transgressor as well as the witness to this transgression turns it into a queer object. This is why, in earlier instances, when user generated pornography emerged, there was an immediate attempt to actually regulate the technological devices and networks rather than the bodies that were occupying these spaces. If queerness is located in dislocating the norm, in exposing the private (Shah forthcoming 2015), in leaking the intimate (Chun forthcoming 2015), in making the bodies we have unfamiliar and erotic (Malhotra 2011), then the mobile is not only something that produces queerness, but is queer in itself. We need to, hence, begin thinking about the regulation paradigms around these devices, not as a value neutral question of spectrum and infrastructure but as a direct intervention in defining and containing queerness and its mobility in the country.

The mobile queer

If the preceding section was about how non-queer bodies get installed with the promise of queerness in their interaction with the mobile, this section proposes that it is possible to decouple queerness from sexual practices and instead imagine it through metaphors of mobility. This is not a call to desexualise queerness, but to reimagine that digital sexuality is more than just the queer marked body and its biological practices. Instead, I propose that the digital queer is that which becomes mobile. A way to understand this relationship between queer and mobility is to understand the digital as constructed of vectors (Kirchenbaum 2012). In Design Thinking, this emerges as vector-space (Capurro et al. 2013). Vector-space foregrounds the fact that the routes of traffic do not precede the movement of the traffic—or that digital traffic does not go on pre-constructed routes. Instead, vectors of traffic, as they emerge in a computational network, generate a range of "edges" or routes which, through repetition, constitute the network.

Thinking of the relationship between mobility and queerness as a vector space proposes that queerness is neither in the body that espouses queer activities, nor in the devices that produce conditions of queerness. Instead, queerness as a vector is a combination of all of it—the dislocation of the body, its movement, its paths, and also its traces. The mobile body that is celebrated in our network societies is a queer body, but it is not merely the combination of the body and the technology. Similarly, technologies of mobility are queer in their operations but they are not queer unto themselves.

Instead, it is possible to think of both of these working together to produce a spectrum of queerness, which is tenuous and tentative. It is the opening of new identity politics that does not accept the "resolved queer" of global identity politics that appropriates and demands a specific kind of body for the reification of the queer. Instead, queerness is a condition of being "doubly broken" (Rege 2006). The queer has to be understood as first broken by its historical disadvantage and discrimination. And it needs to be seen as twice broken by only being conceived in mobility.

Mobility is exciting and seductive, but mobility also produces fragility and precarity. To think of the queer only as a mobile identity, is to disallow it roots, home, and belonging. As a corollary, these characteristics of fragile dislocation and perpetual motion need to be our focal points of understanding queerness. It helps us expand the scope of queerness—looking at other disadvantaged and "broken" identities as also queer, and examining the intersections of power and politics that mobile technologies and mobile metaphors bestow upon them. This is best illustrated in what is now known as the North East Exodus of 2012.

In August of 2012, the city of Bangalore woke up to an expected crisis. In this IT city of India, built by transient bodies of temporary labor, where the migrant population has already surpassed the "local" residents, thousands of people were suddenly fleeing the city. Following an ethnic clash in the North-East Indian state of Assam, where a local ethnic community had entered into a violent encounter with a Muslim immigrant group, there were rumors that the Muslims in Bangalore were going to attack and harm the sizeable population from the North-East Indian states that is culturally marked for a racial difference. As rumors started spreading, through text messages, email chain letters, and on the local digital grapevine, thousands of people started flooding buses, trains, and flights and stampeded to get out of the city.

The mobile intra-networks precipitated a large number of people to leave homes, networks, friends and jobs, and flee, despite the lack of material evidence of threat or the assurances given by the state security authorities because their precariousness was activated by the rumors on the local networks (Liang 2012). The ensuing debates pondered how the mobile networks were indeed responsible for the crisis and it was no surprise that the first regulations tried to control the traffic and censor social media, instead of dealing with the problems of actual migration and exodus.

I propose that we need to read the large numbers of people who were forced into becoming mobile, who were negated their stasis and rendered temporary in their homes, as queer. They were queer because they suddenly found themselves on the fringes. They were queer because the meritocratic IT dreams that brought them to this new city to find work and home betrayed the emptiness of economic development and made them feel unwanted and outsiders. They were queer because they were imagined as permanently uprooted, and this made them leave home, friends, jobs and run away to imaginary homes that they had moved from, in their quest for safety. Just as these otherwise "acceptable" bodies suddenly became queer, we need to understand queerness as mobile. Mobile queerness, as I propose it, is then a process that "activates" different bodies into forced mobility, when intersected by other vectors of discrimination. The mobile queer is a node that is generated through the frisson and the pathos of the excitement of mobility and the denial of permanence that marks our bodies in the global circuits of the digital.

The mobile movement

The emergence of mobile computing technologies, ranging from the state-supported innovation to cheap *jugaad* technologies, has moved many things in India. It has disrupted traditional lines of belonging and possessing. It has escalated the contested engagement with modernity in an India that becomes both the biggest market for mobile consumption, but also the new global workforce that supports mobile infrastructures. With a growing individuation that the mobile necessitates, these dislocations have also led to the visibility of bodies that were not always present in the public spaces and discourse. The mobile revolution, true to its name, has produced movements in many different ways.

The flash-mob, which has become a common spectacle in the urban fabric of the country, stands as a prime example. The first flash-mob which inaugurated the "Uncanny networks" (Sundaram 2001) of connectivity and connections was a great instance of unravelling these paradoxes. The story of the first recorded flash-mob begins with the opening of a flash-site—the first mall that opened in the city of Mumbai, which stipulated that the only people who had free access to this shrine of neo-liberal globalised consumption were people who had cell phones or platinum credit cards. Everybody else—the riff-raff, so to speak—was expected to pay an entry fee of 50 Indian Rupees, which was not redeemable against any purchases. This blatant discrimination, based on economic symbols of success, was challenged and later repealed by the law, despite the mall's argument that opening its doors to "everybody" would be a problem of "safety and security" in the mall where many people might not know how to behave (Shah 2005).

The first flash-mob, then, constituted largely of people who were privileged enough to have access to cell phones, ironically went into the mall, and in the process of dancing, flash-freezing, pretending to sell stocks of the company that owned the mall, and unfurling pink umbrellas before dispersing, did exactly what the owners of the mall were afraid of—they behaved in a way that was not expected and, with their entitled access, they changed the texture of the space, created a certain amount of madness and mayhem, and brought into stark focus the notion of publicness and access in the rapidly changing country. The mobile phone, and its ability to create temporary networks to mobilize flash-mobsters, immediately saw the proliferation of flash-mobs as acts of gamified interventions and orchestrations across the country, leading to many cities banning flash-mobs as potential acts of terror and vandalism. The new generation of flash-mobs, which are often dissociated from this history, concentrate more on choreography and documentation, but they still carry with them the seeds of protest and activism which the mobile ushered into the country.

This is how the mobile became the weapon of choice when the largest people-led nation-wide political protest, dubbed the "India Against Corruption Campaign," came together to demand the appointment of new anti-corruption regulation. This is why the mobile was the device that voiced the horror and rage of the population when a young woman was brutally gang-raped on a moving bus in New Delhi, eventually leading to her death. The mobile also became the witness to the "Radia Tapes" that betrayed the corrupt nexus between policy actors and industrial lobbies that were "leaked" to public outrage. The mobile tablet was the source of embarrassment when three members of the parliament in the Karnataka State Assembly were caught surfing porn while the assembly was in session, trending to vicious derision on the hashtag #PornGate.

The mobile was also present to capture testimonies of thousands of queer identified people, who talked of the indignity, the fear, the harassment and the threat to their lives, as they lived their queer lives under the regime that penalized homosexual activities in the country. The mobile was there to witness the surfeit of joy and wonder, when the Delhi High Court decriminalized homosexuality, and it was also there to mark the tear-stained faces of people who reeled from the blow of having this verdict overturned by the Supreme Court of India when it reinstated the penalization of queerness. The mobile has captured moments of public joys, in individual and collective selfies, and it has also been the intruder that has caught intimate moments of sexual encounters. The mobile has not only moved things, but is also in movement. As it moves, it also creates movements.

The mobile, in the network society, is perverse, in excess, and thriving on an abundance that encompasses piracy, resistance, pornography and the rest of it. It creates bodies as potentially queer, ready to be activated in their acts of transgression and circumventing the expected. Which is why right wing political parties have, at various times, asked for a ban on women's access to the mobile phone, lest it leads them astray. This might also be the reason that men and women, caught sexting across community, religion and caste lines, have been murdered in the name of honor. This is obvious in the human-flesh search engines that enable moral vigilantes to triangulate on "erring" bodies and administer mob-justice to them. This is the reason why the new Prime Minister in India is encouraging his ministers to ban mobile phones from entering their offices. The mobile is queer, it is dangerous, it is disruptive—it is seductive, and exciting and here to stay. The mobile has to die. Long live the mobile.

It has been the scope of this chapter to understand the relationship between the mobile (as a figurehead of mobile digital technologies) and sexuality (embodied in the shorthand of being queer) in order to map the new contours of globalizing India, which are often made invisible in the developmental and economic maps produced for global consumption. I propose that instead of the usual rhetoric of access, usage, penetration, and adoption, it might be more fruitful to think of what the mobile and the queer, as simultaneously emerging in post-information revolutions in India, share with each other. From the queer bodies and their use of mobile technologies, I extrapolate that we need to decouple queerness from sexuality, and look at the mobile as a queer technology, as it transcends, transgresses, and renders different bodies and events queer. I further argue that the way to understand the relationship between the queer and the mobile is to understand it at intersections of disadvantage, discrimination and dislocation, to move away from the almost universal celebration of having mobile bodies, without actually looking at the precariousness and fragility that accompany it.

I want to conclude by positing the mobile as a node, a point of intersection in the networked lives that we live. It is an object, a metaphor, a process and an embodied reality that shapes the social, cultural and political life of defining space, place, bodies and conditions of being governed in emergent economies like India. The mobile has to be imagined as being in motion, as moving, as generating movement, and catalyzing movements, in the process creating conditions of queerness which are not just embedded in sexual choices and practices. Instead the metaphor of the mobile thinks of queerness as a condition of temporary activation, where bodies, in their mobility, accrue queerness, thus creating queerness as a potential radicalism available to us all in our mobile states of being rather than a state of pathology that configures only certain bodies which are marked for punishment and regulation.

Notes

1 A recent study reported a staggering 933 million active mobile connections in the country, with a projected growth of 11 percent in the coming years. Available at: http://timesofindia.indiatimes.com/tech/tech-news/Indias-telecom-subscriber-base-rises-to-933-million/articleshow/35024488.cms (Accessed on December 10, 2014).
2 In 2012, just when India was witnessing an increased visibility of public gender violence, Google Trends reported New Delhi as recording "the highest percentage worldwide for the number of times the word 'porn' was searched online." Available at: http://www.thehindu.com/todays-paper/tp-opinion/freedom-that-must-have-limits/article4665202.ece (Accessed on February 24, 2014).
3 The United Nations reports that India is one of the youngest countries in the world, with 704 million people under the median age of 30 years. Available at: http://blog.euromonitor.com/2012/02/special-report-the-worlds-youngest-populations-.html (Accessed on December 4, 2014).
4 A detailed report of the incident can be found at http://www.yawningbread.org/apdx_2006/imp-249.htm (Accessed on March 6, 2014).
5 An insightful narration and analysis of how the "scandal" was constructed appears here at: http://www.yawningbread.org/apdx_2006/imp-249.htm (Accessed on March 6, 2014).

References

Achuthan, A. (2011) *Re: Wiring Bodies*, Bangalore: The Centre for Internet & Society.
Bagga, R.K., Keniston, K. and Raj Mathur, R. (2005) 'State, ICT and Development: The Indian Context'. In R.K. Bagga, K. Keniston and R. Raj Mathur (eds) *The State, IT and Development*, New Delhi: Sage Publications: 25–36.
Berry, C., Martin, F. and Yue, A. (2003) *Mobile Cultures: New Media in Queer Asia*, Durham, NC: Duke University Press.
Binnie, J. (2005) *The Globalization of Sexuality*, London: Sage Publications.
Bose, B. and Bhattacharyya, S. (eds) (2008) *The Phobic and the Erotic: The Politics of Sexualities in Contemporary India*, London: Seagull Books.
Capurro, R. Eldred, M. and Nagel, D. (2013) *Digital Whoness: Identity, Privacy and Freedom in the Cyberworld*, New Brunswick: Rutgers University Press.
Chun, H. K. W. (forthcoming 2015) *Habitual Media*, Cambridge, MA: MIT Press.
Doron, A. and Jeffrey, R. (2013) *The Great Indian Phone Book*, Cambridge, MA: Harvard University Press.
Franklin, M.I. (2013) *Digital Dilemmas: Power, Resistances, and the Internet*, New York: Oxford University Press.
Ganesh, M. I. and Bhattacharjya, M. (2011) 'Negotiating Intimacy and Harm: Female Internet Users in Mumbai'. In *Erotics: Sex, Rights and the Internet*. Available at: http://www.genderit.org/sites/default/upload/erotics_finalresearch_apcwnsp.pdf#india (Accessed on July 29, 2014).
Görkemli, S. (2014) *Grassroots Literacies: Lesbian and Gay Activism and the Internet in Turkey*, New York: The State University of New York Press.
Gupta, A. (2006) 'Section 377 and the Dignity of Indian Homosexuals', *Economic and Political Weekly*, 41(46): 4815–4823.
Heidegger, M. (1977 [Tr. 1982]) *The Question Concerning Technology*, London: Harper Perennial.
Kavi, A.K. (2009) In Ira Trivedi *India In Love: Marriage and Sexuality in the 21st Century*, New Delhi: Aleph Book Company.
Kirchenbaum, M. (2012) 'Digital Humanities As/Is a Tactical Term'. In *Debates in the Digital Humanities*, Minneapolis: University of Minnesota Press: 415–429.

Liang, L. (2012) 'Strangers in a Place They Call Home', *The Hindu*. Available at http://www.thehindu.com/opinion/op-ed/strangers-in-a-place-they-call-home/article3785965.ece (Accessed on July 24. 2012).

Malhotra, N. (2011) *Porn: Law, Video, Technology*, Bangalore: Centre for Internet and Society.

Martin, F., Jackson, P., McLelland, M. and Yue A. (eds) (2008) *AsiaPacifiQueer: Rethinking Genders and Sexualities*, Urbana and Chicago: University of Illinois Press.

Muñoz, J.E. (2009) *Cruising Utopia: The Then and There of Queer Futurity*, New York: NYU Press.

Narrain, A. (2004) *Queer: 'Despised sexuality', Law, and Social Change*, Michigan: Books for Change.

Narrain, A. and Bhan, G. (eds) (2005) *Because I Have A Voice: Queer Politics in India*, New Delhi: Yoda Press.

Nilekani, N. (2010) *Imagining India: Ideas for the New Century*, New Delhi: Penguin.

Poonam, S. (2012) Casting the Net, *The Caravan*. Available at: http://caravanmagazine.in/reportage/casting-net (Accessed on July 28, 2014).

Radhakrishnan, S. (2011) *Appropriately Indian: Gender and Culture in a New Transnational Class*, Durham, NC: Duke University Press.

Ragneddo, M. and Muschert, G.W. (eds) (2013) *The Digital Divide: The Internet and Social Inequality in International Perspective*, New York: Routledge.

Rajadhyaksha, A. (ed.) (2013) *In The Wake of Aadhaar: The Digital Ecosystem of Governance in India*, Bangalore: Centre for the Study of Culture and Society.

Rege, S. (2006) *Writing Caste/Writing Gender: Narrating Dalit Women's Testimonios*, New Delhi: Zubaan.

Roy, K. (1998) 'Unravelling the Kamasutra'. In J. Nair and M.E. John (eds) *A Question of Silence: The Sexual Economies of Modern India*, New Delhi: Kali for Women: 52–76.

Shah, N. (2005) 'Once Upon a Flash'. In *Sarai Reader 06: Turbulence*, New Delhi: Sarai Publications.

Shah, N. (forthcoming 2015) 'Exposing Porn'. In W. Chun and A. Fisher (eds) *New Media Old Media*, 2nd edn, Cambridge, MA: MIT Press.

Shaikh, D. (2012) Presentation at the *All India Privacy Symposium*, organised by Privacy India. Available at: http://cis-india,org/internet-governance/all-india-privacy-delhi-report (Accessed on February 15, 2014).

Sundaram, R. (2001) 'Recycling Modernity: Pirate Electronic Cultures in India', *Sarai Reader 01: The Public-Domain*, New Delhi: Sarai: New Media Initiatives: 59–65.

25

Isaac Julien's *Ten Thousand Waves*: screening human traffic and the logic of ebbing

Sean Metzger

Perhaps, as Michaeline Crichlow suggests, art might be the best vehicle to apprehend the process of human traffic since it can capture the rich dimensionality of this phenomenon.[1] Whereas journalistic coverage might emphasize economic determinism and the inequities of human rights in terms of both definition and distribution, art foregrounds issues like representation and the conditions that enable intelligibility. How do media forms shift not only the capacity to recollect the experience of traffic, but also the very material mechanics of trafficking? What circuits of power and technologies of visibility enable us to see what are often invisible currents of both documented and undocumented human labor? What sorts of fantasy projection does the dissemination of media networks across the globe enable? What possibilities not only for communication, but also for identification and production of agency (and subjectivity) become available through such networks?

These questions emerge as central in relation to Isaac Julien's nine-screen installation, *Ten Thousand Waves*, first exhibited in 2010. A consideration of Julien's complex project demonstrates surprising relations between form and content, specifically by suggesting ways in which human traffic as transnational circuits of labor might be entangled with particular streams of globalized aesthetic production. Such an analysis illustrates why screen cultures might matter, even for those whose precarious status might seem to position them without access to new media and without relevance to the philosophical debates such technologies engender.[2]

Part 1 Mediating migrants' mortality

The deaths of 23 Chinese workers inspired Julien's artistic endeavor.[3] On February 5, 2004, the families of several cockle pickers working in England's Morecambe Bay heard from their loved ones for the last time. The cell phone calls they placed demonstrate how even those individuals subject to human trafficking engage technology that alters quotidian experience, transforming, for example, even the temporality of death. Rather than a mere post-mortem record, these phone calls capture time immediately prior to loss of life. The disembodied sounds of the victims' voices continue to echo beyond their watery graves. They begin a process that rescripts human subjectivity for those whose conditions of existence have largely rendered them exploited objects as a migrant labor force. The phone calls reverberate with these workers' experiences and generate public interest in the life stories of people otherwise unseen in their English worksite, people who were scarcely recognized as such by British and Chinese authorities alike until their bodies washed ashore.

This situation resonates strongly with Rey Chow's elaboration of Walter Benjamin's writings on the age of mechanical reproduction:

> rather than reality being caught in the sense of being contained, detained, or retained in the copy-image (understood as a repository), it is now the machinic act or event of capture, with its capacity for further partitioning (that is, for generating additional copies and images ad infinitum), that sets reality in motion, that invents or makes reality, as it were.
>
> *(Chow 2012, 4)*

The mediated conversations of the imperiled cockle pickers both testify to their existence and activate processes that restore these individuals' humanity to previously unconcerned publics. In the wake of the news reporting, narrative film, and Julien's own more abstract response to the Morecambe Bay drownings, the victims' life narratives have been reconstructed and circulated to the extent that each individual has achieved far more human recognition after death.[4] Of course, people with access to technology around the world might achieve a certain digital afterlife given everyday exposure on various media platforms. What is interesting about this particular case—and human traffic in general—is that the circuit of traffic enables visualization of the points at which people become visible and invisible in their life trajectories and the public audiences to whom such visibility might matter at any given moment.

To entertain the question of visibility in this case is not to argue that human trafficking might be combated through exposure of unjust practices. Rather I argue that the peculiar alignment of visibility with *victims* of human traffic attributes responsibility to the exceptional case of organized crime rather than the mundane phenomena of hoping and suffering under neoliberal capitalism. Agency in the discourse of human trafficking tends to reside in the hands of the snakehead or his equivalent. In this vein, the Palermo Protocol addressing this matter and issued by the United Nations in 2000 (effective 2003) requires subjects to perform victimhood in order to seek legal redress:

> "trafficking in persons" shall mean the recruitment, transportation, transfer, harbouring or receipt of persons, by means of the threat or use of force or other forms of coercion, of abduction, of fraud, of deception, of the abuse of power or of a position of vulnerability or of the giving or receiving of payments or benefits to achieve the consent of a person having control over another person, for the purpose of exploitation. Exploitation shall include, at a minimum, the exploitation of the prostitution of others or other forms of sexual exploitation, forced labour or services, slavery or practices similar to slavery, servitude or the removal of organs.
>
> *(United Nations 2004, 42)*

A recognizable subject in this discourse depends on victimhood. In other words, the subject must dispossess someone or be the dispossessed. Much of the reporting on the cockle pickers has furthered such a construction. A single moment of recognition, then, can direct how an audience might understand the entirety of someone's life. In this way, the human traffic protocol potentially screens out the very humanity it would seek to protect. For people entangled in human traffic, visibility and recognition come at a cost.

As a riposte to this kind of reductive discourse that would have audiences imagine the cockle pickers as continually subjected to the wills of others, *Ten Thousand Waves* immerses the spectator in an artistic reflection on media, time, phenomenology, and death. Julien's installation brings together folk tales, found footage, reconstructions of Chinese film, and poetry. These convergences constructed through a specific architectural design transform how viewers understand migrant experience. The form of the installation captures some of the fractured experience of migrancy even as it combines several disparate technologies by means of which stories about migration circulate.

Julien's nine-screen work has been altered to fit the places of its exhibition. The most ambitious display to date took place at New York's Museum of Modern Art (MOMA). Museum curators showed *Ten Thousand Waves* in the Donald B. and Catherine C. Marron Atrium, a sixty-foot high space that can be viewed from a number of angles. The double-sided screens were suspended at different levels above a floor covered in blue carpet on which sat four amoeba-shaped chaises and five large, circular ottomans. The film ran on a loop of approximately fifty minutes. In order to see the exhibition from several vantage points, I visited the museum four times in the course of a week in January of 2014. Repeated visits also enabled me to see different audiences engage the work; these spectators included individuals who would lounge on the furniture in order to observe a full cycle of screening and those who passed by or through the installation en route to another gallery.

Given the entry price of 25 dollars and the number of activities that compete with the museum in New York (not to mention the number of exhibitions on display in the museum itself), many visitors saw the actual installation only once and only in segments. However, the exhibition itself includes a placard about the museum videotaping and/or live-streaming the program during its opening hours. To watch this spectacle is to consent to being recorded as part of it. Even as the screens themselves reproduced images, then, the exhibition itself was multiplied both through MOMA's official videography and through the many photos and videos uploaded by museum visitors to various social media sites. In this continual process of reproducing screen images, the installation works within the atrium's architectural specificity even as it constantly transcends it.

Julien himself has expressed an interest in the mobile spectator—an idea he borrows from theater in the sense of wandering through a specific performance space—but Julien multiplies the potential effects of motion and circulation. Again, the audience immerses itself among a physical set of double-sided screens even as this set of participant-spectators might themselves be projected on someone else's online social media network. By looking at Julien's installation, one potentially becomes both an image and image-maker. This facet of the installation materializes Julien's longstanding desires to make "an intervention into the museum and the gallery, an intervention with the moving image" (Julien 2013, 122). Rather than a rarified repository of masterpieces of modern art (MOMA overwhelmingly displays European and American male artists from its permanent collection), this museum exhibit supports individuals that actively or passively partake in the process of *moving* images, of contextualizing Julien's own piece and the sections of MOMA in which it is located in idiosyncratic ways through new placements across various media.

Such sharing of art also offers implicit commentary on visuality itself. Images create different meanings depending on the framing and circumstances of their display. To attempt to document in some pseudo-objective manner the deaths of cockle pickers for the consumption of tourists and art aficionados in New York at 25 dollars a head seems crass. To project spaces of reconstruction and reflection that the audience might augment through their own devices would seem a decidedly more thought-provoking and probably more ethical project. That said, screens conceal as much as they might reveal. Julien's installation does not address the material conditions for victims' families produced in the wake of the incident at Morecambe Bay. For example, a complicated and importantly, informal, system of debt and credit structures the experiences of the families of the cockle pickers.[5] Certainly Julien is quite conscious of the expenses and profit generated by filmmaking, in general, and multi-screen format cinematic experiences designed for prestigious art institutions, in particular. Witness his recent work *PLAYTIME* (2013/2014). But if a critique of art's imbrication with capitalism appears through *Ten Thousand Waves*, it emerges obliquely. Information pertaining to how this artistic work trades on the misfortune of others and the questions about ownership, profit, and responsibility such negotiations might elicit never appear on screen. Nevertheless the very presence of so many projection panels urges audiences to consider what is and is not visible in the juxtaposed elements that assemble its loose and ambivalent narrative structure.

Part II Genealogies of form in Julien's oeuvre

A variety of factors contributed to the aesthetic development of *Ten Thousand Waves*. English national cinema and queer cinema offer useful contexts for engaging Julien's work and also demonstrate some of the political stakes that have informed and continue to animate Julien's artistic projects. And certainly Julien's own efforts in documentary film production and in museum installations provide antecedents that underscore the centrality of the screen to his corpus. Indeed, the continual return to the politics of screening as a mode of capture, a mode of exhibition, and a mode of profitmaking constitutes part of Julien's creative signature.

One might begin the discussion of antecedents for Julien's new media projects with the late 1950s/early 1960s New Wave in England, whose most prolific director was Tony Richardson (*Momma Don't Allow*, 1956). Building on the movement known as the Free Cinema, the British New Wave brought a realist aesthetic to the patriotic masculinities celebrated in WWII that were encouraged, during the war years, by the Ministry of Information's Films Division. To be sure, New Wave films articulated their own sexism and machismo, but they also placed the spotlight on the workers and the social conditions throughout England that produced disenfranchisement. These films, then, projected stories that reflected and shaped contemporary English life in and through the cinema, and they anticipate Julien's focus on the stream of labor, albeit a Chinese immigrant one in this case, that inspired *Ten Thousand Waves*.

Of course, the decidedly English valence of these mid-century films belies the enormous international investment in English cinematic production from as far back as the 1920s onward. It is worth noting, for example, that in 1969 "90 percent of the investment in British cinema came from America" (Petrie 1999, 609). Such investment helped to launch the cinematic career of one the most enduring Cold War figures, James Bond. Although commercial productions like the Bond films shifted attention away from a body of work that might constitute English national cinema, by the early 1980s there was a resurgence of films that returned to the specific landscape of England, especially to the plight of the disenfranchised. Julien also engages this site and theme with *Ten Thousand Waves*, but he demands that the audience consider the transnational currents that shape labor within England today. This move also specifically expands the scope of Julien's earlier efforts with Sankofa.

During the 1980s, Channel 4 (particularly its Multicultural Department) and the British Film Institute funded low budget productions, although they tended to funnel monies to different constituencies.[6] Nevertheless, these monetary sources, along with workshop programs targeting ethnic minorities and the protests against such programs (for tokenism), facilitated the formation of several artist collectives. These included the Black Audio Film Collective and Sankofa, with which Julien was associated. Whereas the former group mainly produced documentaries, Sankofa often worked in the genre of the art film.[7] The legacy of this kind of work—smaller, independent pictures—successfully brought the margins to the center, so that British cinema soon became largely defined, in an international context, by those filmmakers who either emerged or were particularly active during this period: Derek Jarman, Neil Jordan, Sally Potter, Peter Greenaway, and Isaac Julien to name a few. Sankofa depended on streams of public funding. The waning of government support for the arts led many artists to consider more seriously the ways in which they might address a commercialized arts sector. One venue for patronage came in the form of commissions from museums, which arrived, as Julien notes, coeval with pronouncements of the death of cinema (2013, 138).

Rather than subscribe to a hypothesis about the end of cinema, I find it useful to situate Julien within genealogies of cinema that already anticipated transformation of the form. Here Julien's work fits within another genealogy: queer cinema. The new queer cinema was coined in the early 1990s to describe a body of largely American but also some British films that explicitly addressed the subject of sexuality through formal innovations that resisted conventional narrative structures. Queer cinema attempted to debunk the official stories of oppressive governmental regimes. The 1980s, after all, was the decade of new conservatism, of Reagan and Thatcher, and of the AIDS pandemic. The stakes of who could speak were high. Julien's films from this period of the late-twentieth century register concerns over the policing of racialized bodies that were and are always also sexualized. In such a context, Julien's co-directed *The Passion of Remembrance* (1986) and his meditation on Langston Hughes entitled *Looking for Langston* (1989), use pastiche—found objects, old newsreels, stills, experimental fiction, etc.—to index black queer cultural formations across time and space. Such formations counter the official histories promoted by the US and UK governments at the time. They question the legitimacy of nation as the defining rubric under which we talk about culture, in general, and cinema, in particular.

In other words, Julien's films both raise the issue of local racial formation within the national space of England at the same time that they interrogate that frame. His films thus work as a kind of call and response—what I might term an antiphonal aesthetic—that constructs the black, gay British subject at the same time it deconstructs the assumptions that render the articulation of a black, gay Englishman possible. Such antiphonal aesthetics continue in works like *Young Soul Rebels* (1991) and *The Attendant* (1993), which also underscore the role of music in filmmaking and its importance to black expressive culture more generally, even if the latter film also initiated Julien's sustained interrogation of what is possible in the space of the museum. Julien's work within the tradition of queer cinema, finally, is to interrogate form by playing with structures of desire.

The interest in sound and the documentation of aural phenomena that are not, strictly speaking, tangible seems to shape some of Julien's later choices in documentary film production.[8] Both *The Darker Side of Black* (1994) and *BaadAsssss Cinema* (2002) address music and soundscapes as much as they address modes of production largely controlled by black people. This emphasis on sound, the ways in which echoes from the past can haunt the present, seems directly linked to Julien's investigation of the voices accompanying the blurred images of Morecambe Bay in *Ten Thousand Waves*. As an illustration of this aesthetic, instead of helicopter shots providing a bird's eye view with an accompanying sense of visual control, the movement of the camera and the tone of desperation captured in the soundtrack convey a sense of the Chinese laborers' precarious plight. Although it is not always clear who is speaking, the exhibition catalogue attributes the voices to "the woman responsible for the cockle pickers . . . and the rescue workers" (Julien 2013: 204). Whereas the voiceover is often used to establish narrative authority, Julien deploys it in *Ten Thousand Waves* to quite the opposite effect. Although sound often provides a mood for the images throughout this work, it does little to render a coherent narrative.

Unlike the conditions that attend many other film screenings, the continual traffic through and around the exhibition space of *Ten Thousand Waves* further fragments the viewer's experience of narrative. Multiple sounds and sights competed for the attention of MOMA's visitors. Although similar situations might structure spectatorship in relation to many of Julien's museum installations, the acoustics and sight lines in the atrium space intensified the ambient noise and the other components of visual and sensory ambiance that museumgoers experience. This sensorial immersion perhaps provides an aesthetic analogue to the situation of being caught in a physical environment (noting, of course, that the cockle pickers' situation is not an all equivalent to some elective participation in an artistic construction). Nevertheless, the attempt to find various scales of comparison to the events at Morecambe Bay drove Julien to seek various ways of allegorizing them not only through the content of *Ten Thousand Waves* but also through its form.

These efforts recall Julien's previous screen installations for gallery and museum spaces. Giuliana Bruno has written in detail about the methods that Julien employs, especially in the installations *Vagabondia* (2000) and *Baltimore* (2003), to choreograph memory "with a network of performative voices and sounds as well as movements" (2014, 169). According to Bruno, these two pieces work to fold different temporalities in relation to one another and in relation to a set of subjects and objects that creates surfaces of contemplation and encounter. Particular processes of black recollection interrogate archives as acts of remembering and as spatial configurations. In Bruno's analysis, Julien's artworks posit pure "-scapes" through "folds of future mnemonic projection" (Bruno 2014, 181). Bruno does not spend much time pursuing the full implications of this statement; she mentions -scapes particularly in relation to the "total light space" created by sheets of ice in Julien's installation *True North* and links it tentatively to *Ten Thousand Waves* (Bruno 2014, 181).

Nevertheless, Bruno's insistence that Julien spatializes memory (consistent with her citation of the English historian Frances Yates) and disrupts linear time through a folding operation recalls Arjun Appadurai's book *Modernity at Large*. Appadurai is also interested in -scapes and time, although his emphasis is less on aesthetics and subjectivity than Bruno's. However, their different scholarship might intersect in thinking through the ways in which a kind of folding temporality helps bring into relief cultural scenes otherwise rendered opaque in dominant discourses. Following Appadurai, -scapes might further designate "deeply perspectival constructs, inflected by the historical, linguistic, and political situatedness of different sorts of actors" (Appadurai 1996, 33). He deemphasizes the individual, who creates and is enmeshed in "larger formations" including "nation-states, multinationals, diasporic communities, as well as subnational groupings and movements (whether religious, political, or economic), and even intimate face-to-face groups, such as villages, neighborhoods, and families" (33). But the folding of which Bruno writes enables shifts in scale as part of the aesthetic operations of Julien's screen technologies. Appadurai's research offers a means to clarify how the idea of -scape as an aesthetic might also fold in the empirical evidence of Chinese laborers in England.

In my own elaboration of Appadurai's provocation, I have been exploring the idea of the seascape as a heuristic for global studies.[9] The resonances of -scape with the action of "escape" gestures to the ways in which individuals might try to shift their livelihoods and the conditions of possibility for representation. The seascape is particularly relevant to the situation of the cockle pickers, since their representation as subjects in popular media has everything to do with oceanic perils. The aquatic submersion of these individuals paradoxically rendered them hypervisible—too late to render their lives meaningful to the press beyond their positions as victims. Building on Bruno and Appadurai, I argue that Julien's *Ten Thousand Waves* folds together a particularly Chinese Atlantic seascape, one structured by a particular logic of return that I designate with the word "ebbing."

In part "ebbing" designates the actual physical engagement with Julien's installation at MOMA. To see the exhibition required repeatedly turning one's body and adjusting one's orientation to view the circle of screens, sometimes selectively illuminated with images that occasionally ran across several panels (e.g., a car moving from one screen across to another). This sort of movement is literally a process of re-turn (that is, turning again), but I qualify such action with the word ebbing because the film's different scenes advance and transition at a regular and relaxed tempo. Unlike, say, one of the action films for which the film's featured star, Maggie Cheung, is known, the editing in Julien's installation generally does not create suspense or elicit a sensation of extremely rapid movement. The transitions from one sequence to the next allow spectators enough time to shift position at a tranquil pace.

However, the installation nevertheless obliges the spectator to reposition if not relocate the body as no vantage point could afford a full view of the entirety of the film. At the same time, because of the length of the piece, a continual ebb and flow of arrival and departure characterizes the audience as a whole. This phenomenon is in part because a spectator's interest might wane (or ebb). Julien's installation also seems structured so that the spectator will miss something in any given viewing (because it would be impossible for someone to capture all of the images on every screen in any one sitting).

These physical conditions draw the visitor into a consideration of the more metaphorical aspects of the exhibition generated by its visual and aural content. The allusion to the Morecambe Bay incident encourages reflection on what follows in the wake of drowning. In other words, what happens to this labor stream with the ebbing of the tides? Following Bruno's logic, the imagery folds the spectator into interconnecting, perhaps collapsing, time and space. However, the exhibition is quite specific in terms of what sorts of materials it folds together. The fold has, of course, been productively elaborated in the scholarship of Olivia Khoo (and my own ensuing writing).[10] Both of us investigate the fold to think through traveling forms of Asianness. Khoo theorizes the fold as part of a formation she calls the Chinese exotic, which "permits certain images and representations of diasporic Chinese femininity to circulate and become globally visible" (2007, 27). The Chinese exotic structures the legibility of Chinese diasporic femininity and also the experience of that category. As one expression of the Chinese exotic, Khoo looks at a character played by Maggie Cheung, who is, to reiterate, the major star in Julien's *Ten Thousand Waves* (her screen time is comparatively greater than that of Zhao Tao, who plays a ghostly version of Ruan Ling Yu, one of China's most celebrated early celebrities).[11] Extending Khoo's Chinese exotic in relation to Julien's film helps to parse the particularity of his depiction of female Chinese screen icons and may also help to parse the on location filming in China and the variety of other Chinese semiological signs in the installation.

Part III Genealogies of transnational Asian forms

Julien's work draws heavily on Chinese iconography from the urban—including the contemporary Shanghai skyline and reconstructions of a 1930s Shanghai cityscape—to the rural and from linguistic signs rendered in calligraphy (*shufa*) to fantastic embodiments of Chinese mythology. Rather than only revealing the postmodern pastiche of late capitalism, these different components in the show articulate potential agency and the limits to such agency. In this vein, the congeries of Chinese references elaborate what Appadurai refers to as the "imagination as a social practice" (1996, 31). Such practice, in my view, pushes spectators to think differently about the material circumstances for Chinese laborers. Rather than framing the Morecambe Bay incident as a series of human rights abuses, *Ten Thousand Waves* shifts discussion to other factors motivating migration.

According to the press release for the show, the juxtaposition of elements comments on modernization through a specifically Chinese cosmology.

> Following ideas surrounding death, spiritual displacement, and the uniquely Chinese connection with "ghosts" or "lost souls", the film links the Shanghai of the past and present, symbolising the Chinese transition towards modernity, aspiration and affluence. Here, Julien employs the visual language of ghost stories, with recurrent figures and images appearing and disappearing.
>
> ('Ten Thousand Waves' 2010)

This construction of Shanghai is obviously quite specific, ignoring moments in Shanghai's past when the city did not serve as a beacon of China's capitalist development. Moreover, the exact relationship of Shanghai to emigration patterns out of Fujian, the province from which most of the cockle pickers hailed, remains unclear.

But perhaps this lack of clarity is the point, since ghosts represent a problem in terms of visuality (Jacques Derrida (1994), of course, argued this point in relation to the revenant, a spectral figure that begins by coming back; however, the principal ghost in *Ten Thousand Waves* functions in a slightly different fashion, as I will argue). In *Ten Thousand Waves*, the main character is Mazu (Maggie Cheung), a deity thought to exist apart from the dead she calls back. Worshipped widely throughout Greater China and the diaspora, Mazu connotes safe passage for fishermen both in the past and today. However, across various time periods and geographical areas, the particular associations of the goddess have varied.[12] Because she traverses diverse territories, often appearing only briefly before disappearing, she is less a figure that comes back (which often applies attachment to a specific place), than one who manifests as need arises. The desire for safe travel, then, correlates as often to a movement towards a new place as much as a return to one already known. Julie Y. Chu has described the appeal of Mazu as involving a "politics of destination" in this vein (2010, 12). This issue of destination raises the question of why people engage in precarious journeys in the first place. Unlike most human traffic discourse, however, a politics of destination does not necessarily attribute the motivation for travel to the horrible conditions of home, to the imagined opportunities for something better, or to forced migration. Following this politics of destination, the subjective desires of the cockle pickers cannot be reduced to a formula in which they only seek financial opportunity or have been exploited by a snakehead.

Such caveats might well inform how one understands Isaac Julien's Mazu, shown on screen as a retrospective guide. Her appearance follows the death of the cockle pickers, whom she would seem to escort back to China. Her all white costume seems to reinforce this idea. This section of the film ostensibly draws on a folktale from Fujian about Yishan Island, a safe haven to which the deity led several sailors in danger of being swallowed by a storm. After returning to their homes, the mariners can never again locate their insular refuge. Obviously the cockle pickers found themselves with less fortune on their side, and, insofar as the film relates Mazu to their actual experience, she provides a place to harbor their spirits after the end of their mortal lives. This manifestation of Mazu correlates with Avery Gordon's writing about ghosts as embodiments of unresolved social conflicts (2008). Exactly which social conflicts Mazu might represent remains somewhat ambiguous. Certainly, one might read nostalgia in the implicit return of seafarers to China's shores. Flying over China's rural landscape of picturesque mountains and rivers, Mazu provides a romanticized homecoming to China's scenic beauty.

But Mazu also appears in Julien's film flying through Shanghai's post-millenial skyline. This placement of the screened goddess conjures the sorts of phrases that have been used to describe the city in recent years, including the tagline for the Shanghai World Expo in 2010, "Better City, Better Life." What role does the working class have in such a vision? What role does faith? Is spirituality waning under advanced capitalism or merely changing forms? Julien does not answer these questions, but his visual juxtapositions raise them. The film folds such queries together in provocative ways. Perhaps most notably, several sequences depict Cheung in a harness being pulled by assistants across a green screen. Here we might ask: what happens when a society worships screen goddesses whose cosmopolitan mobility is enabled by the labor of usually unseen workers? What is at stake in not seeing the everyday toil that renders the urban environment livable and perhaps even enchanting? Exactly how and for whom does a city generate a better life?

The film continually evokes the tensions between pushing and pulling, ebbing and flowing. These dynamics are in turn expressed as shifting between ostensible traditions and signifiers of modernity. For example, even the calligraphy sequences depict the flow of energy through the hands of a master, Gong Fagen, to create Chinese characters (*fantizi*) on a clear surface. The ink from the written words 萬重浪 (*wan zhong lang*, or ten thousand waves) drips down the transparent screen until being cleaned by a set of anonymous assistants. An aesthetic project, Julien continually reminds the viewer, requires work. Put differently, labor and aesthetics are entwined, folded together in ways that sometimes produce, for example, visions of the Chinese exotic. But such exoticism is often predicated on the disavowal of the blood, sweat, and tears that helped to fashion it.

Following this line of argument, the scenes of 1930s Shanghai play on the seen and unseen. Julien himself has noted the remarkable efficiency of Chinese crews who built for him reconstructions of 1930s Shanghai complete with a trolley. The actress who plays Ruan Lingyu, Zhao Tao, has starred in many of Jia Zhangke's films, works that have frequently depicted the nightmarish aspects of China's modernization projects. Certainly both the allusion in *Ten Thousand Waves* to Ruan Lingyu's film *The Goddess* and the reference to its screen icon of yesteryear both suggest the high cost that urban life can exact on people, particularly women (the film depicts a prostitute, and its lead actress committed suicide at the age of 24). Zhao Tao's temporal placement in this earlier moment of China's cinematic history thus interrogates the lineage of Chinese capitalism. In other words, the star discourse around Zhao Tao suggests one future for 1930s Shanghai: a booming yet in many ways dystopian China.

In these depictions of Shanghai and the layering of Chinese female stars, *Ten Thousand Waves* seems to have moved far from the ostensible event that inspired it. Whither does the installation drive audiences to Morecambe Bay? As much as the screens facilitate a consideration of the seen and unseen, the sound design for the show plays with the heard and unheard. In my own case (and I switch to the first person because I cannot generalize about others' experiences), the direct allusions to the Morecambe Bay incident that punctuated the soundtrack often eluded me. After each visit to MOMA, I found myself contemplating the scale of images, the vastness of projected and actual space. Such considerations of the spectacle, of the immersion in the scene, often inhibited my ability to recollect, for example, narrative sequence or the aural experience of the installation. As I have mentioned, the latter phenomenon also involved the ambient soundscape of the museum itself. In any case, although my research had informed me to expect poetry about Morecambe Bay, I did not process that auditory aspect of the show until months after visiting it. Yet that element is one of the most explicit linkages to the historical event of 2004 and to the subjects of human traffic.

Part IV The ebbing of notoriety

Isaac Julien's *Ten Thousand Waves* was in many ways a collaborative endeavor. Julien's work points the visitor of the installation to other forms of cultural production: the films of its lead actresses, the calligraphy, and the re-contextualization of the installation on various social media sites. In this spirit, I eventually read what I believed I had missed in the exhibition in terms of the literary aspect.

Chinese/American writer Wang Ping wrote a series of nineteen dramatic monologues each labeled as a voice (or as voices) of the deceased. While she penned most of the poems in an individual persona, she marks some of them as couples. The set of verses ends with a "Chorus from All Ghosts" (2014, 82). Over half of the individual poems end with some mention of the North Wales Sea. As the verses reach conclusion, the referent becomes the Yellow Sea and the East China Sea. The poems enact a geographic movement that reflects Julien's use of Mazu as leading the cockle pickers from Morecambe Bay back to China. Because the form of dramatic monologue demands that the reader perform the subject position of the speaker, the poems also produce a certain kind of identification with those who are named in the text. These names correlate with the Chinese laborers who drowned in Morecambe Bay. In this instance, the poems subordinate the details of the human trafficking that preoccupies much of the journalistic coverage and emphasizes the subjectivities of the individuals who died. In this fashion, the poems work as performatives that testify to lives otherwise submerged in the currents of history. I conclude with a brief passage from Wan Ping about Wu Jia Zhen, a cockle picker who died at the age of 36.

> Tides ebb and flow with the moon
> Our house is empty, covered in tall weeds
> I walk on the sand, eyes on the sea
> Who can fill the hollow hearts
> In the bottomless North Wales Sea?
> *(Ping 2014, 77)*

Notes

1 Crichlow 2013.
2 For a very useful elaboration of the term precarious also related to labor but in a different Asian context, I refer the interested reader to Anne Allison's important work (2013).
3 See Julien 2013, 193.
4 The film is Nick Broomfield's *Ghosts* (2006).
5 This statement is derived from Jonathan Watts's work (2014). In order to pay the snakeheads for transportation and other expenses (lodging, food, work documents), each worker borrowed several thousand RMB from relatives, fellow villagers, and other creditors. With interest rates at ten percent or more, the accumulated debt for many families amounts to several hundred thousand yuan on salaries to be paid by households who earn monthly incomes in the triple digits.
6 For an elaboration of this point, see Julien 2003.
7 Although I offer this schematic distinction, other scholarship has pointed to the Black Audio Film Collective's work "as an archaeological excavation into the limits of medial evolution and as a metamedial engagement with the epistemological conditions of the imperial archive" (Eshun 2004, 39).
8 Kahana (2006) offers a useful interrogation of sound in general in Isaac Julien's work, particularly in *Frantz Fanon: Black Skin, White Mask* (1996).
9 See Metzger 2014.
10 See Khoo 2007 and Metzger 2011.
11 Maggie Cheung previously played this role in the biopic, *Center Stage* (Stanley Kwan, 1991). This coincidence for spectators familiar with Cheung's career adds an element of spectrality to Cheung's ghostly character in *Ten Thousand Waves*. She continually returns through different screen embodiments.
12 For specifics, see Tan 2013.

References

Allison, A. (2013) *Precarious Japan*, Durham, NC: Duke University Press.
Appadurai, A. (1996) *Modernity at Large: Cultural Dimensions of Globalization*, Minneapolis: University of Minnesota Press.

Bruno, G. (2014) *Surface: Matters of Aesthetics, Materiality, and Media*, Chicago: University of Chicago Press.

Chow, R. (2012) *Entanglements, or Transmedial Thinking about Capture*, Durham, NC: Duke University Press.

Chu, J. (2010) *Cosmologies of Credit: Transnational Mobility and the Politics of Destination in China*, Durham, NC: Duke University Press.

Crichlow, M. (2013) 'Human Traffic—Past and Present', *Cultural Dynamics*, 25(2): 123–140.

Derrida, J. (1994) *Specters of Marx: The State of Debt, the Work of Mourning and the New International*, (Peggy Kamuf trans.), New York: Routledge.

Eshun, K. (2004) 'Untimely Meditations: Reflections on the Black Audio Film Collective', *Nka: Journal of Contemporary African Art*, 19: 38–45.

Gordon, A. (2008) *Ghostly Matters: Haunting and the Sociological Imagination*, Minneapolis: University of Minnesota Press.

Julien, I. (2003) 'Burning Rubber's Perfume'. In Justin Lewis and Toby Miller *Critical Cultural Policy Studies: A Reader*, Malden, MA: Blackwell Publishers.

Julien, I. et al. (2013) *Isaac Julien: Riot*, New York: The Museum of Modern Art.

Kahana, J. (2006) 'Cinema and the Ethics of Listening: Isaac Julien's *Frantz Fanon*', *Film Quarterly*, 59(2): 19–31.

Khoo, O. (2007) *The Chinese Exotic: Modern Diasporic Femininity*, Hong Kong: Hong Kong University Press.

Metzger, S. (2014) 'Seascape: The Chinese Atlantic'. In Hilary E. Kahn (ed.) *Framing the Global: Entry Points for Research*, Bloomington and Indianapolis: Indiana University Press.

Metzger, S. (2011) 'At the Vanishing Point: Theater and Asian/American Critique', *American Quarterly*, 63(2): 277–300.

Petrie, D. (1999) 'British Cinema: The Search for Identity'. In Geoffrey Nowell-Smith (ed.) *The Oxford History of World Cinema*, Oxford: Oxford University Press.

Ping, W. (2014) *Ten Thousand Waves: Poems*, San Antonio, TX: Wings Press.

Tan, C.-B. (2013) 'Tianhou and the Chinese in Diaspora'. In Tian Chee-Bang (ed.) *Routledge Handbook of the Chinese Diaspora*, New York: Routledge.

'Ten Thousand Waves Press Release' (2010) Available at: http://www.isaacjulien.com/tenthousandwaves/downloads/PRESS_RELEASE_TTW_v3.5.pdf (Accessed September 8, 2014).

United Nations (2004) 'United Nations Convention Against Transnational Organized Crime and the Protocols Thereto'. Available at: https://www.unodc.org/documents/treaties/UNTOC/Publications/TOC%20Convention/TOCebook-e.pdf (Accessed August 1, 2014).

Watts, J. (2014) 'Going Under'. Available at: http://www.theguardian.com/uk/2007/jun/20/ukcrime.humanrights (Accessed July 26, 2014).

Part V

Creative industries: new producers, performativity and production paradigms

26

TV or not TV? Re-imagining screen content in China

Michael Keane and Elaine Jing Zhao

In the People's Republic of China television is a dynamic industry, growing ever more profitable by the day. With a potential viewing population of "over two billion eyes" (Zhu 2013), it would seem that the medium has no obvious limits to growth. Yet fewer people are watching television in the traditional living room mode. Moreover, audiences are less inclined to watch television during prime time.

If people's reception habits have changed so dramatically, how is this impacting on content, its production and delivery mode? Furthermore, what does this mean for the way that the television market works? To answer these questions it is necessary to reframe our understanding of television content and audiences, not just in China but globally. We need to look at what television was, what it is now, and what it might be like in the future. Certainly the technologies of satellite and wireless reception have changed perceptions of the medium's ubiquity, allowing content to be accessible to distant audiences. The term "tele-vision," originally coined to depict the technology of sending moving images over telegraph wires to people in living rooms, is arguably anachronistic, as is the Chinese translation *dianshi* (literally "electric seeing").

In this chapter we examine the convergence of traditional broadcasting and new media in China. We begin with some brief background on television in China in order to illustrate the changes that have been wrought by marketization and technological change. The desire to modernize China's communication system has resulted in a greater degree of political latitude towards new online media companies; these companies are less constrained by the administrative boundaries that pertain to terrestrial broadcasters; moreover their "creative" personnel are less conditioned by traditional ways of imagining content. Yet the challenges facing the new media companies are of a different order: should they form alliances with traditional media or forge a new frontier of content generation?

Our brief background on broadcast television leads us to the advent of satellite television and the ways that satellite channels have looked to initiate brand programming and establish brand identities. The idea of branded channels is explored in the example of Henan Satellite Television, which has identified its offerings as being "cultural" in contrast to the fierce competition from talent and variety shows. In passing we observe the role played by format television, which has introduced new ways of thinking about the relationship between content and audiences, particularly as new celebrity-based formats take advantage of the affordances of new media—including apps that enhance audience engagement and mobile devices that allow content to be viewed (and re-viewed) anytime. With formats increasing the potential for audiences to participate, the entry of online media companies into the production of content further disrupts the dominance of traditional media.

In the final section we illustrate two examples of development that show the integration of technology and culture; the first is an IPTV (Internet Protocol Television) service in Shanghai called BesTV and the second, Mango TV, a website and "over the top" (OTT) subscription service operating from Hunan Province. In the case of IPTV we note the arrival of an alternative technological platform with links to China's second largest media group. BesTV runs on a business model based on advertising and user payment. On the other hand, Mango TV is a website and OTT subscription service offering ad-supported on demand streaming videos of TV shows, movies, as well as short form online dramas called "webisodes," and behind-the-scenes footage from Hunan TV and other content providers.

Background: the revolution will be televised

The first broadcast of a television program in China took place on May 1, 1958 in Beijing. Television's function was to propagate national unity, to educate people in the lessons of history, and above all to instill moral lessons. Audiences were an undifferentiated mass, known as the "people." By 1985, as China edged closer towards becoming a "socialist market economy" it was estimated that ninety-five percent of all urban families owned at least one television (Huang 1994). For people starved of information and curious about the outside world television was a great blessing.

The blessings bestowed by television continued in the 1980s and 1990s; more programs were made, serial drama became the main form of family entertainment, and foreign programming—together with ideas about capitalism—found their way into schedules (see Keane 2015). Despite restrictions on content and genres, the new technologies of broadcasting provided greater access: firstly cable and satellite, and later digital television, smart TV and Internet TV. In the wake of these technological enhancements viewers' understanding of the role of television in China has altered significantly. In the past decade programming genres have changed, international formats have been adopted, and audiences have become sophisticated. Yet the words of the Canadian media scholar Marshall McLuhan ring true. Writing in an era predating the Internet, blogs, and Facebook, McLuhan announced that the "medium is the message" (McLuhan 1967), implying that characteristics of a particular medium, for instance television, are more significant than the content carried.

What are the characteristics of the medium of television today? Where, when, and how are Chinese people watching TV? What are they accessing? In the mid-1990s, despite a wave of commercial reforms in the media, the Chinese television industry differed from its international counterparts in one important way. All television stations were state-owned: with this came a responsibility to disseminate propaganda. Although stations competed for viewers, there was no identifiable industry policy. In 2001, the term "industry" (chanye) began to be widely used to describe the commercialization of China's culture and media (see Keane 2013, 2015). Today the differences, aside from language, are less obvious.

Much of this similarity has to do with changing international business models. Television during most of the twentieth century was a very different medium from cinema: its industrial logic was predicated on advertising. In most international media environments well-made professional content attracted large audiences and increased profits for producers, investors and originators. This content business model has not changed. Terrestrial stations still dominate programming acquisition and success is still predicated on ratings. Globally, however, the media industry has witnessed the impact of convergent technologies over the past two decades. We can now differentiate between "network television" and "networked television." Network television refers to an era dominated by the big commercial networks, when producing hit shows was the primary source of profitability.

Networked television creates a bridge with new media. Enhanced connectivity made possible by convergence impacts upon the abovementioned model of television economics that was underpinned by agencies whose role was to deliver ratings numbers to television executives. The main change, however, is that the consumption of television is no longer tied to prime time. According to Holt and Sanson: "The extension of television entertainment content across screens and platforms, not to mention a socially networked viewership, has again altered textual practices and expanded the space and time devoted to television consumption" (Holt and Sanson 2014, 4). Echoing this transition Michael Curtin uses the term "matrix era" to describe a proliferation of "interactive exchanges, multiple sites of productivity, and diverse modes of interpretation and use" (2009, 13).

Television is more than ever about screens and users. Networked television includes businesses that own infrastructure that enables video content to be pushed from a single point to a large audience (Cunningham and Silver 2014). Multi-channel platforms are providing opportunities for aspiring producers, hopeful of making their ideas accessible to different audiences. Broadband Internet and digital television are widespread as is Internet Protocol Television (IPTV), which allows access to television services via the Internet. Moreover, the advent of digital television has spelt the end of the analog dinosaurs, or has at least disrupted their business models. Television producers have to attend to new challenges coming from "born-online" TV-like companies including YouTube/Google, Amazon, Apple TV and Yahoo. Cross-platform delivery strategies and online marketing have become imperative to the survival of commercial broadcasters.

In China where a large slate of programming is commissioned to please officials, usually historical serials and documentaries, the changes are significant. Despite the truism that television in China now looks a lot like television elsewhere, there is unprecedented change in the way that it is delivered to audiences, which in turn impacts on the commissioning of content. The rapid expansion of digital media is where we see the accelerated evolution of Chinese television. Digitization enables the fulfilment of numerous latent consumer needs in ways that the state-owned traditional media platforms could not offer. As a result, younger audiences who spend little or no time "watching the box" in the living room have adopted digital media.

According to a comparative study of several countries conducted in 2012, online content on TV is viewed most in China—possibly due to consumer interest in viewing foreign programs that may not be available via traditional TV platforms.[1] Evidently fewer people are viewing programs on set screens in their living rooms in "prime time." Data shows that 10.8 percent of persons born in the 1980s watch only television screens (Cui 2013, 304). Most viewers, except for those born in the 1950s and 1960s, are accessing content on TV-pads, iPads, smart phones, digital recording devices, and through computer terminals. Many Chinese are consuming television-like content at times that suit them rather than during scheduled broadcast times.

As audiences have become more fragmented and selective the Chinese television industry has had to reconsider its mode of operation. Format television has played a major role in changing the landscape, bringing international ideas and skills though the licensing of talent and reality shows (see Keane 2015 for a discussion). Format TV, with its penchant for mixing celebrity and "wanna-be celebrity" in turn offers tie-ins with the emerging online companies. The new players in the Chinese television market have names like Youku-Tudou, Sohu, Baidu, IQiYi, LeTV, BesTV, PPS and PPTV. While these names may be unfamiliar much of their content is produced in the same way that characterizes "old TV." As they evolve and stake out their positions traditional incumbents, media institutions, TV channels, production bases and studios are being impacted.

From regional networks to national distribution: the role of satellite TV

Before examining some of these players, it is worth outlining the landscape of the television industry in China. The principal "network" players in China are China Central Television (CCTV), provincial stations (e.g., Guangdong Television) and municipal stations (e.g., Guangzhou Television). The stations are nested within media groups or conglomerates that are intended to be the equivalent of large international players. Each province, and some of the large municipalities, has a media group made up of radio, television and print. Administratively and technologically provincial terrestrial television channels cannot operate at a national level. Indeed, their mandate is to broadcast to their own province and not beyond. Provincial terrestrial channels have seen their share of the television advertising market slipping slightly in recent years and this is related to the changes in satellite television competition. Each media group is allowed one satellite channel with national reach. The exception is Beijing where CCTV has 17 satellite channels and Beijing Television (BTV) two.[2]

Coincident with the conglomeration of networks in the late 1990s producers of television began to diversify by creating branded programs, later extending these to branded channels. The need for brands was an inevitable consequence of a glut of channels and an abundance of look-alike offerings. However, differentiation came up against the widespread practice of copycatting, that is, once a channel came up with something different it was only a matter of time before its competitors would clone their own "version." Because it takes a while for a brand program to establish itself in the market the practice of copycatting conspired against the development of new ideas.

However, despite the problem of duplication competition for hearts and minds among satellite channels inevitably led to brand differentiation. As Wanning Sun writes:

> Voting with their remote controls Chinese viewers may now go to Hunan Satellite TV for entertainment and fashion, Jiangsu Satellite TV for "touchy feely" programs (*qinggan Zhongguo*), Anhui Satellite TV (dubbed "China's mega supermarket for television serials") for dramas, Jiangxi Satellite TV for legends and folktales (*gushi Zhongguo*—narrative China), Hainan Satellite TV for tourism, and Chongqing Satellite TV for history and culture.

(2013, 15)

Another example of an innovative yet traditional approach is Henan Satellite Television. To establish its brand positioning among fellow provincial satellite stations, Henan Satellite TV adopted "culture" as its point of competitive advantage. In 2011 it came up with the slogan of "cultural TV: educate through entertainment" (*wenhuaweishi, yujiaoyu le*). This slogan obviously has appeal to China's regulators, echoing the logic of combining the educational function of TV as mass media, which has a long tradition in China, and the appeal of entertainment which is widely embraced by today's audiences. Since mid-2013, Henan TV has made a number of strategic moves around cultural positioning with the aim of "carrying forward civilization" (*chuancheng wenming*). It collaborated with the online video sharing platform iQiyi in launching a new program *Hero of Chinese Characters* (*hanzi yingxiong*), ostensibly with the aim of bringing people's attention back to the written language and the profound culture behind it in an era of typing and texting. Such positioning around Chinese culture has successfully differentiated the program from the glut of singing and dancing competitions currently on the small screen.

With contestants aged between seven and 17 years old, the program is an apparent attempt at attracting the youth market, a segment that had previously evaded Henan Satellite TV. Of course, the cultural positioning has an appeal to parents concerned with the "excessive entertainment" on screen in recent years. The inter-generational interaction is demonstrated during production, where cameras target parents backstage or in the audience, nervously watching the game or enthusiastically showing their support for the contestants. At the press conference for the launch of the program, when asked the difference between *Hero of Chinese Characters* and *The Dictionary of Happiness (kaixin cidian)* and *A Special Six-Plus-One-Day Performance (feichang liu jiayi)*, two similar Q&A reality game shows broadcast on CCTV, producer Ma Dong explained the main purpose of *Hero of Chinese Characters* is to tap into youth potential and build a platform for parent–child interaction.

Apart from leading the production team, Ma hosts the program. Significantly, he became the chief content officer of iQiyi after quitting his previous role at CCTV as a program host. Such boundary-crossing experience suggests that Ma has insights into both "traditional" TV market and the new frontiers of online screen culture.

The collaboration affords a multiple-screen experience for the audience. After screening on Henan Satellite TV, each episode is distributed on iQiyi, the exclusive online platform for the program with a "window" of about 1.5 hours. iQiyi also supports viewing on mobile devices. Audiences can view various versions: outtakes, uncut versions and mini versions on online and mobile devices. These features allow young people to watch the content of their choice at their own pace and at a time and place of their convenience. In a mobile application launched in association with the program, players can play the game by writing characters based on the questions on the handwriting panel. They can also use the mobile app to interact with the program at the time of broadcasting. Like a lot of game shows there is a competitive element. The top-ranking player emerging from the mobile platform has an opportunity to compete with players on TV for the championship (*zhuangyuan*). The app had received 1.2 million downloads by the end of the first season ('Final of *Hanzi yingxiong*' 2013). Such dynamics between TV and online platforms appeal particularly to young people, who are on their mobile devices almost all the time.

Apart from the non-linear multiple screen experience, the use of cultural celebrities also helps to attract the youth market. Three cultural celebrities joined Ma as the panel of guests, including Yu Dan, a scholar and professor at Beijing Normal University, well known for her populist explanations of the ancient texts of Confucius and Zhuangzi; Gao Xiaosong, a musician and pop icon; and Zhang Yiwu, a professor of Chinese language at Peking University and well-known cultural critic.

Overall, the cultural positioning, the intergenerational twist, the non-linear multiple-screen experience and the use of cultural celebrities have contributed to positive audience reception. The success of the first season of *Hero of Chinese Characters* is demonstrated in ratings, taking third place in nationwide ratings, second only to the *Voice of China (Zhongguo haoshengyin)* and *Happy Boy (kuaile nansheng)*, two immensely popular singing competitions launched by Zhejiang Satellite TV and Hunan Satellite TV respectively ('*Hanzi yingxiong*' 2013).

The success of *Hero of Chinese Characters* has led Henan Satellite TV to launch a sister program *Hero of Chinese Idioms (chengyu yingxiong)*. It has replicated the strategy of using cultural celebrities and facilitating multiple-screen experience through mobile games to attract a young audience. The "you draw, I guess" format of the competition involves teams of two people, three cultural experts as the panel of guests and the former CCTV talk show host Cui Yongyuan who hosts the program. Among the panel of experts is the Taiwanese cartoonist and winner of Taiwan's

Golden Comic Award Tsai Chih-chung, who is well known for popularising the works of Chinese ancient philosophers including *Laozi*, *Liezi* and *Zhuangzi* through use of plain language and humorous cartoons. In the program, Tsai provides advice to contestants on how to use drawings of Chinese traditional culture that can be embedded in the idioms. The appearance of the Taiwanese Tsai in the program can be seen as a footnote to the creative migration of East Asian cultural celebrities to "play to the world's biggest audience" (Curtin 2007).

The collaboration between Henan Satellite TV and iQiyi is a step beyond the usual copyright transaction model observed between TV stations and online video platforms whereby the latter purchases ready-made content from the former. It involves an equal share of investment by each party in addition to co-design and co-production. For iQiyi the collaboration with a TV station is a move to enhance its in-house production strategy, a response to the copyright war waged among online video platforms and a demonstration of its ambition to become a content provider (Zhao and Keane 2013; Zhao 2014). For Henan Satellite TV, the collaboration with the new-generation screen platform assists it in winning over young audiences by appealing to their viewing habits.

BesTV

Whereas the cultural brand positioning is a response to competition among satellite channels, IPTV has followed a different development path. Satellite channels are accessible in a number of ways, primarily as part of a cable TV package. IPTV is contingent on bandwidth and is therefore more local. Whereas conventional television is not affected by how many people are watching, IPTV (user) experience suffers when a large number of people are collecting their packages of information at the same time. This technical bottleneck means that people who can afford faster broadband are the consumer base. IPTV trials began in 2005, concurrent with digital television and the players in the market were China Telecom and China Netcom.

While telecoms fall under the regulatory control of the MIIT, licenses to produce and distribute television-like content come from the State Administration of Press, Publication, Radio, Film and Television (SAPPRFT), which is a result of the merger between the State Administration of Radio Film and Television (SARFT) and the General Administration of Press and Publication in March 2013. The frontrunner in IPTV was the Shanghai Media Group (SMG). Soon after it received its IPTV license from SARFT it spun off one of its production units into two companies, BesTV, now the leading provider of IPTV in China, and the Shanghai Film Radio and Television Production Ltd (FRTP), which produces event television and provides sets for reality TV shows such as *The Voice of China* (*Zhongguo haoshengyin*).

BesTV has a high profile among the new online media companies that are usurping the dominance of the traditional broadcasters. Its slogan is "from watching TV to using TV."[3] The IPO listed company behind this initiative is BesTV New Media Company Ltd, which also has interests in mobile television, smart television, online video, broadcasting integration, as well as movie, television and multimedia production. Like a number of other new entrants it has established relationships with hardware companies, in this case the Chinese computer giant Lenovo. The expansion into smart TV and cloud TV are strategies to monetize "over-the-top" (OTT) content.[4] BesTV offers a range of options for consumers willing to pay, from High Definition Digital TV with a buffet of premium content such as the US National Basketball Association (NBA) and the English Premier League (EPL) without advertising, to Standard Definition Digital services with advertising. In hoping to migrate some of its customers from IPTV to OTT, the company offers a smart TV with both functions. Other dedicated services include apps through which viewers can customize their viewing, allowing family members to simultaneously access programs on tablets and mobile devices, and local community television channels that allow people in the community to receive medical and social security information.

Hunan Satellite TV and Mango TV

If BesTV represents the broadband enabled technological interface, Hunan Satellite TV (HSTV) is a case of a traditional broadcaster trying to commercialize its brand in the face of competition from born-online video companies. Hunan Satellite TV is the most well-known entity in the Hunan Broadcasting System: it is also the most successful satellite channel in the Mainland. Established in 1997, it was the first satellite channel to realize the potential of branding, establishing an image of a youth-oriented network willing to try out ideas, even if this meant plundering them from abroad. As the strongest provincial competitor to CCTV, HSTV has often come under attack from Beijing's regulators for its transgressions, namely appealing to youth audiences in a language and style that is notably different from CCTV.

In an interview in 2010, CEO Ouyang Changlin elaborated on the HSTV brand vision, "Our program strategy is grounded on the 'three locks': locking in entertainment, locking in youth, and locking in a national market" (cited in Zhu 2013, 205–206). A key issue, according to Ouyang, is copyright protection. HSTV's own popular programs had fallen victim to copyright violation, the most conspicuous case being Jiangsu Satellite TV's *If You Are the One* (*feicheng wurao*), a copy of the format that HSTV acquired from Fremantle Media. HSTV's most well-known talent show, *Supergirls* (*chaoji nüsheng*), itself a clone of *American Idol*, was cloned by Shanghai's Dragon TV as *My Hero* (*jia you! haonaner*).

Aware of people's changing viewing habits, HSTV has moved to extract more value from its hit shows by embracing new delivery platforms. As early as 2006 Hunan Happy Sunshine Interactive Entertainment Media Co., Ltd (hereafter referred to as Happy Sunshine) was established as a subsidiary of HSTV with the mission of developing value-added new businesses in digital media. According to Vice-President of Happy Sunshine, Yi Keming, the focus is on developing multiple modes of content delivery through new media. As he explained, the new media platforms under the parent company have more resources compared with independent online video platforms, which means there is no need to explore new forms of businesses from the ground up (Yi 2014). As CEO Ouyang Changlin pointed out in an interview, despite the vicissitudes of working in an uncertain media environment, content is still king: "Content innovation is the only way for HSTV to maintain its edge" (in Zhu 2013, 205–206).

The new media strategy includes an online video platform www.hunantv.com and Internet TV, branded as Mango TV under HBS. Following the logic of building its own platforms by leveraging its premium content, Hunan Satellite TV started broadcasting its hit entertainment shows exclusively on www.hunantv.com and stopped licensing copyrights to other online video websites. These hit shows include *Divas Hit the Road* (*huaer yu shaonian*), *X-change* (*bianxingji*) (Season 8), and *Song of Vengeance* (*changzhanji*). Although the television station had previously received a US$32 (RMB 200) million licensing fee from iQiyi for five of its popular shows (Yi 2014), the management is confident that advertising revenue and subscription fees from users of their own platform will surpass the revenue loss in copyright licensing (Yi 2014).

The strategy of maintaining exclusive rights resulted in a spike in the number of daily unique visitors to Hunan TV's online platform. According to Helen Huang, Happy Sunshine Brand Centre Director, the figure jumped from around 300,000 to a peak of ten million within two months, with a daily average stabilizing at around eight million users (Huang 2014). Originally a target for the end of 2014, the threshold of ten million was crossed half a year in advance. This spike is a vindication that exclusive rights to quality content can strengthen the potency and brand of a platform, at least for the moment. Although a latecomer to the battlefield of online video distribution, HSTV is quickly catching up.

That being said, the strategy of maintaining exclusive rights is still in its early days. The question remains: will this be a sustainable approach for HSTV claw to back its audience from other online video sites? Whether or not a few hit shows can continue to support the growth of the online platform remains to be seen. The drawing power of these programs has so far resulted in a significant increase in users within a short period of time. Continued production of top quality content will be a key condition for this trend to last. Echoing Ouyang Changlin, content is still king. Despite this truism, user experience is the other half of the success equation. Given its target users have already been watching videos on other online video sites for years, Hunan TV needs to deliver at least acceptable user experience on its own site to maintain its newly gained users. So far this has proved a challenge. An example of the task at hand is the Mango TV mobile app. Current versions of the app received only a two-star rating from users. A review of the comments left by users at the app store shows many complaints on issues including frequent pauses, stutters and image quality. It is worth noting that Happy Sunshine has worked on these issues and things have improved significantly after adopting the strategy of maintaining exclusive rights to its original programs. Obviously, the new media arm of HSTV understands the significance of user experience in maintaining users.

Apart from developing HSTV's own online video platform, Happy Sunshine is advancing its options in the Internet TV business. In collaboration with television manufacturers such as Samsung, Changhong and TCL, it delivers television services on smart TVs with built-in set-top boxes. The partnership with set-top box manufacturers brings over-the-top content to audiences. Television content comes from channels under CCTV, provincial TV stations, and local TV channels under Hunan Broadcasting as well as other genre-specific channels such as cartoons and educational content. Apart from close-to-live broadcasting with a window of 30 minutes, time-shifting features allow users to catch up with the content they have missed. Audiences can also review programs broadcast within the last seven days, on-demand. In addition, the service provides access to a library of around 2000 films.

Conclusion

In this chapter we have provided an overview of changes in the way television is produced, distributed and consumed in China. The Chinese television landscape now looks very different to how it did just a decade ago. However, the rate of change since the mid-2000s has been frenetic and new players are changing the structure of the industry, adding to profitability while at the same time drawing advertising income away from traditional channels. The dominance of traditional networks is challenged by the entry of "networked" online companies not tied to geographical administrative boundaries. These have the advantage of knowing their audience more deeply through the exploitation of big data.

Traditional channels and networks like Henan Satellite TV and Hunan Satellite TV are now impelled to consider online strategies, which entail partnering with new media players in rights acquisition, distribution and production. The entry of IPTV and OTT services further extends the need to acquire new forms of branded content that are amenable to delivery on the devices and networks that now underpin the communication system. Strategic alliances have been brought about by the necessity to comply with international intellectual property frameworks. The willingness of the state to validate these alliances is in stark distinction to the administrative boundaries that were imposed on traditional media. Thanks to the expansion of these alternative platforms for accessing, viewing and interacting with content, the boundaries have blurred between traditional and new media, in turn changing the experience of watching television. This is TV but not as we used to know it.

Notes

1 See PR Web Consumers Viewing More Online Video Content on TVs, NPD DisplaySearch Reports. Available at: http://www.prweb.com/releases/NPD/DisplaySearch/prweb9829010.htm (Accessed April 4, 2014).
2 Being the national broadcaster CCTV's channels are accessible nationwide. In addition it operates international language channels.
3 http://www.bestv.com.cn/en/
4 OTT refers to delivery of video, audio and other media over the Internet without a multiple system operator being involved in the control or distribution of the content. See http://en.wikipedia.org/wiki/Over-the-top_content

References

Cui, B. (2013) *Report on Development of China's Media Industries (chuanmei chanye fazhan baogao)*, Beijing: Social Sciences Academic Press.
Cunningham, S. and Silver, J. (2014) *Screen Distribution and the New King Kings of the Online World*, New York: Palgrave Macmillan.
Curtin, M. (2007) *Playing to the World's Biggest Audience: The Globalization of Chinese Film and TV*, Berkeley and Los Angeles: University of California Press.
Curtin, M. (2009) 'Matrix media'. In Graeme Turner and Jinna Tay (eds) *Television Studies After TV*, London: Routledge.
'*Hanzi yingxiong* breaks its ratings record, second only to *the Voice of China* and Happy Boy' (2013) *Chinadaily. com*. Available at: http://www.chinadaily.com.cn/micro-reading/dzh/2013-08-22/content_9931756.html (Accessed July 18, 2014).
'Final of *Hanzi yingxiong* draws near with the mobile app receiving 1.2 million downloads' (2013) *Sohu.com*. Available at: http://roll.sohu.com/20130830/n385454924.shtml (Accessed July 18, 2014).
Holt, J. and Sanson, K. (2014) 'Introduction: getting connected'. In Jennifer Holt and Kevin Sanson (eds) *Connected Viewing: Selling, Sharing and Streaming Media in the Digital Era*, London: Routledge.
Huang, H. (2014) Interview with Happy Sunshine Brand Centre Director, Hunan Broadcasting, Changsha, July 1, 2014.
Huang, Y. (1994) 'Peaceful evolution: the case of television reform in post-Mao China', *Media, Culture and Society*, 16(2): 217–241
Keane, M. (2013) *Creative Industries in China: Art, Design, Media*, London: Polity.
Keane, M. (2015) *The Chinese Television Industry*, London: BFI Palgrave.
McLuhan, M. (1967) *The Medium is the Message*, London: Allen Lane.
Sun, W. (2013) 'Localizing Chinese media'. In Wanning Sun and Jenny Chio (eds) *Mapping Chinese Media*, London: Routledge.
Yi, K. (2014) Interview with Vice-President of Hunan Happy Sunshine, Hunan Broadcasting, Changsha, July 1, 2014.
Zhao, E.J. (2014) 'The micro-movie wave in a globalising China: Adaptation, formalisation and commercialisation', *International Journal of Cultural Studies*, 17(5): 453–467.
Zhao, E.J. and Keane, M. (2013) 'Between formal and informal: the shakeout in China's online video industry', *Media, Culture & Society*, 3(6): 724–741.
Zhu, Y. (2013) *Two Billion Eyes: The Story of CCTV*, New York: The Free Press.

27

New media in Singapore's creative economy: the regulation of illiberal pragmatism

Audrey Yue

The transformation of Singapore as a creative economy in the last fifteen years or so has been enabled by key transformations in the new media landscape. This chapter examines these policy developments and regulations over new media in general, and on television and the Internet in particular. By critically mapping its new media ecology across its creative economy, this chapter has two aims: first, to elucidate the innovations of its new media developments that have earned the city-state the reputation as the world's first cyber-city; second, to demonstrate its distinct mode of regulation through the practice of illiberal pragmatism. Illiberal pragmatism describes the regulatory milieu where new media decentralization and control have occurred concurrently; it is marked by an ambivalent governmental logic of liberalism and non-liberalism; and undergirded by a pragmatism that forms the commonsense ideology of the state's performance principle.

This chapter argues that illiberal pragmatism characterizes Singapore's new media ecology where informational openness is encouraged at the same time that media surveillance has become more pervasive, and where rational judgments about media economics and technological developments are almost always accompanied by an inconsistent and irrational reasoning of state authoritarianism. While illiberal pragmatism has produced a self-regulating and compliant society, it has also created new media ecologies of dissent and alternative self-biographies.

The crucial context in the 1990s

It is important first to situate the economic, political, technological and regulatory conditions of the decade in the 1990s leading up to the implementation of the country's creative industrial development strategy in 2002. During this period, Singapore experienced accelerated economic growth and cemented its status as a leading "Asian tiger economy" alongside Hong Kong, Taiwan and South Korea. The phrase "Asian tiger economy" refers to countries in the Asian region that had achieved exceptionally high annual growth rates of more than 7 percent. Buoyed by the transition from a manufacturing base to a regional hub for financial and high technology industries, Singapore returned an average annual growth of 8 percent between 1989 and 1997 (World Bank 2014). When the Asian financial crisis crippled the region in 1997, Singapore experienced in the following year, for the first time since its postcolonial independence in 1966, negative growth

(−2.2 percent GDP growth) (World Bank 2014). While countries like South Korea rebuilt their economies through developing an urban cyber-ecology (Townsend 2007), Singapore embarked on a creative economic plan.

This period also saw the political rule of Goh Chok Tong who was selected as Prime Minister by his own political party, the People's Action Party (PAP) when Lee Kuan Yew retired in 1990. Goh's tenure between 1991 and 2004 was marked by his open and consultative leadership, and saw Singapore become a more tolerant and liberal country where bohemian enclaves and gay nightlife thrived (see e.g., Yue 2012a). These transformations in economy and culture were also aided by an "Intelligent Island" strategy that was already starting to be put in place in the 1980s.

The "Intelligent Island" strategy aimed to transform Singapore into an information society where pervasive computing infused all aspects of society, from work to schools and at home. Comprising three stages, it sought to build a national information infrastructure, create a population who would use the technology and encourage a local IT industry (Lam 1999). The first stage, the Civil Service Computerization Plan (1981–1985), computerized its public service bureaucracy through networking the infrastructure, developing the capacity for the local IT industry and re-skilling the civil service. The second stage, the National IT Plan (1986–1991), introduced electronic data change between government and industry to facilitate online resource sharing and enhance business efficiency. The third stage, the IT 2000 Masterplan (1992–1999), built the world's first nationwide broadband network that covered 99 percent of schools, homes, offices and public access areas. These developments informatized the country through key growth areas in broadband, wireless and e-commerce, and earned Singapore the reputation as the world's first cyber-city. By 2000, Singapore was one of the top ten most technologically ready and competitive countries in the world (WEF 2000).

Significant here is how the apparent decentralization of information has occurred concurrently with the rise of Internet censorship. In 1996, Singapore became the first country in the world to introduce Internet content regulation. Internet service providers were required to channel all traffic to proxy servers to allow the government to filter or block "prohibited materials." According to its Internet Code of Practice, prohibited material includes: "material that is objectionable on the grounds of public interest, public morality, public order, public security, national harmony, or is otherwise prohibited by applicable Singapore laws" (MDA 2014, 2). The government committed to this law by applying a "light touch" approach. The phrase refers to how the government would: (a) be flexible in applying its law to ensure minimum standards are set for responsible use while offering flexibility for industry innovation; and (b) not censor all sites containing prohibited material but limit itself to a symbolic list of 100 websites in order to safeguard what it deems as society's norms and values. In addition to controlling content, Internet regulation also focused on industry self-regulation and the promotion of media literacy through public education.

The "Intelligent Island" strategy generated scholarly critiques on the contradictory nature of its informational expansion and control. Singapore journalist and media scholar Cherian George (2009) shows how the "light touch" approach is a practice of calibrated coercion that enables the authoritarian government to consolidate its power and rule through strategic self-restraint. According to Asian studies academic Garry Rodan (1998), this form of media control has allowed the government to become more authoritarian through more surveillance. Elaborating the effects of surveillance, media and cultural studies scholar Terence Lee suggests Internet surveillance has created a more self-regulating society (Lee 2001). The engineering of such a compliant society has also prompted others like Chun Wei Choo (1997), an information management scientist, to propose complementing informational intelligence with social intelligence through the development of attitudes, values and social relations so that a community can also build a community of practice that has the agility and capacity to sustain Singapore's competitive advantage. Common to these critiques is how Internet censorship in particular, and new media policies and its program implementations in general, have resulted in a distinct mode of regulation. Oscillating between information control and freedom, this mode of regulation is understood as the illiberal pragmatics of governance (Yue 2011, 2012a, 2012b, 2012c). This process refers to how, in the pragmatic desire to achieve and maintain its performance principle (Chua 2003), the logic and legitimacy of governmental control is concurrently liberal and non-liberal, and rational and irrational. This is evident is all aspects of public and private life, such as, as will be detailed later, across the gay Singapore Internet subculture, where, on the one hand, homosexuality is illegal and homosexual content prohibited, and on the other hand, a gay portal like Fridae.com has flourished to become the regional electronic gateway to gay and lesbian activities in Asia, and one of the most successful and stickiest business websites in Singapore (Yue 2012d).

These economic, political, technological and regulatory factors inform the development and implementation of new media that has flourished with the introduction of the creative industrial development strategy.

New media in the Creative Industry Development Strategy (2002–present)

In 2002, Singapore introduced the Creative Industries Development Strategy (CIDS) (MDA 2002), the first of its kind in Asia, and one of the earliest in the world. Creative industries merge culture and business as a service, usually through technological innovation, as a way to ensure a country's competitive edge within a rapidly integrating global economy. Defining "creative industries" as "those industries which have their origin in individual creativity, skill and talent and which have a potential for wealth and job creation through the generation and exploitation of intellectual property" (MDA 2002: 2), the CIDS aimed to transform a predominantly information-led society into a knowledge creation economy. Following the British model (DCMS 2001), it classified the creative industries into fifteen sectors, under three broad headings of arts and culture, design, and media, and identified detailed institutional and structural reforms in these three domains. In 2002, the creative economy comprised 3.2 percent of the GDP, with a growth rate of 8 percent and employed 4.3 percent of the workforce. This economy has since thrived and a decade later, commanded an annual government budget of S$365 million (MCCY 2012, 89).

Singapore's success has followed the innovation model where the significance is not much in terms of its relative contribution to economic value, but in new ideas or technologies, such as "industrial entrepreneurship operating on the consumer side of the economy" (Potts and Cunningham 2008, 239). Evident through the branding of the city-state (Singapore as New Asia) (Birch 2008; Ooi 2008; Yue 2006) and the development of creative clusters (Boorntharm 2012; Kong 2012), industrial and entrepreneurial innovations to date include the expansion of arts and culture, heritage tourism and the rise of the digital media industry. The building of spectacular monuments such as Theatres on the Bay and the Asian Civilisations Museum, and the wooing of big players in the animation and gaming industries such as the Hollywood-based Lucas Studio and Japanese video game developer Koei Entertainment, for example, are promoted through the appeal of consumerism, with the former creating new spaces of entertainment and the latter bringing its glamorous association with Hollywood to value-add to the newly revitalized city.

Singapore's import of the British model has not gone unnoticed. Landry has noted that the country is better at building the containers for such an economy rather than the content needed to sustain it (Landry 2006, 360). Local critics have also questioned whether creativity can really be nurtured in an authoritarian nation-state (Gwee 2009; Lee 2010; Ramcharan 2006) and criticized the high import of and reliance on foreign talent to create such an economy (Himanen et al. 2011). Whether transplanting "Xerox" policies (a term coined to describe the wholesale copying of the British model) (Pratt 2009) or catching up with the West (Yue 2012b), new media developments are central to the CIDS.

In general, the term "new media" refers to a wide range of digital technologies including cable and satellite television, the cinematic use of special effects, new delivery and display formats, mobile telephony and the Internet. For the CIDS in particular, new media developments are most evident through the industry convergent strategies of its media plans.

The Media 21 plan was the media blueprint for the CIDS. The blueprint established a new statutory agency (Media Development Authority, MDA) formed through the merger of the Singapore Broadcasting Authority, the Films and Publications Department, and the Singapore Film Commission. This merger of regulatory bodies was a response to industry convergence (The Straits Times 2002). MDA oversaw the blueprint's integration into other sectors like information technology and telecommunications development (Infocomm Development Authority of Singapore), trade (International Enterprise Singapore) and industrial infrastructure (Jurong Town Corporation). This whole-of-government approach ensured the sector not only delivered content and hardware, but also increased capacity for its proposed media hub through place making. Its strategies included developing a media cluster (Mediapolis@One-North), positioning Singapore as a place of media exchange and exporting "made-by-Singapore" content. By 2006, the sector earned S$19.5 billion, value-added S$5 billion to the economy, and employed 54,700 workers (MDA 2009, 8).

In 2009, Singapore released an upgraded media strategy, Singapore Media Fusion Plan (SMFP) (MDA 2009). Against the backdrop of the Web 2.0 revolution and rise of Asia (and its media), SMFP continued to consolidate Singapore as a global media city and position the country as a leader in digital media innovation. These included not only making Singapore a center for media business and finance, increasing its critical mass of media talent and building competencies for local media entrepreneurs and world-class infrastructure (MDA 2009, 23), but also incubating research and development to create new value chains in the digital media market. Added to this was also an emphasis on local content development that would tell local stories to engage its own local audience. These strategies supported the SMFP's slogan that situated Singapore as a "Trusted Global Capital for New Asia Media" (MDA 2009, 31).

The following illustrates these practices of media convergence using selected examples across television and the Internet. The aim is to elucidate the illiberal pragmatics of new media regulation. The developments of cross-platform and digital television are critically examined to show how they have created Singapore as a regional media hub and global media city through state-affirming practices that re-regulate the nation-state. The queer blogosphere is also critically examined to show how the Internet has created avenues for participatory voices in spite of the high degree of state regulation.

Television and re-regulation[1]

Television in Singapore is state-controlled despite its mix of public service and pay-TV broadcasting. Its monopoly industry is helmed by Media Corporation Singapore (MediaCorp), which is in charge of the programming for free-to-air public broadcasting while government-linked companies such as StarHub and Singtel provide subscription cable television services. Under the strategic direction of Media 21 and SMFP, television's most significant convergent practices are its technological development of cross-platform and digital television, and institutional collaborations that have earned the country its status as a regional media hub and global media city.

Singapore, eager to maintain its high-ranking world competitiveness reputation, was an early adopter of technological innovation. Even before the 2002 introduction of the CIDS, television has already tapped into its mobile audience market. TVMobile, Singapore's first outdoor digital television channel, was launched in 2001. The first to use Digital Video Broadcast (DVB) technology, it was made available across public transport, academic institutions, shopping malls and food courts. By the time it stopped operating in 2010, Singapore's television landscape had been radically transformed by the developments of cross-platform and digital television.

The mid-2000s were a landmark period for its new mediascape. In 2006, Singapore announced its HDTV trial in a partnership worth S$25 million with Rainbow Media, a subsidiary of Cablevision that owned Voom HD Networks, a suite of twenty-one HDTV television channels. The network was the largest of its kind and the content was produced in high definition (PR Newswire Europe 2005). That same year, MediaCorp also debuted Asia's first-of-its-kind Chinese 3G mobile drama at the Shanghai Television Festival (Channel NewsAsia 2005). By 2007, a two-tier license framework to facilitate the growth of IPTV (Internet Protocol Television) services in the country was established by the MDA (Chia 2007).

Unlike the tight control of broadcasting content, the Class License (or the light touch approach, as elaborated above) is for regulating decentralized, or open architecture services like mobile television platform that can play 3G videos, mobile broadcasting content, and even multimedia broadcasting and multicast services. By 2009, the mobile penetration rate was 136 percent, with subscription of 6.58 million (IDA 2009). In 2012, a national transition to digital TV was announced with the conversion completed by the end of 2013, ahead of the ASEAN analog switch-off time frame of 2020 (Tham 2012). This was aided by the upgrading of the nation-wide broadband network to the all-fibre optical high-speed and pervasive Next Generation National Broadband Network (Next Gen NBN) (capable of delivering speeds of 1Gbps and above) which was completed that same year, and accessible across all homes, schools and offices (IDA 2014). Rather than succumb to globalization's ubiquitous propensity to homogenize content and audiences, Singapore has harnessed its unique geographical location to create new local markets—markets hungry for new media content and services—and foster regional benchmarks, as evident in its institutional transformations.

By 2009, Singapore has become the home to the top fifteen major international and satellite broadcast networks and achieved the reputation as the "broadcast hub of Asia" (MDA 2009: 9). As the regional nexus for television content production, aggregation, distribution and broadcasting, it has collaborated with international media companies to create innovative content in the genres of children's animations (*Dinosaur Train*; *Dream Defenders*), drama (*Stormworld*; *House of Harmony*), lifestyle (*Kungfu Kitchen*; *Kylie Kwong: My China*) and documentaries (*Sumatra's Last Tigers*; *Culinary Asia*), and these are distributed globally across diverse channels in North America, Europe and Asia. When Mediapolis@One North opens in 2015, it will be a 1.5 hectare site which will house MediaCorp in an ecology also comprising "incubators, R&D activities, content development, digital production, broadcasting, industry-responsive education, intellectual property and digital rights management," as well as "shared facilities such as sound stages, advanced digital screen studios, sound recording studios and motion-capture studios" (JTC 2014: n.p.). Institutional transformations have clearly led to new creative and economic capacities as a result of spatial clustering.

Since Porter's (1990) seminal study on how the spatial agglomeration of business clusters can achieve economic efficiency, cluster studies have developed to highlight the specificity of various forms and objectives, as well as intervene in the critique of business, culture, people and resource. The creative media cluster—such as Hollywood, Silicon Valley or the West Coast film cluster across Los Angeles and Vancouver—is, by far, the fastest spatial form that has arisen in recent decades. Defined as "a linked grouping of creative industries, firms or cultural activities which has a spatial concentration and significant growth potential" (Evans and Foord 2005, 26), the creative media cluster has emerged as part of city revitalization projects connecting cultural facilities to new forms of geographies, entrepreneurship, social inclusion and civic engagement. Spatial proximity is important for these clusters, especially small or micro businesses, such as craft or digital work, and those organized around short-term projects or flexible modes of labor. They have three benefits: first, reduce costs; second, increase the circulation of capital and information; and third, enhance sociality (Scott 2000). These benefits extend Porter's business cluster model, which has been criticized for ignoring non-economic and non-material factors, such as the spatial and local contexts of social networks and regulation that shape industries (Pratt 2004).

The development of Singapore as a regional media hub and global media city is driven by these principles; in particular, through how different organizations have come together via partnerships and collaborations to generate new innovation capabilities, such as the creation of new content; and co-location in the city-state, as well as in media precincts such as Mediapolis@ OneNorth, which has the potential for new economic capabilities. While no scholarship has examined the quality of sociality in Singapore's media cluster, it is significant to note that these developments are informed by the state's regulatory mode of illiberal pragmatism.

Existing scholarship on television studies in Singapore has noted the continued restrictive nature of the media despite the apparent expansion and deregulation of information brought about by the implementations of Media 21 and the SMFP. Wong (2001) shows how the media is characterized by "controlled commodification," a practice where the state continues to exert its influence over the media market place through sanctioning the commodification of images and content that reinforces its hegemonic norms and values. This is evident, for example, in Chua and Junaid's (2005) ethnographic analysis of television advertising. Examining the reception of McDonald's television advertisements by children between the ages of four to six in two schools, Chua and Junaid show how these ads not only commodify children's culture and reinforce gender stereotyping, but also promote idealized family values that resonate with the government's pro-family ideology.

Similarly, discussing the state of the public sphere, Birch and Phillips (2003) draw on policies on internal security and broadcasting to show how the government uses the media to "[extend] its power [by] censoring public opposition" (118). The public sphere, they contend, is tightly controlled, both in terms of programming content and through the self-regulation of broadcasters, and thus serves to promote the government's vision of the nation as a homogenous and unified community. Overall, this strand of scholarship reveals how the deregulation of television is not a process of decentralization and liberalization; rather a practice of re-regulation that exposes the tension between civic concerns of nation-building and citizen-making, and the participatory democracy of the civil society (Birch and Phillips 2003, 127).

In discussions on the regionalization and globalization of television industries, scholarship has steered the critique away from state paternalism to the status of Singapore as a media hub (Curtin 2007). Common to this strand of research is the repositioning of national culture, and the introduction of alternative approaches to understanding media imperialism. Lim (2003) examines the import of format television and explores how local knowledge articulates with global templates, giving rise to different strategies of format adaptation, customization and translation of global television formats. Her study focuses on three distinct segments of production, from industry and circulation to local consumption, and highlights how formatting has moved from carbon copying to customizing. It is through the latter, she argues, that shows, such as *Who Wants to be a Millionaire*, imbue the generic with the local through the promotion of shared cultural literacies. This process where the global is localized has been widely discussed through the concept of glocalization (Robertson 1992).

Further examining how Singapore's online communities respond to these game shows, Lim shows how their responses embrace nationalistic sentiments that add to the essence of a national culture. Crucial here is how the national is revealed as a site of racial contestation. One group of responses complains that by launching the Chinese-language version of the show, other non-Chinese language speaking groups (such as Malays and Tamils) are excluded. Another group, responding to the English-language version, lauded the program for not including Indian professionals or Causasians as these groups are stereotyped as better educated, have more competent English-language comprehension, and are deemed to have an advantage over other non-English speaking groups. At the heart of these glocalizing national sentiments is the dominance of Chinese racial hegemony and the way it continues to exclude other officially recognized multilingual groups, such Malays, Tamils and minority others such as Caucasians. By pacifying the Chinese majority, state media also controls the norm. Similarly, Chua (2012) investigates the circulation and reception of East Asian media culture in Singapore and shows how they contribute to the cultural base of national values, in particular, through the promotion of heterosexual family values and the use of the Mandarin language. The latter, he stresses, allows Singapore to support its local Chinese hegemony, as well as belong to a larger Sinophone market. While studies from Lim and Chua focus on television's domestic market, scholarship on television's export market has also stressed the importance of local specificity. The production of global television content, such as the documentaries and animations aforementioned, for example, has been criticized for its lack of local content (Chua 2004) despite the fact that such a trend has helped internationalize emerging talents like Fann Wong. Rather than media imperialism, the cultural flows identified in this strand of research on television industries evince the theses of localization and regionalization, not as forms of resistance to the national, but practices that sustain the nation.

Against the state-affirming tendencies critiqued in both strands of scholarship, it is not surprising thus that studies assessing the telecommunications industry have favored Singapore's planned model of media regulation despite tight content control. Comparing how Hong Kong (which is executive led and has a high freedom of information flow) and Singapore (which is authoritarian and has a high control of information flow) have responded to media convergence, Wu and Leung (2009) praise Singapore's planned economy in implementing reform as more suited to the growth of a progressive media ecology in terms of technological adoption and change.

The following discusses how the Internet has created avenues for queer participatory voices in spite of the high degree of new media regulation.

The LGBT Internet and transgender blogging

The introduction of the nation-wide broadband network has enabled gays, lesbians, and transsexuals (LGBT) in Singapore to go online to seek community support and participate in political activism. In a country where homosexuality is a crime under the Victorian Penal Code 377A, and Internet content subjected to censorship, LGBT groups have thrived online (Yue 2003), raising issues about human rights (Offord 2003a), the Internet's role in making present a conservative discourse of gay activism that fits the patriotic ideology of the nation-state (Tan 2007), and its status as an alternative public sphere for racialized sexual minorities (Philips 2012) as well as a medium for queer social entrepreneurship (Yue 2012a).

Social media has been central in galvanizing the support for the Repeal 377A Campaign (Nichols 2007), spreading the influence of the Pink Dot movement (Philips 2014), and creating the queer Singapore short film genre (Khoo 2014). These activities demonstrate how new media in general, and the Internet in particular, have created avenues for participatory voices in spite of the high degree of state regulation. As argued earlier, key to this is the regulatory mode of illiberal pragmatism. Rather than the re-regulating tendency discussed above about decentralized television's capacity for interpellating patriotic affirmation from the mainstream community, illiberal pragmatism has enabled sexual minorities to carve out new spaces and identities that work with and challenge state affirming discourses.

Elaborating the logic of illiberal pragmatism within the collective gay social movement in Singapore, lawyer and legal scholar Lynette Chua (2012) suggests the movement engage a strategy of "pragmatic resistance" (722). This involves a delicate balance between pushing boundaries and toeing the line, such as obeying the law, making use of legal restrictions, getting around these restrictions, downplaying confrontation and playing up accepted norms such as social stability (723). While Chua describes these tactics as part of the collective action of the gay social movement, its practices are also evident at an individual level, across embodied and everyday life. The online tool of blogging has allowed these tactics of illiberal pragmatism to be enacted precisely because of its personal, diary-like and episodic nature of disclosure and performance (Rettberg 2008). The following discusses one such example of transgender blogging.

Blogging, one of the earliest forms of social media, has been and continues to be highly popular in Singapore. Consider for example, Asia-Pacific's top blogger, Xiaxue, and the world's leading blog advertising company, Nuffnang. Both are direct beneficiaries of the "Intelligent Island" strategy, with the former a part of the digital native broadband generation and the latter an innovative start-up company that has flourished as a result of the boom in social media marketing. This is not surprising as Singapore has an active Internet population (75 percent of the population are active Internet users) (Rock Publicity 2012, 23). In 2012 social media penetration reached 68 percent, with 57 percent of the population reading and/or authoring blogs (Rock Publicity 2012, 21).

One such blogger is Ms Chor Lor (MCL) with her *Blog of a Singaporean Transgender* (2009).[2] The blog started in January 2009, and currently has about 428,814 hits. It is a highly regular blog, with about one to five postings a week. Categories include everyday topics such as "All About Dogs," "comics," "cool," "fiction," "food" and "funny," as well as more specific types relating to the broader discourses of homosexuality, such as "a gay story," "gays," "GLBT" (gay, lesbian, bisexual, transsexual), "lesbians," "health," "Singapore Gay Scene" and "transgender." Of significance here is the category of "A Transgender Story" (ATS), which is serialized into 102 posts. The author calls these posts "chapters," and publishes them at a rate ranging from once every two to three months, to two or three times a month. Each chapter generates between 100 and 1500 views, and attracts between one and ten comments. ATS, which began on March 3, 2009, is an account of the author's life story, from a male childhood, her awareness of her same-sex attracted sexuality, and her transition to a female adulthood.

ATS begins with an account of a working class childhood in one-room flat in a public housing estate. With a father in jail, and a mother working long hours as a hawker assistant, MCL recounts her filial duty (sibling care, cooking and washing) by juxtaposing these with friendships that developed into homosocial bonding and homosexual encounters. These encounters are introduced through a rite-of-passage discourse such as "crush," "first love," "first kiss," "first boyfriend," etc., as well as through a school–work transition, from primary to secondary school, first job, and so on. Replicating the life cycle, this serialized narrative, written in the voice of the first person, follows the structural motif of an autobiographical coming out transgender story.

Trans-femininity, defined as a hybrid of male femininity (Halberstam 1998), is acquired through denaturalizing normative masculinity and performing a femininity that can also be medically enhanced through surgical sexual reassignment. This is evident in ATS through practices of dress, deportment and breast augmentation. In the beginning, as the author comes to realize her same-sex attraction, she begins to reveal her desire for a less masculinized and more feminine body. Using words like "man enough" to describe the ideal masculinity of her boyfriend, she attributes a normative maleness to straight-acting homosexuality, which in turn, calibrates her femininity. As she befriends a group of transsexuals and transgender prostitutes in the northern seaside township of Changi Village, she begins to learn the codes of cross-dressing. When her borrowed dress from her mother is deemed too "aunty" by the group, she learns the finer details of generational femininity, and begins to cross-dress accordingly. She keeps her hair long, learns to put on make-up, and starts to assume the public identity of a woman in everyday life. Made easier by her job as a retail assistant in the fashion industry, these modes of embodiment attest to femininity as a performance that is socially constructed, quickly mimicked and promptly internalized. As she begins to medically transition using hormones, she also recounts how her breast implant surgery is funded by a man she met on the Internet, who wants nothing more than to go with her to Thailand and foot the medical bill. These practices of femininity, from the length of hair to the types of bra, suggest a normative deportment that is also transgressive.

Transgressive femininity is evident in her screen name, Ms Chor Lor. "Chor lor" is Hokkien for "rough" and "unrefined." This pseudonym connotes a femininity that is uncouth and crude. Indeed, she describes this hybrid sexuality as "She's a man. He's a woman." She also rides a bike, burps, talks loudly, eats with her mouth open, and does not wear a skirt and puts on little make-up. Unlike the idealized demure and porcelain Asian femininity of most Singaporean Chinese women, MCL transgresses these stereotypes by heightening the accepted and embodied frames of this femininity. Authenticity is authored into the blog with voice recordings of her drag song performance, and long-framed photos of her in various stages of transition.

In ATS, local spaces such as public housing estates, department stores, shopping malls and military training camps are recoded to fit the tactical cultivation of working class trans-femininity. The void decks and common staircases of public housing allowed MCL to avoid her family when she was growing up. During her time as a sex worker, they double as changing rooms so she can secretly dress up in fetish wear without alerting her family to her abjected profession. Writing of her job experiences at Sogo and Takashimaya department stores, and recounting her introduction to make-up and long hair as a cosmetic retail assistant, and especially how she performs a drag act for the opening of one of the stores, she twists these exemplary spaces of Singaporean modernity with self-styled expressions of trans-femininity. As an army clerk during the two-year compulsory military service, she imbues national masculinity with her hyperfemininity and recodes herself as a "queen" of the camps. Class, sexuality and modernity are embodied in these trans practices that permeate the spaces of everyday life. While subjective and personal, these practices appropriate the institutional and carve out a claim to citizenship based on spatial, cultural and gender rights that facilitate access to trans participation and representation.

In the chapters that chronicle the Changi Village transgender subculture, MCL describes Changi Village from the late 1980s to the late 1990s, and how it was like before and after the tourist development. Before development, the area was known as "Changi Point" by the transgender subculture. "Sistas," as they would call themselves, would rent weekend chalets and hang out together. MCL belonged to one of these sista groups. Their hang out place was a room above a seafood restaurant that was hired to them by the sympathetic owner. In this room, they would learn and perfect dress-ups before parading openly on the streets. They would also stay there and "chit-chat" through the night. Sometimes they also fished at the beach or ate together at the hawker center. Membership was hierarchical. A young cross-dresser would usually join the group from around the age of sixteen, where she would learn how to dress. Older ones would be in various stages of "upgrading," beginning with hormone pills. It was not uncommon for sistas to style and name themselves after Hong Kong and Chinese celebrities. A "mummy" was the most experienced sista, who would also protect them. According to MCL, Changi Point is a "stepping stone," from "andro dressers" to "part-time dressers" to "full-time women."

When Changi Point was redeveloped for domestic tourism, the precinct was renamed "Changi Village," acronymed by the sista culture as "CV." The seafood restaurant was demolished to make way for a bus interchange. As transgender prostitution grew with the increasing commercialization of the area, distinct sista cultures emerged around this interchange. Chinese sistas would ply the trade with Malay sistas, and both groups jostle for clients with those at the back of the interchange ("back sistas") and those at the front ("front sistas"). In the beginning, trade would be quiet on Saturdays and holidays, and the sistas would rest and go clubbing instead. By the time MCL began to work there full time as a sex worker in the mid 1990s, transgender subculture and prostitution had already grown to a daily phenomenon. Amongst the many types of clients encountered in the sex trade is the distinct "ah pong" type, named as such by the sistas to refer to a straight man with a transgender fetish.

While the blog narrates MCL's life biography as a transgender, it links these practices to a larger subterranean collective of transgender lifestyle and activism. Unlike the cool bohemia of gay Chinatown in Singapore consisting predominantly of circuit parties and saunas (see Yue 2012a), this scene is more subterranean and ephemeral. MCL's self-narration gives visibility and voice to a vibrant and established local Singaporean transgender subculture with a distinct place, style and identity. These practices also complement the official narratives of sexual reassignment that was introduced in Singapore's medical history in the 1970s to encourage gender normalization and create Singapore as the sexual reassignment surgery hub of the region. In place of state medical modernity, this transgender subculture reflects an alternative modernity that also arose as a result of cultural liberalism and domestic tourist developments. From clandestine practices and police escapades, to an informal transgender tourist destination, such a culture, although illegal, is unofficially tolerated. Like the cool bohemia of gay Chinatown, queers add diversity (à la Florida), and hence value, to a sleepy seaside resort town.

By linking the CV transgender subculture to other GLBT-related topics in other categories, MCL helps publicize community events such as Pink Dot and IndigNation, and even provides insights into the nuances of gay and lesbian scenes including linking to the sites of local gay activist, Alex Au and global lesbian icon, Jenny Shimizu. Her transgender sexuality is tied to an identity that consists of embodied femininity, as well as allegiance to local and global GLBT communities.

Armstrong (2004) uses the concept of a "subaltern counter public" to show how young feminists use the web "to build networks and create space to articulate their interests and experiences" (92), and argues such tactics constitute a "vernacular feminism" (94). Harcourt (2004) also points to how these platforms are used especially in contexts where women are denied other forms of political participation. Although MCL's blog demonstrates the oppositional discourse of a subaltern counter public, as well as expresses a vernacular trans-femininity, her practices do not challenge the status quo but are more related to the narrations of personal life experiences that underpin the individualization of life politics. In other words, rather than emancipatory politics that reflects the Western post-Stonewall liberationist discourse, MCL's blog shows transgender sexuality as a form of life politics that is part of the commodified discourse of lifestyle.

Powered by Nuffnang and Google, her blog page is surrounded by rows of advertising. Advertising is banner-style and confined to the side menu, and more geared towards the lifestyling of gender transition. Products available include online purchases for male-to-female hormones, voice coaching towards a more feminized voice, and even online psychologist clinics for the treatment of gender dysphoria. Dating links also proliferate on the site. These are ambiguously polysexual, from Asian singles looking for marriage, to heterosexual and gay personals.

Accompanying these are also travel, hotel, car and dining ads that are location-specific to the reader. Two modes of commodification are evident: first, the identity instruments that enable gender transitioning as a lifestyle, from body, voice to sex and relationships; second, the broader niche market of pink tourism that is targeted towards the general readership, identified through the side bar link to Clustrmap, which allows users to track visitor locations.

Outside of Singapore, which forms the majority of the readership, it is interesting to note that most readers come from the USA and Europe rather than the Asia-Pacific region. These advertising banners demonstrate the logic of illiberal pragmatism that not only surrounds new media but also sexual politics. While sexual reassignment and pink tourism are encouraged because they normalize gender identities and add to the income of the economy, transgender rights are invisible and homosexuality is illegal. For MCL, new transgender life politics do not challenge the status quo but are enabled by its queer complicity to the illiberal pragmatism of cultural liberalism that underpins the romance capitalism of the new creative economy.

Conclusion

This chapter has mobilized an interdisciplinary methodology to examine the new media ecologies that have proliferated in Singapore's thriving creative economy. It began by setting the economic, technological and political contexts of the 1990s that have led to the implementation of the creative economy in the early 2000s. In particular, it has shown how these developments have built an "Intelligent Island" infrastructure that is both emancipatory and regulatory. It introduced the concept of illiberal pragmatism as the distinct mode of new media regulation and showed how developments across television and the Internet are subjected to its concurrent and ambivalent forces of liberalism and non-liberalism.

Beginning with media policy and creative industrial analysis, this chapter examined the political economy of cross-platform and digital television, and showed how the new televisual mediascape is a site of nationalist re-regulation. Using discourse and queer subcultural analyses, it further examined the gay and lesbian Internet and showed how transgender blogging is an example where not only can minority participatory voices be heard in a state of high regulation, but these voices provide agency to construct new communities and life biographies that carefully work with and creatively resist heteronormative state ideologies.

Notes

1 An earlier version of this section appears in a longer essay (see Yue 2015, forthcoming).
2 A shorter and earlier version of this analysis appears in Yue 2012c.

References

Armstrong, J. (2004) 'Web Grrrls, Guerilla Tactics: Young Feminisms on the Web.' In D. Gauntlett and R. Horsley (eds) *Web Studies*, New York: Oxford University Press: 92–102.

Birch, D. and Phillips, M. (2003) 'Civic or Civil Contingencies?: Regulating Television and Society in Singapore'. In P. Kitley (ed.) *Television, Regulation and Civil Society in Asia*, London: RoutledgeCurzon, 115–130.

Birch, S. (2008) *The Political Promotion of the Experience Economy and Creative Industries: Cases from UK, New Zealand, Singapore, Norway, Sweden and Denmark*, Copenhagen: Imagine–Creative Industries Research, Copenhagen Business School.

Boontharm, D. (2012) 'The Idea of Creative Reuse Urbanism—The Roles of Local Creativities in Culturally Sustainable Place-making: Tokyo, Bangkok, Singapore'. In L. Hee, D. Boontharm and V. Erwin (eds) *Future Asian Space: Projecting the Urban Space of New East Asia*, Singapore: NUS Press: 73–87.

Channel NewsAsia (2005) '11 media companies to showcase 3G, HD content at Shanghai Television Festival', *Channel NewsAsia*, n.p.

Chia, C. (2007) 'Media mentor: Dr Christopher Chia, Chief Executive Officer, The Media Development Authority of Singapore (MDA) gives Television Asia an overview of media industry advancements in 2007', *Television Asia* 14(10), n.p.

Choo, C.W. (1997) 'IT2000: Singapore's Vision of an Intelligent Island'. In P. Droege (ed.) *Intelligent Environments: Spatial Aspects of the Information Revolution*, Amsterdam: North-Holland: 49–66.

Chua, B.H. (2003) *Life Is Not Complete without Shopping: Consumption Culture in Singapore*, Singapore: National University of Singapore Press.

Chua, B.H. (2004) 'Cultural Industry and the Next Phase of Economic Development of Singapore'. Paper presented at the Workshop on Port Cities and City-states in Asia, Europe, Asia-Africa Institute, University of Hamburg, Germany, November 4–7, 2004.

Chua, B.H. (2012) *Structure, Audience and Soft Power in East Asian Pop Culture*, Hong Kong: Hong Kong University Press.

Chua, L.J. (2012) 'Pragmatic resistance, law, and social movements in authoritarian states: The case of gay collective action in Singapore'. *Law and Society Review* 46: 713–748.

Chua, S.K. and Junaid, A. (2005) 'Hook' em Young: McAdvertising and Kids in Singapore'. In J. Erni and S.K. Chua (eds) *Asian Media Studies: Politics of Subjectivities*, Malden: Blackwell: 37–54.

Curtin, M. (2007) *Playing to the World's Biggest Audience: The Globalization of Chinese Film and TV*, Berkeley: University of California Press.

Department of Culture, Media and Sport (DCMS) (2001) *Creative Industries Mapping Document*, 2nd edn, London: Department of Culture, Media and Sport.

Evans, G. and Foord, J. (2005) *Strategies for Creative Spaces – Phase 1 Report*: Report Commissioned by London Development Agency – Creative London, City of Toronto, Ontario Ministry of Economic Development & Trade and Ministry of Culture.

George, C. (2009) 'Coercion Unmasked: The Counter-Hegemonic Impact of New Media Activism in Singapore'. Paper presented at the 2009 International Communication Association Annual Conference, Communication Law and Policy Division, May 23, 2009.

Gwee, J. (2009) 'Innovation and the creative industries cluster: A case study of Singapore's creative industries', *Innovation: Management Policy and Practice* 11(2): 240–252.

Halberstam, J. (1998) *Female Masculinity*, Durham, NC: Duke University Press.

Harcourt, W. (2004) 'World Wide Women and the Web'. In D. Gauntlett and R. Horsley (eds) *Web Studies*, New York: Oxford University Press: 243–253.

Himanen, P., Au A., and Margulies, P., (2011) 'The new incubators', *World Policy Journal* 28(3): 22–34.

Infocomm Development Authority of Singapore (IDA) (2009) *Statistics on Telecom Services*. Available at: http://www.ida.gov.sg/Publications/20061205165739.aspx (Accessed on December 12, 2009).

Infocomm Development Authority of Singapore (IDA) (2014) *Next Gen NBN*. Available at: http://www.ida.gov.sg/Infocomm-Landscape/Infrastructure/Wired/Next-Gen-NBN (Accessed on September 1, 2014).

Jurong Town Corporation (JTC) (2014) *Mediapolis*. Available at: http://www.jtc.gov.sg/RealEstateSolutions/one-north/Pages/Mediapolis.aspx (Accessed on January 1, 2014).

Khoo, O. (2014) 'The minor transnationalism of queer Asian cinema: Female authorship and the short film format', *Camera Obscura* 85 29(1): 32–57.

Kong, L. (2012) 'Ambitions of a global city: arts, culture and creative economy in "Post-Crisis" Singapore', *International Journal of Cultural Policy* 18(3): 279–294.

Lam, C.L. (1999) 'From Intelligent Island to Global Infocomm Capital', *Infocomm Development Authority*. Available at: http://www.ida.gov.sg/~/media/Files/Archive/News%20and%20Events/News_and_Events_Level2/12164302/CIAPR_Keynote1.pdf (Accessed on September 1, 2014)

Landry C. (2006) *The Art of City Making*, London: Earthscan.

Lee, T. (2001) 'The politics of Internet policy and (auto-)regulation in Singapore', *Media International Australia, Incorporating Culture & Policy* 101: 33–42.

Lee, T. (2010) *The Media, Cultural Control and Government in Singapore*, Hoboken: Taylor & Francis.

Lim, T. (2003) 'Let the Contests Begin!: Singapore in the Global Television Format Business'. In A. Moran and M. Keane (eds) *Television Across Asia: Television Industries, Programme Formats and Globalization*, London: RoutledgeCurzon: 105–121.

Media Development Authority (MDA) (2002) *Creative Industries Development Strategy*, Singapore: Ministry of Trade and Industry.

Media Development Authority (MDA) (2009) *Singapore Media Fusion Plan*, Singapore: Department of Information, Communication and the Arts.

Media Development Authority (MDA) (2014) Available at: http://www.mda.gov.sg/RegulationsAndLicensing/ActsCodesOfPracticeAndGuidelines/Documents/Acts,%20Codes%20of%20Practice%20and%20Guidelines/PoliciesandContentGuidelines_Internet_InterneCodeOfPractice.pdf (Accessed on September 1, 2014).

Ministry of Culture, Community and Youth (MCCY) (2012) *Arts and Culture Strategic Review.* Available at: http://www.mof.gov.sg/budget_2013/revenue. . ./53%20MCCY%202013.pdf (Accessed on December 12, 2013).

Ms Chor Lor (2009) *Blog of a Singaporean Transgender.* Available at: http://mschorlor.com/ (Accessed on February 5, 2011).

Nichols, L. (2007) 'Singapore activists fight sodomy law', *Philadelphia Gay News* 31(41): 17.

Offord, B. (2003) 'Singaporean Queering of the Internet: Toward a New Form of Cultural Transmission of Rights Discourse'. In C. Berry, F. Martin and A. Yue (eds) *Mobile Cultures: New Media in Queer Asia*, Durham, NC: Duke University Press: 133–157.

Ooi, C.-S. (2008) 'Reimagining Singapore as a creative nation: The politics of place branding', *Place Branding & Public Diplomacy* 4(4): 287–302.

Philips, R. (2012) '"Singaporean by birth, Singaporean by faith": Queer Indians, 187 Internet Technology, and the Reconfiguration of Sexual and National Identity'. In A. Yue and J. Zubillaga-Pow (eds) *Queer Singapore: Illiberal Citizenship and Mediated Cultures*, Hong Kong: Hong Kong University Press: 187–196.

Phillips, R. (2014) '"And I am Also Gay": Illiberal Pragmatics, Neoliberal Homonormativity and LGBT Activism in Singapore', *Anthropologica,* 56(1): 45–54.

Porter, M. (1990) *The Competitive Advantage of Nations*, New York: Free Press.

Potts, J. and Cunningham, S., (2008) 'Four models of the creative industries', *International Journal of Cultural Policy* 14(3): 233–247.

Pratt, A. (2004) 'Creative clusters: Towards the governance of the creative industries production system?' *Media International Australia, Incorporating Culture & Policy* 112: 50–66.

Pratt, A. (2009) 'Policy Transfer and the Field of the Cultural and Creative Industries: What Can Be Learned from Europe?' In L. Kong and J. O'Connor (eds) *Creative Economies, Creative Cities: Asian-European Perspectives*, New York: Springer: 9–23.

PR Newswire Europe (2005) '$20 Million USD High-Definition Collaboration by Rainbow HD Holdings LLC, Mega Media Pte Ltd, and Singapore's Media Development Authority', *PR Newswire Europe*, n.p.

Ramcharan, R. (2006) 'Singapore's emerging knowledge economy: Role of intellectual property and its possible implications for Singaporean society', *Journal of World Intellectual Property* 9(3): 316–343.

Rettberg, J. (2008) *Blogging: Digital Media and Society*, Cambridge: Polity Press.

Robertson, R. (1992) *Globalization: Social Theory and Global Culture*, London: Sage.

Rock Publicity (2012) *The State of Social Media in Singapore: The 2012 Rock Publicity Singapore Social Media Study*, Brisbane: Rock Publicity.

Rodan, G. (1998) 'The Internet and political control in Singapore', *Political Science Quarterly* 113(1): 63–89.

Scott, A. J. (2000) *The Cultural Economy of Cities*, London: Sage.

Tan, K.P. (2007) 'Imagining the gay community in Singapore', *Critical Asian Studies* 39(2): 179–204.

Tham, I. (2012) 'TV to go digital next year; move paves way for viewers to get more high-definition and 3D content'. *The Straits Times* (Singapore), Singapore Press Holdings Limited, n.p.

The Straits Times (2002) 'Media competition code to be out by June; it will be enforced by a new statutory board which will ensure fair competition, regulate and develop the industry', *The Straits Times*, n.p.

Townsend, A. (2007) 'Seoul: birth of a broadband metropolis', *Environment and Planning B: Planning and Design* 34: 396–413.

Wong, K. (2001) *Media and Culture in Singapore: A Theory of Controlled Commodification*, Cresskill, NJ: Hampton Press.

World Bank (2014) *GDP Growth: Singapore.* Available at: http://data.worldbank.org/indicator/NY.GDP.MKTP.KD.ZG?page=2 (Accessed on September 1, 2014).

World Economic Forum (WEF) (2000) *The Global Competitiveness Report.* Available at: http://www.cid.harvard.edu/archive/res/gcr_2000_overview.pdf (Accessed on September 1, 2014).

Wu, R.W.S. and Leung, G.L.K. (2009) 'Hong Kong and Singapore: Two models of telecommunications regulations?' *Telematics and Informatics* 26(4): 322–332.

Yue, A. (2003) 'Paging "New Asia": Sambal is a Feedback Loop, Coconut is a Code, Rice is a System'. In C. Berry, F. Martin and A. Yue (eds) *Mobile Cultures: New Media in Queer Asia*, Durham, NC: Duke University Press: 245–266.

Yue, A. (2006) 'The regional culture of New Asia: Cultural governance and creative industries in Singapore', *International Journal of Cultural Policy* 12(1): 17–33.

Yue, A. (2011) 'Doing Cultural Citizenship in the Global Media Hub: Illiberal Pragmatics and Lesbian Consumption Practices in Singapore'. In R. Hegde (ed.) *Circuits of Visibility: Gender and Transnational Media Cultures*, New York: New York University Press: 250–267.

Yue, A. (2012a) 'Queer Singapore: A Critical Introduction'. In A. Yue and J. Zubillaga-Pow (eds) *Queer Singapore: Illiberal Citizenship and Mediated Cultures*, Hong Kong: Hong Kong University Press: 1–25.

Yue, A. (2012b) 'From Gatekeepers to Gateways: Pragmatism, Sexuality and Cultural Policy in Creative Singapore'. In M. Morris and M. Hjort (eds) *Instituting Cultural Studies: Creativity and Academic Activism*, Hong Kong: Hong Kong University Press: 191–212.

Yue, A. (2012c) 'Female Individualization and Illiberal Pragmatics: Blogging and New Life Politics in Singapore'. In Y. Kim (ed.) *Women and Media in Asia*, New York: Palgrave Macmillan: 237–254.

Yue, A. (2015, forthcoming) 'Film and Television in Singapore'. In T. Chong (ed) *A History of Cultural Policy in Singapore*, Singapore: Institute of Policy Studies.

28

Japanese creative industries in globalization

Shinji Oyama

In recent years, the creative industries have become an increasingly important concept in Japan. The focus of many debates is no longer exclusively on manufacturing and productivity, but has shifted to nurturing creativity and culture. Research around Japanese creative industries is growing—however most of them are focused on the popular, but niche, genre of *manga* and *anime*. Much of this research is concerned with so-called "Cool Japan," which is a discourse about the popularity of Japan's content—mostly *manga* and *anime*—in overseas market and a set of economic, political and diplomatic policy to capitalize on it (Daliot-Bul 2009; Condry 2009; Valaskivi 2013). Addressing limitations in existing literature, this chapter seeks to present a complex picture of Japanese creative industries. I will analyze how Japanese creative industries are organized and the uneven impact of globalization felt in different parts of the industries. This unevenness reveals tensions and complexities in Japanese creative industries that, in turn, reconfigure production paradigms.

Japanese creative industries

In Japan, the attention to creative industries is a response to opportunities and risks brought about by globalization. On the one hand, it is a response to the perceived opportunities opened up by media globalization, particularly the Internet, which has enabled Japanese content to penetrate, mostly un-monetized, even the remotest corner of the world at an even faster pace (e.g., Hye-Kyung 2009). On the other hand, fierce competition from other East Asian economies—China, Korea, and Taiwan—has eroded Japan's competitive advantage in manufacturing. A key example is the rise of Samsung that surpasses Japanese giants—Sony and Panasonic—in sales and profits in consumer electronics, a symbolic sector which has long been a source of Japan's national pride and identity (Yoshimi 1999). This example shows clearly how Japan is no longer able to compete on the basis on price and quality alone (Oishi 2009).

The challenge is that Japan, it has been argued, is trapped in a mentality of the manufacturing era (see, for example, Arnaud 2014) or obsessed with the myth of *monozukuri* or "making things." While manufacturing accounted for 35 percent of economic output in the early 70s, in 2011 it was less than 20 percent, and is on an irreversible decline. Yet it is still considered a pillar of the national economy whose interests are usually protected at the cost of other industries.[1] Top economic organizations, such as Keidanren Japan Business Federation, are historically known to serve the interests of big manufacturing companies, with the Federation's chairman being elected from companies like Sumitomo Chemical, Canon, and Toyota. In Japan, creative industries provide one avenue to move away from this problem—the creative industries adding immaterial value to increasingly undifferentiated global products that, in turn, create new sources of economic growth and job creation.

Current shape of Japanese creative industries

What then are the Japanese creative industries? In this chapter I focus mostly on the media and communication industries but conceptually I would like to use the term creative industries to refer to "those industries which have their origin in individual creativity, skill and talent and which have a potential for wealth and job creation through the generation and exploitation of intellectual property" (DCMS 2001, 4). This includes twelve *creative sectors*: advertising; architecture; arts and antique markets; crafts; design; designer fashion; film, video and photography; software, computer games and electronic publishing; music and the visual and performing arts; publishing; television; and radio (DCMS 2001).

The size of Japanese creative industries: Asian perspective

In the context of 20 years of relatively slow growth since 1993, it has become commonplace to talk about Japan's *problems* particularly in terms of its contrast with other Asian countries that are demonstrating accelerated growth. This is evident in relation to China or, more specifically in the context of creative industries, Korea, where some of the country's cultural products increase its presence in the region (Chua and Iwabuchi 2008; Jung 2011). However, it is also important, particularly in the context of this edited volume, to have a perspective on Japanese creative industries.

In many ways, Japan still has the biggest and most developed creative industries in Asia as the following few examples highlight. In recorded music sales, Japan is the second largest market in the world with a trade value of ¥442 billion (US$4,422 million), which is almost the same as the USA (US$4,481 million) and is four times as big as the UK (US$1,325 million). The second largest market in Asia is Korea at US$187 million, about 1/23rd of Japan: third is China at US$92.4 million, which is 1/47th of Japan. In term of advertising spending, which indicates the size of the commercial media market, total ad spending in Asia-Pacific is US$142.4 billion making it the second biggest regional advertising market after North America (US$178.3 billion) and ahead of Europe (US$108.9 billion). [2]

Of the region, Japan is still the biggest spender with US$47.2 billion, followed by China (US$41.7 billion) and then Korea (US$9.0 billion), Indonesia (US$7.6 billion), and India (US$5.8 billion).[3] Generally speaking this is more or less the case with other sectors and genres (Dentsu Sōken 2014). This cursory look indicates that Japanese creative industries are huge. For many years, it has consistently produced highly localized differentiated products for the world's second largest consumer market in fierce domestic competition (for discussion of Galapagosization see Mizukoshi 2014). The market size is declining slowly as the population dwindles, but it is nonetheless worth remembering the sheer size of Japanese creative industries.

The anatomy of Japanese creative industries

In Japan, the term "creative industries" is primarily an administrative term, which is almost never used outside a small community of bureaucrats and scholars even in its translated term *Sōzō Sangyō*. It is far more common to use terms such as *Masukomi gyōkai* (mass communication industries), *Net kigyo* (New media) or *Kontentsu gyōkai* (contents industries) all of which are part of creative industries, but might or might not overlap. Yet the term creative industries has been one of the key concepts for quite some time at the METI—the powerful government body that plans and implements Japan's industrial and trade policies.

Creative industries ≠ cool Japan

On June 8, 2010, the Ministry of Economy, Trade and Industry (METI) established the "Creative Industries Promotion Office" under the Manufacturing Industries Bureau. The METI identifies its role as promoting

> overseas advancement of an internationally appreciated 'Cool Japan' brand, cultivation of creative industries, promotion of these industries in Japan and abroad, and other related initiatives from cross-industry and cross-government standpoints.
>
> *(METI 2104, n.p.)*

It should be stressed that this office was established in order to play a central role in a long-term project "Cool Japan." Cool Japan refers to a discourse about the popularity of Japanese cultural products in overseas markets and a set of economic, political and diplomatic policies to capitalize it. The term first used by American journalist Douglas McGray became a buzzword that circulated in an endless stream of magazine articles, television series, government reports and industry policies. As far as METI is concerned, it seems, creative industries promotion and Cool Japan are one and the same thing (Mihara 2014, 2013).

In METI's definition, along the line of DCMS, creative industries include everything from advertising, movies, music, television, design publishing, software, as well as craft, stationery and furniture. Based on this inclusive definition METI estimates the size of creative industries to be around ¥45.2 trillion and employing 2.1 million people. The office will implement measures to facilitate these industries' overseas expansion, disseminate relevant information in Japan and abroad, and develop human resources. METI also writes that its immediate aim is to capture ¥8–11 trillion (around US$8–10 billion) out of a US$900 billion global market for cultural goods.[4]

In terms of growth and employment, as well as its ambition, it is a little odd that METI only looks at the international development of creative industries and focuses on these eight sectors. Indeed despite all the hype surrounding Cool Japan, Japan is a net importer of pop culture except gaming. Creative industries in America generate more than 17 percent of their annual turnover in the overseas market while Japan's remains low at 2.8 percent. However, if one takes a look at the size of the potential overseas market and actual revenue inflow for Japanese popular culture products they are not large enough or promising enough to realize METI's ambition; characters goods ($6.3 billion / $315 million); game hardware ($13.7 billion / $9.6 billion); game software ($5.8 billion / $4.1 billion); animation ($1.9 billion / $130 million); *manga* ($1.2 billion / $120 million); movies ($200 million / n.a.); television (n.a. / $75 million) and music (n.a. / mostly *anime* related) (METI 2011). On the other hand, despite slow growth there is some room in the domestic market as the Japanese content market is 2.2 percent of domestic output and is significantly smaller than 5 percent in the US. This means there is room for growth both in domestic and international markets.

The way METI identified eight sectors (fashion, foods, content, local produce, houses, tourism, art and design) to which it aims to direct resources most heavily is also odd. Among those eight sectors, only one of them (content) is usually considered part of what scholars like Hesmondhalgh (2007) identify as the core of the creative industries of advertising and marketing, broadcasting, film, Internet and music industries, print and electronic publishing, and video and computer games. In reality, content refers to *manga* and *anime*: very popular in overseas markets and exemplifiers of Cool Japan. Nonetheless in economic terms, as we have seen above, *manga* and *anime* are insignificant relative to the whole of the core of creative industries.

METI policy also does not say anything about new media that have come to have a significant presence in the last ten years within creative industries. If there needs to be growth in creative industries, then a large part of it must be coming from the so-called core, both from domestic and international markets. In short, too much attention both from policy makers and also critical academic research has been fixed on Cool Japan and its usual repertoire of *manga* and *anime*. In the following section, I will look at the core of creative industries and discuss the ways in which different actors are negotiating the effect of globalization differently.

Old media

Let us turn our attention to what in Japan is called the mass communication industry, which in terms of market size contributed the most to creative industries, and which hereafter I will call *old media*. That old media is not considered at all in creative industries and Cool Japan discourse indicates it is operating in a different sphere and politics. To put it bluntly, while Cool Japan is concerned with overseas markets and thus a positive response to globalization, other old media in Japan remains unchanged by globalization—indicative of the complexities and contested ideologies underscoring Japanese creative industries.

Old media consists of old and established companies in what has been usually referred to as the "four media" —broadcasting, publishing, newspaper and advertising. The largest players are NHK (the world's largest public broadcaster) and five big media groups that own television and newspapers through cross-ownership. This includes *Yomiuri* newspaper and Nippon Television; *Asahi* newspaper and TV Asahi; *Sankei* Newspaper and Fuji television; *Mainichi* newspaper and TBS; and Nikkei and TV Tokyo. Add to this, publishers such as Kadokawa and Shogakukan and large advertising agencies such as Dentsu and Hakuhodo. The list of major players has not changed much for well over 50 years. It is these companies in old media that control Japanese creative industries.

Employees at old media have long enjoyed prestige, generous pay, security of lifetime employment and other perks. The job is usually long and tiring but also considered fun and stimulating. The pay is better than large banks or finance and far better than manufacturing companies such as Toyota or Sony. A business journal *Toyo Keizai* publishes the top 300 companies with the highest average salaries. Amongst the top 20, seven are so-called old media companies. Most commercial television companies in Tokyo as well as in Osaka ranked in the top 20, all of them paying close to ¥15 million on average. Fuji has been in the number 1 spot for many years. Large national newspapers and Dentsu also are amongst the top 20 with an average salary over ¥12 million.[5,6]

Naturally there is fierce competition amongst college graduates to get into traditional media companies. There are 300 applicants for each new Fuji television opening. Traditional media is notoriously conservative, and they very rarely hire outside a small number of elite universities. Graduates have to go through the same recruitment process as the manufacturing or banking sectors. This means wearing a dark suit, filling in entry sheets, going through a series of routinized interviews (e.g., "what is your biggest achievement so far?"). The traditional media world is male dominated. Of commercial broadcaster employees, around 20 percent are women and less than 10 percent of employees above manager class are women. NHK, which is public, is worse with 11 percent women and 2.9 percent women above manager class.[7]

In addition, broadcasters generally hire a significant number of graduates based purely on their personal connections. They have close family relationships with large advertisers, other media companies, politicians, regulators, or celebrities. Just take an example from politicians. Many important ruling LDP politicians have their sons and daughters at one of the big old media companies. Acting Prime Minister Shinzo Abe's nephew is now at Fuji television. Former Prime Minister and LDP kingpin Yasuhiro Nakasone's daughter is at NHK, and his grandson at Fuji. Former Prime Minister Keizo Obuchi's daughter, who is now a minister herself, was at TBS; two former governors of Tokyo, Shintaro Ishihara and Naoki Inose, each had their son and daughter working for NTV and NHK. A similar practice is also common in large advertising agencies and newspapers.

These examples demonstrate that old media is blatantly not interested in hiring people with a creative spark but in administrators of creativity. In fact, most of the real creative work is outsourced to a large number of small production companies and independent creators, which do hire the more flamboyant youths that are now commonly associated with Japanese popular culture. The working conditions for the young people in smaller firms in creative industries are dire. The predicament of Japanese animators has drawn the most attention. Seventy-three percent of young Japanese animators earn less than one million yen (or US$10,000) a year. Forty-four percent of them are in their 20s and forty percent of them quit within five years (Mōri 2011).

Similar gulfs in salary and career prospects, stability and social status exist within old media across different sectors. This is the case in other developed countries (e.g., Gill and Pratt 2008) but what is characteristic about Japanese old media is that it is more difficult to *work your way up* as its job market lacks mobility and flexibility. Large companies in old media are quite reluctant to hire mid-career professionals from competitors or smaller companies. In reality the window to join one of them opens just once and that is when one is 20 years old, and from a good university to be allowed to try to get through. This represents a kind of social and cultural status that working in old media represents in Japanese society and its cosy relationship with the establishment.

Content with a large local market, old media has not been concerned much with going global. Japan's biggest media group Fuji Media Holding has an annual turnover of ¥539.6 billion (US$5.3 billion) and led the Japanese television industry with a series of highly successful variety shows and trendy dramas including the famous *Tokyo Love Story* which was consumed widely in Asia (Iwabuchi 2002, 2004). While being the biggest television group in Asia, the group's overseas sales account for less than 1 percent of its total sales. This complete dependence on domestic sales and indifference to the international market is the same at all the major broadcasters, publishers and newspapers.[8] Global media companies such as Time Warner (US$29 billion), or Walt Disney Company (US$40 billion) and News Corp (US$32 billion) are much more internationalized. These giants earn 20–30 percent of their revenue from the overseas market. Even the BBC is commercially more successful internationally through its BBC Worldwide Limited.[9]

Dentsu and Hakuhodo, Japan's largest and second largest advertising agencies, make 14 percent[10] until very recently and 3.3 percent of their business overseas, respectively.[11] Dentsu is the world largest standalone agency, but most of its sales come from following Japanese clients to overseas markets, and not from winning non-Japanese clients.[12] This contrasts sharply with many Western agencies such as WPP, which does 35 percent of its business in North America, 12 percent in the UK, 25 percent in Europe and 28 percent in the rest of the world corresponding roughly to distribution of global GDP.[13]

On home soil old media has stopped Western competitors from challenging their domestic dominance. Western media has so far failed to mount any serious challenge in Japanese markets in broadcasting, publishing, newspapers and/or advertising. It is protected by various regulations and policies including strict resale price maintenance for newspapers, limited membership to news sources and broadcasting law. Overall old media resistance to the effect of globalization at home has been surprisingly successful.

The Japanese government is so far reluctant to do much to change business practices or promote innovation in this highly protected sector that has produced little growth and employment and shown little appetite to go global. For instance, myriad regulations and practices that prevent digital distribution in publishing, broadcasting and/or music from flourishing have been left untouched. The government has done nothing to break Dentsu's monopoly and its abuse of power vis-à-vis media and creators. It does too little to change unfair practices in which television networks exploit numerous small production studios and pay little to no fees for the use of frequencies for which the mobile operators pay hundreds of billions of yen (Ikeda 2006). It effectively banned new entrants and ownership change in the television industries and investment from overseas. This leads to my discussion of new media.

New media

Another huge part of the creative industries that has been missing in the creative industries debate in Japan is new media. In Japan new media is generally considered and called net media (Internet media), and has grown rapidly in the last 20 years, challenging the dominance of old media for the time and attention of half of Japan's 100 million people who are online.

New media is almost by definition much more global. With the benefit of global platforms such as YouTube and apps stores, it is much easier for new media companies to go global than it is for old media, which has many physical and legal boundaries to overcome before bringing its business overseas. Unlike in the world of old media, Google, Facebook, Twitter, Yahoo and other global media players have firmly established their position in the Japanese new media ecology. Yet Japan has also produced home grown new media, which is competing with Western rivals successfully in many areas.

One of the biggest and in many ways representative of the new media players is Yahoo! Japan, which is only 30 percent owned by Yahoo Inc. in America (unlike subsidiaries in other countries that are majority owned) and thus retains substantial autonomy.[14] It offers different services from Yahoo Inc. and is a market leader in many areas ahead of its competitors, including search (well ahead of Google), auction (pushing eBay out of the country), news and other key services. Already a few new media players are amongst the biggest media in Japan. With net sales of ¥38.6 billion Yahoo! Japan is already the third biggest media company in terms of sales, after Fuji Media Holding and Yomiuri Shimbun group (¥42.9 billion),[15] but is by far the most profitable.[16]

Management teams of many new media companies, as well as employees, are generally much younger than old media, and there is significantly more flexibility and mobility in job markets. Yahoo! Japan has 6,291 employees and on average they are 33 years of age, make ¥6.7 million, and staff turnover is 4.7 years—in comparison to 47 years old, ¥14.5 million on average and 20 years at Nippon TV, a broadcaster. Yahoo! Japan's CEO is 47 years old while NTV has a 64-year-old former Yomiuri newspaper reporter as a CEO.[17] Online retailer Rakuten, which is becoming a media company in many ways, was founded by then 30-year-old Harvard Business School graduate, Hiroshi Mikitai. It now has net sales of ¥44 billion, which is more than any old media company, and successfully holds Amazon at bay. It is also accelerating its global operation, entering not only Asia but also Europe and America. It has bought buy.com in America, Canadian e-book reader maker Kobo, Wuaki in Spain, and mobile messaging and VoIP service Viber.

In social media Japan has different ecology from the Western countries (Mizukoshi 2014; Takahashi 2010). Tokyo-based Mixi had been a market leader for a long time before it was taken over by Facebook. In the last five years, mobile-social gaming platforms are the newest players in Japan's new media scene. One of the two major players GREE started its operation in 2004 and its revenue, mainly from controversial *kompu gacha* (random reward system that cost players a large amount of money), surpassed ¥150 billion in 2012 and 2013.[18] Similar social media platform DeNA recorded net sales of ¥202.4 billion and a whopping profit of ¥79.2 billion in 2013 also marketing similarly controversial but hugely profitable games.[19] Both DeNA and GREE invested in foreign markets and M&A. In 2013, there are four Japan-based companies (Gangho, Line, GREE, DeNA, and Supercell owned by Softbank and Gangho) in the world smartphone game category (MIAC 2014). LINE, developed by the Japanese arm of Korean company Naver, is leading the market with its playful messenger based social app. LINE has 400 million users globally, and there are ten countries where it has more than 10 million users including the USA, Indonesia, India, Spain, and Mexico.[20] Other notable Japanese players include Ameba (an aggregate of mostly celebrity blogs with page views of 230 million pages per month) run by Cyberagent, an Internet advertising agency. Niconico, a video sharing platform operated by Dwango, recently merged with Kadokawa, a publisher, a rare case of new media buying major old media.

Large new media companies become popular amongst graduate and mid-career professionals. A few popular magazines report that DeNA, GREE and Cyberagent have become the new top three most popular companies for students at the prestigious University of Tokyo instead of traditional trading companies and big banks.[21] They offer a competitive salary, with opportunities from a significantly younger age when compared to traditional media, along with more "exciting" and entrepreneurial working environments. DeNA hired 28 and Cyberagent hired eight while once revered *Asahi* Newspaper was not able to hire a single student from the University of Tokyo—this made the business journals wonder if this signals a decline of old media vis-à-vis new media

Clearly Japan is more open to global new media companies and local players are also embracing opportunities opened up by globalization. They are competing against Western media fiercely and show more willingness and commitment to overseas markets to a far greater degree than old media. In the midst of the shift in the balance of power old media seems to have mixed feelings consisting of contempt, suspicion, fear toward new media, and reluctance to work with it particularly as in Japan the decline of old media is irreversible, but noticeably slower than in other developed countries (Dentsu Sōken 2014). No incident tells the tensions and complex relationship between old media and new media more vividly than the rise and fall of Livedoor and the lingering legacy its fall has had over new media in Japan.

The Livedoor incident

Livedoor was an Internet start-up founded by a University of Tokyo dropout and serial entrepreneur Takafumi Horie, or Horiemon, the nickname by which he is known to the public with either affection or contempt. Horie started his business in 1996 while still in university and rose to public prominence and gained cult status through a number of widely reported buyouts as much as through his defiant attitude in numerous appearances on national television. He wore jeans, sneakers and spiky hair and is in stark contrast to the dark-suited, middle-aged old media executives. Still he is considered physically unattractive and to share the culture of the young, geeky, unpopular, male Internet users who supported Horie most strongly. He is a ruthless rationalist and free market fundamentalist who denies traditions of many kinds—particularly old, corporate-Japan routines and practices.

Horie listed his company on Mothers, a stock market for start-ups equivalent to Nasdaq in America, and used the newly raised capital to buy Livedoor, a defunct Internet service provider, which he renamed in 2004. Chiefly through financial engineering (he has split its stock 30,000-fold to increase liquidity), and a series of mergers and acquisitions, the capitalization of Livedoor rose to about ¥930 billion (US$9 billion) at its peak in late 2004.[22] The Livedoor business is based on a Yahoo-style portal site, from which visitors are led to different services, including shopping, travel, auction, IP phone or used cars. Traffic to the portal, therefore, is key and he eagerly pursued publicity opportunities such as his failed attempt to buy a professional baseball team.

In February 2005 then 32-year-old Horie mounted a takeover bid for Nippon Broadcasting System (NBS), a radio station, which, because of a complicated system of cross-shareholdings, would have given him control of Fuji Television. What surprised everybody about this deal was that Livedoor, with revenue of ¥20 billion (US$200 million) and a market capitalization of US$2 billion was able to raise the ¥80 billion needed for the acquisition. Infamous American investment bank Lehman Brothers gave Livedoor the money in exchange for the issue of Moving Strike Convertible Bonds, which, to put it simply, gave Lehman a sure way to make a huge profit at the expense of other shareholders.

Led by then 65-year-old CEO Hisashi Hieda, who is a representative of old media in terms of his advanced age,[23] resistance to change, and hostility to the logic of American financial capitalism, Fuji Television fought a melodramatic battle over the airwaves and in court against what it saw as the juvenile fraudster, destroyer of the old system. On the other hand, Livedoor fought by basically playing by the rules (of global financial capitalism) and buying shares during after-hours trading, which enabled it to avoid disclosure. The two-month conflict—a national media event in which every move and detail was reported minute by minute—was resolved in April 2005, through a forced settlement in which Livedoor sold its stake in Fuji for a handsome profit, and, in return, Fuji made an investment in Livedoor.

In this national media frenzy, Livedoor and new media in general were accused of being "kyogyō" a term that is used pejoratively to refer to an industry that does not create tangible goods or serve important public interest (like journalistic old media) and thus does not ultimately hold any value.[24] Livedoor and new media were also represented as contaminated too much with American style capitalism. Television and newspaper accused them of putting shareholders' interest and profit before those of audiences or employees. Horie's personality did not help either. He owned a private jet that he reportedly used to travel to exotic South Pacific resorts with young models and made frequent remarks boasting how money can buy everything (Horie 2011, 2004).

Another term that has been frequently used by both parties and media during the row is "convergence between telecommunication and broadcasting." Media convergence had been a technological possibility for broadcasters, and they had the luxury to decide when and how much to converge on their terms. With Horie, the old media was chilled to know what media convergence really means, and to encounter the cold logic of global capitalism, comically embodied in Horie, who said he would lower the salary significantly and other perks enjoyed by television employees for decades as he has done to many companies that he bought.[25]

While the battle ended amicably, Horie had infuriated the old media and old system including the prosecutors who are closely inter-connected. In January 2006, his home and office in prestigious Roppongi Hills were raided in front of the cameras of all the national television stations that had been tipped off and briefed by the authorities. In March the following year he was convicted of fraud and sentenced to two-and-a-half years in jail—this surprised many observers as being overly harsh.[26] On the date he was imprisoned, he was taking interviews wearing a black t-shirt, which had "Go To Jail" in big white letters on it and listed all the major old corporations involved in similar but far larger corporate crime but not prosecuted at all, in a last-ditch attempt to criticize the establishment.[27]

Livedoor and Horie's fall tarnished the image of new media and decreased the risk appetite of young people.[28] The Mothers index was crushed at the news of the Livedoor raid and lost more than 90 percent of its value, going from its peak of 2800 to hovering at around 300 for much of the last ten years. Nikkei had to close early on the following day. Livedoor was delisted on April 14, 2006, before the prosecution even started.

The early 2000s were usually considered the third wave of the start-up boom. Many start-ups were launched in universities and by university students. The number of university start-ups peaked in 2004 with 247, with 128 in 2007. The number of IPOs was 204 in 2000 but was 20 in 2009. While there are many reasons contributing to this, industry observers cite the Livedoor incident as a defining moment. GREE, DeNA or Cyberagent may attract students from top universities, but they need to pay significantly more starting salary to attract them; other smaller new media companies still struggle to recruit employees and funds. There are reports that young people are more risk averse. A government-published report says the turnover rate was much lower in 2009 than in 2003, and more students say they would like to continue their first job until they retire, and the lowest number say they would like to switch job for better opportunities.[29] The Livedoor incident has had a long-lasting, dispiriting effect on entrepreneurship within the creative industries and played a powerful role in the development of the relationship between old media and new media.[30]

Conclusion

As this chapter has sought to demonstrate, there is a great deal of diversity within Japanese creative industries that has been overshadowed by the disproportional attention to Cool Japan and its *manga* and *anime*. In making sense of the relationship between Japanese creative industries and globalization it is important to attend to the ways globalization is distributing opportunity and risks, prestige and predicament unevenly across industries, companies and individuals. While this chapter has been an attempt to identify one such line of demarcation in terms of (perhaps too general and mechanical) old media and new media, it goes some way to explain how it is not unfolding within predictable discursive frameworks of neoliberalism or technological determinism but in very specific local and historically contingent developments in creative industries, policy and regulation. All this has created, and is creating, a distinct form of creative industries, and a highly original "Galapagos"-style popular culture in Japan, which has had a significant influence on the ways creative industries, and popular culture, have developed in other countries in Asia. While the peculiarity of Japanese creative industries might run counter to business rationalization and the benefits of convergence, I leave it up to the reader to decide whether that is a bad thing for the diversity of global popular culture and new media ecology.

Notes

1 'Creative Industries Save Japan!' *Diamond Online*. Available at: http://diamond.jp/articles/-/1657?page=3 (Accessed September 20, 2014).
2 'Regional Economic Woes Drag Down Worldwide Total Media Ad Spend Growth'. Available at: http://www.emarketer.com/Article/Regional-Economic-Woes-Drag-Down-Worldwide-Total-Media-Ad-Spend-Growth/1009974 (Accessed September 20, 2014).
3 'The world music market nation-by-nation top 20 2012'. Available at: http://10rank.blog.fc2.com/blog-entry-205.html (Accessed September 20, 2014).

4 'Cool Japan and Creative Industries Policy', *METI*. Available at: http://www.meti.go.jp/policy/mono_info_service/mono/creative/ (Accessed September 20, 2014).

5 'Saishin Heikin nenshū rankingu toppu 30', *Toyo Keizai Online*. Available at: http://toyokeizai.net/articles/-/13896?page=5 (Accessed September 20, 2014).

6 'Nenshū 1000 manen ijō no kaisha wo sagasu', *Kyuuryou.com*. Available at: http://kyuuryou.com/w2867-2013.html (Accessed September 20, 2014).

7 Available at: http://www.gender.go.jp/research/kenkyu/media_resarch.html (Accessed September 20, 2014).

8 'Terebi bangumi kuuru japan no ochikobore'. Available at: http://blogos.com/article/50003/ (Accessed September 20, 2014).

9 Annual Review 2013/14. Available at: http://www.bbcworldwide.com/annualreview (Accessed September 20, 2014).

10 Although if its acquisition of UK Aegis group is reflected it will increase significantly to about 40 percent.

11 *Hakuhodo Annual Report*. Available at: http://www.hakuhodody-holdings.co.jp/ir/library/sfr/HDYir120207_01.pdf (Accessed September 20, 2014).

12 'Dentsu no ei kigyo baishū ni mittsu no gimon: nihon kigyō no kaigai M&S no kansei'. Available at: http://judiciary.asahi.com/fukabori/2012092000008.html (Accessed September 20, 2014).

13 Available at: http://www.wpp.com/wpp/investor/financials/reports/ (Accessed September 20, 2014).

14 This is because Tokyo-based Softbank Corp has been the biggest shareholder of both Yahoo! Japan and Yahoo Inc.

15 'Shimbunsha uriage rankingu'. Available at: http://sougouranking.net/uriageranking/info_np_fy2012.html (Accessed September 20, 2014).

16 Dentsu is excluded because it treats billing as sales, which is not compatible with other accounting systems.

17 'Nihon terebi holding no heikin nenshu to gyōseki suii'. Available at: http://nensyu-labo.com/kigyou_ntv.htm (Accessed September 20, 2014).

18 'GREE Gyōseki Hairaito'. Available at: http://corp.gree.net/jp/ja/ir/highlight/highlight.html (Accessed September 20, 2014).

19 'DeNA IR Gyōseki hairaito'. Available at: http://dena.com/ir/finance/higlight.html (Accessed September 20, 2014).

20 LINE official blog. Available at: http://official-blog.line.me/ja/archives/1001168643.html (Accessed September 20, 2014).

21 'Gekihen Tōdaisei no shūkatsu: shingosanke wa kono sansha'. Available at: http://toyokeizai.net/articles/-/34081 (Accessed September 20, 2014).

22 'The Invented Here'. *The Economist*. Available at: http://www.economist.com/node/10169932 (Accessed September 20, 2014).

23 At 77 years of age Mr. Hieda is still acting CEO of Fuji Media Holding at the time of writing this chapter (August 2014) and is close to acting Prime Minister Shinzo Abe.

24 'Livedoor jiken ni manabu netto kigyō no honshitu'. Available at: http://japan.cnet.com/sp/column_ncompany/20099534/ (Accessed September 20, 2014).

25 This was not the only case where television was protected from outside takeover. In 1996 Softbank (Yahoo! Japan's parent company) and Rupert Murdoch made a joint and ultimately failed bid to take over TV Asahi. The broadcast law was changed to restrict foreign investors' stakes in Japanese broadcasters to less than 20 percent. Another Tokyo-based station TBS was rescued from Rakuten in a similar situation in 2005 by government that changed the law further to protect existing broadcasting companies from any takeover bids.

26 'Not Invented Here'. *The Economist*. Available at: http://www.economist.com/node/10169932 (Accessed September 20, 2014).

27 The interview Horie gave before being imprisoned can be seen in full on YouTube. Available at: https://www.youtube.com/watch?v=C-ck1H80H2k (Accessed April 27, 2015).

28 'Livedoor jiken ni manabu netto kigyō no honshitu'. Available at: http://japan.cnet.com/sp/column_ncompany/20099534/2/ (Accessed September 20, 2014).

29 'Shinki gakusotsusha no rishoku jyoukyou ni kansuru siryo ichiran'. *Ministry of Health, Labour and Welfare*. Available at: http://www.mhlw.go.jp/topics/2010/01/tp0127-2/24.html (Accessed September 20, 2014).

30 'Livedoor jiken ni manabu netto kigyō no honshitu'. Available at: http://japan.cnet.com/sp/column_ncompany/20099534/2/ (Accessed September 20, 2014).

References

Arnaud, R. (2014) 'Monozukuri shinko ga nihon wo dame ni suru', *Newsweek Japan*.

Chua, B.-H. and Iwabuchi, K. (eds) (2008) *East Asian Pop Culture: Analysing the Korean Wave*, Hong Kong and London: Hong Kong University Press.

Condry, I. (2009) 'Anime Creativity: Characters and Premises in the Quest for Cool Japan', *Theory, Culture & Society*, 26: 139–163.

Daliot-Bul, M. (2009) 'Japan Brand Strategy: The Taming of "Cool Japan" and the Challenges of Cultural Planning in Postmodern Age', *Social Science Japan Journal*, 12.

DCMS (2001) *The Creative Industries Mapping Document 2001*, London: UK Department of Culture, Media and Sports.

Dentsu Sōken (2014) *Jōhō media hakusho 2014* [*Annual Report on Information Media 2014*], Tokyo: Diamond Publishing.

Gill, R. and Pratt, A. (2008) 'In the Social Factory? Immaterial Labour, Precariousness and Cultural Work', *Theory, Culture & Society*, 25: 1-30.

Hesmondhalgh, D. (2007) *The Cultural Industries*, London: Sage.

Horie, T. (2004) *Kasegu ga kachi zero kara hyakuokuen ore no yarikata* [*Make Money! From Zero to 10 Billion Yen: How I Did It*], Kobun-sha.

Horie, T. (2011) *Ookane wa itsumo tadashii* [*Money Is Always Right*], Futaba-sha.

Ikeda, N. (2006) *Denpa Riken* [*The Vested Interest of Airwave*], Shinchō-sha.

Iwabuchi, K. (2002) *Recentering Globalization: Popular Culture and Japanese Transnationalism*, Durham, NC and London: Duke University Press.

Iwabuchi, K. (ed.) (2004) *Feeling Asian Modernities: Transnational Consumption of Japanese TV Dramas*, Hong Kong: Hong Kong University Press.

Jung, S. (2011) *Korean Masculinities and Transnational Consumption: Yonsama, Rain, Oldboy, K-Pop Idols*, Hong Kong: Hong Kong University Press.

Lee, H.-K. (2009) 'Between Fan Culture and Copyright Infringement: Manga Scanlation', *Media, Culture and Society*, 36: 1011–1022.

Mihara, R. (2013) 'Shiron: kūru japan to tsūsho seisaku [An Essay on Cool Japan and Trade Policy]', *RIETI Discussion Paper Series*, 13.

Mihara, R. (2014) *Kūru Japan ha naze kirawarerunoka: nekkyō to reishō wo koete*, Chūo Kōron.

Ministry of Economy, Trade and Industry (METI) (2011) *Kūru Japan senryaku suishin jigyō saishū houkousho* [*Cool Japan Strategy Promotion Project Final Report 2011*].

Ministry of Economy, Trade and Industry (METI) (2014) 'Cool Japan/Creative Industries Policy', http://www.meti.go.jp/english/policy/mono_info_service/creative_industries/creative_industries.html.

Ministry of Internal Affairs and Communications (MIAC) (2014) *Jōhō tsūshin Hakusho* [*White Paper 2014: Information and Communications in Japan*], Tokyo: Ministry of Internal Affairs and Communications.

Mizukoshi, S. (2014) 'Is Japan the "Galapagos Islands" of Social Media?', *Global Asia: The Power of Social Media to Transform Asian for Better or Worse*, 9: 36–39.

Mōri, Y. (2011) 'The Pitfall Facing the Cool Japan Project: The Transnational Development of the Anime Industry under the Condition of Post-Fordism', *International Journal of Japanese Sociology*, 20: 30–42.

Oishi, Y. (ed.) (2009) *Nihon kigyō no gurōbaru mākethingu*, Tokyo: Hakuto Shobō.

Takahashi, T. (2010) 'MySpace or Mixi? Japanese Engagement with SNS (Social Networking Sites) in the global age', *New Media & Society*, 12: 453–475.

Valaskivi, K. (2013) 'A Brand New Future? Cool Japan and the Social Imaginary of the Branded Nation', *Japan Forum*, 1.

Yoshimi, S. (1999) '"Made in Japan": The Cultural Politics of "Home Electrification" in Postwar Japan', *Media, Culture & Society*, 21: 149–171.

29

Globalization of the privatized self-image: the reaction video and its attention economy on YouTube[1]

Yeran Kim

Globalization has shifted the ways in which people experience privatized self-images through media. YouTube, as its slogan of "Broadcast yourself" demonstrates, has become one of the most conspicuous platforms on which young people mutually produce, consume, and circulate their privatized self-images (Light et al. 2012). The present study focuses on "reaction videos" on You-Tube. Reaction videos are a vernacular form of visual production where people use a webcam to record themselves while watching certain media content (Kim and Gang 2012; Ramstad 2012). The name "reaction video" refers to the portion of the video where the producer reacts to the content being watched.

Reaction videos have become popular, particularly among fan groups of certain cultural genres, enabling fans to confirm that they are not lone consumers of the particular contents and, thus, constructing a collective fan identity in the digital era (Gray et al. 2007; Pearson 2010). Because of this reason, reaction videos on YouTube are a significant form of cultural practice through which one can see how, in the global context of the digital mediascape, a certain genre of culture consumed in private spaces and made available using sequential processes of popular networks of intermission—production, distribution, and consumption—emerges as a particular collective form of fandom culture.

The current study aims to account for the cultural implication of the term "reaction" in the contemporary global, and apparently active and interactive, digital mediascape. In tackling this question of "reaction" in the contemporary visual culture, an emergent visual culture called "reaction video" is focused on. The notion of the reaction video can seem contradictory in that "reactive" is discursively manifested, even when, as Carpentier points out, reactive with its implication of passiveness is an apologetic word in the contemporary visual culture where "activeness" of audience is normalized in the digital interactive media pervasive environment (Carpentier 2011). Reactors in reaction videos, then, may be seen as against the dominant norm of activeness or interactivity. The role of reactors in reaction videos, in fact, is doubled: in terms of interpretative position, a reactor takes the reactive position of appreciating the ready-made visual product, but, in terms of productive action, the reactor is a "produser" (Bird 2011; Bruns 2008) that not only consumes ready-made media products but also makes and distributes self-reactive images. In short, reactors in reactive videos are those who "actively" create visual products of a "reactive" self-image.

In approaching reactive videos on the global visual network, forty reaction videos on You-Tube, specifically videos reacting to Korean popular music videos (hereafter "K-Pop reaction videos"), and viewers' discourses presented along with the videos are analyzed. This selection has been made based on the consideration that K-Pop reaction videos show how the emergent culture of K-Pop has been able to draw the attention of a globally networked "attention economy" (Goldhaber 1997) in the intertwined dynamics of active/reactive, production/consumption in visual practices. The methodology of multimodal analysis is adopted to handle the digital visual and textual materials in integration. Multimodality analysis is useful in the interpretation of literal and visual texts in integration with the discursive interactions made among many anonymous producers and users on YouTube from a social semiotic perspective (Lim 2007; O'Halloran 1999).

The emergence of the attention economy of reaction videos

If one reaction video is fun and the reactors are conceived to be devoted to the production of reaction videos, YouTube audiences may, in turn, request the reactor to produce another reaction video of certain media content or of the stars they like. Consequently, it is not surprising that an interactive relationship of supply and demand is sometimes built between reactors and viewers. This develops to become what is known as "attention economy." Attention economy is, according to Goldhaber (1997), a new form of economy generated in the digital era where attention is seen as property. Differentiated from information which is abundantly available, attention is a scarce resource and is exchanged in exclusive and competitive relation. Thus, contestation and rivalry are strengthened among those who intend to obtain and sustain the limited currency of attention.

Reaction videos, the subject of the current research, are notable in that they have a formative effect on the attention economy by means of shifting attention from the K-Pop stars in the music videos to ordinary people in reaction videos. Some reactors are seen to obtain their own recognition and reputation among YouTube audiences, as certain groups of video clips produced in variety by particular reactors are saliently found to be available for consumption on the Internet. It is common for these reactors to achieve a certain degree of popularity among YouTube audiences. YouTube audiences' responses, such as, "We are watching not music videos but reaction videos," are sometimes found, suggesting reaction videos have established their own area of attention economy independent from K-Pop professional musicians.

In this way, the consistent circuit of supply and demand is made between reactors and YouTube audiences, resulting in the emergence of a genre form in the global networked media environment. For the reactors deliberately create a series of reaction videos with a self-styled aesthetics in the procedure of selecting K-Pop stars, applying technical methods, performing reactions to the chosen music videos, editing and polishing, and completing the video works. They are also distributors who are in charge of building a regular schedule of providing them to a certain group of imagined audiences and mediating K-Pop culture and global cultural consumers.

> My first reaction to Brown Eyed Girls, Abracadabra. . . . One of my favorite K-Pop videos of all time. First reaction video, new reactions out every week, with reviews out every Monday starting next week. Leave which songs you would like me to review in the comment section BELOW.
>
> – Ka✶✶✶✶✶

The area of reaction videos is thus established as an independent attention economy having its own circuits of production and consumption between reactors as providers and YouTube audiences as consumers.

While the process further develops and stabilizes, the reactors are seen to build up a kind of authorship with their unique filmography and appreciate fandom to a certain degree. Britani is one of the examples. She looks ambiguous in sex to the extent that questions asking whether Britani is a woman or man sometimes appear on YouTube. She differs from the typical glamorous star image one may imagine to garner a great fandom on the Internet: short hair, short-sleeve T-shirt, and casual pants over a chubby figure, she performs reaction with an impassive poker-face. In fact, it may be her very plain appearance that brings her a high degree of fandom as a reactor.

> BRITTANY ALL THE WAY !!!!! She seems so BAD ASS! And I like her input on reaction videos. She tells it like it is, whether she liked the video or not, she'll say it straight up XD Brittany is my FAV reactor !!! <33 TEAM Brittany :P
>
> *— funn*★★★★★

YouTube audiences do not always respond positively to reactors. When a reaction video looks quite similar to another reactor's video, a plagiarism debate may appear in the comments. The author of the reaction video in question is expected to give an account.

> You copied hellopopfriend
>
> *— Fish*★★★★★

> I like the idea, it doesn't mean that I copied it. I showed my dad her videos, and he said that it'd be cool if we did something like that, so we did. A lot of people make reaction videos, is it so bad that I made one with my family?
>
> *— oliv*★★★★★ *to Fish*★★★★★

In this respect, various threads of attention traffics are intertwined in the formation of the attention economy through the global practices of reaction videos. To begin with, the reactors often take on multiple roles. A reactor in a reaction video is simultaneously a consumer of the ready-made visual content of the music video, a producer and performer of the self-made reaction video. In other words, the reactor is the subject who represents the objectified self. The reactor, as both consumer and producer, may be called a "produser" in Bruns's terms (2008). Furthermore, the reactors are also intermediaries, as they exercise the authority of selecting particular stars and programs, guide how others should appreciate and react to their selections, and then review the stars' performances for anonymous YouTube audiences. The reactors are also playing an educational role, as they are often asked by potential reaction video producers to teach complicated advanced editing technology that will assist in the production of others' reaction videos. In short, the reactors are the core node of the operation of reaction videos: they are consumers of the original music videos, performers in reaction videos, critics of music and stars, and distributors of their own reaction videos. Thus significantly, reactors may be said to become active produsers not because they are engaged in the virtual space on the Internet with an unlimited amount of *information*, but because they succeed in pillaging a certain degree of recognition from the well-known stars in the mass media industry markets and build up their own positions in the cultural network of *attention* economy.

Secondly, a reaction video is a combination of the ready-made visual content and of user-generated content. Reaction videos are thereby "spreadable media" (Jenkins et al. 2013) that transmutes "stick media," or a ready-made media product and in this particular case the K-Pop music videos, disseminating and sharing it among many viewers within the YouTube network. The audiences of reaction videos on YouTube are simultaneously the consumers of both the ready-made visual content and the reactions portrayed in reaction videos and the producers of discursive elements in the global practices of K-Pop culture. Hence, the binary oppositions of active/reactive, producer/consumer, original creator/editorial intermediary, and stickiness/spreadability are blurred and interwoven in the social network of reaction videos.

Thirdly, reaction videos are seen to contribute to the formation of a cultural sphere which is related to, but autonomous from, the media industries mostly led by major corporations. The formation of cultural sphere reveals the nature of social constitution and contextualization underlying the attention economy operating in the global digital era. The activation of attention economy is not limited to the functioning of digital media in a technical sense, but also always and already realized through the human performance of cultural signification and collective engagement and expansion of its social meanings. This is illustrated in the interactive relationship between author, distributor, performer, and critic on the part of the reactors and consent, expectation, support and even criticism on the part of YouTube users. The consistent circuits of supply and demand can also develop and sustain not only on the basis of media technical facilities but also in the context of aesthetic principles, cultural tastes and social conventions that are generated and shared among the communities. It is noteworthy that the attention economy is in the social and cultural process of interactive performances in the mediated cultural milieu rather than simply given as the technological structure. Such process is initiated by the human agency having specific social orientations and cultural values pursuing self-expression and communitarian sharing, and predicated on popular participation and collective engagement for the subsequent development and expansion.

The aesthetics of reaction videos: ordinariness, naturalness, and self-immersion

In general, the aesthetics of user-created videos are concerned with "experimentation with the video forms" (Burgess and Green 2009, 52). Burgess and Green find the logic of cultural value embedded in user-created videos is mostly around "novelty and humor" (Burgess and Green 2009, 53). Reaction videos have a unique format of the novelty and humor, which originates in their fundamental element of being "reactive."

The standard K-Pop reaction video consists of three parts. In the first part, the reactors introduce themselves to the audiences on YouTube. They voice the motive for the production of the present reaction video, and then give a short explanation of the ready-made content to which the reactors will react. The second part follows with the ready-made content, which is the music video of K-pop. During this part, some reaction videos show only the reactors' reactions while others, with an application of more advanced visual technology skills, show both the reactions and the ready-made content being viewed by the reactors. In the former situation, the reaction videos provide only K-Pop music sound and a view of the reactors while in the latter situation, the audiences of reaction videos can watch both the reactors and the K-Pop musicians, along with hearing the song from the ready-made music videos. The third part consists of concluding remarks from the reactors, including their opinions of the music videos, any promises to provide additional reaction videos, and farewell greetings to the audiences.

The key aesthetics of reaction videos are ordinariness, naturalness, and self-immersion. These features differ from the observation of the YouTube meme proposed by Shifman (2012), where the "vernacular creativity" featured in incompleteness and fun are emphasized. In comparison with the amateur style of humor and vitality as generally assumed on YouTube, reaction videos are characterized with own unique cultural codes: the peculiarity of K-Pop reaction videos is focused on the visual expression of reactive passiveness, which comes to be concretized in the performative styles of ordinariness, naturalness, and self-immersion.

Regarding ordinariness, reaction videos are contextualized in ordinary people's everyday life and their habitual behaviors. Reactors can present themselves in a video as an individual or as a group. Reactors normally are situated in a personal place, such as one's bedroom or living room, wearing casual clothes. The atmosphere of a reaction video hence appears to be privatized and intimate. The reactions that reactors perform are easy body gestures and frank feelings expressed in simple words. Exaggerated movements and overstatements are quite often lamented in the audiences' responses. Naturalness is another characteristic of reaction video aesthetics. A reaction video showing a young girl around five years old with almost no gestures is welcome among the audiences as "one of the cutest reaction videos that I have ever seen." The responses to an overweight, middle-aged father's inarticulate reactions include, "Your father is really cute." Reaction videos in their literal sense show people's natural states when presented with the ready-made content. Reaction videos also featured self-immersion as an aesthetic. According to Burgess and Green (2009), the aspect of co-presence and conversation in "phatic" communicative function (Miller 2008) is highlighted in most content on YouTube. In contrast to the assumedly generalized feature of collectivity and connectivity of the youth culture on the Internet (Light et al. 2012), reaction videos have an obvious division between the section of distanced reaction and that of phatic action. This deliberately designed structure highlights the attribute of self-immersion in the way in which apart from the first and third parts where reactors are actively addressing the audience, reactors in the main part appear to be entirely occupied by one's own self-interiority while simply watching the K-Pop music videos. Their attention is focused on the music video to such an extent that no attempt at eye contact with the imaginary audience on YouTube is made while viewing the ready-made content.

Thus the reaction video, with its features of ordinariness, naturalness, and self-immersion, is formulated in the unique order of attention. That is, the attention of obliqueness. Avoiding the 'norm' of the conversational active (van Dijck 2009), dual desires to watch and to be watched are simultaneously drawn in and slantingly slide by. The reactors are watching K-Pop stars while, at the same time, they are being watched by YouTube audiences in a voyeuristic position. The binary attitudes of activeness and passiveness are combined, shared but also twisted in reaction videos. The complication of the structure of seeing of reaction videos is rooted in the reactors' ambivalent subject position of being active and passive "interactively or interpassively" (Wilson 2003; Žižek 1999) in the way that they produce their self-images to gain attention, but immediately deflect the attention by their presentation of reactive passiveness.

Cultural diversity in K-Pop reaction videos

The specific glocal (i.e. global and local) context the current study explores is reaction videos on Korean pop music, or K-Pop. K-Pop has become dramatically popular within the last few years in the global music scene (Kim 2011; Shin 2009). K-Pop is a relatively new and local genre of popular culture, in contestation with the conventional and universalized Western-white-centered visual culture (Evans and Hall 1999) or the global dominance by American-European and Japanese music industries. K-Pop is noted for its particularity in the process of its global development. It has become diffused globally not least through the anonymous users' horizontal interactions of exchange and sharing through the Internet rather than heralded by the established mainstream media institutions.

The multimodal analysis of reaction videos of K-Pop and popular discourse around them as appeared on YouTube suggests an interpretation of how, in accordance with the gradual emergence of the attention economy over K-Pop, global audiences initially come to adopt, become accustomed to and negotiate with a relatively new genre, such as K-Pop, and how individuals construe and identify themselves as fans of a new genre. Fans' online discussions reveal how the "emergent" genre exercises cultural influences on YouTube audiences concerning ethnicity, gender, race, and subcultural fashion and style, in articulation and differentiation from Western "dominant" culture (Williams 1977). In other words, the process of the formation of attention economy of K-Pop reaction videos is correlated with that of K-Pop achieving cultural recognition and reputation in the global cultural sphere.

The reaction videos on YouTube create a discursive space in which, concerning various aspects of the K-Pop phenomenon, reactors and audiences have conversations on diverse issues related to gender, sexuality, race, generation, and subculture. For example, a collaborative work by father and daughter on UKiss's (a K-Pop teen idol group) *Forbidden Love* was popular among the audience. The audience's responses to their reaction videos voice how K-Pop, a relatively new genre, is articulated or disarticulated within the Western patriarchal family structure.

> damn ur dad is cool.
>
> My dad doesn't even care.. he calls them Chinese and just ignores everything. My mom really likes miss a and 2ne1 tho and even urges me to play their songs for he[him] its cool!
>
> I love this video, I think they did a really good job in Forbidden love.
>
> *– Mari* ★★★★★

> your dad is cool! My dad would kill me for showing him the mv especially when they danced =. He said it's inappropriate =. =
>
> *– Fore*★★★★★

> This has got to be the cutest and most adorable reaction video I've ever seen. OMG I WANT DAD!!!! Not that way . . . He is toooo cool! AWWWW . . . Really loved this. Great vid!!!!!
>
> *– saku*★★★★★

Most reaction videos on K-Pop are produced, circulated, and consumed in the context of English. Responses written in Korean, Chinese, or Japanese are rarely found. Despite the dominance of English in the literary aspect, the visual images remain prevalently multicultural and multiracial. The ethnicity of reactors in groups is particularly diverse and the topics discussed on the reaction videos' sites are predominately Korean-oriented subcultural particularities. Questions asking the meanings of certain Korean words included in the lyrics of the songs are raised and speculated on among audiences, as well as exchanging information about K-Pop idol groups and their fashions. For instance, Big Bang (one of the most popular K-Pop idol groups) members' fashion styles, such as tattoos and hairstyles, are explored and this knowledge gradually develops into "subcultural capitals" (Thornton 1996). Gay and lesbian codes, which are, if any, too subtle and hardly perceptible in the original content of K-Pop music videos, are freely and divergently explored and explicitly appreciated among the YouTube viewers.

The popular practices of the attention economy pertaining to K-Pop reaction videos are articulated with specific geopolitical contexts of gender, race, ethnicity and generation in various ways and generate diverse social implications. In addition, peculiar cultural elements of subcultural knowledge, interest, and consumer desire for exotics are interwoven in the discursive construction of K-Pop culture. Alongside the convergence between the attention economy as communicative mode and discursive practice as cultural signification, K-Pop as an emergent culture newly achieves scarcity values in contestation with the previously Western-dominant attention economy of global popular music.

Normalization of reactive in communicative capitalism

As discussed in the aesthetics of reaction videos, reactors voluntarily undertake the work of re-creating and distributing the original K-Pop music videos. K-Pop reaction videos are the product of "fandom as free labour" (Kosnik 2013; Terranova 2004) through which fans' affection and passion are harnessed in the expansion of a local cultural industry or K-Pop towards the global market of popular culture. Significantly, to be reactive, which is traditionally seen as an opposition and inferiority to the norm of activeness regarding contemporary cultural consumption, is persistently capitalized on and exploited in the attention economy of reaction videos. In other words, fan labor invested in reaction videos takes the form of voluntary activeness to be reactive. The active voluntarism is also supported by the anonymous people's requests and responses rather than in oligopolistic control by major media corporations. This means that the human action of being reactive is motivated and captured in the global attention economy of reaction videos.

Being watched as one is being reactive in this sense becomes a type of "work" to rephrase Andrejevic's expression: "the work of being watched" when speaking of reality TV (Andrejevic 2004). The performance of passiveness may, then, be the cutting edge of creative labour "involving human contact and interaction" (Hesmondalgh and Baker 2010, 159) in the global visual network of YouTube. Reaction videos are in this respect a kind of emotional labor but having its own distinctive peculiarity. Most "emotional labour" is characterized by the presentation of excessive self-consciousness and hyperbolic narcissism in the attempt of inducing or suppressing feeling thereby creating and drawing affective attention (Hochschild 1983). In comparison, the simplicity of doing nothing other than being reactive is normalized as a deliberate, audacious strategy to present oneself in reaction videos. In the perspective of the ideology of demotic ordinariness (Turner 2009), reaction videos are the crux on which even the human naturalness of passivity, in the name of reaction, is commodified as global entertainment content.

Reaction videos as fan labor can be perceived in two ways; that is, the moral economy of a fan culture on the one hand and the critical assessment from a political economic perspective on the other. The first perception indicates that reactors offer a "gift" to the YouTube audience, the reward of which is obtained not in economic but in symbolic forms. The attention economy of reaction videos is fused with moral economy, in which "informal relationships . . . generate meaning through the exchange of media" (Jenkins et al. 2013, 61). The moral economy on the web is "based on reputation or status, competition and 'bragging rights,' mentorship and learning and the exchange of curatorial expertise and fan mastery" (Jenkins et al. 2013, 61).

Nevertheless, the moral economy "coexists and complexly interacts with commercial economy" (Jenkins et al. 2013, 61). Thus in terms of political economic account of reaction videos, the realm of reaction videos signifies a "communicative capitalism" (Dean 2010) in which human cognition, emotion, and knowledge are monetized as commercial information and culture. Reactors' labor to supply their passiveness is a part of "servile labour" (Marazzi 1994) to the anonymous Internet users in keeping their promises to produce sequences of their natural appearances. To this point, providing reaction videos is not merely meant to celebrate K-Pop stars, or to offer the audiences gifts. The active voluntarism involved in the production of K-Pop reaction videos is in the pursuit of self-branding, thereby promoting the self as a potential star in the global cultural network. The reactors are at once ambitious and exploited affective workers as their work to be reactive is seduced to become a part of the derivative loops of K-Pop industries and contribute to the global expansion of commercialized cultural consumption.

In short, reacting as a kind of fan labour has contradictions and complexities: it originates from "fan volunteerism" (Kosnik 2013) with the expectation of symbolic and material compensations while at the same time adding surplus value to the global market of K-Pop industries.

Conclusion

The notion of reaction is explored in relation to the presumed conceptual opposition of production/consumption and activeness/passiveness. Instead of reinforcing the separation, this study highlights the ambivalence and complexity embedded in the globally networked popular culture. It is argued that the diversification of global cultural sphere is realized through the popular participation in the attention economy from production and distribution to consumption, thereby the multilayered conjuncture and disjuncture are articulated in the emergence of K-Pop culture.

The developmental process of reaction videos of K-Pop as an emergent culture is identified with that of the attention economy of K-Pop in articulation with the diverse social and cultural relations and the various discourses of ethnicity, gender, sexuality, and subcultural practices. More significantly, the popularization of reaction videos reveals the process in which the natural form of a reactive private image of the self is publicly visualized and commercialized. The cultural activity of reaction is transformed into the economic logic of "immaterial labour," especially in the aspect of "cultural content" in Lazzarato's terms. According to Lazzarato (1996), the aspect of cultural content of immaterial labour concerns "a series of activities involved in defining and fixing cultural and artistic standards, fashions, tastes, consumer norms, and, more strategically, public opinion" (132). Reaction videos are seen to use or exploit human reaction as immaterial labor which creates symbolic (reputation and fame) and economic (market values of K-Pop) capitals. Thereby, "forms of life" of reaction are modified to the "source of innovation" (Lazzarato 1996, 145). The immaterial labor of being reactive reevaluates the prior perspective of the human natural passiveness and presents it as a commodity in the global communicative network. Reactive passiveness, which has been shunned in the interactive digital media environment, has been inverted and is now celebrated as a creative code of self-visualization.

YouTube allows the "performance of the self" (Goffman 1959), a type of "presentational media" (Marshall 2010), to prosper and to be driven to the pervasiveness of "the private self for public presentation" (Papacharissi 2010) in virtual space. In particular, this study suggests that the reactive images of the publicly privatized self are enthusiastically and hedonistically branded, celebrated and promoted in the globalized public network of attention economy. The human naturalness of reaction is mediatized in the digital mode, presented to attract anonymous attention, and exploited for the perpetual generation of pleasure in "communicative capitalism" in Dean's terms (Dean 2010). Reaction videos, then, represent a critical aspect of communicative capitalism. The contradiction between narcissistic desire for self-expression via active production and the human nature of reactive in passive consumption is combined to be modulated as the labor force of attention economy. The popular drives for active production and reactive consumption of the self altogether are coercively and impulsively produced, distributed, and consumed in the global, digital-mediated and post-capitalist cultural sphere.

Note

1 An earlier version of this paper is published with the title 'Reaction video and its attention economy: global production and consumption of K-Pop' (in Korean) in *Studies of Broadcasting Culture*, 24(2) in 2012, Seoul, Republic of Korea.

References

Andrejevic, M. (2004) *Reality TV: The Work of Being Watched*, Lanham, MD: Rowman & Littlefield.

Bird, S.E. (2011) 'Are we all produsers now?' *Cultural Studies*, 25(4–5): 502–516.

Bruns, A. (2008) *Blogs, Wikipedia, Second Life, and Beyond: From Production to Produsage*, New York: Peter Lang Publishing.

Burgess, J. and Green, J. (2009) *YouTube: Online Video and Participatory Culture*, Cambridge: Polity.

Carpentier, N. (2011) 'Contextualising author–audience convergences', *Cultural Studies*, 25(4–5): 517–533.

Dean, J. (2010) *Blog Theory: Feedback and Capture in the Circuits of Drive*, Cambridge: Polity.

Evans, J. and Hall, S. (1999) *Visual Culture: The Reader*, London: Sage Publications.

Goffman, E. (1959) *The Presentation of Self in Everyday Life*, New York: Doubleday.

Goldhaber, M. (1997) 'The attention economy and the net', *First Monday*, 2(4). Available at: http://firstmonday.org/ojs/index.php/fm/article/view/519/440 (Accessed on July 27, 2014).

Gray, J., Sandvoss, C. and Harrington, L. (eds) (2007) *Fandom: Identities and Communities in a Mediated World*, New York: New York University Press

Hesmondalgh, D. and Baker, S. (2010) *Creative Labour: Media Work in Three Cultural Industries*, London and New York: Routledge.

Hochschild, A.R. (1983) *The Managed Heart: The Commercialization of Human Feeling*, Berkeley: University of California Press.

Jenkins, H., Ford, S. and Green, J. (2013) *Spreadable Media: Creating Value and Meaning in a Networked Culture*, New York and London: New York University Press.

Kim, S. and Gang, J. (2012) 'Transmedia strategies in K-Pop industry: a case study of Gangnam Style', in *Korean Society for Journalism & Communication Studies Conference*, 2012, Autumn Conference.

Kim, Y. (2011) 'Idol republic: the global emergence of girl industries and commercialization of girl bodies', *Journal of Gender Studies*, 20(4): 333–345.

Kosnik, A. (2013) 'Fandom as free labour'. In T. Schotz (ed.) *Digital Labor: The Internet as Playground and Factory*, New York: Routledge: 98–111.

Lazzarato, M. (1996) 'Immaterial labour'. In P. Virno and M. Hardt (eds) *Radical Thought in Italy: A Potential Politics (Theory Out of Bounds)*, Minneapolis: University of Minnesota Press: 33–147.

Light, B., Griffiths, M. and Lincoln, S. (2012) '"Connect and create": young people, YouTube, and graffiti communities', *Continuum*, 26(3): 343–355.

Lim, V. (2007) 'The visual semantics stratum: making meaning in sequential images'. In T. Royce and W. Bowcher (eds) *New Directions in the Analysis of Multimodal Discours*, London: Lawrence Erlbaum Associates: 195–214.

Marazzi, C. (1994) *La svolta linguistica dell'economia e i suoi effetti nella politica*, Edizioni Casagrande; trans. G. Mecchia (2011) *Capital and Affects: The Politics of the Language Economy*, Los Angeles: Semiotext(e).

Marshall, P. (2010) 'The promotion and presentation of the self: celebrity as marker of presentational media', *Celebrity Studies*, 1(1): 35–48.

Miller, V. (2008) 'New media, networking and phatic culture', *Convergence,* 14(4): 387–400.

O'Halloran, K.L. (1999) 'Interdependence, interaction and metaphor in multisemiotic texts', *Social Semiotics*, 9(3): 317–354.

Papacharissi, Z. (2010) *A Private Sphere: Democracy in a Digital Age*, Cambridge: Polity.

Pearson, R. (2010) 'Fandom in the digital era', *Popular Communication: The International Journal of Media and Culture*, 8(1): 84–95.

Ramstad, E. (2012) 'Reaction vids get a pop with "Gangnam Style"', *Korea Real Time: The Wall Street Journal Asia*. Available at: http://blogs.wsj.com/korearealtime/2012/08/06/reaction-vids-get-a-pop-with-gangnam-style/ (Accessed on July 27, 2014).

Shifman, L. (2012) 'An anatomy of a YouTube meme', *New Media & Society*, 14(2): 187–203.

Shin, H. (2009) 'Have you ever seen the *Rain*? And who'll stop the *Rain*?: The globalizing project of Korean pop (K-pop)', *Inter-Asia Cultural Studies*, 10(4): 507–523.

Terranova, T. (2004) *Network Culture: Politics for the Information Age*, London and Ann Arbor, MI: Pluto Press.

Thornton, S. (1996) *Club Cultures: Music, Media, and Subcultural Capital*, Middletown, CT: Wesleyan University Press.

Turner, G. (2009) *Ordinary People and the Media: The Demotic Turn*, London: Sage Publications.

van Dijck, J. (2009) 'Users like you? Theorizing agency in user-generated content', *Media, Culture & Society*, 31(1): 41–58.

Williams, R. (1977) *Marxism and Literature*, Oxford: Oxford University Press.

Wilson, L. (2003) 'Interactivity or interpassivity: A question of agency in digital play'. Available at: http://hypertext.rmit.edu.au/dac/papers/Wilson.pdf (Accessed on July 27, 2014).

Žižek, S. (1999). 'The interpassive subject'. Available at: http://www.egs.edu/faculty/slavoj-zizek/articles/the-interpassive-subject/ (Accessed on July 27, 2014).

30

Public broadcasting, the Korean Broadcasting System (KBS), and its online services

Hye-Kyung Lee

The impact of new media, convergence culture, and participatory cultural consumption have so far been examined mainly from the perspective of commercial cultural business by scholars in cultural studies, media and communications, marketing, and management. It is not until recent years that we began realizing the above forces would also heavily affect public cultural institutions ranging from public service broadcasters, museums to theatres, which are endowed with educational missions and the status of national institution, and are usually financed publicly. While trying to adjust to the new media environment by introducing online platforms to widen the audience base and deepen their engagement, these public institutions are likely to undergo a complicated process of transformation, the nature of which we have yet to explore.

As part of this transformation, institutions face a series of fundamental questions on their rationale, identity, remit, and relationship with the public. For instance, the key public cultural institutions in London—such as the National Gallery, the British Museum, and the National Theatre—are questioning how to extend their public service remit to online spaces, how to balance existing and online services, what kind of relationship to establish with online audiences, and how their authoritative voice, derived from the existing expert knowledge, can coexist with cultural content generated by the audience (King's Cultural Institute 2011). Public cultural institutions' embrace of online and digital technologies would not only reshape their delivery of existing public service but also introduce a pressing need for the institutions' reconfiguration of their identity and function. As seen from the debate around the BBC's online strategies, this could remold the broader ecology of cultural industries by affecting business models and technological developments of commercial cultural providers in varying ways. By looking into the case of the online strategies of the Korean Broadcasting System (KBS),[1] this chapter argues that the transformation is heavily tied to the institution's path that has been conditioned by the political and social landscape of the country and its own understanding (or lack of it) of its public service remit.

This chapter shows that the KBS has suffered from Korean society's absence of clear vision of public service broadcasting and, consequently, maintains a weak social legitimacy (Cho 2012; Kim 2001; Park 2007), which is affecting the orientation of its online strategies. That is, the underdevelopment of consensus on the broadcaster's public responsibilities deters it from actively "imagining" online activities as an expansion of public service delivery. Rather than exploring online spaces' potential to form a public mediasphere, the KBS is using them mainly as platforms to promote its existing programs and provide program-specific information. The commercialism that characterizes the country's mediascape today heavily informs the broadcaster's view of online services. Under the rhetoric of audience engagement and participation, its online spaces imitate popular cultural spaces, such as online portals or fansites, and indicate a strong interest in valorizing program content, such as TV drama and entertainment series.

When the broadcaster is concerned primarily with the existing "audience" in its narrow sense or "fans" of its program content (Cho 2005), there is little attention given to "the public" that the broadcaster is expected to serve: inform, educate, entertain, challenge, engage, and collaborate with. The limited public service orientation of online spaces and the accommodation of commercial imperatives are not an issue for the KBS alone. This is because the shift from political to market parameters without serious reflection on public and civic roles of culture has characterized Korean cultural—both arts and media—policy and management since the 1990s. This chapter proposes that now is the time to scrutinize the commercial framework of the KBS's online strategies and the embrace of market-oriented discourses. Debating the KBS's online remit brings us back to the fundamental question of the broadcaster's identity as a "public broadcaster," the idea of which was never fully explored and has never generated social consensus since the broadcaster's inception (Cho 2012).

Public culture and public service broadcasting

Public service broadcasting (PSB) resides at the heart of a society's public culture. This chapter broadly defines public culture as a collection of cultural, artistic, and media infrastructure, services, and programs that contribute to the public benefit and cultural well-being, especially those created, circulated, displayed and/or communicated primarily for such purposes. From an economic perspective, public culture is seen as a type of "public good": it is normally financed and provided publicly as its non-exclusivity and non-rivalry make it widely accessible to members of society so privatizing it would be problematic. It is also suggested that society is willing to maintain, advance, and protect public culture from market pressures as it serves as a merit good, a current and future resource for members of society, and a source of positive externalities.

Taking the perspective of public policy, we focus primarily on government and public sector organizations' cultural services and infrastructures that aim at enhancing cultural well-being and the quality of life of the public. The sociocultural perspective that public culture consists of particular activities and services to which a society collectively assigns cultural value allows us to view this culture as a public good and service. The spectrum of public culture would be unfixed as its core constituents may change over time and differ across societies because cultural values would be relative and specific temporally. This implies that public culture inherently entails both cultural consensus and the challenges to it. Its content and boundaries, therefore, are subject to constant questioning and debating, and, perhaps, such processes would be an essential part of public culture itself. Public cultural institutions would play crucial roles in advancing and sustaining the ecology of this type of culture.

In the past, public culture was likely to be defined by the cultural authority held by the state, elite classes, and cultural experts while its elitism and paternalism were criticized by popular culture and alternative cultural practices. In spite of the prevalence of postmodern, relativist, and market-centered perspectives of culture nowadays, many societies try to redefine public culture rather than simply giving up such an idea. This context presents the rise of digital technologies and online communications as a new opportunity to reconfigure public culture by allowing public cultural institutions' deeper, wider and more direct engagements with members of the public and by democratizing cultural production and distribution. This opportunity, however, is causing some fundamental tensions to arise as the democratization of culture necessitates the decentralization of symbolic resources such as the expert knowledge traditionally held by cultural institutions and experts.

The question is then how to redistribute these resources between existing cultural producers and members of the public who are active in creating and communicating their own culture online, and what roles public cultural institutions could play to strengthen the public elements of our everyday culture when it is increasingly individualized and decentralized with online social networks becoming hot spots for cultural dissemination and consumption. Discovering ways to redefine and enrich public culture is an important policy agenda given the penetration of commercial imperatives in everyday culture and cultural industries' attempt to capitalize on consumers' creativity via actively sharing symbolic resources with them (van Dijck 2009). Under this new media and cultural landscape, cultural policy's traditional agenda, including accessibility, participation, and excellence, would be given new, currently undetermined, meanings.

One can argue that PSB is well situated to play decisive roles in reconfiguring public culture. This is because PSB is a popular, accessible, and ubiquitous medium that delivers a wide range of program content and is already an essential part of most people's cultural life. The idea and institution of PSB were born in a Western European context with strong political and professional consensus that public broadcasting is best delivered when the broadcaster's independence of political and commercial pressures is guaranteed, and when PSB can provide universal service for all members of the public and not just particular sections of it. Although PSB has never been free from the accusation of being elitist or commercialized, it has long been seen as a democratic medium that addresses issues that are important for wider society and provides diverse programs, from education to information to entertainment, including programs that target minority groups in society. While pursuing cultural diversity, PSB programs are expected to contribute to the support of social cohesion, fostering shared public life, and reflecting and cementing public opinion (Freeman 2008, 147–148 cited in Tunstall 2010).

Like many other counties, Korea has looked westward at the BBC as a model for its public broadcasting since the 1990s (Cho 2012, 41). What is often overlooked, however, is the fact that the BBC's creation was rooted firmly in the British society's cultural consensus, led by the cultural hegemony of middle classes who also constituted the core of British civil society, although this consensus has been questioned heavily. Meanwhile the German PSB system is based on strong corporatist consensus between the state, the business sector, and social groups, as seen in the country's two public broadcasters' governance where a range of social and interest groups' participation in decision making is structurally guaranteed. Additionally, the reliable and consistent public funding in the form of license fees attributes to the success and achievements of British and German PSB.

PSB going online and its key issues

The rise of new media, online platforms, convergence culture, and participatory consumption has seriously challenged PSB as a one-to-many broadcasting of predefined quality programs. It has been widely reported that young audiences today prefer to access specific content on non-traditional broadcasting platforms such as a PC, mobile phone, tablet PC, game console and MP3 device at their chosen moment. The traditional linear model of broadcasting may no longer be sustainable and, consequently, many broadcasters are now developing on-demand services that are accessible through multiple platforms—the BBC's *iPlayer* is the most successful example. As proven by the YouTube phenomenon, cultural consumers today have a strong tendency to exercise active agency in media making and disseminating, and are not simply satisfied with the program content provided by professional media producers and companies. Remaking and recreating media content is becoming a part of everyday culture, where cultural production and consumption converge, making obsolete the traditional distinction between providers and users, companies and markets, and broadcasters and audiences.

Today's media environment and consumption presents a series of serious questions about PSB. First, the fact that the traditional service of PSB is a small section of the ever-enlarging and complicated media ecology and its diminishing audience size and ratings tend to undermine the existing rationale of PSB (serving all members of the public) and its public funding. Facing the proliferation of free online platforms such as YouTube (global) and Youku (Chinese) where audiences' free choice of programming is seen as democratic and empowering, PSB is pressured to reconsider its top-down, centralized, paternalistic nature of program delivery. The dominant discourse on PSB seems divided broadly into two themes: PSB reduction and PSB expansion. The first discourse is informed by the aforementioned trends and derived from the view that PSB is an obsolete institution technologically and socio-culturally, since broadcasting service is no longer tied to airwaves that used to be regarded as a scarce public resource; additionally, free audio and video content is now available on multiple channels for various devices.

When considering this phenomenon in terms of consumer sovereignty, one can say that it would be irrational for consumers to continue to support PSB, which requires a license fee, when they prefer YouTube to PSB usage. This argument fits within the broader discourse of the marketization of the broadcasting sector. It further includes the view that existing regulations on commercial terrestrial broadcasters—for instance, commercial terrestrial channels must provide a certain type and amount of PSB content—should be reduced given that other commercial (online) platforms operate without the same restrictions, and the commercial terrestrial broadcasters are only one of many such providers available today.

Meanwhile, the discourse of PSB expansion argues that the existing PSB needs to expand into new media so high-quality PSB content can be produced and made accessible for the public (Jakubowicz 2010). This view suggests that embracing new technologies and converging existing broadcasting services with new media could reconfigure public culture and serve as a node for public knowledge and information, and provide a space where expert knowledge and collective intellect validate each other, leading to both democratic and critical production of knowledge. Tension and debates arising would be part of this new public culture.

Public broadcasting in the South Korean context

It is crucial to note that the idea of public service broadcasting, which is embedded in Western European public broadcasting, has not been fully explored and implemented in South Korea (hereafter Korea). In this sense, the Korean Broadcasting System (KBS) is better defined as a "public broadcasting corporation" rather than a "public service broadcaster," because its public service remit is not as clear as its legal status as a public corporation. The *Korean Broadcasting System Act* (1972–2000) did not give a definition for public broadcasting.[2] The new *Broadcasting Act* (2000), which incorporated the *Korean Broadcasting System Act*, states in its 44th clause that KBS (1) has "public responsibilities" that would implement "broadcasting's public responsibilities" (the 5th clause) and realize "broadcasting's impartiality and public benefits" (the 6th clause), (2) should provide universal service of quality programs, (3) should develop new broadcasting programs, services, and technologies that are beneficial to its audience, and (4) should develop and broadcast programs that advance national culture and promote national cohesion. In addition, the KBS's current website says that its public remit includes monitoring and critiquing the social environment and forming public opinion. Nevertheless, there has traditionally been weak consensus on the interpretation of the above wording and on the relationship between the broadcaster, government, and public. It is within this context that, in summer 2014, the new president of the KBS promised to end the continuing debate on the broadcaster's lack of impartiality and prove its status as a public broadcaster (KBS 2014).

The KBS started as a government-owned and managed broadcaster (*gukyeong bangsong*) when the Republic of Korea was born in 1948 after the 35 years of Japanese colonial rule until 1945 and the three years of American military army occupation afterwards. The government maintained a tight grip on the KBS and a strong belief that broadcasting, like other governmental activities and public services, should play parts in the country's ideological and political endeavor to counter the communist regime in North Korea and forge social cohesion (Ministry of Culture and Public Information 1979, 191). The broadcasting sector was monopolized by the KBS until the mid-1950s when religious and commercial broadcasters came into being. The KBS's TV service began in 1961, followed by commercial TV.

In 1973, the KBS became a public corporation that delivered publicly managed broadcasting (*gongyeong bangsong*) soon after President Park Chung Hee's implementation of the October Reform (*Siwol Yousin*) to strengthen his political power and make his presidential tenure permanent. According to the government, the main reason for the transformation was the existing system's problems, such as bureaucracy, low flexibility, and difficulty in recruiting talented professionals (Ministry of Culture and Public Information 1979, 201). The *Korean Broadcasting System Act* (1972) defined the KBS as a state key broadcasting system (*gukga gigan bangsong*) and required it to actualize the impartiality of broadcasting, delivery of public benefits, and provision of high-quality broadcasting that is accessible by all citizens. Unfortunately, there was neither society-wide discussion nor consensus on what public broadcasting (*gongyeong bangsong*) would mean and should deliver, and this situation continued.

Throughout the 1970s and the first half of the 1980s, the country saw a stark power imbalance between the dictatorial government and the almost non-existent civil society, implying that there was little social or civil force that could play active roles in determining the nature of public broadcasting. Similarly, the broadcasting reform in the 1980s, which resulted in the incorporation of four commercial radio stations and the commercial TBC TV into the KBS and the KBS's acquisition of 65 percent of MBC (Munhwa Broadcasting Corporation) shares, took place without public consultation as the government wanted better control over the sector. The KBS's mixed financing also raised questions on its identity as a public broadcaster. Initially, the KBS relied solely on license fees; however, a gap between income and expenditures caused by the introduction of color TV allowed the KBS to raise money via advertising in 1980. Since then, the proportion of advertising income to its total income gradually increased, indicating that the KBS could not be free from commercial influences even during the three successive military governments until 1993. Considering these circumstances, defining Korea's public broadcasting as "public service broadcasting" could be misleading.

Despite being a public broadcaster, KBS was continuously susceptible to political pressures from the government. The noticeable political bias in programs such as news reports caused high frustration and anger among audiences to the point that some of them launched a nationwide "license fee refusal" campaign in the mid-1980s (see Cho 2012 and Kim 2001 for detailed accounts of the campaign). It was not a mere tax resistance but a political protest against the broadcaster's subordination to governmental imperatives. The protest triggered KBS workers' self-reflection and the formation of a trade union, which believed that democratic and independent broadcasting would be a key driving force of a society wide democratic movement (Cho 2012, 48). The KBS's commercialism and the declining quality of children's programs further exacerbated Korean society's distrust of the KBS.

During the 1990s, the KBS gained more independence from political imperatives while commercialism rose as a new control mechanism of it (Kim 2001, 99). The emergence and expansion of the civil sector influenced the broadcaster's programming via monitoring and auditing. For instance, civil groups protested against the decline of children's programs and program quality. While the key issue for civil groups in the 1980s was promoting independent journalism, the main concern for them in the 1990s was increasing commercialism of the sector. The emerging multichannel environment (cable and satellite TV were introduced in 1995 and 2002, respectively) meant that the KBS was in fierce competition with other channels for audiences as well as advertising income. The proportion of advertising income of the broadcaster's total income in 2003, 2008 and 2012 was 54.95 percent, 41.8 percent and 41 percent, respectively (KBS 2013) though the KBS stopped advertising on the main KBS1 TV and KBS 1 Radio in 1994 to strengthen these main channels' public nature. The KBS's overall market orientation has resulted in a lack of distinction between its program content and that on other channels. For instance, although KBS1 TV is keen on broadcasting educational and informative programs (*gyoyang program*), its drama and entertainment programs compete fiercely with other TV programs for a share of the audience.

The Korean society's concern with political and market imperatives explains why the KBS license fee has been frozen at 2,500 Korean won (approx. US$2.5) per month for the past 33 years with the public's heavy opposition against a fee raise. For many Koreans, a fee raise is not a condition for achieving PSB; rather, they see concrete evidence of the KBS's transformation into an independent broadcaster as an essential condition for a fee raise. The two consecutive conservative governments (2008–2013 and 2013–2018) and the weakened political independence of the broadcaster apparently lead Koreans to prioritize independent journalism and political impartiality as key issues while leaving questions on the broader meaning of public broadcasting unasked.

The KBS and its online services

Currently, all three main terrestrial broadcasters in Korea—KBS (public), MBC (non-profit), and SBS (commercial)—are providing online services, including on-demand audio/video available via streaming and downloading. The broadcasters launched websites where they began online services in the 1990s and expanded the range of offerings for audiences by setting up subsidiaries dedicated to Internet services. The KBS was at the forefront of this development, launching its homepage in 1995 and offering real-time streaming in 1996. Its video-on-demand news program started in 1997 and extended to include other programs in 1998. The main purpose of the KBS website was promoting the broadcaster and its programs domestically and abroad (mainly for overseas Koreans), and there was little consideration about the potential of Internet services for public broadcasting and consequent financial implications (Yoo 2004, 46–47).

The broadcaster's plans to utilize the Internet for public broadcasting purposes was announced in the 1999 "Promise to Viewers and Listeners" (March 3, 1999), where it promised to: provide publicly beneficial programs; be responsive to and reflect audience's views; provide precise, impartial, and reliable news; improve the quality of entertainment and drama programs; strengthen programs for children, young people, and marginal groups; promote environmental protection; strengthen Korean cultural identity and develop cultural diversity; promote and protect the Korean language; broadcast digitally; and innovate with management (Cho 1999). Yet, the Promise's understanding of the Internet was limited: the Internet would be a means to communicate with audiences, disseminate information on its key programs, offer the KBS publications electronically, and strengthen the KBS website's section for disabled audiences. The subsequent development of the KBS online strategies lacked clear guidelines for public broadcasting, and this, combined with the shortage of funding, resulted in the prevalence of commercialism.

The KBS website soon became popular and attracted a growing audience (the number of daily visits to the website on October 4, 2000 was ten million and the number doubled in one year) thanks to the penetration of high-speed broadband and the PC in Korean households (Yoo 2004, 48). This trend encouraged the KBS to create Crezio.com, a joint commercial venture between the KBS and KT, the biggest telecommunications company in the country, in 2000. Crezio ran the KBS website—and the homepages for its programs—where programs were live-streamed and their video-on-demand was available for four weeks. Crezio also experimented with producing online-only programs, such as online daily sitcoms and the broadcasting of Internet game matches on the KBS website, browsing potential business models. Nevertheless, offering online-only content was not successful in terms of attracting a critical-mass audience, and this meant Crezio's main income was the fee from the KBS for running its website. In 2003, the website surpassed 834,000 members and thereby proved its ongoing popularity (An and Lee 2012).

When Crezio.com was renamed KBS Internet in 2002, its commercial business model was strengthened. In the same year, it began running Conpia.com (Content Utopia, a commercial digital content distribution website) and launched various commercial activities including caller ring, character, and shopping businesses. The biggest change, however, was the commodification of the KBS programs. That is, while the KBS homepage continued to provide a free catch-up service for a reduced period (two weeks), Conpia began commercial video-on-demand services in 2002. The KBS chose this "indirect" commercialization strategy via an external website to satisfy its status as a public broadcaster. The year 2002 marked the start of commercialization of SBS and KBS program content on the Internet, and this trend was soon followed by the non-profit MBC. At the same time, these three broadcasters began discussing the potential to develop Conpia into a commercial hub of terrestrial broadcasting content (KBS Internet 2003), albeit without a concrete outcome. The move to commercial online services did not spark debate within the KBS as there was a widely shared concern about the shortage of income and online sales of its programs were seen as a new way to raise additional financial resource (Interviewees 1 and 2).[3]

With a weak consensus on whether or not the Internet should be included in the remit of public broadcasting and how it should be financed, different sections of the KBS had different ideas about its Internet presence (Interviewees 1 and 2). For example, policy makers at the KBS saw the Internet as a new platform to offer public broadcasting programs for free without engaging commercial activities while those working at KBS Internet, which was the broadcaster's commercial subsidiary, saw it as a space where profit-generating activities would be carried out. This explains the broadcaster's ultimate failure to keep the website free of advertisement despite its repeated assertion that its programs on the website would be free of commercialism indefinitely.

For instance, in 2003 the KBS promised free provision of program content and the removal of all commercial activities, including advertising, sponsorship, and content sales, from its website (Yoo 2004, 50). The statement led to the broadcaster's subsequent announcement of a KBS homepage reform ("clean homepage") on March 3, 2004, which would remove advertising and commercial business and develop the website into the "third" public channel (after the existing two channels, KBS1 and KBS2). Advertisements, however, began to reappear in autumn the same year and became a continuing trend (Interviewee 1). In 2006, the website removed commercials and created homepages for the disabled, KBS e-cinema, and an online TV museum to enhance its public service roles. Nevertheless, it reintroduced commercial advertisements soon thereafter.

Despite the KBS's repeated promises to keep its programs free and reflect the spirit of public broadcasting in its management of online services, there has not been a solid understanding on whether the online services would be a core of public broadcasting or auxiliary services;

further, discussions at practical levels took place between those at the KBS and KBS Internet, which is commercially operated (Interviewee 2). Amid audiences' suspicion about the KBS's commercialism, the broadcaster defined itself as one of many service providers in the market, meaning that its public service remit would include the provisioning of program information, live streaming, and low-quality video-on-demand services only. With the merger between KBS Media and KBS Internet in 2011, the broadcaster developed more concrete and coherent content business models based on "one source, multi uses" across online and offline channels. In 2009, the three terrestrial broadcasters created a joint venture, Conting, to prevent their content's unauthorized distribution online and supply one-spot video-on-demand services for TV audiences (Interviewee 2). Currently, the KBS website offers low-quality videos (300K) only, while standard (500K) and high-quality videos (2M) are sold on Conpia and Conting in various paid packages. These commercial websites' free content consists of a limited number of episodes of ongoing drama series and a larger number of episodes of a single educational program.

The KBS website's layout and content look similar to other broadcasters' websites, although it more actively introduces select key programs, including news and documentaries. These websites' main components are news reports, information on entertainment and drama, and popular videos. Even in the case of the KBS, it is difficult to see how the broadcaster selects website content based on what criteria or how public service remit affects related decisions. The overall layout implies that the broadcaster offers a range of popular programs and information so its audience can decide what to view. The broadcaster's cultural authority and expert knowledge, the legitimacy of which has been questioned along with its susceptibility to political pressure, seems to be decentralized within the commercial framework.

Conclusion

The KBS launched online services as early as the mid-1990s, ahead of its time not only with the application of online communications technologies, but also by experimenting with the production and broadcasting of online-only program content. Its initial belief was that the Internet would be a distinct space to deliver online-only, unique content; however, it is difficult to say that this experiment was successful as the Internet has become an additional outlet for rebroadcasting existing TV and radio programs. With an absence of contemplation and debate on the public broadcasting roles of KBS online services, the continuous license fee freeze and financial constraints have encouraged the broadcaster to pursue a commercial approach with online services. In a way, this strategy can be seen as something in between PSB reduction and PSB expansion: PSB expansion driven by commercialism. The long-standing public opinion is that a license fee raise should come after the broadcaster's genuine demonstration of "public broadcasting," especially showing its programs' political impartiality and independence of governmental influence. Consequently, the broadcaster is finding it hard to argue for the potential centrality of online services based on the provision of public broadcasting and this has led to the deepening of commercial oriented development of its online strategies.

In the current discourse of public broadcasting in Korea, new media and online services are not seen as key determinants of the future of the KBS as a public broadcaster. Facilitating debate and forming consensus on the aims, uses, content, and financing of KBS online services is as politically important as the long-standing and re-occurring issue of independent journalism; however, a widely held view within the KBS and civil society is that achieving the latter is a prerequisite for addressing the former. It is unfortunate that as Korea's recent discussion of public broadcasting is almost solely tied to independent journalism and impartial news reports, there is little scope to explore the broadcaster's wider roles in reconfiguring the country's public cultural landscape and bringing public cultural elements to online spaces does not draw public attention.

Notes

1 KBS consists of three TV channels (KBS1 TV, KBS2 TV, and KBS World), seven radio channels (KBS1, KBS2, KBS3, KBS FM1, BS FM2, Korean Nation, and KBS World Radio) and four terrestrial DMB channels. In addition, it provides data broadcasting and new media services.
2 *The Korean Broadcasting System Act* (1972–2000) only states the aim of KBS as contributing to the development of broadcasting culture and the improvement of public welfare by effective broadcasting for domestic and overseas audiences and making the whole nation accessible to broadcasting. It asks KBS to clarify its aims in its constitutional document, implying that the actual meaning of public broadcasting would depend on the broadcaster's interpretation. KBS was expected to operate within the framework of broadcasting ethics set by the *Broadcasting Act* (1973): respect for human rights, fairness, national spirit of independence (*jucheseong*), national culture, guiding children and young people, and public morality. The law did not define public broadcasting.
3 The author interviewed two professionals who worked at KBS Internet in the mid-2000s. The interviews took place at their offices in KBS on July 31 and August 4, 2014.

References

An, J.-H. and Lee, S.-Y. (2012) 'A study on case analysis and construction situation of KBS Internet broadcasting (*Internet bansongui guchughyeonhwanggwa seongjanggwajeoge gwanhan yeongu: KBSreul jungsimeuro*)', *Hangukjisikgisuljeongbohakoe nonmunjib*, 7(3): 1–6.
Cho, E. (2005) 'An analysis of the producers' responses on the opinions of viewers through the program website (*Bangsongjejakjinui sicheongja uigyeon suyong hyeongtaee daehan yeongu*)', *Hangugeonnonhakoebo*, 49(1): 57–81.
Cho, H. (2012) 'An historical study on the licence fee of public service broadcasting in Korea (*Hanguk-gongyeongbangsongui susinlyo munjee daehan yeoksajeong gochal*)', *Bangsongmunhwayeongu*, 24(2): 37–70.
Cho, S.-H. (1999) 'A study on the way of evaluation for "Promises to viewers and listeners" of KBS (*KBSui sicheongjae daehan yagsog ihaeng pyeongga bangan yeongu*)', *Sahoegwahak*, 11: 225–246.
Jakubowicz, K. (2010) 'PSB 3.0: reinventing European PSB'. In *Reinventing Public Service Broadcasting Communication: European Broadcasters and Beyond*, Basingstoke: Palgrave Macmillan: 9–22.
KBS (2013) 'Report to National Assembly National Audit (Committee for Korea Communications Commission) (*Gukjeonggamsa yogujaryo, miraechangjoguahakbangsongtongsinwiwonhoe*)', Seoul: KBS.
KBS (2014) *KBS Company Newsletter*, 576, Seoul: KBS.
KBS Internet (2003) *Rapid commercialization of the Internet sites of three broadcasters* (*Bangsong 3sa Internet site, yuryohwa geupjinjeon*). Available at: http://www.crezio.com/notice (Accessed on July 30, 2014).
Kim, Y. (2001) 'The broadcasting audience movement in Korea', *Media, Culture & Society*, 23(1): 91–107.
King's Cultural Institute (2011) *Creative Futures Symposium Summary*, London: King's Cultural Institute.
Ministry of Culture and Public Information (*Munhwagongbobu*) (1979) *The 30 Years of Culture and Public Information* (*Munhwagongbo 30nyeon*), Seoul: MCPI.
Park, I. (2007) 'Korean public service broadcasting's social roles and its performance evaluation (*Internet gongyeongbangsongui yeokalgwa geu suhaengui pyeongga*)', *Hyeonsanggwa insig*, Spring/Summer.
Tunstall, J. (2010) 'The BBC and the UK public service broadcasting'. In *Reinventing Public Service Broadcasting Communication: European Broadcasters and Beyond*, Basingstoke: Palgrave Macmillan: 145–157.
van Dijck, J. (2009) 'Users like you: theorizing agency in user-generated content', *Media, Culture & Society*, 31(1): 41–58.
Yoo, Y. (2004) 'Comparative Study of BBC and KBS on their Strategies of Managing Internet Services (*BBCwa KBSui Hangug seobiseu unyeongjeonlyag bigyoyeongu*)', Seoul: Department of Mass Communication, Sogang University, Korea (MA dissertation).

31

The struggle between subaltern nationalisms and the nation-state in the digital age: China and its ethnic minorities

Kwai-Cheung Lo

The Internet is generally considered as the core of radical politics in the digital age and is believed to have the capacity to mobilize oppositional forces to resist against dominant power structures. In the 2011 Arab Spring, the Internet's role was perceived to be central in this series of movements for political reform and regime change (Rane and Salem 2012). However, the prediction that the Internet may have democratizing effects on contemporary Chinese society has not yet come true.

Technology-determined understandings of how the Internet can change society are usually not very accurate since the Internet's impacts are always filtered through the structures and contexts of a particular society. Technological determinism tends to be flawed because it is more often the way in which a society receives and makes use of technologies that defines their technological significance. Perhaps, the Internet should not be simply treated as a transforming agent of society but more importantly as a channel for understanding the functioning of power and struggle in a given society.

This chapter examines at least four aspects of struggle and power relations in connection to the uses of new media in a contemporary Chinese multi-ethnic context. Firstly, new media study is often thought of as a story about control and emancipation. While attention has been primarily paid to how the Chinese government restricts the influences of the Internet and what the new media may mean for China's democratization, the ethnicity issue in such contested sites is relatively overlooked.

Secondly, the notion of time in relation to the Internet may generate more in-depth conceptualization when both the state appropriates the new media for nation-building and modernity project, and the ethnic groups for identity reflection or re-articulation. Thirdly, the dissemination of ideas and information by digital means may lead to a further reinforcement of the centralization of power and knowledge as well as some new challenges to the top-down organization of the transmission of knowledge and information. Fourthly, the Internet is playing an ambivalent role of encouraging dialogue among ethnic communities but also of promoting ethnic separatism or sectarianism.

Control and emancipation

Different technologies—suffice to say—comprise part of processes of emancipation and control in the ongoing mutation of worldwide capitalist modernization. The mechanization and industrialization of the earlier waves of modernity since the nineteenth century already enabled drastic structural changes in many Asian countries, while the digitalization also comes with very different processes of liberation and domination in twenty-first century China. The common use of telegraphy in nineteenth-century China already demonstrated how Chinese people employed such a new communication technology of the times to participate in politics.

While the telegraph overcame vast distances and connected the whole country on an instant basis, the imperial government of the Qing Empire (1644–1911) tried to regulate and control this media (Zhou 2006). The physical presence and penetration of telegraph, railway, and steamship have generally undermined Chinese sovereignty since many of these new technologies were introduced to the Chinese lands without the authorization of the Qing government. That explains why the Chinese authorities took a rather hostile position towards these technologies even though they were well aware that these major symbols of modern progress and national strength would benefit China's future development. The Internet in China's politics is obviously a different story.[1] The Chinese state over the last two decades has efficiently employed the Internet to develop the economy and strengthen governance if not entirely to suppress political democratization.

If the Internet is the new media that triggers off new hopes for real changes, as well as drives for strengthening control in contemporary Chinese society, China's ethnic minorities also play the role of "new media" for the nation to consider what it means to be "Chinese" and how the nation-state, national identity, and nationalism should be defined. Ethnic minority became a new issue in the early twentieth century for many Asian countries when they tried to establish themselves as modern nation-states based upon the notion of one race, one language, and one culture. Although ethnic minorities only make up about 9 to 10 percent of the Chinese population, they occupy almost two-thirds of the territories that the People's Republic of China (PRC) has primarily inherited from the Qing dynasty.

More importantly, these borderlands populated by ethnic minorities are the military-strategic areas key to the national security and the resource-rich parts of the country. Managing ethnicity and constituting a cohesive sense of national identity has become the primary task for the PRC since its establishment in 1949. The Chinese state has been persistently working hard to downplay ethnic conflicts, promote an image of ethnic harmony in China, and mold public opinions on ethnic issues domestically and internationally. Although the Internet may serve as one of the efficient propaganda tools to manage ethnic affairs, it also brings a host of new challenges to the state's domination of ethnic representations.

Despite authorities' efforts to maintain the peace-and-stability image of Tibet, many Chinese tourists to Tibet from 2011 to 2012 have uploaded hundreds of images that document the harsh security measures implemented in a highly militarized Tibet by the Chinese regime. These Chinese tourists' expressions of shock and even fear at the "war zone" atmosphere in Tibet were posted on social media though being quickly deleted by the censor (Samphel 2014). On the other hand, China is also using fake Twitter accounts bearing false Western names accompanied by profile pictures to promote the state's propaganda on Tibet and Xinjiang tailored to Western audiences. The tweets from the bogus accounts have not only portrayed Tibet as a contented and idyllic Chinese province and disseminated upbeat news about these ethnic regions, but also posted English-language articles that attacked the Dalai Lama. Although it is difficult to judge if those counterfeit twitter accounts that spread pro-Chinese propaganda are making any desired impact, many of them have genuine followers, apparently believing the accounts belong to real people (Jacobs 2014).

Perhaps the nature of the modern Chinese nation-state is far from being natural (the so-called organic whole) and it is hard to envision it as an integrated whole no matter how incessantly the regime has tried to do so. China's ethnic mosaic is anything but a harmonious totality. Indeed, it is an internally conflicted political economy at odds with itself from the very beginning of the national formation. It may be tempting to see the ethnic mosaic as multiple, decentered, rhizomatic—the features attributed by the optimists to the Internet. But it is the ruling regime that perceives the new media as something too dangerous to be left for free development and thus it immediately grasps its potential by turning it into a powerful homogenizing and standardizing machine. In a similar mode, the Han-dominated Chinese government nominally grants ethnic minorities autonomous rule, but many of its ethnic policies aim at enhancing integration for fear that the high degree of autonomy would give rise to breakaway states. The lack of true autonomy (in the sense that ethnic minorities do not have the genuine opportunity and power to shape the policies that directly affect them) becomes a significant cause of antagonism in China's ethnic politics, especially when the rapid economic developments fail to bring adequate benefits to the ethnic communities but intensify the income inequities between Han and non-Han.

Since the Internet appeared in China in the mid-1990s, digital activism from the civil society and cyber policing of the state both have been gaining their momentum and adapting to rapid changes. As the history of popular protest (including ethnic protest) and the history of state control are equally strong in China, the creative and flexible online activism has encountered the highly adaptable state governing in the twenty-first century. While the authorities are actively blocking websites, filtering keywords, monitoring online postings, harassing dissidents, hiring paid bloggers to influence online discussions, and launching mass campaigns to guide online expressions, Internet activists also creatively bypass the censorship firewalls to disseminate banned information and mobilize online/offline action.

As the Chinese state in recent years inclines to take a soft-power approach[2] to Internet governance by co-opting and channeling online protests to its advantage rather than completely eradicating them, some room seems to be opened to social advocacy and civic engagement (such as food safety, environmental protests, citizen's rights, etc.) as long as they are not confrontational to the government (Yang 2014). However, the Chinese state takes a zero tolerance policy towards the digital dissenters who call for direct political opposition and regime change, as well as the ethnic activists who aspire for more political autonomy and even outright independent status. A few days after the violent Urumqi unrest in July 2009, the Chinese state did not hesitate to cut off the whole of Xinjiang from all access to the Internet and international communication for almost a year.[3]

In the digitalized societies of control, new media or technology is an expression of such given social form. Unlike those in the disciplinary societies, people in the societies of control are believed to be more undulatory than linear, in circling orbit, or in a fluid network surfing. Not only does the state manipulate the Internet. The governed people in the society also actively make use of the new media to empower themselves and to enhance a larger degree of liberalization that does not necessarily require any structural change of the political system. The politics of new media in multi-ethnic China suggests possible strategies to resist new techniques of control enabled by those technologies, although the newer modulatory mode of power could actually function at the same time as the older disciplinary mode of power.

Conflicting temporalities: nationalist conservatism and ethnic anachronism

The Chinese state does not simply intend to control the dissemination and content of the Internet, but also aggressively promote it for its own interests by establishing some controlled public space and attempting to channel political discourse in the way the regime most desires. In addition to the pervasive censorship-cum-surveillance, commercialization also greatly shapes the constitutive components of the Internet in contemporary China. Indeed, economic growth is a means for the Chinese one-party state to maintain its legitimacy and preserve political stability. The proactive policy of the Chinese authority has simultaneously allowed phenomenal Internet growth for economic development and exerted tight control over the new media. Undoubtedly, the Chinese government attempts to use digital technologies and computer-mediated communications as an institutional basis of its power.

While a new politics, one not necessarily focused on identity politics, is emerging through the new media that focuses on articulating post-national or supranational identification, new (or recurring) forms of organizing and (re-)constructing national, ethnic, or religious identity are also empowered by new technologies that many domestic and diasporic ethnic groups use to resist against the hegemonic ideology imposed by the Chinese sovereign state. The local identity empowerment and ethnic-consciousness raising are increasingly connected with planetary configurations of the new media. Far from dissolving the particular ethnicity into the united national identity, the Internet enables ethnic minorities to link with one another wherever they are. The Chinese Islamic community (the Hui) is one example that successfully negotiates between the assertion of the Chinese state sovereignty and the connection with the global Muslim brotherhood network through the cyber media (Ho 2010).

Internet studies of ethnic minority may help us reflect if these users would stand for an agent of time in the sense that minority groups are always seen as synonymous with untimeliness, non-synchronicity, or non-contemporaneity. Here untimely, at the surface, may mean that the ethnic minorities, under the scrutiny of the linear evolutionary epistemology, are the people who fail to catch up with the advanced and enlightened Han, and those who can never be completely modern. As the Internet facilitates China to be further immersed in the global standard time or the abstract standard of world time measurement within which every action and event is "subject to a single, quantifiable chronology" (Harootunian 2000, 49) of capitalist modernization, the non-Han ethnic groups as the elements of anachronism are destined to remain in the time of the primitive, beyond the trajectory of progressive time. However, from a different angle, China's ethnicity issue designates a multiplicity of temporalities, of which some are repetitions of the past, while others produce fissures, fractures or wrinkles in the era of homogeneous totality.

As nationalism plays a major role in the Chinese politics of ethnic relations, we may be able to see how universalism reconciles and runs into conflict with the concrete, particular temporalities. Historically, the modern Chinese nation was a product of the great capitalist transformation that dismantled every traditional structure and dissolved all ancient, backward and isolated communities into an industrial society that requires some kind of solidarity built upon a shared culture and a common identity. But, in the long process of the state-led modernization, the violence of the socio-political mechanism has deprived ethnic minorities of equal entrance into the largely Han-created elite national culture. In other words, all nationalities in China might have experienced industrial modernization in similar ways, yet they did not experience it in common. This led to the ethnic minority groups being confronted with drastic changes in their struggle for life, to search for their own commonality which is translated as shared habits of everydayness, shared cultural identity, and eventually shared political vision.

The state suppression of the ethnic nationalism and separatist movement within China has driven the diaspora community leaders to reify their ethnic identity as a unified whole in order to represent a distinct image to the rest of the world for their political cause. Xinjiang Uyghur Autonomous Region, formed in 1955, is the largest administrative region in the PRC, but the name "Uyghur" (or Uighur, "weiwuer" in Putonghua) itself does not correlate to a unified cultural Uyghur identity since it is an arbitrary label dating back to the Tang Dynasty (618–907) and has been re-appropriated by the Chinese Communist regime for the purpose of administrative classification and management of the very diverse groups of indigenous peoples in the region. Although the ancient Uyghurs and modern Uyghurs are not necessarily identical, the leaders of the Internet-Uyghur movement depict their ethnic community as the legitimate descendants of this history in order to claim Eastern Turkistan as a unified nation. The very creation of Uyghur as a "minzu" (nationality) was a deliberate attempt to enhance state control over the non-Han peoples by dividing them into accepted categories of ethnicity and to discourage pan-Turkic movement. The imposed identity for contemporary Uyghurs, however, also becomes "the vehicle for rallying support in order to establish a Uighur nation" (Petersen 2006, 65).

Not all diasporic Uyghur organizations advocate independence on their websites, though many of them quest for real political change in the region. Both separatist and information-based diasporic Uyghur websites remain critical of the Chinese state policies in Xinjiang. These websites usually report human rights violation, environmental degradation, economic inequalities, restrictions on religious freedom, and they also offer alternative histories of the region. Since most of these websites are blocked in China, very few of them have been deliberately created with the purpose of reaching the Uyghurs in China, as few of their languages are in Chinese and Uyghur (Gladney 2007). The nationalistic drive of these disaporic Uyghur websites is not in sync with their compatriots since the Internet is yet to reach out to their own people living in their native land, let alone successfully agitating them into mass sentiment or even social movement.

Subaltern nationalism is usually the defensive weapon resorted to by the subordinated ethnic groups to fight against the unwelcome domination of the authoritarian regime. Unlike the exiled groups that openly pursue separatist goals, the domestic ethnic websites carefully support the unity of China, although they also appropriate the notion of subaltern nationalism (or ethno-nationalism) for empowering their ethnic community. For example, a Chinese-language website, newtibet.com, created by Tibetans inside China, had critical online discussions on the problems of modernity and Tibetan cultural changes. While cautiously keeping the sensitive political issues at bay in the forum, the participants—who are mostly bilingual and bicultural young Tibetans brought up under the rule of the PRC—unwittingly engaged in promoting the concept of "Xizang" (the Chinese term for Tibet) in order to include all Tibetan-speaking peoples into their ideal ethnic community (Rabgey 2008).

The Chinese official view only refers to the Xizang Tibet Autonomous Region, which is the second-largest province created by the PRC in 1965, and it includes about half of the ethno-cultural Tibet. However, Tibet in the Tibetans' own perspective consists of all areas inhabited by Tibetans, covering the provinces of Qinghai, Gansu, Sichuan and Yunnan. Though not speaking of independence, such a claim for a greater Tibet has already got on the nerves of the Chinese regime since the concept itself constitutes a threatening historical-political agency to the existing ruling structure and its assimilation policy. The online discussants of newtibet.com could also be trapped into a confining vision that the notion of nation (or the model of nationalism based on unified ethnicity, language, culture, religion, and/or territory) is the only way for them to imagine community. Indeed, subaltern nationalism is "a double-edged sword" (Hardt and Negri 2000, 106). Its progressive nature is the legitimate defense against the domination of more powerful external forces, the right to self-determination and the demand for autonomy and equality. But it can easily manifest its reactionary and regressive aspects in the way that the multiplicity of the community itself is always negated. Perhaps nationalist sentiments for building an imagined community are only truly productive if they do not continue beyond a certain period of existence. Chinese nationalist revolution itself is one good example: as soon as the nation becomes a sovereign state, its progressive revolutionary qualities rapidly fade away, and it erects its own severe structure of domination.

Therefore the ethnic struggle is always a struggle on two fronts. While resisting the oppressive domination of the Chinese state, the ethnic activists also have to be aware of the reactive dimension of asserting the univocity (uni-vocal representation) of their community that would suppress its genuine multiplicity. Very often an imagined unified ethnic identity has been reified by the diasporic or exiled group so as to portray a legitimate ethnic history and collectivity that it claims to represent as a significant antagonist against the Chinese state. The Internet always becomes a crucial means for the elite émigré leaders of the independence movement to usurp the modern united identity and orient its goals in their chosen direction.

Meanwhile, patriotic frenzies were frequently expressed on the Internet and in public demonstrations against foreign countries in China recently. Combined with nationalistic victim narrative, the state and popular discourses about the rise of China have promoted Chinese exceptionalism, emphasized China's own path to modernity, invoked nostalgia for imperial greatness, instigated the revival of militarist spirit to confront foreign enemies, and encouraged a new interpretation of Chinese history from a victim perspective in order to rewrite the wrongs of a century of national humiliation but that also radically simplifies the complex past (Callahan 2012; Hughes 2011). Ironically, it is the nationalist conservatives who create an anachronistic view of Chinese history by reordering and selecting the bygone facts. As mentioned earlier, the Han majority, while acknowledging their temporal coexistence, tend to preempt the possibility of coevalness with the ethnic minorities so as to reinforce their backwardness and unmodern-ness in relation to the Han's superiority and advancement. However, while the Han nationalist conservatives cherish the grandeurs of imperial China and strive to conjure them up in their present conception of a single uniform and unidirectional temporality of the international world, time in the digital media has been reconceived as something multiple that is outside the sequence of linearity and that repeats the past as a form of present yet in a different time and in an undetermined way.

The slogans of "Chinese dream" (*Zhongguo meng*) and "the great revival of the Chinese nation" (*Zhonghua minzu de weida fuxing*) tossed around by the Communist regime under President Xi Jinping can be considered as a call for a return journey to the greatness of the past after recovering from the long century of humiliation. While summoning a national dream along the road back to the old glories (which is a move radically divergent from the socialist revolutionary tradition of repudiating the feudal past), the state agenda also pushes forward, deepening developmental trajectories in order to compete with the modern West.

In other words, the temporality of China's conservative currents is both an anachronistic projection (onto a past that has been vigorously reinterpreted) and a linear model (emphasizing developmentalism and catching up with the West). The so-called China model of modernization remains captive to the logic of emulation and could not be genuinely free from the constraint of a Western model based upon progressive development. In truth, time is never and cannot be a homogeneous totality such as the Chinese state tries to impose on the nation. Although the Chinese authorities see the Internet as an instrumental superhighway linear spatial form of the virtual that can accelerate the country to grand economic success and political power, the Internet time confronts us with an incessantly growing multiplicity of temporal events that connect a multitude of players in same and different places of the network and render the pasts as if they were always present.

Top-down or divergent disseminations

The Chinese authoritarian regime has made unprecedented efforts to spend huge resources with technological sophistication to selectively censor online activities and expressions within the national boundaries in order to limit freedom of speech and to prevent potential collective action against the state.[4] It is actually very difficult for China's ethnic minorities to employ the Internet for their political activism. The statistical report on Internet development by China Internet Network Information Center (CNNIC) in 2014 specifies the numbers of Internet users by provinces, but the penetration rate of the Internet in Xinjiang, Inner Mongolia, Tibet, Guizhou and Yunnan are only 49 percent, 43.9 percent, 37.4 percent, 32.9 percent and 32.8 percent respectively, indicating that the ethnic regions' Internet users are not as many as those in Beijing, Shanghai, Guangdong, and other major provinces where the penetration rates are above 60 percent.

It is also generally believed that the ethnic minorities living in these regions are comparatively poor and would have proportionally less access to the limited Internet resources than their Han compatriots. Given the fact that most digital activists in developing countries are the people with the ability to pay a monthly subscription fee for Internet access, to afford high-speed connection and to work in white-collar jobs where Internet access is common (Fenton 2012, 155), it could be expected that the figures of ethnic minorities inside China engaging in digital activism would be negligent. While the minority peoples in China may not actively participate in restructuring digitally the transmission of knowledge because of the inadequate resources in their communities, their actual experiences and affects which are under the increasing influences of the new media may still form the potential sources of emancipation and the motivations of striking for equality.

Since 2000, websites about ethnic minorities have begun to emerge in China, for instance, Zhuang (www.rauz.net.cn), Hui (www.huizucn.org), Tibetan (www.tibetcul.com), Manchu (www.manjusa.com), Miao (www.3miao.net), Mongol (www.mgwhw.com; www.mongol.cn), Qiang (www.qiangzu.com), Yi (www.yizuren.com), and so on. In the beginning, there were about 20 ethnic groups having their own websites out of the officially recognized 55 nationalities (Shi 2001). Many of them were established by central or regional governments and institutions with official backgrounds in order to promote ethnic policies and foster economic development and tourism of the ethnic regions. While ethnic academic institutes built websites to create communication channels for publicizing ethnic cultures, a few individuals or private groups also opened blogs and launched their websites to express their own ethnic identity consciousness, improve their self-representation, and encourage solidarity in their communities. It is expected that, along with the explosive constant increase of the Chinese Internet population (618 million in 2013), China's ethnic websites will also have an exponential growth, though no statistics can be found about their exact numbers.

However, since several violent ethnic conflicts have happened over the last few years, some of these ethnic websites, particularly those related to Tibetans and Uyghurs, have been shut down by the Chinese authorities. The most prominent one is Uyghur Online (*weiwuer zaixian*), Uighurbiz.net, operated by Ilham Tohti who was an economics professor at Minzu University of China at Beijing and an outspoken critic of the shortcomings in the state governance of the Uyghur homeland of Xinjiang. The Chinese-language Uighurbiz.net was a platform that promoted understanding between Han Chinese and Uyghurs, and watchfully monitored the developments in Xinjiang, but it has been blocked and closed by the Chinese government after some years of operation. Tohti was later arrested and charged with separatism though he never openly advocated Uyghur independence.

The new media bears witness to the struggle against the model that politics can only be taught to the common people by the elites through institutional transmissions. In 2006, the fourteenth Dalai Lama from the Tibetan government in exile in India requested Tibetans to stop wearing pelts of endangered animals in order to launch a wildlife conservation campaign. In response to the Dalai Lama's summons, many Tibetans living in China gathered at various open spaces to publicly burn their pelts which were worth of millions of US dollars in total. The Chinese government, infuriated by the Tibetans' loyalty to the Dalai Lama, contradicted its own law on the protection of endangered species by coercing Tibetan government employees to wear pelts of animals in television broadcasts and at public events (Environmental News Service 2006). The incident, on the surface, appears to be the antagonistic struggle between the exiled Tibetan government and the Chinese state for the sovereignty over the governed people, in which Tibetans had been manipulated for conflicting political agendas.

China's renewed emphasis on the economic development of its northwest in the twenty-first century has sparked the influx of Han immigrants to Tibet, Xinjiang, and other adjacent provinces as well as accelerated tourism and further commodification of Tibetan and other ethnic cultures. Different local governments in Tibetan areas competed for promoting exotic images to tourists by organizing festivals and encouraging Tibetan participants to wear jewelry and pelts at those events in order to show off the regions' wealth and development status. Condemning the relentless economic campaign that might drive Tibetan traditional culture to disappear, the Dalai Lama has given speeches on various occasions in India to state that wearing pelts and expensive jewelry disgraced the environmental protection image of Tibetans. The speeches circulated very quickly through old and new media: video and audio tapes, broadcast from Voice of America and Radio Free Asia. The following burnings of pelts by the Tibetans in PRC were mainly distributed through Internet sites. The online video clips of the burning incidents further convinced more people to participate. The digital videos of the burnings circulated through the web-based social media were meant to deliver to the Dalai Lama the message that Tibetans in China still follow his teachings and also to show to the world audience that Tibetans are environmentally conscious in comparison to other ethnic groups (Yeh 2013, 328).

Although the acts of burning the pelts were not directly instructed by the Dalai Lama, the Tibetans' decision to destroy by fire the expensive clothing lined with endangered animal skins was understood, from the Chinese official point of view, to be a manifestation of their national loyalty to their exiled religious leader. Apparently it looked like a social movement piloted by the Tibetan government in exile to challenge the legitimacy of the authoritative Chinese state. However, a close analysis reveals the acts of burning actually convey multiple motivations and meanings far beyond the original message in the Dalai Lama's speech. As evidence shown by this researcher's interviews and online discussions, the pelt burnings have generated many different arguments and views, some of which are even congruent with the policy and perspective of the Chinese state (Yeh 2013, 332–337). Some Tibetans see the burning as a move to reduce visible economic inequality among the Tibetans and to construct a harmonious society as promoted by the state. Other Tibetans rebuke the spectacular burning as a terrible waste of valuable resources and as a violent act associated with the Cultural Revolution and lament it as a way to speed up the demise of Tibetan cultural identity when Tibetans give up their traditional clothing for casual jeans. Even though being understood as a protest, the burning is regarded by some radical Tibetan intellectuals as a nationalist wakening to democracy and modernity, rather than a blind obedience to the diasporic spiritual leadership.

Dialogues and separatism

Beyond the conflicts perpetuated between the Chinese state and the Tibetan government in exile, there have been new media attempts to reconcile the ethnic tensions and help the Han majority understand more about the Tibetans. Writer Wang Lixiong[5] began to promote a direct dialogue between the Han Chinese and the Dalai Lama through Twitter (which is called "weibo" in China) in 2010. After the Tibet uprising in March 2008 that happened a few months before the Beijing Olympics, Tibetans in China started a wave of self-immolation protests in order to draw global attention to the Chinese government's increasingly heavy-handed domination over

Tibet. The graphic images of the protesters, while burning or afterwards, have been transmitted over the Internet to news media and supporters. Such a dramatic form of resistance, however, further made the Chinese authority adopt more restrictive measures against any non-governmental contact between minority groups (specifically Tibetan and Uyghur) and Han Chinese.

Wang Lixiong and his wife, Woeser,[6] thus have established a website *"minjian zangshi"* (unofficial affairs about Tibet), http://tibet.woeser.com, after the Tibetan riots in order to open up a space for Chinese netizens to discuss about, and to have a better understanding of, Tibet. It aims at collecting discussions on current Tibet from Tibetan and non-Tibetan bloggers in China and gathering information from diverse sources so as to generate perspectives different from that promoted by the state propaganda on the region. As the Chinese state has shut down its dialogue with the Tibetan government in exile, the website takes up the mission to create opportunities for the conversations between Tibetans and Han Chinese at the level of civil society, because Wang and Woeser foresee that, without mutual understandings among the different ethnic groups, even the future democratization of China could not resolve the ethnic antagonisms planted by the insensible policy of the authoritarian regime.

While the Chinese government has adopted a harsher and harsher policy on Tibet, the official meetings between the Dalai Lama and the Chinese authorities have come to a halt, and the spiritual leader of the six million Tibetans has been demonized by Chinese officials as "a wolf in monk's robes" and his clique has been blamed for dividing China. Given the fact that ordinary Chinese people do not query the government's view on the Dalai Lama and they know very little about the conditions in Tibet, in May 2010, Wang organized a Twitter conversation between netizens in China and the Dalai Lama. Actually it was an indirect online exchange; Wang brought the most popular questions about Tibet to the Dalai Lama in person to New York. Through the Google moderator, 1,253 net users in China submitted 289 questions and 12,473 voted for the most popular questions to the Dalai Lama including: how the Tibetan spiritual leader looked at the reincarnation problem; why the meetings between the Chinese regime and the Tibetan government in exile could not lead to any positive results; how the growing tensions between Tibetans and Han Chinese can be resolved; what Tibet's future would be, and so on and so forth.

While the Dalai Lama was frankly and explicitly stating his views on these questions from Chinese netizens, Wang in real time posed them on Twitter with 7,000 to 8,000 followers and also contacted his friends to retweet the messages. In the end, there were about 10,000 netizens in China witnessing the interview through their microblogs. The full record of the conversations was later uploaded on Wang's own website (wanglixiong.com) under the title of "Ethnic Dialogue and New Media" (*zuqun duihua yu xin meiti*). In January 2011, Wang again launched a live Skype video conference with the Dalai Lama in India from his Beijing home with two Chinese human rights lawyers, Teng Biao in Shenzhen and Jiang Tianyong in Beijing, to continue the dialogue and to raise with the Dalai Lama those unanswered questions of the Chinese netizens from the last Twitter conversation. The entire video conference has been filmed by Wang Wo and made into a documentary entitled *The Dialogue (Duihua)* which is being circulated online.

Such an Internet dialogue event, in relation to ethnic minorities, only takes place sporadically, and the Chinese government has quickly cracked down on it. Perhaps what is more significant is to examine how the ethnic groups inside China make use of the cyber communication technology in their daily lives to construct, negotiate and redefine identity for themselves, and to achieve greater social equity as a way to exert agency for shaping their futures despite tight government control. One thing that triggers ethnic minorities to further reflect on their identity is the reactions coming from the Han majority. Ethnic designations remain strong on the Internet even though the utopian view would want us to believe that the new media can function as a social equalizer, in which class, race, age and gender no longer matter. In fact, ethnic slurs are easily found on the Internet no matter how hard the party state since the Mao era has tried to curb Han chauvinism and discourage local ethnic nationalist sentiment from its minority groups. But such a policy went awry in the post-Mao era when the state heavily relied on patriotism for its legitimacy. The oft-cited victimization narrative of Chinese sufferings at the hands of Western and Japanese imperialists in many nationalistic outbursts against the West and Japan seems to have spilled over to the Han's perception of their relation to the ethnic minorities domestically.

In a study of Han supremacists on the Chinese Internet, James Leibold examines how some vocal groups of Chinese youth use the Internet as a powerful outlet by creating websites focusing on Han ethnicity (such as www.hanminzu.com, www.tianhan.com.cn) to mobilize "the ancient Han ethnoym to seek redress for what they perceive to be the marginalization and discrimination of the vast majority of Chinese citizens within the party-state's multicultural mosaic and national imaginary" (Leibold 2010, 541). As the Chinese Communist Party has implemented some preferential treatment towards the ethnic minorities in order to alleviate inequalities and ethnic sentiments,[7] the bloggers on the Han websites have complained that the Han majority has been reversely discriminated and become second-class citizens. The main minority group these Han supremacists target is the Manchu, who established the last feudal dynasty Qing in Chinese history and were the ruling class in China for more than 250 years. The Hanist bloggers, with conspiracy theory in mind, attacked the Manchu for their plot to restore the Qing dynasty which constituted "a bigger threat to Chinese sovereignty than the Tibetan, Taiwanese or Uyghur separatists" (Leibold 2010, 554). They entirely negate the contributions made by the Manchu and other ethnic minorities, and equate the Han ethnic group to the Chinese, disdaining the state policy of upholding a multi-ethnic nation. These Han supremacists in the online forums blame the Manchu invasion and contamination of China for China's failure to compete with the West since the eighteenth century, eulogize pre-Qing imperial China as progressive and advanced, and politically advocate an authoritarian and centralized state based upon imperial Chinese institutional structure (Chew and Wang 2012). Ridiculous as these online comments may sound, and they seem to be easily dismissed as some irresponsible speeches made by angry youths, such ethnic bigotry against domestic minorities actually is a part of China's conservative nationalistic trends.

The Chinese state at the moment seems to gain the upper hand by using the new media as a modern form of mass persuasion and control to gather popular support and mold public opinion into accepting the existing system. Ethnic inequality, injustice, and lack of ethnic autonomy could not be effectively alleviated in the name of national security and stability maintenance. However, it will be the ethnic issue that serves as the "new media" to push China toward real change in the long run. The politics of new media should be judged not by what has been determined, but by the becoming of its unpredictable potentials and of its universal striving.

Notes

1 The first railway in China, the Woosung Railway, built illegally in the nineteenth century by Western companies to connect the foreign concessions at Shanghai and Woosung, a port at Yangtze River was purchased and then destroyed by the Qing government. The removal of the railway was seen as a symbol of the Qing's conservatism and backwardness. But the official who ordered the railway destroyed was a modernizer, Shen Baozhen (1820–1879) who was well aware of the long-term benefits of railway. His action suggested his main concern for the Western infringement of the Chinese sovereignty and the threats of that railway might bring to the social and political order without a commensurate amount of advantages (Pong 1973).

2 Joseph Nye's concept of soft power has been enthusiastically received in China, especially by the policy community, where its interpretations somewhat differ from the original formulation in the way that the soft power approach, beyond the realm of foreign relations, has been incorporated into the domestic governance like pursuing nation-building objectives and fostering social cohesion (Edney 2012).

3 The Uyghurs in Urumqi, the capital of Xinjiang province, took to the streets to protest against Han Chinese factory workers in the southern province of Guangdong of ethnic violence against Uyghur co-workers in 2009. The demonstration immediately turned into ethnic violence. Uyghurs vented their anger against non-Uyghurs in Urumqi. As a result, it was reported that more than 150 people were killed and hundreds more injured.

4 See, for instance, the very large scale study of censorship in China's social media by King, Pan, and Roberts (2013). But such extensive effort to censor and closely watch human expressions in social media is not confined to the Chinese state. Edward Snowden, a former Central Intelligence Agency employee, has disclosed operational details of the global Internet surveillance run by the United States government, along with many commercial and international partners. The scale of such Internet surveillance is perhaps even much larger than that carried out by the Chinese government.

5 Wang is the author of the political novel *Yellow Peril* (*Huanghuo*), a book about Tibet, *The Sky Burial* (*Tianzang*), and a book on Xinjiang, *My West China, Your East Turkestan* (*Wo de Xiyu, ni de Tongtu*). Wang is considered as one of the most outspoken democracy activists in China, and is famous for his provocative writings about China's ethnic issues.

6 Tsering Woeser is a Tibetan poet, blogger, and democracy activist in China, receiving various human rights awards from different international organizations.

7 China's ethnic minorities are notably exempted from the population control of the one-child policy, admitted to college with lower test scores, and allowed to take the national college entrance examination in their own ethnic languages, etc. Autonomous ethnic regions are provided with preferential economic aid, and are guaranteed to use and develop ethnic languages, and to maintain their own cultural and social customs. Politically, ethnic groups are represented in the National People's Congress as well as governments at the provincial and prefectural levels.

References

Callahan, W.A. (2012) 'Sino-speak: Chinese exceptionalism and the politics of history', *The Journal of Asian Studies*, 71(1): 33–55.

Chew, M. and Wang, Y. (2012) 'Online cultural conservatism and Han ethnicism in China', *Asian Social Science*, 8(7): 3–10.

China Internet Network Information Center (CNNIC) (2014) *Statistical report on Internet development in China*. Available at: http://www1.cnnic.cn/ IDR/ReportDownloads/201310/P020131029430558704972.pdf (Accessed on July 7, 2014).

Edney, K. (2012) 'Soft power and the Chinese propaganda system', *Journal of Contemporary China*, 21(78): 899–914.

Environmental News Service (2006) *Tibetans set endangered animal pelts ablaze, rousing Chinese ire*. Available at: http://www.ens-newswire.com/ens/feb2006/2006-02-24-01.asp (Accessed on July 3, 2014).

Fenton, N. (2012) 'The Internet and radical politics'. In J. Curran, N. Fenton, and D. Freedman (eds) *Misunderstanding the Internet*, New York and London: Routledge.

Gladney, D.C. (2007) 'Cyber-separatism, Islam, and the state in China'. In J.C. Jenkins and E.E. Gottlieb (eds) *Identity Conflicts: Can Violence Be Regulated?* New Brunswick, NJ: Transaction Publishers.

Hardt, M. and Negri, A. (2000) *Empire*, Cambridge: Harvard University Press.

Harootunian, H. (2000) *History's Disquiet: Modernity, Cultural Practice, and the Question of Everyday Life*, New York: Columbia University Press.

Ho, W.Y. (2010) 'Islam, China and the Internet: negotiating residual cyberspace between hegemonic patriotism and connectivity to the Ummah', *Journal of Muslim Minority Affairs*, 30(1): 63–79.

Hughes, C. (2011) 'Reclassifying Chinese nationalism; the *geopolitik* turn', *Journal of Contemporary China*, 20(71): 601–620.

Jacobs A. (2014) 'It's another perfect day in Tibet!' *New York Times*. Available at: http://www.nytimes.com/2014/07/22/world/asia/trending-attractive-people-sharing-upbeat-news-about-tibet-.html?_r=1 (Accessed on July 22, 2014).

King, G., Pan, J. and Roberts, M.E. (2013) 'How censorship in China allows government criticism but silences collective expression', *American Political Science Review*, 107(2): 1–18.

Leibold, J. (2010) 'More than a category: Han supremacism on the Chinese Internet', *The China Quarterly*, 203: 539–559.

Petersen, K. (2006) 'Usurping the nation: cyber-leadership in the Uighur nationalist movement', *Journal of Muslim Minority Affairs*, 26(1): 63–73.

Pong, D. (1973) 'Confucian patriotism and the destruction of the Woosung railway, 1877', *Modern Asian Studies*, 7(4): 647–676.

Rabgey, T. (2008) 'newtibet.com: citizenship as agency in a virtual Tibetan public'. In R. Barnett and R. Schwartz (eds) *Tibetan Modernities: Notes from the Field on Cultural and Social Change*, Leiden: Brill.

Rane, H. and Salem, S. (2012) 'Social media, social movements, and the diffusion of ideas in the Arab uprisings', *Journal of International Communication*, 18(1): 97–111.

Samphel, T. (2014) 'Tibet tweets to China and China tweets back', *The Huffington Post*. Available at: http://www.huffingtonpost.com/thubten- samphel/tibet-tweets-to-china-and_b_5230511.html (Accessed on July 2, 2014).

Shi M.M. (2001) 'Zhongguo minzulei wangluoziyuan dasaomiao (Survey on China's ethnic website resources)', *Zhongguo Minzu* (China Ethnicity), 1: 31–32.

Yang, G. (2014) 'Internet activism and the party-state in China', *Daedalus*, 143(2): 110–123.

Yeh, E.T. (2013) 'Blazing pelts and burning passions: nationalism, cultural politics, and spectacular decommodification in Tibet', *The Journal of Asian Studies*, 729(2): 319–344.

Zhou, Y. (2006) *Historicizing Online Politics: Telegraphy, the Internet, and Political Participation in China*, Stanford: Stanford University Press.

32

Mainland Chinese women's homo-erotic databases and the art of failure

Katrien Jacobs

This chapter looks at mainland Chinese women's online micro-fictions and do-it-yourself (DIY) comics based on the Japanese animation genre of Boys' Love (in Chinese called *danmei* 801 or simply "BL"). This genre refers to female-authored narratives about homosexual love affairs that involve emotional hardship and include hard-core sex. Just like the Japanese fans of Boys' Love, Chinese women who devour the genres and sub-genres of Boys' Love have labeled themselves with the ironic self-description of "rotten girls" (the Japanese term is *fujoshi* and the Chinese term is *Funu*) or "rotten families" to distinguish themselves from the well-behaved moral mainstream. The stories are divided into classical Chinese stories, modern stories and fantasy stories, focusing on the interplay of "sweet love" and "abuse" between the two male characters. They also consist of esoteric fantasies about gay sex, such as the existence of a specific male genital entitled 801, "Boys' Love ana (801)," which would be located between the penis and the anus and can be thought of as a male vagina.

Chinese women's attachment to stratified databases around these genres will be related to the theme of "art of failure," as they develop an imaginative type of non-normative sexuality and artistic expressivity that challenges China's totalitarian policies towards obscenity legislation and its overall crackdown on dissident pop cultures and openly queer art forms.

Boys' Love fans as database animals

The online circulation of micro-fictions and visually oriented *manga* constitute an unusual type of feminine erotica that is aligned with browsing behavior, corporeal sensations and a tendency towards post-narrative consumption. These collections of explicit love stories remain true to the original meaning of Japanese genre *yaoi*, or fan-made gay fictions that have "no climax, no ending, and no meaning." They do not develop into full-scale romantic narratives and proudly claim the status of debased "low art." They exhibit a proud veneer of imperfection, but are indeed also distributed on well-organized media portals that follow the neatly ordered structure of a "database imagination" (Manovich 2001, 218). They are divided into a wide range of genres and categories that include character types, s/m relationship types, genres centered on specific taboos such as incest, or oddball genres such as "male pregnancy." Browsers get immersed in the narratives of these stories, while performing other functions such as searching and navigating, collecting and archiving, downloading or uploading collections.

Japanese theorist Hiroki Azuma views new media users as postmodern "database animals" whose art works have melded into multiple databases of genres and characters and who sacrifice a search for greater significance for instant gratification. According to Azuma, they are "satiated by classifying characters from stories according to their traits and anonymously creating databases that catalog, store, and display the results. In turn, the database provides a space where users can search for the traits they desire and find new characters and stories that might appeal to them" (Azuma 2009, xvi).

In Azuma's theory, the database instinct does not merely refer to being hooked on computer programs or browsing behaviors, but rather it is a "model or a metaphor for a worldview of 'grand non-narrative' that lacks the structure and ideologies that used to characterize modern society" (Azuma 2009, xvi). Azuma explains that the loss of grand narrative in literature and cinema culture has made way for a specific type of fragmentation and erotic attachment ("moe") to archives and databases. The database instinct is driven by an urge to endlessly classify stories and characters who within their fictional worlds often represent post-human figures such as androids and dolls who have given up their roots to humanity. This lack of human origin in characters also reflects a loss of originality in these works, which are highly derivative and part of a chain of infinite imitations and piracy.

Susanna Paasonen in her study *Carnal Resonance: Affect and Online Pornography* has equally applied a notion of post-narrative consumption to ways of sensing and consuming the database arrangements of online pornography. Pornography as a post-cinematic media form has been defined by a lack of mainstream cinematic narrative and by poor technical or aesthetic quality. People who watch online pornography are not motivated by storytelling or a voyeurism of narrative cinema, but generally are exploring a new rhythm of sensing media selections which Paasonen calls "resonance"—as somatic and somewhat involuntary moments of proximity with serialized images that produces by a specific type of feeling of directness between these fictional scenes and viewers. Viewers experience resonance as moments of repetition and novelty according to a personalized rhythm (Paasonen 2011, 186).

In both these theories, there is contradictory impulse in consumers of cultivating deep empathy for characters whilst also coldly decontextualizing, classifying and objectifying them. What rotten girls and porn users may have in common is the fact that they have given up narrativity and use search engines to endlessly browse and archive specific types of celebrity, or body types, pairings, sex acts, orientations and fetishes. While the theory of dabatase animals comes primarily from an analysis of male subcultures, women in East-Asian pop culture and globally have joined the database imagination by building and endlessly replicating stories around characters or their specific attributes.

Chinese women's tendency to browse such databases and look for erotic stimulation will now be posited as an "art of failure," a positive claiming of unorthodoxy and artistic-sexual literacy. Jack Halberstam's *Queer Art of Failure* provides an insight into how we can recuperate this type of productivity within social media platforms—as novel languages of sex and culture that are critical of normative measures of success or failure within the literary arts or within the traditional patriarchal Chinese family. Halberstam's notion of "low theory" will be used to validate these micro-fictions as "a counterhegemonic form of theorizing . . . the theorization of alternatives within an undisciplined zone of knowledge production" (Halberstam 2011, 18). These online databases and micro-fictions could easily be brushed aside, either by traditional Chinese morality or by neo-liberal standards of success within the creative industries.

However, they are a good example of how to remain self-consciously "irrelevant" and "whimsical," using their unique styles to pester and poke fun at mainstream society. Halberstam explains this kind of reflection as a new kind of "low" theory to be distinguished from overly serious academic "high" theory. As she explains:

> I believe in low theory in popular places, in the small, the inconsequential, the anti-monumental, the micro, the irrelevant; I believe in making a difference by thinking little thoughts and sharing them widely. I seek to provoke, annoy, bother, irritate, and amuse; I am chasing small projects, micropolitics, hunches, whims, fancies.
>
> *(Halberstam 2011, 21)*

The notion of failure can also be related to self-conscious attitudes of "being distracted" while consuming fictions, by rewriting, revising, appropriating, "slashing" or debasing works of art. Japan's leading Boys' Love Scholar Kazumi Nagaike places the origin of Boys' Love storytelling in a little girl's "wandering mind." She refers to Anna Freud's reading of her father Sigmund Freud's famous article about masochism in "A Child is Being Beaten" (Nagaike 2012, 2). In the daughter's reading of the iconic psychoanalyst's work, a little girl is day-dreaming while reading a story about a knight and his slave, her mind drifting between their martial bond and the manufacturing of a love affair. While the original story sets up a boundary between master and slave, the girl slashes the story by imaginatively interpreting mutual desire and a sexual vibe between these two characters. For Nagaike, here lies one of the seedbeds of the Boys' Love fantasy, which is to challenge social hierarchies by eroticizing role reversal and emotional interdependency.

Boys' Love explosion and criminalization in mainland China

In the People's Republic of China the influx of Japanese *manga* began in the 1990s and has been more tightly controlled by the government and publishers who are instructed to reduce the Japanese influence and produce Chinese-style comics and animation. Major cities in mainland China such as Beijing and Shanghai are now centers for ACG genres and products, and a large part of their popularity is due to the easy availability of pirated materials. Ng writes that the role of China has become very important since it is the largest supplier of pirated products. Ironically enough, Hong Kong people consume Japanese ACG not directly from Japan but indirectly through China and Chinese websites that offer localized products in terms of language, genre and content (Ng 2010, 474).

Mainland Chinese fans who frequent Boys' Love portals have to be very careful in posting their gay-themed erotica and utilize various strategies in order to circumvent censorship: all Internet traffic is monitored by government agents; the posting of any sexually explicit materials is prohibited by law; and discussions of queer or alternative sexualities are discouraged. As a result, most fans express their fantasies as micro-fictions, rather than sexually explicit visuals, and they self-censor and use code words to refer to sex acts. Of course these stories have similar themes of taboo love and the quest for consummation, but they do not visualize, nor elaborate on descriptions of the sex scenes.

As is explained by Mark McLelland elsewhere in this volume (see Chapter 10) the reason why sexualized Boys' Love *manga* have expanded and flourished in Japan is directly related to a more lenient censorship legislation. In Japanese depictions of obscenity it is the degree of precision with which sexual acts are rendered visible that becomes the mark of censorship, hence sexually explicit videos or drawings and even sexual violence, rape or group sex can be permitted as long as genital areas and pubic hair are blurred or blanked and an appropriate age rating is published on the cover. While Boys' Love *manga* as a kind of feminine-oriented pornography have been attacked in Japan, they were also revalidated and redeemed by free speech feminists who were able to successfully protect these materials from further persecution. The mainland Chinese anti-obscenity laws do not make distinctions between types of media or artforms as they rely on ancient laws that can be used at will to clamp down on any and all types of media and expressions. Since government appointed censors and automated filters are used to routinely scan sexually explicit audio-visual materials on the Chinese Internet, the laws are also used to detain commercial porn producers and netizens who are active uploaders within sexual subcultures and web communities. Under these circumstance, as equally observed by McLelland, it is quite a surprise that Chinese Boys' Love materials are still blossoming and able to resist the pressure to normalize the perverse edge of these materials.

Mainland Chinese media at first were curious and supportive of the Boys' Love fad, but they began to shift their focus to Boys' Love's supposedly evil impact on youth as the subculture became more popular. At some point the state media started to frame these comics "peppered with Japanese flavors" as malevolent forms of cultural imperialism and a threat to Chinese youth:

> The popularity of these pornographic pocket comics will interrupt their academic study, distract these innocent kids, lower their moral standards, and weaken their legal sense. . . . Comics peppered with heavy Japanese flavors, values and concepts will bring more damage to students. It is "cultural hegemony" endangering Chinese kids.[1]

As for the persecution of Boys' Love fandom in 2010, Erika Junhui Yi provides an insider's point of view as a Boys' Love fan and a scholar of the genre. She explains that a major crackdown of websites and fan forums, instigated by homophobic arguments, happened in 2010, and saw well-known newspaper columnists and bloggers such as Dou Wentao denouncing the subculture. In 2011 the Zhenzhou police arrested 32 slash fiction writers, and this news was widely commented on through statements and cartoons on Sina Weibo (Yi 2013). Many of these commentaries suggested that the subculture is vast and robust and would be able to resist censorship. In one of the fan comics, an imprisoned girl cannot decide which genre-specific cell to enter. Despite the humorous and supportive tone of these commentaries, Yi describes a chilling effect produced by the 2010 crackdown, showing that many Boys' Love fans have resorted to ways of hiding their "inclinations." At the same time, some of the news items surrounding Boys' Love started going viral and netizens showed their support by fantasizing about "all going to jail together."

The most severe crackdown happened in April 2014 when 20 *fujoshis* were arrested once again for "spreading pornography." The incident sparked reactions in the foreign and Chinese news media and netizens reacted by means of extensive debates as well as fantasized comics and micro-fictions about their lives in jail. An article in the *New York Times* by Didi-Kirsten Tatlow was translated and tweeted by a well-known Communist Chinese newspaper *CanKaoXiaoXi* then was retweeted 3,000 times and received hundreds of comments, many of them in favor of the subculture (Tatlow 2014).

One of the major targeted websites in 2014 is called Jinjiang, which was established in 2003 and boasts five million registered users and over 300,000 registered writers. Besides Jinjiang there are sites such as Lucifer Club and the Fictions Website of Tanbi, the latter of which places on its homepage a call for stories "without descriptions of sexuality and violence."[2] This is the website's attempt to self-censor Boys' Love's tendency towards violent and pornographic description. It has also built a webpage where fans themselves can self-censor their fictions for sensitive content. The page has installed filters for sensitive keywords similar to those employed by government censors, and in this way fans can pre-scan their stories. But since fans realize that descriptions of sex and violence are essential to the genre and are increasingly popular, they also try to invent coded language ways to continue their "peppered" fictions. They may recompose the sex scenes in a euphemistic or literal manner and avoid the use of taboo words. Or they may use code words such as "OO" instead of anus or anal intercourse, just as in heterosexual fictions XXOO can mean "to make love," XX means "penis," and OO can mean "vagina." Sometime they may use spaces and slashes around the taboo words to avoid censorship; as shown in the following graphic, the sensitive words are divided by the symbols 【 】

The website Jinjiang used to allow its authors to post their uncensored stories in a special section of the site named "the author's words," while publishing self-censored versions in the "general" section. However, because of the authorities imposing tougher policies for online materials, this section of unabridged stories had to be closed down. Finally, some authors from mainland China chose to publish their works on websites in Taiwan, whose regulating system and censorship are much looser than in mainland China. Unfortunately, few authors have easy access to the Taiwanese sites as they would need a VPN to jump across the Great Firewall and access those sites.

The BL new wave and the art of failure

As will be further shown, Chinese *fujoshis* are database animals who do not embrace polished narratives and art forms but who project desire onto multiple types of genres, characters and character-pairings. In terms of physical attributes of these characters, *fujoshis* have overall upheld an idealized notion of "beautiful" masculinity (*bishonen*), though in recent years there is a wave of stories about characters with imperfect bodies, as well as mental and physical dysfunctions. Kazumi Nagaike explains that in Japan the tendency to focus on "failure" is part of a larger trend towards diversifying the male lead characters. In her recent talk "For Liberation or Moe: The decline of *bishonen* and the emergence of new types of protagonists in contemporary BL," she argues that that the subculture has been moving away from its obsession with *bishonen* characters, or love between two idealized beautiful and effeminate males. She describes the new BL wave in Japan as one not so concerned with good-looking characters, as with the love shared between a younger and older male (*oyaji*) who is average looking and cast in the submissive position (*uke*). She sees this tendency to adore physical weaknesses and *moe* or the cultivation of strong attractions towards such characters as a moment of sexually queer emancipation (Nagaike 2014).

The obsession with failure also becomes apparent in a new wave of DIY *manga* that depict "loser" type characters whose experiences include sexual disorders and impotence. In this sense Boys' Love can be seen as a counter-pornography focusing on physical, sexual and emotional distress. If typical pornographic fantasies depict a healthy and animalistic sexual body that can easily and repeatedly experience physical sexual climax, here women fantasize about the various human incompetencies that would prevent such endeavor. A compassion for failure is cultivated through characters that cannot live up to conventional beauty norms, such as mediocre-looking men (in Japanese *oyaji uke*) who are past their prime and are coupled with arrogant dominant youths.

I will examine the treatment of this "loser" type by looking at a collection of BL fictions about sexual disorders and Chinese DIY *manga* (in Japanese called *dōujinshi*) based on the popular Japanese *anime* TV series *Tiger and Bunny*. The chapter will end with an analysis of interviews with fans of Boys' Love in Guangzhou. The Guangzhou interviews focus on women's fantasies of sexual traumas and masochism—or a tendency towards processing eroticism through empathy with the submissive character. The tendency for women to imagine loser-types and bottoms is seen as an intervention in patriarchal morality, as it is a way to create a distance between describing their own "normal" private desires and their need for love.

I searched for Chinese "new wave" micro-fictions detailing aspects of failure. And indeed some new databases have emerged which share characteristics of protagonists who are all somewhat "abnormal"; for instance, they are physically handicapped, sexually impotent, or simply social outcasts and losers. On Sina Weibo, a user posts a collection of "high quality BL" fictions that are divided by "illness": HIV, leukemia, problems with the brain, other diseases, disabled hands or legs, weaknesses, diseases of the five internal organs, mental problems, sexual disorders, and disabled facial features.

The reason why her database did not get deleted by censors is that she used pictures of the Chinese language text, rather than the actual text, which is another common anti-censorship device. This genre presents failure (under the search term "sick beautiful men") in one character as a plot device that requires the other character to take notice and empathize. In almost all cases, these disabilities are neither profound nor permanent, and they can be fixed. If a person has a permanent disability, the story unfolds around the person that takes care of his lover and who even finds erotic pleasure in nurturing the deformed body. But, most commonly, "failure" points to the value of the social outcast and pre-sets a social gap within the gay couple, an economic disparity or class difference that cannot be easily crossed but can lead to love.

As far as sexual impotence goes, about 50 percent of the stories are "classical," set in Chinese imperial history. Indeed Chinese BL fiction has spawned a unique sub-genre centering on a love affair between the emperor and his beloved eunuch. For instance, there is a story by Shangguan Chen, entitled *Time-travel to be a eunuch*, which casts a submissive character Xie Dongjun as *uke* who serves the emperor Xuanqiu Puyang as *seme*. It is a typical "ancient-background" fiction involving a hero who witnesses an epoch that he is not familiar with. This journey also includes trauma and physical pain:

> After a long time in the darkness, he wakes up with great pain, only to find his penis removed—it seems that he travelled from modern times to ancient China, and became a person who had been sent to a palace to be a eunuch! He is very angry, telling himself that this is a dream and tries to "wake up," but it doesn't work. Life always gives him the opposite of what he wants, he has to accept the facts: now he is a 9-year-old boy named Xie, waiting to serve as a eunuch. (Other little boys died in the operation because of the great pain, but he was the only one who survived.)

After several years go by, the two men develop a very close relationship and then they fall in love and occasionally have sex. Xie is very shy at the first time and doesn't want Xuanqiu to looks at the scar in his groin, but Xuanqiu thinks it is beautiful and kisses it. As the story goes:

> His underwear has been taken off, and Xie twists his legs trying to hide his body, while he covers his hands covering his red face. He feels just like an ostrich, and doesn't dare to look into Xuanqiu's eyes. Because there is a pink scar between his legs, not the penis that should be here. It is covered by flabby skin, and there is an orifice's or a little hole. Around the hole, a scar blossoms like a rose. The color of it is not so much deep red, but light pink. In Xuanqiu's eyes, it is so attractive.
>
> He can't help to touch it, which makes Xie tremble for a second.
>
> "Don't . . . stare at it . . ."

> The reddening on Xie' face spreads towards his neck. This is the most shameful moment that he has experienced in years. Even Xie himself didn't have the courage to look at it carefully, but now Xuanqiu does.
>
> "How could I. . . . You'll never know how beautiful it is" Xuanqiu says, who can't help but kiss it.

The eunuch's penis removal does not only produce a scar, but also becomes eroticized as a specific type of genital or "erogenous zone." The area causes psychological distress but is also recuperated because it is an attractive kind of deformity, a body part that is different and can be adored—as a matter of fact it is described as a beautiful flower.

The recuperation of failure also involves the redrawing of gender boundaries and experiences of transsexualism. Just as the eunuch's scar is described as a vagina, other stories focus on mental illness in which a male experiences a dissociated personality and a female alter ego. An example of these stories concerns a male who suffers from familial abuse, but he has a feminine alter ego who is able to express her hidden feelings. When the protagonist attempts to commit suicide and finds himself lying in a hospital bed, his female alter ego finds peace. At that moment he is visited by his mother and by a boyfriend who both lovingly pay attention to him.

These fantasies show that illnesses can be recuperated and lead to happy endings, as the "bottom" gains power through his specific style of submission and sex appeal. There is a transfer of power as the dominant character becomes aware of his limitations, or is suddenly smitten by unspeakable love. In each case, failure is used to shake up engrained social divisions and to assert the power of eroticism. In the article "Forbidden Love: Incest, Generational Conflict, and the Erotics of Power in Chinese Boys' Love Fiction," Xu and Yang come to a similar conclusion when analyzing large collections of women's incest fantasies, or more particularly love stories between fathers and sons. The authors view these stories, which are common amongst BL fans, as a feminine attempt to tackle taboos and to re-order power structures within the family and within Chinese society at large.

To give an example, one of the most popular stories, *Father and Son*, features a 15-year-old boy who is sold by his evil mother to his stepfather, who also treats him badly but who eventually develops empathy and love for him. According to the authors, the permeable role of "ice-cold tyrant in need of love" is a direct comment on the Chinese totalitarian state. The stories also cast parents who, as a generation, have been deprived of rights and sexual satisfaction and who reverse the Oedipus complex by projecting libidinous desires onto their children. Similarly, the submissive character endures emotional distress or physical disability but eventually permeates the ice-cold tyrant with a sexual chemistry that eventuates into an enduring kind of love (Xu and Yang 2013).

Oyaji Uke: the middle-aged male as bottom

Tiger & Bunny is a 2011 Japanese *anime* television series produced by Sunrise under the direction of Keiichi Satou. The series features the young and fetching TV celebrity Barnaby Brooks (or "Bunny"), who is forced to collaborate with an older and more experienced colleague Kotetsu T. Kaburagi or "Tiger." In the DIY comics, the youthful blond develops a crush on the older male, who is "passive," un-attractive and sexually challenged (often nicknamed "the old man"). It is set in a futuristic city called Sternbild (based on New York City) and focuses on the two superheroes who participate in a reality TV show, *Hero TV*, where they are sponsored by companies to solve crimes.

The transnational fandom around this TV series has settled on gay love and hard-core sex between these two men as their own recreation of the series. I made a selection of Japanese and Chinese DIY comics (*dōujinshi*) to see how the issue of sexual attraction and failure was further treated by these fans. In 2010 I visited a enormous convention in Tokyo solely devoted to *Tiger & Bunny dōujinshi*. Interestingly enough, the *dōujinshi* collections were spread out over two large rooms of the Ikebukuro convention center. The biggest sales-room was reserved for stories with Bunny as the dominant lover, and the smaller sales-room for Tiger as dominant lover. I perused the different collections and specifically those that had an "R 18" or adult only sign on the cover. After visiting this *Tiger & Bunny* convention, I perused a much larger collection of *Tiger & Bunny* online comics that had been scanlated into English. And then finally I also looked at sexually explicit Chinese-language *dōujinshi* of *Tiger & Bunny* that were mostly produced by mainland Chinese fans.

In order to find collections of Chinese *Tiger & Bunny dōujinshi*, I searched the promotion website Tianchuang X Bangumi, searching under the tag "Tiger and Bunny" and easily found examples of sexually explicit *manga* which I then also easily found for sale for on Taobao.com. In *Drunk Moment*, Tiger and Bunny have had wine and are frolicking in bed, where Tiger is recuperating from a severe chest injury. Bunny gets turned on and wants to give Tiger an orgasm by inserting a finger in his anus. Tiger protests yet cannot control his orgasm. The comic ends on a humorous note showing the little boy "Dragon Kid" in bed next door, complaining that he cannot sleep due to all the orgasmic noises.

The theme of Tiger's submission to Bunny is again emphasized in *35.7 degrees* by K.I (King Indigo) a DIY *manga* author from Hong Kong. On a hot day, Bunny and Tiger end up in a shower together. Tiger's facial expression is one of shame and panic, showing his concern about having sex with the younger man. But Bunny makes up for this feeling by showing extreme "sweetness" and even servitude towards Tiger and his body—licking him all over and thoroughly washing the lower regions of Tiger's body. Tiger gets turned on and as he ejaculates he has a pained expression on his face. In the comic *Temperature* by Michun, Tiger is seriously ill with a high fever. Bunny becomes his nurse, getting into bed with him and sharing moments of passionate intimacy, such as pouring cold water directly into Tiger's mouth, then getting turned on and wanting to make love with him.

On the front covers of both these comics, Tiger is depicted as an ill person with a thermometer stuck in his mouth, while Bunny stands next to him as his young and sexy nurse. If the older character is depicted as loser, the younger person is a consistently pestering force who nonetheless wants to love and heal "the old man." In this way the fandom depicts tops and bottoms as loving individuals who are sexually needy and who do not shy away from getting aroused by physical abnormality and illness.

Art of failure amongst BL fans in Guangzhou

I was invited to Guangzhou, China by Professor Song Sufeng at Sun-Yat Sen University, who hosts the university's well-established Sex and Gender Education Forum, which deals extensively with research into sexual minorities and *tongzhi* activism. In this sense, the women who participated in my workshop were also tuned into discussions of queer sex culture. The city of Guangzhou, located in South China, is only a two-hour train ride from Hong Kong, but the city itself is a typical Chinese sprawling metropolis—a motley grid of highways and factories that has erased the older city architectures and produced the endemic air pollution of all China. The university itself has maintained a measure of distance and respite from the city as it is housed in older Ivy League-type mansions surrounded by trees and lawns. Professor Song has successfully managed to gather 25 women to attend a special session dedicated to Boys' Love narratives. They represent undergraduate and graduate students from different departments, as well sex activists and academic faculty who are interested in the topic, some of whom have volunteered to be simultaneous Chinese/English translators.

The women are again mostly students who belong to different age groups, some identifying as *fujoshis* while others have a more basic knowledge of Boys' Love culture and have decided to participate out of curiosity. Overall the discussion is highly spirited and provokes rich dialogues and creative reactions to the themes discussed in this chapter. I asked the women to engage in a collective brainstorming and storytelling exercise. This type of storytelling experiment is also consistent with their specific media landscape as Boys' Love culture in mainland China mainly consists of "online Boys' Love fictions" or the exchange of written stories on websites.

When asking what kinds of erotic entertainment the participants are into, I receive all kinds of answers—some women prefer "pure" (soft-core) Boys' Love stories while others see themselves as "senior *fujoshis*" who have grown up on Boys' Love culture since primary school or high school and now are into the more extreme or hard-core subgenres. As explained by one of the participants:

> I started my Boys' Love reading when I was twelve years old in primary school. The first one I read was hard-core pornographic, so my taste is rather strong.

Another male participant reacts by saying that the issue is not one of "hard-core" versus "soft-core" imagery but that there should be a "love-core"—it is important that the love story is well-developed and that the sex scenes are not "gratuitous" and explains "why the characters are falling in love." Other participants are into watching gay pornography rather than Boys' Love animation or stories. One woman states that she likes gay porn because she hates heterosexual Japanese porn in which "the female is always serving the male." Other participants express that gay sex scenes can be favored by men and women who are feminists and looking for alternative options.

After this we embark on the topic of masochism and failure in Boys' Love narratives. I asked the question why Boys' Love fans identify so much with the masochistic *uke* character. Again I receive different answers which indicate that women are looking for an escape from heterosexual relations. The decision to eroticize the bottom goes along with role reversals and a love of failure:

> [Fujoshi 1] And maybe we have a kind of maternal feeling about him.

> [Fujoshi 2] Actually I think that many of us prefer to see a struggle between two strong characters. In this way there is more tension in the relationship. As a matter of fact, we like it when the *uke* switches roles in the end, so we like the strong character to suffer as well.

> [Fujoshi 3] For example, I read a story of a policeman who tortures a schoolboy, and afterwards they develop some kind of "brotherhood." Then the policeman commits a crime and he himself is imprisoned. The schoolboy then helps him to take care of his parents. So there is a kind of a reversal of power or a "sweet" ending after the power game has ended. I think that this could be a kind of feminist response to a mainstream patriarchal society, just the way women could imagine new endings to these kinds of power games.

At the end of this discussion session, a woman posits a more direct connection between the theme of masochism and "art of failure." The art of failure means to her that these characters emanate vulnerability while practicing non-normative sexualities. The theme of masochism is used to express a position of marginalization that can become one of empowerment:

> It is like the mixture of power and vulnerability. In mainstream society, these males would be a "failure" as they are not straight men who are dominant towards the female. It is like the two men are finding their own ways of pleasure and subvert the mainstream notion of pleasure. Happiness is related to pain and failure. For me this is much more pleasurable than other kinds of eroticism because I enjoy this kind of mixture of strong bodies and vulnerability.

Women like to identify with the *uke* in order to eroticize vulnerability and empowerment alongside the details of sexual conquest. In this way they can project their joyful imagination onto loser characters. Moreover, fans want to empathize with the suffering *uke* as a uniquely Chinese way of processing the psychology of abuse, as explained here by one of the fans:

> We like to develop dark themes of sadism and torture because it gives us a sense of superiority and strength. In terms of masochism, there is strong emphasis in Chinese entertainment in general on a psychology of martyrdom or suffering, which will make us "stronger," "greater" and "more respected" as individuals. The idea is that there is nothing wrong with being a victim and it gives us psychological strength. But it is also an issue of feminism. By reading and writing Boys' Love stories women also express and hijack the desires of men and they don't even have to feel shameful about it. Some Boys' Love works have "bottom" characters who in terms of sex are just like "traditional Chinese women," but in the newer stories we also have "bottoms" who seek sexual pleasure more actively. In any case we can cast these male "bottoms" as a kind of "prey" and it is powerful. That is why we win the game. And I think this is also one reason that most Boys' Love fans have a preference for the "bottom" rather than the "top" character.

Just as in the Tiger and Bunny stories, the *uke* is an older man who is seduced by a younger adorable and beautifully looking male colleague or *homme fatal*. The older male is also ridiculed and stands for an old-fashioned patriarchal authority figure who has lost his sex appeal. Fans want to re-educate this worn out figure of authority by pairing him with a younger man who teases him yet also loves and heals him, thus inspiring a fuller sexual performance and orgasm.

Conclusion

This chapter delves into the database imagination and erotic philosophies of mainland Chinese women who have projected fantasies of sexual climax and failure onto sexually explicit homo-erotic narratives. They distribute sexually explicit micro-fictions and *dōujinshi* on social media platforms and specialized databases. While they visit these highly structured or "pigeon-holed" databases, just as browsers of porn genres would do, the stories themselves are counter-pornographic and focus on failure and the complicated sex affairs between the characters.

There is a further tendency to identify with stories of martyrdom and abuse as a feminist strategy of "time traveling" to ancient imperial histories in order to imagine stories of emperors who are abused yet humanized by their underlings. In these stories the boundaries of the traditional notions of patriarchal authority and filial piety are tested and sexualized by female fan authors who thereby tacitly express anger and frustration at patriarchal institutions, or express a willingness of "not belonging" to mainstream society. The writers of these fictions are heavily persecuted in ongoing government crackdowns, but they use methods of self-censorship and persist in sharing materials on databases of non-normality and sexual abundance.

Acknowledgement

The research for this article was funded by a Chinese University of Hong Kong General Research Fund grant 14404514 Trans-Asian Women's Forum on Erotic/Pornographic Media and Cultural Affect.

Notes

1 Media report quoted by Tina Liu in 'Conflicting Discourses on Boys' Love and Subcultural Tactics in Mainland China and Hong Kong'. In Mark McLelland (ed.) (2008) "Japanese Transnational Fandoms and Female Consumers," *Intersections: Gender, History and Culture in the Asian Context*, 20.
2 The URLs of these websites are Lucifer-club http://www.lucifer-club.com/login.php, Jin Jiang http://www.jjwxc.net/ and Chinese Fictions Website of Tanbi http://www.52blgl.com/ (Accessed April 8, 2014).

References

Azuma, H. (2009) *Otaku: Japan's Database Animals*, Minneapolis: University of Minnesota Press.
Halberstam, J. (2011) *The Queer Art of Failure*, Durham, NC: Duke University Press.
Manovich, L. (2001) *The Language of New Media*, Cambridge, MA: MIT Press.
Nagaike, K. (2012) *Fantasies of Cross-dressing: Japanese Women Write Male–Male Erotica*, Leiden: Brill.
Nagaike, K. (2014) 'For Liberation or Moe: The decline of *bishonen* and the emergence of new types of protagonists in contemporary BL', Lecture delivered at Modern Women and Their Manga conference, Comix Home Base, Hong Kong, March 24, 2014.
Ng, W.M. (2010) 'The Consumption and Perception of Japanese ACG (Animation-Comics-Games) among Young People in Hong Kong', *International Journal of Comic Art*, 12(1).
Paasonen, S. (2011) *Carnal Resonance: Affect and Online Pornography*, Cambridge, MA: MIT Press.
Tatlow, D.-K. (2014) 'Why Many Young Chinese Women Are Writing Gay Male Erotica', *New York Times*. Available at: http://sinosphere.blogs.nytimes.com/2014/05/21/why-many-young-chinese-women-are-writing-gay-mal erotica/?_php=true&_type=blogs&_r=0 (Accessed July 11, 2014).
Yi, E. (2013) 'Reflection on Chinese Boys' Love Fans: An Insider's View', *Transformative Works and Cultures*, 12.
Xu, Y. and Yang, L. (2013) 'Forbidden Love: Incest, Generational Conflict, and the Erotics of Power in Chinese BL Fiction', *Journal of Graphic Novels and Comics*, 4(1): 30–43.

Part VI

Mobile, play and game ecologies in Asia

33

Game industries in Asia: towards an Asian formation of game culture

Anthony Y.H. Fung and Vicky Ho

Asia is a fast growing region in the global game market. According to a report by the marketing research company Newzoo, Asia will account for 82 percent of the US$6 billion global game revenue growth in 2014 (Takahashi 2014a). The same report estimated that as the global game market will grow 8 percent to US$81.5 billion in 2014, Asia will see a faster growth rate and thus increase its global market share from 42 percent to 45 percent (US$36.8 billion). North America is expected to take up 27 percent (US$22.2 billion) of the global market in the same year, while Europe, Middle East, and Africa (EMEA) will be 24 percent (US$19.1 billion). "Consuming 'Asia'" has emerged as a gaming phenomenon and is becoming more and more prevalent both within and outside the region (Hjorth 2011).

Game studies in the Asia-Pacific region can be considered the most developed in terms of regional studies on gaming outside the oft-cited US and UK contexts (Aslinger and Huntemann 2013). Indeed, the Asian game industry is significant as it manifests a regional formulation and the locative politics of different places within. As diverse production and consumption practices exist among the intra-regional and transnational flows of game cultures, the specifications of Asian modernity can be illuminated (Hjorth and Chan 2009). Hjorth and Chan suggested that the Asian gaming cultures provide insights for ways to re-imagine "Asia" as a region that has an "affect" which informs experiences and networks of production, circulation and consumption, while also offering emotive registers of performativity, subjectivity and community. Therefore, when examining the game industry in Asia, the questions of how much it informs us about an Asian formation, and how much it manifests "multiple localities of divergent soft power" (Hjorth 2011) are in mind. This chapter will present and discuss the current scene of the Asian game market.

Japan, Korea and China are the three major players in the game industry in Asia. The former two have been considered two prime examples of the Asia game industry. Hjorth (2008) pointed out that Japan and Korea—based on the differing technological, economic, political, social and cultural contexts—have developed their gaming industries in two opposing directions, representing "two futures" (Hjorth 2011) for gaming: while Japan has been the pioneer in mobile (privatized) convergent devices and thus mobile gaming, Korea has emphasized online MMO games played on PCs in public spaces. On the other hand, Cao and Downing (2008) proposed that Korea and China serve as the "twin towers" of game centers in Asia, as China is gaining increasing importance in the Asia gaming scene. In the special issue on Asia gaming in *Games and Culture*, Hjorth (2008) considered these three major players as a "three-stage gaming paradigm" in which she suggested that economic, cultural, and ideological weights have been shifting from Japan as the "geo-imaginary center" to Korea in the rise of the Korean wave, and today further shifting to burgeoning China. However the relations of these three major players are conceptualized, the authors of this article contend that all the three of them still cast a strong influence in the Asia gaming scene. This will be especially evident if we benchmark the development of games in these countries with some of the key insights for global games development.

As highlighted in PricewaterhouseCoopers' *Global Entertainment and Media Outlook 2014–2018* (PricewaterhouseCoopers 2014), first, online gaming has opened up markets previously considered lost to piracy, and the micro-transaction model rather than the subscription model will attract more gamers to online games. China is the second largest market for online gaming (US$4.2 billion in 2013 with a 7.9 percent CAGR from 2013–2018). Online game development has been the strong suit of Korea, but China is clearly catching up. Second, the *Global Entertainment and Media Outlook* projects that mobile is delivering a new generation of gamers. Global mobile games revenue is forecasted to reach US$15 billion in 2018, rising at a CAGR of 9.6 percent. China, Japan and the US are key markets. Indeed, all three major players in Asia are increasingly devoting energy to developing the mobile game market. Third, social and casual games will continue to grow by attracting non-gamers. Unlike their Western counterparts for whom the market may be difficult to monetize, Japanese and Korean companies have found this to be a profitable turf in the game market. Fourth, new features will renew and sustain consumer interest in console gaming, while improved online offerings through online console games stores will drive digital console games revenue. At the same time, console gaming companies will target emerging markets such as Brazil and India, as shown, for example, in Sony's opening of a manufacturing plant in Brazil. The revival of console gaming might be a positive signal for Japan.

In the following sections we will first present an overview of the market situation of different countries in Asia as well as some observations related to game consumption and player practices. The chapter will conclude with discussions on the implications for an Asian formation of game culture.

Japan: shifting to social games

Japan's superiority in developing console-based videogames culture can be dated back to the 1980s, with companies such as Atari and Nintendo dominating the game market. In her article about console games and global game companies, Consalvo (2006) spelt out how transnational corporations contributed to the formation of a hybrid game culture that mixes Japanese and American cultural essences. Today, the two remaining console platform companies in Japan are Nintendo and Sony Computer Entertainment. After the release of their handheld console platforms in 2004, both companies were able to ride on their consoles and software to increase sales between FY 2006 and FY 2009. However, the shift of game consumption to the online market in recent years returned the revenues of the companies to the pre-NDS or pre-PSP levels (Eurotechnology Japan KK 2014). Yet Sony's PlayStation has done quite well lately. While Microsoft's Xbox had dominated Europe and the US, PS3 had enjoyed the highest sales volume in the console market in Asia. In 2013, PS4 even out-sold Xbox One in the US. According to industry data, PS4 sold seven million units, compared with five million for Xbox One, while Wii U was not selling as well and added pressure for Nintendo's downward business (Fritz and Olivarez-Giles 2014). Sony now plans to re-enter the console market in China by forming joint ventures after its initial attempt in early 2004 (Inagaki 2014).

Social game has become the single largest segment of the Japanese game market. The social game market was almost the same size as the market for console games or portable games in 2010. The social game market in Japan reached US$2.5 billion in 2011 (Yano Research Institute 2012) and in 2013, it already surpassed the US$4 billion domestic console market (Toto 2014b). Our research report on the Japanese social game industry shows that the Japanese video game industry is going through a transition from relying on traditional video games to the rise of social games. Social games attract not only teenagers, but also "non-players" like office ladies, businessmen in their 20s to 40s, and even people over 50. Social games work by a free-to-play, micro-transaction model. Players can play games for free, while the premium purchase of services or items in the game generates revenue for businesses. Japan is a pioneer when it comes to mobile phone technology and usage. The function of mobile phones goes far beyond simply making calls. Also known as "feature phone" or "Galapagos *keitai*" in Japan, they integrate features such as Internet browsers, high-resolution cameras, television, digital wallets, and train passes. Japanese are able to access the Internet via their mobile phones thanks to high-speed Internet access and flat-rate data service in the country. Most social games can be played on these feature phones, and Japan is the only country in the world with a sizable market for feature phone gaming.

According to Japan's Computer Entertainment Supplier's Association's (CESA) 2014 Games White Paper, feature phone games saw a US$1.6 billion market in Japan in 2013 (Toto 2014b). However, if we compare it with the US$2.2 billion market in 2011, we can see feature phone gaming is shrinking. At the same time social games on smartphones are on the rise. According to a report by CyberZ, the Japanese market for smartphone games was worth US$5.4 billion in 2013, making up about 50 percent of the Japanese gaming industry overall, which is sized at US$10.8 billion in 2013. To compare it with the scenario in the previous year, the smartphone games market was less than 30 percent of the overall game market in Japan in 2012. Thus a marked growth of the smartphone game market can be seen. Furthermore, the smartphone game segment is expected to grow to US$6.5 billion in 2014 and even reach US$8.1 billion in 2016 (Toto 2014a).

Even though PricewaterhouseCoopers' global insights on gaming consider social and casual gaming as a sector "difficult to monetize" (PricewaterhouseCoopers 2014), Japanese game publishers' ability to monetize on social games seems to amaze Western game experts. As mentioned, integrating different features into their mobiles is a habit of the Japanese phone users. In other words, they have long been conditioned to pay for add-ons on their phones. According to a report from Enterbrain, the average time for a Japanese user between starting a social network game and making a first purchase is 140 days. The average first purchase is about US$16. Eighty percent of premium content purchasers will make additional purchases, with 50 percent being frequent purchasers. Overall the comfortable spending level for consumers is about US$18 a month (Wireless Watch Japan 2012). Our research shows that people in the 30–40 age group have the highest average spending on online games compared with other age groups. The success of online games can also be shown in the daily earning of US$4.1 million in October 2013 of Japan's GungHo Online Entertainment Inc., thanks to its biggest revenue source *Puzzle and Dragons* (Mayumi 2013).

The success of the Japanese game industry is owed a mostly to market forces, rather than to deliberate government efforts. For example, Koichi Prefecture, together with Shikoku Bank and Kouchi Bank hosted the first local social network game design contest in 2011 with the aim of acquiring promising game scenarios and game characters. They also provided help to local companies in terms of social game development techniques and know-how, fundraising, marketing, and Intellectual Property (IP) management support. The government, on the other hand, does not provide much formal support to the game industry. The government has begun supporting the video game industry at a national level only since 2006 (Ministry of Economy, Trade and

Industry 2006). Regarding other sub-sectors of the games industries, such as the social game industry, there is currently no explicit national policy to promote them. Speaking overall, the government's role is more one of maintaining the regulatory and legal environment of a society for its mature and thriving game industry to grow healthily and sustainably, while minimizing the harm caused by game addiction and virtual crime. There are a few local level policy initiatives aimed at developing the game industry though. Fukuoka city attempted to form its own cluster of game companies, outside of Tokyo, by lowering office rental. It managed to attract quite a number of social game companies also due to its relatively lower cost of living and the city's easy access to other Asian countries via its transportation network.

Korea: expanding game exports

Korea is well-known as a key player in the global online game industry as well as the Asian game hub. Gaming has become a mainstream social activity in Korean society with its own TV channels dedicated to games and a vibrant E-sports and pro-gamer celebrity culture. Government policy and the social context are some of the key contributing factors in the growth of the Korean game industry. For example, Korea's *PC bangs* have been widely discussed as a "third space" functioning between work and home spaces and an influential factor in the development of the game culture in Korea (Chee 2005; Hjorth 2006; Huhh 2009).

Comprehensive and steadfast government support has a major role to play in the international ascendance of the Korea game industries. As identified by the Korea Game Development Promotion Institute (KGDPI), the development of the Korea game industries can be conceptualized into three stages: stage of importation (1980s); stage of import substitution (1990s); and the stage of ascendance (2000 onwards). As mentioned, the Korea government has played a decisive role in helping the local game industries to pick up and become an international success.

The year 1997 marked a watershed for the Korean game industries. In January 1997, the Korean government announced a scheme to boost the local game industries, which included a plan to set up a Korean Game Promotion Centre (KGPC). This not only put the development of the Korean game industries into the policy agenda, but also set in motion a series of related state initiatives. The game industries scene in Korea was pretty much dominated by imported products from the US and European markets until this point. In 1998, the development of the game industries had officially been grouped into that of the cultural industries. This move elevated the status of game industries to go beyond entertainment and become part of the national cultural arena. The move also showed the Korean government's foresight in understanding the cultural pervasiveness of the game industries in the international cultural psyche.

The launching of KGPC in July 1999 and its Japan branch two months later marked another major step of progress in the government's plan to nurture the local game industries. KGPC's mission was to provide the industry with the needed technological innovation and support, overseas market information, and to provide venue and facility support.[1] KGPC served as a strategic platform between the government and the industry. As such, it enabled the government to grasp the market pulse directly, while also facilitating industry practitioners to get the best needed and timely technological and market advice from the government.

The inauguration of the Ministry of Culture and Tourism (MCT) in 1998 and the transfer of the cultural assets policy portfolio, including the game industries, into MCT's jurisdiction served to enhance the industries' booming as a Korean cultural asset proper.[2] The launching of Cyber Korea 21 in 1999 accelerated development of the game industries, in particular the online game industries, by speeding up broadband technology development, rapidly increasing the number of Internet users in Korea and enhancing national Internet education on both the positive and dysfunctional sides of cyber development. To nurture talents for the booming game industries, the Korean government started the Game Academy in November 2000. A game investment association and a game investment valuation association were also established in December 2000 and June 2001 respectively to nurture talents and mature venture funding and investments to meet the needs of the rising game industries.[3] KGPC was transformed into Korea Game Industry Agency (KOGIA) in no more than two and a half years of operation.

Moreover, the launch of the Korea Content Agency (KOCCA) in 2009 also played a role in boosting the Korean game industries. KOCCA is an overarching state agency whose composition is specified in Article 31 of the Framework Act on Cultural Industry Promotion. It combined the works of the Korea Broadcasting Institute, Korea Culture and Content Agency, Korea Game Industry Agency, Cultural Contents Centre, and the Digital Content Business Group of Korea IT Industry Promotion Agency. As an agency dedicated to the promotion of all areas of content, KOCCA provides a comprehensive support system that aims at developing Korea into one of "the world's top five contents powerhouses."[4] The game industry is amongst the content industries to be supported by KOCCA. Other industries to be supported include *manga*, animation and music. KOCCA provides the identified industries with the needed support which includes equipment rental, investment, technological training, international marketing strategy advice, research support on medium- and long-term development, and to develop strategic partnerships with overseas buyers and suppliers.

According to the 2013 White Paper on Korean Games (KOCCA 2013), the Korean online game market ranked second in the world in 2012, accounting for 28.6 percent of the world market. The first place in the world online game market continues to be held by China and the gap between China and Korea in the online game market is increasing, as ever. However, Korea managed to widen the gap with the US, which maintains the third place in the world. Korea also continues to expand its share of the world mobile game market, recording a 5.1 percent share in 2012.

The exports of Korean games broke through US$1 billion in 2008 (40.1 percent growth from 2007) and soared from US$1.6 billion to US$2.4 billion between the years 2010 and 2011 (a 48.1 percent growth). As of 2012, exports surpassed US$2.6 billion while growth has slowed down. As for the share of exports by platform, online games was by far the leader, recorded at US$2.4 billion or 91.4 percent of the total game exports. Mobile games exports grew significantly, recording close to US$170 million, which is almost a fivefold growth from the previous year. Total domestic game exports in 2013 were forecasted to reach approximately US$2.9 billion. China is the largest export market for Korean online games yet the penetration is shown to have slightly slowed down.

In 2012, the game production/distribution companies in normal operation in Korea numbered 957 and 14,782 PC rooms were in operation. The total number of workers in the 2012 game industry was found to be 95,051, up 1.2 percent from the previous year. Roughly 55 percent of them work at game production and distribution companies, while the rest are retail and consumption business workers.

The platform with the greatest growth now in Korea is the mobile platform. Games distributed through the messaging app KakaoTalk have a crucial role to play in energizing the Korean mobile game market. The most successful games sold through KakaoTalk were casual games that could be enjoyed with simple controls. For example, *Cookie Run*, released in April 2013 on Kakao, was the most downloaded game in Korea in 2013 (Cheng 2014). People enjoy these games as they can play them easily when they are on the go. The easy exchange of items or gifts also appeals to users as it enables them to manage their personal connections through these simple games. *Cookie Run* has now reached 52 million downloads across Asia, and tops the charts in Japan, Taiwan and Thailand, by continuing to work closely with messaging apps like WeChat,

Kakao and Line. Devsisters, the Seoul-based start-up that developed *Cookie Run*, generated about US$60 million in revenue in 2013, and another US$20 million in the first quarter of 2014.

As for user trends, online games (38.7 percent) is chosen to be the most commonly used game platform by Korean gamers, followed by mobile games (33.1 percent) (KOCCA 2013). Respondents felt that mobile games will be the platform to lead the future domestic game market and "role playing" is thought to be the genre to lead the future.

China: progressing in game development

As mentioned, China is rising to become one of the major players in the Asian as well as the global gaming industry. As a market, playing video games has displaced TV watching to become a major leisure activity among the young generation in China. In terms of the industry, China's Tencent, the majority owner of *League of Legends* creator Riot Games, is the largest game company in the world with its revenue from games of over US$5.3 billion in 2013 (Takahashi 2014b).

Cao and Downing (2008) sketched the development of the game industry in China. The game industry in China has developed from the arrival of arcades and home console games in the early 1980s, through the rapid growth of PC games in the late 1990s and early 2000s, to the boom of online games after 2000. Today online gaming has become the most profitable Internet market in China. Arcades arrived in China in the early 1980s after its post-Mao economic reform and opening policy. But as concerns about gambling and illegal activities in the game rooms built up, the government started to suppress these arcades through a series of administrative measures. Along with the decline of game rooms and arcade games, home game consoles became popular. Parents were willing to invest in the so-called "study consoles," which were believed to be education aids for their children to improve academic performance and to keep them away from game rooms. Into the late 1990s and early 2000s, given the economic development of the country, domestic PC ownership grew rapidly, which contributed to the growth of stand-alone PC games. Japanese and Taiwanese games were popular, later followed by US and European games, but they were largely consumed in pirated forms. While many players switched to online games in the next decade, those who continue to play PC games mostly prefer Western games of the first-person shooter, RTS, and racing and sports genres.

Online games took over the Chinese game market after the 2000s, thanks to the significant progress in broadband penetration and the popularity of Internet cafés. For Chinese urban youngsters who are single children, these online games, especially MMOGs, meet their needs of peer interactions. The number of online gamers in China grew by three times from 26 million in 2006 to 86 million in 2010. The online game market in China grew from US$0.7 billion in 2006 to US$5 billion in 2010. China was the largest online game market in the world and represented 89 percent of the market in Asia in 2011 (PricewaterhouseCoopers 2011).

Chinese online gamers have a preference for Korean and Chinese MMOGs over popular global online games. Chinese online games are usually PVP (player versus player) oriented, characterized by graceful movements and community interactions. These are more appealing to Chinese gamers when compared with the PVE (player versus environment) oriented Western online games. Chinese gamers also show a strong identification with storylines associated with Chinese dynastic history or legends such as Kung Fu romances. Korean firms used to play a major role in China's online game market, but Chinese game companies have evolved from licensing Korean games to developing games for the domestic and export market. In 2003, among the top ten online games in China, seven were from Korea, and none from China. Only a year later, Chinese firms were able to produce four out of the top ten online games, leaving Korea with five and Japan with one (*Business China* 2005).

However, the popularity of smartphone games in late 2012 has presented fierce competition to online games in China. Smartphone penetration quickly increased in China between the years 2012 and 2013. As users migrate to 3G and faster networks for their mobile devices, they find that mobile games are delivering increasingly engaging experiences of play. The sales revenue of the mobile game market in China showed an increase of 90.6 percent in 2012 as compared with the previous year (IDC 2013). In 2013, there were more than 80,000 development studios in China working on mobile games, releasing 100+ games per day (Research and Markets 2013).

Market forces including domestic private capital and non-state enterprises are the major players in the development of the game industry in China while the state maintains regulating and facilitating roles (Cao and Downing 2008). Ernkvist and Ström (2008) detailed the ways the Chinese government has set out techno-nationalistic policies aimed at increasing the economic growth of Chinese developed games and other policies designed to curb the social effect of online games, control the ideology in game content, and vigorously promote nationalistic propaganda. State intervention in terms of protective measures actually did help the local industry to grow (Chung and Fung 2013). Although foreign online games are allowed to be imported they are often screened out by content censorship procedures, leaving more room in the market for local games. With government intervention as such, transnational companies are bound to be less influential in the Chinese game industry as compared with the early development stage in the early 2000s.

Southeast Asia: emerging high-growth markets

Collectively, Southeast Asia serves as a promising region for the game industries to grow. ASEAN Economic Community (AEC) is the central governing office working on a pan-Southeast Asian strategy. The AEC's policy, *ASEAN ICT Master Plan 2015*, identifies the development of ICT as an agreed area of growth for ASEAN's member nations. The video game industries of Singapore, Malaysia, Indonesia, the Philippines, Thailand and Vietnam have reached and are projected to sustain an annual compound growth rate of 17.4 percent from 2011 to 2016 (Mead 2012). By 2016, the region is expected to reach a market size of 117 million gamers. The rapid increase in the number of gamers will generate over US$1 billion market revenue. Although the region constitutes only 9 percent of the world's total population, Southeast Asia has attracted multinational game companies to settle there partly due to the access to an abundant pool of skilled workers, and in some instances, partly in response to incentives given by individual government. Generally speaking, the region has the comparative advantage of having creative talents who can communicate in English and are receptive to Western game art and storytelling. This makes it easy for overseas game developers to overcome the barriers regarding the language and content localization.

Individually, each Southeast Asian country is in different stages of economic development, which also impacts the development of their respective game industries. Singapore stands out as a more developed economy, while Malaysia, Indonesia, the Philippines, Thailand and Vietnam are less developed but with a middle class on the rise. In 2012, the total inflow of foreign direct investment (FDI) to Southeast Asia was US$56.1 billion in US dollars. Among all the nations, Singapore received more FDI capital than the other five countries (Malaysia, Indonesia, the Philippines, Thailand and Vietnam) combined (*cogitAsia* 2012). Southeast Asia is also going through a process of social transformation as the result of the rise of its newly "rich" middle class. It is reported that the collective middle class population in the region in the five fastest-growing Southeast Asian countries (i.e., Malaysia, Indonesia, the Philippines, Thailand and Vietnam) will grow from 90 million people in 2011 to 150 million people within the next five to ten years

(PricewaterhouseCoopers 2011). This directly adds to the size of the gamer population in the respective countries. While Singapore, Malaysia and Thailand form one interconnected game market, the Philippines, Indonesia and Vietnam will constitute three single markets on their own (Grubb 2012).

Disparity also appears in ICT infrastructure among Southeast Asian nations (Ang and Loh 1996). Singapore and Malaysia have developed a high degree of Internet household penetration, reaching 133 percent and 90 percent respectively. However, Vietnam, the Philippines, Thailand and Indonesia still lag behind the global average of 45 percent (Kim et al. 2011). The low growth in Internet penetration slows down the region's collective competitiveness in the global game scene. Internet connectivity in Southeast Asia is expanding at a pace that is slower by more than six times than in the country with the world's fastest connection, South Korea. Within-country disparity also exists. For instance, Indonesia has 11 percent of ownership of home computer in 2009, while the rural area has only 2 percent (*Audiencescape* 2010). In some cases, the relatively high production cost incurred by charges of broadband service providers serves to constrain the development of the game industry.

Most of the global game companies set up their studios in Southeast Asia due to the region's cheap cost in skilled talent. Such companies include Electronic Arts, Lucasfilm, Koei, Gevo and Ubisoft in Singapore; Codemasters Studios in Malaysia; Square Enix and Gameloft in Indonesia; Activision, Bioware, Bungie and Eidos in the Philippines; and Gameloft in Vietnam. The problem of rampant piracy imposes barriers for most international game publishers endeavoring to distribute products in Southeast Asia.

Most of the local game developers in the Southeast Asian region are small and medium-sized companies. These companies are either companies that started in the 1990s or 2000s, and grew from contractual work they accepted from international game companies seeking to outsource projects, or as start-ups that produced small budget games like mobile and flash games. These local game companies produce quality art assets for global titles. They hone their expertise in cross-platform production to excel in console, PC and mobile and casual game development.

Game publishers in Southeast Asia focus instead on online game publishing. These companies include Thailand-based Asiasoft, Singapore-based Infomcomm Asia Holdings and Malaysia-based Cubinet and E-Club. Local publishers that publish games only within a single nation are a rare situation, except in Vietnam. While most publishers see Southeast Asia as an integrated single market for game publishing, Vietnam remains restricted to them, because of barriers to foreign imports due to censorship imposed by the Vietnamese government.

In the policy aspect, among the six Southeast Asian governments, Singapore, Malaysia and Thailand have adopted an activist approach by playing a crucial role in formulating cultural policies pertinent to their emerging cultural industries. These three governments tend to grow local start-ups by matching global capital with local game development projects. Thus, local game industry players in these countries tend to be sub-contractors of major international game developers, and most local production of game components tends to be for export. In Singapore, global game companies such as Electronic Arts, Lucasfilm, Koei and Ubisoft establish their studios with the incentive of accessing regional creative talents in Southeast Asia.

Singapore has an ICT policy, *iN2015 Digital Media and Entertainment*, created to respond to a fully integrated Southeast Asia in 2015. The plan considers digital gaming as one of the country's core sectors in creative industry development. It constitutes a strategy demonstrating Singapore's ambition to use ICT in order to build the country's leadership in the region as an intelligent nation in Southeast Asia (*eGov* 2006). Similarly, countries such as Malaysia, Indonesia and Thailand have also adopted the ICT approach as they compete with each other to become the hub of digital content in Southeast Asia. In Malaysia, for example, the government has formulated its game development policy based upon the plans of *Multimedia Super Corridor* and *Economic Transformation Programme*.

Practices of play in Asia

After an overview of the market situation in Asian countries, we now turn to some observations about the practices of play among Asian players. Generally speaking, play practices are very narrowly understood in dominant discourses about video games (Shaw 2010). Academics and journalists tend to express a tension between the stereotype and "reality" of gaming. Apart from questioning such stereotypes that game playing is a male-dominant, addictive, violent and dysfunctional behavior, it is important to understand the ways computer games as a new media form provide new kinds of involvement and engagement. Humphreys (2005) posits that computer games have an emergent structure that draws on their players' participation and inputs. Computer games involve play and interaction that configure the text and make it different every time it is played. The trajectory of the game text is thus contingent upon the particular dynamics and action generated by shifting combinations of players. In particular, MMOG typifies a new level of player productivity as players actively devote their time to forming coalitions, strategically coordinating for more efficient game combat, and managing group dynamics and tensions for better in-game performance. The community and networks of relationships are both structural and textual to the game, and these social aspects of the game are integral to the constitution of the emergent and mutable game text. In Asia, we can observe some different forms of involvement and engagement by these "productive players."

First, practices of play in the prevalent MMORPGs illustrate salient developments of techno-sociality in Asia. In-game social relations are shown to be connected with relationships in the real world. Players of the game *Online Jinyong* in Hong Kong, for example, actively devote energy in building relationships with others whom they see as sharing the same values through acts of communication, consolidation, confirmation and consumption in the game (Fung 2006). Players gain support through engaging in the game and these relations might compensate real life relationships. And yet, online community relations must be sustained by offline communication and resources as well. Furthermore, online games have become more than spaces for play and social interaction. In discussing two incidents of in-game protests in Chinese MMORPGs, Chan (2009) asserted that online games work as sites for different types of collective group action and social engagement that manifest serious issues such as patriotism and public morality. Online game protests are seen as constitutive of "a new field of struggle," although the coalition may be contingent and transitory.

Second, as social games tap new market segments, practices of these previously non-players in different age and gender groups also merit attention. For example, the game *Happy Farm*, played through SNS such as Renren and Kaixin, attracts users of all age groups in China. In *Happy Farm*, players acquire, raise, and sell farm produce while chatting with neighbors, and exchanging gifts and favors. Players are also entitled to steal other people's produce when they are offline, but those who are stolen from are compensated with "pious" points, constituting win-win transactions rather than causing harm. Hjorth and Arnold (2013) noted that *Happy Farm* provides a place for nostalgia in which one can own one's own farm and build capital by working hard. These SNS games are also much more casual in their demands on engagement, but they manage to attract the parents and even grandparents of the urban young population in China. After teaching their parents and grandparents to use the Internet, children use these SNS games to connect with their family. These social media games therefore facilitate players' "playful socialization" on a micro level, and a cross-generational new media literacy in China on a macro level. Another interesting case is the rise of a romance game genre for female social game players in recent years in Japan. This genre is probably hardly known to Westerners. But with the good-looking male characters, attractive voices, and beautiful graphics in the games, it fulfills Japanese female players' fantasies of having an ideal virtual male partner who can keep company with them anytime and anywhere.

The consumption of "cute" also adds to the gameplay culture in Asia. Chen (2013) considers the "cute" culture as a new entertainment concept created to appeal to child and female players in Asia. An abundance of cute characters and aesthetics in girls' games is consumed in association with the yearning to be comfortable and soothed. The cuteness also creates a new game space that is non-confrontational, non-offensive and non-competitive for child and female players. For example, the well-known and classic Japanese game *Mario* captures a nostalgia for childhood experiences that is characterized by innocence. Players' identification with the cute avatars can also be explained as a pursuit of "playful possibilities" through games, as shown in the South Korean game *Kart Rider* (Hjorth 2006). While the "cute" culture might be a peculiar phenomenon to Western gamers, it may provide a point of interest for us to address the specific socio-cultural contexts that shape this specific cultural practice of play.

Asian formation and East Asian dominance

In the last section of this chapter, we would like to discuss the implications of the current market situation for an Asian formation of game culture. In general, an intra-Asian games network is said to be formed on the basis of distinctive intra-Asian games design and marketing (Chan 2008). It involves the use of a unique set of regional aesthetic and narrative forms in game content and regionally focused marketing and distribution initiatives. For example, Japanese developers are well known for using "a unique aesthetic, an approach to iconography, character design and structure that is unfathomable to studios in the West" (*The Guardian* 2009). Games in the region often draw on or cross-reference the plots and characters from other popular cultural forms such as comics, animation and fantasy novels. Regional cultural signifiers—such as Asian antiquity/fantasy and Chinese wuxia-themes—often become common reference points for the narratives, characters and imagery of many Asian MMORPGs. These versions of so-called traditional Asian culture are then marketed to the audience to invoke a sense of regional identification. However, the perceived cultural proximity in Asia games today is largely based on the three major players: Japan, Korea, and China. These three countries are themselves large-scale markets and industry data shows that they are trying to expand further in each other's market. While we can see that Southeast Asian countries will emerge as high-growth markets, the East Asian players will continue to dominate the playing field exactly by exploiting these potential markets. Such dominance by East Asian players is what we would like to bring into the discussion of the Asian formation of game culture.

As a matter of fact, the Asian game markets are clearly filled with products from the three dominant players. In 2012, 177 Chinese online game titles were exported, with 133 exported to the Greater China area (Taiwan, Hong Kong, Macau) and 110 to Southeast Asia. Seventy-nine titles (44.6 percent) were exported to Japan and Korea and Chinese game companies plan to further expand the Korean market (*Chinatimes* 2013). In reverse, China was the largest export market for Korean games, accounting for 38.6 percent of total Korean game exports in 2012, according to KOCCA. The second was Japan, accounting for 26.7 percent of the total exports; followed by Southeast Asia (18.8 percent). As for exports to each country by platform, online game exports to China and Japan were the greatest. Japan (25.1 percent) was also the second largest export country for Korea in mobile game exports (while the US came first with 58.0 percent).

Chinese games are popular not only in the Greater China area, but also in Southeast Asian countries. In Malaysia, for example, although the Chinese population only represents 30 percent of the country's population, Chinese gamers have become the major source of income for game publishers. The Chinese community is generally more knowledgeable and more exposed to the Internet. According to an interview with a Malaysian online game publisher,[5] because most of the paying customers are Chinese gamers, publishers mostly offer gaming environments in the Chinese language. Despite the government's effort to promote racial harmony under the "One Malaysia" plan's title, this emphasis reveals a potential problem in the lack of development and publishing for local content that exist for all races in the country. In addition, a clear disconnection exists between Malaysian game developers and publishers, as game development concentrates on producing content for the global market while game publishers import competitive Chinese games for the Chinese ethnic community in the domestic market. While games with "Chinese" art styles and centered on Chinese cultures may not be attractive for the non-Chinese gamers in Malaysia, Korean games such as *Lineage 2* are getting very big and becoming a lot more approachable for Malaysians, which again illustrates the dominance of East Asian games.

We believe that Japan still maintains a strong presence in the scene because players in certain markets such as Taiwan and Korea, where they seldom play English games, do have a preference for Japanese games. Besides, social game companies from Japan have been making efforts to expand their operations both regionally and globally. For example, DeNA acquired US mobile game company Ngmoco for US$400 million (Parkin 2010), and GREE bought OpenFeint for US$104 million (Caoili 2011). Other forms of expansion include overseas subsidiaries, partnerships, joint ventures and platform localizations in the US, Europe, Latin America and Asia. Within the region, target locations include China, Korea, Singapore and Vietnam. Japanese game developers offer comprehensive training for the local staff in Southeast Asian countries by either sending the local staff to be trained in Japan or sending experienced programmers, designers and artists to train the staff in those Southeast Asian locations.

One example of the expansion of Japanese social games is the partnership between GREE and Tencent. The Japanese SNS platform GREE has approximately 30 million users, and was hoping to extend its reach to over 120 million Chinese mobile game users by partnering with Tencent, the largest online service provider in China. The social game platforms of the two companies were made compatible with each other, so that games can be easily imported, exported and distributed between the two countries. Through this platform, Japanese game developers Taito and TECMO KOEI have been able to release their games to Tencent, based on the ones they previously developed for the GREE smartphone platform.

Although Chan (2008) noted that the localization practices of game companies do prove the diversity of Asian audiences in the intra-Asian games network, we may want to further question how much of the significance of the local can be truly reflected in this Asian formation. Indeed, the diversity of the cultures of smaller Asian countries can rarely be featured in original game design. A game company owner in Malaysia told us that it is difficult for smaller Southeast Asian countries to incorporate cultural elements in game development.[6] He felt that these smaller countries do not have the long history which can become a source of inspiration for games, plus games with nation-specific elements would not be profitable because they could only appeal to a very small domestic market. It is also difficult for smaller countries to flow their products reversely to East Asian markets. He said that even though they are aware of the vast potential of the China market, they are limited by the lack of understanding of the Chinese culture and language in order to tap the most current trend and thus break into that market. In this regard, they are already at a disadvantage when competing with domestic games developed within China.

To conclude, given the fact that the presence of the East Asian powers is strong, what we are proposing here is that they are casting a homogenizing effect on the gaming scene in Asia. Neither are we content with the conclusion that the plurality of cultures in Asia has already been reflected. What we would like to bring forth, though, are questions about a desirable vision/version of an Asian formation. Or, more precisely, if the Asian formation of game culture we now observe is characterized by the entrenchment of East Asian cultural capital currencies, what will become of "Asia games"? And how desirable is that vision/version of Asian formation?

Acknowledgement

This work was fully supported by a grant from the Research Grant Council of Hong Kong Special Administrative Region (Project no. 4001-SPPR-09).

Notes

1 科技發展政策報導, Sci-Tech Policy Review (in Chinese) SR9209 (2003): 711–720.
2 2013 White Paper on Korean Games: Guide to Korean Games Industry and Culture. Available at: http://kocca.kr/knowledge/publication/indu/__icsFiles/afieldfile/2013/11/19/UM3mpLQqzHbm.pdf (Accessed on July 25, 2014).
3 科技發展政策報導, Sci-Tech Policy Review (in Chinese) SR9209 (2003): 711–720.
4 KOCCA's website is available at: http://www.kocca.kr/cop/main.do (Accessed on April 4, 2015).
5 Personal interview conducted in Kuala Lumpur, October 22, 2012.
6 Personal interview conducted in Kuala Lumpur, October 23, 2012.

References

Ang, P.H. and Loh, C.M. (1996) 'Internet Development in Asia'. Available at: http://www.isoc.org/inet96/proceedings/h1/h1_1.htm (Accessed on April 14, 2015).
Aslinger, B. and Huntemann, N.B. (2013) 'Introduction'. In N.B. Huntemann and B. Aslinger (eds) *Gaming Globally: Production, Play, and Place*, New York: Palgrave Macmillan.
Audiencescape (2010) 'World Bank Knowledge for Development: Indonesia'. Available at: http://www.audiencescapes.org/country-profiles/indonesia/country-overview/internet/internet-132 (Accessed on September 12, 2013).
Business China (2005) 'Keep It Remote and Pre-paid', 31(5), February 28: 5.
Cao, Y. and Downing, J. (2008) 'The Realities of Virtual Play: Video Games and Their Industry in China', *Media, Culture and Society*, 30(4), 515–529.
Caoili, E. (2011) 'Japan's Gree Acquires Mobile Social Gaming Network OpenFeint for $104M'. Available at: http://www.gamasutra.com/view/news/34258/Japans_Gree_Acquires_Mobile_Social_Gaming_Network_OpenFeint_For_104M.php (Accessed on July 28, 2014).
Chan, D. (2008) 'Negotiating Online Computer Games in East Asia: Manufacturing Asian MMORPGs and Marketing "Asianness"'. In A. Jahn-Sudmann, and R. Stockmann (eds) *Computer Games as a Sociocultural Phenomenon: Games Without Frontiers: War Without Tears*, Hampshire and New York: Palgrave Macmillan.
Chan, D. (2009) 'Beyond the "Great Firewall": The Case of In-Game Protests in China'. In L. Hjorth and D. Chan (eds) *Gaming Cultures and Place in Asia-Pacific*, New York and Oxford: Routledge.
Chen, L.C. (2013) 'What's the Cultural Difference Between the West and the East? The Consumption of Popular "Cute" Games in the Taiwanese Market'. *New Media & Society*, August 2, 2013: 1–16.
Chee, F. (2005) 'Understanding Korean Experiences of Online Game Hype, Identity, and the Menace of the "Wang-tta"'. Proceedings of DiGRA 2005 Conference: Changing Views—Worlds in Play, Digital Games Research Association (DiGRA).
Cheng, J. (2014) '"Cookie Run" Game Sweetens Messaging Apps', *The Wall Street Journal Asia*, July 2, 2014: 1.
Chinatimes (2013) 'Proportion of Chinese Game Export and Upcoming Focus on the Korean Market'. (In Chinese) Available at: http://www.chinatimes.com/realtimenews/20131123001561-260412 (Accessed on July 25, 2014).

Chung, P. and Fung, A. (2013) 'Internet Development and the Commercialization of Online Gaming in China'. In N.B. Huntemann and B. Aslinger (eds) *Gaming Globally: Production, Play, and Place*, New York: Palgrave Macmillan.

cogitAsia (2012) 'By the Numbers: Foreign Direct Investment in Southeast Asia'. Available at: http://cogitasia. com/by-the-numbers-foreign-direct-investment-in-southeast-asia/(Accessed on April 14, 2015).

Consalvo, M. (2006) 'Console Video Games and Global Corporations: Creating a Hybrid Culture', *New Media and Society*, 8(1): 117–137.

eGov (2006) 'Singapore iN2015 Masterplan Offers A Digital Future For Everyone', Media Release. Available at: http://www.egov.gov.sg/media-room/media-releases/2006/singapore-in2015-masterplan-offers-a-digital-future-for-everyone (Accessed on July 25, 2014).

Ernkvist, M. and Ström, P. (2008) 'Enmeshed in Games with the Government: Governmental Policies and the Development of the Chinese Online Game Industry', *Games and Culture*, 3(1): 98–126.

Eurotechnology Japan KK (2014) 'Japan's Game Makers and Markets'. Available at: http://www. eurotechnology.com/store/jgames/ (Accessed on July 30, 2014).

Fritz, B. and Olivarez-Giles, N. (2014) 'Microsoft Xbox Losing Gamers to Sony's PS4', *Wall Street Journal*, June 9, 2014: B1.

Fung, A. (2006) 'Bridging Cyberlife and Real Life: A Study of Online Communities in Hong Kong'. In D. Silver and A. Massannari (eds) *Critical Cyber-Culture Studies*, New York and London: New York University Press.

Golub, A. and Lingley, K. (2008) '"Just Like the Qing Empire": Internet Addiction, MMOGs, and Moral Crisis in Contemporary China', *Games and Culture*, 3 (1): 59–75.

Grubb, J. (2012) 'Southeast Asian Gaming Firms Expect Huge Growth in the Region Through 2016'. Available at: http://venturebeat.com/2012/11/30/southeast-asian-gaming-firm-expects-huge-growth-in-the-region-through-2016/ (Accessed on April 14, 2015).

Hjorth, L. (2006) 'Playing at Being Mobile: Gaming and Cute Culture in South Korea', *The Fibreculture Journal*. Available at: http://eight.fibreculturejournal.org/fcj-052-playing-at-being-mobile-gaming-and-cute-culture-in-south-korea/ (Accessed on July 4, 2014).

Hjorth, L. (2008) 'Games@Neo-Regionalism: Locating Gaming in the Asia-Pacific', *Games and Culture*, 3(1): 3–12.

Hjorth, L. (2011) 'Gaming in the Asia-Pacific: Two Futures for Gaming – Online Gaming versus Electronic Individualism'. In *Games and Gaming: An Introduction to New Media*, Oxford and New York: Berg.

Hjorth, L. and Arnold, M. (2013) 'Playing at Being Social: A Cross-Generational Case Study of Social Gaming in Shanghai, China'. In N.B. Huntemann and B. Aslinger (eds) *Gaming Globally: Production, Play, and Place*, New York: Palgrave Macmillan.

Hjorth, L. and Chan, D. (2009) 'Locating the Game: Gaming Cultures in/and the Asia Pacific'. In L. Hjorth and D. Chan (eds) *Gaming Cultures and Place in Asia-Pacific*, New York: Routledge.

Huhh, J. (2009) 'The "Bang" Where Korean Online Gaming Began: The Culture and Business of the PC *bang* in Korea'. In L. Hjorth and D. Chan (eds) *Gaming Cultures and Place in Asia-Pacific*, New York: Routledge.

Humphreys, S. (2005) 'Productive Players: Online Computer Games' Challenge to Conventional Media Forms', *Communication and Critical/Cultural Studies*, 2(1): 37–51.

IDC (2013) 'Web Games Help China's Game Export Grow 57.5% to RMB 3562.5 Million in 2012, According to IDC'. Available at: http://www.idc.com/getdoc.jsp?containerId=prCN24141413 (Accessed on July 25, 2014).

Inagaki, K. (2014) 'Sony's PlayStations Headed Back to China', *Wall Street Journal*, May 27, 2014: B3.

Kim, C., Hong, D., Winterle, D. and Zhao, A. (2011) *The Future of Content: Southeast Asia. A Bain and Company Study for the World Economic Forum*. Available at: http://www3.weforum.org/docs/WEF_MEI_The_Future_of_Content_Report_2011.pdf (Accessed on April 14, 2014).

KOCCA (2013) 'White Paper on Korean Games: Guide to Korean Games Industry and Culture'. Available at: http://kocca.kr/knowledge/publication/indu/__icsFiles/afieldfile/2013/11/19/UM3mpLQqzHbm. pdf (Accessed on July 25, 2014).

Mayumi, N. (2013) 'Japan: Land of the Rising Game—Mobile Publishers Master the Psychology of Payments in a Country Conditioned to Buy on Phones', *Wall Street Journal*, December 11, 2013.

Mead, N. (2012) 'OECD: South-east Asian Economic Outlook to Return to Pre-Crisis Levels', *The Guardian*. Available at: http://www.guardian.co.uk/global-development/datablog/2012/nov/18/oecd-south-east-asia-economic-outlook (Accessed on April 12, 2013).

Parkin, S. (2010) 'Japanese Social Gaming Giant DeNA to Buy Ngmoco For $400 Million'. Available at: http://www.gamasutra.com/view/news/30916/Japanese_Social_Gaming_Giant_DeNA_To_Buy_Ngmoco_For_400_Million.php (Accessed on July 28, 2014).

PricewaterhouseCoopers (2011) *The Southeast Asian Tigers Roar Again: This Time For Real.* Available at: http://www.pwc.com/en_US/us/forensic-services/publications/assets/marketmap-southeast-asia.pdf (Accessed on July 11, 2014).

PricewaterhouseCoopers (2014) *Global Entertainment and Media Outlook 2014–2018—Video Games.* Available at: http://www.pwc.com/gx/en/global-entertainment-media-outlook/segment-insights/video-games.jhtml (Accessed on July 11, 2014).

Research and Markets (2013) 'China's Mobile Game Market Report 2013'. Available at: http://www.researchandmarkets.com/reports/2639645/chinas_mobile_game_market_report_2013#pos-3 (Accessed on July 4, 2014).

Shaw, A. (2010) 'What is Video Game Culture? Cultural Studies and Game Studies', *Games and Culture*, 5(4): 403–424.

Takahashi, D. (2014a) 'Asia Will Account for 82 Percent of the $6B Global Game-Market Growth This Year?' Available at: http://venturebeat.com/2014/05/23/asia-will-account-for-82-percent-of-the-6b-global-game-market-growth-this-year/ (Accessed on July 24, 2014).

Takahashi, D. (2014b) 'The DeanBeat: How Far Will the Advantage Swing to Asia in Games?' Available at: http://venturebeat.com/2014/05/23/the-deanbeat-how-far-will-the-advantage-swing-to-asia-in-games/ (Accessed on July 24, 2014).

The Guardian (2009) 'Is Japan "Finished" in the Games Industry?' Available at: http://www.the guardian.com/technology/gamesblog/2009/sep/30/games-gameculture (Accessed on July 7, 2014).

Toto, S. (2014a) 'Japan's Smartphone Game Market Worth US$5.4 Billion in 2013, Accounts for Half of All Games'. Available at: http://www.serkantoto.com/2014/03/25/japan-smartphone-mobile-game-market/ (Accessed on July 25, 2014).

Toto, S. (2014b) 'Japan's Console Game Market Down 15.7% in 2013, Mobile Games Bigger'. Available at: http://www.serkantoto.com/2014/07/30/japan-gaming-market-size-statistics/ (Accessed on July 30, 2014).

Wireless Watch Japan (2012) 'Japan Mobile Social Game Market—2012'. Available at: http://wirelesswatch.jp/2012/08/14/japan-mobile-social-game-market-2012/ (Accessed on July 25, 2014).

Yano Research Institute (2012) ソーシャルゲーム市場に関する調査結果 2011. (In Japanese). Yano Research Institute Ltd.

34

Online games and society in China: an exploration of key issues and challenges

Matthew M. Chew

It is well known that the market size, revenue, profits, and production volume of the Chinese online games industry is impressive, rivalling global market leaders including the US (Chung and Fung 2013). The small but growing field of Chinese game studies has already provided much information on the business and industrial aspects of Chinese online games (Chen 2009; Chung and Yuan 2009; Kshetri 2009; MacInnes and Hu 2007). However studies into the social aspects of Chinese online games still remains a relatively underdeveloped subfield. What are the social impacts of online games in China? What are the socio-political contexts of online gaming in China? How do online gaming culture and gamer communities interact with Chinese society? Do online games generate implications for class, race and gender in China? Broad questions such as these surely cannot be comprehensively answered here. Answers for these questions require us to consolidate the large number of empirical studies that examine various socially relevant aspects and problematics of online gaming in China. This chapter identifies and briefly explores some of these issues raised in the various literature. It is meant to serve as an invitation to further research and inquiry.

Six key social issues associated with online games in China will be overviewed in this chapter. They include virtual property, gold-farming, game addiction, collective action of gamers, women and online games, and the Chinese state's relationship with online gaming. The choice of these six issues is made on the basis of their social relevance, theoretical interest, and their potential to advance studies on the social aspects of Chinese online games. There are additionally different specific reasons for choosing each issue. The first issue, virtual property, is one of the most mainstream problematics in English-language studies on online games. The very different virtual property culture, relevant game design, and relevant government policies in China provide data that are likely to yield fruitful comparisons with those of North American and Europe. The second issue, gold-farming, is selected because it is the most well studied (and, by the way, the only well studied) social aspect of Chinese online games. A report on key social issues of Chinese online games will not be complete without a review of current theoretical thinking about gold-farming.

The third issue to be discussed in this chapter, game addiction, is selected mainly because it has been regarded by the Chinese public—including that in mainland China, Hong Kong, and Taiwan—to be the most serious social problem entailed by online gaming. This issue is especially interesting because it is less discussed in the West as the main negative social effect of online gaming. The fourth issue, collective action of gamers, is chosen because it is theoretically intriguing. The terms "collective action" and "online games" are seemingly oxymoronic; it is rare for anyone to argue that online game entertainment generates socio-political activism. Nonetheless, although gamer collective actions are rarely observed in the West, they have occurred in China in many different forms including virtual world protests and real world violent actions. The fifth issue, women and online games, is covered mainly for its social significance. It is understood that online games and especially traditional MMORPGs are less congenial to women than many other pop cultural genres. How this social inequality transpires in China differently than it does in the West is worth exploring for feminists as well as game studies scholars. The sixth issue, the Chinese state's relationship with online gaming, is selected because authoritarian state control is a powerful determinant of Chinese media. Given that most other major online game markets in the world do not experience strong state control, the Chinese case should provide valuable data for international comparisons.

This chapter will reflect upon the overview of the six aforementioned issues. Because a number of English-language studies on the first two issues already exist, overviews of these two issues will be mainly composed of clarification and critical commentaries of current studies and secondary reports. Overviews of the other four issues do not contain many commentaries on or citations of current studies however, for such studies are few. Discussion under these four issues is organized instead around: i) identification and clarification of the issue's social significance; ii) a brief discussion of primary data; and/or iii) preliminary analysis of the theoretical implications of locally specific China data for international comparisons.

Virtual property

Virtual property is one of the earliest research foci of English-language online game studies. Virtual property is a new type of economically valuable and exchangeable goods created through massively multi-player online gaming. Current studies examine the economic consequences, legal implications, and social issues associated with virtual property (e.g., Castronova 2002, 2006; Grimes 2006; Lastowka and Hunter 2004). There are articles that explore virtual property in China from business and technical legal perspectives, but few approach the topic from a social angle apart from gold-farming (Chew 2011).

It is remarkable that many studies that explore the legal implications of virtual property in the US allude briefly to China. These allusions focus on an intriguing legal case in China that was ruled in favor of gamers instead of game corporations in regard to virtual property ownership (e.g., Fairfield 2005). It is therefore well understood that the socio-legal context of virtual property in China is different than that in the US or Europe. But research on why and how they are different is still lacking. A tentative and brief exploration of this problematic, one that incorporates insights of current English-language studies, Chinese-language data, and a stakeholder analysis framework, is offered here as an invitation to further research.

The most relevant stakeholders of virtual property in China include gamers, game publishers, the state, and the legal system. Numerous surveys and polls show that Chinese gamers and the Chinese public overwhelmingly believe that virtual property should be considered private property, that laws need to be set up to protect virtual property rights, and that gamers have much more rightful claim than game corporations or the state to virtual property created through their avatars (Chew 2011). There is also an overwhelming consensus among Chinese lawyers that specialized legislature and law enforcement units should be established to protect gamers' virtual property. I find that out of the more than a hundred scholarly articles published by Chinese legal scholars and lawyers on virtual property since the early 2000s, less than a handful advocate pro-corporate views or a neutral stance regarding virtual property ownership.

Because of China's communist past and current authoritarian political structure, (non-state owned) corporations have never been as powerful as those in the US and Europe and lobbies are entirely absent. The absolute majority of Chinese game developers and publishers are non-state owned and recently founded. It is therefore not surprising that Chinese game corporations do not receive favorable treatment from the Chinese legislators, courts, and police for their claim to virtual property ownership.

Virtual property theft presents a much more serious challenge to gamers in China than that in the West. There are criminal operations that systematically steal from millions of game accounts annually. Moreover, surveys inform us that Chinese gamers themselves are unscrupulous about breaking into acquaintances' game accounts (Chew 2011). In the early 2000s, the Chinese police rejected gamer victims' pleas for recovering their stolen virtual property on the grounds that there were no laws against the stealing of virtual game items. But beginning from the mid-2000s, the Chinese police proactively fought against virtual property theft as relevant laws and a specialized police sub-section were established.

Real money trading (RMT) of virtual property emerged in China among gamers in the early 2000s. A part of it developed into an export industry that real money trades gold-farm produced virtual property, while another part turned into RMT among gamers through ad hoc means and domestically oriented gold-farms. Quantitative estimates on the size of RMT in China are completely lacking. But it appears that RMT among gamers has remained limited in comparison to export-oriented gold-farm RMT, mostly because Chinese game publishers do not support it (even though they tolerate it).

The social impact of virtual property in China seems to be transforming into a different form in the 2010s. Virtual items and currency in many newly developed games becomes much less exchangeable and real money tradable. It is because varieties of MMO games other than MMORPGs are popularized, mobile and console online games adopt new business models and game mechanics, and pay-to-win games dominate the market. These changes effectively let game publishers monopolize the RMT of virtual property and turn virtual property trading into a regular part of their business model. Additionally, the emergence of virtual currencies entirely unconnected to gaming (such as bitcoin) undermines the real world economic impact of game virtual property. Virtual property related legal cases, virtual property disputes among gamers, and virtual property theft have become fewer and less publicized. It has also become less urgent to establish additional virtual property laws in China as the court and legal enforcement have recognized the protection of gamers' virtual property as part of their routine work. How exactly the new, corporate-controlled virtual property trade will generate social implications in China will be an interesting problematic.

Gold-farming

Gold-farming refers to the work of generating real money, tradable virtual property through operating online game avatars. "Gold-farmers" refers to individuals who do this type of work and gold-farms are the workplace of gold-farmers. Gold-farming became a large industry in China in the mid-2000s and it supplied a large portion of global demand. Gold-farming is the most well-researched topic in the field of Chinese online game studies. The study of no other social aspect of Chinese online gaming has received the attention of as many global scholars and reporters. This section reviews the current approaches to studying gold-farming and then identifies some research gaps and future research directions.

A richly developed approach to gold-farming problematizes the class-based exploitation aspect of gold-farming. A number of scholarly works, serious journalistic reports, and documentaries focus on the question of whether one should interpret gold-farms as an internet-assisted institution that socioeconomically empowers gold-farm workers, or an unconventional yet still exploitive type of sweatshop. Different arguments are mobilized to support the former position (Anon. 2006; Barboza 2005; Dibbell 2007; Jin 2006; Russell 2004). It is argued that gold-farm workplace environments are more similar to typical offices than manufacturing plants and are hence much more safe and comfortable than the typical sweatshop. For example, air-conditioning is often equipped because the numerous computers in a gold-farm need cooling. Online skill training is provided to gold-farmers, a significant number of whom were rural migrants who lack online skills and who would not otherwise have received training in a typical sweatshop workplace. Some make the contextualist argument that although gold-farms are exploitive according to the wage standards of developed economies, they offer valuable job opportunities to unskilled workers in underdeveloped parts of China, who would otherwise remain unemployed or be forced to work in sweatshops. It is also argued that the wages of gold-farmers are higher than typical sweatshop wages in China.

Arguments that interpret gold-farms as fundamentally exploitive are not less persuasive. It is found that gold-farm owners make enough profits to sustain a middle class lifestyle, while gold-farmers normally enjoy wages that are only slightly higher than factory workers (van Luyn 2006). If the socioeconomic differential between gold-farm owners and gold-farmers constitutes a classic Marxist critique, that between Western gamers and Chinese gold-farmers is formulated into a global Marxist critique (Chan 2006). Gold-farmers, living in underdeveloped parts of the world system and under working class conditions, co-inhabit game virtual worlds with Western gamers who come from middle class backgrounds and the center of the world system. While gold-farmers are there to work and serve, gamers are there to play. To add insult to injury, Western gamers despise what gold-farmers do even though they are the main subscribers of gold-farm services. My ongoing research finds that gold-farmers have extremely long work hours (i.e., 12 hours a day for the absolute majority of gold-farms) and that most gold-farmers are allowed only a day or two of holiday each month. Because gold-farms' dormitories are often extremely unhygienic and overcrowded, their living conditions are more similar to that of workers in sweatshops than that of low-income white collar workers.

A minor approach to understanding gold-farming and exploitation analyzes dimensions of exploitation that are not mainly class-based. For example, some young gamers in China were manipulated by gold-farm managers to do gold-farming work (Chew 2006). While these children thought they were helping out a fellow gamer or their clan, they were actually made part-time gold-farmers without getting any wages. Prisoners in China constitute another group that is turned into gold-farmers without wages. Reports in the Chinese media claim that prisoners find gold-farming work much more preferable than conventional hard labor. But ethical questions remain. Incidentally, there are reports of similar work arrangements for prisoners in the US.

Yet another social inequality issue associated with gold-farming is racism (Nakamura 2007; Nardi and Kow 2010; Steinkuehler 2005; Yee 2006). Because the majority of the world's export oriented gold-farms were located in China in the 2000s, Western gamers tend to interpret gold-farmers as exclusively Chinese. Stereotyping of the racial characteristics of Chinese gold-farmers can be easily found in game forums, in-game conversation among gamers, and machinima. Racial hatred can be observed through organized activities that harass Chinese gold-farmers. For example, powerful gamers band together to visit spots in the game world where gold-farming is usually carried out and to kill gold-farmers working there.

A relatively optimistic approach to gold-farming interprets it in terms of ICT4D (information and communication technology for development) (Heeks 2008). Gold-farming is effective in facilitating development because it offers employment to inexperienced workers, trains workers in upgradable skills, and operations can be set up even in rural locations. At the same time, gold-farming avoids the major shortcomings of conventional ICT4D initiatives. Gold-farm operations are financially self-sustainable and profitable; whereas conventional ICT4D operations are seldom profitable. Additionally, the founding of them requires very little financial overhead. Gold-farms are also technically self-sustainable in the sense that they do not rely heavily on computer technicians for daily operation. Moreover, gold-farms do not require government support.

A few research gaps can be identified in current gold-farming studies. First, basic quantitative data on the industry is extremely lacking. Macro level data on the size of the industry, the global market share, size of workforce, or output volume are non-existent, for instance. Even rough estimates are rarely attempted because there is too little reliable data to work with. Micro level quantitative data on wages of gold-farmers and revenue of individual gold-farms have been provided. But different scholars and reporters supply considerably different numbers. Second, in-depth and thick ethnographic details of gold-farms are lacking. Scholarly studies have not been more informative than journalistic reports and video documentaries in this regard. Participant observation of gold-farming work has not been carried out. Without detailed data, difficult questions such as whether gold-farms should be seen as sweatshops cannot be meaningfully deliberated. Third, gold-farming work provides research directions apart from exploitation and racism (e.g., Lee and Lin 2011; Nardi and Kow 2010). These directions have not been well explored and there is much room in them for further studies.

Game addiction

Game addiction has not been seen as a serious and controversial social problem among the public in the US or Europe. It is much less discussed than other negative implications of gaming including violent and sexual game contents. But game addiction has come to be regarded as the most serious social problem associated with online games by the public in mainland China, Hong Kong, and Taiwan. There are around a dozen English-language studies on game addiction in China. Almost all of them focus on quantitative data analyses that demonstrate how heavily Chinese gamers are psychologically addicted (Chiu et al. 2004; Peng and Liu 2010). The findings of these studies are questionable given the highly contested definition of addiction and strong arguments made against addiction measurements used by psychologists (Trent 2015, forthcoming; Williams et al. 2008). A small number of scholars do not take for granted Chinese public perceptions of game addiction, and instead problematize why game addiction is socially constructed as a social problem and how game addiction treatment generates illiberal social consequences (Golub and Lingley 2008; Trent 2013). This section will identify and briefly examine some intriguing aspects of the phenomenon of game addiction in China. These aspects also represent promising directions for future research.

Parents constitute the social group that most adamantly opposes game addiction in China. The tracing of how Chinese parents organize among themselves, persuade officials, and influence the wider public to collectively act against game addiction is a worthwhile research project. Chinese parents in effect initiate a relatively successful social movement against online games; similar social movements are not reported elsewhere in Asia or other regions.

Analysis of how online games is represented and framed in contested ways in Chinese media is also a meaningful project, though current studies have done relevant work. Various mass media channels including official government television joined forces to demonize online games. The negative image of games as addictive and lethal became widespread since the mid-2000s. Gamers and young digital natives fought back, creating well-made and widely circulated machinima and videos that deconstruct demonized image of online games.

The state's position on game addiction is also worth studying. Under the pressure of parents and public opinion, it established statutes that restrict online gameplay time of under-aged gamers. All Chinese gamers are impacted as operationalization of the statute requires gamers to provide personal identification information. Some games even forbid gamers of all age groups to log on for more than a few consecutive hours. Consequently, many Chinese gamers protest against state intervention on gaming. It remains unclear whether the Chinese state intends to limit gamers' freedom or it is merely reacting passively to the Chinese public's concern for game addiction.

A peculiar institution, game addiction treatment clinics, emerged after game addiction was perceived as a serious social problem in China. This institution deserves as much scholarly attention as the phenomenon of addiction (Trent 2013). These clinics adopt brutal procedures including electric shock to 'cure' youths' addiction to games. Treatment service was in great demand. Such clinics were enthusiastically supported by parents and founded across many cities in China. A dramatic change of public opinion towards these treatment clinics was brought about by a few scandalous incidents that involved the violent deaths of patients. Social confrontations broke out between critics and supporters of these clinics. How much these events serve as an opportunity for the public to reflect on game addiction as a social problem and revise the demonized perception of gaming is a good topic for further study.

Collective action of gamers

How online gamers initiate and participate in socio-politically relevant collective action is an issue that receives much less attention than it deserves in the game studies field. There is greater potential for online gamers than other entertainment audience groups to engage in collective action because gamers form persistent and closely knit virtual communities. There is also empirical evidence that indicates the presence of gamer collective actions. Examples range from discursive petitions against game developers on game balance issues to the staging of in-game protests against particular wars.

There are reports on how Chinese gamers engage in socio-politically relevant collective actions (Jenkins 2006), but there are very few attempts to theorize or analyze such collective action (except for Chew 2008). An important reason is that scholars have not looked beyond gamer collective action that directly concerns conventional sociopolitical issues such as class, race, and gender inequalities in the offline world. Gamer collective actions that problematize in-game inequality issues or collective protests against game corporations are overlooked, although these types of collective actions are not really socio-politically irrelevant. This section will show how gamer collective actions in China can offer useful data on the basis of which promising research directions can be opened up.

A distinctive type of gamer collective action in China is violent protests that storm game publishers' offices. There were several protest incidents of this sort in the early 2000s. Groups of gamers, ranging from several to over a hundred in different cases, travel to game publishers' offices to debate with company representatives, negotiate for settlement, fight against company security guards, camp overnight inside the offices, and/or destroy office facilities. Gamers are reacting against unjust permanent banning of their game accounts in most of these cases. While these protests could be categorized as nimbyist, they cannot be easily dismissed as socio-politically irrelevant.

There are numerous forms of gamer collective action in China apart from violent offline protests and there are a wide variety of game-related issues that spark gamer collective action. Aside from virtual property disputes, Chinese gamers have for example protested on game server instability, premature termination of game publication, game bots, and game masters' abuse of in-game privileges.

The most remarkable aspect of Chinese gamer collective action is probably not the quantity and variety of protest incidents though, but the gradual transformation of disconnected protest incidents into something that demonstrates characteristics of a social movement. By the late 2000s, Chinese gamers have formulated a collective action frame that assists gamers in all fronts of the struggle against game corporations. The frame is "gamer rights protection" (*wanjia weiquan*). This term came from a frame bridging effort that combined the politically endorsed collective action frame of "consumer rights" with the widely socially accepted collective action frame of "rights protection."

The protest against Chinese styled pay-to-win game design can be seen as the branch of gamer collective action in China that came closest to a direct addressing of social inequality in the offline world. An in-depth journalistic report published in 2006 argues that Chinese pay-to-win games construct a deceptive system through which great profits are extracted from gamers and that these games represent a virtual social environment that reproduces and encourages the unjust socioeconomic hierarchy of contemporary Chinese society (Cao et al. 2007). The report went viral, arousing the attention of both gamers and non-gamers. Although it did not lead to much protest action, it provides a critical discursive basis for the public and especially non-gamers to think about online gaming.

Women and online games

Gender issues have been regarded as an important research direction in game studies. Many of the manifestations of gender inequality in Western online game contents, game worlds, and gamer behavior are found to be present and similar in China. For example, female gamers are often considered less serious gamers than male ones, game contents tend to be male-oriented, and the sexual content in games and game commercials objectifies women more than men. This section focuses instead on aspects of game content, game worlds, and gamer behavior that generate gender inequality issues that are distinctive to China.

Virtual marriage is a locally distinctive game design feature commonly found in online games developed in China. It consists of dating and marriage rituals for avatars and it gives in-game rewards and/or special virtual items to the married avatars. Many Chinese MMORPGs have this feature. Additionally, there are MMOs and casual games that specialize in marriage and dating gameplay without offering conventional PVP and PVE contents. The social implications of this design feature for women have been examined in two English-language works (Lo 2009; Wu et al. 2007). Both studies recognize the liberating potential of virtual marriage for women: it offers to an extent an alternative marriage partner and family system for women, especially for married women. But these studies also identify a darker side in virtual marriage. Their main argument is that many patriarchal elements can still be found in game marriage systems and that these design features disadvantage women and other sexual minorities through reproducing online the patriarchal marriage system found in the real world. For example, online marriage in the majority of games does not permit marriage between avatars of the same sex.

A gender relevant and locally distinctive gamer behavior in China is that there is a large number of male gamers who prefer to play their game with female avatars instead of male ones. This gamer behavior has not been discussed by scholars and there is no quantitative data to elaborate to what extent this preference diverges from that of Western gamers. But Chinese gamers are aware of it. Future research may approach the phenomenon through at least three inter-related problematics. First, scholars may investigate the reasons and social contexts that bring about this gender-crossing preference. Second, accounts of how exactly male gamers experience their virtual cross-gender behavior are needed. Third, scholars may explore whether this gamer behavior can be interpreted as a cross-gender act that contributes to subverting reified conceptions of masculinity and femininity or not.

I observe that in a small number of online games in China, female gamers become as high profile, numerous, and respected as male ones. Although scholars have not yet paid attention to them, research on these games promises to contribute to understanding of games related gender issues. One of these games is *Audition Online*, a Korean dance game that was localized by Chinese gamers into a dating platform. Data that I have collected show that female gamers behave in a very proactive role in courting dates and initiating friendships in the game. It is also found that *Audition Online* gamers form women-only Internet chat groups to discuss game strategy as well as dating strategy. Interviews with female gamers from rural areas reveal that they use the game as a relatively safe, non-discriminatory, and affordable channel to experience urban popular culture, nightlife, and fashion. It is likely that future research on this and other women-friendly games will reveal female gamers' agency and the potential for games to help subvert patriarchal social structures.

The Chinese state and online games

In contrast to most major online game markets in the world, gaming contents and market in China are not only determined by gamer preferences, technology, creativity, and corporate imperatives. They are also significantly influenced by an authoritarian state that has been eager to control and censor all aspects of mass media including computer games. This fact is well understood and there are a few studies dedicated to examining how legislature, policies, and administrative structures were developed by the state to regulate online games (Ernkvist and Patrik 2008; Tai 2010). These studies are informative in that they clarify state actions and imperatives from a top-down perspective. Yet the field has still not provided information on how these laws, policies and structures actually affect game culture, game design, and social actions of gamers. This section will explore whether and how a bottom-up perspective can yield deeper understanding and alternative interpretations of the political context of online gaming in China.

The 'Ethnic Online Games Project' is a well-publicized and well-financed program devised by the state to facilitate and regulate domestic game production. This Project is cited in every study that discusses Chinese game policies and it deserves frequent citation. Yet how exactly the Project has influenced game contents produced in China remains an entirely unexplored question. Inferring from the Project's name, one may think that it has encouraged Chinese game developers to add Chinese cultural elements into gameplay, graphics, and storylines. Interview data that I collected from Chinese game developers show, however, that the Project hardly affected their creative decisions because almost any game produced by domestically owned companies in China could qualify as "ethnic games." This suggests that the state did not try to micro-control game content. The primary objective of the Project may instead be to resist the domination of domestic game markets by Japanese, Korean and Western products.

The "Game Addiction Prevention System," a statute announced to the game industry in 2007, sets a limit to the consecutive and cumulative number of hours that non-adults can play a particular game in a day. A side effect of this System is that both adult and non-adult gamers are required to register their real names and ID card numbers before they can play any game. Adopting a top-down interpretation, this statute reflects the paternalistic and authoritarian nature of the Chinese state and its powerful and illiberal control of gamer behavior. A bottom-up view could yield a different interpretation, however. What really happens is that Chinese gamers effortlessly bypass the System through registering with the real names and ID card numbers of their adult friends or any random adult Chinese citizen. Game publishers do not monitor the System with any seriousness and the state has not ruled against the use of certain ID card numbers by a huge number of gamers across different games. This state of affairs suggests that the System is not primarily established for paternalistic control of gamer behavior or illiberal infringement on gamers' privacy. One may even read the state as an unwilling and passive party— it founded the System only to fulfill the anti-game addiction demands of Chinese parents and mainstream public.

In my observation, the main current means through which the Chinese state influences gamers, game contents, and gaming culture is the production of games that help propagate official ideologies. Such influence cannot be observed through policies; it can be examined only through detailed examination of game content and gamer actions. Currently there is only one study to explore this topic (Nie 2013). The overlooking of this topic is understandable given that state-produced online games are not present in most of the other online game markets in the world. The most successful examples of such games are developed by ZQ Games, a state-operated listed company that specializes in what it calls "red games." Its flagship online game *War of Resistance against Japan* enjoyed a wide audience and earned good profits. It contains many nationalist and pro-government design features, some of which are more subtle than others (Nie 2013). For example, gamers can only play as a Communist Chinese soldier and not Nationalist Chinese soldiers or Japanese ones. Data I collected from playing the game *War of Resistance* suggest that a significant minority of gamers actively resist the game's nationalist and pro-government messages. For instance, they explained to other gamers how the Communist army in history actually avoided the War of Resistance and left most of the major battles against the Japanese occupation to the Nationalist army. Some other gamers name their avatars with Japanese names even though their avatars represent the Chinese side. Despite subversive gamer actions, ZQ Games' products still play a role in serving the state's ideological goal, especially as nationalism has partially replaced Marxism as the mobilizing ideology of Chinese society since the late 1990s.

Conclusion

There are a number of other socially relevant issues associated with Chinese online games that deserve as much scholarly attention as the six previously discussed ones. Although this chapter cannot discuss them because of the limitation of space, a few of them deserve to be briefly mentioned. The first of them involves social class. The majority of China-designed online games adopt heinous pay-to-win design features that force gamers to spend (real-world) money rather than utilize intellect, time, or skills to achieve in-game success. Game communities, game culture, and gamer interactions in Chinese games are consequently much more heavily affected by real world social class than those in the West.

The second issue that is worth mentioning is secondary industries. Local specificities of the Chinese context have generated a range of secondary industries of online gaming that are not present in North America and Europe. Gold-farming is the most well understood of them but there are others (Zhang and Fung 2014). For instance, commercialized gamer clans, specialized customer service personnel, and Internet café campaign promoters are some of the locally distinctive parties that play crucial roles in the domestic marketing of Chinese online games. And they have gradually been formalized into secondary industries in the past several years.

The third issue concerns homosexual groups and online gaming. Because of the harsh social, political, and legal pressures against homosexuality in China, gay and lesbian individuals in China rely much more heavily than those in the West on the internet's virtual world as a social interaction and community formation platform. Gay game clans and groups, specialized games for gays, and interactions between homosexual and heterosexual individuals in game communities are some of the many examples of promising research topics in this regard.

This chapter has overviewed several ways in which online games generate social implications in China. A few important observations can be made despite the brevity of the overview. Online gaming generates social implications for Chinese society in a broad range of disparate ways. The implications involve serious issues including gender inequality, class-based exploitation, digital labor, social activism, state censorship, etc. Online games' multifarious social implications are still scarcely analyzed by scholars. Chinese data on online games' social implications are theoretically valuable to global game studies in at least two ways: they provide alternative data for international comparison and they alert scholars to issues that are not salient in Western contexts. Based on these observations, we may conclude that studies of the social aspects of Chinese online gaming is an important field for further analyses and that such a field will not only enrich Chinese but also global online games studies.

References

Anon. (2006) 'Is mining virtual gold exploitative?' *Music Television Channel*. Available at: http://www.mtv.com/overdrive/?id=1545907&vid=120059 (Accessed November 25, 2010).

Barboza, D. (2005) 'Ogre to slay? Outsource it to Chinese', *New York Times*, Dec 9.

Cao, Y., Zhang, C., and Wang, S. (2007) '"Xitong" (The System)', *Nanfang Weekend*. Available at: http://ohmymedia.com/2007/12/23/736/ (Accessed November 25, 2010).

Castronova, E. (2002) 'On virtual economies', *CESifo Working Paper Series* No. 752.

Castronova, E. (2006) 'A cost-benefit analysis of real-money trade in the products of synthetic economies', *Info*, 8(6): 51–68.

Chan, D. (2006) 'Negotiating intra-Asian games networks: on cultural proximity, East Asian games design, and Chinese farmers', *Fibreculture Journal*, 8. Available at: http://journal.fibreculture.org/issue8/issue8_chan.html (Accessed November 12, 2011).

Chen, L.C. (2009) 'The value chain in the Asian online gaming industry: a case study of Taiwan', PhD Thesis, University of Westminster.

Chew, M.M. (2006) 'Policy implications of massively multiplayer online games for Hong Kong', Occasional Papers no. 176, Hong Kong Institute of Asia Pacific Studies.

Chew, M.M. (2008) 'Virtual-world unrest and the gamer rights protection movement in China', paper published in the proceedings of The Sixth Annual Chinese Internet Research Conference, The University of Hong Kong, Hong Kong, June 13–14.

Chew, M.M. (2011) 'Virtual property in China: the emergence of gamer rights awareness and the reaction of game corporations', *New Media and Society*, 13(5): 722–738.

Chiu, S.I., Lee, J.Z., and Huang, D.H. (2004) 'Video game addiction in children and teenagers in Taiwan', *CyberPsychology & Behavior*, 7: 571–581.

Chung, P. and Fung, A. (2013) 'The Internet development and the commercialization of online gaming industry in China'. In Huntemann, N. and Aslinger, B. (eds) *Gaming Globally: Production, Play & Place*, New York: Palgrave.

Chung, P. and Yuan, J. (2009) 'Dynamics in the online game industry of China: a political economic analysis of its competitiveness', *Revista de Economía Política de las Tecnologías de la Información y Comunicación*, XI(2).

Dibbell, J. (2007) 'The life of the Chinese gold farmer', *New York Times Magazine*, June 17.

Ernkvist, M., and Patrik, S. (2008) 'Enmeshed in games with the government: governmental policies and the development of the Chinese online game industry', *Games and Culture*, 3: 98–126.

Fairfield, J. (2005) 'Virtual property', *Boston University Law Review*, 85: 1047.

Golub, A. and Lingley, K. (2008) '"Just like the Qing Empire": Internet addiction, MMOGs, and moral crisis in contemporary China', *Games and Culture*, 3(1): 59–75.

Grimes, S. (2006) 'Online multiplayer games: a virtual space for intellectual property debates?' *New Media and Society*, 8(6): 969–990.

Heeks, R. (2008) 'Current analysis and future research agenda on "Gold Farming": real-world production in developing countries for the virtual economies of online games', *IDPM*, University of Manchester: Manchester, UK. Available at: http://www.sed.manchester.ac.uk/idpm/research/publications/wp/di/index.htm (Accessed November, 2008).

Jenkins, H. (2006) 'National politics within virtual game worlds: the case of China'. Available at: www.henryjenkins.org/2006/08/national_politics_within_virtu_1.html (Accessed November 25, 2010).

Jin, G. (2006) 'Chinese gold farmers in the game world', *Consumers, Commodities, and Consumption: A Newsletter of the Consumer Studies Research Network*, 7(2). Available at: https://netfiles.uiuc.edu/dtcook/www/CCCnewsletter/7-2/jin.htm (Accessed June 30, 2008).

Kshetri, N. (2009) 'The evolution of the Chinese online gaming industry', *Journal of Technology Management in China*, 4: 158–179.

Lastowka, G. and Hunter, D. (2004) 'The laws of the virtual worlds', *California Law Review*, 92(1).

Lee, Y and Lin, H. (2011) '"Gaming is my work": identity work in internet-hobbyist game workers', *Work, Employment and Society*, 25(3): 451–467.

Lo, K. (2009) 'The web marriage game, the gendered self, and Chinese modernity', *Cultural Studies*, 23(3): 381–403.

MacInnes, I. and Hu, L. (2007) 'Business models and operational issues in the Chinese online game industry', *Telematics and Informatics*, 24(2): 130–144.

Nakamura, L. (2007) *Digitizing Race: Visual Cultures of the Internet*, Minneapolis: University of Minnesota Press.

Nardi, B. and Kow, Y.M. (2010) 'Digital imaginaries: how we know what we (think we) know about Chinese gold farming', *First Monday*, 15(6–7).

Nie, H.A. (2013) 'Gaming, nationalism, and ideological work in contemporary China: online games based on the War of Resistance against Japan', *Journal of Contemporary China*, 22(81): 499–517.

Peng, W. and Liu, M. (2010) 'Online gaming dependency: a preliminary study in China', *Cyberpsychology, Behavior, and Social Networking*, 13(3): 329–333.

Russell, M. (2004) 'New industry: scavengers collect virtual booty in online games and sell it for real cash', *Newsweek International*, October 11.

Steinkuehler, C.A. (2005) 'Cognition and learning in massively multiplayer online games: a critical approach', PhD Dissertation, The University of Wisconsin, Madison.

Tai, Z. (2010) 'Setting the rules of play: network video game policies and regulations in China', *Iowa Journal of Communication*, 42(1): 45–72.

Trent, B. (2013) *Youth and Internet Addiction in China*, London: Routledge.

Trent, B. (2015, forthcoming) '"Internet Gaming Disorder" in China: biomedical sickness or sociological badness?' *Games and Culture*.

van Luyn, F.J. (2006) *Cyberkoelies* (video documentary). Available at: http://www.vpro.nl/metropolis/speel.WO_VPRO_043588.html (Accessed January 11, 2011).

Williams, D., Yee, N. and Caplan, S. (2008) 'Who plays, how much, and why? Debunking the stereotypical gamer profile', *Journal of Computer-Mediated Communication*, 13(4): 993–1018.

Wu, W., Fore, S., Wang, X. and Ho, P.S.Y. (2007) 'Beyond virtual carnival and masquerade: in-game marriage on the Chinese internet', *Games and Culture*, 2(1): 59–89.

Yee, N. (2006) 'Yi-shan-guan', from the the Daedelus Project. Available at: http://www.nickyee.com/daedalus/archives/001493.php (Accessed December 8, 2008).

Zhang, L. and Fung, A. (2014) 'Working as playing? Consumer labor, guild and the secondary industry of online gaming in China', *New Media and Society*, 16(1): 38–54.

35

The globalization of game art in Southeast Asia

Peichi Chung

This chapter studies the globalization of Southeast Asian game art. In particular, it explores the circumstances of Southeast Asian identity formation as it takes place in the domain of video gaming. It analyzes the visual aesthetics of Southeast Asian games in order to examine the characteristics of Southeast Asian popular game culture. Southeast Asia has become a geographic region with growing power in new media production and consumption. The popularity of video games in this region demonstrates the emerging global circulation of new media content in Asia's south. In 2013, Southeast Asia was home to a total of 130 million Internet users, among whom 85 million were gamers. The region forms a game market worth US$661 million revenue. Those numbers will continue to grow: By 2017, analysts expect Southeast Asia to have 132 million users generating US$1.2 billion in revenue. The global game market will aim at market growth of more than US$100 billion in 2017.

A cultural analysis of Southeast Asian game production and consumption raises the issue of global media circulation in video games. Scholars in media studies have long discussed the interconnected power networks that transnational media companies in the US have advanced. There is no doubt that global media has now become an enabler of cross-border cultural exchange, producing globalization whose effects now influence politics related to media, power, and society. This is relevant to debates about media globalization concerning the "de-Westernization" of media studies.

One debate revolves around the argument that the "West vs. rest" framework requires a theoretical justification sophisticated enough to incorporate national and regional politics in order to better understand the multifaceted aspects of globalization (Ho 2013). Another debate focuses on the previously under-explored research area about the "global north–south divide" (Curran and Park 2000). Soft power in India, for example, has risen to complicate the dominant paradigm of global communication—a framework that questions unequal relationships between the over-powerful media producers in the global north and the under-privileged media consumers in the global south.

In game studies, global powers such as Electronic Arts, Ubisoft, Microsoft, Sony, Nintendo, and Sega display similar corporate dominance as gaming empires. Analysts find that major game companies have employed capitalist ideological control to standardize the worldwide console game market (Dyer-Witheford and de Peuter 2009). They exploit global networks of production and distribution while facing few regulatory restrictions. Culturally, global game companies create cross-border entertainment content that naturalizes gaming pleasure based upon social conventions that carry ambiguous gender, racial, and national stereotypes (Nichols 2010). Economically, the global game industry has divided into a two-tiered world system.

On the one hand, major products in both hardware and software production are designed in developed countries; on the other hand, these producers outsource production to independent studios in developing countries because of the cheaper labor and closer markets (Kerr 2013). The increasing concentration and consolidation of game development scatters the geographic locations of independent development studios, in particular to those developing countries that strive to outgrow their outsourcing status such as Mexico and China (Kerr 2006). It is this concern with the "global north–south divide" that contextualizes the significance of locating a new geography of independent game studios in Southeast Asia.

This chapter explores the multiple cultural genealogies that independent game studios refer to in the process of creating globalized local game art. It first uses the concepts of cultural adaptation and internal hybrid culture to examine the region's converging game art and then explores its digital socio-cultural space. It analyzes selected transnational Southeast Asian games based upon selections drawn from among independent entrepreneurs in the ASEAN 6 nations—Singapore, Malaysia, Indonesia, the Philippines, Thailand, and Vietnam. Next, the chapter reviews game genres that are emerging across networked and PC-based platforms. The conclusion discusses how contested subjectivities collectively re-imagine Southeast Asia's regional identity through game art. It ends by determining that Southeast Asian hybridity reflects multiple localities in the process of forming a regional gaming culture in the age of game globalization.

Literature review

Discussion of media production and consumption in Southeast Asia addresses the hybridity of regional media, which transcend national media industries. Southeast Asian media arguably developed its crossover reception due to the influence of local politics in regulating the accessibility of media content to national audiences (George 2012). Whether imported from the United States or East Asia, notable international film and television programs have widely circulated through Southeast Asian media distribution channels. Popular foreign content from the East Asian region includes Japanese *anime* and *manga*, Korean television drama and popular music, and Hong Kong kung fu movies (Otmazgin 2005).

Among Southeast Asian producers, the influence of international media results in the production of adapted content (Chung 2013). Studies of cultural producers who use international production formulas include the makers of *telenovela* (TV drama) in the Philippines. Southeast Asian cultural producers follow the production formula of global popular media to achieve "niche globality" (Tolentino 2013). Similar forms of internationalization are also seen in the transcultural practice of casting Asian film stars in Hollywood movies. Film stars like Michel Yeoh adopt an accented English in order to conform to the marketable semiotic system of "Asian imagery" that global Hollywood reproduces (Khoo 2013). However, local political culture determines the specific elements of East Asian popular cultures that can enter the nation, so it is practiced differently in other parts of the region. In Indonesia, for example, during the Suharto New Order era, the Indonesian government favored popular Hong Kong and Taiwan films in order to help stabilize the country's internal racial politics and distract Chinese Indonesians from connecting with communist China (Kusno 2013).

A notable sense of nationhood has been gradually disappearing and replaced by a new form of localism, in which Southeast Asian media producers are internationalizing their production to accommodate global consumption patterns. Zulkarnain (2014) calls this disappearance and re-appearance of nationhood in online games in Indonesia "playable nationalism" in Indonesia. To Indonesian players, digital nationalism reproduces everyday forms of nationalism. Playing the online, historical, multiple-player role-playing game *Nusantara Online*, for example, allows Indonesian gamers to engage in a form of open-ended storytelling about historical reconstruction.

Two concepts explicate the reappearance of this new form of localism in the mediated game space of Southeast Asia. The first is *cultural adaptation*. Entertainment media adaptation demonstrates a complex, multilayered cultural selection process wherein particular effects and consequences transcend simple imitation (Moran and Keane 2010). O'Hagan and Mangiron (2013) call this diversification of game versions through cultural adaptation a process of rewriting in game localization.

As video games have become an integral part of global popular culture, rewriting game text has grown important along with it. Game designers tend to localize game narratives and adjust gamer tastes in order to ensure success in target markets. Similarly, in Southeast Asia, as game developers continuously rely on outsourcing models in order to cultivate game-development expertise in storytelling, visual game art has naturally acculturated to reflect the creative style of the global corporate system (Chung 2013; O'Hagan and Mangiron 2013). A review of the Korean global games *Lineages* shows an integrated cultural space in which local authentic Korean culture is repackaged into a new form to fit into the global gaming market (Jin 2010).

The second concept is a form of *ambiguous hybridity* reflected in Asian digital culture. In *Hybrid Culture*, Spielmann argues that intercultural mixing defines the hybrid aesthetics of Japan's hi-tech digital art (Spielmann 2013). Japan's digital culture is rooted in traditional Japanese popular culture where both *anime* and *manga* influence the aesthetic perception of Japanese artists. The idea of ambiguous hybridity goes against the perception of global culture that is based upon a belief in a two-way power relationship between the West and non-West. Spielmann proposes replacing the identification of the non-West with an in-between zone, in which we can observe globally interconnected cultural practices in Japan's technical-innovative mediative space. "Hybrid culture refers to [the] aesthetic-creative praxis of media arts, where culture and science meet to be recognized in in-between zones" (ibid.). This aspect allows media cultural analysis to concentrate on media art. It also provides a legitimate gateway through which one can observe the internal dynamics that result from multilayered cultures in Southeast Asian games.

Southeast Asian digital space

The digital space of Southeast Asia is a growing interconnected space that allows media production and consumption to cross national borders. Southeast Asia is currently undergoing a rapid technological transformation, which has produced an ever-changing difference in the scale of Internet development among the region's nations. As of November 2013, the number of Internet users in Southeast Asia reached 130 million. However, the disparity of Internet growth still exists. For example, among the six economically advancing Southeast Asian countries, Singapore has the highest rate of Internet penetration (70 percent), reaching 3.5 million users. Indonesia, by comparison, has a penetration rate of only 9 percent, the region's lowest, despite its total user population of 22 million.[1]

Table 35.1 The demographic statistics of digital media development in Southeast Asia (via Internet, mobile, online, and social media platforms)[2]

	Singapore (million)	Malaysia (million)	Indonesia (million)	Philippines (million)	Thailand (million)	Vietnam (million)
Total population	5.14	29	240	103	67	92
Internet population (penetration)	4 (80%)	17 (66%)	42 (16%)	39 (39%)	19 (28%)	39 (43%)
Mobile population (penetration)	7.7 (150%)	35 (124%)	220 (92%)	90 (99%)	77 (115%)	121
Online game population	1.3	5.8	14.8	12	6.4	12.4
Social media (Facebook)	1.5	5.2	4	5.2	10.2	N/A

Table 35.1 provides an overview of the stages of technological development in Southeast Asian digital space, in order to show the differences among nations. Despite the fact that technological, political, and economic disparities still exist among members of the ASEAN 6, the demographic scale of gamers who participate in reconstructing the social imaginary of new forms of localism in Southeast Asian games is increasing. According to a Nicko Partners market report,[3] the potential for growth of the online gaming space expands when the market scale of the region grows to US$661 million in revenue. In 2013, the Southeast Asian game market reached 85 million online gamers and achieved 246 percent in market growth. Table 35.1 also shows that mobile platforms have a higher rate of penetration than web penetration in most countries. This is an indicator that explains application games, with an emphasis on development in the region. The table also presents a game market that prioritizes online games because the number of online gamers surpasses the number of social media users, with the exception of Singapore and Thailand.

Economically speaking, Southeast Asian digital space indicates an open-market environment in which consumers welcome foreign imports of all kinds in the area of social media. Platforms like Facebook, LinkedIn, Twitter, Zynga, and the Korean social-networking site CyWorld are widely popular among online users all over the region, except in Vietnam where the government restricts the entry of foreign media companies. While, most of the time, online consumers in Southeast Asia follow the social and collective culture of their societies, they easily follow foreign technological trends and accept the main forms of online activities, like watching videos and playing games online.[4] The political scene, however, reveals the major challenge of new localism that is presented through digital gaming due to censorship control. Most Southeast Asian governments employ regulations to restrict online user ability to upload content that includes statements such as anti-government messages.

For example, in the Philippines, the government uses Internet laws like Section 114 A of the revised Evidence Act of 1950 and the Cybercrime Prevention Act of 2012 to restrict the circulation of political messages. Malaysia, Singapore, and Indonesia also employ strict regulations that punish government critics. Thailand's Criminal Code of 2012 is considered as the most severe regulation against political criticism, with its punishment for anti-royal insults. These factors contribute to an overall regulatory environment that shapes the Southeast Asian game development environment and, of course, the games it produces.

The globalization of Southeast Asian games

Southeast Asia's regional imaginary can be examined through the representation of a new form of localism found in made-in-Southeast Asian games. The techno-cultural spaces that Hjorth and Chan (2009) describe provide us a gateway to understand the multiple contested localities of gaming cultures in the Asia-Pacific region. This section analyzes Southeast Asian games in two categories, for the purpose of presenting the multiple layers of subjectivities in gaming cultures that develop from different distribution networks. The first category includes application games that circulate globally through the mobile distribution systems of Apple iTunes and Google Play.

The second category includes Massively Multi-player Online Role Playing Games (MMORPGs) that circulate locally in domestic markets through broadband connections. The application games that receive detailed analysis in this chapter include those that have achieved recognition in the international gaming community, such as *Autumn Dynasty* (Singapore),[5] *Ravenmark* (Singapore),[6] *Flappy Bird* (Vietnam),[7] *Flying Bomoh* (Malaysia),[8] *Ong Bak Tri* (Thailand),[9] and *Majapahit Online* (Indonesia).[10] This section also includes analyses of blockbuster MMORPGs that are tested in the market, such as *Nusantara Online* (Indonesia),[11] *Narusuan Online* (Thailand),[12] *400* (Thailand),[13] and the PC game *7554* (Vietnam).

One of the techno-cultural spaces that contributes to the globalization of Southeast Asian games is the growing social connectivity made possible by Internet technology. Because networked spaces nowadays have replaced nations as the basic geographic units of cultural analysis for the study of globalization, the dynamic trajectories of supranational communicative structures have opened up complex forms of time-space distanciation that help us understand local diversity (Volkmer 2012). Naturally, Internet distribution has made independent Southeast Asian game developers search for ways to break the monopoly of global video-game players in the console distribution system. Southeast Asian independent game companies enter the global game market through the publishing platforms of iTunes and Google Play. Most Southeast Asian developers produce 2D flash games due to low production costs and easy access to the application game sector.

For example, the ease of application game development creates the opportunity of entrepreneurship for passionate young talents to explore the global casual-game market. This emerging market contributes to the niche globality already achieved by the game industry of Singapore, an industry where the government offers its full support by providing an innovative technological and business environment for local independent game developers. A review of one government supported website, Singapore Gamebox (http://singaporegamebox.com/), shows the varieties of genres among made-by-Singapore games.

Altogether, these games demonstrate the globalized scale that Southeast Asian game developers are able to achieve by publishing games on mobile platforms. Singapore's independent game developers experiment to produce local narratives for their globally niched gamers. For example, *Yusheng Rush* is a free application game downloadable through iOS.[14] The game targets casual gamers who are interested in gaining knowledge about bank management through game play. The storyline that supports this kind of gameplay environment focuses on lifestyle and cultural traditions among Southeast Asian Chinese. The game narrates the story of Chinese celebrating the lunar New Year. *Kopi Tiam* is another free application game showcasing the societal customs of Singapore.[15] The game aims at Facebook users and capitalizes on a theme that shows Singapore's multicultural society. This niche globality through game production enables producers to present a grassroots form of nationhood in the global game market. This presence demonstrates a new localism that global, blockbuster-game developers rarely explore when they produce games that include Southeast Asia.

Another type of niche globality in Southeast Asian game art includes social games such as *Autumn Dynasty* and *Ravenmark*. Both games utilize iOS distribution to achieve their international releases. The cultural characteristics of the region are revealed whenever game developers win awards in international game-developer festivals. For example, the Singaporean game *Autumn Dynasty* is a networked game developed by a small company called Touch Dimension. *Romans in My Closet* is another Singapore game developed by Witching Hour Studios; it won an award for best game art in the 2014 Casual Connect Asia game festival. The game developers focused on innovation that has international appeal in independent game festivals.

Figure 35.1 shows the innovation skills that the developer of *Autumn Dynasty* reflects in its visual narrative. The game uses a brush-style calligraphy graphic to create artistic impact in its depiction of a battle in ancient China. The game is rich in interactive storytelling content, combining game development technology and visual presentation skills to an iPad platform in order to present an East Asian visual feature that mixes the drawing styles of Japanese and Chinese games. While the narrative depicts a Chinese story, the drawing style resembles Japanese real-time strategy games such as *Three Kingdoms* and *Dynasty Warriors*.

Another type of globalized game art supported in the application game category is the cute and culture-free visual style that developers use in telling local stories. Some game developers use their applications to address social issues. One of the best examples of this phenomenon is the Vietnamese application game *Flappy Bird*, which once was a globally successful game because of the wide popularity of mobile-phone downloads among global players. The Vietnamese game developer, Dong Nguyen, produced *Flappy Bird* as a simple game that adhered to the marketable gaming concept of *Angry Bird*. The developer twisted the design concept to produce a game that is difficult in scoring points. Because of this design concept, *Flappy Bird* once was the number-one most downloaded application game worldwide (Kushner 2014). The game's contribution

Figure 35.1 Visual aesthetics about battle and war in Ancient China. Represented in *Autumn Dynasty*

can be seen in YouTube videos; a game critic of *Flappy Bird* has received more than 19 million views since January 2014.[16] The viral circulation of *Flappy Bird* shows the game's reach into the global gaming community, particularly the teenage gamer group. The game has created a popular gaming culture and formed a genre of its own based upon the craze of fans for the game. Its global success has inspired fan-game development, prompting international game developers to produce similar games such as *Floppy Bird*, *Snappy Bird*, *The Impossible Flappy Game: Night Adventure of a Tiny Bird*, *Twitchy Hop*, *Maverick Bird*, *Grumpy Beaks*, and *Delirious Bird*, in dedication to the design concept behind *Flappy Bird*.

In addition, *Flying Bomoh* is a Malaysian application game created to function as social commentary for gamers who wish to respond to local politics in Malaysia. The game is based upon a news event, in which a well-known Malaysian shaman, Bomoh, offers to perform a public ritual in order to assist the search for missing Malaysian Air flight MH370. The act triggered a mixture of outrage among Malaysian social media users because the broadcast of the shaman (wielding coconut and bamboo binoculars) spread internationally. This event added to local embarrassment about the government's inability to resolve the country's political crisis in the international community.

However, the timely release of the application game *Flying Bomoh* further demonstrates the internal racial and religious conflicts in the country. The developer of *Flying Bomoh* rides on global popular culture as mediated through news media. The company capitalizes on gamers who respond to entertainment in the global media-scape and reacted to the hype about the missing Malaysian plane. Like *Flappy Bird*, *Flying Bomoh* also has generated a transnational game craze because of the niche globality the game has been able to achieve through the iOS distribution system. Similar games such as *Bomoh* and *Bomoh MH370* also appear in the same market that formed the *Flying Bomoh* genre.

With the publishing of social commentary games like *Flying Bomoh*, a techno-cultural space appears in game play, through which racial and religious tensions appear. The game narrative shown in Figure 35.2 presents extensive layers of political discourses that contest the legitimacy of the new localism in social commentary games. Though media entertainment oftentimes easily misleads the public into overlooking tensions mounting in society because of stereotypical images, *Flying Bomoh* presents a repackaged religious representation of Muslims in the form of an entertaining Malay shaman. A critical reading of Figure 35.2 demonstrates the problem with popular entertainment, as gaming and play become the main forms of media usage yet also underestimate the problem of internal racial conflict in Malaysia's troubled multicultural society.

Yinglack vs. Suthep is another social commentary game that uses play to connect the public to Thailand's divided politics.[17] The company Debuz published the game in May 2014, and executed a timely marketing promotion as Thai society underwent protest and division on the streets of Bangkok in early 2014. *Yinglack vs. Suthep* is a poker game in which gamers must be able to identify politicians whose images appear virtually before them to pair in the card play. The game provides a techno-cultural space for gamers to participate in Thai politics. It also offers international gamers a media channel through which to consume news about Thailand's politics other than international news agencies like CNN and the BBC. Because the visual presentation of the poker game requires further understanding of local politics, the storytelling of *Yinglack vs. Suthep* relies on a simple, universally accessible narrative that enables global gamers to bypass language barriers. This process of creating a simplified understanding of Thailand's political culture illustrates the complexities of nationhood built into the globalized distribution system of an application game.

Unlike the niche globality presented in Southeast Asian application games, MMORPG game art focuses on the history genre to present their ideas about a contested regionalism. Most

Figure 35.2 Visual representations of local cultural practice and ethnic politics in the Malaysian application game, *Flying Bomoh*

history-genre games are developed to target the national audience in a specific Southeast Asian country. All developers aim at showing the legitimacy of leadership from the historical past, when their country was at war with other Southeast Asian countries. There is a collective form of niche regionalism that these historical genre games form. These MMORPG games were enabled by national broadband infrastructure, so they adopt similar narratives to build national identity. However, the specific story shapes the complexity of contested localism as gamers play to consume "national sovereignty" when they build the world of virtual nationalism on their own. These games altogether form multiple layers of subjectivities that present the complex nature of regional identity in Southeast Asian games.

In the history genre, *King Narusuan Online* (KNO) is a game in which players contest for the leadership of Thailand among Southeast Asian countries. The company, Prommitr Production, produces the game to promote the Thai government's creative industry policy project, *Creative Kingdom*. The developer presents the story of ancient Thai King, Narusuan, who realized Thailand's (then called Siam) greatest territorial extent and influence during the sixteenth century. The game receives support from Thailand's largest online game publisher, AsiaSoft. Developers of the game rely on marketing resources from AsiaSoft to incorporate the most updated gamer background for game development in the local market.

Compared with imported MMORPG games, *King Narusuan Online* (KNO) is a Thai-language online game that is built upon the free-to-play revenue model. The game has more than 1,000 game-related items, included to provide gamers with the ability to make in-game purchases. The story of *King Narusuan Online* promotes Thailand's cultural heritage dating back to the time before the arrival of Western colonial powers (Boonnoon 2010). The visual presentation of *King Narusuan Online* provides an overall storytelling narrative that is similar to most online history games produced in Korea and China. As AsiaSoft publishes major Korean and Chinese online games in the region, gamer demographics collected for *King Narusuan Online* reflect the design style preferred by Thai gamers. Local cultural traits are shown by visual representations of images like temples, architecture, elephants, and armor.

Figure 35.3 compares the visual aesthetics of three history-genre games.[18] The image includes the representation of national heroes who led the country to safeguard the motherland during wartime. A comparison of the visual styles of game heroes in three MMORPG games shows that national identity transformed into a context in which visual representations of heroes reflect strong gamer tastes long cultivated by imported games. The Indonesian history game *Nusantara Online* emphasizes the imaginary virtual world of the Malay kingdoms in the pre-national stage of history. Visual representations of the Indonesian nation focus on historical cultural symbols such as traditional rural clothing, kampong housing, and national language.

Similarly, the 3D MMORPG game, *Four Hundred*, from Thailand, also heavily features cultural symbols that reaffirm a nationalist gaming environment. The game tells a war story from the Siam historical era. *Four Hundred* is a successfully marketed MMORPG game characterized by the game's use of 3D technology to present a realistic cinematic effect. It refers to the American war film *300* (2006) in its graphic art style. The theme is developed by a war narrative, which corresponds to the strategic use of cultural adaptation in presenting cultural content displayed by most Southeast Asian popular cultural producers.

In addition to games from Thailand and Indonesia, contested subjectivities through multiple genealogies in networked space also appear in the historical game space of Vietnam. *7554: Glorious Memories Revived* is a first person shooting war game whose story takes place during the Franco-Vietnamese War of 1946–1954. The game creates an imagery of nationhood that allows gamers to play without being "the other" as they typically must do in most Vietnam War games produced in the West. The producer Emobi developed *7554* to target Vietnam's domestic

King Narusuan Online	
Nusantara Online	
400 Online	

Figure 35.3 A comparison of national heroes represented in three Southeast Asian online games

market. The game sold only about five thousand copies due to piracy problems in Vietnam. However, it won a Reader's Choice Award from the game magazine of *PC World Vietnam* in 2012, although it received negative reviews from major English game magazines for the low quality of English translation and visual narrative design.

Sequence	Image	Narrative
1		The game starts with introduction of geographic locations on a map of Vietnam in each section. It also introduces the historical context for each gaming section.
2		The image shows the battle scene with the Vietnamese flag waving in the background. This scene demonstrates a positive depiction of the Vietnamese army from the perspective of a Vietnamese player.
3		The image shows the surrender of French soldiers. This is the final scene of the last section under the title, "global shock," in the walkthrough section.

Figure 35.4 Visual narrative of the Vietnamese victory in the Franco-Vietnamese War of 1954[19]

Like most war-game titles, including *Battlefield Vietnam*, *Call of Duty*, *Air Conflict Vietnam*, and *Wings Over Vietnam*, *7554* provides two types of narrative in which to construct its gaming environment. *7554* imitates the production formula used in the popular game, *Call of Duty*. The historical moment is set in between 1946 to 1954 during the Franco-Vietnamese War. The Vietnamese aspect can be seen in Figure 35.4 when vernacular language, character, national flag, and victory in the battle of Dien Bien Phu construct a local narrative about national sovereignty. The game changes its storytelling perspective between black-and-white documentary videos and colorful gaming environment to constitute Vietnam's perspective on the Franco-Vietnam War. The visual image of Vietnamese soldiers and other national symbols presented in Figure 35.4 shows a narrative contrast in *7554* compared with most war game titles that are produced by US game companies.[20]

Conclusion

This chapter contends that internal politics arise from multiple social groups and genealogies, which constitute the multi-layered subjectivities that structure Southeast Asian game art in global game development. On the one hand, the gradual appearance of political and cultural voices in the region diversifies potential cultural content beyond the current East Asia-emphasized popular culture in Asia.

This unpacking of the hybridized discourses that represent Asia provides the opportunity to analyze deeper layers of contested identity politics among politically, culturally, and socially divided groups. It is through the understanding of problematic identity politics that local games like *Flying Bomoh* serve, that a point of entry into understanding ethnic politics in Malaysia opens. The meaning of techno-nationalism in the case of Singapore is then challenged with a critical cultural analysis of the award-winning game, *Autumn Dynasty*, as the game presents the outward-looking search for cultural identity that has international appeal and technologically represents the nation. Game art in Southeast Asia demonstrates bourgeoning techno-cultural spaces that narrate hybrid local stories. This form of contested hybridity altogether creates a global niche for Southeast Asian game art in global game development.

On the other hand, another layer of regional narrative also arises within the networked spaces of broadband MMORPG games. Digital regionalism has become apparent particularly in the history gaming genre, as regional game developers create their own national MMORPG narrative to make claims over the historical legacy of the region. Consequently, digital globalism opens up a possibility for further cultural analysis of the competitive regional-identity politics that shapes the diversity of new voices in Asian popular gaming culture as expressed within Southeast Asia. It is not coincidental that developers create heroism and follow a global popular production formula due to the marketability of history online games.

The articulation of Southeast Asian regionalism based upon the competitive subjectivities demonstrated in the case studies shows the new sense of nationhood enabled by Southeast Asian game producers. Their game art reveals a form of inwardness in the globalization process, where national narratives are crafted and shared based upon the pre-existing global gaming culture that is so popular as a form of piracy culture throughout the Southeast Asian region.

It is therefore important to question the rationale that certain images from Southeast Asia travel transnationally, while others have faced rejection from global gamers in Apple's and Google's new content distribution systems. As political and economic dynamics contribute to the representative discourses of popular Southeast Asian game art, it is also important to further understand how globalization opens up a new channel of investigation that shows the potential restriction that the gaming context can place on identity politics.

Notes

1 MVF Global Customer Acquisition. 'Online Lead Generation in Southeast Asia'. http://www.mvfglobal.com/south-east-asia (Accessed on July 3, 2014).

2 From online sources at http://www.mobilemonday.net/reports/SEA_Report_2012.pdf (Accessed on April 22, 2015) and http://www.mvfglobal.com/south-east-asia (Accessed on April 22, 2015).

3 Online document available at: http://nikopartners.com/southeast-asian-games-market-revenue-expected-to-double-reach-1-2-billion-by-2017/ (Accessed on April 22, 2015).

4 'Surfing Southeast Asia's Powerful Digital Wave'. Online document available at: http://www.accenture.com/sitecollectiondocuments/pdf/accenture-surfing-asean-digital-wave-survey.pdf (Accessed on April 22, 2015).

5 The game is available at: http://www.autumndynasty.com (Accessed on April 22, 2015).

6 The game is available at: http://mercs.ravenmark-saga.com (Accessed on April 22, 2015).

7 The android version of the game is available at: http://www.getflappybirdandroid.com (Accessed on July 17, 2014).

8 The games are created in response to the Bomoh incident, which happened in the wake of the MH370 air tragedy. Developers responded to the religious acts of Malaysian leaders. Currently in the game market there are more than 40 versions of Bomoh-related apps games circulating on the Internet. One of the Android versions, *Flying Bomoh*, is available at: http://www.seriously.my/flyingbomoh/ (Accessed on April 22, 2015).

9 The game is not yet released but some of the screen shots are available online at https://www.facebook.com/ongbakgame (Accessed on April 22, 2015).

10 The game is available at: https://id-id.facebook.com/MajapahitOnline (Accessed on April 22, 2015).

11 The game is available at: http://nusantararising.com (Accessed on April 22, 2015).

12 The game is available at: http://kno.playpark.com (Accessed on April 22, 2015).

13 The game is available at: http://fourhundred.gameindy.com (Accessed on April 22, 2015).

14 The game is available at: https://itunes.apple.com/sg/app/yusheng-rush/id591359577?mt=8 (Accessed on April 22, 2015).

15 The game is available at: https://play.google.com/store/apps/details?id=com.afzane.kopitiam&hl=en (Accessed on April 22, 2015).

16 The video is available at: https://www.youtube.com/watch?v=lQz6xhlOt18 (Accessed on April 22, 2015). The title of the video is "Flappy Bird: Don't Play This Game". It has attracted more than twenty million views within eight months from the publication of the video on YouTube.

17 The game is available at: https://itunes.apple.com/th/app/id845214784 (Accessed on April 22, 2015).

18 Information about the three games include: (a) distributor: Play@Park; title: King Narusuan Online; release date: December 2011; URL: http://kno.playpark.com/item_shop.aspx (Accessed on April 22, 2015); (b) distributor: Behance; title: *Nusantara Online*; release date: July 2011; URL: https://www.behance.net/gallery/9235991/Nusantara-Online (Accessed on April 22, 2015); (c) distributor: Game Indy; title: *400*; release date: 2012; URL: http://fourhundred.gameindy.com (Accessed on April 22, 2015).

19 Information about the game includes: distributor: Emobi Games; title: *7554*; release date: December 2011; URL: http://7554.vn (Accessed on April 22, 2015).

20 Detailed visual narrative can be seen in the YouTube video about the final section of *7554*, when the sequence titled "global shock" describes the victory of Vietnam in the Battle of Dien Bien Phu over France. The video is available at: https://www.youtube.com/watch?v=n8EWYV56PCE (Accessed on April 22, 2015).

References

Boonnoon, J. (2010) 'Online Game to Give Players an Insight into Thai History', *The Nation*. Available at: http://www.nationmultimedia.com/home/2010/01/08/business/New-game-to-give-players-an-insight-into-thai-hist-30119908.html (Accessed on April 22, 2015).

Chung, P. (2013) 'Co-Creating Korean Wave in Southeast Asia: Digital Convergence and Asia's Media Regionalization', *Journal of Creative Communication* 8(2&3): 231–246.

Curran, J. and Park, M.-J. (2000) *De-Westernizing Media Studies*, London: Routledge.

Dyer-Witheford, N. and de Peuter, G. (2009) *Games of Empire: Global Capitalism and Video Games*, Minneapolis: University of Minnesota Press.

George, C. (2012) 'Silence and Protest in Singapore's Censorship Debates'. In N. Otmazgin and E. Ben-Ari (eds) *Popular Culture and the State in East and Southeast Asia*, London: Routledge: 191–202.

Ho, A.-M. (2013) 'Southeast Asia Has More than 130 million Internet Users'. Available at: http://www.techinasia.com/southeast-asia-Internet-infographic/ (Accessed on April 22, 2015).

Hjorth, L. and Chan, D. (2009) *Gaming Cultures and Place in Asia-Pacific*, New York: Routledge.

Jin, D.J. (2010) *Korea's Online Gaming Empire*, Cambridge, MA: MIT Press.

Kerr, A. (2006) *The Business and Culture of Digital Games: Gamework / Gameplay*, London: Sage Publications.

Kerr, A. (2013) 'Space Wars: The Politics of Games Production in Europe'. In N. Huntemann, B. Aslinger (eds) *Gaming Globally: Production, Play, and Place*, New York: Palgrave Macmillan: 233–250.

Khoo, O. (2013) 'On No Longer Speaking Chinese: Crossover Stardom and the Performance of Accented English'. In S. Khorana (ed.) *Crossover Cinema: Cross-Cultural Film from Production to Reception*, New York: Routledge: 66–82.

Kushner, D. (2014) 'The Flight of The Birdman: Flappy Bird Creator Dong Nguyen Speaks Out: How Did a Chain-Smoking Geek from Hanoi Design the Viral Hit Flappy Bird—and Why Did He Walk Away?', *Rolling Stone*. Available at: http://www.rollingstone.com/culture/news/the-flight-of-the-birdman-flappy-bird-creator-dong-nguyen-speaks-out-20140311 (Accessed on April 17, 2015).

Kusno, A. (2013) 'Master Q, Kung Fu Heroes and the Peranakan Chinese Asian Pop Cultures in New Order Indonesia'. In N. Otmagin and E. Ben Ari (eds) *Popular Culture Co-Productions and Collaborations in East and Southeast Asia*, Singapore: NUS Press: 185–206.

Moran, A. and Keane, M. (2010) *Cultural Adaptation*, London: Routledge.

Nichols, R. (2010) 'Target Acquired: America's Army and the Video Games Industry'. In N. Huntemann and T. Payne (eds) *Joystick Soldiers: The Politics of Play in Military Video Games*, Routledge: New York: 39–52.

O'Hagan, M. and Mangiron, C. (2013) *Game Localization*, Amsterdam: John Benjamins Publishing Company.

Otmazgin, N. (2005) 'Japanese Popular Culture in East and Southeast Asia: Time for a Regional Paradigm', *Journal of Asia-Pacific Journal*. Available at: http://www.japanfocus.org/-nissim_kadosh-otmazgin/2660 (Accessed on April 22, 2015).

Spielmann, Y. (2013) *Hybrid Culture: Japanese Media Arts in Dialogue with the West*, Cambridge, MA: MIT Press.

Tolentino, R. (2013) 'Niche Globality: Philippine Media Texts to the World'. In N. Otmagin and E. Ben Ari (eds) *Popular Culture Co-Productions and Collaborations in East and Southeast Asia*, Singapore: NUS Press: 150–168.

Volkmer, I. (2012) 'Deconstructing the "Methodological Paradox": Comparative Research Between National Centrality and Networked Spaces'. In *The Handbook of Global Media Research*, Malden, MA: Blackwell Publishing: 110–122.

Zulkarnain, I. (2014) '"Playable" Nationalism: Nusantara Online and the "Gamic" Reconstructions of National History', *Sojourn: Journal of Social Issues in Southeast Asia* 29(1): 31–62.

36

From a cottage to the symbol of creative industries: the evolution of Korea's online game industry

Dal Yong Jin

Introduction

> Online gaming has been taking the world by storm since the 1990s and Korean developers have been among the leaders. While Korean games are successfully exported to China, Japan, US and other Asian countries, highly-developed manufacturing nations such as the US, Japan and several countries in Europe struggle to develop an identity in the online gaming space. The spectacular growth of online gaming marks a new chapter in the history of game industry.
>
> *(Wi 2009, 1)*

Korea has rapidly developed its online games and exported them to the global markets in the early twenty-first century. Although several leading countries, such as the US and Japan, are still major players in the digital game industries, including console, PC, and mobile games, Korea has produced several successful online games to become a global leader. With several MMORPGs (massively multi-player online role playing games), including Lineage [I], Lineage II, and Aion, Korea has penetrated the Western game markets as well as the Asian game markets.

It was not long ago that the Korean game industry was a cottage industry because video games were not considered as a major part of culture or business. During the late 1980s and early 1990s, a small industry of about two dozen computer game companies developed video games to serve the Korean market. However, since the late 1990s, the Korean game industry suddenly developed video games, particularly online gaming, although the early stage of the development of online games during the 1990s was closely related to social milieu, including several cases of censorship and regulation. The game industry has become one of the fastest growing sectors in the early twenty-first century and has enjoyed its status as the most significant cultural form, representing Korean popular culture in terms of both foreign export and domestic use. Online game firms have rapidly become symbols of the creative industries due to the nature of creativity, youth culture, and the export-driven digital economy.

This chapter is an overview of key issues relating to the growth of Korea's online games in tandem with the creative industries. By employing social constructivism theory as a theoretical framework, it historicizes the remarkable growth of Korea's online game industry, and it discusses several key factors, such as political, cultural and financial elements, for the evolution of the online game industry. It especially analyzes an interplay between the government and online game corporations so that the readers are able to understand the primary players in Korea's online game industry, which has rapidly become part of the global digital game industries.

The social construction of technology in digital games

Two major theoretical frameworks in interpreting the perceptions and uses of technologies are technological determinism and social constructivism. As technological determinism advanced, social constructivism, known as the social construction of technology (SCOT), emerged later as an alternative perspective of technological determinism. Technological determinism refers to the belief that technology advances along a path of its own creation, once introduced into society, and inevitably and irreversibly takes an active predicate and progress along the way (Marx and Smith 1994, xi). Meanwhile social constructivism advocates that people shape new technologies, instead of technologies shaping society that technological determinism advocates (Winner 1993; Mackenzie and Wajcman 1999). As Brey points out;

> social constructivism includes a conception of technological development as a contingent process, involving heterogeneous factors. Accordingly, technological change cannot be analyzed as following a fixed, unidirectional path, and cannot be explained by reference to economic laws or some inner technological logic. Rather, technological change is best explained by reference to a number of technological controversies, disagreements and difficulties, that involve different actors or relevant social groups, which are groups of actors that share a common conceptual framework and common interests. These actors or groups engage in strategies to win from the opposition and to shape technology according to their own plan.
>
> *(1997, 4)*

In other words, social constructivism implies that technological change does not occur because new devices and processes demonstrate their clear-cut superiority over other ways of doing things (Mackenzie and Wajcman 1999).

As Feenberg (1992) argues, constructivism means that technologies are underdetermined by scientific and technical criteria. Concretely, this means two things: first, there is generally a surplus of workable solutions to any given problem, and social actors make the final choice among a batch of technically viable options; and second, the problem-definition often changes in the course of solution. Therefore, social constructivists' perspectives (Volti 2008; Bijker et al. 2012) envision that technological design is especially a function of interconnected social, cultural, technical, and economic factors. Technological artifacts thus result from a complex interaction between technical capabilities and the interests and values of many individuals, groups, and organizations. As Bijker et al. point out, "technological artifacts are culturally constructed and interpreted" (2012, 40). Since the presence of interest groups and unequal distributions of power are fundamental aspects of every society, social constructivists are interested in delineating the main actors involved in the development and selection of particular technologies (Volti 2008, 39).

As Thomas Hughes (1994, cited in Volti 2008) points out, social, political, and economic forces are likely to exert the greatest influence when several alternative technologies emerge at about the same time. It is necessary to understand several players both included and excluded, because this comprehensive interpretation provides the reasons as to why some players cannot be the major players as the result of unequal power relations between several actors.

In fact, technology is no longer an isolated area of study, and it is essential to enter into a discussion of the emerging online game sector through utilizing social constructivism theory. Several previous works already developed their research on this particular perspective. Richardson (2012, 135) argues that the heuristic understanding of the nexus of the cultural, organizational and technological aspects is necessary in order to map out the emergence of new technologies. Hjorth (2012, 194–195) also gives an insightful interpretation of mobile gaming using social constructivism theory. She states that the manner in which technology is deployed is not only a matter of simplistic understandings of technologies and users, but also a matter of conceptualizing the dynamic relationship between the user and their technologies. Using smartphone games in Korea as an example, Jin et al. (2014) also found that the recent growth of Korea's mobile game culture primarily relied on the interplay of several socio-cultural and political initiatives. What we emphasize is that online games must be defined based on the sociocultural specificity of Korea's digital media. Through this sociotechnical examination of online game culture, we hope to illuminate some of the complexities inherent in examining online game platforms as they have manifested—and continue to manifest—in Korea.

In the Korean context, beginning in the early 1990s, many corporations and developers have started to create online games. However, because relevant social actors cannot have equal power or opportunities, it is critical to comprehend who takes a potentially important choice that never surface as matters for debate and choice (Winner 1993, 369). In other words, instead of simply adopting social constructivists' perspectives on the role of relevant social actors, I critically address different abilities of members who influence the outcomes of development and adoption, as Winner (1993) argues. This means that the early stage of the growth of online gaming in Korea needs to be carefully examined not only by understanding the role of socio-economic factors but also by mapping out the crucial role of major players, including game developers, game corporations, and government agents.

Evolution of the Korean online game industry in the 1990s

The growth of Korea's digital games traces back to the mid-1970s. The history of video games in Korea began in 1974, when small stationeries in Korean villages started to install one or two arcade games (Yoon et al. 2012). Of course, there were a few games before 1974. First, when Korea opened the first Children's Center in Seoul in 1970, the center installed several game machines, although they were not electronic but mechanical. The exhibition room was also called 'Science Game Room,' which aimed to provide scientific knowledge; therefore, it was not the contemporary form of digital games (*Maeil Economic Daily* 1970, 1975). Second, between 1970 and 1975, several Pong machines entered into Korea for American soldiers who resided in different parts of the country, but they were not used for the general people. Third, Korea permitted electronic game rooms by law in 1973, which means that the country started to have the old form of arcade rooms, but they were banned one year later in the name of energy saving (Korea Game Culture Association 2014).

Right after, in 1975, the *Midopa* Department Store in Seoul, which was one of the largest department stores at the time, installed three units of the Pong machine (clone), known as "Computer TV," which was developed in the US. According to *Maeil Economic Daily* (1975), it was called TV game, and from the outside it looked like a TV set. This was assumed to be the first official game machine imported to Korea, and later domestic corporations, including Olympus, started to produce locally made arcade games. Olympus exported its own video game console titled GAMATIC 7600 to several countries, including Germany, Denmark, Sweden, Thailand, Canada, and Chile before its sale in the domestic market (*Maeil Economic Daily* 1975, 1976). This

Figure 36.1 A Pong console game machine known as the first commercial game in Korea
(*Maeil Economic Daily* 1975)

implies that game producers did not find it to sell their games in Korea in the 1970s due to several regulations based on moral and economic reasons.

In the early 1980s, although the fact was not well publicized, some corporations imported video game consoles like the Atari VCS and Colecovision to Korea, but only insiders knew about them. There were a few large corporations who jumped into the video game industry. For example, Goldstar (now LG) announced in 1984 that the company would invest 200 million Korean Won in the development of a game console until the end of the following year, although the claim was never followed up on in any further news (Derboo 2014). Since *Midopa* and Goldstar were two of the largest corporations back then, this indicates that Korean digital game industries would have been driven by large corporations, if these investments had been made.

Most of all, the Korean digital game sector moved into the arcade age in the late 1970s. It cannot be traced accurately when exactly video game arcades entered Korea, as they typically evolved out of slot machine or pinball rooms. The first accounts are in fact news about crackdowns on the aforementioned illegal establishments. Up until the end of the 1970s, electronic entertainment rooms (*Jeonja Oraksil*) quickly spread around the country, despite fierce opposition by conservative parents and media in a still somewhat Confucian society due to potential game addiction (Derboo 2014). However the arcade games in *Jeonja Oraksil* had grown substantially and the first generation of gamers in the Korean context started to enjoy video games with several arcades games in the late 1970s and the early 1980s. Although *PC bangs* in the early twenty-first century is here very similar to *Jeonja Oraksil*, this form of entertainment room typically had several arcade games, which worked as the main part of the gaming culture until the very early 2000s when Korea substantially started to develop online gaming. *Jeonja Oraksil* also became one of the first forms of bang culture, including *PC bang* and video bang, which has been rampant in Korea.

Based on the growth of these early forms of video games, Korea has become one of the fastest countries in the world in developing new media, including online gaming. There are several significant new media technologies representing Korean information and communication technologies, such as high-speed Internet, smartphones, and telecommunications equipment; however, the online gaming industry stands apart in Korea. In online gaming, Korea is now the market leader rather than the follower, both in terms of production and consumption. The first major online game, *Ultima Online*, was American in origin but was commercialized and marketed by Koreans. Online gaming is a field where "Korea no longer is forced to compete on price, but on technology and service" (Wi 2009, 1–2). Around the 1990s, several local developers were also creating video games, but primarily focused on Multi-User Dungeons (MUDs), which are text-based online games, in which a group of users simultaneously participate within a shared virtual world, typically a role playing game. MUDs, which are devoid of graphics and are played solely via reading and inputting text, first appeared in Korea with the launch of *Jurassic Park* in 1994. This was just over a decade after MUDs had originally been developed and released in the Western world.

This form of game helped to originate the contemporary online games industry in Korea (Nam 2011, 12; Jong 2009).

> The early stage of the development of online games during the 1990s was closely related to Korea's rather unique social environment. Back then, computer networks could be found only within a couple of elite universities, including Korea Advanced Institute of Science and Technology (KAIST) and Seoul National University, which had access to broadband communications networks.
>
> (*Nam 2011, 12–13*)

Some younger people could not image this kind of limited service in the 1990s. The MUD phenomenon appeared in Korea in the early 1990s as part of a student project at KAIST in which several computer science students converted a popular open source codebase called DIKU MUD that could be used to develop MUD games into a Korean version. The revamped Korean version became popular among university students at KAIST. A start-up company called Samjung Data Systems published the first commercial MUD to appear in Korea, a game called *Jurassic Park*, in which players battled both dinosaurs and other players in an attempt to "restore" the fictional dinosaur park popularized in Michael Crichton's novel. The game was launched in 1994 as proprietary software offered on two PC communication networks popular with students, Challion and Hitel (Casper and Storz 2013; Jong 2009, 87). Jae-kyung Jake Song who developed *Lineage* later also had participated in the development (Yoon et al. 2012). "The success of *Jurassic Park* quickly led to other MUDs being marketed, such as *Land of Dangun* and *Ghost Fortress*" (Wi 2009, 83). By 1996 over 200,000 individuals played MUDs on a variety of Korean Internet Service Providers (ISPs) that were being launched in the country (Casper and Storz 2013).

Text-based MUDs were a technologically primitive form of online game that nevertheless attracted large numbers of Korean users. Having to take in all of the information from the game via text and input commands in English was inconvenient for users though. In 1996, Nexon released *The Kingdom of the Winds* (*Baramae Nara* in Korean), which is loosely based on Korean mythology and on a series of graphic novels by an artist named Kim Jin—the first MUD to include graphic content (referred to as a MUG, or Multi-User Graphic) (Wi 2009, 83).

While the Korean game market prior to 1996 was heavily concentrated on the arcade sector, a few game developers were pouring their efforts into developing PC package games. The overall market was small, but for PC games, illegal duplication of software left the game development market on the verge of collapse, despite the few but quality games including *The War of Genesis* and *White Day*. The solution to such problems was NEXON's *The Kingdom of the Winds* (Eun 2010).

The Kingdom of the Winds had especially surpassed the symbolic meaning of the first graphic-based online game to change the entire paradigm of the Korean game market. The environment that forced users to play only by connecting directly to the server imposed numerous restrictions on illegal duplication, which was forcing the game market off the cliff. In addition, the new billing system of receiving a fixed monthly service fee from the users created a stable business structure promoting steady sales. *The Kingdom of the Winds* had become a new role model of the game market. The early success of *The Kingdom of the Winds* breathed new life into the Korean game development market, which had been constantly stagnant (Eun 2010).

Although several companies were involved, the early development of the online gaming sector in Korea can be largely traced to a small number of entrepreneurs, the most important of which was Jae-kyung Jake Song. At Nexon, Song led a team of three engineers to develop both the *DOOMVAS* engine and a game using it called *Nexus: Kingdom of the Winds*, which became one of the first MMORPGs to use a graphics engine. It was launched a few months after the release of *Meridian 59*, the first Internet-based online role playing game using graphics to be launched in the US, and about a year before *Ultima Online*, a similar game to *Kingdom* that established the online RPG genre in the US. *The Kingdom of the Winds* was loosely based on Korean folklore. It allowed players to assume one of a number of character classes (knights, wizards, etc.) who would complete a variety of in-game quests. Again, it was initially made available for testing through the Internet Service Provider Challion, then released as an Internet–based game in 1996 (Casper and Storz 2013). "While *The Kingdom of the Wind* would eventually become a commercially successful product with over a million users, its initial version attracted no more than a few hundred hard-core gamers. Nexon needed to take on a variety of web development contracts to stay afloat and fund its game development" (Jong 2009, 94).

Two years after *The Kingdom of the Winds* had its breakthrough, *Lineage* launched its official services in 1998. *Lineage* provided the future direction of online games. *Lineage* borrowed the world view of its original cartoon, and also paved the systematic foundation of the MMORPG genre. Moreover, it fundamentally utilized the principle that online games should be based on exchange and competition between the users (Eun 2010). In late 1997, Song was hired by NCsoft, a start-up focused on online games founded by Tak Jin Kim. *Lineage* included player-versus-player combat centered around a castle siege system in which groups ranging in size from five to 100 players could bond together into guilds (Casper and Storz 2013; Park 2005, 303).

While a few Korean developers and game corporations started to develop their unique online games, Korea had no technical capability and expertise in consumer electronics that served as a critical foundation for the early development of platforms, unlike the Japanese video game industry (Aoyama and Izushi 2003, cited in Johns 2006). The Japanese software industry draws upon the *manga* (the Japanese word for comic book) and animation films industry to provide creative and innovative inputs (Johns 2006, 173); however, Korea has not had these cultural traditions, with some exceptions. Although Hae Kyung Lee (2001, 22–23) argued that "early Korea's online games shared its cultural origins with animation, *manga*, character as the major reason for the growth of online gaming in the Korean context," Korea has advanced its online game sector with no substantial help from either *manga* or animation, which makes Korea's online gaming distinctive, while Japan has developed console and *manga* (or animation) almost identically.

Game industries in the cultural economy in the early twenty-first century

The game industry has suddenly become one of the fastest growing sectors in the creative industries in the early twenty-first century and has enjoyed its status as the most significant cultural form representing Korean popular culture in terms of both foreign export and domestic youth culture. In 1998, online gaming accounted for only less than 1 percent in Korea's video game industry, while arcade gaming consisted of 75 percent; however, with the introduction of *PC bang* and *Lineage* in 1998, the situation was dramatically changed, because the growth rate of online gaming in 1999 was 228 percent, and it was again 400 percent in 2000. During the same years, the growth rate of the global online game industry was only 36 percent in 1999 and 44 percent in 2000 (Lee 2001), while the market share of Korea's video gaming globally was only 1.7 percent in 2000 (Ministry of Culture and Tourism 2002, 461–462).

The Korean game market has furthermore increased over the last several years. The global market size of Korea's video gaming accounted for 6.3 percent in 2012; however, within online gaming Korean products consisted of as much as 28.6 percent, behind only the Chinese market (Ministry of Culture, Sports and Tourism 2013). Korea was the largest online game market in the world until 2008; however, due to the soaring Chinese online game market, the Korean online game market in 2010 made up 25.9 percent of the world's online game market, behind China at 30.4 percent (Ministry of Culture, Sports and Tourism 2012, 363).

The Korean game industry especially generates more export revenue than all other Korean cultural industries combined. In 2003, Korean game companies exported a total of US$182 million, which accounted for 39 percent of cultural exports. However, in 2013, the country exported as much as US$2.98 billion. Korea expects to export US$3.4 billion in 2014, which will account for 60 percent of cultural exports (Ministry of Culture, Sports and Tourism 2014). During the period 2002–2013, the export figures increased by about 20 times, while the level of imports increased by only 1.25 times. In 2013, the gross market value of gaming, including console/handheld, online, mobile, arcade, and PC games, had grown to US$10.8 billion (Ministry of

Culture, Sports and Tourism 2014). Unlike the early years of the 2000s, the online game industry accounted for around 90 percent, followed by mobile and console/handheld games.

In Korea, young people are likely to enjoy online games, although some of them are now switching to mobile games with the rapid growth of multi-functional and speedy smartphones. More than half of the online population in the country is between the ages of 11 and 34, and with such a youthful group of Internet mavens, it's no surprise that Korea's gaming culture is growing (*emarketer* 2012). Korea has developed online games based on the improved broadband services, and local online games are currently well received in many parts of the world. The online game industry as the largest sector in the Korean digital game industries consisted of 97.2 percent of game exports in 2009. However, the proportion of online gaming has continuously declined to 96.2 percent in 2011 and again to 91.4 percent in 2012 primarily due to the recent growth of mobile games in the smartphone era (Kim 2014; Ministry of Culture, Sports and Tourism 2012).

Unlike other cultural sectors in which East Asia has become a major target region, the Korean game industry has penetrated the Western markets relatively well, although it is seasonally fluctuating based on the development of globally successful MMORPGs. In other words, while Asia, including China, Japan and Taiwan, has continued its dependency on Korean online games, Western countries have increased their imports of Korean games. In 2003, for example, China accounted for as much as 62.1 percent of Korea's gaming exports, and other regions were relatively small, with North America at 5.7 percent, Japan at 5.6 percent, and Europe at 2 percent. North America and Europe together consisted of only 7.7 percent of the total. As with many other cultural forms, such as television programs and films, the Korean game industry had very little penetration among Western countries. This situation continued to 2004 when North America (6.1 percent) and Europe (3.5 percent) together accounted for 9.6 percent, although Korea ranked as the second largest online game import country for the US during the same year. The environment surrounding the export of the Korean game industries has fundamentally changed since 2005, when the US suddenly increased its imports of Korean games to 15.7 percent of the total. Including Europe, these two Western regions accounted for 20.7 percent of the export of domestic games that year, and the trend has continued to very recent years (Korea Game Development and Promotion Institute 2008, 53). In 2010, North America and Europe accounted for 17.8 percent, and this figure was much higher than that of popular music (1 percent) and television programs (3.16 percent).

For Korean online game publishers and developers, the US market is crucial because online gaming is getting bigger and bigger as people increasingly have access to high-speed Internet. During 2011, the majority of game users in North America enjoyed console games at 46.7 percent, while 28.6 percent of users played online games; however, it is expected that by 2016, the number of online game players (37.8 percent) will surpass the number of console gamers (36.7 percent). The online game market in North America grew by 10.6 percent in 2011, while its counterpart in console games decreased 5.6 percent. Growth in the online game market has been driven by an increase in broadband subscribers, by transition to the current generation of consoles, and by the growth of social games (PriceWaterhouseCoopers 2012, 358). This suggests that Korea is likely to increase its penetration in the North American market, which is rapidly growing.

Meanwhile, online gaming is a mainstream youth culture in Korea. Professional game players become national idols, commanding the same popularity as K-pop (Korean popular music) stars. Korea's online games are the primary part of youth culture because Korean youth enjoy online gaming more than other activities, although mobile gaming in the early part of the 2010s has rapidly grown and gradually replaced online gaming due to the heavy use of smartphones in their daily activities. The majority of Koreans play online games, much as many Americans go to watch a movie. As online games allow players to interact with other players wherever they can connect, gaming in the home on a static player will become more and more outdated (Jin 2010; *emarketer* 2012). In other words, as online gaming can be accessed anytime from anywhere, Korea's online games have played a major role as part of global youth culture.

As such, primarily due to its significance in both global trade and youth culture, online gaming has become a symbol of Korea's creative industries. While Korea has initiated its growth of creative industries, such as film, broadcasting, animation, and popular music (K-pop) as leading export items in the twenty-first century, online gaming has continuously led other creative industries, making itself the most important digital technology and culture.

Socio-economic elements for the growth of the online game industry

There are several significant factors contributing to the growth of online gaming in Korea; favorable government policy, timely emergence of infrastructure to support the game sector, the formation of a workforce of skilled programmers and network engineers required to develop online games, and the 1997 economic crisis. In fact, there were early market conditions surrounding the offline game industry, including infrastructure developments such as *PC bangs* (Internet cafés) and broadband Internet access (Wi 2009, 111–112). These socio-economic elements have greatly supported the growth of Korea's online games, in particular, in a certain period of time. As noted, social, political, and economic forces are likely to exert the greatest influence when several alternative technologies emerge at about the same time, and it is crucial to understand the complex interplay of these factors in the development of the early state of new technologies, in this case, online gaming.

To begin with, it is interesting that the history of the console game market influenced the spread of online gaming in the Korean context, because online gaming is expanding most rapidly in parts of the Asian market where console gaming has not yet made strong inroads. Markets with a long history of console game playing, such as the US and Japan, are seeing much slower growth in online gaming (Wi 2009). Console games are the most popular sector of the global game market; however, unlike in many other countries, online games are far more popular in Korea than the console variety because the country had little exposure to console games. As explained, several domestic capitals, including Goldstar planned to develop console games several decades ago; however, console gaming never took hold in Korea to the same extent it did in the US and Japan. The Korean console game market began to develop in 1989 when Samsung and Sega joined forces to market their 8-bit Aladdin Boy console. Other companies, including Hyundai Electronics and LG Electronics entered the console gaming market. Hyundai Electronics collaborated with Nintendo to create and market 8- and 16-bit game consoles. Regardless of these corporate efforts, the Korean console market was stagnant, and these corporations decided to cancel production of their console games in the latter part of the 1990s (Wi 2009, 114).

The status of Japanese game consoles as contraband until the late 1990s was a significant factor for the weakness of console games in Korea. Up until 1998, the Korean government banned Japanese cultural products which included console games, film, and music due to the Japanese colonial experience. With the ban lifted, Korea gradually opened the market to Japanese culture, with console games from the country making their appearance in the Korean market by 2002 (Chan 2008). Japanese companies that anticipated generating huge profits through gaining access to the Korean game market found the endeavor generated a negligible amount of revenue. Through its subsidiary company, Sony experienced a net loss in 2004 and 2005 when it began its sale of PlayStation 2. It subsequently delayed its launch of PlayStation 3 in Korea (Cho 2007).

Nintendo also sold only 40,000 consoles during the same period, while it sold 24.4 million consoles worldwide excluding Korea (Shim 2008). With Japanese console manufacturers (including Nintendo and Sony) experiencing such difficulties in penetrating the Korean video game market, the Korean online game industry has been able to utilize the opportunity to develop its own online games (Jin 2010). Accordingly, "Korean gamers became immersed in online text-based MUDs to a much larger degree than in the two major console nations" (Wi 2009, 113). "The weakness in console gaming was a boon for the nascent online gaming industry" (Wi 2009, 114).

Secondly, the Korean online gaming industry's growth has been driven by the existence of a strong infrastructure, including the entry and growth of *PC bangs*. *PC bangs* became a cultural venue for teenagers and college students, and promoted the formation of intra-game communities (Wi 2009, 121). *PC bang* played an imperative element in generating the Internet boom and the swift deployment of broadband services, primarily because many Korean users, especially young people, were first exposed to high-speed Internet access in Internet cafés (Jin 2010). The *PC bang* later played a crucial role "in shaping and forming the socio-cultural context and business for Korean online gaming" (Huhh 2009, 103). *PC bang* can be described as a business model in which constant access to the Internet is open to the public through leased lines for 24 hours without closing. *PC bangs* are equipped with high-speed lines and multimedia computers and offered high-speed access to the Internet at almost one dollar per hour as of the end of 2002, and as low as 73 cents per hour in 2007 due to severe competition among *PC bangs* (Korea Game Industry Agency 2008). *PC bangs* have since evolved as places for Internet use among the population to send e-mails, chat, research information, and so on at any time of the day and night (Lee et al. 2003; Jin 2010).

In fact, the introduction and development of *Lineage* in 1998 as well as *Starcraft* developed by an American company is closely related to the growth of *PC bangs*. Since the high-speed Internet network of present times was not widely distributed to individuals back then, many people sought *PC bangs* to enjoy online games. Amidst such a background, online games including *Lineage* and *Starcraft* as well as *PC bangs* grew together by providing synergy effects to one another. Counted to be around only 3,000 in 1998, the number of nationwide *PC bangs* rose rapidly to 21,460 in 2000 (Ministry of Culture, Sports and Tourism 2013; Eun 2010). However, the number of *PC bangs* has substantially decreased in the early 2010s. In 2009, the amount was still 21,547; however, it decreased to 19,014 in 2010, and again to 13,796 in 2013 (Korea Creative Content Agency 2014, 248). This means that *PC bangs*, which were one of the major reasons for the growth of online gaming in the early twenty-first century, cannot play the same role as they did a decade ago. While there are several reasons for the recent decline in the number of *PC bangs*, the most significant reason is the end of *Starcraft* which was the most popular online game for Korean users until several years ago. Many Korean gamers enjoyed *Starcraft* at *PC bangs*; however, it disappeared on December 17, 2012 after its final game. Although *PC bangs* currently offer several games, including *League of Legend* developed by Riot Games, their popularity is not comparable to *Starcraft*. The surge of smartphone use since 2009 and the switch to mobile games have also negatively influenced *PC bangs*, while a new government policy designating *PC bangs* as non-smoking facilities in 2013 also partially caused the decline in the number of *PC bangs*.

Thirdly, government policies have promoted the growth of the online game industry since the 1990s. "As online gaming grew and became viewed as an actual industry, the government began to institute policies fostering it and encouraging its growth" (Wi 2009, 131). The government put the game sector in the center of cultural policy as a major part of digital economy and culture. The government has wanted to develop communication businesses and information technologies to establish a high-tech industrial base, and the Korean government has begun to support the booming online game industry primarily with legal and financial forces, due to gaming's influence on young people who are major consumers, as well as its relevance to youth culture (Jin and Borowy 2014). Some early policies proved very useful in propelling the industry's rapid growth. The building of high-speed communication networks was essential for the growth of online gaming (Wi 2009).

More specifically, the Korean government first established the Integrated Game Support Center in 1999, which changed its name to the Korean Game Development and Promotion Institute (KGDI) in 2000, in order to develop the domestic game sector into a strategic export-oriented cultural industry. It has changed to the Korean Game Industry Agency since 2007. In 2004, the Korean government announced the so-called "Long-term Promotion Plan of the Game Industry." According to the Plan, the government was willing to support the game industry to become one of the three game-empires in the world by increasing its market size to US$10 billion by 2007, while increasing the number of employees in the game industry to 100,000 (Ham 2003). As part of this plan, the government invested US$13.5 million for the growth of the game industry and the creation of a game culture in 2006. Although the amount of this particular investment is inadequate when compared with actual costs, it illustrates the intention of the Korean government to deliver on its promise of keeping to its policy (Jin and Chee 2009).

The Korean government also enacted the Relevant Implementation Order and Implementation Rules for the Game Industry Promotion Law in 2006 to protect the game industry by differentiating it from speculative games, including poker games. The Promotion Law clearly claims that "the game industry is the core industry of the next generation, which yields additional economic values"; therefore, the government wanted to develop an environment of growth for the game industry by providing legal supports, such as tax breaks and copyrights. The online game industry is still a cottage industry with fewer than 30 employees per company on average. Therefore, when they cannot make revenues, the new tax-related law exempts 50 percent of corporate tax of game corporations for the next three years (Jin and Borowy 2014).

Last, but not least, the emergence of publishers since the late 1990s has become a crucial factor for the growth of online gaming in the early twenty-first century. As the game industry has been growing, game corporations need to secure talented game developers. However, both production and marketing costs have soared, and mid-sized and small-sized game corporations could not find enough investment. Large corporations, such as Hangame and Netmarble, also needed to secure many games in order to compete with other leading game corporations. Therefore, they provide some funds to small game developers and let them use their own game portal, while distributing the profits. The introduction of this type of publishing system has greatly contributed to the growth of online gaming (Yoon et al. 2012).

As such, several socio-economic factors have played key roles for the growth of Korea's online gaming. As technologies cannot be separated from society, the surge of Korea's online gaming as the main part of Korea's youth culture and foreign export has been the result of the interplay of growing infrastructure, such as high-speed Internet and *PC bangs*, favorable cultural and/or new media policies, and the historical factor that explains the weakness of console games in the Korean context. In addition, several online games, both foreign-origin and domestic-origin, such as *Starcraft* and *Lineage* games, certainly influenced the growth of Korea's online game market, which is one of the largest and most vital in the global digital game markets.

Conclusion

The Korean video game industry, and particularly the online gaming sector, has rapidly grown and expanded the export of online games in the global markets. Since the early 2000s, the Korean game industry has swiftly developed its unique online games, in particular, MMORPGs, to become the market leader among video games in Korea and has exported them to both neighboring countries and Western countries. Although the degree of penetration in the Western market is not phenomenal, at the very least, it is not dicey to say that the local online game industry has proved the possibility of a leading role for non-Western countries in the global markets. Korea's online gaming industry has transformed from a cottage industry in the 1990s to the symbol of creative industries in the twenty-first century.

While there have been several socio-cultural elements expediting the growth of Korean online gaming, government policies, historical background, and the surge of *PC bangs* all played key roles in the Korean context. Korea's online gaming industry is no longer an isolated area, and the heuristic understanding of the nexus of the cultural, organizational and technological aspects has worked for the emergence of new technologies (Richardson 2012). As Hjorth (2012) points out, the manner in which online gaming is deployed is not a matter of simplistic understandings of games and users, but a conceptualizing of the dynamic relationship between the game user, cultural context and their technologies, as well as changing government policies. In particular, the rapid growth of online gaming in the Korean context proves that several social, political, and economic forces exert the greatest influence when several alternative technologies emerge at the same time. Although console and arcade games as well as PC games emerged almost at the same time, Korea selected online gaming based on not only its infrastructure but also its historical background.

This implies that the nascent development of Korea's online gaming has relied on the complex interplay of several socio-cultural and political initiatives. The substantial growth of infrastructure, in particular, high-speed Internet, which is the highest in the world in terms of penetration rate and the surge of *PC bangs* right after the 1997 economic crisis, has become the undisputable background of the development of Korea's online game industry. Unlike Western countries, Korea had no experience of console games due to its historical relationship with Japan; therefore, the game users in Korea just started to enjoy online games, including *Starcraft*, followed by several MMORPGs. At the same time, the Korean government has supported the online game industry with its legal and financial arms. As Volti (2008) and Bijker et al. (2012) argue, the growth of Korea's online gaming proves that social structures and processes have affected choices of technologies, in this case, online gaming. Technological artifacts thus result from a complex interaction between technical capabilities and the interests and values of many individuals, groups, and organization (Bijker et al. 2012). The perceptions and uses of Korea's online games are socially constructed as the result of the interplay of several socio-cultural as well as economic factors.

The Korean online game industry has been challenged by a few emerging markets as well as the uprising of mobile games on smartphones in the 2010s. Therefore, the continuing growth of the Korean online game industry will be relying on whether domestic online game firms can massively penetrate Western markets as well as regional markets, because several countries, including China, have also substantially developed their own games. Due to heavy competition in the same region, the Western markets have become significant for Korea's game firms and developers. This implies that the next generation of Korea's online games will be heavily influenced by the role of Western users, and therefore, it is crucial to develop games that Western users enjoy.

Korea's online game corporations also need to adjust to the smartphone era. Although mobile games and online games are different in their platforms and major game genres, people heavily use smartphones these days, and mobile games have gradually replaced online games. Since Korea is a test bed for digital games, the same phenomenon will be followed globally. In short, the future growth of Korea's online gaming will be the result of the interplay of several video game platforms and governmental and corporate initiatives, and how to adjust to the changing socio-economic milieu is the most important task for Korea's game developers and publishers.

References

Bijker, W., Hughes, T. and Pinch, T. (2012) *The Social Construction of Technological Systems*, Cambridge, MA: MIT Press.

Brey, P. (1997) 'Social Constructivism for Philosophers of Technology: A Shopper's Guide', *Society for Philosophy and Technology*, 2(3/4). Available at: http://www.utwente.nl/bms/wijsb/organization/brey/Publicaties_Brey/Brey_1997_Social-Constructivism_PoT.pdf (Accessed on July 29, 2014).

Casper, Steve and Cornelia Storz (2013) 'Entrepreneurial Communities and the State: The Emergence of Korea's On-line Gaming Industry'. Paper presented at the 2013 Industry Studies Association Conference Kansas City, MO, May 2013

Chan, D. (2008) 'Negotiating Online Computer Games in East Asia: Manufacturing Asian MMORPGs and Marketing Asianess'. In Sudmann, A.J. and Stockmann, R. (eds) *Computer Games as a Sociocultural Phenomenon: Games without Frontiers: War without Tears*, New York: Palgrave: 186–196.

Cho, J.S. (2007) 'Hangame Meets Japanese Taste', *The Korea Times*, December 17.

Derboo, S. (2014) 'A History of Korean Gaming'. Available at: http://www.hardcoregaming101.net/korea/korea.htm (Accessed on July 20, 2014).

emarketer (2012) 'Mobile Leads Gaming Charge in South Korea'. Available at: http://www.emarketer.com/Article/Mobile-Leads-Gaming-Charge-South-Korea/1009541 (Accessed on December 13, 2013).

Eun, M. (2010) 'The Rising Representative Contents of Korea, Games', *Aving Global Networks*. Available at: http://us.aving.net/177840 (Accessed on July 13, 2014).

Feenberg, A. (1992) 'Subversive Rationalization: Technology, Power, and Democracy', *Inquiry: An Interdisciplinary Journal of Philosophy*, 35(3/4): 301–322.

Ham, S.J. (2003) 'Domestic Game Market to be $10 Billion: The Government Announced the Long Term Plan', *Hangaeyae Shinmun*, November 13, 31.

Hjorth, L. (2012) 'iPersonal: A Case Study of the Politics of the Personal'. In Hjorth, L., Burgess J. and Richardson, I. (eds) *Studying Mobile Media: Cultural Technologies, Mobile Communication, and the iPhone*, London: Routledge: 190–212.

Hughes, T. (1994) 'Technological Momentum', in Smith, M.R. and Marx, L. (eds) *Does Technology Drive History?: The Dilemma of Technological Determinism*, Cambridge, MA: MIT Press: 99–113.

Huhh, J.S. (2009) 'The Bang Where Korean Online Gaming Began: The Culture and Business of the PC Bang in Korea'. In L. Hjorth and D. Chan (eds) *Gaming Cultures and Place in Asia-Pacific*, London: Routledge: 102–116.

Jin, D.Y. (2010) *Korea's Online Gaming Empire*, Boston, MA: MIT Press,

Jin, D.Y. and Chee, F. (2009) 'The Politics of Online Gaming'. In Hjorth, L. and Chan, D. (eds) *Gaming Cultures in the Asia-Pacific Region*, London: Routledge: 19–38.

Jin, D.Y. and M. Borowy (2014) 'Political Culture of Gaming in Korea amid Neoliberal Globalization'. In Kleinman, D. and Moore, K. (eds) *Routledge Handbook of Science, Technology and Society*, London: Routledge: 189–203.

Jin, D.Y., Chee, F. and Kim, S. (2014) 'Transformative Mobile Game Culture: Socio-cultural Analysis of the Korean Mobile Gaming in the Smartphone Era', *International Journal of Cultural Studies*.

Johns, J. (2006) 'Video Games Production Networks: Value Capture, Power Relations and Embeddedness', *Journal of Economic Geography*, 6(2): 151–180.

Jong, H.W. (2009) *Innovation and Strategy of Online Games*, London: Imperial College Press.

Kim, S.U. (2014) 'Game Hallyu 11 Times Higher Than K-pop', *Yonhap News*, April 14.

Korea Creative Content Agency (2014) *2014 Korean Games White Paper*, Seoul: KOCCA.

Korea Game Development and Promotion Institute (2008) *2008 Korea Game Whitepaper*, Seoul: Korea Game Development and Promotion Institute.

Korea Game Industry Agency (2008) *2008 Korean Game Whitepaper*, Seoul: Korea Game Industry Agency.

Korea Game Culture Association (2014) 'Game Industry History Charts', Seoul: Korea Game Culture Association. Available at: http://kgca.kr/xe/menu12 (Accessed on April 21, 2014).

Lee, H. J., Robert, M. O' Keefe, R. M. and Yun, K. L. (2003) 'The Growth of Broadband and Electronic Commerce in South Korea: Contributing Factors', *The Information Society*, 19(1): 81–93.

Lee, H. K. (2001) 'The Current Affairs and Problems of Korea's Online Game Industry', *Information, Telecommunication and Broadcasting Policy*, 13(5): 20–37.

Mackenzie, D. and Wajcman, J. (1999) *The Social Shaping of Technology: How the Refrigerator Got its Hum*, 2nd edn, Philadelphia, PA: Open University Press.

Maeil Economic Daily (1970) 'Children Like Science Game Room', 25 July.

Maeil Economic Daily (1975) 'Computer TV Introduced by Midopa Department Store', 29 January.

Maeil Economic Daily (1976) 'Export 6,000 Video Game Machine', 13 November.

Marx, L. and Smith, M. (1994) 'Introduction'. In Smith, M. R. and Marx, L. (eds) *Does Technology Drive History?: The Dilemma of Technological Determinism*, Cambridge, MA: MIT Press: ix–xv.

Ministry of Culture, Sports and Tourism (2012) '2012 Game Industry Whitepaper', Seoul: MCST.

Ministry of Culture, Sports and Tourism (2013) '2013 White Paper on Korean Games', Seoul: MCST.

Ministry of Culture, Sports and Tourism (2014) '2014 Contents Industry Report', press release, 5 February.

Ministry of Culture and Tourism (2002) 'Cultural Industries White Paper', Seoul: MCT.

Nam, Y. (2011) 'The Origin of Korean Online Game Industry: Networks of Butterflies', *Science and Technology Studies*, 11(2): 1–30.

Park, K. H. (2005) 'Internet Economy of the Online Game Business in South Korea: The Case of NCSoft's Lineage'. In Singh, V. P. and Kehal, V. (eds) *Digital Economy: Impacts, Influences and Challenges*, Hershey, PA: IGI Global.

PriceWaterhouseCoopers (2012) *Global Entertainment and Media Outlook 2012–2016*, New York: PriceWaterhouseCoopers.

Richardson, I. (2012) 'Touching the Screen: A Phenomenology of Mobile Gaming and the iPhone'. In Hjorth, L., Burgess, J. and Richardson, I. (eds) *Studying Mobile Media: Cultural Technologies, Mobile Communication, and the iPhone*, London: Routledge: 133–153.

Shim, H. Y. (2008) 'Sony-Nintendo Competes in Korea', *Digital Times*, March 15.

Volti, R. (2008) *Society and Technological Change*, 6th edn, New York: Worth Publishers.

Wi, J. H. (2009) *Innovation and Strategy on Online Games*, London: Imperial College Press.

Winner, L. (1993) 'Upon Opening the Black Box and Finding it Empty: Social Constructivism and the Philosophy of Technology', *Science, Technology & Human Values*, 18: 362–378.

Yoon, H. S., Kang, J. W. and Park, S. Y. (2012) *The History of Korean Games*, Seoul: Book Korea.

37

Getting a life: expatriate uses of new media in Hong Kong

Meaghan Morris with Elaine Lally and Catherine Driscoll

"Medium" signifies first of all an intermediary. The import of the word "means" is the same. They are the middle, the intervening, things through which something now remote is brought to pass. Yet not all means are media. There are two kinds of means. One kind is external to that which is accomplished; the other kind is taken up into the consequences produced and remains immanent in them. . . . [The] moment we say "media," we refer to means that are incorporated in the outcome.

(Dewey 2005, 204–205)

What does it mean to "share" thought and experience in contexts enabled by new media platforms?[1] In a usage dominant on social network services that "spread" existing media content (Jenkins et al. 2013), sharing blurs into a gesture of display for mostly unspecified friends who may easily miss or ignore it. In contrast, this chapter exists because three women shared time, ideas and activities in the practical sense of developing a five-year project (2009–2014) shaped by a more or less equal division of labor and an ethic of reciprocity when circumstances allowed. Our focus was the Zynga games (*Farmville, Cityville, Castleville, Farmville 2*) that we played together during those years. However, with Meaghan Morris living in Hong Kong for much of that time while Elaine Lally and Catherine Driscoll worked at different universities in Sydney, our collaboration was made materially possible by the *affordances* of Facebook (Inbox and a closed group page where we posted materials, ideas and chat about our gaming), supplemented by email, SMS, Dropbox and a sporadic use of Pinterest as well as of pubs, cafés and conference presentations.[2]

Changing over time, this varied but purposeful engagement with new media affordances—that is, the aspects and properties of technological environments that allow users to appropriate their utility for specific situations and needs—shaped a sense of the *formative* uses of new media in social experience that this chapter explores. The situation considered here is that of a white Western "expat" working without Chinese language skills in a predominantly Cantonese-speaking university environment in Hong Kong. This is Meaghan's life experience, shared with Elaine and Catherine only in the form of stories. Accordingly, the text is written in Meaghan's first person and deals with media uses other than playing Zynga games. The chapter itself, however, draws substantially on talks with Elaine and Catherine and their knowledge of digital media and game studies. This is a text with one authorial voice produced between three contributors. If this may be a little unusual, we think it is consistent with the kind of sharing that new media afford us amidst the diasporic work that grounds this chapter's themes.

The perspective taken here is historical in the sense that it deals with "old" new media uses informing some aspects of the 2014 "Umbrella Movement" that attracted world-wide attention between September 26 and December 15 when pro-democracy protesters occupied key sites in Admiralty, Mongkok and Causeway Bay ('2014 Hong Kong Protests' n.d; Leong and Lee 2014). In global coverage the digital and artistic creativity of the movement (Martel 2014) and the "surprise" (Shultziner 2014) of civil disobedience erupting on this scale in Hong Kong aroused as much interest as the political issues involved. Yet social movements have a deep history in Hong Kong (Chiu and Lui 2000) and, as Szeto (2014) demonstrates, their forms of creativity are shaped by the intense conditions of Hong Kong urban life. This chapter is a small contribution to exploring some of those forms.

Sleepless in transit: navigating Hong Kong

> I feel lost in Hong Kong. I don't know how you'd write about it, it's impenetrable.
>
> *Paul Theroux (McHugh 2014, 19)*

There are few more solitary times in the daily life of a Hong Kong foreign resident than spending a crammed double decker bus ride as the only person awake. Given to late nights and long working days, Hong Kong people of all ages have an uncanny ability to nap on public transport whenever chance affords and to snap awake at the last second to get off at the right stop—as though most of the city's seven-plus million inhabitants are born with a bio-rhythmic alarm system attuned to GPS. Before the mid-2000s, when the rapid spread of smartphones multiplied ways to make travel time productive, this communal conversion of a bus or MTR (rail) carriage into a dormitory could occur at any time of day. New media have to some degree attenuated the practice of "catch-up sleep efficiency"; when recently I saw a mother and daughter jump up cursing as their stop flashed by they were both playing *Candy Crush Saga*, an "addiction" (Griffiths 2013) across the city in 2013. However, the sleep-through still prevails over texting, talking, snapping, filming, swiping and gaming on early morning commuter rides and there are always people dozing at other times.

For some years I valiantly tried to adopt local custom on the 40 minute trip between Hong Kong Island and Tuen Mun in the far north-western New Territories where I worked from 2000 to 2012. Even when I managed to nod off (a challenge for one raised in country Australia to rise at cock-crow and pass out soon after dark), my own inner alarm would jerk me bolt upright with anxiety about snoozing past Lingnan University to find myself lost in a remote high-rise forest where not a soul would speak English and my Cantonese insults and food requests would be no help at all. Yet the coming of an iPhone with location services did little to further my efforts despite giving me navigational means. I finally accepted failure one day when a large man who snored loudly every morning—so heavily that being near him was like sharing a bed with a relative—snorted violently and fell sideways to the floor of the moving bus. As his neighbors gently pulled him up and rescued his bag and he started snoring again, I realized that lacking a habitual sense of Hong Kong transport rhythms was a minor aspect of my exclusion from the dormitory. It wasn't about timing and bus stops at all. Rather, I could not achieve that man's incorporated, intimate trust in the urban communal *spaces* he inhabits. Trained from childhood in watchfulness near strangers, I would never risk falling asleep on the familiar routes of my home town of Sydney.

Any smartphone has the potential to act externally as what the American philosopher John Dewey called a "means" to orient a person in transit. First published in 1934, Dewey's *Art as Experience* distinguishes between, on the one hand, "external or *mere* means" that enable an accomplishment but are separable from it and could be replaced (by a paper map and a watch alarm in my example), and, on the other hand, the special kind of means that, like the water or oil colors in a painting and bricks or stone in a building, "coalesce" with the ends they accomplish and are intrinsic to its effects. Dewey (2005, 205) calls these *media* and their immanence to what they enable defines an "esthetic" effect (while "externality may even be regarded as a definition of the non-esthetic"). Crucially, though, as Deen (2011, 4) points out, for Dewey there is a fundamental continuity between art and everyday life. This means that such activities as study or travel may be conducted in aesthetic as well as instrumental ways and that the quality of our *use* of means (as "when we journey for the delight of moving about and seeing what we see" (Dewey 2005, 205)) transforms mere means into media. In this sense there may be an aesthetic "coalescence" of the *form* of a mesmeric puzzle game such as *Candy Crush* with the snatching of pleasurable moments from daily life in a work-driven, time-poor economy such as Hong Kong's.

Of course, one must first have those means. When I moved to Hong Kong in 2000 I did not own a mobile phone. Scarred by years as a film critic with distributors pestering me to join publicity stunts (how about a submarine ride in Sydney Harbour for *Raise the Titanic?*), I could not bear to have an untethered phone following me about. I held out for six months until the night of June 4, when, on my way home after failing to find my friends in the vast crowd gathered in Victoria Park to commemorate the 1989 massacre in Tiananmen Square, I got hopelessly lost in an insalubrious mall while trying to find my bus stop. It was late, shops were shut, triad men were coming out of the narrow walkways, and I felt very . . . visible as a lone *gwei por* ("white ghost woman") wandering in circles with a handbag. Hong Kong is a fairly safe city when it comes to opportunistic crime but away from Central on Hong Kong Island its footpaths winding through cramped and visually saturated mall-scapes are hard to navigate if you don't read Chinese. That night I extracted myself using Australian bush skills, noting characters on signs as I would a branch or leaf, but in the process I learned that a mobile phone can be a saviour as well as a stalker. I bought a Nokia 8210 the next day.

Beginning with the animated conversations that my choice provoked (why not the 8110 model from the film *Matrix* choreographed by Hong Kong's Yuen Woo-ping and partly shot in Sydney?) this changed my life, opening my social existence unexpectedly to new qualities of experience, or "consequences" in Dewey's terms. For just as "mobile games are becoming seamlessly incorporated into the day-to-day activities of people across diverse cultures and contexts" (Hjorth and Richardson 2014, ch. 1, loc. 88–89) so, too, may this *kind* of incorporation more broadly enable not only new daily activities but cross-cultural "outcomes" (Dewey 2005, 205) that might not otherwise have occurred. New media helped make me a Hongkonger and later I consider some of the "particular genres of use" (Miller 2011, x) that Cantonese people shared with me. To call these genres "particular" is not to make a claim about exclusive features of Hong Kong culture. My perspective is formed by that small but historically obdurate aspect of the city's social mix that is the expatriate condition, of which it is a given that "the processes of forming identity and forging self-identification are fundamentally relational" (Hjorth and Chan, 2009, 79). However, as Miller (2011) argues in his Trinidad-centered study of Facebook, the "emergent heterogeneity" of media platforms themselves derives from the way their value and impact for different people and places is inflected by the latter's distinctive histories, economies and social practices—that is, in continuity with the mixed stuff of a way of life that involves but is not reducible to the media uses it shapes.

The stuff of life: Hong Kong working time

> I don't use email; I phone and fax. I think people who are hunched over their computer screens all day should get a life.
>
> *Joan Collins ('Get A Life Quotes' 2014)*

What, then, is a way of life? For Cultural Studies, following Williams's (1958, 4) insistence that culture involves both "special processes of discovery and creative effort" in art and thought *and* the common meanings shared across a "particular way of life, whether of a people, a period or a group" (Williams 1976, 80), this is a question for social and historical research as well as aesthetic enquiry. Discussions of new media often prefer an ethical question—"what is a *good* way of life?"—to which the cultural premises for an answer are taken for granted as shared. As Shaw (2010, 411) argues, in video game studies this takes the form of a normative emphasis on how people spend their time and what sorts of interactions they have. While few workers today could share Joan Collins's assumption that computers are just a "means" of communication, the ease with which many feel licensed to spend their own time online ordering others to "get a life!" if they post nerdy videos or leave traces of gaming in a social network feed derives from that strange moral fantasy of norming intimacy (Morris 2009) that prompts earnest debate about whether Facebook friends are "real."

Transposed across social formations, this regulatory impulse generates sentimental fiction. Western anglophone accounts of new media use presume a symbolically American context in which modern middle class urban virtues such as sociability and a busy diary are, as Taylor (2009, 70) notes, idealized as good for all. In his comic confession of addiction to "stupid games," Anderson (2012) adds nostalgia for the good life of Hollywood family sit-com memory: "I was playing when I should have been doing dishes, bathing my children, conversing with relatives, reading the newspaper" and even "after learning that my dog . . . was probably dying of cancer." I lived a bit like that in 1960s Australia, although we had to chop wood first to heat the water, but in middle class Hong Kong today a domestic helper might do the childcare as well as the housework, conversation is inescapable when families are squashed in a very small flat, a newspaper is grabbed off the street on the rush to work and beyond expat enclaves the rare sight of a dog sends people swerving in fear. The gamer of anglophone imaginaries also inhabits a specific architecture of daily life. An ironic portrait cited by Juul (2010, 28–29) situates the ideal hardcore player in a computer-equipped "home" that is spatially distinct from a workplace or school, unlike the millions of people worldwide who work or study where they live, using a phone or a café to play (Lai 2014). He/she also has a private bathroom to forgo using (extra space that is not a given even in European cities) and a "weekend" free as a norm. Most workers of the world do not have two days off and those working online anywhere may have none at all (Gregg 2011).

Diversified by ethnicity and religion (Erni and Leung 2014), violent class and gender inequalities (Chiu 2003; Choi and Cheung 2012), contested sexualities (Kong 2012b; Leung 2009; Yau 2010), and a porous but fractious divide between "rural" New Territories villages and the hyper-urban zones of Kowloon and Hong Kong Island (Chiu 2002; Hayes 2006), Hong Kong ways of life are massively dominated by work. Within a political economy of urban density (Rooney 2003), this is no less true for the elderly, disabled and destitute who suffer from lack of work. Inhabiting one of the world's most extreme wealth gaps (Gu 2014) almost a fifth of Hong Kong's people live in poverty (CASD 2012) despite a generally low unemployment rate (3.3 percent in 2012). Hongkongers are often derided as money hungry, with a persistently poor showing in sex satisfaction surveys prompting ritualized media jokes ('Why?' 2014). However, within a polity dominated by the interests of a small group of tycoons with influence in Beijing (Chen 2012; Hajari 2014; Yan 2014), lack of money brings dire living conditions in a city where property prices, always high, have doubled since 2009 (Hu and Yun 2013) and the waiting time for public housing is about three years. A middle class wage-earner now struggles for 14 years merely to save a deposit on a 40 square meter flat (Tsang 2014), leaving young adults to live indefinitely with their parents (Timmons 2014). Adding to the squeeze, 14.2 percent are over 65 (CASD 2014) and, in the Hong Kong Chinese version of the good way of life, children should work to support their parents in the absence of a comprehensive social welfare system (Chan and Lee 1995, 89).

Hongkongers work the longest hours in the Asia-Pacific (Lu 2010; Hudson 2012) with little real regulation. While 48 paid full-time hours was officially the average in 2011, "uncompensated" overtime in service and professional sectors adds at least nine hours a week (Labour Department 2012, 128). In reality, with wages pegged to performance targets rather than to time, people "hunched over their computers" work as much as 70 hours a week for modest pay. Whereas in mainland China a "double leisure day" (weekend) was introduced by state policy to foster consumption in 1995 (Wang 2001, 77–78), 15 years later only 45.7 percent of Hong Kong's already-consumerist employees had been offered a five day week (Ng 2010, 1). For most of the 89.5 percent of residents who speak Cantonese (GovHK 2014), the proximity of extended family in the city adds to the schedule a thick layer of ethically pressing obligations to attend reunions during festivals and family gatherings on Sundays.[3] The latter may combine with the major cultural activities of eating, shopping, sight-seeing in malls and walking in country parks.

These cramped spatio-temporal conditions give a poignant immediacy to Taylor's (2009, 59) argument that new media affordances such as game spaces "offer interesting possibilities to undo some of the constraint produced by traditional families and localized friendship pools." Hong Kong family affect is powerful in complex registers. Escaping the constraint of "quantity time"[4] with relatives may certainly be a goal: during the 2009 craze for *Happy Farm*, a Chinese online multi-player simulation game allowing players to steal each other's vegetables (Lai 2010; see Hjorth and Richardson 2014, ch. 9), I heard Hong Kong youth accused of threatening family values by staying home on Sunday to protect their crops. However, "getting a life" is commonly a dream of spending *more* time with family (Ng 2010, 11). As a participant observer in the 2002–2006 period Chan (2008, 182) studied working mothers who hunched over the Hong Kong Chinese parenting website *Happy Land* "to bring domesticity via virtual space into the workplace," enacting their gender roles from the office. More recently, while diners using mobile phones at the table provoke an anglophone etiquette storm (Dewey 2014), in Hong Kong this may as easily involve an intimate experience of being together while working late on separate jobs as an escape from each other's company. Conversely, the widespread aesthetic passion for using photo apps such as Instagram to "share" a meal brings family and friends together temporally in social conditions that render spatial proximity hard to achieve with any frequency.

Expatriates drop in to this life in isolating ways that make "getting a life" a challenge. In a local usage shaped by past realities of colonial administration, "expats" are usually Westerners earning high incomes in business, education or civil service. With Hong Kong now saturated in images of Chinese wealth, stereotypes of expat luxury attach to the *idleness* of "wives" living "a charmed existence made up of cocktails by the pool and an army of staff" (Expat Explorer 2010) in spacious and subsidized housing. Where such privilege still exists (notably in the financial sector), that army is composed of other foreign workers, women from the Philippines and South East or South Asia, who for six long days a week do "labour intimacy" (Chang and Ling 2011; Constable 2007) for Hong Kong families of all kinds but do not count socially as expats.[5] The expat breadwinner enters a maelstrom of work that fills evenings with obligatory functions from which partners are excluded; presumed to be male, "his" version of cocktails by the pool involves clustering with compatriots in raucous bars and exclusive clubs. In these ways the "ugly" expat

(Foley 2011) avoids Cantonese life. Yet the vibrancy of that life, evident everywhere on the streets and pervasive Chinese media—radio in taxis, MMOB ("Multi-Media On Board") loops in public transport, big screens on towers—is largely closed to newcomers by the long hours, the work/family divide, small flats making hospitality impractical and the "code-switching" fatigue that falls most heavily on Cantonese asked to use Mandarin and English all day with little reciprocity.

Writing of the transformative power of mobile networked technologies, Hjorth and Richardson (2014, ch. 1, loc. 172–174) remind us that place is constructed "by an ongoing accumulation of stories, memories, and social practices" (see Massey 2005). Accumulation takes time, however, and some expats quickly leave with only personal memories of work and anomie. I was fortunate to arrive with Hong Kong stories already in my memory, thanks to the great "vernacular modernism" (Hansen 1999) of Cantonese cinema with its genius for remixing elements of transnational media culture with local stories and concerns (Morris 2005, 2013). So my expat luxury in the early 2000s was watching the Hong Kong films then lying by the thousand in cheap heaps at stalls and pop-up stores, thanks to the novel (to me) technology of VCD (Video Compact Disc). It took years, an epidemic and the arrival of smartphones before I learned that this genius was active all around me in everyday life.

Genres of use: the Hong Kong milieu

> A child in the dark, gripped with fear, comforts himself by singing under his breath. He walks and halts to his song. Lost, he takes shelter, or orients himself with his little song as best he can. The song is like a rough sketch of a calming and stabilizing, calm and stable, center in the heart of chaos.
> *Deleuze and Guattari (1987, 311)*

Singing, for Deleuze and Guattari (1987, 311), is a way of organizing and inhabiting space; "one ventures from home on the thread of a tune." Home in this perspective is not a point of origin but something we make in the middle (*le milieu*) of everyday practices like humming over the housework (Morris 2006, 187–201) or, let's say, playing on a mobile phone. One tune rich with homely associations for Hongkongers is "Under (or Below) the Lion Rock," the 1979 theme song, performed by Roman Tam, of a long-running TV series of dramas about the joys and sorrows of ordinary Hong Kong lives meeting under the lion-like rock that rears above Kowloon (Ma 1999, 122–133; Mak 2013; 'Simon' 2009). A sense of belonging under the Lion Rock myself came in the midst of work one day in 2003 when I saw a crowd huddling in the office, listening to the off-key notes of a warbling of *Moon River* (a tune I played on a recorder as a child) we had endured the night before at a graduation dinner. Giggling, people scattered as I approached and there, on the flashy new laptop a colleague had been waving around at my table (showing it off, I thought), was a film of Professor Morris furtively pouring whisky from a hip-flask into the horrid sweet cordial served on such occasions while covering up by telling students their fellow was "murdering that song." I was the star of a Hong Kong comedy! With no thought of violated privacy (this felt like a family joke) I laughed until the tears ran down my bright red cheeks.

At this time we were still forced to use transparencies in the classroom and a version of Web-CT so clunky that a technician took an hour to explain almost none of its use. My first contact with a built-in camera brought home the tension between the swift creativity of Hong Kong people as they not only "make do" but make *joy* out of "what they have" (de Certeau 1984, 18) and the stifling resistance to change in the institutions ordering Hong Kong lives. 2003 was a threshold for articulating that tension. With the sorrow of the SARS epidemic (Erni 2006; Morris 2004) followed by a July 1 march of half a million people protesting "Article 23," a proposed national security law threatening free speech, the popular aesthetic use of media for high-speed politics as well as communal solace presaged forms of the Umbrella Movement more than a decade later (Grace 2014, 29). Subversively reworked film stills, cartoons and complex calligraphic puns pillorying government figures flew thickly around the Internet, between phones enabled for MMS (Multimedia Messaging Service) and were posted on walls, lifts and doors. Dynamically neophile when it comes to brands and models, Hong Kong vernacular culture avoids the wasteful snobbery of disdaining "old" technologies, turning any available material into means for producing media.

SARS forced me to begin practicing a little fast creativity myself. Asked to teach with damp surgical mask fluff backing down my throat, I used group email instead, discovering that my ICQ-trained students who froze in front of a Word file and sometimes cried if asked to speak by a foreign professor could pour their hearts out in English online about their reading. I had resented ICQ, the first stand-alone instant messenger; students who chatted all night fell asleep in class. Chan and Cheuk (2009, 14) show, however, that ICQ was valued by Hong Kong youth not only for the privacy and friendship it afforded them in cramped familial space but for improving their "typing skills." My students' fluency of expression on the unwieldy email interface was far greater than mine and with shame I learned that their engagement with their studies was deeper than I had known as a technologically conservative teacher. At the same time, any rosy new media utopianism was checked as I fielded the terrifying rumors spread daily by SMS and Internet throughout the student body, often with malicious intent and some emotional harm. This intensive training in the arts of digital combat for a public sphere in which anonymous accusation, "big character poster" style (Leijonhufvud 1990), is seen as a legitimate mode of dissent also imbued me with a more nuanced and thus durable sense of Hong Kong community.

The urban social forces shaping these earlier uses of new media intensified during the rapid uptake of smartphones after 2007 in Hong Kong. A 63 percent penetration rate (230 percent with multiple ownership; Budde 2014) was achieved by 2013 (StartupsHK 2013), with 96 percent of users going online every day and 84 percent making photos or video ('Smartphone Usage' 2014).[6] Some recent research suggests that Hong Kong people primarily use social media to "maintain" existing relationships, acting as "passive social media participants rather than content creators"; this is ascribed to a "highly collective culture" and a Cantonese orientation to "extremely contextual communication practices which online interaction is unable to foster" ('Digital Media' 2012). Maintaining relationships is indeed an art in Hong Kong for reasons I have described, but an ideological association between individualism, context abstraction and content creativity cannot explain why the city was heralded for "an artistic and digital revolution" (Martel 2014) just two years later. Fung (2006, loc. 2570–2594) provides a much more solid basis for grasping this when he shows in a study of cyber-café culture in the early 2000s that online communities in Hong Kong's "hectic and crowded" environment are "often actually closely connected to one another through real-life identities" and locales such as schools and homes.

In other words, new media *add* social spaces and potentials, including the escape hatch of "time out" from work, developing on a continuum with everyday life rather than offering virtual alternatives to it (Lehdonvirta 2010). This is exactly how a smartphone became my magic carpet for fully getting a life in Hong Kong. I bought a smartphone on the advice of my trainer when I joined a gym, adding a local milieu to my workplace, home and desktop/mobile networks. Rapidly exceeding its pedagogical use for showing me videos of my movement errors, the smartphone was a portal to what Jenkins et al. (2013, 263) call, following Pratt (1991), the "arts of the contact zone" in Hong Kong's polyglot life. Discussing "the unexpected mingling and mixing of cultural materials" with "multiple points of entry" informally spread by new media practices, they stress the diverse literacies active in "exchanges" between countries. Their analysis also works for a linguistically complex city.

In business terms, Hong Kong's social media ecology can be seen as "fragmented" between US-based platforms such as Twitter and China's Weibo and Jiepang ('Digital Media' 2012). The fact that Facebook maintains a big lead as the most used social network ('Infographic' 2011; Steimle 2014) suggests that Hong Kong users who want to switch languages and thus filter audience contexts easily have a different ecological perspective. Historically rich in Chinese dialects as well as "ethnic minority" languages (CASD 2011), Hong Kong life flows around two official spoken languages, Cantonese and English, and two written, Chinese and English (Morris 2010). Anglophones can live there indefinitely while experiencing Chinese as only a sonic and visual background. As Fung's (2006) research predicts, however, once placed in a social assemblage within the mixed local space of a gym, my smartphone vastly increased my Hong Kong *cultural* literacy as people shared news, comedy and entertainment clips from the Chinese websites of *Yahoo! HK*, *Apple Daily* and *HKGolden.com* (Siu 2014) through Whatsapp while standing next to me or texting later to explain them. In return I gave nuance on request to Australian natural disaster, politics and sports scandal news.

The gym milieu shaped new media practices that "intervened" for me in many ways. Given a multi-media player to put action movies on my treadmill, I learned to run for the first time since childhood, eventually doing it outside with apps such as Instagram and Runkeeper to "maintain friendship" with my trainer. In theory, I might have done this with other means. The aesthetic force of these practices as immanent to the life they enabled derives, however, from the access they brought to Hong Kong "genres of use" (Miller 2011, x). Genres are collective forms of practice that are recognizable as such to members of a community. "Navigating" is a genre in this sense, practiced with smartphones by 76 percent of Hong Kong users ('Smartphone Usage' 2014) while "working" or "maintaining friendships" are purposes for which genres may be used. Another genre organizes the pragmatic use of new media affordances for advancement in a highly commercial society: students use ICQ to improve their typing, personal service professionals keep clients interested with Facebook, YouTube and Whatsapp. A more complex view of this emerged for me when for a period I found myself endlessly playing Zynga's mobile *Words with Friends* with Chinese friends and *their* friends wanting to improve their English. This was fun, an escape hatch and also informally a transaction: the game gave me a sense of social connection and my friends a free language lesson (a well-established "genre of use" for Hong Kong parents showing Disney films to their children; Choi 2010). Resonating with the "catch-up sleep efficiency" of commuters, making the most of even tiny amounts of time involves a *creative maximisation* of time's value in Hong Kong lives.

By separating an external realm of disposable tools from the subjective pursuit of "delight," Dewey's (2005, 205) distinction between instrumental and aesthetic means for doing things tends to break down at this point. Driscoll (2012) points out that even in the designer space of Zynga's casual simulation games (*Farmville 2*, for example) there is no clear line between "self-expression" and the "self-promotion" necessary to play the game. Moreover, in Hong Kong's stressed conditions the act of *sharing* delight in self-expression has a collective value that is instrumental in maintaining community. The collective itself moves quickly between passions and investments: during the brief period when Hong Kong friends played Zynga's time-soaking desktop games (an immersive pursuit I share durably with Australians), they switched so fast from *Farmville* to *Cityville* after the latter's launch in December 2010, leaving dead farms in their wake, that the moment felt like living through the depopulation of the countryside in a textbook on urbanization. However, while games, apps and even platforms quickly go in and out of favor, remaining in this sense "external" for their users, the *genres* of use endure and coalesce with maintaining community.

One genre that strikes me as significant for social creativity is the way of remixing materials for Hong Kong contexts that I have elsewhere called "fashioning" (Morris 2005, 30–31). Only in part a variation on what scholars of global culture (Crane et al. 2002) commonly call localization, fashioning is a dynamic way of evolving a locality-based frame of reference that is also a stable field of parochially shared *affect* that happily absorbs ideas from all over. This certainly draws on Hong Kong's deep tradition in cinema, television, music, theatre, visual arts and design of retooling foreign cultural goods for local purposes and tastes. However, fashioning is a street-level art rather than a mode of industrial production, and affect-sharing begins on the scale of a neighborhood, group or locale within the city. In his history of the Hong Kong uptake of Japanese combat games, Ng (2006, 5) shows how in the 1980s a player-driven hybridization of Japanese game texts with Cantonese argot and subcultural "rules of behaviour" created a "unique arcade game culture" amongst youth that spread into daily life and language, influencing Hong Kong comics, and over 20 years becoming "part of the collective memories of Hong Kong players."

Fashioning also exceeds localization by renewing images, music, film or TV moments and (with YouTube) daily practices such as preparing recipes and herbal medicines from the Hong Kong Chinese past, while diverting the value of mundane consumer goods too costly for ordinary people. Choi (2012, 390) describes how families visiting Hong Kong Disneyland in 2005–2007 invented "ways to consume Disney fantasy without paying," using merchandise stores "as a playground" for taking photos with their children, touching toys, wearing characters' wigs and often leaving without buying a thing. Such photos then created family and friendship affect when posted on Chinese album-sharing sites with links circulated on the once ubiquitous MSN Messenger, "*the way* to socialise before Facebook, Twitter and WhatsApp" (Billington 2014; see Sheer 2010). From MSN, too, I discovered that a popular pastime was to turn up at a boutique opening (festive occasions in Hong Kong) to take photos with creatively denatured commodities. I have special fondness for an image of a tea cozy in an Australian home-ware shop being worn upside down as a hat.

As a genre of new media use, fashioning creates social networks of cultural practice joyfully bringing popular localization, memory work and impromptu performance art on to the same plane of rapidly changing consensus about what matters in Hong Kong life. The full aesthetic power of this practice touched me when, with the album affordance of Windows Live Messenger, I saw a spectacular series of photos featuring a friend inserting himself seamlessly into the celebrity history depicted at Madame Tussauds on Victoria Peak, where the chance to pose with the Queen, Andy Lau, Mao Tse-tung and David Beckham all in one day is an attraction. Most people do this, portrait style, as "themselves." Carl Kwok-Leung Chan's series owed more to the historical revisionism for which Hong Kong people loved *Forrest Gump* (1994), but rather than intervening as one character he used facial and bodily gesture to melt perfectly into each waxwork tableau, becoming (for example) an utterly credible Chinese fifth Beatle. For me his artistry recalled Cindy Sherman's black and white *Untitled Film Stills* (Galassi 2003) but without the medium nostalgia (Chan's colors were vibrant) or the institutionally oriented self-consciousness as art. Thus is "content creativity" practiced daily in Hong Kong's "highly collective" and contextually sensitive culture.

Postscript: umbrellas under the Lion Rock

> We have always maintained we are not here because there is hope; we are here, therefore there is hope.
>
> (*The End of the Umbrella Revolution' 2015*)

In some ways Deleuze and Guattari's (1986, 17) theory of the creativity of "minor literature" as shaped by "cramped space" is ideal for thinking about Hong Kong new media practices. Analogies leap from their account of Kafka's use of German as a Prague Jewish writer for whom fascism and communism were "knocking on the door," given Beijing's increasingly overt pressure in Hong Kong affairs, the stress on the urban fabric exerted by rampant development and massive mainland tourism—40.7 million arrivals in 2013 from a total of 54 million tourists (Tourism Commission 2014)—and a perceived official attempt at "minoring" Cantonese language and heritage in the city (Chow 2014), as Mandarin promotion converges with continual carping at Hong Kong's richly distinctive English (Bolton 2002), However, Deleuze and Guattari are concerned with how collective conditions for creativity in *literature* shape an exemplary artist's imagination. Irreducibly collective in expression, Hong Kong new media practices require a more concrete description to grasp their formative force.

For Dewey (2005, 204–205), means and media bring things "now remote" to pass. The uses of media I have discussed all played a role in the unexpected movement that took its name from a rapid crowd re-purposing of the umbrellas everyone carries in the wet season to afford protection from the tear gas fired at protestors by police on 28 September 2014. As photos, videos and personal stories poured through the city and into the world outside China (Boehler 2014) through social media networks, with dedicated pages, hashtags and Whatsapp groups (Szeto 2014) set up, the "invisible violence" (Lam, O. 2014) of digital combat saw pro-government hackers repeatedly attack independent media sites and university servers. Correspondingly the mesh networking app Firechat (Bland 2014) allowed people to find friends, request supplies, disseminate warnings and navigate *together* via Bluetooth if the mobile network and Internet went down.

For almost three months, the fashioning of many thousands of digital and material art works, now lovingly "preserved" through Instagram and curated more formally by an artist collective with an archive on Facebook and Twitter (Chan 2014), showed Hong Kong people's creativity at its most affecting and dynamic ('Art' 2015). Pop stars and indie bands took part (Meigs and Fan 2014), writing new songs and reviving Canto-classics for a new generation. Among the icons of the Movement was the Lennon Wall developed on the Hong Kong Central Government Offices in a cumulative mass creation of continuity with the Prague Spring of 1968 ('Lennon Wall' 2014) combined with a "big character poster" practice using thousands of small, vividly colored sticky notes. The occupation itself involved the production of real locales, as Fung's (2006) argument again predicts. Humanizing with tent villages the normally choked crossroad and flyover spaces that give primacy in the city to vehicular traffic (Lam, J. 2014), the protesters built a different Hong Kong, including a fancy women's toilet and a "study hall" for students, while providing civic services such as garbage collection. Perhaps the most dramatic fusion of new media with physical space was the filmed performance art of "Hong Kong Spidey," a group that climbed the Lion Rock to unfurl a huge banner, visible for a day across the city, declaring "I Want Real Universal Suffrage." With a wink to Marvel comics along with the singing of Roman Tam, the video prolongs this event online and the vertical yellow form of the banner with black characters continues to pop up on pins and stickers around the city (Tharoor 2014).

Drawing on earlier scholarship about media rituals in his discussion of social gaming, Burroughs (2014, 155) suggests that we think of these rituals not as extensions of a pre-existing order but as "performances that help construct and coconfigure new possibilities of social order," melding "the real world . . . with the game space in new and meaningful ways." While my argument has been that this socially formative potential of new media practices has historical depth in Hong Kong's everyday life (even for expats), the events of late 2014 suggest that Burroughs is right to stress their capacity to produce new possibilities. We have just begun to imagine what these ways of sharing new media might accomplish in future.

Notes

1 My thanks to Graham Meikle for a conversation about 'sharing' that led me to think about this.
2 Versions of material in this chapter were presented by the three contributors in 'Games People Play: Genre, Style and Temporality in Zynga Community-building' at *ACS Crossroads in Cultural Studies 2012*, Nouvelle Sorbonne, Paris, July 2–6; and at *Cultural Studies Association of Australasia 2012* conference, University of Sydney, December 5, 2012.
3 Recently scholars have argued that while Hong Kong "families provide the empirical, middle-ranged setting within the concrete set up of everyday life" (Chan and Lee 1995, 87) this is a product of British colonialism (Kong 2012a; Law 2009) rather than of Chinese tradition. Interacting with a strict control of the land supply (Tse 2010, 52) that kept living spaces tiny and real estate profits vast, "familialism" gave a principle of social order to indirect colonial rule.
4 I owe this wonderful expression to Kimburley Choi Wing-yee.
5 The categorical separation of foreign domestic helpers from the rest of the population runs deep. In government statistics relating to ethnic minorities, for example, "foreign domestic helpers" are treated for all issues as a distinct group (CASD 2011).
6 In a significant but little remarked upon qualification of this embrace of smartphones, only 22 percent of Hongkongers interviewed would rather give up their television set while only 17 percent would give up PC desktops and tablets ('Smartphone Usage' 2014).

References

'2014 Hong Kong Protests', n.d. *Wikipedia* (Accessed on January 23, 2015).
Anderson, S. (2012) 'Just One More Game . . . Angry Birds, Farmville and Other Hyperaddictive "Stupid Games"'. Available at: http://www.nytimes.com/2012/04/08/magazine/angry-birds-farmville-and-other-hyperaddictive-stupid-games.html?pagewanted=all&_r=0 (Accessed on April 28, 2012).
'Art of the Umbrella Movement', *Wikipedia*. Available at: http://en.wikipedia.org/wiki/Art_of_the_Umbrella_Movement (Accessed on January 16, 2015).
Billington, J. (2014) '10 Things We Remember about MSN Messenger'. Available at: http://www.news.com.au/technology/online/things-we-remember-about-msn-messenger/story-fnjwnhzf-1227043994803 (Accessed on September 9, 2014).
Bland, A. (2014) 'Firechat—The Messaging App that's Powering the Hong Kong Protests', *Guardian*, 30 September.
Boehler, P. (2014) 'Record Censorship of China's Social Media as References to Hong Kong Protests Blocked', *South China Morning Post*. Available at: http://www.scmp.com/news/china-insider/article/1603869/record-censorship-chinas-social-media-references-hong-kong (Accessed on January 25, 2015).
Bolton, K. (2002) *Hong Kong English: Autonomy and Creativity*, Hong Kong: Hong Kong University Press.
Budde, P. (2014) 'Hong Kong—Mobile Communications—Market Overview, Statistics and Forecasts'. Available at: http://www.budde.com.au/Research/Hong-Kong-Mobile-Communications-Market-Overview-Statistics-and-Forecasts.html (Accessed on January 16, 2015).
Burroughs, B. (2014) 'Facebook and FarmVille: A Digital Ritual Analysis of Social Gaming', *Games and Culture* 9(3): 151–166.
Census and Statistics Department [CASD] (2011) Government of the Hong Kong Special Administrative Region, *2011 Population Census Thematic Report: Ethnic Minorities*, Hong Kong: CASD.
Census and Statistics Department [CASD] (2012) Government of the Hong Kong Special Administrative Region, *Poverty Situation Report 2012*, Hong Kong: CASD.
Census and Statistics Department [CASD] (2014) Government of the Hong Kong Special Administrative Region, 'Hong Kong: The Facts', June. Available at: http://www.gov.hk/en/about/abouthk/factsheets/docs/population.pdf (Accessed on November 4, 2014).
Chan, A. H.-N. (2008) '"Life in *Happy Land*": Using Virtual Space and Doing Motherhood in Hong Kong', *Gender, Place and Culture* 15(2): 169–188.
Chan, H. and Lee, R.P.L. (1995) 'Hong Kong Families: At the Crossroads of Modernism and Traditionalism', *Journal of Comparative Family Studies* 26(1): 83–99.
Chan, M. (2014) 'The Umbrella Archives: Hong Kong Artist Collective Fights to Preserve Protest Art', *Art Radar*. Available at: http://artradarjournal.com/2014/10/24/the-umbrella-archives-hong-kong-artist-collective-fights-to-preserve-protest-art/ (Accessed on December 24, 2014).

Chan, Z.C.Y. and Cheuk, W. (2009) 'An Exploratory Study on Adolescents' Experiences of Using ICQ (I Seek You)', *The Qualitative Report* 14(1): 1–19. Available at: http://www.nova.edu/ssss/QR/QR14-1/chan.pdf (Accessed on December 23, 2014).

Chang, K.A. and Ling, L.H.M. (2011) 'Globalization and its Intimate Other: Filipina Domestic Workers in Hong Kong'. In M.H. Marchand and A.S. Runyan (eds) *Gender and Global Restructuring: Sightings, Sites and Resistances*, 2nd edn, London and New York: Routledge.

Chen, T.P. (2012) 'Hong Kong's Tycoons Under Attack', *Wall Street Journal*. Available at: http://online.wsj.com/articles/SB10000872396390444230504577615212739865968 (Accessed on November 8, 2014).

Chiu, F.Y.-L. (2002) 'Combating the Double Processes of Decolonisation/Recolonisation in Hong Kong, or, "Postcoloniality" as a Double-pronged Politics', *Cultural Studies Review* 8(2): 33–61.

Chiu, F.Y.-L. (2003) *Colors of Money, Shades of Pride: Historicities and Moral Politics in Industrial Conflicts in Hong Kong*, Hong Kong: Hong Kong University Press.

Chiu, S.W.-K. and Lui, T.-L. (eds) (2000) *The Dynamics of Social Movements in Hong Kong*, Hong Kong: Hong Kong University Press.

Choi, K.W.-Y. (2010) *Remade in Hong Kong: How Hong Kong People Use Hong Kong Disneyland*, Saarbrücken: Lambert Academic Publishing.

Choi, K.W.-Y. (2012) 'Disneyfication and Localisation: The Cultural Globalisation Process of Hong Kong Disneyland', *Urban Studies* 49(2): 383–397.

Choi, S.Y.-P. and Cheung, F.M. (eds) (2012) *Women and Girls in Hong Kong: Current Situations and Future Challenges*, Hong Kong: Hong Kong Institute of Asia-Pacific Studies.

Chow, V. (2014) 'Speaking up for Cantonese, a Tongue in Peril', *South China Morning Post*. Available at: http://www.scmp.com/news/hong-kong/article/1603994/speaking-cantonese-tongue-peril?page=all (Accessed on January 21, 2015).

Constable, N. (2007) *Maid to Order in Hong Kong: Stories of Migrant Workers*, 2nd edn, Ithaca: Cornell University Press.

Crane, D., Kawashima, N. and Kawasaki, K. (eds) (2002) *Global Culture: Media, Arts, Policy and Globalization*, London: Routledge.

de Certeau, M. (1984) *The Practice of Everyday Life* (S.F. Rendall tr.), Berkeley and London: University of California Press.

Deen, P.D. (2011) 'Interactivity, Inhabitation and Pragmatist Aesthetics', *Game Studies* 11:2. Available at: http://gamestudies.org/1102/articles/deen (Accessed on August 24, 2014).

Deleuze, G. and Guattari, F. (1986) *Kafka: Toward a Minor Literature* (D. Polan tr.), Minneapolis: University of Minnesota Press.

Deleuze, G. and Guattari, F. (1987) *A Thousand Plateaus* (B. Massumi tr.), Minneapolis: University of Minnesota Press.

Dewey, C. (2014) 'Why You Should (Really, Seriously, Permanently) Stop Using Your Smartphone at Dinner', *Washington Post*. Available at: http://www.washingtonpost.com/news/the-intersect/wp/2014/07/14/why-you-should-really-seriously-permanently-stop-using-your-smartphone-at-dinner/ (Accessed on November 12, 2014).

Dewey, J. (1934; Perigree edition 2005) *Art as Experience*, New York: Penguin.

'Digital Media in Hong Kong' (2012) Singapore Management University, wiki article. Available at: https://wiki.smu.edu.sg/digitalmediaasia/Digital_Media_in_Hong_Kong (Accessed on January 15, 2015).

Driscoll, C. (2012) 'The Style of Play: Economy, Community, and Social Gaming', *Cultural Studies Association of Australasia 2012* conference, University of Sydney, December 5. Publication forthcoming.

Erni, J.N. (2006) 'SARS, Avian Flu and the Urban Double Take'. In D. Davis and H. Siu (eds) *SARS: Reception and Interpretation in Three Chinese Cities*, New York and London: Routledge.

Erni, J.N. and Leung, L.Y.-M. (2014) *Understanding South Asian Minorities in Hong Kong*, Hong Kong: Hong Kong University Press.

Expat Explorer (2010) 'Expat Women Series: Challenging Expat Women Stereotypes'. Available at: http://expatexplorer.blogspot.com.au/2010/12/expat-women-series-challenging-expat.html (Accessed on September 21, 2014).

Foley, M. (2011) 'Become an Ugly Expat in 12 Easy Steps'. Available at: http://iwasanexpatwife.com/2011/02/27/become-an-ugly-expat-in-12-easy-steps/ (Accessed on September 22, 2014).

Fung, A. (2006) 'Bridging Cyberlife and Real Life: A Study of Online Communities in Hong Kong'. In S. Jones, D. Silver and A. Massanari (eds), *Critical Cyberculture Studies*, New York: NYU Press Academic. Kindle Edition.

Galassi, P. (2003) *Cindy Sherman: The Complete Untitled Film Stills*, New York: Museum of Modern Art.

'Get A Life Quotes' (2014) *BrainyQuote*. Available at: http://www.brainyquote.com/quotes/keywords/get_a_life.html (Accessed on December 2, 2014).

GovHK (2014) 'Hong Kong—the Facts', updated October. Available at: http://www.gov.hk/en/about/abouthk/facts.htm (Accessed on November 7, 2014).

Grace, H. (2014) *Culture, Aesthetics and Affect in Ubiquitous Media*, London and New York: Routledge.

Gregg, M. (2011) *Work's Intimacy*, Cambridge: Polity.

Griffiths, M. (2013) 'Bitter Sweet? A Brief Look at "Addiction" to Candy Crush', *Gamasutra*. Available at: http://www.gamasutra.com/blogs/MarkGriffiths/20131029/203442/Bitter_sweet_A_brief_look_at_addiction_to_Candy_Crush.php (Accessed on October 27, 2014).

Gu, W. (2014) 'Hong Kong Protests Also Fueled by Widening Wealth Gap', *Wall Street Journal*. Available at: http://online.wsj.com/articles/hong-kong-protests-also-fueled-by-widening-wealth-gap-1412860304 (Accessed on November 4, 2014).

Hajari, N. (2014) 'To Save the Rich, China Ruins Hong Kong', *BloombergView*. Available at: http://www.bloombergview.com/articles/2014-08-29/to-save-the-rich-china-ruins-hong-kong (Accessed on August 30, 2014).

Hansen, M.B. (1999) 'The Mass Production of the Senses: Classical Cinema as Vernacular Modernism', *Modernism/Modernity* 6(2): 59–77.

Hayes, J. (2006) *The Great Difference: Hong Kong's New Territories and Its People 1898–2004*, Hong Kong: Hong Kong University Press.

Hjorth, L. and Chan, D. (eds) (2009) *Gaming Cultures and Place in Asia Pacific*, New York and London: Routledge. Kindle Edition.

Hjorth, L. and Richardson, I. (2014) *Gaming in Social, Locative and Mobile Media*. Palgrave Macmillan. Kindle Edition.

Hu, F. and Yun, M. (2013) 'Hong Kong Poverty Line Shows Wealth Gap with One In Five Poor', *Bloomberg*. Available at: http://www.bloomberg.com/news/2013-09-29/hong-kong-poverty-line-shows-wealth-gap-with-one-in-five-poor.html (Accessed on November 6, 2012).

Hudson report (2012) 'Hong Kong Employees Work Longest Hours in Asia-Pacific'. Available at: http://www.apsco.org/article/hong-kong-employees-work-longest-hours-in-asia-pacific-649.aspx (Accessed on October 28, 2014).

'Infographic: Asia-Pacific Social Media Statistics' (2011) *Digital Buzz Blog*. Available at: http://www.digitalbuzzblog.com/infographic-asia-pacific-social-media-statistics-stats-facts/ (Accessed on August 27, 2014).

Jenkins, H., Ford, S. and Green, J. (2013) *Spreadable Media: Creating Value and Meaning in a Networked Culture*, New York: New York University Press.

Juul, J. (2010) *A Casual Revolution: Reinventing Video Games and Their Players*, Cambridge, MA: MIT Press.

Kong, T.S.K. (2012a) 'A Fading *Tongzhi* Heterotopia: Hong Kong Older Gay Men's Use of Spaces', *Sexualities* 15(8): 896–916.

Kong, T.S.K. (2012b) *Chinese Male Homosexualities: Memba, Tongzhi and Golden Boy*, London and New York: Routledge.

Labour Department, HKSAR (2012) *Report of the Policy Study on Standard Working Hours*. Available at: http://www.labour.gov.hk/eng/plan/pdf/swh/swh_report.pdf (Accessed on October 28, 2014).

Lai, Y.-K (2010) 'Log On and Veg Out', *YoungPost*. Available at: http://yp.scmp.com/article/1326/log-and-veg-out (Accessed on November 14, 2014).

Lai, Y.-K. (2014) 'Young in Hong Kong More Likely than in West to Use Mobile Internet Devices', *South China Morning Post*. Available at: http://www.scmp.com/news/hong-kong/article/1643349/young-hong-kong-more-likely-west-use-mobile-internet-devices (Accessed on November 30, 2014).

Lam, J. (2014) 'Protesters Build Makeshift Communities at Occupy Sites', *South China Morning Post*. Available at: http://www.scmp.com/news/hong-kong/article/1630823/protesters-build-makeshift-communities-occupy-sites?page=all (Accessed on January 20, 2015).

Lam, O. (2014) 'The Invisible Violence of Cyber War in Hong Kong's Umbrella Revolution' (L. Chu and R. Yick tr.), *Global Voices*. Available at: http://globalvoicesonline.org/2014/10/06/the-invisible-violence-of-cyber-war-in-hong-kongs-umbrella-revolution/print/ (Accessed on October 7, 2014).

Law, W.-S. (2009) *Collaborative Colonial Power: The Making of the Hong Kong Chinese*, Hong Kong: Hong Kong University Press.

Lehdonvirta, V. (2010) 'Virtual Worlds Don't Exist: Questioning the Dichotomous Approach in MMO Studies', *Game Studies* 10(1). Available at: http://gamestudies.org/1001/articles/lehdonvirta (Accessed on August 24, 2014).

Leijonhufvud, G. (1990) *Going Against the Tide: On Dissent and Big-Character Posters in China*, London: Curzon Press.

'Lennon Wall in Hong Kong: A Post-it Mosaic of Freedom' (2014) *Prague Freedom Foundation*. Available at: http://www.lennonwall.org/en/site/article/133/Lennon-Wall-in-Hong-Kong-A-Post-it-Mosaic-of-Freedom.htm (Accessed on December 24, 2014).

Leong, J. and Lee, L. (2014) 'Hong Kong: Occupy Central', *People and Power* program, Al Jazeera English. Available at: http://www.aljazeera.com/programmes/peopleandpower/2014/10/hong-kong-occupy-central-201410151493427300.html (Accessed on October 28, 2014).

Leung, H. H.-S. (2009) *Undercurrents: Queer Culture and Postcolonial Hong Kong*, Seattle: University of Washington Press.

Lu, J. (2010) 'Hong Kong Workers Getting Less Time Off', *China Daily*. Available at: http://www.china-daily.com.cn/hkedition/2010-01/01/content_9253840.htm (Accessed on November 6, 2014).

Ma, E.K.-W. (1999) *Culture, Politics and Television in Hong Kong*, London and New York: Routledge

McHugh, F. (2014) 'Stranger than Fiction', *South China Morning Post Magazine*, November 30: 19–21.

Mak, S.Y.T. (2013) 'Everyday Imaginings Under the Lion Rock: An Analysis of Identity Formation in Hong Kong', PhD thesis, University of California eScholarship database. Available at: http://escholarship.org/uc/item/6dd1s8sj# (Accessed on January 15, 2015).

Martel, F. (2014) 'Hong Kong, une révolution artistique et numérique', *Slate* December 7. Available at: http://www.slate.fr/story/95479/hong-kong-revolution-artistique-numerique (Accessed on December 10, 2014).

Massey, D. (2005) *For Space*, London: Routledge.

Meigs, D. and Fan, M. (2014) 'The Umbrella Movement Playlist', *Foreign Policy*. Available at: http://foreignpolicy.com/2014/10/09/the-umbrella-movement-playlist/ (Accessed on October 13, 2014).

Miller, D. (2011) *Tales from Facebook*, Cambridge: Polity Press.

Morris, M. (2004) 'Participating from a Distance'. In K. Iwabuchi, M. Thomas and S. Muecke (eds) *Rogue Flows: Trans-Asian Cultural Traffic*, Hong Kong: Hong Kong University Press.

Morris, M. (2005) 'On the Future of Parochialism: Globalization, *Young and Dangerous IV*, and Cinema Studies in Tuen Mun'. In J. Hill and K. Rockett (eds), *Film History and National Cinema: Studies in Irish Film II*, Dublin: Four Courts Press.

Morris, M. (2006) *Identity Anecdotes: Translation and Media Culture*, London: Sage.

Morris, M. (2009) 'Grizzling about Facebook', *Australian Humanities Review* 47. Available at: http://www.australianhumanitiesreview.org/archive/Issue-November-2009/morris.html (Accessed on November 2, 2014).

Morris, M. (2010) 'On English as a Chinese Language: Implementing Globalization'. In B. de Bary (ed.) *Universities in Translation: The Mental Labor of Globalization*, Hong Kong: Hong Kong University Press.

Morris, M. (2013) 'Media and Popular Modernism around the Pacific War: An Inter-Asian Story', *Memory Studies* 6(3): 359–369.

Ng, B.W.-M. (2006) 'Street Fighter and The King of Fighters in Hong Kong: A Study of Cultural Consumption and Localization of Japanese Games in an Asian Context', *Game Studies* 6(1). Available at: http://gamestudies.org/0601/articles/ng (Accessed on August 24 2014). Revised in Hjorth and Chan (2009).

Ng, W. (2010) *The State of Work–Life Balance in Hong Kong 2010 Survey*, Hong Kong: Community Business. Available at: http://hkupop.hku.hk/english/report/WLB12/content/resources/summary.pdf (Accessed on November 4, 2014).

Parker, E. (2014) 'Social Media and the Hong Kong Protests', *The New Yorker*. Available at: http://www.newyorker.com/tech/elements/social-media-hong-kong-protests (Accessed on October 9, 2014).

Pratt, M.L. (1991) 'The Arts of the Contact Zone'. In P. Franklin (ed.) *Profession 91*, New York: Modern Language Association of America.

Rooney, N. (2003) *At Home with Density*, Hong Kong: Hong Kong University Press.

Schulzke, M. (2014) 'The Critical Power of Virtual Dytopias', *Games and Culture* 9(5): 315–334.

Shaw, A. (2010) 'What Is Video Game Culture? Cultural Studies and Game Studies', *Games and Culture* 5(4): 403–424.

Sheer, V.C. (2010) 'Hong Kong Adolescents' use of MSN vs. ICQ for Developing Friendships Online: Considering Media Richness and Presentational Control', *Chinese Journal of Communication* 3(2): 223–240.

443

Shultziner, D. (2014) 'Hong Kong's Umbrella Movement', *Open Democracy*. Available at: https://www.opendemocracy.net/civilresistance/doron-shultziner/hong-kong%E2%80%99s-umbrella-movement (Accessed on January 23, 2015).

'Simon' (2009) 'Under the Lion Rock', *Simontalks.com*. Available at: http://simontalks.com/2009/02/13/under-the-lion-rock (Accessed on December 1, 2014).

Siu, P. (2014) 'How Social Media Shapes Occupy: Web Forum HKGolden.com Takes Off', *South China Morning Post*. Available at: http://www.scmp.com/print/news/hong-kong/article/1628549/how-social-media-shapes-occupy-web-forum-hkgoldencom-takes (Accessed on November 2, 2014).

'Smartphone Usage in Hong Kong—Statistics and Trends' (2014) *Go-Globe Hong Kong*. Available at: http://www.go-globe.hk/blog/smartphone-usage-hong-kong/ (Accessed on January 15, 2015).

StartupsHK (2013) 'Google Reveals That 96% of Hong Kongers Never Go Without their Smartphones and Browse the Internet Daily, Highest Rate in Asia'. Available at: http://www.startupshk.com/google-reveals-that-96-of-hong-kongers-never-go-without-their-smartphones-and-browse-the-internet-daily-highest-rate-in-asia/ (Accessed on January 16, 2015).

Steimle, J.J. (2014) 'An Introduction to Social Media in Hong Kong', *Clickz*. Available at: http://www.clickz.com/clickz/column/2381245/an-introduction-to-social-media-in-hong-kong (Accessed on January 20, 2015).

Szeto, M. (2014) 'Rereading Hong Kong Coloniality through the Cultural-Spatial Turn of Social Movements', paper delivered at *Hong Kong as Method* conference, University of Hong Kong, 7–9 December, forthcoming.

Taylor, T.L. (2009) *Play between Worlds: Exploring Online Game Culture*, Cambridge, MA and London: MIT Press.

Tharoor, I. (2014) 'Hong Kong's Protesters Climb City's Iconic Mountain', *Washington Post*. Available at: http://www.washingtonpost.com/blogs/worldviews/wp/2014/10/23/hong-kongs-protesters-occupy-citys-iconic-mountain/ (Accessed on October 24, 2014).

'The End of the Umbrella Revolution: Hong Kong Silenced' (2015), *Vice News*. Available at: https://www.youtube.com/watch?v=_wXUulAG5z4 (Accessed on January 25, 2015).

Timmons, H. (2014) 'Hong Kongers' Miserable Sex Lives Are Making a Baby Drought Worse', *Quartz*. Available at: http://qz.com/271236/lack-of-sex-is-to-blame-for-hong-kongs-baby-drought/ (Accessed on November 7, 2014).

Tourism Commission (2014) Commerce and Economic Development Bureau, Government of the Hong Kong Special Administrative Region, 'Tourism Performance in 2013'. Available at: http://www.tourism.gov.hk/english/statistics/statistics_perform.html (Accessed on September 4, 2014).

Tsang, E. (2014) 'Build Hostels for Young While They Save for Costly Housing Deposits: Think Tank', *South China Morning Post*, 27 November. Available at: http://www.scmp.com/article/1648543/build-youth-hostels-young-people-who-cant-afford-homes-says-hong-kong-think-tank (Accessed November 27, 2014).

Tse, D.S.T. (2010) 'Tung Lo Wan: A Lesbian Haven or Everyday Life?' In C. Yau (ed.) *As Normal as Possible; Negotiating Sexuality and Gender in Mainland China and Hong Kong*, Hong Kong: Hong Kong University Press.

'Why Is Hong Kong's Libido So Low?' (2014) *Time Out Hong Kong*. Available at: http://www.timeout.com.hk/feature-stories/features/52502/why-is-hong-kongs-libido-so-low.html (Accessed on November 7, 2014).

Wang, J. (2001) 'Culture as Leisure and Culture as Capital'. *positions: east asia cultures critique* 9(1): 69–104.

Williams, R. (1958) 'Culture is Ordinary'. In R. Gable (ed.) (1989) *Raymond Williams: Resources of Hope*, London: Verso.

Williams, R. (1976) *Keywords: A Vocabulary of Culture and Society*, Glasgow: Fontana.

Yan, S. (2014) 'Hong Kong has a Tycoon problem', *CNN Money*. Available at: http://money.cnn.com/2014/11/02/news/economy/hong-kong-tycoons/ (Accessed on November 4, 2014).

Yau, C. (ed.) (2010) *As Normal as Possible; Negotiating Sexuality and Gender in Mainland China and Hong Kong*, Hong Kong: Hong Kong University Press.

38

The everydayness
of mobile media in Japan

Kyounghwa Yonnie Kim

The existence of mobile media nowadays is so conspicuous that we could hardly imagine every-day life without it. Mobile media, like other media technologies, has firstly presented itself as a device with certain social contexts and functional roles, extending upon those practices of the landline phone. However mobile media has expanded the ranges of the social application and cultural customization beyond the expectation of the technological developers, reaching the significant level of universal presence.

The meaning of this significant phenomenon might be inquired from two different points of view. The first view is to pay attention to the quantitative aspect of its social deployment. Although there is still a gap in terms of the technological sophistication between advanced coun-tries and developing countries, it seems clear that mobile media is becoming a necessity in the globe. We could call this new materiality unprecedented, since there has been no such media so widely consumed globally. It is the first media technology to realize the new materiality of the *technology everywhere*, as even the landline telephone and television, which had been considered as the most successfully deployed media technology before the mobile phone, could reach far behind the diffusional level of mobile media (Castells et al. 2007).

Secondly, we need to take consideration of its qualitative aspect in terms of the penetration into one's personal life. When Katz and Aakhus (2002), Ling (2004), and Katz (2006) argued the social impact of wireless communication in various contexts, they were timely and right in a sense that mobile media was a successor of the landline telephone. However, the perspectives of first generation mobile researches need to be requestioned, as mobile media is no longer dragging on the practices of the telephone, but expands its usage to *wide-ranging practices in every moment*. It is now obvious that mobile media is not just a communication tool, but also a versatile platform to deal with numerous practices, contexts and content. We could collect and transfer information, consume contents, create works, manage daily schedules or even calories, listen to music, watch movies, play games, and so on, by using only a mobile phone. It seems obvious that we could no longer understand the social essence of mobile media merely in the dimension of communica-tion and social relations.

Taking into account both quantitative and qualitative aspects of mobile phenomena nowadays, the most challenging aspect to question mobile media might be how to deal with its *everydayness* rather than its social novelty. As Koskinen addressed for the case of camera phone practices, we are now encountering "the mundane as a problem" (2007, 63) within the aesthetics and ideologies informing the mobile media. Regarding this perspective could be applicable to other various behaviours with mobile media, Hjorth's (2009) suggestion to interrogate the dynamism of mobile media within creative practices in various cultures is worthwhile paying attention to. The question of *mobile creativity* rather than *mobile communication* may provide us a wider and fundamental approach to understand it in terms of the converged consequence of technological innovation and cultural interpretation. In other words, by suggesting new questions, mobile media could be re-situated as a multi-dimensional substance of technological novelty and cultural banality.

In this chapter, I will raise the question of the *everydayness* of mobile media with the Japanese example. As the earliest and mostly wirelessly connected country in the world, Japan unfolds the richest contexts of the mobile technologized society, both in positive and negative senses.

"Unexciting" mobile media in Japan

In Japan, mobile media is no longer an exciting matter. It may be suggestive that when Apple introduced its advanced and ambitious model of the smart mobile phone, Japanese consumers were somewhat cool and showed a lack of interest toward the iPhone. Unlike the enthusiastic responses from the rest of the world, an inspirational reaction that was able to be called an "iPhone boom" never occurred in Japan, because the smartphone seemed neither fresh nor "smarter" than *keitai* (Japanese-styled mobile phone, meaning "portable") that they had been carrying around for more than a decade. When NTT DoCoMo launched i-Mode, the world's first mobile broadband service in 1999, Japanese society was already ready to adopt a highly advanced mobile technology into every corner of life. Moreover, after flat-rate packet billing for data telecommunication was introduced in 2004, the number of mobile broadband subscribers sharply increased to exceed 69 million at the end of the year, which formed more than 77 percent of mobile phone users (Ministry of Public Management, Home affairs, Posts and Telecommunications 2005). From the early stage of the twenty-first century, Japanese metropolis was equipped with a close-woven wireless network to enable city dwellers to browse and search Internet from everywhere, to buy tickets, to involve the online community or even to bank online while moving around.

For the younger generation in Japan, mobile media and ubiquitous accessibility was *something always there* from their childhood. According to Hashimoto et al.'s (2010) based on a long-term quantitative survey and cohort analysis, the allegedly *86-generation*, designating people born after the year 1986, has a distinguishably different interpretation in information behavior and media perception from the previous generation. For example, they definitely feel more comfortable with mediated literary communication via either mobile or PC than face-to-face communication. They also favor *writing on mobile* and *reading on PC*, feel the PC monitor is *too big* rather than that the mobile screen is *too small* to use, which presents just the opposite to what the previous generation feel. Contrary to general expectations of the ubiquitous network and placeless use of mobile Internet, data on this generation clearly shows that the time to access mobile broadband at home is from two to three times longer than the time to access outdoors. It seems obvious that, for Japan's younger generation, mobile media is an all-too-familiar commodity, and mobile accessibility is a mundane convenience.

Ambivalent discourses

Meanwhile, a techno-nationalistic discourse has repeatedly been spoken in the region. The role of the telecommunication industry has been emphasized to gain leadership in the IT revolution and to promote Japan as a high-tech nation (Ito et al. 2005, 33). The term *gara-kei*, a shortened form of *Galapagos keitai*, addresses the peculiar type of the mobile media circulated within Japan. Although the word is now being used as an endearment for domestic handsets, it was originally coined in order to problematize the situation of Japan's highly advanced mobile technology evolving in isolation from the rest of the world. As it first appeared in a government document, the word used to have techno-nationalistic nuances intended to press Japanese telecommunication industry players to make a harder effort in overseas markets (Kita 2006). As a rightward shift has become notable in the political flux after the great earthquake and the following failure of the post-controlling of the Fukushima nuclear plant crisis, techno-nationalism is even intensifying. Although a meaningful change in civic movement in line with social media practices has been reported in the region, the social discourse still strives to criticize the Japanese industry's absence from the smartphone market.

On the other hand, there have been deep-rooted antagonisms against the rapid technological progress in the region and mobile media is a typical case reflecting ambivalent and contradictory feelings towards the most high-end technology. In particular, there have been worrying and controversial discourses on youngsters' use of mobile phones. From the late 1990s, the general public has criticized mobile media as young people's devices for poor communicational manners, superficial relationships and problematic and deviant social behaviors in Japan (see Ito et al. 2005; Matsuda 2010).

It is emblematic that the local assembly of the Ishikawa prefecture officially enacted "The general regulation for children in Ishikawa" in 2010, whereby parents and school teachers were obligated to require children and teenagers in high schools *not to own* mobile phones. Although the purpose of the regulation was explained as cultivating a better understanding of mobile devices and promoting the appropriate use of them, the measure was underpinned by a criticism against mobile technology viewing it as a social evil, something to protect against in order to keep young people safe.

In summary, the discourses in Japan contain an ambivalent evaluation of the social role of mobile media. On the one hand, it is a symbolic achievement to display the image of high-tech Japan in the globe; on the other hand, mobile media is viewed as harmful and implicated in social problems and deviances, especially in relation to younger generations. This situation might result from the Japanese context in which domestic technologies have played a key role since 1970, in terms of both the contribution to rapid economic growth as well as the constitution of the image of the nation as a technological power. While a growing expectation of the IT industry surpassed the social anxiety on the dramatic change in the media landscape, there was no room for forming a social consensus surrounding the social application of the mobile media. A techno-centric approach driven by the IT industry apparently has been overwhelmed in the region.

Yet, despite this controversy, it is obvious that Japanese society has gone through the cycles of birth, growth, maturity of mobile technology, and moreover is now observing the decline of its domestic prototype in the sense that *gara-kei* is being swiftly replaced by import smartphones. Undoubtedly it is the region with the richest contexts regarding mobile media in socio-cultural situations, raising the question of how we could/should estimate a new media landscape in the era of the *everydayness* of the mobile.

How to grasp the *everydayness* of mobile media

Based on a critical awareness of the problems identified so far, I will suggest how we can capture the social presence of mobile media and map out the concept of media creativity for the case of mobile technology. A new vision of media literacy and the role of mobile media practices is a crucial theme, and necessary to explore. As previously mentioned, one of the key issues for the integral understanding of mobile media in Japan may be how to grasp the *everydayness* of its practice as an actual form. This is a problematic issue to encounter, because it specifically raises a cognitive issue. Behaviors and activities with mobile media often become "invisible," because they are too natural and therefore tend to be unconsciously conducted. Thus, even researchers would fail to unveil the actual experiences with the mobile media if they depend merely on a questionnaire survey and a verbal interview (Kim 2010).

In relation to the *everydayness* of the mobile media, it is not a coincidence that there is a comparatively active movement towards interdisciplinary approaches in Japan. Various types of action research have been attempted in an effort to capture the various and hidden dimensions of ordinary people's mobile practices (Mizukoshi 2007). I have also worked on several action research projects in Japan which were critically related to the pursuit of solving the problem of how to grasp the *everydayness* of mobile media. In a different paper (Kim 2013), I linked them to a reflexive approach to build the "differentiating" or "de-familiarizing" moment about media experiences, suggesting a possible way to excavate a new knowledge and to provide the positive outlook toward a new concept of media literacy.

In order to gain insights about some necessary modes of media awareness and literacy through those action research projects, I will give an example of the case project conducted in Niigata prefecture in 2012. I will especially focus on what kinds of new understanding and knowledge were deliberately generated through the activities, and how those aspects could be related to the concept of new media literacy. The program was carried out as an educational scheme rather than for an investigational purpose; the workshop sought to cultivate a comprehensive understanding of mobile media as a cultural medium. In the workshop, various cultural probes such as the historicization of mobile technology, an auto-storytelling activity, social drama production and so on were incorporated to encourage participants to recollect and visualize their own image of mobile media. They will be subsequently introduced and respectively discussed afterwards.

The case of Niigata University students

Niigata city is one of Japan's main cities, with a population of more than 2.3 million. It is not only the seat of a local government of the Niigata prefecture, but also the center of industry and transportation of the northern region of the main island of Japan. Although the size and scale of the urban area are quite small compared with commercially prosperous cities such as Tokyo, the general cityscape is similar to the capital's urbanity. In particular, as the diffusion rate of mobile media per population exceeded 90 percent already in 2009, mobile media usage and cultural trends show little difference from those of young dwellers in the capital city.

From August 7 to 10, 2012, I conducted an intensive educational course in Niigata University with a group of eight students (two males and six females) aged between 20 and 27. Titled "Expression and Media Activities," the course was designed to gain comprehensive understanding of information society and mobile media literacy. It consisted of four full-day workshops including several types of reflexive activities regarding mobile media, on top of a lecture on the history of media technology that was given on the first day of the course by the author. The results of those activities are the main focus of the following discussion, as an example to imply different ways to elicit a new awareness and creativity about mobile media.

The revelation of personal memories

The first session of the workshop was a storytelling practice, wherein students were asked to find a unique topic recalling their experience and memories with a mobile phone and to make a brief presentation consisting of an oral storytelling with a performance photo created for them. Mobile media is ordinarily considered as a device for communication, not as an object for communication. The reaction from students to this first assignment was thus embarrassment rather than accommodation; however, it ended with an unexpected report of trivial but noteworthy findings around mobile media. The activity could be understood as similar to what Denzin (2003) called an auto-ethnographic performance, whereby texts allow the subject to confront and interrogate the cultural logics about things that matter in everyday life. Storytelling about mobile media could be regarded as the point of departure for re-discovering and re-questioning the media in one's actual life stories.

Moreover, this process was also related to the issue of how to visualize the "invisible" mobile practice in everyday routines. After the presentation, many students reflected upon their activity, noting that it was their first time seriously thinking about their involvement with mobile media. Some even noted that they actually re-discovered a new aspect and meaning of the media to associate with daily practices and personal customization.

For example, a female student made a presentation on her unique interpretation of *keitai* as a spiritual charm (Figure 38.1). Having a physical handicap in one leg, she carried her *keitai* with her all the time in case of needing assistance. She told us that her *keitai* was more than just a tool for communication but an essential item in order to survive. She even regarded it as if it had a spiritual power to protect her, calling it a good luck charm (*o-mamori*). Her introspection actually has in common with the identification of *keitai* as a cultural locus in which Japanese subcultures were revealed and integrated (Fujimoto 2005, 87). In this case, mobile media was less about social behaviors and external contacts but more about the personal emotion and self-confidence within oneself.

Figure 38.1 *Keitai* as a spiritual charm

Figure 38.2 Lurking *keitai*

Meanwhile, another female student spoke on how she made use of a tactic to keep her *keitai* close with her. She showed a picture (Figure 38.2) whereby she hid her *keitai* behind her pencil case during the class so to be out of the lecturer's sight. She usually kept the *keitai* in a hidden position because, despite the implicit prohibition, she couldn't relax unless her *keitai* was in constant eye contact. While her story typically connotes disapproval of mobile media in educational events, it also reveals that the visibility and materiality of mobile media is also important for users. Mobile media as a gateway to ubiquitous access and networkability has been noted in numerous studies (see Ling and Campbell 2009; de Souza e Silva and Frith 2012, etc.). Yet, as seen in her case, such practices as carrying, hiding out of others' sight or physical involvement with the media are also crucial factors in maintaining the forms of etiquette in social place.

Auto-ethnographic activities offer an opportunity for students to recall their personal memories with mobile media, as well as to listen to others' vivid narratives about the media. It not only works as a process to encourage a storyteller to find the mode of personal customization in various contexts but also helps her/him to understand the diversity of cultural displays of the media. Even though mobile media had become such a universal commodity, individual narratives and personal memories around the mobile were surprisingly different and diverse. The activity allowed students to learn the essence of a highly individualized device as a form of actual narrative about everyday lives. In other words, it was another way to read various displays of the *everydayness* of the mobile media.

The recollection of everyday experiences

The second session of the workshop activity was the production of a visual performance on and through mobile media. In Japan, there have been some fairly active attempts to apply the visualizing method in the study of mobile media. For example, Kato (2005) examined the image and representation of mobile media via the analysis of student-produced dramatic visual themed *keitai*. Emphasizing the embedded and mundane characteristic of the *keitai* experience, Kato tried to pay attention to the representation of the *keitai* via student-produced narratives, rather than a direct questioning of mobile experiences. On the other hand, Ito (2007) attempted a cross-cultural analysis of the mobile media through a comparison of the bodily performances made by dwellers in Tokyo and Helsinki, of which the approach had been situated as a form of *performance ethnography*. Performance ethnography is a term coined by Victor Turner (1987), a cultural anthropologist well known for his works on symbols and rituals. As an originally pedagogical offer for students, it offers ethnographers the opportunity to "experience" other cultures via bodily performances rather than just "describe" them through a literal expression. Ethnographers could gain an "inside view" in and through performance and it would engender a comprehensive critique of how cultural events and symbolic structure are internally constituted.

This logic of the "inside view" of cultural anthropology seems to be applied in the case of mobile media, not only in a way to aid the understanding of different cultures, but also as a way onto gaining an insight to "differentiating" one's own experience through the reflexive cycle of re-discovering things that matter in everyday life. Regarding an actual topic for performance production, I reused Ito's frame of "visualize a typical scene of the city," because the regional context was important for students to lead their lives in the university. As a result, I asked students to create a short story to show the typical scene of the use of mobile media in Niigata city. Students decided on the narrative of the stories themselves, and developed their works through group discussion, rehearsal and staging. The assignment was conducted by two groups of four members each.

One story titled "A day with *keitai*" described a typical daily routine of a college student. The main character was an ordinary male student. He woke up with an alarm call on the mobile phone, sent a message to a friend, or secretly chatted with friends during the lecture. Also, he pretended to look in the mobile phone when a person seeking to distribute a leaflet approached to him (Figure 38.3), browsed the Internet to search the location of ramen restaurants nearby, and

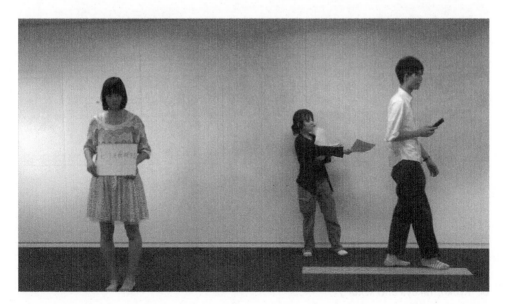

Figure 38.3 The use of *keitai* as a sign of implicit refusal in a public space (a scene from "A day with *keitai*")

published a photo of his own cooking dish via the SNS. The described practices were normal but essential activities in their usual lives. From morning until midnight, *keitai* was a casual but indispensable companion in numerous contexts of social practices in both personal needs and interactive behavioral arrangement.

Meanwhile, "Kyoko, Takuya and *keitai*" was a cute puppy love story between Kyoko (female name) and Takuya (male name). This story paid more attention to the inter-personal and inter-relational contexts of mobile media, whereas the previous story focused more on the personal context and actions solitarily conducted. As both Kyoko and Takuya were newly enrolled students of Niigata University, they met on the first day of campus life and soon became friends. They gradually got closer through campus happenings such as lectures, a midterm examination, a student festival, summer holidays, a leisure club event, Christmas party and so on, and *keitai* played cupid as an important tool bringing them together. The highlight of the story is the last scene in which Kyoko confessed her interest in Takuya by showing her *keitai* screen with a message "I like you" (Figure 38.4).

Although these performances seemed to contain much that showed ordinary practices carried out with mobile media in general, they cannot be dealt with as a direct reflection of the mobile use. It would be proper to understand them as the representation of the image that students had regarding mobile media. In other words, these works should be positioned as a reflexive object to reveal social representation as well as a typical level of the consciousness of students. The actions that appeared in these two stories are very typical forms of Japanese twenties' use of mobile media: they start a day with the alarm of the mobile, gauge inter-personal relationships through frequent wireless communication, spend time playing with *keitai* in the physical space,

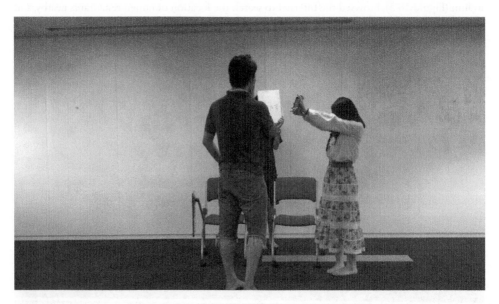

Figure 38.4 Showing the *keitai* screen meant opening one's mind to the other (the last scene of "Kyoko, Takuya and *keitai*")

express opinions or emotions by uploading contents to social media, and eventually end the day by setting an alarm for the next morning.

There might be no peculiar findings in terms of the newness of these practices. However, through the process of recalling, reenacting and visualizing them onto the stage, performers usually have an illuminating moment of some of their unconscious behaviors and trivial practices with the media. In the other words, performance ethnography evokes a reflexive moment and lets a performer become aware of practices beyond their thorough and clear perception. Through auto-ethnography (the first session) and performance ethnography (the second session), students had an opportunity to rediscover how their own lifestyle is tightly tied to *keitai*, and to start to understand the actual essence of the mobile media in everyday life.

The visualization of imagination

Finally, the last session of the workshop activity was the production of a visualized image of mobile media in the future. The purpose of this final activity was to let students transform their reflexive insights into the concrete idea of the future media through the visualization. More specifically, I asked students to conceptualize a prototype for future mobile media with desirable functions and designs inferred from personal memories, auto-storytelling narratives, performance ethnography, and the staged performances. Thus the prototype would contain insights and understandings gained through the activities so far. Because of the limited time and materials that could be used within a classroom and workroom, the visualized image was made into the form of a promotional poster of the future handsets. Students worked in groups of the same members as the previous activity.

The first group presented *Pipeta* (Figure 38.5), the idea of a pet-like mobile media. It had a cute and small-animal-like shape with the soft surface and cushioning texture to allow a favorable sense of touching a living pet. The tactile preference was taken into great consideration to design *Pipeta* as a whole. For example, the buttons set on top of the belly of this impersonated device would rise automatically for a touch, while they were hidden beneath the surface of soft skin while not being used. Moreover, *Pipeta* could be carried and hung around with in a quite interesting mode; it was no more necessary for the owner to be anxious on forgetting her/his media, because it would stick to her/his body without leave. It was the same group that made the performance "A day with *keitai*" in which the customization of mobile media inside personal contexts was emphasized. The idea of *Pipeta* seemed to reflect an insight into the portable materiality of the media and different ways of customization to bring it into one's personal intimacy.

Meanwhile, the second group demonstrated quite a different concept. The *With* (Figure 38.6) was mobile media for couples or groups; it had a variety of interfaces for pairing and grouping including a token sticker that enabled users to share the resources of their devices, a three-dimensionally projected screen by which several people could watch images together, as well as the easily removable decorations for a couple and so on. It seemed to convey a somewhat subversive thought against the concept of *keitai*, being painstakingly designed as a device for an individual. It was still an individual device, but every feature of the media was designed to take account of the possibility of using it with someone else or sharing it. This group made the performance of "Kyoko, Takuya and *keitai*". It seemed the prototype reflected the group's criticism of the concept of personal media designed for the solitary user alone.

Figure 38.5 Pipeta: a pet-like mobile media with a cute appearance and soft feel

Figure 38.6   With: mobile media with an interface for sharing

Drawing the future: towards mobile creativity

The exploration of the *everydayness* of mobile media eventually settles onto the question of how we perceive our usual experiences in respect of a better and more creative media environment. It is notable that participants in the workshop frequently mentioned the material presence of media on their palms, and deliberately linked it into their affective moments. The variety of experiences with mobile media actually surmounts the dimension of the mere media use; it rather embraces un-technological aspects, such as an obsessional sense of its materiality, the indifference and ignorance of mobile technology and even the denial of mobile communication on occasions. It seems obvious that these un-technological aspects and varieties are also important constituents of the reality of mobile media nowadays.

On the other hand, it is also noteworthy that performance activities engendered reflexive moments in which the workshop participants recollected and rethought their own experience, which usually went unnoticed. Taking the form of integrated tacit knowledge, the activities worked to open a way into a critical self-awareness, creative inquiry and, moreover, the further mode of understanding. These user-expressed texts have authorized themselves as a method to evoke a creative moment in which self-reflection and personal aesthetics could contribute to the imaginative and productive transformation of mobile media; that is to say, they envisaged a new type of creative mobile literacy.

The rapid progress of mobile technology and following techno-centric discourses, often urged by techno-nationalistic patriotism, discourages people from questioning the state of technology in their own lives, and rather enforces a consideration of it as a "black-boxed" given. However, in the era of the *everydayness* of mobile media technology, it does not only mean the way in which information is "mediated" or "consumed," but also expands upon the way information is to be "created" and "constituted." The crucial point is to encounter technology as a flexible and usable platform for oneself in everyday life, and consequently to create a positive circuit for social transformation and innovation, rather than how to use mobile media or how to associate it with professional knowledge. Creativity is thus an essential part.

Japan is a convincing example to show the complex and contradictory reality of a highly technologized society. How to overcome the *everydayness* of the technology becomes a critical point to produce a creative and positive flow in society. Different from a conventional notion of media literacy, defined by the capability of understanding, estimating, and utilization of various media forms and genres, this new awareness insists on accountability to both introspective findings and the technologically constituted outer environment. It is thus necessary to establish a reflexive and dialogic circle within which self-understanding and social reflection could accompany introspection. This is not mere functional and technological knowledge but a creative awareness based on self-reflection and a voluntary willingness towards a better media landscape.

References

Castells, M., Fernández-Ardèvol, M., Qiu, J.L. and Sey, A. (2007) *Mobile communication and society: A global perspective*, Cambridge, MA: MIT Press.

Denzin, N.K. (2003) *Performance ethnography: Critical pedagogy and the politics of culture*, Thousand Oaks: Sage.

de Souza e Silva, A. and Frith, J. (2012) *Mobile interfaces in public spaces: Locational privacy, control and urban sociability*, New York: Routledge.

Fujimoto, K. (2005) 'The third-stage paradigm: Territory machines from the girls' paper revolution to mobile aesthetics'. In M. Ito, D. Okabe and M. Matsuda (eds) *Personal, portable, pedestrian: Mobile phones in Japanese life*, Cambridge, MA: MIT Press.

Hashimoto, Y., Dentsu Innovation Institute, Oku, R., Nagao, Y. and Shono, T. (2010) *Neo-dejitaru-neitibu no tanjo: Nihon dokuji no shinka o togeru net sedai* [*A birth of neo-digital natives: How Japanese net users are different*], Tokyo: Daiyamondo.

Hjorth, L. (2009) *Mobile media in the Asia-Pacific: Gender and the art of being mobile*, New York: Routledge.

Ito, M. (2007) 'Keitai no hukei wo enjiru [Performing *keitai*]. In S. Mizukoshi (ed.) *Komunaru na keitai [Communal Keitai]*, Tokyo: Iwanami.

Ito, M., Okabe, D. and Matsuda, M. (eds) (2005) *Personal, portable, pedestrian: Mobile phones in Japanese life*, Cambridge, MA: MIT Press.

Kato, H. (2005) 'Japanese youth and the imagining of *keitai*'. In M. Ito, D. Okabe and M. Matsuda (eds) *Personal, portable, pedestrian: Mobile phones in Japanese life*, Cambridge, MA: MIT Press.

Katz, J.E. (2006) *Magic in the air: Mobile communication and the transformation of social life*, New Brunswick: Transaction Publishers.

Katz, J.E. and Aakhus, M. (eds) (2002) *Perpetual contact: Mobile communication, private talk, public performance*, Cambridge: Cambridge University Press.

Kita, S. (2006) 'Keitai denwa sangyo no kokusai kyousouryoku kyouka enomichisuzi [A way to strengthen the international competitiveness of mobile phone industry]', *Knowledge Creation and Integration*, 14(11): 48–57.

Kim, Y.K. (2010) 'Performance ethnography shuhou wo mochita Keitai kenkyu no kanousei [The possibility of performance ethnography in mobile studies: The implication of cultural anthropological approaches]', *Joho Tsushin Gakkai-shi*, 95: 75–85.

Kim, Y.K. (2013) 'An insider's view in media studies: Performance ethnography of mobile media'. In R. Rinehart, K. Barbour and C. Pope (eds) *Ethnographic worldviews: Transformation and social justice*, Dordrecht: Springer.

Koskinen, I. (2007) 'Managing banality in mobile multimedia'. In R. Pertierra (ed.) *The social construction and usage of communication technologies: European and Asian experiences*, Diliman: The University of the Philippines Press.

Ling, R. (2004) *The mobile connection: The cell phone's impact on society*, San Francisco: Morgan Kaufmann Publishers.

Ling, R. and Campbell, S.W. (2009) *The reconstruction of space and time: Mobile communication practices*, New Brunswick and London: Transaction Publishers.

Matsuda, M. (2010) 'Japanese mobile youth in the 2000s'. In S.H. Donald, T.D. Anderson and D. Spry (eds) *Youth, society and mobile media in Asia*, New York: Routledge.

Ministry of Public Management, Home Affairs, Posts and Telecommunications (2005) *2004 White Paper: Information and Communication in Japan*. Available at: http://www.soumu.go.jp/johotsusintokei/whitepaper/eng/WP2004/2004-index.html (Accessed on July 20, 2014).

Mizukoshi, S. (ed.) (2007) *Komunaru na keitai [Communal Keitai]*, Tokyo: Iwanami.

Turner, V. (1987) *The anthropology of performance*, New York: PAJ Publications.

Notes on contributors

Genevieve Bell is an anthropologist and research fellow at Intel. Her expertise in ubiquitous computing is displayed in her co-authored book (with Paul Dourish), *Divining a Digital Future: Mess and Mythology in Ubiquitous Computing*.

Tripta Chandola is an urban researcher based in Delhi. Her research explores the everyday materiality and negotiations of identity, rights and citizenship(s), especially amongst the marginalized and the disenfranchised. Drawing from her ongoing, decade-long research engagement with the slums of Govindpuri, she has published several peer-reviewed journal articles and book chapters.

Kakit Cheong is a graduate student at the Department of Communications and New Media, National University of Singapore. He studies the use of mobile technologies by migrant workers. His current research work explores how technologies can be designed to support family storytelling for domestic helpers.

Matthew M. Chew is an Associate Professor at the Sociology Department of Hong Kong Baptist University. His research interests include cultural sociology, social theory, sociology of knowledge, globalization and sociology of popular culture. He currently works on empirical data that deal with online games, dress and the night-time economy. He has published over 50 articles in journals including *New Media and Society*, *International Sociology*, *Cultural Studies* and *Positions*.

Leo T.S. Ching teaches Japanese and East Asian cultural studies at Duke University. He is the author of *Becoming Japanese: Colonial Taiwan and the Politics of Identity Formation*. He is completing a manuscript on anti-Japanese sentiments in post-war, postcolonial East Asia.

Younghan Cho is Associate Professor at Hankuk University of Foreign Studies (Seoul, South Korea). His current research interests are nationalism, pop culture, modernity and neoliberalism in East Asian contexts. He is co-editor of many special issues including *Glocalization of Sports in Asia*, *Colonial Modernity and Beyond* and *American Pop Culture*.

Rey Chow is Anne Firor Scott Professor of Literature at Duke University. Among her numerous book publications are *The Rey Chow Reader*, ed. Paul Bowman and *Entanglements, or Transmedial Thinking about Capture*. Her writings have appeared in over ten languages.

Peichi Chung teaches at the Department of Cultural and Religious Studies at the Chinese University of Hong Kong. Her research interests include creative industry policy, digital media production and popular culture in Asia. She has studied comparative game industry dynamics in East and Southeast Asia since 2006.

Gloria Davies is Professor of Chinese Studies at Monash University and an Adjunct Director of the Australian Centre on China in the World at the ANU. Her publications include *Worrying About China: On Chinese Critical Inquiry* and *Lu Xun's Revolution: Writing in a Time of Violence*.

Stephanie Hemelryk Donald is Head of the School of the Arts and Professor of Comparative Film and Media, at the University of Liverpool. She is currently finishing a book, *The Dorothy Complex*, on migrant children in world cinema.

Catherine Driscoll is Professor of Gender and Cultural Studies at the University of Sydney. Her research focuses on rural cultural studies, youth and girls studies, media and popular culture, and cultural theory and cultural studies. Her publications include *Girls*, *Modernist Cultural Studies*, *Teen Film: A Critical Introduction* and *The Australian Country Girl: History, Image, Experience*.

Anthony Y.H. Fung is Director and Professor in the School of Journalism and Communication at the Chinese University of Hong Kong. He obtained his PhD at the School of Journalism and Mass Communication at University of Minnesota. He is also a Pearl River Chair Professor at Jinan University at Guangzhou, China. His research interests and teaching focus on popular culture and cultural studies, popular music, gender and youth identity, cultural industries and policy, and new media studies. He has published widely in international journals, and authored and edited more than ten Chinese and English books.

Helen Grace is currently an Associate at the Department of Gender & Cultural Studies and Research Affiliate at the Sydney College of the Arts. She is the author of *Culture, Aesthetics and Affect in Ubiquitous Media: The Prosaic Image* and co-editor of the forthcoming *Technovisuality: Cultural Re-enchantment and the Experience of Technology*.

David Kurt Herold lived in China for nine years, before joining the Hong Kong Polytechnic University. His research focuses on the Chinese Internet, in particular the impact of the Internet on offline society. Herold's most recent publication is the edited volume *China Online: Locating Society in Online Spaces* (in press).

Larissa Hjorth is an artist, digital ethnographer, Professor and Deputy Dean in R&I in the School of Media & Communication, RMIT University. Since 2000, Hjorth has been researching the socio-cultural dimensions of mobile and play cultures in the Asia-Pacific – these studies are outlined in her books, *Mobile Media in the Asia-Pacific*, *Games & Gaming*, *Online@AsiaPacific* (with Michael Arnold), *Understanding Social Media* (with Sam Hinton) and *Locative, Social and Mobile Games* (with Ingrid Richardson).

Vicky Ho is a PhD graduate in the School of Journalism and Communication at the Chinese University of Hong Kong. She is teaching at Hong Kong Baptist University on the area of creative industry.

Heather Horst is Associate Professor and Director of Research in the Design & Social Context College at RMIT University. Horst is a sociocultural anthropologist who joined the School of

Media and Communication at RMIT University as a Vice Chancellor's Senior Research Fellow in September 2011. She has written many of the key texts in mobile media including *The Cell Phone* (with Daniel Miller).

Katrien Jacobs is Associate Professor in cultural studies at the Chinese University of Hong Kong. She has lectured and published widely about pornography, censorship and media activism in Hong Kong and global media environments. Her most recent book *People's Pornography: Sex and Surveillance on the Chinese Internet* investigates Hong Kong and mainland China's immersion in new erotic/porn trends and anti-censorship activism. Her work can be found on www.libidot.org/blog.

Dal Yong Jin finished his PhD degree from the Institute of Communications Research at the University of Illinois at Urbana Champaign. His major research interests are on game studies and new media, globalization and media, transnational cultural studies, and the political economy of media and culture. He is the author of several books, including *Korea's Online Gaming Empire*, *De-convergence of Global Media Industries* and *Hands On/Hands Off: The Korean State and the Market Liberalization of the Communication Industry*.

Fumitoshi Kato (PhD, Communication Studies) is currently working as a Professor at the Faculty of Environment and Information Studies, Keio University, Japan. His research interests include communication theory, media studies, socio-cultural impacts of new technologies, qualitative research methods, and experiential learning theory and practice.

Michael Keane is Professor of Chinese Media and Cultural Studies at Curtin University, Perth, Australia. Michael's research interests include China's cultural and media policy, creative industries in China and East Asia, and East Asian cultural exports. His current funded researched with the Australian Research Council concerns audio-visual media collaboration in East Asia with a focus on Mainland China. He is author or editor of 15 books on China's media and creative industries.

Olivia Khoo is Senior Lecturer in Film and Screen Studies at Monash University, Australia. She is the author of *The Chinese Exotic: Modern Diasporic Femininity*, co-author (with Belinda Smaill and Audrey Yue) of *Transnational Australian Cinema: Ethics in the Asian Diasporas*, and co-editor (with Sean Metzger) of *Futures of Chinese Cinema: Technologies and Temporalities in Chinese Screen Cultures* and (with Audrey Yue) *Sinophone Cinemas*.

Kyounghwa Yonnie Kim is an Assistant Professor at the Kanda University of International Studies, Chiba, Japan. She has worked for media companies in South Korea and Japan since the middle of the 90s, of which extensive media experiences are outlined in her writings *Media in Social History*. As a skilled ethnographer and lecturer on media studies, she is doing research with a special interest on mobile media and cultural practices in East Asian context, with a combination of cultural anthropological perspective.

Yeran Kim is Associate Professor in the School of Communications, Kwangwoon University, Seoul, South Korea. Her current research focuses on the popular cultural practices of digital communication. She has published several papers and books, including 'Idol Republic: Global Emergence of Girl Industries and Commercialization of Girl Bodies', *Faces of Word* and *Mobile Girl@Digital Asia* (co-authored).

Love Kindstrand is a doctoral student in anthropology at the University of Chicago, interested in online counterpublics, populism and the legitimacy of dissent.

Machiko Kusahara has extensively written, lectured, curated and served as a jury member internationally in new media art since the early 1980s. Her research explores media art and media archaeology with a focus on the correlation between art, technology, and culture. Kusahara is currently a professor at Waseda University in Tokyo.

Elaine Lally is Associate Professor of Communication Studies at the University of Technology Sydney. She researches in the areas of creative practice and digital culture, drawing on the fields of cultural studies, material culture, consumption and everyday life, and the sociology and philosophy of technology. A monograph on home recording and online musical collaboration, *Making Music in the Cloud: Creativity, Collaboration and Social Media* is currently in progress. She is co-editor of *The Art of Engagement: Culture, Collaboration, Innovation* and is the author of *At Home with Computers*.

Pui-lam Law received his PhD in sociology from the University of New South Wales, Australia. He is currently Assistant Professor in the Department of Applied Social Sciences of the Hong Kong Polytechnic University. His research interest is on modernity and social development in China.

Hye-Kyung Lee is based at Cultural, Media and Creative Industries at King's College London and researches on cultural policy, industries and consumption within both global and East Asian contexts. She co-edited *Cultural Policies in East Asia* and is writing *Cultural Policy in South Korea*.

Susan Leong is an Early Career Research Fellow with Curtin University. She is the author of *New Media and the Nation in Malaysia: Malaysianet*. Her current project, 'Belonging at the Borders: Diaspora Business in the Age of the Internet', focuses on provisional business migrants from Mainland China.

Sun Sun Lim (PhD, LSE) is Associate Professor at the Department of Communications and New Media and Assistant Dean for Research at the Faculty of Arts and Social Sciences, National University of Singapore. She studies the social implications of technology domestication by young people and families, charting the ethnographies of their Internet and mobile phone use. Her recent research has focused on understudied and marginalized populations including youths-at-risk, migrant workers and international migrant students. Her forthcoming book *Mobile Communication and the Family: Asian Experiences in Technology Domestication* will be published Fall, 2015.

Kwai-Cheung Lo, Professor in the Department of Humanities and Creative Writing, and Director of Creative and Professional Writing Program at Hong Kong Baptist University, is a specialist in trans-Chinese cinemas and cultural studies. He is the author of *Excess and Masculinity in Asian Cultural Productions* and *Chinese Face/Off: The Transnational Popular Culture of Hong Kong*. His other ongoing project is about the notion of Asianism, and he is the editor of a Chinese-language anthology entitled *Re-Sighting Asia: Deconstruction and Reinvention in the Global Era*.

Ani Maitra is Assistant Professor of Global Film and Media at Colgate University. Maitra's teaching and research interests span the fields of post-colonial and diaspora media cultures and gender and sexuality studies. His essays have appeared in journals such as *Camera Obscura*, *Continuum* and *Jindal Global Law Review*.

Chris Marmo has a PhD from RMIT University. He is co-founder of Paper Giant.

Mark McLelland is Professor of Gender and Sexuality Studies at the University of Wollongong and was the 2007/08 Toyota Visiting Professor of Japanese at the Center for Japanese Studies at the University of Michigan. He has published widely about gender and sexuality in Japan in books such as *Queer Japan from the Pacific War to the Internet Age* and *Love, Sex and Democracy in Japan during the American Occupation*.

Sean Metzger is an Associate Professor in the UCLA School of Theater, Film, and, Television. He is the author of *Chinese Looks: Fashion, Performance*. His co-edited volumes include *Embodying Asian/American Sexualities* and *Futures of Chinese Cinema: Technologies and Temporalities in Chinese Screen Cultures*.

Meaghan Morris is Professor of Gender and Cultural Studies at the University of Sydney, Distinguished Adjunct Professor at Lingnan University, Hong Kong, and Chair of the Inter-Asia Cultural Studies Society. The author of *Too Soon, Too Late: History in Popular Culture* and *Identity Anecdotes: Translation and Media Culture*, her most recent book is *Creativity and Academic Activism: Instituting Cultural Studies* (co-edited).

Keiko Nishimura is a doctoral student in Communication Studies at University of North Carolina at Chapel Hill, interested in the new media technology and its cultural signification.

Kana Ohashi is a doctoral student at the Graduate School of Media and Governance, Keio University, Japan. Ohashi has research interest in how people experience mobility and how people use social media on the move. She has published co-authored papers in *Digital Creativity* and in *The Journal of Quality Education*.

Nissim Otmazgin is a Senior Lecturer in the Department of East Asian Studies, the Hebrew University of Jerusalem. He is the author of *Regionalizing Culture: The Political Economy of Japanese Popular Culture in Asia* and co-editor (with Eyal Ben-Ari) of *Popular Culture and the State in East and Southeast Asia* and *Popular Culture Co-production and Collaboration in East and Southeast Asia*.

Shinji Oyama is Lecturer in Japanese Media and Cultural Studies in the Department of Film, Media and Culture Studies at Birkbeck College, University of London. His research interests include Japanese creative industries, brand and globalization. He has ten years of industry experience divided evenly between old media and new media.

Becky Pham is currently a Master of Arts candidate at the Department of Communications and New Media at the National University of Singapore. Pham has a keen research interest in studying how young people appropriate new media and technology, and how their technology engagement shapes their worldview. Her other research interests include media and migration, and human–computer interaction.

Sarah Pink is a Professor at the Design Research Institute and the School of Media & Communication RMIT University. She is a global authority on digital visual and sensory ethnographic methodologies and has published over a dozen monographs on the topic.

Jack Linchuan Qiu is Associate Professor at the School of Journalism and Communication, the Chinese University of Hong Kong. His publications include *World's Factory in the Information Era*, *Working-Class Network Society* and *Mobile Communication and Society* (co-authored).

Nishant Shah is a Professor in Digital Cultures at the ICAM, Leuphana University, Germany. He was the co-founder and Director-Research at the Centre for Internet & Society Bangalore, India, where he now serves on the board. He is the editor of the four-volume anthology *Digital AlterNatives with a Cause?* and works at the intersection of technology, gender, sexuality and governance.

David H. Slater is Professor of Cultural Anthropology at Sophia University, Tokyo, working on issues of capitalism, disaster, media and political mobilization. His recent publications include *Japan Copes with Calamity*, co-edited with Tom Gill and Brigitte Steger.

Sophie Ping Sun is a PhD student in Chinese University of Hong Kong. Her research interests concern new media, ICTs and global communication. Her main publication is *The History of Journalism in China* (co-authored).

Jo Tacchi is Director of Research, RMIT Europe in Barcelona. A media anthropologist, Tacchi's research is mostly concerned with media, communication and development. She has developed methodologies that combine ethnographic principles with action research cycles (ear.findinga-voice.org), and her latest co-authored book is *Evaluating Communication for Development*.

Denise Tse-Shang Tang is Assistant Professor in sociology at the University of Hong Kong. She is the author of *Conditional Spaces: Hong Kong Lesbian Desires and Everyday Life*. Her articles have been published in *Sex Education* and *GLQ: A Journal of Lesbian and Gay Studies*. Current research interests include queer youth and self-harm, celebrity culture and civic engagement.

Lina Tao is an HDR candidate at UNSW. She has previously worked in policy portfolios for the EU and Singapore in Beijing, and for the China Policy group, also in Beijing. In 2013 she was selected to take part in the Australia-China youth dialogue in Canberra and Melbourne.

Shobha Vadrevu is a Doctoral Candidate with the National University of Singapore's Department of Communications and New Media. Her work has appeared in *Science, Technology and Society* and *Learning, Media and Technology*. Her research interests include critical new media theory, ICTs and pedagogy, political communication, and youth and citizenship.

Miao Xiao graduated from School of Journalism, Fudan University. She now works at *Tencent*, one of China's largest Internet companies.

Audrey Yue is Associate Professor in the Screen and Cultural Studies Program at the University of Melbourne, Australia. Her recent publications include *Sinophone Cinemas* (co-edited with O. Khoo), *Transnational Australian Cinema* (co-authored with O. Khoo and B. Smaill) and *Queer Singapore* (co-edited with J. Zubillaga-Pow).

Elaine Jing Zhao is a Lecturer in Public Relations and Public Communications in the School of the Arts and Media, Faculty of Arts and Social Sciences at the University of New South Wales, Australia. Zhoa has been researching and publishing on digital media, creative economy, user co-creation, informal media economies, and their social, cultural and economic implications. Her publications on these and other topics include contributions to *International Journal of Cultural Studies, Media, Culture & Society, Global Media and Communication* and *Convergence: the International Journal of Research into New Media Technologies*.

Baohua Zhou is Professor and Director of the New Media Communication master program at School of Journalism, Fudan University, China. He is also a Research Fellow of the Center for Information and Communication Studies and Associate Director of Media and Public Opinion Research Centre of Fudan University. His research focuses on new media, media effects and public opinion. His research has been published in *Asian Journal of Communication, Chinese Journal of Communication* and various communication journals in China.

Index

Page numbers in italics refer to figures. Page numbers in bold refer to tables.